Fifth Edition

World War II
A Short History

Michael J. Lyons
North Dakota State University, Emeritus

Prentice Hall

Boston   Columbus   Indianapolis   New York   San Francisco   Upper Saddle River
Amsterdam   Cape Town   Dubai   London   Madrid   Milan   Munich   Paris   Montreal   Toronto
Delhi   Mexico City   Sao Paulo   Sydney   Hong Kong   Seoul   Singapore   Taipei   Tokyo

In Loving Memory of Joan

VP, Editorial director: Leah Jewell
Executive editor: Charles Cavaliere
Project manager: Rob DeGeorge
Editorial assistant: Lauren Aylward
Production liaison: Denise Forlow
Editorial/production supervision:
  Laserwords Maine: Bruce Hobart

Senior operations specialist: Mary Ann Gloriande
Cover design director: Jayne Conte
Cover designer: Bruce Kenselaar
Cover art: U.S. Marines under Japanese fire during the
  invasion of Peleliu Island. National Archives and
  Records Administration

Credits and acknowledgments borrowed from other sources and reproduced, with permission, in this textbook appear on appropriate page within text.

Library of Congress Cataloging-in-Publication Data

Lyons, Michael J.
  World War II : a short history / Michael J. Lyons.—5th ed.
     p. cm.
  Includes bibliographical references and index.
  ISBN-13: 978-0-205-66056-8
  ISBN-10: 0-205-66056-8
1. World War, 1939–1945. I. Title. II. Title: World War Two.
2. III. Title: World War 2.
  D743.L96 2009
  940.53–dc22

                                   2009014304

15 14 13 12 11 10 9 8 7

ISBN 10 0-205-66056-8
ISBN 13 978-0-205-66056-8

Contents

Preface

When the first edition of *World War II: A Short History* appeared in 1989, the conflict had already inspired over 70,000 volumes. The number has risen steadily since then. In this fifth edition, I again have incorporated material from the vast array of new literature, along with suggestions from readers. In particular, I have changed the format of the book in three important ways. To provide greater continuity to the narrative of the war in the Pacific, the material in former Chapter 24, covering the period from early 1943 to mid-1944, is now to be found in Chapter 15, entitled "America Gains the Initiative in the Pacific." It follows three chapters dealing with the earlier stages of the Pacific conflict. Similarly, I have placed the section on the 1942 German offensive in Russia and the Stalingrad debacle in new Chapter 16, entitled "The Tide Turns in Russia: Stalingrad and Beyond," which also includes the material in former Chapter 21, detailing the events on the Eastern Front during 1943–1944. Finally, the period of the North African war, from the summer of 1942 to the German surrender in Tunisia, is to be found in new Chapter 17, "The Tide Turns in North Africa: El Alamein to Tunisia."

The new edition places greater emphasis on the ideological aspects of the German war against the Soviet Union, including the notorious "Commissar Order," as well as the complicity of the Wehrmacht in Nazi atrocities on the Eastern Front. It also pays more attention to Stalin's initial failure to react to the invasion and the Soviet murder of German prisoners. I have increased coverage of the Holocaust, including a consideration of the reasons why the Western Allies were not able to intercede in behalf of the European Jews. I have also stressed the coexistence of collaboration and resistence in occupied countries and have raised the question of whether resistence was always worth the price.

Another change poses the question of whether the United States made a mistake in linking its interests too closely to those of China during the diplomatic crisis that culminated in the Japanese attack on Pearl Harbor. Still another gives greater credit to U.S. lend-lease aid to Russia than was the case in earlier editions. I have also modified my appraisal of the Battle of Midway. While still emphasizing its importance, I demonstrate that until late 1943, the U.S. and Japan continued to struggle to gain the initiative in the Pacific.

Among the multitude of other changes throughout the book, I have contrasted the war aims of Germany and Japan, elaborated on the divisions in French society before and during the German invasion, corrected the erroneous notion that Patton and Montgomery engaged in a "Race to Messina" during the Sicilian campaign, focused more on the myriad of problems confronting Eisenhower in making the decision as to when to invade Normandy, and emphasized the effects of the war on decolonization in Africa and the Middle East. I have also done my best to eliminate any mistakes from the following pages.

My basic purpose in this edition is still the same as that which prompted me to write the first: to satisfy the needs of the college student in the classroom as well as those of the general reader. At the same time, I have sought to provide a relatively brief synthesis of the work of other scholars that the professional historian will find useful. With these aims in mind, I have endeavored neither to overestimate the reader's knowledge of the subject nor to insult his or her intelligence by being too elementary. In pursuit of this elusive goal, I have attempted to fashion a book that is readable, informative, understandable, and interesting. Each reader will determine how well I have succeeded.

Though focusing primarily on the Second World War, I have examined the many factors that combined to cause that terrible calamity as well as the most significant effects of the conflict. Obviously, in a work of this scope, it has been necessary to deal selectively and summarily with the highly complex history of the decades preceding the outbreak of hostilities in 1939 and the period that followed the defeat of Germany and Japan in 1945. I have also striven to present a balanced account that does justice to both the European and Pacific theaters of operations and the connections between them. The global conflagration gave birth to innumerable controversies, and I have done my best to analyze the most important of these while often presenting my own views as to the best interpretations to place on them.

Any author incurs numerous debts in writing and publishing a book. Mine start with the late Professor Harold C. Deutsch, whose masterful course at the University of Minnesota kindled my fascination with the Second World War. Thanks also go to the many students who enrolled in my own World War II course at North Dakota State University during a period of over two decades. Their obvious interest helped stimulate my dedication to this project. Professor Archer Jones offered encouragement and advice during his years as dean of the College of Humanities and Social Sciences. I must also acknowledge my discussions, not to mention arguments, with Professor James D. Sadkovich, that helped to alter my view of Italy's performance in the war to some extent. My good friend and colleague Professor David B. Danbom provided me with inspiration by example as well as strong personal support. I also greatly appreciate the encouragement and suggestions of Professor A. Harding Ganz.

I am indebted, too, for the many valuable suggestions offered by the readers who found my manuscript worthy of publication. These include James P. Shenton, Columbia University; Joseph W. Bendersky, Virginia Commonwealth University; David Detzer, Western Connecticut State University; John A. Maxwell, West Virginia University; Robin F. A. Fabel, Auburn University; Donald L. Layton, Indiana State University; Robert Maddox, Pennsylvania State University; Charles L. Ponce de Leon, SUNY Purchase; Nancy Wingfield, Northern Illinois University; Neil Heyman, San Diego State University; Mary Kathryn Cooney, Lourdes College; Christopher J. Fischer, Indiana State University; and Roger Lotchin; University of North Carolina at Chapel Hill.

My gratitude for their encouragement also goes with much affection to my children—Mary, Mike, and Nancy. Finally, I must pay tribute to my late wife, Joan, who was a constant source of support during my labors on the first three editions.

Michael J. Lyons

CHAPTER ONE

World War I: The Great Turning Point

Some readers may wonder why a book on World War II begins with a chapter on World War I. There is a good reason for this, however. Without at least a brief consideration of the first conflict and its momentous effects, it is extremely difficult, if not impossible, to understand why World War II came to pass. The two wars were closely linked. World War I dragged on for four bloody years and resulted in enormous political and economic upheaval in Europe and, to some extent, the world. Governments and peoples struggled throughout the 1920s and 1930s to solve the many problems created by the conflict. Most of their efforts failed, and this failure contributed significantly to the outbreak of World War II.

World War I erupted directly out of a crisis triggered by the assassination of the Archduke Franz Ferdinand, heir to the thrones of the dual monarchy of Austria-Hungary, by a Bosnian Serb terrorist on June 28, 1914. Within a month this crisis led to war between Austria-Hungary and Serbia. All of the Great Powers of Europe as well as Japan soon found themselves drawn into the struggle, and eventually the United States followed their lead.

Europe Prior to World War I

World War I has aroused more controversy regarding its origins than any other war. Although the crisis that followed the assassination led directly to the conflict, many factors helped create an atmosphere of tension in the decades before 1914. Some historians consider these factors as more important than the crisis itself and view the war as the inevitable result of their interaction.

Among the factors that contributed to World War I was the growth of nationalism throughout the nineteenth century. This process affected not only the Great Powers—Britain, France, Germany, Austria-Hungary, and Russia—but many smaller countries as well. Early twentieth-century nationalism tended to be of a narrow, selfish, and strident type. Rabid nationalists saw their own nations as superior and looked toward other countries with contempt and hostility. To be sure, most people were not so extreme in their outlook. But many took great pride in their nation and often exaggerated its accomplishments. Governments were willing to go to the brink of war or beyond to safeguard what they considered to be "national interests" or to avenge supposed insults to national honor.

This burgeoning nationalism coincided with large-scale industrialization in much of Western and Central Europe and to a lesser extent in eastern portions of the continent. The nineteenth century also experienced a vast increase in population and the transformation of society in many countries from one that had traditionally been rural and agrarian to one that was largely urban and industrial. These changes occurred with relative speed and contributed to the erosion of traditional values, including religious beliefs, among many people. To some, nationalism became a sort of secular substitute for religion. The concentration of large portions of the population in cities and the development of more efficient communications and a popular press facilitated the dissemination of nationalistic propaganda.

The nineteenth and early twentieth centuries also witnessed the growth of representative political institutions in many countries and the extension of the right to vote in parliamentary elections to the poorer classes of society. The development of a system of mass education, at least at the primary level, played an important role in this democratizing trend. But at the same time, wealth and the actual exercise of political power remained concentrated in a small percentage of the population. The landowning aristocracy, which had dominated Europe for centuries, retained its importance and tended to merge with the wealthy capitalists, who controlled large industries, and directed powerful financial institutions. Industrial society held the promise of a better life, but to the poorer classes, expectations often proved greater than achievements. Although the standard of living rose, millions still remained victims of poverty. And while countries such as Britain and France had become democracies, the political systems of Germany and Austria-Hungary had the appearance of democracy but lacked the substance. Their elected parliaments possessed only limited power, while the heads of state and their ministers controlled the formation and implementation of policy. In Russia, there was not even the appearance of democracy.

Many members of the industrial working class turned to labor unions and socialism as a way out of their dilemma. These movements opposed nationalism and appealed to the international solidarity of the workers. They also preached the need to preserve peace and opposed expenditures on armaments. Many Socialists subscribed in theory to the Marxist doctrine of revolution to overthrow the existing political and economic system. But in practice most of them were moderate and willing to work peacefully for reforms. Radical parties appealed to many from the lower middle class, especially small businessmen and independent craftsmen who felt threatened by Big Business and Big Labor. Others found solace in the emotional stimulus of nationalism, which cut across class lines.

Industrialization accelerated economic competition among European powers, which vied for markets and raw materials. But at the same time, they continued to enjoy a large volume of trade with one another. This tended to reduce the intensity of their competition. As patterns of trade became extensive within Europe and between the continent and other parts of the world, however, the economy grew more complex, international, and interdependent. Economic rivalry also provided an impetus to a new flowering of imperialism among the Great Powers in the late nineteenth

century. They engaged in a scramble to acquire colonies in Africa, Asia, and other parts of the "underdeveloped world." Although imperialistic rivalry led to some heated disputes, the powers had settled most of them well before 1914. But some of them had profound and ongoing effects.

The Growth of National Rivalry

The development of two rival alliance systems in the years prior to 1914 proved especially critical. The first of these, the Triple Alliance, was the creation of Otto von Bismarck. As minister-president of Prussia, Bismarck had been primarily responsible for combining the various German states in a united Germany and became the country's first chancellor in 1871. The new Germany represented the greatest triumph of nineteenth-century nationalism and became the leading military and industrial power in Europe. But Bismarck had made enemies during the unification process, most notably France, which Prussia had defeated in the Franco-Prussian War of 1870–71. This conflict eliminated French resistance to German unification and forced France to give up two provinces, Alsace and part of Lorraine, to Germany. To provide his country with security against a possible French attempt to gain revenge and destroy his achievement, Bismarck set out to acquire allies.

His quest led to the formation of the Triple Alliance during the period 1879–82. This defensive alliance linked Germany, Austria-Hungary, and Italy. In the event that an outside power should attack one of the members of the alliance, the other two would be obligated to go to war. Bismarck also attempted to maintain a close relationship with Russia by negotiating a separate treaty with that country. But after his retirement in 1890, his successors allowed the agreement to lapse, fearing that it conflicted with Germany's other commitments. This action provided France with an opportunity to pursue friendlier relations with the Russians. These efforts culminated in a defensive alliance in 1894. Russia's need for capital to finance its industrialization program and France's willingness to provide the funds contributed to this agreement.

Britain later overcame its traditional dedication to what it called "splendid isolation" and made separate agreements with France in 1904 and Russia in 1907. Each of these agreements merely settled colonial issues that had caused problems in the past, but in the following years, Britain drew closer to both countries. This three-cornered relationship became the Triple Entente and served as a counterweight to the Triple Alliance.

The British tightened their connection with France largely because of their growing fear of Germany. The decision of the German emperor, Wilhelm II, and Admiral Alfred Tirpitz to increase greatly the size of Germany's navy, starting in 1898, contributed significantly to that concern. Britain had long possessed the world's largest navy. As an island nation dependent on massive imports of food and raw materials, it viewed any threat to its naval supremacy as a danger to its existence. But Wilhelm and Tirpitz considered a large fleet necessary for a world power and questioned Britain's right to dictate naval strength.

The rather truculent nature of German foreign policy also alarmed the British, especially in connection with two crises over the North African territory of Morocco. In the first of these in 1905, Germany challenged France's efforts to transform Morocco into a protectorate, which Britain had sanctioned in their 1904 agreement. German leaders believed that if confronted by such a crisis, Britain would desert France, and this would wreck their newly formed friendship. But contrary to German expectations, the British supported the French and even initiated military staff talks with them. During the second crisis, in 1911, Germany again pressured France over its encroachment on Morocco, and again Britain sided with the French. This time, the two powers began naval staff talks. These ongoing discussions led to the development of plans to coordinate their armies and navies in case of war with Germany. In 1914, shortly before the outbreak of war, Britain and Russia inaugurated conversations between their naval staffs.

European powers also increased their military and naval strength and devised strategic plans that they intended to put into operation in case of war. New technology facilitated the creation of weapons of increasing sophistication and destructiveness, and industrialization enabled their mass production. As in the case of their alliances, the powers contended that these military and naval

forces were necessary to defend them from aggression. But their staff officers drafted strategic plans that were offensive in character. In case of war, they intended to put them into operation as quickly as possible. They considered speed to be essential. In a crisis situation, demands for swift mobilization could create intolerable pressure on civilian officials to resort to war rather than wait for the other side to strike first.

The Seeds of Conflict in Europe

During the decade before 1914, the powers focused their attention to a large extent on the Balkan area of southeastern Europe, where a number of crises erupted. Austria-Hungary and Russia had long been rivals for political and economic influence in the Balkans. The emergence of nationalism among the various Balkan peoples complicated this rivalry. These national groups had been subject to the rule of the Ottoman Turks for centuries. But during the late nineteenth and early twentieth centuries, the Ottoman Empire declined to such an extent that it earned the unenviable reputation as the "sick man of Europe." The Balkan nationalities took advantage of this weakness gradually to win their independence. By 1913, the Turks had lost all of their Balkan holdings except for the predominantly Turkish area bordering the straits that linked the Black Sea with the Mediterranean.

Among the states that emerged from this long process was Serbia. Its existence posed a special problem for the dual monarchy of Austria-Hungary, which was a glaring exception in an age of nation-states. It was a multinational empire, consisting of minorities that differed from one another in language, customs, historical development, and religion. In fact, the two dominant nationalities—the Austrians, who were ethnically German, and the Hungarians—comprised less than half the population. The Austro-Hungarian government had long viewed nationalism as a force that could lead to the country's disintegration into its component national parts. Among the dual monarchy's nationalities was a Serbian minority that lived in territories bordering Serbia. The Serbian government hoped eventually to absorb these kinsmen into a "greater Serbia." To complicate matters even more, Russia treated

Serbia as a client state. Both the Russians and Serbs were Slavic peoples. In the early twentieth century, Austria-Hungary became obsessed by what it viewed as "the Serbian menace." This menace materialized with the creation of a secret Serbian nationalist society that took the name Union of Death or the Black Hand. It was this organization that carried out the assassination of Franz Ferdinand in 1914.

The Austro-Hungarian government responded to the assassination with outrage; however, it could not decide how it should deal with Serbia. At this critical point, Germany pledged to support whatever action the dual monarchy deemed necessary, even if it meant war with Serbia's protector, Russia. Armed with this "blank check," Austria-Hungary finally issued an ultimatum to Serbia that, if accepted, would have reduced the nation to a virtual satellite state. Although the Serbs agreed to comply with most of the ultimatum's demands, they balked at certain points that they felt were incompatible with their independence. Austria-Hungary responded by declaring war on July 28, hoping to deal with Serbia in isolation.

The War Spreads

But Russia rallied to Serbia's aid by mobilizing its reserves, an act preparatory to military action. Since the Russians assumed that war with Austria-Hungary would also mean war with Germany, they had only one plan, which provided for mobilization against both countries. Germany, taking for granted that a conflict with Russia would also embroil it in hostilities with France, issued ultimatums to both. Germany asked Russia to cease mobilization and France to declare neutrality in case of war between Germany and Russia. Neither agreed, and by August 3 Germany was at war with both powers.

Despite its close relationship with France, Britain hesitated at first but entered the conflict when Germany sent forces into tiny Belgium. This violated an agreement that the Great Powers had made in 1839 to guarantee Belgium's permanent neutrality. The British had traditionally opposed any power that attempted to seize this area because of its location across the channel from Britain. Germany justified its aggression on grounds of military necessity. Its strategic plan provided for an invasion of France by way of Belgium. The British responded to this action by declaring war on Germany.

Italy refused to support its partners in the Triple Alliance, contending that Austria-Hungary and Germany were the aggressors. Italy pointed to the fact that its only obligation was to take action in case of an attack on one of them. The Italians remained interested onlookers until April 1915, when they sided with the Allies—Britain, France, and Russia. They did so in return for Allied promises of compensation at Austria-Hungary's expense as well as in the Middle East and Africa. Japan also declared war on Germany but confined its efforts to the Far East and Pacific, where the Japanese quickly seized a number of German colonial outposts. The Central Powers—Germany and Austria-Hungary—managed to lure Turkey and Bulgaria into the conflict on their side.

The war that came in 1914 was not inevitable. To be sure, conflicting national interests and the existence of the alliances contributed to the outbreak of hostilities. But the war was nevertheless the result of the inability of the powers to solve the 1914 crisis. This failure was due to human error, especially Germany's blank check, Austria-Hungary's belief that it could localize the war, and Russia's decision to mobilize. It does not appear that any of the Great Powers desired a general conflict, but once the Austro-Hungarians issued their ultimatum to Serbia, the crisis took on a momentum of its own. The necessities of mobilization and strategic plans quickly swept Europe into war.

Civilians and soldiers alike greeted the outbreak of war with nationalist pride and enthusiasm. To them, it was a great adventure. Millions lined the streets to cheer and throw flowers to the brave warriors as they marched through Berlin, Vienna, and Paris. One young German recruit was so overjoyed when he received his uniform and weapons that he shouted, "War is like Christmas!" The mood soon changed.

Miscalculations and Illusions

At first, none of the European powers realized the type of conflict they had unleashed. Most leaders seriously underestimated the length of the war, its costliness in lives and wealth, and its impact on the very foundations of European politics and society. They expected a short war, basing their assumption on the fact that since the defeat of Napoleon in 1815, most European wars had been brief, lasting only a few weeks or months. They also anticipated that the development and mass production of powerful new weapons in the years leading up to 1914 would give the advantage to the offense rather than the defense. It seemed obvious that the side that possessed the greatest offensive strength would win.

The Central Powers especially counted on a short war because a long conflict was almost certain to go against them. The Allied countries possessed larger manpower reserves, greater industrial strength, and access to the resources of the rest of the world. They also used their superior naval strength to impose a blockade that cut off the Central Powers from the other continents. The Allies virtually encircled their enemies, with Britain and France on the west, Russia on the east, and Italy on the south. Despite the fact that German armies operated within the borders of both France and Russia from 1914 on, the Central Powers were in effect the besieged nations, at least until the collapse of Russia late in the war.

Germany, the most powerful of the Central Powers, had taken a two-front war for granted in its long-range military planning. But the Germans realized that they could not win such a conflict unless they defeated France and Russia one at a time in quick, decisive fashion. Their strategic plan, which aimed at accomplishing the first stage of this task, was not new. It was the work of General Alfred von Schlieffen, who had retired as army chief of staff in 1906. Schlieffen called for the Germans to concentrate powerful forces in the west while remaining on the defensive against Russia. He envisioned a thrust through neutral Belgium that would avoid the fortifications along France's northeastern border. German troops would then swing into France, led by an overwhelmingly powerful right wing that would advance to the southwest of Paris before wheeling to the east. If all went according to plan, the Germans would encircle the main enemy armies and force France to capitulate within six weeks. After this great victory, Germany would shift its strength eastward to deal with the Russians.

When the war began, General Helmuth von Moltke, who had taken over as chief of staff, put the Schlieffen plan into effect. At first, all went well, and the Germans were nearing Paris by early September. But Moltke had reduced the striking power of the right wing to strengthen his forces along the German border where he anticipated a French attack. He also shifted additional troops to the eastern front to help resist an unexpected Russian offensive. As a result, the German spearhead did not have sufficient strength to execute its turn to the southwest of Paris. Instead, it had to shorten its front and wheel to the northeast of the capital, and as it did, the French counterattacked the German flank.

In the desperate struggle that followed, the Allies forced the Germans to halt their offensive. This First Battle of the Marne proved to be the decisive encounter of the war. It denied Germany a quick victory and condemned it to fight a prolonged two-front conflict. Although Moltke received the blame for the German failure, it appears that the Schlieffen plan had little chance of success under any circumstances. It was far too ambitious and would soon have encountered such extreme supply problems that it would have failed even if Moltke had attempted to carry out Schlieffen's instructions to the letter. In fact, a stronger right wing would have compounded these logistic difficulties.

A Long and Bloody Deadlock

As the short-war illusion faded, hostilities on the western front degenerated into a bloody war of attrition. The two sides began to dig in and gradually created opposing systems of trenches, extending across southwestern Belgium and northern France from the English Channel to the Swiss border. The front had no flanks, and thus for the next four years both the Allies and Germany tried to break the deadlock by means of direct assaults using millions of men. Unfortunately, the new and terrible weapons, which the Great Powers had developed prior to the war, proved especially well suited for defensive warfare. They included vastly improved rifles, the machine gun, and artillery of tremendous range and velocity. This concentrated firepower prevented either side from gaining a breakthrough and inflicted hundreds of thousands of casualties in each major offensive.

Another deadlock developed on the eastern front, even though this vast area provided far greater room for maneuver. After halting Russia's offensive in the great Battle of Tannenberg in August 1914, the Germans carried out a major offensive in 1915 that drove the enemy out of much of its western territory. The Russians suffered appalling casualties, and the Germans captured over a million prisoners. But despite this demoralizing setback, Russia refused to make peace. This confronted the Germans with a dilemma. Should they continue to advance deeper into the vast expanse of Russia or halt their operations and concentrate on the western front during 1916? After considerable debate, they chose the latter solution.

The man responsible for this decision was General Erich von Falkenhayn, who had succeeded Moltke as chief of staff. Falkenhayn devised a master plan to win the war in the west during 1916. It involved a huge offensive against the French fortress city of Verdun with the purpose of inflicting such heavy losses that France would be forced to leave the war. This assault, designed to "bleed France white," began in February and continued for months. It did cost the French 375,000 casualties, but the Germans suffered 335,000 of their own, and France did not make peace.

Britain was active, too. It had started the war with a small volunteer military force but resorted to conscription early in 1916 and by the summer had created a mass army. General Sir Douglas Haig, commander of the British Expeditionary Force, opened an offensive along the Somme River in July 1916 with French assistance. But his hopes for a major breakthrough proved as illusory as Falkenhayn's dream of victory at Verdun. The Battle of the Somme continued until November. When it ended, the British had sustained 420,000 casualties, the French 200,000, and the Germans 450,000. This fearful carnage had resulted in no appreciable change in the battle line.

The Russians also returned to the offensive in the summer of 1916. Under the leadership of General Alexei Brusilov, they scored impressive early successes against the Austro-Hungarians, but, as usual, their drive eventually stalled. Again, casualties were high for both sides, the Russians suffering most with close to half a million dead, wounded, and missing and another 400,000 prisoners. Hundreds of thousands of others deserted.

The horrible events of 1916 struck the belligerent powers with stunning psychological impact. Verdun, although a French victory, left the army on the verge of rebellion. When France resorted to another suicidal offensive in the spring of 1917, large-scale mutinies actually took place. The British had to shoulder most of the burden during the remainder of the year, while the French restored order and morale among their forces. The Brusilov offensive had virtually finished both the Russian and Austro-Hungarian armies as important factors in the war. Even the proud German army was never quite the same after Verdun and the Somme and found itself stretched too thin in too many places.

On the home front, war weariness increased, and support for peace grew among the civilian populations. The winter of 1916–17 was particularly harsh, adding to the suffering. Both sides toyed with the possibility of a negotiated settlement, but neither was willing to settle for a peace without compensation.

The Resort to Total War

Instead of peace, the new concept of "total war" gradually took shape. It focused on the relationship among war and politics, technology and the economy, and the need to mobilize, not only the armed forces, but the civilian population as well in an all-out effort to gain victory. The ability to achieve this goal varied considerably from country to country. The Western Allies and Germany gained the most success in this endeavor. They also resorted to stronger leadership completely dedicated to victory. In Britain, David Lloyd George, a fiery Welshman, became prime minister in December 1916. The equally combative Georges Clemenceau, who had earned the nickname "the Tiger," took over as premier of France in 1917. The governments of both countries assumed virtual dictatorial power and subordinated everything to their war efforts, but at least civilian officials remained in charge.

Europe, 1914 - 1918

Allied and Associated Powers
Central Powers and their allies
Neutrals
———— Political boundaries, 1914
– – – Boundary between Austria and Hungary
• • • • Greatest advance by Central Powers
•••••• Greatest advance by Allies
■ Battle sites

Europe, 1914–18

In Germany, the military increasingly dominated the government. Field Marshal Paul von Hindenburg succeeded Falkenhayn as chief of staff after the failure at Verdun. He and General Erich Ludendorff pressured Chancellor Theobold von Bethmann-Hollweg out of office in 1917 when he appeared too receptive to a negotiated peace. Bethmann's successor, Georg Michaelis, proved to be little more than a puppet for Hindenburg and Ludendorff.

The governments of all three countries concentrated their economies almost totally on the war effort. They allocated resources as well as labor and coordinated production to an unprecedented

degree. Their achievements were remarkable. The war's insatiable demand for manpower on the battlefield quickly led to a shortage of male workers in munitions plants. Women in accelerating numbers took their place, especially in France and Britain. This pattern was to be repeated in World War II. The task of large-scale economic mobilization proved far more difficult for Austria-Hungary, Italy, and Russia. Their less well developed economies and weaker governmental structures left them more dependent on aid from their allies. Again women replaced many male workers in war industries. Russia's isolation from the Western Powers also sharply limited the

FIGURE 1-1   Allied troops advance on the western front. *(National Archives and Records Administration)*

amount of assistance it could receive. All the warring countries appealed to their peoples for support and continued sacrifice.

The European powers had blundered into the conflict so unexpectedly in 1914 that they initially had few, if any, clear war aims. All of them believed they were fighting in defense of their national independence or at least national interests. None of them considered itself to be the aggressor. Of the major powers, only Italy entered the war with definite aims. Soon after hostilities began, however, other belligerents formulated specific war aims. With the realization that the struggle was going to be long and bloody, leaders and important segments of the public concluded that it must result in gains that would help justify the terrible slaughter and the strain on their economies.

The Territorial Imperative

On the Allied side, France hoped from the start to regain Alsace-Lorraine. But as time passed, French leaders began to covet Germany's coal-rich Saar, a small area bordering France on the northeast. They also favored removing German control over the Rhineland, the region to the west of the Rhine River, and establishing an independent Rhenish

state. This would create a buffer between France and Germany. The French also hoped to weaken Germany to such an extent that it would be unable to make war on France in the future. And they hoped to acquire German colonies in Africa as well as Turkish possessions in the Middle East. Britain had no territorial ambitions in Europe but, like France, desired colonial compensation at the expense of Germany and Turkey.

Russia expected to oust Turkey from control of the straits. This cherished dream had long been contrary to the interests of both Britain and France, which had desired to keep Russian naval power out of the Mediterranean. But in 1915, fearing that Russia might make a separate peace, the Western Powers conceded to Russia control over the straits after the war. Italy had entered the conflict to obtain territory along the Austrian border—the Trentino on the north as well as the port city of Trieste and the peninsula of Istria to the east. Italy also desired a sizable strip of Austria's coastline along the Adriatic Sea.

As for the Central Powers, Austria-Hungary had been confused from the start about what it expected to gain from the conflict. In fact, Hungarian leaders had agreed to war only on condition that Austria-Hungary would not acquire any Serbian territory. They believed that the absorption of additional Serbs would only create greater internal problems. And the Austro-Hungarians immediately suffered defeats at the hands of not only the Russians but the Serbs as well. This ominous beginning seemed to indicate the wisdom of seeking a quick end to the war. Instead, they continued to persevere, and Germany came to their rescue with the 1915 offensive, which drove the Russians deep into their own territory. The Germans also directed a campaign in which their troops joined with those of Austria-Hungary and Bulgaria to crush Serbia. But this salvation ultimately proved fatal to the dual monarchy because the war became more and more unpopular with the subject nationalities, kindling desires for independence. Austria-Hungary's increasing reliance on its ally also transformed the empire into a German satellite. As the war continued, its primary aim came to be one of self-preservation.

By far the most extensive aims were those of Germany, although these fluctuated according to the fortunes of war. They provided for absorption of an additional iron-rich slice of French Lorraine as well as Luxembourg and either annexation of Belgium or its conversion into a satellite state. The Germans harbored far greater ambitions in Eastern Europe. These included acquisition of almost all of Russia's western territory—the provinces bordering the Baltic Sea, Poland, and the vast area of the Ukraine. Germany's intentions in these areas are not clear, but it certainly planned some annexations and the establishment of satellite states. The Germans also anticipated establishing a sphere of influence in the Balkans. They visualized creating a German-dominated European customs union that would make them economically supreme. In addition to this vast increase of German power in Europe, they also proposed to take over a number of French, British, and Belgian colonies in Africa.

Revolution in Russia

As the war continued, the pressures on each of the powers increased steadily. Russia was the first to crack under the strain. Although the Russian economy had experienced some industrialization in the years prior to 1914, it still remained primitive compared to those of Germany and Britain. It proved quite inadequate to supply the needs of both the armed forces and the civilian population. Shortages of all kinds developed early and became more pronounced as the conflict continued. The Russian transportation system also broke down under the unprecedented demands of modern warfare. To make matters worse, the government of Tsar Nicholas II was inefficient, corrupt, and unpopular. War weariness grew steadily.

Early in March 1917, a revolt broke out in Petrograd, the capital. It started as demonstrations against the food shortage that soon became riots. Workers showed their sympathy by going on strike. The government ordered the city's army garrison to put down the unrest, but the soldiers deserted to the rebels. Revolution spread rapidly to other cities, and it soon became apparent that virtually no one was willing to defend the discredited regime. Within a week, Nicholas II had bowed to increasing demands for his abdication, ending the 300-year rule of the Romanov dynasty.

The weak Russian parliament now established a provisional government to lead the country until a constituent assembly could draft a constitution for a permanent political system. But the provisional government was reluctant to hold elections for the assembly in the unsettled atmosphere and also refused to seek a negotiated peace. This obstinate policy eroded the government's support. Its failure to enact a land reform program also alienated the peasants. Workers and soldiers increasingly rallied to the Bolsheviks, a revolutionary Marxist Socialist party.

Under the leadership of Vladimir Lenin, the Bolsheviks sought to win control of the soviets, councils that workers and soldiers had organized early in the revolution. The soviets had remained in existence despite the formation of the provisional government and represented a threat to its rule. By October, the Bolsheviks had gained a majority in the soviets of Petrograd, Moscow, and several other industrial cities. In early November, they moved against the provisional government and quickly gained control of much of European Russia.

Lenin had promised to secure peace if the Bolsheviks came to power and now set out to fulfill that pledge. It proved difficult because the

Germans insisted on exceedingly harsh terms. It was not until March 1918 that the Bolsheviks finally agreed to the Treaty of Brest-Litovsk. This settlement, required Russia to give up most of its Baltic provinces, much of Russian Poland, and the Ukraine, as provided in the German war aims. Germany also extracted such far-reaching trade concessions that Russia became a virtual economic dependency.

The War Outside Europe

Although Europe remained its epicenter, the conflict was, nevertheless, a "world war" with hostilities in far-flung theaters of operations. In addition to Japan's seizure of German possessions in East Asia and the Pacific, Allied forces conquered Germany's colonies in Africa and engaged in an ill-advised, long, bloody, and unsuccessful attempt to seize the Turkish straits linking the Black Sea with the Mediterranean. They also drove the Turks out of Palestine, Syria, and Mesopotamia (later Iraq) with long-lasting repercussions.

The Allies also received help from their overseas empires. Canada, Australia, New Zealand, and South Africa, which had become self-governing dominions within the British Empire, all contributing troops. India, which did not enjoy dominion status, also provided soldiers. In addition, both Britain and France utilized colonial contingents from their possessions in Africa. Not surprisingly, these contributions kindled expectations among the peoples of both empires that they would gain concessions from London and Paris after the war.

The U.S. Role

Meanwhile, the United States had entered the war on the side of the Allies in April 1917. Many Americans had been sympathetic to the Allied cause from the start of the war. They had much more in common with democratic Britain and France than with the more authoritarian regimes of the Central Powers. They also were appalled by the German shooting of Belgian hostages in reprisal for civilian attacks on soldiers, the shelling of the beautiful Gothic cathedral at Reims, France, and the sinking of the British

ocean liner *Lusitania* with the loss of over 1,000 lives, including 128 Americans. Allied propaganda proved especially effective at portraying the Germans as barbaric "Huns." And American loans to Allied powers created an economic stake in their victory.

But the primary factor that brought the United States into the war was Germany's policy of unrestricted submarine warfare, which resulted in the sinking of several American ships in early 1917. This policy was a calculated risk designed to force Britain out of the war. The Germans realized that the British were dependent on large-scale imports of food and other supplies. They hoped that they would be able to starve Britain into submission by sinking large numbers of both Allied and neutral ships in the waters around the British Isles. The gamble failed. Not only did it bring the United States into the war, but also the British were able to combat the submarine menace and continue the struggle.

Despite a large population and great economic resources, America was a negligible military power in early 1917, with only 110,000 men under arms. Before the United States could help in the actual fighting, it had to raise a mass army through conscription, train it, and transport it to France. This new and powerful force was not ready for action until the summer of 1918. In the months that followed Russia's departure from the war, Germany attempted to defeat the British and French before America became a factor. The Germans unleashed a series of offensives between March and July 1918, but the Allies managed to hold out, and during the last offensive, fresh American divisions began to make a major contribution. After stopping the final German drive, the Allies took over the offensive and applied unrelenting pressure. On August 8, "the black day of the German army," the whole enemy front began to fall back. German military leaders realized that they had lost the war.

An End to the Nightmare

Soon afterward, dramatic events unfolded far to the southeast. An Allied army had been encamped in northern Greece since 1915, when it had arrived too late to prevent neighboring Serbia from being overrun by the Central Powers.

But in September 1918, it went over to the offensive. By the end of the month, it had forced Bulgaria out of the war. Turkey, now isolated to the southeast, capitulated a month later as Allied troops pushed into Serbia.

In late October, Italian forces also won a major victory over the Austro-Hungarians in the Battle of Vittorio Veneto. Confronted by these two critical developments, Austria-Hungary's army disintegrated, and the various subject nationalities began to declare their independence. The dual monarchy signed an armistice on November 4. Soon afterward, Charles, the last emperor of the Hapsburg dynasty, which had ruled Austria since 1276, abdicated.

Germany's position was now hopeless. With its army in full retreat and its allies gone, morale began to crack. Naval mutinies and sporadic civilian revolts broke out. Demand for an end to the war and even to the monarchy grew ever more insistent. Emperor Wilhelm II, realizing the weakness of his position, abdicated and fled into exile in neutral Holland. On November 11, a new republican government accepted an armistice.

The long nightmare was over. But although the Allies had defeated the Central Powers, in a larger sense none of the European belligerents had really won. The war had cost the lives of at least 10 million soldiers and had left another 20 million wounded. There were few families that did not mourn the loss of loved ones. An atmosphere of gloom and uncertainty persisted long after the fighting stopped. The war had also seriously disrupted the European economies. Overseas markets were gone, and all the belligerents were deeply in debt. Devastation abounded in many parts of the continent. And although peace had returned, wartime hatreds lingered. So did the questions. How could it have happened? How could the leaders have allowed it to continue for so long? What did it accomplish? Could anything be worth the price? Among the casualties was the old confident Europe, long the focal point of the world. It was gone, perhaps forever.

CHAPTER TWO

The Legacy
of World War I

Although the war had ended, turmoil still afflicted much of Europe. The Austro-Hungarian Empire had vanished from the map. A jumble of small, weak states had taken its place, creating a vacuum of power. In Russia, the Bolsheviks had not been able to savor their victory over the provisional government for long. Various anti-Bolshevik forces had challenged their right to rule, and civil war had erupted during the summer of 1918. It continued to rage in the aftermath of World War I. Defeat had reduced Germany to a state of shock, bitterness, and disillusionment. And while Britain, France, and Italy engaged in victory celebrations, mourning for millions of dead, who had paid the price for this triumph, tended to restrain their joy. Now that they were free from the grim reality that had haunted them for four long years, Europeans looked to the future with both hope and uncertainty. But hatred of recent enemies persisted.

The Peace of Paris

It was in this atmosphere that the victorious Allies met in January 1919 to draft the settlement that liquidated the war—the Peace of Paris. They refused to invite either Germany or Russia to attend the conference. After four years of bitter warfare, the European Allies, especially the French, had little inclination to sit across the bargaining table from the despised Germans. Resentment over the Bolshevik government's separate peace with Germany and fear of its doctrine of world revolution prompted the decision to bar Russia from participation. The outcome of the Russian civil war was also uncertain, and the Allies hoped that the anti-Bolshevik forces would win. They had even intervened in the civil war during 1918. British and French forces had

landed at Russian ports on the Arctic and Black Seas, ostensibly to prevent war materiel, which the Western Allies had sent to the provisional government, from falling into the hands of the Germans. But they also provided aid to the anti-Bolshevik forces. American and European units had gone ashore at Vladivostok in East Asia to help the escape of Czech prisoners of war who intended to join the Allies. With the end of World War I, the original justification for intervention was no longer valid, and the Western Allies withdrew during 1919. Japan had also sent troops to Vladivostok in an attempt to increase its influence in East Asia.

Delegations representing 27 nations convened in Paris, but the leaders of the Great Powers actually made the major decisions. They started as the Big Four, consisting of President Wilson of the United States, France's Premier Clemenceau, British Prime Minister Lloyd George, and Italian Premier Vittorio Orlando. But Orlando walked out of the conference in protest when the Western Powers refused to grant Italy the extensive compensation it had expected along the Adriatic Coast. They were not impressed with Italy's performance in the war, and Wilson was opposed to giving the Italians territory that contained predominantly South Slav populations. As a result, they agreed to grant only the Trentino, Trieste, and Istria. Although Orlando did return later, the Big Three—Wilson, Clemenceau, and Lloyd George—essentially molded the settlement.

The most important portion of the Peace of Paris was the Treaty of Versailles, which provided the settlement for Germany. It represented a compromise, essentially between the views of Wilson and those of Clemenceau. Wilson desired a peace of reconciliation that would be lenient with the Germans and, he hoped, they would accept as final. He had issued a statement of war aims—the Fourteen Points—in January 1918. His position was highly idealistic and included such unselfish aims as the creation of an international peace-keeping organization, disarmament, the securing of the right of all peoples to govern themselves. He could afford to be unselfish. The United States had suffered far less from the war than had the European Allies. In fact, it had taken over markets that the European powers were not able to supply due to their concentration on the war and had achieved a highly favorable balance of trade in the process. The European Allies had also turned to the United States for loans to help them finance their war efforts. In 1919, they were all deeply in debt, whereas America had become a creditor nation on a massive scale.

Wilson firmly believed that the United States had a special calling to lead the world into a new age of peace and democracy. He looked with disapproval at the traditionally cynical attitude of European countries in the realm of power politics. Wilson wanted to build an international system based on liberal capitalism, free trade, and democracy, with a League of Nations dedicated to preserving peace as its cornerstone.

At least some of Wilson's Fourteen Points differed rather dramatically from the war aims of the European Allies. Britain and France agreed to the Fourteen Points as the basis for negotiation but not as a hard-and-fast blueprint for settlement. But the German government accepted the armistice in the belief that Wilson's proposal would be the framework for a lenient peace. Actually, the Germans were unduly optimistic about the Fourteen Points, which contained a provision for an independent Poland with access to the sea. This meant that Germany would lose territory to the new Polish state, including a corridor to the Baltic Sea that would divide Germany into two parts, something extremely unpalatable to most Germans.

Clemenceau, above all else, desired a settlement that would safeguard French security from another German attack. In pursuit of that goal, he sought to deprive Germany of some territory, dramatically reduce the size of the German armed forces, and require heavy payments for war damages. He also hoped to bind France, Britain, and the United States in a peacetime alliance that

FIGURE 2-1   Victorious Allied troops march through London. (*National Archives and Records Administration*)

would protect his country from the possibility of renewed German aggression.

Lloyd George started out as an advocate of a harsh peace, but by the time the conference opened, he had modified his approach. He became something of a mediator between the more extreme views of Wilson and Clemenceau and performed capably in this role. As he later commented, "I think I did as well as might be expected, seated as I was between Jesus Christ and Napoleon Bonaparte."

The Treaty of Versailles, which was the fruit of the Big Three's labors, was a compromise settlement. Both Wilson and Clemenceau yielded on many points to obtain what they considered essential. Wilson won approval for his League of Nations. Clemenceau gained restrictions on Germany that he considered necessary to safeguard France's security. Certainly the treaty was not nearly as severe as the peace that the Germans would have imposed had they won the war. The Treaty of Brest-Litovsk forced upon Russia in 1918 had been the first installment of that projected "peace of iron."

By comparison to Brest-Litovsk, the territorial provisions of the Versailles treaty were, for the most part, fair. As everyone expected, France regained the provinces of Alsace and Lorraine. Belgium also received minor border changes in its favor, and a plebiscite resulted in Denmark gaining a slice of Danish-populated territory along Germany's northern border. In the case of the coal-rich Saar, the peacemakers provided a temporary compromise settlement. Clemenceau wanted to annex the area to France as compensation for the destruction of French coal mines during the war. But Wilson and Lloyd George withheld their approval. Instead, the three men agreed to place the area under the administration of the newly established League of Nations for 15 years and provided for French operation of the coal mines during this period. But the agreement stipulated that the population, which was solidly German, would have the right to determine the permanent fate of the Saar by plebiscite in 1935.

A much more important provision concerned the Rhineland. In keeping with French war aims, Clemenceau favored its separation from Germany and the establishment of an independent Rhenish state. Again, Wilson and Lloyd George refused and secured another compromise. Under this agreement, the Rhineland remained part of Germany, but the Allies were to maintain troops there for 15 years. When this period expired, they were to withdraw their forces, and the entire area was to remain permanently demilitarized, along with a 50-kilometer-wide strip on the Rhine's east bank. The Big Three hoped that this solution would provide a buffer area that would shield France and Belgium from a possible German invasion. To reconcile Clemenceau to this compromise, Wilson and Lloyd George made a remarkable commitment to safeguard French security. If Germany attacked France, this "guarantee treaty" bound the United States and Britain to support the French militarily. It represented a significant departure from the traditional peacetime policies of both countries.

But by far the most extensive and controversial territorial changes took place in the east. In keeping with Polish national aspirations and Wilson's Fourteen Points, the Big Three agreed that Germany must surrender a substantial amount of territory to the revived state of Poland. This included the province and city of Posen (Poznan in Polish) and, most important, a strip of land that linked the major portion of the new country with the Baltic Sea to the north. Without this "Polish corridor," Poland would be a landlocked state, and its only access to the sea would be through Germany. Unfortunately, the corridor also divided the bulk of Germany from the province of East Prussia, which was certain to anger the Germans. This territory contained a majority of Poles, although large German minorities were present as well. Farther south, the industrial area of Upper Silesia also proved troublesome. Again, the population was mixed, and the Big Three ordered a plebiscite, which resulted in less than half the disputed area going to Poland.

Wilson, Clemenceau, and Lloyd George found it far less easy to justify the detachment of the large city of Danzig from Germany. Danzig's population was German, but since it was the only major port in the vicinity of the Polish corridor, the Poles coveted its harbor facilities. Another compromise provided a solution of sorts. Danzig and the surrounding area became a free state under League of Nations supervision, but Poland received the right to unrestricted use of the port.

Separation of the smaller port of Memel in extreme northeastern East Prussia also proved difficult to justify. Memel, like Danzig, was a German city, but the border strip extending to the south contained a predominantly Lithuanian population. Again, the treaty placed the entire area under League administration. But the new state of Lithuania, small though it was, took advantage of Germany's weakness to seize Memel in 1921.

The treaty also provided for the total dismantling of Germany's overseas empire and the distribution of its colonies to various Allied powers as "mandated territories" under League of Nations supervision. In theory, the occupying powers were to prepare their mandates for eventual independence. But in practice, they governed most of them as colonies. Britain and France were the principal beneficiaries in Africa, while Japan gained Germany's enclaves along the coast of China as well as the Marshall, Caroline, and Mariana island chains in the Pacific. These islands were to become important Japanese bases during World War II.

Territorial Settlements in Europe, 1919 - 1926

Areas lost:
- by Germany
- by Austria-Hungary
- by Russia
- by Bulgaria

········· Boundaries of 1914   ——— Boundaries of 1926

Demilitarized areas (Rhineland, the Straits)

Allied Occupation Zone (Rhineland)

Territorial Settlements in Europe, 1919–26

France, of course, was determined to weaken Germany's ability to make war. The Allies agreed to limit the German army to a volunteer force of only 100,000 men and prohibited the existence of any kind of reserve. Tanks, heavy artillery, and other offensive weapons were banned. The Big Three also ordered the dissolution of the general staff, the war academy, and the cadet schools, which they considered breeding grounds for Prussian militarism. The German navy received bad news, too. It was to consist of only six warships, none of which was to be over 10,000 tons, and there were to be no submarines. Finally, the treaty prohibited Germany from maintaining a military air force.

To compensate Allied powers for damages inflicted by German forces during the war, the treaty provided that Germany pay reparations. This

FIGURE 2-2   The Big Four at the Paris Peace Conference. From the left: Vittorio Orlando (Italy), David Lloyd George (Britain), Georges Clemenceau (France), Woodrow Wilson (U.S.). (*National Archives and Records Administration*)

was not unusual. Germany had imposed a heavy war indemnity on France after the Franco-Prussian War and on Russia in the Treaty of Brest-Litovsk. Clemenceau and Lloyd George originally asked that, in addition to paying for civilian damages, reparations cover all Allied costs in fighting the war. Wilson blocked this proposal as much too extreme but did allow inclusion of the cost of war pensions for Allied soldiers. At the same time, he renounced any American claim to reparations. The peace conference did not establish the final amount.

Instead, the Big Three appointed a commission to study the problem and set the total. Germany was to pay $5 billion in cash and commodities during the interim period. The Reparations Commission announced the final bill in May 1921 as $33 billion in gold. It set annual payments of about $500 million for 66 years. American experts considered the burden to be considerably beyond Germany's ability to pay. The great British economist John Maynard Keynes agreed and attacked it in the most scathing terms, predicting that it would unhinge the postwar economy. The Germans were even more critical. Although, in proportion to values at the time, the amount was

equivalent to the indemnity imposed on France in 1871, they greeted the announcement with a wave of protest.

In an effort to justify reparations, the Allied leaders inserted a clause in the treaty that became known as the "war guilt" clause, and the Germans found it highly unfair. It did not actually contain the term *guilt* or specifically blame the Central Powers for starting the war. But it did charge them with responsibility for the "loss and damage" suffered by the Allies and referred to "the aggression" of Germany and its partners. The Germans interpreted this to mean guilt.

In addition to the German settlement, the treaty contained the covenant that established the League of Nations. The covenant created a League assembly to which every member nation would belong. The assembly had the right to consider all issues, but the actual decision-making power, in most cases, lay with the League council. The council would include five permanent members—Britain, France, Italy, the United States, and Japan—as well as four nonpermanent members that the assembly would select for limited terms.

The covenant declared that members must submit all disputes for investigation, arbitration, and settlement. If a member ignored this obligation and went to war, the League could take action against the aggressor power. But the question of what this would entail proved difficult. Clemenceau insisted that the only way to secure meaningful collective security was the creation of an international army that could enforce League decisions. But Wilson and Lloyd George refused to agree to such a far-reaching commitment. Ultimately, the only coercive power that the League possessed was the authority to impose economic sanctions. This involved cutting off trade between League members and the aggressor power. The Big Three refused to allow either Germany or Russia to join the organization, a decision which undermined the validity of the League.

Despite Wilson's dream, the United States also did not become a member of the League. This was due to a quarrel between the president and Republican leaders in the Senate who refused to accept the League without modifications that they considered necessary to safeguard American sovereignty. But Wilson refused to compromise, and the Treaty of Versailles failed to obtain the two-thirds majority necessary for ratification. The Senate finally passed a resolution in 1921 accepting all provisions of the treaty except those establishing the League.

The British had never shared Wilson's enthusiasm about the League and now saw considerably less reason for optimism. The French had been even more skeptical of the League and viewed America's withdrawal from Wilson's commitment with alarm. Of far greater concern to them, however, was the failure of the Senate to act on the guarantee treaty, which would have provided for Anglo-American support for France if attacked by Germany. Britain subsequently used the American failure to act as grounds for abandoning its own commitment.

Other Peace Treaties

Two other treaties recognized that Austria-Hungary had ceased to exist and that a number of new countries had come into being in Central Europe. Even the Austrians and Hungarians had severed the connection between themselves and created separate states. This necessitated individual agreements—the Treaty of St. Germain with Austria and the Treaty of Trianon with Hungary.

The disintegration of Austria-Hungary led to the formation of two other new countries—Czechoslovakia and the Kingdom of Serbs, Croats, and Slovenes, which later became Yugoslavia. All of Czechoslovakia's territory had formerly been part of Austria-Hungary. Yugoslavia consisted of a merger of prewar Serbia and Montenegro with the portions of Austria-Hungary that had contained Serbs, Croats, and Slovenes.

Czechoslovakia based its independence on a union of the Czechs, who lived in the western provinces of Bohemia and Moravia, and the Slovaks, who inhabited the eastern area of Slovakia. Although the two groups were related Slavic peoples, the Czechs were considerably more numerous and more advanced politically and economically. They played the predominant role in the new state. The country also included substantial German, Hungarian, and Ruthenian minorities. The Germans were the largest and most important of these, numbering over 3 million. The bulk of them resided in the frontier areas of Bohemia and Moravia. This border region came to be known as the Sudetenland.

The Serbs, Croats, and Slovenes of Yugoslavia also were related Slavic peoples. But the Serbs outnumbered the others and had previous experience governing Serbia. They dominated the new state from the start, much to the chagrin of the Croats, the second largest group, who considered themselves culturally superior to the Serbs. A religious difference also increased antagonism between the two peoples. The Serbs were predominantly Orthodox, while the Croats were Catholic.

Another national group, the Poles in Galicia, the extreme northeastern portion of Austria-Hungary, joined their kinsmen in territories formerly under German and Russian domination to create the independent state of Poland. Unfortunately, eastern Galicia contained a majority of Ruthenians, who now found themselves under Polish rule. To the southeast, the Rumanians in the provinces of Transylvania and the Banat joined the prewar state of Rumania. But these areas also contained Hungarian and Yugoslav minorities. Finally, the Italians in the Trentino, Trieste, and Istria merged with Italy. Here, too, other nationalities were present—Germans in the southern Trentino, Slovenes in Trieste and Istria.

The creation or enlargement of all of these states posed major problems. Most of them were small multinational states and were not remotely strong enough to be great powers. Each of them also had internal problems. As a result of these factors much of central Europe became a "power vacuum." This posed the danger that at some time in the future stronger outside nations would attempt to move into the area and fill the vacuum. Finally, the small countries engaged in a myriad of border disputes with their neighbors. The peacemakers established commissions to help adjust borders as much as possible in keeping with national aspirations. But this proved a formidable task due to the mixed population patterns of the region, and in some cases, countries would not be economically or strategically viable if they did not include territories inhabited by minorities.

The Sudetenland, much of which contained a predominantly German population, provided the most notable example of this. It was vital to Czechoslovakia because the northern and western portions contained important industries and natural resources. Much of it also contained hilly and heavily wooded terrain that served as an easily defensible border. In view of these factors, Wilson, Clemenceau, and Lloyd George agreed that the Sudetenland must go to Czechoslovakia rather than to Austria or Germany. The Big Three also violated the principle of national self-determination in regard to Austria. Many Austrians doubted that their severely truncated state would prove economically viable and asked that they be allowed to merge with their fellow Germans across the border. Allied leaders rejected this request because they opposed any increase in Germany's size. Both decisions held the potential for trouble. By the late 1930s, most of the Sudeten Germans were unreconciled to their position as citizens of Czechoslovakia, and many Austrians continued to favor union with Germany.

The Paris Peace Conference played only a minor role in the settlement for Eastern Europe. With its defeat at the hands of the Allies, Germany had to relinquish control over the territories it had wrested from Russia at Brest-Litovsk. Since the Russian civil war prevented the Bolshevik government from retaking these areas, various national groups established independent states. These included Finland in the far north and three small countries along the shore of the Baltic—Estonia, Latvia, and Lithuania. The region inhabited by Poles became a part of the new Poland, and the people of the Ukraine established still another new state. Finally, Rumania annexed Bessarabia, an area of mixed Rumanian and Ukrainian population.

In most cases, the peacemakers took no action in regard to these territories other than to recognize their independence. But the British foreign secretary, Lord Curzon, did propose an eastern border for Poland that roughly followed the linguistic division between Poles to the west and Belorussians and Ruthenians to the east. The Poles were not at all interested in the "Curzon line" and demanded restoration of their eighteenth-century boundary. This would have included most of the Ukraine as well as Belorussia just to the north. They went to war to enforce this claim in 1920 but ultimately had to settle for a line about 150 miles east of the Curzon line.

The Big Three were pleased by the changes in Eastern Europe, because the new nations were all anti-Russian and anti-Communist. It became customary to refer to this entire tier of countries as the *cordon sanitaire*, a barrier that helped sanitize the West from the spread of communism. But it was a weak barrier. None of the new states was strong, and all of them feared the revival of Germany and Russia, both of which dreamed of revising the Eastern European settlement. One of the fledgling countries, the Ukraine, failed to maintain its independence for long. By 1920, the Russian government had reasserted its control over Ukrainian territory.

Two additional treaties dealt with the minor members of the Central Powers—the Treaty of Neuilly with Bulgaria and the Treaty of Sèvres with Turkey. The Bulgars lost a strip of territory along the coast of the Aegean Sea to Greece and two small border areas to Yugoslavia. The Allies forced Turkey to relinquish all of its remaining Balkan territory to Greece with the exception of the great city of Constantinople (soon to be renamed Istanbul). Greece also gained the right to administer a substantial amount of territory on

Turkey's Asian coastline. Although there were Greeks in this area, the majority of the population was Turkish. The treaty also took away all of Turkey's Arab-inhabited lands. Only Saudi Arabia gained independence; France received Syria and Lebanon, and Britain won Palestine, Transjordan, and Iraq, all as mandates.

Loss of territory to the Greeks was too much for Turkish nationalists. General Mustapha Kemal carried out a coup, overthrew the decrepit government of the sultan, and established a republic. Turkish troops soon began to drive the Greeks out of their Asian foothold. Stability did not return to the area until the powers reached another agreement in 1923, the Treaty of Lausanne, which deprived the Greeks of most of their original gains. It also prepared the way for a massive deportation of the Greek population from Asia Minor to Greece and the Turkish minority from Greece to Turkey.

Reactions to the Treaties

Although Wilson, Clemenceau, and Lloyd George were all more or less satisfied with the Peace of Paris, not everyone agreed with them. Germany's new democratic government only accepted the Treaty of Versailles because it had no alternative. Germans in general, many of whom had favored extensive territorial and economic gains for their own country, considered the treaty to be an outrageously unfair and humiliating dictated peace. They believed Germany had entered the war to defend itself from the encircling Allied powers. They also found it difficult to accept that Germany had really suffered defeat. Allied troops had not reached the German border before the conflict ended. There were few signs of destruction in Germany. The armistice had provided for Allied occupation of the Rhineland and a few bridgeheads on the Rhine's east bank, but most of the country remained unoccupied.

Indeed, the story was already circulating that the German army had not actually been beaten. According to this account, the new republic had betrayed the army by hastily accepting the armistice. This "stab in the back" legend was to plague the republic throughout its existence and contributed to the German refusal to accept the treaty as final. Ironically, the republic's first

chancellor, Friedrich Ebert, unwittingly provided impetus to the legend when he greeted German troops arriving back in Berlin in November 1918 with the words, "As you return unconquered from the field of battle, I salute you."

Most Germans considered the "war guilt" clause to be a gross distortion of reality. Their anger over this made them highly resentful of the large reparations bill. The Germans also found the disarmament provisions unfair and degrading to a great power, especially one in which the army had enjoyed such enormous prestige. They argued that only if the Allies undertook disarmament themselves could they justify the restrictions they had placed on Germany's armed forces.

Germans also detested the territorial changes, especially the loss of Danzig and the lands to Poland as well as the separation of East Prussia from the rest of Germany due to the Polish acquisition of the Polish Corridor. They looked forward to the day when their country could revise these provisions. Both the refusal of the Allies to allow the union of Austria with Germany and the incorporation of the Sudetenland into Czechoslovakia struck the Germans as hypocritical. It seemed to them that the peacemakers were interested in the principle of self-determination only if they could use it against the Germans.

In general, the abrupt end to the war, hatred of the treaty, and the stigma of the "stab in the back" legend helped create a depressing malaise among the German people that contrasted dramatically with the apparent solidarity and confidence with which many of them had greeted the outbreak of war in 1914. It did not bode well for the future of Germany or Europe.

To the British, it also appeared that the treaty was too harsh. Many agreed with Keynes that Germany was incapable of paying the reparations bill. They came to view the French as vindictive. Opinion also turned against the prewar connection with France, which many believed had dragged Britain into the conflict at the cost of 750,000 dead and the undermining of the country's economic stability. The British were determined to avoid any kind of arrangement in the future that might have the same effect and preferred a policy aimed at reconciliation with Germany.

The war also resulted in greater independence for territories of the British Empire that had become self-governing dominions during the late nineteenth and early twentieth centuries. Canada, Australia, New Zealand, and the Union of South Africa had all gained control of their own domestic affairs before the war. But they had still been technically dependent on Britain in foreign affairs. All of them had joined Britain in the conflict and had suffered heavy casualties. As a reward for their services, they had each received separate representation at the peace conference as well as in the League of Nations. The dominions, henceforth, were virtually independent. This fact played a prominent role in the transformation of the empire into the Commonwealth of Nations during the postwar period and meant that Britain could not be certain of the support of the dominions in case of another war. British awareness of this changed relationship furthered the pursuit of a conciliatory policy toward Germany.

The debilitating effects of the war had also made Britain less certain of its hold over parts of the empire that had not gained the right of self-government. In some of them, most notably India, nationalist movements favored independence. This, too, contributed to the cautious British policy in Europe.

In America there appeared to be general acceptance of the treaty at first, but enthusiasm soon waned. Many became disillusioned, not only with the peace settlement but also with the war itself. To them it seemed that Britain and France had lured the United States into a typical European power struggle. It appeared that despite Wilson's idealistic rhetoric about a peace of reconciliation, the settlement represented a cynical division of spoils. With the Senate's refusal to approve entry into the League of Nations, America returned to its traditional policy of isolation from European political affairs. But it was never complete isolation. The United States continued to play an active role in efforts to solve the related economic problems of European war debts, reparations, and currency stabilization but remained totally opposed to participation in any collective security arrangements.

Despite criticism of their alleged vindictiveness from friend and foe alike, the French were not happy with the peace settlement either. France had survived, but the war had taken the

lives of 1,300,000 of the nation's soldiers, in proportion to population the heaviest loss suffered by any of the Great Powers. The northern provinces lay in desolation after four years of trench warfare and massive artillery barrages. And the war had left deep psychological wounds on the national spirit. The compromise peace had not brought France the security it had sought. To the French, the peace, far from being too harsh, was much too lenient.

Not surprisingly, the French feared a revival of German power and remained acutely concerned about their own security. Their wartime losses compounded the problem of a declining birth rate, which had been a source of worry even before the war. France's population in 1921 totaled only 39 million compared to Germany's 60 million. France also suffered from deep divisions between social classes, which were reflected in the republican political system. The Third Republic had come into existence in 1870 as a result of the French defeat in the Franco-Prussian War. Instead of a system of two major political parties, such as characterized both Britain and the United States, the Third Republic had developed a multiparty system. This made the French cabinet dependent on maintaining the support of a majority coalition of parties in parliament. Since these coalitions usually did not hold together for long, cabinets also did not remain in power for long. As a result, the system became chronically unstable, making it extremely difficult to deal with controversial issues.

The failure to achieve an alliance with Britain and the United States led the French to turn to lesser countries for help. During the early 1920s, they secured defensive military alliances with Belgium, Poland, and Czechoslovakia, all of whom shared France's dread of a revived Germany. They also made agreements with Rumania and Yugoslavia, which bound the partners to consult in case of a threat to their independence. But this system of collective security was a poor substitute for the wartime relationship between France, Britain, and America. As a result, France assumed primary responsibility for enforcing the peace settlement. It soon proved to be a task beyond the nation's capabilities.

Italy also bitterly assailed its wartime Allies for disavowing their promises regarding Italian compensation in the Adriatic, the Middle East, and Africa. A chorus of nationalistic disapproval forced Orlando out of office, and the desire to revise the peace settlement remained strong.

Russia, only marginally affected by the Paris peace settlement, harbored resentment over the territorial losses that had originated with the Treaty of Brest-Litovsk. But even when the civil war ended, the Russians were not in a position to do much about these changes. Nevertheless, like Germany and Italy, Russia hoped to revise this settlement sometime in the future. The Bolshevik government retained a deep distrust of the Western Powers, which had recognized the new countries of Eastern Europe. It also did not forget the Allied intervention in the civil war.

Economic Repercussions

European recovery from World War I proved elusive during the 1920s. The continent's economy was far from healthy. The conflict had disrupted the old prewar patterns of trade, and European countries encountered difficulty regaining their former shares of the world market. To compound their problems, the United States raised tariffs on imported goods, making it more difficult for the debtor nations of Europe to sell products in the American market. They retaliated by increasing import duties to protect their own domestic industries from foreign competition. This mutual protectionist approach increased the strain on the international economy.

With the exception of Britain, the belligerent countries had financed their war efforts in large part by printing paper money that did not have gold backing. This led to serious inflation while the war was in progress, but tighter government controls managed to keep it within reason. In the postwar years, however, the inflationary spiral increased. By 1926, the French franc had fallen to 10 percent of its prewar value. In Germany, the situation was far worse. Before the war, 4.2 German marks possessed a value equivalent to 1 U.S. dollar. By January 1923, it had skidded to 18,000 to the dollar. And this was only the beginning of an even more disastrous slide.

The related problems of war debts and reparations added to the economic dilemma. The United States had refused a British and French request for a temporary suspension of war debt payments during the peace conference. But America actually demanded little more than token payments during the 1920s. The problem of reparations was more serious. The French were desirous of securing early and regular payment of reparations to aid them in rebuilding their devastated areas. But they obtained relatively little. At first, they received payment in commodities such as coal and timber, but the German government did all it could to avoid meeting its obligation. Although the French protested, the British from the start sympathized with Germany and urged France to make concessions. The British hoped that a reduction of reparations payments would aid the German economy and stimulate trade. Finally, in late 1922, Germany defaulted on its obligation altogether.

In early 1923, French Premier Raymond Poincaré responded vigorously to this action. His government ordered troops into the Ruhr, Germany's most important industrial area, just to the east of the Rhineland. The French hoped to force German compliance on reparations and, in the meantime, planned to operate the mines and railroads of the Ruhr for their own use. But German workers resorted to strikes and delaying actions. The German government subsidized the workers, and the French accomplished little. This Ruhr crisis lasted for almost a year while Germany's inflation soared out of control. By November, the mark's value had fallen to the amazing figure of 4.2 trillion to the dollar. Salaries, savings, pensions, and insurance became worthless while debtors easily paid off loans and merchandise purchased on the installment plan.

Germany had no choice but to abandon its policy of promoting passive resistance, and the French agreed to submit the whole question to an international commission, chaired by the American banker Charles Dawes. In April 1924, the Dawes Commission agreed that reparations payments should be based on Germany's "index of prosperity." This had the effect of reducing payments by half with the prospect for gradual increases in the future. The Dawes plan also urged an international loan to Germany to help stabilize the currency and promote prosperity. American financiers provided more than half of the subsequent loan, which began a pattern of

U.S. financial assistance to Germany during the next five years.

This influx of foreign capital contributed to a remarkable economic recovery in Germany. German leaders also introduced a new currency based officially on gold, which halted the inflation. In 1929, another committee of international financial experts, headed by the American Owen Young, scaled down the total German reparations bill to a mere $9 billion. But Germany never came close to paying this amount because the nation soon felt the impact of a far worse economic catastrophe—the Great Depression. In reality, during the 1920s the United States and, to a lesser degree, the former European Allies provided more than twice as much money to Germany's recovery than Germany paid in reparations.

Political Realignments

The failure of the Ruhr occupation to secure German compliance on reparations led to France's realization that it could not enforce the Paris peace settlement alone. So France turned instead to cultivating better relations with Germany. Foreign Minister Aristide Briand was the architect of this policy. Germany's foreign minister, Gustav Stresemann, also followed a friendlier approach to France, hoping to gain a revision of the peace settlement in the process. The chief result of their efforts was yet another treaty in 1925, negotiated in the Swiss resort town of Locarno. The Treaty of Locarno was a curious document. It merely reaffirmed the provisions of the Versailles settlement that applied to Germany's western boundaries as well as the future demilitarization of the Rhineland. But the treaty was silent on the question of Germany's eastern borders, which, in effect, indicated that Germany did not consider them permanent.

During the next few years, observers spoke of a "spirit of Locarno," which supposedly represented the beginning of a new, more peaceful era in European affairs. Other agreements followed. In 1926, Germany entered the League of Nations. In 1928, American Secretary of State Frank Kellogg and Briand drafted a treaty that renounced war as an instrument of national policy. Sixty-five nations, including Germany, eventually signed the Kellogg-Briand Pact. Unfortunately

it provided no means of enforcement. Finally, the Young Committee, in addition to lowering Germany's reparations bill, also provided for the end of the Rhineland occupation in 1930, five years ahead of schedule.

Meanwhile, throughout the 1920s, Germany had been violating the disarmament provisions of the peace settlement. General Hans von Seeckt, who served as chief of the army command from 1920 to 1926, led the way. Seeckt maintained the outlawed general staff in existence by dividing its functions among various governmental bodies. He also created a reserve of 70,000 men that he disguised as a special labor force and later as a security organization. Seeckt made an agreement with the Krupp munitions firm to provide designs for artillery as well as working models in the company's affiliated plants in Sweden. Other Krupp affiliates in Spain and the Netherlands produced submarine models and torpedoes.

Germany also cultivated closer relations with Russia in the early postwar period. Both countries hoped to escape from their diplomatic isolation. Seeckt started this process by making a secret agreement with the Russian general staff in 1921. It granted the German army permission to establish illegal tank and artillery units as well as aviation schools on Russian soil. Germany also gained the right to manufacture prototypes of aircraft, tanks, and artillery and to experiment with poison gas. Seeckt reciprocated by training Russian soldiers and providing a financial subsidy. In 1922, the two governments startled the world by signing a treaty of friendship in the Italian city of Rapallo. This agreement provided mutual diplomatic recognition and renunciation of war claims. Neither side really trusted the other, but both believed that they would benefit from the new relationship.

The Western Powers also came to the conclusion that their attempt to keep Russia in isolation was self-defeating. Although they feared the spread of communism, they also coveted the Russian market as an outlet for their hard-pressed economies. Britain took the initiative in 1921 by signing an agreement that reestablished diplomatic relations and trade between the two powers. Other Western countries followed a similar policy during the next few years. But despite these efforts, no real friendship blossomed, and distrust continued.

The Rise of Japan

The United States was not the only non-European power to benefit from World War I. Japan, the sole industrialized country in East Asia, had also taken advantage of the inability of European powers to supply their former markets. Japan could not match American commercial expansion because of its less well developed industry, but the island nation did improve its competitive position significantly. The Japanese also gained strategically important territories on China's coast and in the Pacific at Germany's expense.

When the war ended, few obstacles seemed to prevent still greater Japanese expansion. Russia, a longtime rival for influence in China, suffered from the accumulated effects of World War I, the revolution, and the civil war. Britain and France possessed colonies in East Asia along with economic and political interests in China. But they, too, focused their attention on recovery and the multitude of European problems that followed the war. The United States, although deeply interested in trade with China, was far away. In fact, much of Japan's relative importance was due to the nation's remoteness from other major powers.

Although some Japanese leaders looked longingly on Russia's East Asian territories, Japan's primary interest lay in China. Inferior in size only to Russia and Canada, China possessed the world's largest population as well as vast natural resources. But it had long suffered from political weakness and economic backwardness. During the nineteenth century, China fell prey to various Western powers, which forced the Chinese government to grant concessions. These included economic privileges and the right of extraterritoriality for European residents in China. This right made them immune from Chinese law and subject only to the legal jurisdiction of their respective countries. Some of the European powers also leased ports along the Chinese coast.

When Japan experienced the startling transformation to a major world power in the late nineteenth century, it, too, began to encroach on China, gaining economic concessions and extraterritoriality for Japanese citizens. As a result of victory over China in the Sino-Japanese War of 1894–95, Japan obtained control of the island of Formosa (Taiwan), strategically located off the Chinese mainland. In the aftermath of this conflict, the Japanese competed with Russia for political and economic influence in Korea and the adjoining Chinese province of Manchuria.

This rivalry led to tension between the two powers and played an important role in Japan's decision to sign a defensive military alliance with Britain in 1902. At that time Britain had not yet entered into the Triple Entente with France and Russia and was concerned about Russian expansion in East Asia. Under the terms of the Anglo-Japanese alliance, Britain would remain neutral if Japan were attacked by another power and would actually aid the Japanese if they fell victim to aggression by two powers. This agreement heralded the arrival of Japan as a major factor in world power politics and encouraged Tokyo to pursue its ambitions in Manchuria and Korea despite Russian opposition. Relations between the two powers steadily deteriorated and culminated in the Russo-Japanese War of 1904–05. Japanese forces defeated the Russians on land and sea. In the peace that followed, Japan replaced Russia as the predominant power in both Manchuria and Korea and took over Russian leases on the ports of Dairen (Talien) and Port Arthur (Lüshun). Japan annexed Korea in 1910.

Early in World War II Japan attempted to capitalize on China's internal weakness and Western preoccupation with the European conflict to pressure the Chinese to grant a number of concessions known as the 21 Demands. These gave the Japanese a privileged economic position in China, although they were moderated to some extent in the face of American opposition.

At the Paris Peace Conference, Japan vigorously pushed for retention of China's Shantung peninsula, which it had taken from Germany during the war. To accomplish this, it needed to overcome China's insistence that it be returned to its complete sovereignty. Japan also set out to gain inclusion of a clause proclaiming racial equality in the Covenant of the League of Nations. The latter reflected Japanese concern over American discrimination against immigrants from Japan. Although the clause proposal gained a majority of the votes in the committee considering it, President Wilson, who served as its chairman, ruled that passage required a unanimous vote. In doing so, he bowed to British and especially Australian opposition.

Outraged by this humiliating defeat, the Japanese insisted on having their way on Shantung and threatened to pull out of the conference unless this were granted. In the end, they won out over violent Chinese protests and Wilson's principle of self-determination.

The Question of China

Japanese ambitions encountered opposition from a Chinese nationalist movement that had overthrown the decadent Manchu dynasty in 1911 and established a republic. But the revolution did not lead to Chinese unity or greater freedom from foreign exploitation. Rival governments came into being in the north and south and vied for authority, while warlords, who had little or no allegiance to either regime, dominated many Chinese provinces. It was not until 1928 that the southern regime, dominated by the Kuomintang party, emerged triumphant in this struggle. Led by Chiang Kai-shek, a skillful and ruthless young general and politician, the Kuomintang officially ruled most of China, but its actual control was tenuous.

The Kuomintang regime was a corrupt military dictatorship that rested on a narrow base of support among the landowning peasantry and wealthy banking and commercial interests. Landless agricultural workers, who comprised the country's largest social class and had long been subject to the merciless exploitation of the landlords, felt little allegiance to the government. Many of them found more in common with the Chinese Communist party. The Communists, under the leadership of the determined and brilliant Mao Tse-tung (Mao Zedong), had cooperated with the Kuomintang until Chiang tried to crush them in 1927. Although some of them fell victim to this purge, Mao and many others escaped to Kiangsi province in southeastern China, where they established a Soviet-style regime in defiance of the Kuomintang.

Chiang and the Kuomintang demanded foreign recognition of China's full sovereignty as well as an end to the privileges and immunities enjoyed by other powers. They also attacked the Treaty of Versailles' assignment of Germany's possessions in China to Japan. Chiang particularly hoped to tighten his authority in the northeastern province of Manchuria, where the warlord Chang

Hsueh-liang had recognized his sovereignty. But the Japanese viewed this as a direct threat to their own strong economic and political influence in Manchuria.

Western powers shared Japan's fears over China's revisionist policy. Britain grew especially concerned because, along with Japan, Britain had the largest investments in China and the most to lose from the establishment of complete Chinese sovereignty. The United States was also deeply interested in China, but for reasons that were less well grounded than those of Britain and Japan. Although its trade with China had never been extensive, the seemingly unlimited potential of the Chinese market exerted a powerful attraction. America opposed the exploitation that other powers pursued in China and remained faithful to the Open Door policy proclaimed at the turn of the century. This doctrine sought to maintain equal access to the Chinese market for all nations while maintaining China's sovereignty and territorial integrity. But America always emphasized the free trade aspects of the policy rather than defense of China's sovereignty.

Seeking Balance between East and West

When World War I ended, Japan and Britain were still linked by the alliance that they had negotiated in 1902. Originally intended to resist Russian encroachment on Manchuria, the pact had also facilitated British and Japanese penetration of China. The United States disliked this agreement and opposed its renewal in 1921. America preferred multinational agreements that would maintain existing foreign interests in East Asia while upholding China's sovereignty and equal access to the Chinese market for all powers. British leaders especially desired to remain on good terms with America in the uncertain aftermath of World War I. Canada also strongly favored such an Anglo-American relationship and pressured Britain to drop the Japanese alliance.

But American leaders were also concerned about the growth of Japanese naval power. Although Japan's navy ranked third behind those of Britain and the United States, all of it operated in East Asian and Pacific waters. The American fleet, on the other hand, divided its attention between the Pacific and the Atlantic, as did Britain's Royal Navy, which also had obligations in the Mediterranean and the Indian Ocean. American proponents of a huge two-ocean navy demanded a great increase in battleship strength, and 15 new capital ships were already under construction. This program alarmed the Japanese, who responded by laying down the keels of eight powerful battleships. Many American leaders feared the economic and political consequences of a naval race and urged an agreement that would prevent this. Britain was still the world's leading naval power, but most of its battleships were aging. Entering into an ambitious new naval building program would place a tremendous burden on the already ailing British economy.

Mutual concern over the prospect of a ruinously expensive naval race led to the decision to convene a conference in Washington to seek limitation of battleship strength. But the Washington conference of 1921–22 also considered the questions of the Anglo-Japanese alliance and the future of China. Representatives of the United States, Britain, Japan, France, Italy, and several lesser powers attended the conference, which resulted in three treaties. The first of these, a naval agreement, placed limitations on battleships and battle cruisers. It provided for a ratio of strength of 5 to 5 to 3 to 1.75 to 1.75 for the United States, Britain, Japan, France, and Italy, respectively. This ratio reflected the size of the navies at that time. The treaty also placed limitations on total tonnage of aircraft carriers but not of cruisers, destroyers, or submarines.

In the second agreement, the Four-Power Treaty, the United States, Britain, Japan, and France vowed to respect each other's possessions in the Pacific and refer disputes to mediation. This arrangement replaced the Anglo-Japanese alliance. All the countries represented at the conference signed the final pact, the Nine-Power Treaty. This document upheld China's sovereignty and territorial integrity while recognizing the right of all nations to equal economic opportunity in the Chinese market. Britain and Japan also agreed to return their possessions on the Shantung Peninsula to Chinese control. The treaty represented formal acceptance of the Open Door policy, and the agreement to restore Shantung to Chinese sovereignty was clearly a hopeful sign.

The naval limitation treaty made sense at the time and prevented a capital ship construction race during the 1920s. But it met with bitter criticism from both U.S. and Japanese naval leaders. Japanese civilian nationalists also reacted angrily to the naval restrictions. One of them went so far as to assassinate Premier Takashi Hara who had diligently tried to enforce them. As for Britain, acceptance of parity in capital ships with the United States ended a long tradition of supremacy on the high seas, a clear indication of Britain's diminished power.

Soon after the furor over the naval limitations, a much more widespread wave of anger swept over Japan as a result of passage of the U.S. Immigration Act of 1924. Among other things, this act totally barred Japanese immigration into America. The Japanese people in general viewed it as a deliberate insult, and the government declared the date the legislation took effect to be a national day of humiliation.

Ironically, the failure of the naval treaty to agree on a formula for limiting cruiser construction opened the way for the major powers to build cruisers in large numbers. This in turn led to attempts to halt the new race, culminating in the London Naval Treaty of 1930. In this understanding, the United States, Britain, and Japan agreed to limit construction of both cruisers and destroyers. Again this agreement did not set well with many Japanese naval leaders and civilian nationalists. This time the hostility led to the assassination of Premier Yuko Hamaguchi whose government had accepted the new limitations.

A Gloomy Outlook

Despite the good intentions and positive aspects of the settlement regarding China, the long-term outlook was not promising. China remained unstable and victim to internal conflict, while rival Chinese and Japanese ambitions in Manchuria clearly posed the danger of a collision.

To be sure the late 1920s had witnessed other promising developments. Europe's economy, though far from restored to health, had at least rallied encouragingly from the dark days of the immediate postwar era. The French and Germans had abandoned their mutual hostility in favor of a policy of cooperation. In the process, Germany had escaped from its role as an outcast and had become a member of the League of Nations. The League itself, while still not tested by a major crisis, had at least won general acceptance. And despite the United States' failure to join the League, the Americans had shown their willingness to work with European countries on economic problems. The early fears of a spread of communism over the continent had proved unfounded, and the Soviet Union concentrated on internal problems. In East Asia, most of China was at least nominally under one government.

But the partial economic recovery and political reconciliation of Europe were extremely fragile, as was the great power cooperation and relative tranquility in East Asia. Gloom, anxiety, and a loss of faith in the long cherished idea of progress permeated the philosophical, literary, and artistic works of the period and cast doubt on the future of humanity. There was good reason for this pessimism. Economic catastrophe and a great wave of political extremism lay just ahead. Another and even greater war would not be far behind.

CHAPTER THREE

The Rise of the Dictators

In the aftermath of World War I, many observers believed that a new age of democratic government had dawned. Wilson had proclaimed that the war's great aim was to "make the world safe for democracy," and the democratic Western Allies had emerged victorious. All of the new states of Central and Eastern Europe became democracies. Even Germany, a former bastion of authoritarian rule, adopted this form of government. In East Asia, Japan also appeared to be making the transition to democracy. Although the Bolsheviks had created a dictatorship in Russia, they supposedly intended it to be temporary, in keeping with Marxist doctrine. But during the 1920s the democratic flame began to flicker, and in the 1930s it threatened to die out almost completely. Instead of an age of democracy, the interwar years, to a large extent, became an era of dictatorship.

They also became an era of conflicting ideologies. Ideology played a vital role in all the major dictatorships that came into being in Europe during this period—communism in the Soviet Union, fascism in Italy, and Nazism in Germany. Belief in the necessity of territorial expansion formed a key aspect of fascism and especially Nazism. It also reflected the deep-seated desires of Benito Mussolini in Italy and Adolf Hitler in Germany. Both fascism and Nazism were also at odds with the democratic outlook of Britain, France, and the United States as well as the communist ideology of the Soviet Union. The ambitions of Hitler were virtually boundless, deeply influenced by his racial ideas, and more than any other factor were to lead Europe into World War II. Those of Mussolini were to lure him into ever closer relations with Hitler and ultimately into war on Germany's side.

The Marxist ideology of the Soviet regime called for the spread of communism throughout the world, but when Josef Stalin came to power he deferred this goal. He preferred to focus instead on consolidation of his personal dictatorship and a massive expansion of Soviet industry, although he hoped eventually to regain the territory lost in World War I, and perhaps to acquire more. His insistence on making the Soviet Union a great industrial power would pay handsome dividends during World War II.

In Japan, ideology played a lesser role. The militaristic circles that came to dominate the country remained essentially faithful to traditional Japanese conservative values, although they did champion the pan-Asian concept of a new East Asia Order. They hoped that this would rally the peoples of East Asia to Japan's side. In part, this approach reflected the belief of some that Japan must distance itself from Western influences, which they feared were deflecting the Japanese people from their cultural traditions. In practice, however, it came to represent a justification for Japanese expansion on the Asian continent.

The Emergence of Totalitarianism

The immediate postwar atmosphere did not prove conducive to the survival of democracy in many countries. None of the new nations had any experience with this type of government, and cleavages between social classes soon became reflected in multitudes of quarreling political parties. The new governments proved unable to fashion solutions to the problems that confronted them, including severe economic distress. Disillusionment over the war and the peace settlement also gripped defeated Germany, Austria, and Hungary, and even victorious Italy. After the brief interval of partial recovery in the late 1920s, the Great Depression plunged the continent once again into economic chaos. It also spawned a growing reaction against the democratic governments. By 1938, almost all of the hopeful fledgling democracies of Central and Eastern Europe had become dictatorships, and Japan had followed a similar course.

In three countries—the Soviet Union, Italy, and Germany—the dictatorial regimes became totalitarian. Although autocratic governments had been in existence for many centuries, totalitarianism was a development of the twentieth century. Totalitarian political systems were much more thoroughgoing in their efforts to control the individuals and groups that made up their populations than was the case with older forms of autocracy. In each of the three totalitarian states, the catalyst of the dictatorship was a political party that viewed itself as an elite group devoted to the commands of a single leader. The party also paid allegiance to an ideology that rejected much or all of the previous social and political systems and projected a utopian vision of the future. The leader became so central to the party and system that there soon developed a "cult of personality" that portrayed the leader as larger than life and the virtual embodiment of the nation.

Although none of the three parties originally had the backing of a majority of its people, after securing power each of them rapidly gained a large measure of popular support. To some extent, fear underlay this acceptance. Control of the army and the creation of a secret police force provided the bases for fear. Domination of the means of mass communication and the development of a sophisticated system of propaganda, which preached the glories of the party, the leader, and the nation, contributed to the growth of popular enthusiasm. Exploitation of the educational system to indoctrinate the young with the party ideology provided the basis for extending this support into the future.

Each of the totalitarian states also proclaimed the need for a centrally controlled and directed economy. But in reality, only the Communist regime in the Soviet Union provided a totally state-dominated economy. In both Italy and Germany, the dictatorships came to terms with the established capitalistic system, though subjecting it to a certain amount of governmental direction.

Popular disillusionment with the previous political systems and despair over economic conditions helped ease the way for the acquisition of power by the totalitarian parties. All of them promised revolutionary change and, in varying degrees, made good on their pledges.

Lenin and the Bolsheviks

Russia created the first totalitarian regime following the Bolshevik victory in the revolution. The Bolsheviks, though a small fraction of the population, gained control of the government because of their superior organization and Lenin's brilliant leadership.

Lenin believed strongly in a small, tightly organized party composed of professional revolutionaries. He remained faithful to the Marxist doctrine of revolution when many others were turning to a more moderate type of socialism that sought reforms by working through the established system. But he departed from Marx's belief that a revolution would only come in a highly industrialized country when conditions were favorable for success. Clearly, Russia's industrialization had not progressed to a point that would make it a candidate for revolution by this standard. Lenin considered it possible to speed up the process, using the party as the vanguard of the revolution and mobilizing the discontented groups in society.

When the Russian Revolution began in March 1917, Lenin was in exile in Switzerland. He returned to Russia in April. Lenin believed from the start that the provisional government was weak and that if the Bolsheviks gained control of the soviets, they could topple it from power. By the fall of 1917, it was clear to Lenin that the time to strike was at hand. The Bolsheviks followed their quick seizure of Petrograd with the capture of Moscow, and within a month most of the cities of European Russia were under their control. But once they had overthrown the provisional government, the Bolsheviks faced the immense problems of consolidating their power and restoring Russia to some semblance of order and economic well-being after the years of war and revolution. The outbreak of civil war in 1918 created still more chaos.

Soon after coming to power, Lenin tried to establish strong popular support for Bolshevik rule by holding elections for the constituent

FIGURE 3-1   Tsarist troops disperse demonstrators in Petrograd during the "July Days" of 1917. (*UPI/Corbis/Bettmann*)

assembly that the provisional government had promised. The elections proved a great disappointment to the Bolsheviks, who gained only 25 percent of the seats in the assembly. Lenin solved the problem by dissolving the assembly after its first meeting and creating a Bolshevik dictatorship. He and his comrades visualized a temporary dictatorship in keeping with Marxist doctrine. This regime would take over the means of production in the name of society as a whole and provide an equitable redistribution of wealth. It would also create a classless society in which all persons were equal and no one would prosper at the expense of others.

But the outbreak of civil war soon made the survival of the regime the first order of business, and for a time it appeared that the anti-Bolshevik (White) forces would actually win. At the low point of the Bolsheviks' fortunes, they controlled only the central portion of European Russia, including the cities of Petrograd and Moscow. (Lenin had moved the capital from Petrograd to Moscow early in 1918.) This desperate situation called for extreme measures. One of these involved the development of an effective military force to fight the White armies. Lenin's brilliant

colleague, Leon Trotsky, was the driving force in the development of the new Red Army. He provided both organizational and leadership ability, and utilized the talents of former tsarist officers and noncommissioned officers to train and direct the army.

The Bolsheviks benefited from a lack of unity among the Whites, who consisted of various groups with differing political views. Their military forces lacked coordination, and their generals frequently regarded one another as rivals.

Lenin and the Bolsheviks also faced a serious economic dilemma. The war had revealed the inadequacies of both Russian industry and the transportation system. With the coming of civil war, the situation deteriorated still more. The government had to provide weapons, equipment, food, and other supplies to the army while feeding the civilian population as well. To achieve this, the Bolsheviks resorted to emergency measures, which became known as "war communism." These included the forced requisition of grain, livestock, and other commodities from the peasants, who had taken over the holdings of the large landowners during the revolution, and the nationalization of industry. Although these actions contributed to victory and the salvation of the regime, they also caused much confusion and even more dissatisfaction. The peasants resented the forced requisitions, and many of them preferred to burn their crops and slaughter their livestock rather than allow them to fall into the hands of the government. Workers also protested the stringent production demands and regimentation that the government had imposed on them.

By the end of 1920, the Red Army had effectively defeated the Whites, but the economy was in deplorable condition. Widespread devastation, rampant inflation, and shortages of all kinds were the order of the day. The peasantry and workers were so hostile that another rebellion seemed highly possible. To add to the critical situation, the combination of shortages created by peasant resistance to the requisition policy and crop failures led to an appalling famine in 1921, which took the lives of 3 million people.

Lenin recognized that he must relax controls in an effort to gain the support of the peasants and workers. In 1921, he instituted the New Economic Policy (NEP), which eliminated forced requisitions and enabled the peasants to sell their surplus crops on the open market. Lenin retained government control of large-scale industry but allowed smaller operations to revert to private ownership. The NEP created a mixed system that included elements of both private enterprise and government control. But Lenin viewed the NEP as a stopgap measure. As he said at the time, "It is sometimes necessary to take one step backward in order to take two steps forward."

In 1923, the Bolsheviks reorganized the country as a federation of republics—the Union of Soviet Socialist Republics (USSR or Soviet Union). Each republic represented an area whose population consisted primarily of a specific ethnic group. This action recognized the fact that the country contained various nationalities, although the ethnic Russians were by far the most numerous. Their republic, the largest, included not only European Russia but most of Siberia as well and dominated the others.

The Bolsheviks established a hierarchical system of soviets ascending from rural and urban localities through the levels of the territories and provinces to that of the republic itself. Despite this elaborate government structure, real power lay with the party, which officially became the Communist party in 1918. It was the only political party, and Lenin still viewed it as an elite group. The party's organization was similar to that of the soviets, with local, territorial, provincial, and republican levels. At its summit was the Party Congress, which met in Moscow. The Congress selected a Central Committee, which included three smaller bodies, the Politburo, the Secretariat, and the Organizational Bureau. In reality, the Politburo was the governing body of the country. But the Secretariat, headed by a general secretary, was also important. The general secretary became increasingly powerful. The Politburo made the decisions, and they were carried out at each level of the Union and party hierarchies.

As early as December 1917, still another party organization came into operation—the secret police. Its duty was to hunt down and eliminate enemies of the party and the state, and it carried out this mission with enthusiasm and efficiency.

The Stalinist Era in the USSR

Lenin suffered a series of strokes, starting in May 1922, and died in January 1924. Long before his death, it became apparent that a power struggle was developing among Communist leaders for the right to succeed the architect of the Bolshevik dictatorship. The two principal figures were Trotsky and the general secretary of the party, Iosif Dzhugashvili, who had taken the name Stalin, derived from the Russian word for steel.

Stalin was born to peasant parents in the region of Georgia in the Caucasus Mountains. He had entered a seminary as a youth but soon turned to revolutionary socialism. Unlike Lenin and many other Bolshevik leaders, Stalin did not go into exile and, in fact, had never ventured out of Russia. He became involved in conspiratorial activity and in the process became an astute organizer. From an early age, he betrayed symptoms of ruthlessness, cruelty, and an excessive desire for power. Although overshadowed by Lenin, Trotsky, and others during the revolution, he emerged as a major figure in the civil war and its aftermath.

Trotsky and most other Soviet leaders were international in their outlook. They believed that the Bolshevik success in Russia would be followed by revolution in other parts of Europe. To promote this goal, they developed an organization that would coordinate Communist movements in other countries—the Communist International or Comintern. Stalin was much less dedicated to the exportation of revolution. He believed that the Communists had enough to do in Russia itself. Stalin not only headed the Secretariat as general secretary but led the Organizational Bureau as well, which gave him control over the party machinery and personnel. He also proved exceptionally skillful at political infighting and repeatedly outmaneuvered his rivals. By 1928 he had succeeded in purging all of them and had emerged as the undisputed leader of the party and the country.

Stalin now felt strong enough to launch a massive program to nationalize the economy and transform Russia into a first-class industrial power as quickly as possible. He decided to bring the entire economy under state control by nationalizing all industry and abolishing private ownership of land in favor of a system of collectivization. To accomplish this, he launched a series of five-year plans, the first of which went into operation in 1928. It set sharply increased production goals for both agriculture and industry.

In agriculture, peasants were required to merge their holdings in large collective farms that the state would supervise and provide with mechanized equipment. But the program soon encountered resistance from the kulaks, a class of peasants who had acquired large land holdings under the NEP. The kulaks burned their crops and slaughtered livestock. Stalin responded with ruthless measures. Secret police and army units intervened, killing large numbers of kulaks and rounding up many others for shipment to Siberia. Peasant resistance, coupled with a crop failure in 1932, led to another terrible famine in 1932–33. Although reliable statistics are not available, Stalin himself later admitted that 10 million persons died as a result of collectivization and famine. Contrary to Stalin's hopes, agricultural production did not reach the level of 1928 until as late as 1937. Stalin persisted in his program, however, and, by 1939, fully 95 percent of agricultural land had come under collectivization. But many peasants remained both unhappy and uncooperative, and production continued to fall short of his goals.

The First Five-Year Plan also emphasized the development of heavy industry—steel mills, power plants, chemical factories, and large-scale machinery. Although industrial output increased substantially, the concentration on quantity led to problems in quality control. It was not until the Third Five-Year Plan in the late 1930s that quality improved to a satisfactory level. Expansion of heavy industry was costly, and the state could finance it only by diverting capital away from other areas of the economy such as light industry and agriculture. Wages and the standard of living remained low. But many peasants, who had suffered from much worse conditions in the countryside, found jobs in industry and became relatively better off. Many women also secured employment and were able to supplement the incomes of their families.

Meanwhile, Stalin consolidated his own personal power, but his ruthless tactics increased opposition within the party as well as within the hierarchy of the army's officer corps. In the mid-1930s, Stalin moved against his enemies in a series of massive purges. He ordered many "old Bolsheviks" arrested and tried for various crimes against the state and party. Among those found guilty was Trotsky who had fled the country, but an assassin tracked him down in Mexico and murdered him in 1940.

Not content with eliminating these leaders, Stalin cast his net much farther and ordered thousands of lesser party and military officials either shot or imprisoned in Siberian labor camps. In all, perhaps 800,000 party members died in the purges, which also decimated the officer corps of the army. Stalin replaced the purged officials and army officers with men whom he trusted.

Despite Stalin's ruthless policies and the dictatorial nature of his system, by the late 1930s a new generation had grown up under the Communist regime. Its members had no ties to the prerevolutionary era and were proud of the achievements of the Soviet Union. Many of them had received technical, administrative, or scientific training and had found attractive positions in industry, government, the party, and the professions. This new intellectual elite felt a deep sense of loyalty to the system.

But the system was far from the one that Karl Marx had envisioned in his dream of a classless society. Instead, party and government officials, industrial managers, technicians, and professional people enjoyed much higher salaries and prestige than the majority of the population. And far from the state withering away, the dictatorship of the Communist party, under Stalin's iron control, had become permanent. Nevertheless, Stalin had transformed the Soviet Union into an industrial giant. This was to prove a vital factor in its ability to emerge triumphant in World War II.

Fascism in Italy

Soon after the victory of Communist totalitarianism in Russia, fascism triumphed in Italy with startling speed. When the Fascist movement began in 1919, it lacked both an efficient organization and a definite ideology. It did not even become a formal political party until 1921. Nevertheless, by October 1922, Benito Mussolini, the Fascist leader, had become premier of Italy and within a few years had created a dictatorship. A multitude of problems that afflicted Italy in the immediate postwar period contributed greatly to this remarkable success story. These included a general sense of dissatisfaction in the aftermath of the war. Italy had gained little from the conflict, at the cost of almost 500,000 dead. Italian nationalists felt a special sense of frustration and betrayal. Returning war veterans were angry over a lack of appreciation for their services, and many of them found it difficult to obtain jobs. Their troubles reflected the dislocation that plagued Italy's economy. Many blamed the democratic government for not achieving more at the peace conference and for failing to solve the economic dilemma.

Italy had only adopted manhood suffrage in 1912, and the system had proven unstable, being characterized by a multitude of parties and dependence on coalition government. Not only did the government provide no solutions to the persistent economic problems, especially reducing Italy's debts and curbing inflation, but it also failed to carry out promises made by the wartime government to adopt a land reform program that would help the country's peasants. Similar pledges to aid the working class also went unfulfilled. These failures led to unrest both in the cities, where strikes became common, and in the countryside, where peasants frequently took matters into their own hands and seized land from the large landlords.

Economic unrest reached a climax in 1920 when industrial workers, inspired by the Socialist party, briefly occupied many factories in the industrial north by means of sit-down strikes. The takeover of the factories and the peasant revolts convinced many of the property-owning classes that there was a real danger of a Socialist revolution. The specter of the Bolshevik victory in Russia haunted them, and they feared that the government would be too weak to cope with such a development. Ironically, the Socialists had reached their peak during the factory takeovers and soon fell victim to internal divisions.

It was against this chaotic background that Benito Mussolini and the Fascists came to power. Mussolini's father, a blacksmith and a Socialist, named him after the Mexican revolutionary leader Benito Juárez. The young Mussolini acquired a deep resentment of the privileged classes and the clergy from his father. But his devout mother sent him to a Catholic school, which he soon came to hate. He especially disliked the upper-class students, and when he attacked one of them with a pen knife, the administrators expelled him. After an unsuccessful career as a teacher, he turned to socialism and rose rapidly in the Socialist party leadership. Mussolini became editor of the party newspaper and initially preached the Socialist doctrine of internationalism and opposition to war. But a few months after the outbreak of World War I, he suddenly urged Italy's entry on the side of the Allies. This heresy outraged his fellow Socialists and led to his ouster from the party. When Italy did enter the conflict, Mussolini joined the army and served capably, seeing action and rising to the rank of corporal before being wounded when a grenade launcher blew up, showering him with fragments.

In the immediate aftermath of the war, many disgruntled veterans and ardent nationalists organized a number of fighting groups in various parts of Italy. One of these bands was led by Mussolini, who gradually won the allegiance of the others and formed the nucleus of the Fascist party. His movement gained its name from the fasces, a symbol of authority during the Roman Empire, consisting of a bundle of rods surrounding an ax. The fasces also became the Fascist insignia. Mussolini combined the movement's fighting units into a paramilitary force known as the *squadristi* or Black Shirts.

The various Fascist groups had little in the way of a common policy, except for their superheated nationalism but it soon assumed an anti-Socialist guise and posed as the great opponent of "Red revolution." The Black Shirts spent much of their time fighting Socialists and other opposing groups in the streets, frequently forcing large doses of castor oil down the throats of those who fell into their hands. But the Fascists were less adept at winning parliamentary elections, failing to gain even one seat in 1919 and capturing only 35 in 1921.

Fascist leaders soon became more aggressive. Black Shirts forced many Socialists out of local government councils and even seized a number of railroad stations and telegraph offices. Despite the obvious illegality of such actions, the government refused to move against the Fascists and tended to look upon them as a bulwark against socialism. Considerable support for fascism also existed in both the officer corps of the army and the court of King Victor Emmanuel III. All of this encouraged Mussolini and other Fascist leaders to attempt to seize power by sending the Black Shirts to march on Rome in October 1922. The government finally awoke to the danger and urged the king to sign a declaration of martial law. But Victor Emmanuel refused, and the cabinet resigned. Instead, the king asked Mussolini to become premier in a coalition cabinet. He took this action in large part because he feared civil war, but he also remembered Mussolini's recent declaration that he favored continuation of the monarchy.

Technically, Mussolini had come to power through constitutional means, but his threat of force had cleared the way for his appointment. Although he intended ultimately to impose a dictatorship, he approached this task cautiously. Mussolini indicated his willingness to preside over a coalition government in which the Fascists would have only three posts. In return, the democratic parties supported his request that he be granted full government powers for a year. During the following months, he appointed Fascists to key local and national positions and transformed the *squadristi* into a national militia. In the 1924

parliamentary election campaign, the Fascists resorted to intimidation and violence. When the balloting ended, a list of Fascist and non-Fascist candidates that Mussolini had endorsed had won 65 percent of the vote.

Now armed with a massive majority, the Fascists applied pressure to other political parties and the press. They even murdered the most outspoken critic of fascism, Giacomo Matteotti, in June 1924. This incident created a serious crisis. A wave of revulsion gripped non-Fascist Italians, and members of the democratic parties walked out of parliament in protest. They hoped that their action might rouse the king to dismiss Mussolini, but Victor Emmanuel took no action. Despite his initial concern, Mussolini actually benefited from the crisis, because the withdrawal of the democratic parties from the Chamber eliminated the last source of opposition.

In 1925 and 1926, Mussolini forced non-Fascists out of the cabinet, dissolved all other parties, and imposed tight censorship on the press. He also banned trade unions and secured his total control over local government. A Fascist secret police came into existence in 1926. By the end of 1926, Italy had become a one-party dictatorship.

The parliament remained in existence but henceforth had little to do while Mussolini ruled by decree. Victor Emmanuel III remained head of state, but though technically superior to Mussolini, the king deferred to the premier. As in the Soviet Union, the party was the actual center of power. Mussolini preferred his party title, Duce (leader), to that of premier and dominated both party and state. At the party's summit, Mussolini established the Fascist Grand Council, consisting of 20 to 30 top party leaders, which loyally approved his decrees.

With power secured, the Fascists belatedly formulated an ideology that remained their official creed until the party's downfall in 1943. It denounced democratic government as corrupt and inefficient. Fascism, according to this argument, protected the interests of the community as a whole through strong, efficient leadership that subordinated selfish interests to those of the state. In reality, in the following years, members of the party proved quite attracted to self-interest and corruption.

The Fascists also adopted the doctrine of corporativism, which supposedly furthered understanding between industrialists and workers while eliminating the selfish individualism that had characterized the capitalistic economy. It provided for the division of economic activity into seven categories—industry, commerce, banking, agriculture, internal transport, the merchant marine, and the intellectual community. A corporation was to represent each of the seven, and a Ministry of Corporations came into existence in 1926 to coordinate them. In theory, this organization became the basis for a "corporative state." But in reality, corporativism was a fraud that masked a cynical deal between Mussolini and Italian industry in 1925. This arrangement granted the industrialists a privileged position in return for their support of the regime.

The industrial workers were not so fortunate. The government denied them the right to strike and forced them to join a Fascist-dominated organization. They came under the joint control of their employers, the party, and the state. The regime made similar preferential agreements with organizations of large employers in both commerce and agriculture. The propertied classes had come to terms with the Fascist state, and Mussolini had suppressed his long-standing hatred of the privileged groups in Italian society.

Fascism also exalted the importance of nationalism, imperialism, and militarism. Mussolini spoke in grandiose terms of Italy's right to achieve its national destiny through the creation of a large empire in the Mediterranean and Africa. Clearly, a powerful war machine was mandatory to attain this goal. To instill a warlike spirit in the Italian people, the Fascists argued that pacifism was a cowardly doctrine, whereas war unleashed the noble human virtues—patriotism, self-sacrifice, and courage. Mussolini posed as a man of action, often appearing in uniform and given to much strutting and posturing. Unfortunately for Mussolini and the Fascists, Italy's armed forces and industry were insufficient to accomplish their grandiose ambitions. Nevertheless, Mussolini would eventually seek to fulfill them. This quest would ultimately lead him and Italy into World War II.

By the early 1930s, Mussolini's government had gained general acceptance. To many Italians, its emphasis on order and discipline was a welcome relief from the instability of the democratic system. But support for the Duce and fascism was actually passive rather than enthusiastic. There appeared to be no alternative, and if one conformed, it was possible to live with relatively little interference from the state.

It is actually questionable to what extent the Fascist regime was totalitarian. To be sure, it was a one-party state and abounded with organizations designed to bring all aspects of life under its scrutiny. But in reality, it had preserved much of the old system—the monarchy, the catholic church, capitalism, and the large landowners. And each of these enjoyed a certain amount of independence.

The Fascist dictatorship was much milder than the Nazi regime that came into existence in Germany in 1933. Like Italian fascism, Nazism was largely the creation of its leader, Adolf Hitler. And also as in Italy, conditions in Germany provided the opportunity for Hitler and the Nazis to come to power.

Hitler and the Nazis in Germany

Adolf Hitler rose from rather modest origins, though not as humble as those of Mussolini and Stalin. His father was a minor customs official in the village of Braunau, Austria, where Adolf was born in 1889. Hitler was an indifferent student and dropped out of school at 16. He dreamed of becoming an artist or an architect but failed to gain admission to either the Vienna Academy of Fine Arts or the Vienna School of Architecture. He remained in Vienna for six years, however, living an aimless life and making ends meet primarily on inheritance money and an orphan's pension. In 1913, Hitler moved to Germany, taking up residence in Munich. When World War I broke out the following year, he joined the German army and served as a dispatch runner at the front. He was wounded twice and earned five decorations, including an Iron Cross, First Class, a rare honor for a common soldier. Despite his exemplary record, he never rose above the rank of lance corporal.

When the war ended, Hitler was in a hospital, recovering from the effects of a poison gas attack that had left him temporarily blinded. The news of the armistice filled him with a deep sense of shame. He readily accepted the "stab-in-the-back" story and felt intense hatred for the German republic that embraced the "dictated peace." After leaving the hospital, he returned to Munich, where he became a member of the German Workers' party, one of the many small extremist political groups that hatched in the aftermath of Germany's defeat.

Hitler soon revealed an exceptional gift for oratory and an astonishing ability to dominate his fellow party members by sheer force of personality. He also demonstrated considerable organizational and leadership skill. In 1921, the party, now renamed the National Socialist German Workers' (Nazi) party, voted him the official title of Führer (leader) with virtually dictatorial powers. In its original form, the party drew most of its members from manual laborers, but it soon attracted many former soldiers as well as various adventurers and misfits. The Nazis were violently nationalistic, anti-Semitic, and totally opposed to the democratic republican government, which they considered guilty of treason.The party also organized a paramilitary force, the *Sturm Abteilung* (SA), or storm troops, in 1921.

Although the republic that the Nazis so detested came into existence with the fall of the monarchy in November 1918, it did not receive its constitution until August 1919. Since the constitution was proclaimed in the city of Weimar, the government became known as the Weimar Republic. The constitution provided for an elected president as head of state, a cabinet led by a chancellor, and a two-house parliament. The most important parliamentary body was the democratically elected Reichstag. As in the parliaments of the French Third Republic and early postwar democratic Italy, the Reichstag came to be characterized by a multiparty system, and the cabinet was dependent on the backing of a majority coalition. The Weimar Republic was beset by a number of enemies—various ultranationalist and conservative groups on the right and the Communists on the left. The right-wing parties favored either a restoration of the monarchy or some other kind of authoritarian regime, while the Communists looked forward to a Soviet-type system.

During its first few years, the republic contended with the difficult economic problems that followed the war, especially the disastrous inflation. It also had to withstand a number of revolts.

The earliest of these, a Communist uprising in January 1919, forced the government to seek protection from the army, which easily put down the revolt with the help of the *Freikorps,* unofficial bands of former soldiers similar to those that developed in Italy. The army proved less reliable in the case of right-wing revolts. In 1920, a conservative ultranationalist group used one of the *Freikorps* to seize Berlin for a time, but the army refused to move against it. Fortunately, the rebel forces were weak and collapsed entirely when the Social Democratic party and the trade unions called a general strike, which paralyzed the capital.

The last of these revolts came in 1923 and became known as the Beer Hall Putsch because its preliminaries took place in a Munich beer hall. It involved a Nazi attempt to seize the state government of Bavaria, to be followed by a march on Berlin, but it failed miserably. The authorities arrested Hitler and several other party leaders and tried them for high treason. Although it appeared as if this fiasco had dealt the Nazis a death blow, they had suffered only a temporary setback. In fact, during the trial Hitler became a national figure for the first time. He took full responsibility for the putsch and turned his defense into a dramatic appeal to German nationalism. The court was sympathetic and administered the most lenient possible sentence, five years, of which Hitler actually served only nine months.

While in prison, Hitler dictated the first volume of *Mein Kampf* (*My Struggle*), a poorly written, bombastic, and self-serving book in which he expressed his major views. Among the most important was his belief in the superiority of what he referred to as the Aryan race. During the nineteenth century, a number of theorists of dubious qualifications had expounded on the supposed existence of such a race, notably the Frenchman Count Arthur de Gobineau and the Englishman Houston Stewart Chamberlain. Generally, they referred to the Aryans somewhat imprecisely as the inhabitants of northwestern Europe and considered them superior to other races. Chamberlain saw the Germans as the purest form of Aryan. Hitler identified all the Germanic peoples as Aryan. In addition to the ethnic Germans, these included the Dutch, the Flemish-speaking Belgians, the Scandinavians, and the English. He believed that the Aryan Germans must avoid interbreeding with lesser peoples, which would pollute Aryan blood and weaken the race.

In Hitler's scheme of things, the most loathsome of these lesser breeds were the Jews. To him, they were not only inferior but a sinister influence as well. He associated them with Marxist socialism and the Weimar Republic, both of which he detested. Karl Marx had been a Jew, as had a number of other Marxist leaders, including some of the founders of the republic. Marxism, with its emphasis on the international solidarity of the working class, ran counter to his own nationalism, and, of course, he blamed the republic for selling out the army and making a shameful peace.

Mein Kampf was also full of scorn for democracy and parliamentary institutions. Hitler much preferred the rule of one man, and, of course, he visualized himself in this role. To him, leadership was primary and decisive, providing order, discipline, and purpose in contrast to the confusion and drift he saw in democracy.

Finally, *Mein Kampf* expressed Hitler's views on foreign policy, including his call for an end to the limitations that the peace settlement had imposed. He also insisted on the need for Germany to absorb the ethnic Germans of Austria, the Sudetenland, Danzig, and Poland. But his ambitions did not end there. His ultimate goal was the conquest of *Lebensraum* (living space) for the German people in the Soviet Union. He looked with special longing to the vast area of the Ukraine with its rich agricultural land and natural resources. Few people read *Mein Kampf* when it first appeared in 1925, and many of those who did refused to take it seriously.

While in prison, Hitler also acquired the conviction that the Nazis must come to power legally through the electoral process of the Weimar Republic. There would be no more attempts to overthrow the government by force. But to win power legally would necessitate appealing to larger segments of the population, thereby creating a mass following. To accomplish this, the Nazis, who were primarily a regional party, needed to create a nationwide organization and make skillful use of propaganda to attack the republic and offer a popular alternative.

Propaganda was particularly important to Hitler's approach, and in Joseph Goebbels he found just the man to head the party's new propaganda division. Goebbels, who walked with a limp as the result of a deformed foot, had considered entering the priesthood but earned a Ph.D. from Heidelberg University instead. Goebbels soon recognized Hitler's political genius and became a devoted follower. He proved a master of persuasion and of the art of using the mass media for the greatest impact.

Another of Hitler's chief lieutenants was Hermann Goering, an air ace who had shot down 22 Allied planes during World War I. He had served as the last commander of the legendary Baron von Richthofen's Flying Circus and deeply coveted fame, wealth, and power but held few ideological convictions. Able but intensely vain, Goering had commanded the SA before fleeing the country following the Beer Hall Putsch. He returned in 1928 and eventually became second only to Hitler in the Nazi leadership and commander of the Luftwaffe (air force).

Despite the efforts of Hitler and other Nazi leaders, the party's outlook was far from bright. The prosperity that Germany enjoyed during the second half of the 1920s strengthened the republic, as did Gustav Stresemann's foreign policy achievements. In the Reichstag elections of 1928, the party won only 12 seats. But Hitler remained confident that his chance would come.

Opportunity beckoned with the advent of the Great Depression in 1929. Despite the prosperity of the late 1920s, the world economy had not recovered completely from the disruptive effects of World War I. Britain never regained prewar production levels, and unemployment remained a chronic problem throughout the 1920s. Germany's remarkable economic comeback rested to a large extent on foreign loans. World agriculture did not share in the prosperity of the late 1920s because commodity prices remained low. The related problems of war debts and reparations also continued to be a source of concern.

In the postwar economy, the position of the United States was of special importance. Any sharp reversal in its economic fortunes was sure to have great impact on the rest of the world. Although prices on the American stock market began to rise dramatically in 1928 and continued upward during the next year, there was actually little reason for optimism. Not only was U.S. agriculture depressed, but also industrial production edged downward during 1929. When the spectacular rise of the stock market abruptly ended in October 1929, stock values skidded catastrophically. The crash ruined many investors and destroyed the confidence of others. Industrial production plummeted; banks failed and unemployment soared. Aftershocks of this disaster spread rapidly as American financiers cut off loans to Germany, creating a severe shortage of capital. German production declined precipitously, businesses failed, and unemployment rose alarmingly.

The Weimar Republic in Crisis

The Weimar Republic found itself in a dilemma, with sharply declining revenues and increasing demands for unemployment assistance. Business interests opposed any increase in these payments, while organized labor refused to support any reduction. The cabinet, unable to agree on a solution, resigned in March 1930. The new chancellor, Heinrich Brüning, actually favored a restoration of the monarchy. His authoritarian views made him acceptable to a number of generals who were influential with President Hindenburg, the World War I military leader. Although a monarchist at heart, Hindenburg had remained loyal to the oath he had taken to uphold the republic when he became president in 1925. But he was 82 years old and susceptible to his military advisers, who had recommended Brüning's appointment.

Brüning adopted a program that called for tax increases and reduction of expenditures in an effort to restore the financial stability of the government. The Reichstag voted against his program, but Brüning asked Hindenburg to put the program into effect by decree. Under article 48 of the Weimar constitution, the president had the power to enact programs by decree in time of emergency. Brüning's action marked the end of parliamentary democracy in Germany and launched a three-year period of rule by presidential decree. The chancellor also called a parliamentary election for September 1930, hoping that he could convince the electorate of the soundness of his program.

Unfortunately, the election of 1930 proved a disaster for both Brüning's hopes and the republic. The extremist parties, the Communists and Nazis, scored major gains. But the Nazis were especially successful, winning 107 seats, which gave them the second largest Reichstag delegation. Brüning now had no chance of creating a majority coalition but refused to resign. Instead, he continued to rely on presidential decree powers and clung to his rigid fiscal policy while the depression worsened. Unemployment had hovered around 3 million when he came to power. By the end of 1930, it had risen to 4,380,000 and a year later reached 5,615,000. The popularity of Brüning, now referred to as the "hunger chancellor," declined steadily.

By the spring of 1932, Brüning was losing the confidence of both Hindenburg and General Kurt von Schleicher, the army's liaison man with the government. In May, the chancellor bowed to their pressure and resigned. Schleicher now persuaded Hindenburg to appoint Franz von Papen as his successor. The general thought that he could dominate Papen, a second-rate figure with no strong personal following. Both Papen and Schleicher hoped to lure Hitler into accepting Nazi participation in a coalition cabinet. They believed that the need to share responsibility for government decisions would undermine Hitler's appeal with the voters. But Hitler had no intention of falling into their trap. He did agree not to oppose Papen in the Reichstag, however. In return, the chancellor agreed to call another parliamentary election in July.

While Hitler concentrated on more traditional campaigning, the SA, under the leadership of Ernst Röhm, engaged in a struggle for "control of the streets." Storm troopers battled Communists and Social Democrats and resorted to acts of terrorism. Röhm, an army officer during World War I, had recruited many members of the *Freikorps* into the SA in its early days. But he had abandoned the party after the failure of the Beer Hall Putsch, serving for a time as an officer in the Bolivian army. Hitler had enticed him back in 1930 to reorganize the SA. By the end of 1932, Röhm commanded a force of over 400,000 men.

Far less conspicuous at this time but destined for much greater importance in the future was the *Schutz Staffel* (SS), which began as Hitler's bodyguard and consisted of less than 300 men in 1929. In that year, Heinrich Himmler, a former operator of a poultry farm, took command of the SS and began to increase its size and functions.

Himmler appeared to be anything but the ideal Aryan. Of modest stature with a flabby body, he wore pince-nez glasses, which gave him the appearance of a pedantic schoolmaster. But behind his unimposing facade lay burning ambition and totally ruthless dedication. He became a devoted disciple of Hitler but at the same time constantly sought to aggrandize his own power.

When the election took place, the Nazis captured over 37 percent of the vote and increased their Reichstag delegation to 230, making them the country's largest party, but they were still far from a majority. Hitler now felt strong enough to demand the chancellorship for himself, but Schleicher, Papen, and Hindenburg refused to go along with this. Papen offered him the vice chancellorship instead, but Hitler declined and withheld Nazi support for the government in the Reichstag. His action forced Papen to call another election in November, but this time the balloting resulted in a major setback for the Nazis. They lost 2 million votes, and their Reichstag delegation fell to 196, although they remained the largest party. It looked as if the Nazis had definitely passed their peak. They were also deeply in debt because of the expense involved in waging three major election campaigns in one year.

Papen and Schleicher soon split over how to solve the government's continuing dilemma, and Schleicher persuaded Hindenburg to dismiss the chancellor. In the absence of another acceptable candidate, Schleicher became chancellor himself, but Papen remained active behind the scenes and worked out a deal with Hitler. Under its terms, Hitler would become chancellor while Papen would take the vice chancellorship. Papen also promised to use his connections with important bankers and industrialists to help the Nazis with their financial problems. In return, Hitler agreed that Papen and his associates could choose the great majority of the cabinet members. Hindenburg did not relish the prospect of Hitler in power, but he finally bowed to Papen's pressure. On January 30, 1933, he appointed Hitler chancellor. Papen was delighted. As he commented to a friend shortly afterward, "We have hired him!" He told another, "Within two months we will have pushed Hitler so far into the corner that he'll squeak!"

The Third Reich Takes Form

Hitler had no intention of allowing Papen or anyone else to dominate him. Instead, he set out to outmaneuver Papen and the cabinet. His first step was to gain agreement for an immediate dissolution of the Reichstag and the calling of a new election in March. He hoped to gain an absolute majority for the Nazis. This would be an important step toward obtaining the two-thirds majority necessary to enact legislation that would authorize him to rule by personal decree for four years. To facilitate his goal, he took measures to curtail freedom of the press throughout the country.

In February, Hitler's hopes rose still higher when the Reichstag building burned down. Clearly arson, it is still not certain who actually set the fire. The Nazis blamed the Communists and used this charge as a pretext not only to crack down on Communist party officials but to suspend civil rights as well. Armed with this authority, the Nazis interfered with the activities of opposition parties. But despite all these advantages, Hitler found the election results disappointing. Although the Nazis won 288 seats, they were still short of a bare majority, not to mention the two-thirds needed to pass the enabling bill. Hitler now resorted to intimidation to gain the necessary support. On the day that the vote took place, SS personnel surrounded the building in which the Reichstag met, while SA troopers stationed themselves inside and chanted, "We want the bill or fire and murder!" Under such pressure, only the Social Democrats had the courage to vote against the bill, which passed by a margin of 347.

Hitler was not yet the complete dictator of Germany, but he was well on his way. To finish the process, he embarked on a policy of *Gleichschaltung* (coordination). This included bringing the state governments under Nazi control. Hitler also eliminated all other political parties, ousted unacceptable members of the cabinet, and merged the labor unions in a new, Nazi-directed German Labor Front. Industrial workers lost their rights to engage in collective bargaining and to strike. The Reichstag continued to exist, but only as a Nazi-dominated assembly that listened to Hitler's decrees and roared back its total, slavish approval.

FIGURE 3-2   Nazi party comrades salute Adolf Hitler in Haltzburg, Germany. *(AP/Wide World Photos)*

Soon after coming to power, the Nazis brought the educational curriculum from the elementary through the university level in line with Nazi ideas. The Nazis also absorbed all the country's many youth organizations into the Hitler Youth. This movement fostered love of the Führer, obedience to the party and state, and exaltation of warlike virtues.

Hitler referred to Nazi Germany as the Third Reich, the Third German Empire. The first Reich had been the medieval Holy Roman Empire, the second the imperial system that World War I had destroyed. Hitler predicted that the new Reich would last for a thousand years.

As soon as they gained power, the Nazis began to move against political opponents, especially the Social Democrats and Communists. A secret police organization, the Gestapo, relentlessly tracked down enemies of the regime. In 1933, both SA and SS units established concentration camps. Dachau, near Munich, became the largest and served as a model for other camps. In 1934, the SS gained control over all of them and reduced their number to three—Dachau, Buchenwald, and Sachsenhausen. After the outbreak of World War II, the influx of political prisoners

from occupied countries necessitated the creation of several new camps, including Bergen-Belsen. Special units known as "Death's Head Formations," staffed the camps, treating inmates with utmost cruelty. The Nazis also quickly began to persecute the Jews. They purged them from the civil service and universities and subjected them to discrimination and violence. At first, these measures were unofficial and somewhat random in nature, but in the following years they became much more formal and increasingly restrictive.*

By 1934, Hitler had essentially completed his revolution. Only two potential sources of opposition still existed—the army and the SA. Military leaders listened with pleasure as Hitler promised to increase the size of the army and provide it with modern equipment. But the generals were alarmed by the rapid expansion of the SA, whose ranks had swollen to over a million men. They also were troubled by reports that Röhm hoped to merge the army with the SA. Hitler shared their

---

*Nazi persecution of the Jews is covered in greater detail in Chapter 11.

concern over Röhm's intentions and feared that the SA leader might attempt to seize power. In June 1934, at the urging of both the army and Himmler, Hitler ordered the purge of the SA. SS troopers took Röhm and many other SA leaders by surprise and executed them without trial.

Shortly after this purge, remembered as the "Night of the Long Knives," President Hindenburg died, and Hitler announced that the offices of chancellor and president were now combined in his new position as Führer and Reich Chancellor. The army agreed to support his acquisition of the presidential powers and swore an oath of allegiance to him. In return, Hitler affirmed the army's position as the sole bearers of arms in the nation. But while the army officers felt honor-bound to remain loyal to their oath, Hitler soon violated his part of the bargain. He recognized the SS as the SA's replacement with the right to form actual combat troops. In the following years, the SS grew rapidly and, under Himmler's leadership, became the chief instrument of internal Nazi power. By 1936, Himmler had gained control over all German police, including the Gestapo. Later Himmler created special military units, the *Waffen SS* (armed SS), which were separate from the army. During World War II they were to receive preferential treatment, including the finest equipment available, much to the army leaders' disgust.

The Führer at the Helm

Hitler now wielded absolute power over both party and state and contended that he embodied the aspirations of the entire German people. Whatever their original misgivings, a majority of Germans soon began to accept the Führer's rule as beneficial. Hitler received credit for Germany's economic recovery from the depression and the great reduction in unemployment. Although recovery actually began before he came to power, his policies certainly contributed significantly to the process and gave the people a new sense of pride and achievement. They included an ambitious program of public works and rearmament.

Despite the power wielded by Hitler and the Nazis, the system lacked the complete coordination of all levels of government from the top that is usually associated with totalitarianism. Instead,

a good deal of confusion, duplication of effort, and competition characterized relations between party and state. Hitler retained the governmental departments of the republic as well as most of their personnel, who tended to be of high quality. The most notable new department, the Propaganda Ministry, staffed by Nazis and headed by Goebbels, performed its functions of spreading lies and promoting hatred with chilling efficiency. But Hitler provided no systematic machinery for coordinating the policies of the departments. The Führer also had a fondness for creating special authorities and agencies to deal with problems that existing ministries could have handled with greater efficiency. These bodies proliferated alarmingly and tended to compete not only with the ministries but also with each other.

In part, this duplication and the resulting jurisdictional rivalries stemmed from Hitler's own deliberate efforts. By dividing his underlings, he maintained unquestioned ascendancy over all of them. But despite this confused reality, Nazi propaganda effectively portrayed the regime as one of totalitarian order and efficiency to the German people and the outside world. The 1936 Olympic Games in Berlin seemed to confirm this view when Germany swept 33 gold medals, compared to only 24 for the United States. Oddly enough, two Jews competed for the German team, one winning a silver medal in fencing.

The Transformation of Japan

In East Asia, dictatorship also came to Japan, but the form of oppression and the manner in which it developed differed from the models of Russia, Italy, and Germany. The driving force behind this transformation was not a political party or a single leader but the army. Japan possessed an ancient military tradition that had originated in a period of civil war between rival feudal clans, starting in the twelfth century and continuing until the 1500s. Throughout this period, a succession of emperors presided over the Japanese government. Although the emperor claimed divine origin as the descendant of the Sun Goddess, he actually played a minor role in the political system. Imperial power, such as it was, lay in the hands of the shogun, a military regent who ruled in the name of the emperor.

Despite the turmoil of those centuries, Japan maintained a highly developed civilization and a thriving commercial economy. The prestigious landowning clans, supported by armed retainers called samurai, dominated Japanese society, followed at a respectful distance by the wealthy merchant class. The landlords mercilessly exploited the peasantry, which comprised the overwhelming majority of the population. One of the clans, the Tokugawa, gradually gained control over Japan in the late sixteenth and early seventeenth centuries and acquired the office of shogun. For the next 250 years, Tokugawa shoguns governed the country as a military dictatorship. They maintained the feudal system but dominated the feudal lords.

The Tokugawa feared foreign influence and isolated the country from most contacts with the West. The Japanese looked inward and became exceedingly nationalistic. Starting in the eighteenth century, however, signs of change became evident. The wealthy merchant class rose steadily in importance and the impoverished landless peasantry grew restless. In 1853, an American fleet under Commodore Matthew Perry forced its way into Yedo (later Tokyo) Bay. Perry demanded that the Tokugawa enter into commercial relations with the United States and other Western powers. In the years that followed Perry's brusque visit, Japan agreed to a series of treaties with various Western countries. These were similar to the ones that China had made with European powers, complete with trade concessions and grants of extraterritoriality.

These concessions angered some of the great clans who defied the authority of the shogun and resorted to attacks on foreign ships in Japanese harbors. The rebels enlisted the support of the emperor, who now loomed as a counterweight to the shogun. This antiforeigner movement backed down, however, when in 1864 a Western fleet, containing warships from four nations, bombarded Japanese shore batteries and sent a landing force ashore to seize them. But this crisis ignited a period of internal strife and weakened the Tokugawa. In 1867, Shogun Keiki resigned in favor of restoring the imperial dignity in the person of 16-year-old Emperor Musuhito who had only recently succeeded to the throne. The young emperor applied the name Meiji (Enlightened Government) to his reign. During the next few years, the great clans surrendered their feudal fiefs to the emperor, and in 1871 an imperial decree abolished feudalism and created a system of centralized administration. The new government turned to Western technology and organizational methods in an effort to resist Western domination. In keeping with this approach, they reorganized the administrative and legal systems and encouraged industrial and financial modernization. Japanese business groups invested in manufacturing enterprises and rapidly increased production while seeking foreign markets.

The new regime created a modern army, patterned after Prussia's military establishment, and transformed the samurai into an officer corps. Somewhat later, a navy, modeled after Britain's, also came into existence. By the early twentieth century, Japan had shaken off Western domination and had emerged as an important power. Its new war machine won victories over China in 1894–95 and Russia in 1904–05. In the latter conflict, a Japanese fleet under Admiral Heihachiro Togo scored a major success in a surprise attack on a Russian squadron at Port Arthur before war had been declared. This decisive victory made a lasting impression on Japanese naval leaders and appears to have ultimately influenced development of the strategy that resulted in the surprise attack on the U.S. Pacific fleet at Pearl Harbor during World War II. Secure in their newly established position of power, the Japanese engaged in the same type of imperialistic activity in China that they had resisted in their own country.

Despite this startling transformation, Japan's traditional social structure continued largely unchanged. Landlords retained their control over the peasantry. The industrial and commercial groups had grown wealthier, but a few great families dominated the economy through giant trusts. And the industrial working class remained thoroughly subordinate to management. Japan's culture also continued in its age-old form, except for the government's campaign to reduce the power of the Buddhist religion and to encourage the Shinto cult, which worshiped the emperor as the descendant of the Sun Goddess. Shinto, meaning "the way of the gods," was an ancient form of religion, which originally focused on the worship of a vast array of spirits or gods personifying aspects of the natural world. It had virtually disappeared as a separate religion by the ninth century but experienced a revival during the eighteenth century. In its revised form, Shinto stressed ancestor worship and complete obedience to the emperor and in effect, through him, the state. It also contended that the Japanese were superior to other peoples because they had descended from the gods.

Japan based its government on a constitution drafted in 1889. It vested authority in the emperor, but in reality, the premier and his cabinet ruled in the emperor's name, while the emperor existed in a state of exalted aloofness. A small electorate, based on property ownership, chose the members of the Diet, the Japanese parliament. Cabinet ministers were responsible to the emperor rather than to the Diet, but since the emperor remained above political affairs, they ruled with virtual freedom from civilian limitations. But they did have to contend with the army and the navy, which wielded enormous influence. High-ranking officers on active duty headed the war and navy ministries, and either minister could bring down the cabinet by resigning. The services could also block the formation of a cabinet not to their liking by refusing to designate officers to fill these positions. Both services even refused to provide information to the cabinet on the pretense of the need to protect military secrets.

Despite the traditional importance of the military, a movement toward liberalization of the system produced remarkable results during the 1920s. Western-style political parties and trade unions developed, and in 1925 Japan adopted manhood suffrage as the basis for parliamentary elections. There was even an attempt to reduce the influence of the army and navy in the realm of foreign affairs. The most notable examples of this were the commitments that Japanese officials made at the Washington and London conferences to limit naval strength over the vehement protests of many navy leaders. To a large extent, the liberalization movement found its strength in the relative economic prosperity that Japan enjoyed during the 1920s. But beneath the surface, the traditional social system still remained largely unchanged, and powerful forces objected to the innovations in the political system.

Japan Moves toward Military Dictatorship

With the coming of the Great Depression, Japan encountered severe economic problems that discredited the civilian government and provided the opportunity for the military to reassert its power. Army leaders took the lead by insisting that the country must seek expansion on the Asian mainland as a way out of the economic dilemma. In particular, they demanded aggressive measures in Manchuria. Junior officers became active in secret organizations that resorted to the assassination of government officials. Their first victim was Premier Hamaguchi, whose government had negotiated the London Naval Treaty in 1930. These violent tendencies culminated in an attempted coup by a group of fanatical army officers in 1936. Although they failed in their bid for power, the rebels did succeed in assassinating several cabinet ministers.

The actions of these junior officers reflected the paradoxical nature of the Japanese army. Despite the ability of top-ranking generals to manipulate cabinets, they were not successful in controlling their own subordinates, who often acted in a startlingly independent manner. This was in keeping with the Japanese tradition of *gekokujo,* which involved open defiance of senior officers by juniors, a frequent occurrence in Japan's history. Army authorities often overlooked such glaring breaches of military discipline. In large part this was due to the fact that senior officers often sympathized with the motives of their subordinates. Even when they did not, they admired their spirit. Indeed, Japanese military doctrine considered fighting spirit the decisive element in war and regarded cautious officers as cowards. All of this was indicative of an irrational element in the army's outlook, which focused on a willingness to undertake military action without due regard for the consequences. It also took the form of fanatical devotion to military honor, fighting to the death in hopeless circumstances, and an insistence on suicide rather than surrender.

These tendencies reflected the centuries-old code of Bushido ("the way of the warrior"), which originated with the samurai of feudal Japan and extolled such virtues as duty, courage, self-discipline, endurance, and especially devotion to the emperor.

Bushido dictated that the soldier must fight until victory was achieved or until he met his own death. Surrender was not an option. Instead, the soldier must commit suicide to preserve his honor. To be taken prisoner was the ultimate disgrace.

Japan's military leaders encroached steadily on the government during the 1930s, and the promising liberalization movement of the 1920s withered away. Civilian authorities buckled under to the army's demand for territorial expansion in China, and the more conservative civilian political groups shared this desire. Japan gradually took on the characteristics of a military dictatorship. But in many respects, the transition was more subtle than in Italy or Germany. There was no mass political movement, no charismatic leader, no revision or suspension of the constitution. But there was steady erosion of civil liberties, encroachment on freedom of the press and other forms of expression, and imprisonment of critics of the regime. The government undermined the powers of the Diet and gradually outlawed opposing political parties.

In Japan, as in Germany and Italy, the expansionist ambitions of the dictatorship along with a willingness to go to war to achieve them formed a dangerous and explosive combination. During the 1930s the foreign policies of all three dictatorships moved steadily in the direction of war. In fact, the consolidation of the dictatorship in Japan was largely a product of a war that the Japanese unleashed against Chinese rule in Manchuria as early as 1931. This aggression marked the start of an accelerating Japanese military involvement in China during the next few years. By 1937, Japan and China were locked in a war that would not end until 1945. By 1939, Hitler had plunged Europe into war as well. The two widely separated struggles ultimately blended into the global conflict we call World War II.

CHAPTER FOUR

The Road to War

World War II, far more than World War I, deserves to be called a global conflict. Although the 1914–18 war involved operations in Africa and the Middle East, in East Asia, and on the high seas, Europe remained its focus from start to finish. Europe also felt the war's impact much more profoundly than any other part of the globe. But World War II really consisted of two parallel though interconnected conflicts of major proportions—one in Europe and the Atlantic, the other on the Asian mainland and in the Pacific.

The earlier war plainly began in 1914; the start of the second struggle is not as easy to determine. Most accounts state that it commenced with the German invasion of Poland in September 1939. But others contend that it really began when Japan and China launched their prolonged hostilities in July 1937. Still others move the date as far back as September 1931, when the Japanese embarked on the conquest of Manchuria. Clearly, the European hostilities led to far greater immediate complications and the eventual joining of the two conflicts. Just as certainly, the first shots were fired in East Asia at least two years before.

It is also clear that Germany's aims in the conflict differed considerably from those of Japan. The Japanese operations in Manchuria and China were more traditional in their motivation than the grandiose and apocalyptic vision that motivated Hitler. They were in keeping with the imperialistic policies that, not only Japan, but European powers as well pursued in the period before World War I—territorial expansion and economic exploitation. To be sure these were also present in the aims of Hitler. Indeed his appetite for expansion was prodigious. But he added an ideological dimension that was missing from the Japanese approach—intense racism, reflecting his hatred of the Jews and contempt for the Slavic peoples of

Eastern Europe. This became the cornerstone of his expansionist policy and ultimately led to genocidal action against both Jews and Slavs. This is not to say that the Japanese were not guilty of appalling atrocities against those peoples who fell under their domination, but they never carried this to the extremes employed by the Nazis, and their crimes were not part of an overriding ideological concept such as that fashioned by Hitler.

A Decade of Crises

The decade of the 1930s witnessed a long series of crises that marked the world's gradual descent into war, both in East Asia and in Europe. These crises unfolded against a background of economic distress created by the Great Depression and the rise of political extremism that was to a large extent the result of these economic problems. Hitler rose to power primarily as a result of the disastrous condition of the German economy in the early 1930s. He promised that he and the Nazis would revive the economy, and revise the peace settlement in Germany's favor. After coming to power, he set out to do just that. The Japanese military leaders exploited the economic turmoil in Japan to push for ever greater penetration into China in pursuit of raw materials and a huge market for Japanese goods.

The other major powers also wrestled with the demoralizing effects of the depression and, although concerned about the German and Japanese threats to the status quo, were divided and uncertain on how to deal with the troubling developments of the 1930s. And, for good measure, all of the Western powers as well as Germany and Japan feared the spread of communism under Soviet leadership. Britain and France were reluctant to pursue policies that might embroil them in another world war. Memories of the ghastly loss of life in World War I as well as the economic, social, and political upheaval that followed in its wake were still fresh. And, although the German people also did not look forward to another conflict, their Führer saw war as the ultimate key to his expansionist dreams.

Japanese Aggression in China

The first crisis, which jarred the world out of what was left of the fragile hopes of the 1920s, began when soldiers of the Japanese Kwantung Army blew up a small section of railway track near the Manchurian capital of Mukden. This incident triggered Japan's escalating involvement on the mainland of Asia, which ultimately led to the outbreak of World War II in the Pacific.

In the late 1920s and early 1930s, Japanese military leaders grew concerned about the northward expansion of Chiang Kai-shek's Kuomintang regime in China. They were especially distressed when the Manchurian warlord Chang Hsueh-liang recognized the Kuomintang's authority over Manchuria. Manchurian officials had even gone so far as to boycott Japanese goods and interfere with the activities of Japanese citizens. The Chinese had also built railroads that challenged the monopoly on rail transport that Japan had enjoyed in Manchuria since the end of the Russo-Japanese War.

All of this clearly threatened Japan's political and economic position in Manchuria at the same time that the Great Depression had unhinged the economy at home. Officers of the Kwantung Army, which defended Japanese interests in Manchuria, believed that drastic measures were necessary. But the war ministry hoped to secure Japanese interests through diplomacy. When this failed, the Kwantung officers decided to take matters into their own hands.

After blowing up the railway track, they blamed Chang's troops for the blast and used the incident to attack his forces. These actions represented a classic example of *gekokujo* and were taken without the war ministry's approval. The Japanese government quickly moved to put an end to the incident and received the army high command's support. But the Kwantung Army ignored instructions to cease operations and continued to advance. When confronted by this defiance, the army leaders in Tokyo gave in and approved the actions in Manchuria. The cabinet now realized that it had no choice but to go along with the army.

With all restraints removed, the Kwantung Army completed the conquest of Manchuria by January 1932. It was an easy victory because the Chinese did not seriously resist. Instead, Chiang reserved most of his troops for a showdown with the Chinese Communists. Although Chiang was not oblivious to the threat posed by the Japanese, he considered it less serious than the internal challenge of the Communists. He also recognized that his own control over Manchuria was tenuous at best and that his army was weak. Chiang preferred to invoke the support of the League of Nations, but the League merely called upon the Japanese to withdraw their troops. It avoided sanctions of any kind, although it did create a commission to investigate the situation. The United States, Britain, and France deplored Japan's aggressive actions, although they agreed that Chinese encroachments on Japanese treaty rights in Manchuria had provoked this extreme response. The Soviet Union was concerned about these developments on its eastern border but was in the midst of the internal struggle with the kulaks and in no condition to intervene.

In September 1932, the Japanese established a puppet state in Manchuria, which they renamed Manchukuo. Japan retained control over the country's military and foreign affairs. Soon afterward, the League commission issued its report, which called for an autonomous Manchurian government under Chinese sovereignty but with safeguards for Japan's special interests. Although the report was quite moderate, Japan withdrew from the League in protest. Almost simultaneously, the Kwantung Army moved into China's Jehol province, southwest of Manchuria. Again the Chinese government offered no serious resistance, and the Japanese incorporated Jehol into Manchukuo. In May 1933, Kwantung forces invaded China's Hopei province, and Chiang, with his attention focused on the imminent start of a new military campaign against the Communists, agreed to a truce. Under this arrangement, China recognized Japanese control over Manchuria and Jehol and also granted Tokyo extensive rights in Hopei. The failure to prevent Japan's conquest of Manchuria and Jehol represented a severe blow to the League's prestige and clearly revealed its basic weakness.

During the next four years, East Asia was relatively quiet, but remained tense. Chiang continued to view the Communists as the primary enemy and tried repeatedly to eliminate their stronghold in Kiangsi province. Although these efforts failed, they weakened Mao's forces. The Communist leader feared that another offensive would be fatal, and in 1934 he ordered his troops to seek refuge in the remote northern province of Shensi. To accomplish this, the Communists carried out an agonizingly difficult fighting withdrawal of 6,000 miles. Only 20,000 of the 90,000 men who started this legendary Long March reached Shensi, but once there, the mountainous terrain shielded them from Chiang's forces.

Many Chinese nationalists believed that Chiang was prepared to sacrifice the country to Japanese domination while he pursued his obsessive desire to crush communism. The forces of Chang Hsueh-liang, which had fled from Manchuria in 1931, were especially resentful. Reports of this disaffection alarmed Chiang and prompted him to visit Chang's headquarters in December 1936 to seek a reconciliation. While he was there, a group of Manchurian officers took him prisoner. In return for his release, Chiang reluctantly agreed to end his anti-Communist crusade and cooperate with Mao Tse-tung to strengthen China against the Japanese. Chiang was never really committed to this agreement, however, and continued to be reluctant to risk war with Japan.

War came nevertheless. It began in July 1937 with a skirmish at the Marco Polo Bridge south of the major city of Peiping (now Beijing) in Hopei province. Although it is not clear which side actually initiated hostilities, neither government really desired a full-fledged conflict at that time. But heavy fighting followed, and the war quickly escalated. By the middle of August, the Japanese were in control of Peiping. Soon afterward, they besieged the great port city of Shanghai at the mouth of the Yangtze River far to the south. After a bitter struggle lasting seven weeks, Shanghai fell, and the Japanese advanced up the Yangtze Valley. In December, they captured Nanking, the Kuomintang capital, which lay virtually defenseless. General Iwane Matsui, the Japanese commander, ordered his troops to treat the Chinese people with kindness and respect in an effort to gain their trust and cooperation. The soldiers, deaf to his entreaties, engaged in what became known as "the rape of Nanking" instead. They killed 20,000 men of military age by machine gun fire, by bayoneting, and even by dousing some with gasoline and then setting them afire. They raped, murdered, and mutilated 20,000 women and for good measure robbed and killed many other civilians. When the horror finally ended, one-third of the city lay in ashes and at least 200,000 persons had lost their lives, perhaps as many as 300,000.

Alarm increased in the West as it became clear that the Japanese intended to dominate China, a development that threatened European and American economic interests. Japan also aroused disgust by the bombing of open cities and especially the rape of Nanking. Tension mounted in December as the Japanese seized a British gunboat and sank the American gunboat *Panay*, both on the Yangtze River. Although London and Washington protested, they were reluctant to take any steps that might lead them into war.

Japan hoped to force Chiang to accept a dictated peace, but when these efforts failed, Japanese troops seized China's remaining seaports in 1938 and continued their offensive up the Yangtze. Despite these setbacks, Chiang refused to capitulate and moved his government to the ancient city of Chungking much farther up the Yangtze. Chungking was so remote and surrounded by such rugged mountains that the Japanese realized an advance in its direction was impractical. Chiang now prepared to wait until the enemy agreed to negotiate a reasonable peace or other powers came to China's aid. By the end of 1938, Japan held almost all of China's major cities and the railroads that linked them. But it could not control the vast countryside, where Communist guerrillas became active. Clearly, the Japanese had embarked on a task that was beyond their capabilities. They could neither destroy the enemy nor end the war through negotiation.

Meanwhile, relations between the Kuomintang and the Communists deteriorated. Despite the 1936 agreement, there was little cooperation, and frequently armed clashes broke out between the two rival forces. As the years passed, the Kuomintang regime became more corrupt, and its army did little actual fighting against the Japanese. At the same time, Mao's troops increased in strength and offered considerably more resistance to the invader. While the war dragged on into 1939, 1940, and beyond, the Chinese people, no strangers to suffering, continued to endure the horrors of enemy occupation and intermittent fighting. Many of them were homeless, destitute, and victims of recurring famine. The economy was in disarray, and the traditional structure of Chinese society and civilization began to break down.

Hitler's Plans for Europe

Despite the importance of the violent events unfolding in East Asia, to a large extent world attention during this period focused on Europe, where another drama was taking shape and led to the outbreak of war in 1939. Although many factors contributed to the coming of this conflict, the foreign policy of Hitler's Germany was the catalyst. Some historians contend that Hitler had no long-range foreign policy goals and was essentially an opportunist who took advantage of the weakness of other countries and the lack of resolve and unity of the Western Powers and the Soviet Union. They dismiss the views that he expressed in *Mein Kampf* as daydreams not to be taken seriously. Relatively few observers agree with them. The signs of continuity between *Mein Kampf* and Hitler's later policies were simply too great. Indeed, the Nazi leader reaffirmed and elaborated on his *Mein Kampf* program in a second book manuscript, which he wrote in 1928 but never published. Its existence came to light only after the war, when it appeared under the title *Hitler's Secret Book*. Numerous statements, which the Führer made to Nazi officials both before and during the war, also remained faithful to his original statement of intent.

To be sure, Hitler was an opportunist and a skilled liar. If it served his immediate purpose, he would make agreements with countries he ultimately planned to destroy. He also repeatedly assured the Western Powers that he merely desired a revision of the peace settlement to correct injustices to Germany. But it is difficult to avoid the conclusion that he planned from the start to dominate Europe, to create *Lebensraum* for the German people in Eastern Europe, and to accomplish this ultimately by resorting to war. He also planned to solve the "Jewish question," although the ultimate nature of that solution does

not appear to have taken final form until well after the outbreak of the war.

Hitler was violently anti-Semitic. His anti-Semitism was reinforced by a strong belief in the superiority of the Aryan race. In his view, only the Germanic peoples possessed pure Aryan blood, and he warned that they must not interbreed with inferiors, particularly the Jews but also the Slavs. He was less certain about the Latins (the French, Italians, Spanish, Portuguese, and Rumanians). He considered them to possess some Aryan blood, but unfortunately, the mixture of other blood lines had seriously reduced the Aryan content.

Closely identified with Hitler's racism was his view that the meaning of history lay in a struggle for existence among peoples or nations. He saw the object of this struggle as the acquisition of land, which was both limited and necessary to sustain the nation. Although he was certain that the Aryan Germans were the strongest nation and would ultimately win this struggle for *Lebensraum,* he saw the Jews as a potential obstacle. Hitler considered the Jews to be a special case because they were a people with no territorial base of their own, no real homeland. Thus, they were international in outlook rather than nationalistic. In Hitler's view, they sought to denationalize the world through the process of the interbreeding with and the bastardization of other peoples. He saw this as an interference with the struggle for existence, and if history were to unfold as he thought it should, it was necessary to crush the Jews. This would enable the German people to pursue their struggle for *Lebensraum* to a victorious conclusion.

The concept of *Lebensraum* had been present in the aims of some German nationalists during the late nineteenth and early twentieth centuries. It was also in keeping with the traditional German interest in expansion to the East that had existed for centuries. Hitler's interest in *Lebensraum* found much of its inspiration in geopolitics. Geopolitics, which involves the application of geographic principles to political problems, became quite influential in the early twentieth century. Hitler took special interest in the theory of Karl Haushofer, which stressed the importance of the Eurasian landmass. Haushofer believed that the nation that controlled what he referred to as the "heartland" of that vast area would be the dominant power in the world. The heartland included most of the Soviet Union.

Hitler believed that Germany was in a highly vulnerable position because of its location in the center of Europe, with a hostile France to the west and the Soviet Union on the east. Although he considered the Slavic Russians to be *Untermenschen* (subhumans) and much inferior to the Germans, he believed that they were capable of using German technology and organizational methods to strengthen the Soviet Union. This, combined with the USSR's enormous landmass and huge population, would eventually enable the Soviets to crush the German people, with their limited population and territory. To prevent such a catastrophe, Hitler insisted that Germany must greatly increase its population, but he warned that there was a limit to the number of people that the country could support within its present borders.

Thus, Germany had to expand its geographic base. The first step would involve taking over bordering territories that contained ethnic Germans—Austria, the Sudetenland, Danzig, Memel, and the areas ceded to Poland. Hitler assumed that to carry out even this limited expansion, it would be necessary to wage war against France. The Führer hoped to persuade Britain to remain neutral or even to entice the British into friendship with Germany. He also desired an alliance with Italy, despite its dubious Latin racial credentials. But Hitler contended that Germany's ultimate salvation lay in expansion eastward into the USSR. The Germans must colonize this area while enslaving most of the Slavs and deporting or exterminating the remainder. He also visualized the ouster—possibly the liquidation—of the Jews from both Germany and the areas to be conquered.

How could he accomplish this grandiose scheme in view of German weakness? Obviously, Germany would have to rearm in violation of the Treaty of Versailles. But if Britain and France intervened militarily to prevent this, the result would be disastrous. Hitler felt confident that they would not resort to such drastic action, however, and for a long time his optimism proved well founded.

Reactions of Other Powers

The British and French were far from united in their attitude toward Hitler and Nazi Germany.

Indeed, their own peoples were not in agreement on this question. In both countries, substantial numbers saw Hitler as a bulwark against the spread of communism and westward expansion by the Soviet Union. In France, many conservatives, including army officers, looked with special concern at the development of a large Communist party in their own country. And although the French government viewed any increase in German power as a threat to national security, they remembered the failure of their unilateral intervention during the Ruhr crisis in 1923. They were reluctant to undertake any similar action without British cooperation, but they realized that there was little chance of obtaining this. In fact, many members of the dominant British Conservative party sympathized with the German desire to revise the peace settlement and did not believe that this could be avoided for long.

A strong current of pacifism was also present in both countries, stemming largely from haunting memories of the horrors of World War I. The ghastly losses it had inflicted on their youth were hard to forget. Both nations hoped above all else to prevent another bloodbath, and this would play a major role in their response to Hitler's aggressive actions.

The pressing economic problems created by the Great Depression also distracted the British and French. Although Britain began to make a partial recovery in 1933, France, with a more diversified economy, did not really feel the full impact of the depression until 1934, and recovery did not start until late 1938. The governments of both countries were reluctant to embark on rearmament programs that would be enormously expensive and would place a tremendous strain on the financial stability of their governments. Britain was especially sensitive to the wishes of the self-governing dominions, which also suffered from the depression and wanted desperately to avoid war. The Western Powers also knew that they could not count on the United States to contribute to the collective security of Europe.

At first, the Soviet Union followed a policy of aloofness from European affairs but when the Russians did offer to cooperate with the West, starting in 1934, they made little progress. Britain and France were dubious about the seriousness of the Soviet commitment to collective security and were not certain that they wanted to ally themselves with Moscow under any circumstances. Stalin, for his part, continued to fear the possibility of a deal between the Western Powers and Hitler that might turn Germany's ambitions eastward at the USSR's expense. When Stalin launched his great purges in the mid-1930s, the British and French looked on with horror. Italy appeared a much better prospect for an alliance in the early 1930s. Mussolini feared the possibility of German expansion into Austria and the Balkans, where the Italians also had interests. But Italy's ambitions in Africa soon turned Mussolini away from the Western Powers and toward closer relations with Germany.

British and French leaders also misinterpreted Hitler's intentions. They tended to believe that he merely desired to end the restrictions that the peace settlement had placed on Germany. It was not until 1939 that they began to comprehend that his ambitions went beyond this and that he actually might contemplate the domination of Europe.

Ploys and Counterploys

The first major problem that confronted Hitler in foreign affairs was the question of how to circumvent the disarmament provisions of the Treaty of Versailles. An international conference had convened in Geneva in 1932 to consider the possibility of general disarmament. After coming to power, Hitler set out to sabotage this conference by demanding the end of all restrictions on German armaments. When France refused to agree, he withdrew Germany's delegation from the conference in October 1933. He used the same occasion as a pretext for terminating German membership in the League of Nations. Up to this point, Hitler had been reluctant to engage in rearmament on a large scale because he feared French opposition, but when the Western Powers reacted meekly to his withdrawal from the disarmament conference and the League, he became less cautious.

He secretly ordered a sharp increase in arms production during 1934 and by 1935 was finding it difficult to disguise these violations. Early in March, Hitler decided to gamble by announcing that Germany already had an air force in being. A week later, he revealed his intention to reintroduce

conscription and increase the German army to 550,000 men. The French and British could have responded by sending troops into Germany or by imposing an economic blockade. They did neither. Instead, they merely protested and took the matter before the League of Nations, which condemned Germany for violating the treaty but took no further action.

Even before Hitler announced rearmament, the first cracks began to appear in France's system of collective security in Eastern Europe. Polish leaders were concerned about their country's precarious geographic position between Germany and the Soviet Union and questioned France's willingness to honor its commitment to Poland if a crisis should arise. They decided that Poland would benefit from better relations with Germany while maintaining the French alliance. Hitler welcomed the opportunity to weaken the Franco-Polish alliance. In January 1934, Germany and Poland signed a ten-year nonaggression pact.

Hitler looked forward to the eventual union (*Anschluss*) of his native Austria with his adopted Germany. But prospects were not bright. Austrian chancellor Engelbert Dollfuss, who had established a dictatorship in March 1933, strongly opposed *Anschluss*. He was also antagonistic to the Austrian Nazi party, which had close ties to its German namesake. France was certain to be hostile to any attempt at union, and it was by no means certain that Britain would approve. Italy looked on Austria as a client state, and also opposed *Anschluss*.

Despite these obstacles, the Austrian Nazis attempted to overthrow the government in July 1934. Although the putsch failed miserably, it did result in the assassination of Dollfuss. It is not clear to what extent Hitler was actually involved in the plot, but once it failed, he denied any complicity. The assassination outraged Mussolini, who dispatched troops to the Austrian border as a deterrent to any German attempt to intervene. Hitler now recognized that *Anschluss* must be postponed. Kurt von Schuschnigg succeeded Dollfuss as chancellor and continued his predecessor's dictatorship as well as his dedication to maintaining Austrian independence.

Contrary to their initial passive response to Hitler's rearmament announcements, Britain, France, and Italy soon took steps toward what appeared to be a system of collective security. Representatives of the three powers met in the Italian resort town of Stresa in April 1935 and agreed to work together to oppose future treaty violations. Observers spoke of a "Stresa front" against Hitler.

The situation looked even more encouraging when France and Russia signed a defensive military alliance in May 1935, but Franco-Russian solidarity was more apparent than real. French foreign minister Jean Louis Barthou had launched negotiations for the alliance in 1934 and had tried to breathe new life into France's Eastern European alliance system, with the USSR as the chief bulwark. But he had fallen victim to assassination in the fall of 1934. His successor, Pierre Laval, was not enthusiastic about close relations with the Soviets. He made the pact virtually inoperable by adding stipulations that required the approval of the League of Nations as well as Britain and Italy before France could take action in cooperation with the Soviets. In this form, the pact never became a factor of any importance.

Russian willingness to make an alliance with France was indicative of a new Soviet policy that Stalin put into effect in 1934. Hitler's ruthless treatment of the German Communist party and his nonaggression pact with Poland had convinced Stalin that Nazi Germany posed a threat. He now attempted to build a collective security system that would seek to block German aggression. As the first step, the Soviet Union accepted membership in the League of Nations, and Foreign Commissar Maxim Litvinov became an outspoken advocate of collective security. In addition to the Franco-Russian alliance, Russia signed a mutual defense pact with Czechoslovakia in 1935. But the Soviets revealed their distrust of the French by stipulating that they were only obligated to aid the Czechs if France honored its alliance with Czechoslovakia first. The Comintern also instructed Communist parties in Western Europe to cooperate with the socialists and liberals in "popular fronts" against the Nazi menace. In 1936, popular front governments came to power in both France and Spain.

Despite these promising developments, Britain weakened prospects for a meaningful system of collective security by making a naval agreement with Germany in June 1935 without consulting either France or Italy. The British hoped to limit Germany's naval construction, which they expected Hitler to accelerate along with his military and air power. Under this arrangement, Britain recognized Germany's right to build up to 35 percent of British surface tonnage and 60 percent of British submarine strength. But in view of German naval weakness, Germany could not reach either level for years and, thus, in the meantime, could build without any limitations. Although the agreement applied only to naval strength, in a broader sense it essentially sanctioned German rearmament.

The End of the Stresa Front

Mussolini's expansionist ambitions dealt the Stresa front a fatal blow. Continuing economic problems and increasing working-class unrest contributed to his decision to seek a cheap victory in Africa. He hoped that this would distract attention away from internal discontent. The Duce had been planning an invasion of the East African country of Ethiopia since 1932. Italy had attempted to conquer Ethiopia in 1896 but had suffered a humiliating defeat. The memory of this disgrace had rankled Italian nationalists for 40 years. In late 1935, Mussolini sent his troops across the border from neighboring Italian Somaliland and Eritrea. The ensuing Italo-Ethiopian War ruined relations between Italy and the Western Powers and opened the door to Italian cooperation with Germany.

Initially, the British government of Prime Minister Stanley Baldwin and Premier Laval's French cabinet supported sanctions by the League of Nations against Italian aggression. But they did not relish a breakdown of relations with Italy, and British foreign secretary Sir Samuel Hoare and Laval worked behind the scenes to arrange a solution acceptable to Mussolini. The Hoare-Laval plan proposed that Ethiopia cede territory along the borders of Eritrea and Italian Somaliland to Italy and grant significant economic concessions as well. But when news of this proposal leaked to the press, it triggered an outburst of popular indignation in both countries. Hoare and Laval felt compelled to resign soon afterward. Sobered by this experience,

Britain and France reaffirmed their support for the League's policy of sanctions. Unfortunately, these sanctions did not extend to the sale of such vital commodities as oil and proved inadequate to prevent the Italians from completing their conquest of Ethiopia in 1936.

Mussolini reacted angrily to what he considered a breach of faith on the part of Britain and France. Hitler had been cool to Italy's invasion, but at least he had not participated in sanctions. Perhaps even more important in Mussolini's mind was the feeble quality of Anglo-French opposition, which cast doubt on their strength as allies. All of this contributed to a reappraisal of Italian foreign policy, and in February 1936 Mussolini informed Hitler that the Stresa front was dead. The failure of sanctions also delivered a serious blow to the League's prestige. Little faith remained in its ability to deter aggression.

Hitler believed that with their attention focused on Ethiopia, Britain and France would be less inclined to resist a German attempt to remilitarize the Rhineland. He knew that Italy would not interfere. Accordingly, he sent troops into the Rhineland on March 7. The Führer pointed to the French parliament's ratification of the Franco-Russian alliance in late February as justification for his action. He contended that the pact was a direct provocation. His generals had advised him against the operation. They felt certain that the French, who were still militarily superior to Germany, would resist. But France did not intervene. French army leaders, who were in a strongly defensive frame of mind, advised the government against military action. They believed that the German force was much stronger than it really was and insisted that France would have to mobilize a million reservists if it were to intervene. The cabinet was reluctant to resort to such a drastic measure as mobilization. Britain opposed military intervention, considering it out of the question to prevent the Germans forcibly from occupying their own territory. The British and French contented themselves with referring the matter to the League, which again condemned Germany for its treaty violations but took no further action. Once again, Hitler's gamble had succeeded.

It probably would have been more difficult for France to oust the Germans from the Rhineland than was once believed, and such an attempt would likely have meant war. But the French were certainly strong enough to have accomplished the task. Vigorous military action on their part also could have dealt a serious blow to Hitler's prestige. By failing to act, the French conceded Germany a victory of crucial importance. The occupation of the Rhineland deprived France of a buffer zone against German aggression and badly undermined faith among France's allies in French determination to resist German aggression. Shortly afterward, Belgium renounced its defensive treaty with France and declared neutrality.

Civil War in Spain

Four months after the Rhineland occupation, civil war erupted in Spain. Revolutionaries had overthrown the Spanish monarchy in 1931 and had established a democratic republic. But the new republic encountered some of the same problems that democracy had faced in Italy and Germany—lack of a democratic tradition, economic problems, and an even more chaotic array of political parties, complete with extremists on the left and the right. When a "popular front" Socialist-Communist coalition took power in 1936, a revolt in Spanish Morocco by troops under the command of General Francisco Franco triggered the civil war.

Oddly enough, Franco had little in the way of strong political convictions and was a latecomer to the military conspiracy that fostered the revolt. He had seen action against Moroccan rebels and gained a reputation for bravery as well as caution. Although originally shy, introverted, and unpopular, he rose rapidly in rank, becoming one of the youngest generals in Europe and eventually chief of staff. His decision to assume command of the revolt was due to his growing concern over the breakdown of order under the popular front government and the growth of radical leftist activity.

Franco's hopes for the conquest of Spain depended on the availability of aircraft to transport his troops across the Strait of Gibraltar. He appealed for aid to both Mussolini and Hitler, who, recognizing the advantage of another dictatorship on France's southern flank, agreed to supply the necessary planes. Although Franco hoped to extend his power rapidly over all of Spain, the republic proved stronger than he had expected. Franco's Nationalist troops managed to gain control over roughly the western half of the country while Republican forces held the remainder. Both Italy and Germany soon contributed manpower and other aid to the Nationalists. By early 1937, almost 50,000 Italian troops were serving in Spain. Hitler sent the so-called Condor Legion, which consisted primarily of planes and pilots, and some soldiers and tanks. Hitler deliberately limited aid to Franco in an effort to prolong the conflict. He wanted to keep British and French attention focused on Spain while he built up his military strength at home. To some extent, the war did provide the opportunity for Germany to test new weapons in combat, including bombers and dive bombers as well as the use of both high-explosive and incendiary bombs in combination.

Stalin countered Hitler and Mussolini by dispatching aid to the popular front government. But he sent no troops, only military advisers and equipment, including tanks and aircraft. The Comintern also sponsored the creation of volunteer units from various countries, which came to be known as international brigades. At their peak, these forces may have reached 18,000. The largest influx of Soviet assistance came during 1936 and early 1937. But in late 1938, Stalin terminated his efforts, apparently sensing the defeat of the Republicans. Britain and France refused to support either side. Despite the fact that a French popular front government had come to power in May, it was split over the question of aid to the republic. Baldwin and his British colleagues were totally opposed to intervention, although they actually favored the Nationalist cause and feared the leftist tendencies of the republic. Britain and France also opposed Soviet aid to the republican government. This increased Stalin's growing suspicion that the Western Powers were not really serious about resisting Hitler and Mussolini and, in fact, were more hostile to him. To prevent escalation of the war, Britain and France sponsored the Nonintervention Committee. This organization consisted of representatives from 27 countries, including Italy and Germany, which cynically participated despite their policy of aid to

Franco. The committee accomplished little and became a symbol of hypocrisy.

Although the Republican forces fought gallantly against increasing odds, they lost ground steadily during most of 1938, and their last strongholds capitulated in March 1939. Franco had benefited greatly from Italian and German support, but his interests did not necessarily coincide with those of Hitler and Mussolini. During the conflict, he had identified his regime with the Falange, a fascist party that had sided with the Nationalists. But this connection was never more than a disguise for what was essentially a traditional authoritarian government. Franco was also determined to maintain his freedom of action in foreign affairs.

Germany on the Offensive

The Spanish civil war inevitably brought the Germans and Italians into closer cooperation. Hitler had expected the conflict to make Italy more dependent on Germany, and his assumption proved correct, although Mussolini still hoped to make his way without becoming too closely tied to Berlin. It was the Duce, nevertheless, who promoted the drafting of a vaguely worded agreement in October 1936 that provided for cooperation between the two countries in the future. On November 1, Mussolini referred publicly to the existence of a "Rome-Berlin Axis."

Hitler also moved in the direction of closer relations with Japan in 1936. Despite the obvious fact that the Japanese were not Aryans, they won the Führer's admiration. He viewed them as a people in quest of *Lebensraum* on the Asian continent and respected their opposition to communism and antagonism toward the Soviet Union. In November 1936, Germany and Japan signed the Anti-Comintern Pact, binding the two countries to benevolent neutrality if one of them became involved in a war with the Soviet Union. A year later, Italy adhered to the pact.

During 1937, Hitler made no aggressive moves, other than to continue his aid to Franco. But in November, he informed Foreign Minister Konstantine von Neurath and his chief military leaders that his long-range goal was the creation of *Lebensraum* in Eastern Europe and warned that this would eventually mean war with France and

Britain. He indicated that his first goals were *Anschluss* with Austria and the destruction of Czechoslovakia.

Hitler's bluntness worried Field Marshal Werner von Blomberg, the war minister, and General Werner von Fritsch, the commander in chief of the army. Both men pointed out that Germany was far from strong enough to provoke a war, and Neurath also expressed doubts. Their lack of enthusiasm disturbed Hitler, and early in 1938 he replaced Neurath with Joachim von Ribbentrop. A member of the Nazi party since 1932, Ribbentrop was slavishly devoted to the Führer's ideas. He had started his career as an importer of wine and spirits and had no training in foreign affairs. But he endeared himself to Hitler because of his knowledge of languages and air of self-assurance. With the exception of Hitler, virtually all German leaders detested Ribbentrop.

Blomberg and Fritsch also gave up their posts under intense pressure. Hitler abolished the war ministry and replaced it with the High Command of the Armed Forces (*Oberkommando der Wehrmacht*, abbreviated OKW). General Wilhelm Keitel headed the OKW with General Alfred Jodl as his chief of staff. Keitel, a particularly spineless individual, had earned the contempt of his fellow officers, who referred to him as a lackey and a lickspittle. Jodl was a man of considerable ability who fell under Hitler's spell. As Fritsch's successor, the Führer chose another officer who was not likely to stand up to him—General Walther von Brauchitsch.

It was also in February 1938 that Hitler invited Austrian chancellor Schuschnigg to his retreat at Berchtesgaden in the Bavarian Alps. At this meeting, he subjected Schuschnigg to unbearable pressure and threats, demanding that he appoint a number of pro-Nazis to his cabinet. The most important of these, Arthur Seyss-Inquart, would become minister of the interior with control over the police. Schuschnigg realized that this would be a prelude to a Nazi takeover of Austria but finally yielded. After his return to Vienna, he resorted to a desperate gamble that he hoped might foil Hitler's plans. On March 9, he announced his intention to hold a plebiscite four days later in which the Austrian people could vote for or against *Anschluss*. Schuschnigg expected the plebiscite to result in a sizable majority in favor of continued independence.

Hitler apparently agreed and realized that such an outcome would undercut any contention that the Austrians desired absorption by Germany. The Führer reacted quickly and decisively. His

FIGURE 4-1   Adolf Hitler and Benito Mussolini inspect an Italian honor guard during a meeting in Venice. (*AP/Wide World Photos*)

first step was to promote demonstrations by Austrian Nazis. He also demanded Schuschnigg's resignation and the appointment of Seyss-Inquart to the chancellorship. The alternative would be an immediate German invasion. Schuschnigg, realizing that he had lost his gamble, complied. Seyss-Inquart became chancellor and, in his first official action, requested that Germany send troops into Austria to assist in the restoration of law and order. German forces crossed the border on March 12, and Hitler annexed Austria to Germany the following day.

These ruthless actions confronted British and French leaders with an accomplished fact. They could only change the situation by war and were not willing to resort to such drastic measures. In fact, both had assumed for some time that *Anschluss* would come eventually. The British believed that there was nothing intrinsically wrong with the merger of the two German peoples, but they were not happy with the tactics Hitler had employed.

Soon after the *Anschluss,* Hitler turned his attention to his next victim, Czechoslovakia. The issue, at least initially, was the German minority that lived in the Sudetenland. On March 28, he instructed Konrad Henlein, the leader of the Sudeten German party, to seek talks with the government in Prague on the question of autonomy for the Sudeten Germans within the Czech state. Henlein's party shared the Nazi goal of uniting the Sudetenland with Germany. Hitler did not want these talks to culminate in an agreement but planned to use them to create a crisis. He instructed Henlein to keep increasing his demands if the Czechs offered concessions. Once Henlein had convinced President Eduard Beneš and the Czech government to begin negotiations, Hitler launched an elaborate propaganda campaign that charged that the Czechs were mistreating the Sudeten Germans. He inferred that if this continued, Germany would have no choice but to intervene. In May, Hitler told his top generals of his "unalterable decision to smash Czechoslovakia by military action in the near future." In June, he selected October 1 as the day of reckoning.

The Dilemma of Czechoslovakia

The crisis posed serious problems for the Western Powers and the USSR. Both France and the Soviets had military alliances with Czechoslovakia. Britain had no obligation, but British leaders feared that if war came, they would become involved on the side of France. Both of the Western Powers considered the possibility of war with the utmost reluctance. They had little faith in Czechoslovakia's ability to repel a German invasion, despite the fact that the Czechs possessed a strong defensive line in the Sudetenland as well as an army of 35 divisions. Of even greater importance to them was the ominous fact that since the *Anschluss,* German territory flanked Czechoslovakia on three sides.

France, as the power with the most definite commitment to Czechoslovakia, felt a special sense of dilemma. It was still suffering from the belated effects of the depression and was in poor condition to embark on a major rearmament program. French generals also indicated that the army would not be able to undertake offensive action against Germany for another two years.

Premier Edouard Daladier, who came to power in April 1938, was convinced that France could not undertake a war without British support and had little faith in the possibility of such aid. Daladier had been premier twice before and had served as war minister since 1936, a position he continued to hold as premier. He had earned the reputation for possessing greater skill as a politician than as a statesman.

Daladier was quite right in expecting no help from Britain. Neville Chamberlain, who had succeeded Baldwin as prime minister in May 1937, favored a policy of appeasement. The British had been highly conciliatory toward Hitler's early violations of the peace settlement. But it was only with Chamberlain's advent to power that appeasement took on the guise of a thoroughgoing policy. A veteran of several cabinets, Chamberlain had little experience in foreign affairs, but he was determined personally to mold Britain's policy toward Hitler. He approached his task with a self-confidence bordering on arrogance.

The prime minister and most of his cabinet felt that the peace settlement had artificially relegated Germany to the role of a third-rate power and that Hitler was merely attempting to restore his country's former greatness. They also sympathized with his desire to absorb fellow Germans into the Reich. In fact, when Chamberlain first came to power, he had been willing to negotiate a general agreement that would have given Hitler a virtual free hand in Austria, the Sudetenland, and Danzig. He believed that the areas in question were not vital to British interests and thus hardly a suitable cause for war. He also did not want to jeopardize Britain's partial recovery by approving huge defensive expenditures. British service chiefs also produced gloomy appraisals of the country's military and naval capabilities and greatly exaggerated German strength.

As for the USSR, soon after the *Anschluss,* Litvinov appealed to Britain and France to cooperate with the Soviet Union in case of continued German aggression. But the Western Powers declined. They were suspicious of Soviet intentions, particularly because the USSR did not border either Czechoslovakia or Germany. The Russians could aid the Czechs only by moving troops through Poland, but the Poles, who also had territorial claims on Czechoslovakia, were hardly likely to grant permission.

Ironically, German generals dreaded the prospect of war and believed that France was far superior militarily to Germany. They also feared the formidable Czech defenses in the Sudetenland. When it became clear that Hitler planned to take military action, General Ludwig Beck, chief of staff of the Army High Command (*Oberkommando des Heeres,* abbreviated OKH), protested in the strongest terms. He even tried to persuade his colleagues to join in a general strike if the Führer persisted. Although Brauchitsch, the army's commander in chief, shared Beck's misgivings, he was not the man to challenge Hitler. In July, Beck resigned in frustration. General Franz Halder, who succeeded him as chief of staff, also was appalled by the prospect of war. Halder joined with Beck and several other generals in a conspiracy to arrest Hitler if he carried out his war plans and if the Western Powers resisted. To what extent the conspirators were determined to act will never be known because the necessary prerequisite, Western intervention on behalf of Czechoslovakia, did not materialize.

Negotiations between the Czechs and Sudeten Germans dragged on throughout the spring and summer. But matters came to a head in early September, when the British pressured Czechoslovakia to grant autonomy to the Sudeten Germans. Hitler now changed his strategy. He ordered Henlein to break off the talks and delivered a speech in which he denounced the Czechs and emphasized his willingness to go to war to settle the Sudeten issue.

At this point, Chamberlain attempted to reach a settlement with Hitler through personal diplomacy. He flew to Germany and asked the Führer what he really desired. Hitler for the first time specified German annexation of the Sudetenland. Chamberlain agreed to this in principle and returned to London, where he gained the support of his own government. Next he persuaded Daladier and the French cabinet to agree. Beneš, recognizing that a refusal would leave Czechoslovakia to confront Germany alone, also reluctantly consented. Chamberlain returned to Germany to report the good news to Hitler, but the Führer had now decided that this generous settlement was not enough. He insisted that the Czechs must also satisfy Polish and Hungarian demands for border revisions as well as a Slovak request for autonomy. Finally, he required the immediate German occupation of the designated areas.

Chamberlain's first response was anger, but by the time he had returned to London, he had decided to accept Hitler's terms, however insulting they might be. But his foreign secretary, Lord Halifax, believed that Britain could not ask the Czechs for any additional sacrifices. Daladier also insisted that France would not accept these demands, and a number of British newspapers attacked Chamberlain's policy. With his support dwindling, the prime minister reluctantly agreed to aid France militarily if that nation honored its commitment to Czechoslovakia. War appeared imminent.

But Chamberlain had not abandoned his efforts. He now sought Mussolini's help in arranging another conference. The Duce realized that Italy was not prepared for war and was more than pleased to play the role of peacemaker. Hitler also had second thoughts and reluctantly decided that it would be best to accept a bloodless conquest. This time, a four-power meeting convened in Munich on September 30, with Hitler, Mussolini, Chamberlain, and Daladier all in attendance. Neither Czechoslovakia nor the Soviet Union received an invitation. During the conference, Chamberlain and Daladier essentially accepted Hitler's original demands. They approved German annexation of the Sudetenland with a brief post-ponement of the actual occupation of some of the territory. Czechoslovakia had no choice but to accept the agreement. Hitler had won total victory; in addition to absorbing 3 million Germans, he had acquired important natural resources and industrial centers, including the huge Skoda armament works. Soon after the Munich agreement Beneš resigned as president and went into exile in Britain. The aged Dr. Emil Hácha succeeded him.

A Change of Policy in the West

Upon his return to London, Chamberlain jubilantly told a cheering crowd that he had secured not only "peace with honor," but "peace in our time." Winston Churchill, a dissident member of the prime minister's own party, was not so sure. He glumly proclaimed that "We are in the midst of a disaster of the first magnitude." As it turned out, Chamberlain had only postponed the coming of war for 11 months. Hitler had no intention of allowing the rump Czecho-Slovak state to survive and merely waited for the right opportunity to strike. It came in March 1939 in the form of squabbling between the Czechs and the Slovaks. Hitler urged Slovak extremists to demand independence and pressured President Hácha to agree to this as well as to accept a German protectorate over Bohemia and Moravia. The alternative was an immediate invasion. Hácha gave in on March 15, and German troops quickly occupied the two provinces. Hitler now recognized the independence of Slovakia, which agreed to become a German protectorate. Hitler also granted Ruthenia, the extreme eastern portion of Czechoslovakia, to Hungary. The Czecho-Slovak state had ceased to exist, and Hitler had fallen heir to vast quantities of military equipment that substantially augmented his still incomplete rearmament program.

By ruthlessly destroying the remnant of Czechoslovakia, Hitler clearly revealed that his goal was not merely to absorb fellow Germans into the Reich. He increased tension still more by seizing Memel from Lithuania on March 23. Chamberlain now reluctantly changed his policy, and on March 30 Britain extended a guarantee to Poland that assured the Poles that if Germany attacked them, they could count on British support. France joined in this guarantee and also reaffirmed its original alliance.

Chamberlain's action represented a startling reversal in British policy. The prime minister was convinced that Britain must take a much firmer approach to Hitler. But he had not ruled out the possibility of a negotiated settlement over Danzig and Poland. It appeared to him that a show of determination would be more likely to bring Hitler to the bargaining table. But if such an approach were to have any chance of success, it required significant preparations for war and immediate efforts to coordinate military planning with the Poles. Little of this followed. Although the British introduced conscription on a limited basis, and both Britain and France strengthened their forces, they took only the most halting measures to cooperate with the Poles. None of this was sufficient to persuade Hitler that they were really serious.

Actually, Hitler had originally hoped to achieve an alliance with Poland for use against the USSR. He had broached such an arrangement as early as 1935 and again in 1937. In return for concessions to Germany on Danzig and the Polish corridor, he held out the prospect of territory for Poland in the Ukraine. The Poles declined. They feared both Germany and the Soviets and were reluctant to become too closely associated with either. Instead, they tried to maintain a precarious balance between the two.

Ribbentrop, the Nazi foreign minister, revived this proposal in October 1938 and again in January 1939. He requested Polish approval for German annexation of Danzig and the construction of an extraterritorial road and railway across the Polish corridor to link East Prussia with Germany proper. He also asked that Poland adhere to the Anti-Comintern Pact. The Poles refused, fearing that acceptance would convert their country into a German satellite. In April, soon after the Anglo-French guarantee to Poland, Germany brusquely renewed these demands. Again the Poles refused. This signaled the start of a new crisis, which continued throughout the spring and summer while the Germans launched another propaganda barrage, accusing the Poles of mistreating the German minority in Poland. In April, Hitler ordered preparations to begin for an invasion of Poland in September.

Crisis over Poland

Hitler looked to Mussolini for support as German relations with Poland and the Western Powers deteriorated. Although the two dictators had grown closer since the outbreak of the Spanish civil war, the Duce had attempted to improve relations with Britain as a counterweight to the Rome-Berlin Axis, but nothing substantial came from his efforts. The Italian dictator also resented Hitler's escalating importance and his own relegation to junior status in the Axis. On April 7, 1939, Italian forces seized little Albania, across the Adriatic Sea from southern Italy. This change was less dramatic than it appeared because the Italians had exercised strong political and economic influence over Albania since 1926.

Despite Mussolini's dream of pursuing a middle course in foreign policy, he concluded an actual alliance, the "Pact of Steel," with Germany on May 22. This agreement bound the two partners to provide full assistance to each other in case of war, regardless of the circumstances. But Mussolini recognized that Italy would not be ready for war until 1943, and his foreign minister, Count Galeazzo Ciano, had so informed Ribbentrop during the negotiations. But the text of the pact made no reference to this. Hitler apparently assumed that Italy would enter the war when he attacked Poland, even though he kept his ally in the dark regarding his plans until late in the crisis. When he did finally confide in the Duce that a military showdown was imminent, Mussolini surprised him with the news that Italy could not join in hostilities for the foreseeable future.

With the deepening of the Polish crisis, the role of the Soviet Union loomed especially large. As Poland's neighbor on the east, the USSR was in a position either to aid the Poles in the defense of their country or to side with the Germans in its destruction. Britain and France recognized that an alliance with the Soviet Union would be the best way—perhaps the only way—to deter Hitler from attacking Poland.

They began diplomatic discussions with the Soviets in April, but these proved indecisive. Military staff talks did not start until early August and quickly took on an aura of unreality. Both Britain and France found it difficult to abandon their distrust of the Russians, and Stalin was perhaps even more suspicious of the Western Powers. He was far from impressed with their military strength and feared a possible Western deal with Hitler which would enable Germany to crush Poland and then turn against Russia without interference from Britain and France. The memory of the Munich agreement was still fresh in his mind. The whole question of an alliance became moot when Poland announced that it would not allow Soviet troops to enter its territory. The Poles feared Russia at least as much as they feared Germany.

It now appeared to Stalin that a deal with Hitler provided his best option, at least for the present. It offered security from a German attack in the near future as well as the possibility of pushing the USSR's borders farther to the West, thus providing a buffer zone against an invasion, if and when it finally came. In fact, Stalin had considered an agreement with Hitler even before the start of talks with the Western Powers. He made his first approach to Berlin in April and in May replaced Foreign Commmisar Litvinov with Vyacheslav Molotov, his oldest and closest associate. Litvinov, a Jew with an English wife, symbolized Soviet support for collective security. Molotov, blessed with nerves of steel and an imperturbable temperament, was devoted to Stalin.

Despite his aversion to the Soviet Union and communism, Hitler also could see the obvious benefits to be gained from an agreement. In late May, talks began on economic issues and culminated in an agreement on August 19. Under its terms, the Soviets were to supply the Germans with raw materials, and Germany would extend credits to enable Russia to purchase German capital goods and war materiel. But what Hitler wanted most was a political arrangement, and he pressed Stalin to receive Ribbentrop on August 23 to discuss such an understanding. The result was the Nazi-Soviet Nonaggression Pact, which Ribbentrop and Molotov drafted that same day. Under its terms, the two powers vowed to remain neutral if either of them became involved in a war. They also concluded a secret protocol that provided for German occupation of the western half of the country while the Soviets claimed the eastern portion. Germany also recognized the predominance of Soviet interests in Finland,

Europe on the Eve of World War II, August 1939

Estonia, Latvia, and the Rumanian province of Bessarabia, reserving Lithuania for its own sphere of influence.

When Germany and the Soviet Union announced the signing of the nonaggression pact, the news created a sensation throughout the world and came as a great blow to the British and French. It meant that Hitler would be free from the need to fight a two-front war once he had defeated Poland. But despite this great advantage, Hitler viewed the pact primarily as a mechanism for assuring the neutrality of Britain and France.

Without Soviet support, he expected the Western Powers to back down and desert Poland as they had abandoned Czechoslovakia. This would enable him to deal with the Poles in a localized war. Much to his surprise, however, the British and French did not back down. Despite this inconvenience, at dawn on September 1 Hitler sent his forces into Poland. The Western Powers declared war on Germany two days later. The conflict, which Hitler had hoped would be an unequal struggle between Germany and Poland, had become World War II.

CHAPTER FIVE

Blitzkrieg in the East, *Sitzkrieg* in the West

Unlike 1914, no great demonstrations of frenzied enthusiasm greeted the outbreak of war in September 1939. Instead, silent resignation prevailed in London, Paris, and even Berlin where American foreign correspondent William L. Shirer observed a mixture of apathy, astonishment, and depression on the faces of German civilians in the streets. The specter of the hideous bloodbath of World War I still loomed over the continent. Britain and France were slow to honor their commitments to Poland. The British did not declare war until 11 A.M. on September 3 when their ultimatum demanding the evacuation of German troops from Poland expired. The French did not follow suit until another six hours had elapsed. In his speech to Parliament that day, Chamberlain glumly declared, "Everything I have worked for, everything I have hoped for, everything I have believed in has crashed in ruins." There was even less reason for jubilation in Poland where the Poles faced the full brunt of the German attack completely alone.

Differing Approaches to War

During the opening period of World War II, from September 1939 to November 1941, Germany won a series of spectacular victories and conquered much of Europe. These successes stunned the world and gave the illusion of overwhelming strength. The Germans failed only in their attempt to crush Britain in 1940, but this defeat came in the air. They remained invincible on land.

Despite appearances, Germany's triumphs were not due to overwhelming strength. Hitler's army was formidable, but considering his ambitious war aims, it was not enormously large. Much of its equipment, including tanks, was not of the highest quality and not especially plentiful.

Ironically, the Germans, who revolutionized warfare through mechanization during the 1930s, were short of motorized transport. Only a few of their infantry divisions were motorized. They also faced a serious shortage of trucks for supply purposes, and the mass of their army depended on horse-drawn vehicles to transport supplies. The actual keys to Hitler's success during the first two years of the war were the ways in which German leaders used their forces and took advantage of their opponents' mistakes.

Germany's approach to war was in large part predicated on Hitler's intention of dominating Europe and creating *Lebensraum*. He could accomplish this only by taking the offensive. But despite Hitler's dedication to offensive warfare, most German generals in the period between the wars expected to fight the next conflict as they had waged World War I—with mass infantry attacks. They were by no means convinced that the tank and the airplane were the weapons of the future.

During the interwar years, most French and British generals were also conservative and unimaginative in their outlook, but unlike the Germans, they were committed to defense and, in particular, fixed fortifications. They had learned what seemed to be the major lesson of World War I—the fact that victory had been won in large part by defensive firepower. Indeed, they had learned it too well.

Ironically, the French had been enthusiastic advocates of offensive warfare before and during World War I. The more optimistic of them believed that fighting spirit was the most important factor in war and that an army that possessed sufficient spirit could defeat any defensive force, no matter how powerful. The French put this suicidal doctrine into practice during World War I and tried repeatedly to break the stalemate by means of

European Theater, 1939–42

mass attacks. Each time, they failed while suffering huge casualties. This experience led to a revulsion for this type of warfare among postwar French leaders, especially Marshal Henri Pétain, who had opposed the prevailing offensive creed even before 1914 and commanded the French forces that stopped Germany's repeated attacks against the fortress city of Verdun in 1916. In the postwar era, he continued to champion defensive warfare. British military leaders shared the French devotion to the defense. They also had undertaken massive offensives during World War I that had resulted in meager gains at a terrible price in lives.

But there was one lesson of World War I that most French and British generals had not learned—even

though the defense had been supreme during most of the conflict, it was offensive power that eventually won the war. The Germans had failed to stop the Allied offensive during the summer and fall of 1918 and had fallen back steadily, although they had prevented a breakthrough. The Allies had employed large numbers of tanks in this operation. Unfortunately, these armored vehicles, ponderous and slow, had suffered heavy losses, convincing many French and British leaders that the tank would never be a decisive weapon.

Not all French and British military men were wedded to static defensive warfare in the postwar period, however. In France, General J. B. E. Estienne, the creator and leader of the French World War I tank force, believed that the key to the next war would be fast-striking offensive operations featuring large tank formations supported by aircraft. Estienne influenced a young colonel, Charles de Gaulle, who expounded similar views in a book he published in 1934. The politician Paul Reynaud shared their belief in the importance of mobile offensive warfare. Unfortunately, Estienne, de Gaulle, and Reynaud won few followers, and the static defensive mentality remained dominant. In Britain, General J. F. C. Fuller, who had served as chief of staff of the Royal Tank Corps in 1918, insisted that the tank, operating in large formations, was the weapon of the future. His most important convert was B. H. Liddell Hart, an infantry captain whose army career had ended when he was gassed during the Battle of the Somme. Liddell Hart developed the "expanding torrent" theory of deep, swift penetration by armored units as the key to breaking a static defensive line. But he was also a strong believer in defense and contended that powerful tank forces should be used in a defensive role to counterattack enemy offensive formations. Fuller and Liddell Hart failed to convince Britain's senior military leaders of the crucial role of armor, but Liddell Hart's views on the importance of defense served to reinforce the British defensive bias.

Ironically, it was the Germans who learned from the Western advocates of armored warfare. They had been slow to appreciate the value of the tank in World War I, but during the 1930s they created large armored (panzer) formations, which France and Britain ignored. The man most responsible for this transformation was Heinz Guderian, a relatively junior officer who did not become a general until 1938. Guderian had witnessed the appalling slaughter at Verdun, which convinced him that Germany must avoid the horrors of such static warfare in the future. During the 1920s, he fell under the influence of British advocates of armored warfare, especially Liddell Hart. Guderian concluded that powerful concentrations of fast-striking, well-armored, and heavily armed tanks, closely supported by aircraft and other motorized troops, would determine the outcome of the next conflict. Guderian found it difficult to overcome the resistance of the more conservative senior generals, but he did win Hitler's support as early as 1933. He published a book in 1937 that explained his theory of armored warfare and

presented what amounted to a blueprint for the future *Blitzkrieg* (lightning war). But Guderian was not alone. General von Fritsch, the former army commander-in-chief, and General Beck, the erstwhile chief of staff of the Army High Command, had developed the concept of "combined arms," which was crucial to the success of the German *Blitzkrieg*. This concept would also ultimately form the key component of Allied success later in the war.

The intent of the *Blitzkrieg* was to gain victory as quickly, as decisively, and with as few German casualties as possible. To accomplish this, powerful panzer forces would smash through opposing border defenses and encircle large concentrations of enemy troops. The panzer divisions themselves were balanced formations of all arms—tanks, mechanized infantry in armored halftracks, and mobile artillery. "Motorized infantry" traveling in trucks, would follow behind the armor and consolidate the initial gains while the tanks dashed deeper into the interior. Next, the traditional mass of infantry, marching on foot, would relieve the motorized infantry, allowing it to keep pace with the panzers. Meanwhile, the Luftwaffe would destroy the enemy air force, ideally catching many planes on the ground. Once they had accomplished this, German aircraft would attack enemy communications and troop formations. Tanks, motorized infantry, and airpower would all work in harmony to crush the enemy.

But while the Germans staked their future on the *Blitzkrieg,* the French carried their defensive doctrine to its ultimate manifestation, the construction of the Maginot line, the greatest system of fixed fortifications ever built. It consisted of massive concrete and steel forts housing guns of tremendous range and power, casements and pillboxes containing smaller guns, and shell and bombproof underground facilities. Although the line was incredibly strong, it had one glaring weakness: it extended only from the Swiss frontier to a point just beyond the convergence of the borders of France, Luxembourg, and Belgium. Unfortunately, the likely route for a German invasion was through Belgium to the northwest of the Maginot line. This would enable the enemy to outflank its powerful fortifications.

Several factors contributed to the French failure to continue the line along the Belgian border to the sea. Such an extension would have been extremely expensive and would have run through heavily industrialized urban centers. The high water table in the extreme western portion of the border area also posed problems for underground construction. And France was concerned that the Belgians might consider the extension of the line an indication that the French would not aid their country against a German invasion but would merely wait behind their defenses. Finally, the French visualized the Maginot line as only a partial defense. In case of a German attack by way of Belgium, they intended to send troops to aid the Belgians. They hoped that these forces, anchored on the Maginot line to the south, would be sufficient to stop a German offensive before it reached French soil. By pursuing such a defensive strategy, France hoped to fight a war of "limited liability" and avoid a repetition of the horrible casualties of World War I.

Britain, too, had opted for a war of limited liability, to an even greater degree than France. The British armed forces clearly reflected this decision. As an island power, Britain's first line of defense was the Royal Navy, still by far the largest in Europe. The Royal Air Force received second priority but only slowly increased in strength during the 1930s. The army came in a poor third, even after the introduction of conscription shortly before the outbreak of war. Although Britain sent an expeditionary force to France in the fall of 1939, it numbered only 250,000 men and contained just one armored division.

Despite his aggressive foreign policy and determination to take the offensive, Hitler actually had also committed Germany to a war of limited liability. He was confident that he could gain victory through a series of swift, decisive *Blitzkrieg* offensives that would not require full mobilization of the economy. Contrary to the view that prevailed in Britain and France, the Führer had not carried out a sweeping reorganization of the German economy; in reality, much of German industry still concentrated on the production of consumer goods.

Hitler had chosen a policy of rearmament "in breadth" intended to provide the armed forces with sufficient weapons to enable them to win a series of lightning campaigns. He did not anticipate a long war and, thus, did not favor an intense mobilization of the economy to provide rearmament "in depth." Such an approach would have concentrated first on expansion of Germany's heavy industry—a vast increase in steel production and construction of additional facilities to enable the manufacture of huge quantities of war materiel. A policy of this type would have necessitated postponing war until at least 1943 and would have assumed a lengthy conflict.

Strengths and Weaknesses

In 1936, Hitler established the Four-Year Plan, under Goering's leadership, aimed at making Germany as self-sufficient as possible and ready for war within four years. The plan had only indifferent success. It did not expand German industry; it merely brought existing production facilities up to full capacity. Hitler and Goering hoped to make Germany independent in materials that the nation could produce. This would enable them to conserve foreign currency reserves for the purchase of food and raw materials that could not be produced domestically. The Four-Year Plan emphasized production of synthetic materials. Goering projected that by 1939 German synthetic production would provide 100 percent of its oil needs and half of its rubber. But in 1939 it actually accounted for only 20 percent of Germany's oil and less than 15 percent of its rubber. Two-thirds of Germany's total raw materials still came from foreign countries. The Germans also had to import 20 percent of their food.

Germany did have some advantages, however. It had the potential to expand its industrial capabilities greatly if necessary. With the absorption of Austria and the Sudetenland, Germany's population had reached 80 million, providing a good manpower pool for both industry and the armed forces. And the Russo-German economic agreement of August 1939 promised a steady flow of food, oil, and other raw materials. Hitler also expected to extract ample booty from the countries that fell under German control as a result of his *Blitzkrieg*.

Britain, with a population of 46 million, could not match Germany either in manpower or in its industrial base, but Britain did possess access to the resources of the rest of the world.

The Commonwealth itself was a storehouse of raw materials. The British colony of Malaya alone produced 58 percent of the world's rubber. Britain, of course, could cut off Germany from overseas sources of supply by virtue of superior naval strength. Whether this would be sufficient to cause Germany critical problems was questionable in view of the 1939 Russo-German trade agreement. Hitler also had access to the resources of southeastern Europe, including Rumania's oil fields.

Britain's Achilles' heel was its dependence on large-scale imports of food and raw materials. To pay for them, the British had to maintain a high level of exports and services, such as shipping and insurance, as well as overseas investment. World War I had seriously disrupted all of these economic activities. Clearly, the outbreak of war in 1939 promised even more disastrous injury to the failing economy. In view of this dilemma, the British were reluctant to embark on an ambitious rearmament program during the 1930s. Although they finally made belated preparations for war, the results were far from impressive. The creation of new cabinet posts for supply, shipping, and food in 1939 helped lay the framework for a thoroughgoing war economy but led to little initial progress. Of more immediate importance, the British had begun to produce two excellent new fighter planes, the Hurricane and the Spitfire.

France, too, still suffered from the impact of the Great Depression. Its population of 42 million was much smaller than Germany's and even less than Britain's. France's industrial base was also much smaller than that of both countries, but the French had made some progress. Premier Daladier had appointed Paul Reynaud minister of finance in November 1938, and Reynaud had eased restrictions on investment credit and stimulated rearmament. Industrial production rose by 20 percent during the next ten months. It is indeed remarkable that France was able to enter the war on an equal basis with Germany in some respects, most notably in tanks and artillery. But the key to Anglo-French hopes for winning the war was time. If they could force Germany into a long war, their chances of victory would increase greatly. It soon became apparent, however, that time was a luxury that their alliance did not enjoy.

The First *Blitzkrieg*: Germany's Invasion of Poland

Germany first tested the *Blitzkrieg* in the invasion of Poland in September 1939, with spectacular results. The Poles never had a chance. Their antiquated army was at a great disadvantage in both men and equipment. The Germans committed 52 divisions (roughly 1 million men) to the campaign, including six panzer and four motorized divisions. German armor, for the most part, was not of high quality. The most numerous tank was the Panzer I, but its armament consisted of only two machine guns. The next most plentiful armored vehicle was the Panzer II, which carried a weak 20-millimeter cannon. Some higher-quality Panzer IIIs and Panzer IVs were available, but in small numbers. The Panzer III mounted a 37-millimeter gun, while the Panzer IV wielded a short 75-millimeter cannon. In all, the Germans used 1,500 tanks, not a particularly large force, but together with their relatively few motorized divisions, it was more than sufficient to overwhelm the Poles.

On paper, Poland, with a population of 35 million, was capable of fielding an army of over 2 million men, but the Poles delayed mobilization until August 31 to avoid providing the Germans with an excuse for aggression. When the invasion began the following day, only 600,000 men were available. Most of this force consisted of infantry and cavalry. Poland's military leaders were exceptionally proud of their cavalry, but it was hardly a match for German armor. The Poles had only 310 tanks, most of them obsolete. They reduced their striking power still more by scattering them among infantry divisions. The Polish army had little else in the way of mechanized forces. Germany enjoyed a big advantage in air power, with 850 bombers and 400 fighters. Poland could muster a total of only 400 first-line planes, just 36 of which were modern.

Since the destruction of Czechoslovakia, German troops flanked Poland on three sides. This placed the Poles in a highly vulnerable position. Logic seemed to dictate that Polish forces should take up positions to the east of the barrier created by the Narew, Vistula, and San rivers. But this would necessitate abandoning much of western Poland, including the country's most important industrial areas. Polish leaders refused to take such drastic action. Instead, they concentrated one-third of their strength in the general area of the Polish corridor and another third in reserve between the capital, Warsaw, and the industrial city of Lodz to the southwest. They stretched the rest of their forces dangerously thin to protect the remaining border areas.

Germany divided its invading forces into Army Group North, which included two armies under the command of General Fedor von Bock, and Army Group South, consisting of three armies commanded by General Gerd von Rundstedt. Bock and Rundstedt were both Prussian aristocrats and the sons of generals. Each had served capably during World War I. At 64, Rundstedt was the

senior general in the German army and highly respected for his ability as a field commander. He had actually retired in 1938 but returned to active duty a few months later. Bock's most noteworthy qualities were determination and hard work rather than brilliance. An extremely arrogant man, he was utterly devoted to the army. General Halder's OKH staff drafted the operational plan for the invasion, which was given the code name Case White. It called for the destruction of the bulk of the Polish army to the west of Warsaw by means of a pincers movement in which elements of Army Group North would swing southeastward to link up with Army Group South, which was to strike northward. Additional troops from Army Group North were to smash across the base

The German and Soviet Invasion of Poland, September 1939

of the Polish corridor into East Prussia, cutting off the enemy forces to the north.

The *Blitzkrieg* began on September 1. German armored forces quickly broke through Poland's border defenses and penetrated deep into the interior. Meanwhile, the Luftwaffe attacked the Polish air force, but contrary to a persistent myth, it did not destroy most of it on the ground. In fact, Polish planes resisted fiercely during the first few days and many Polish pilots demonstrated great heroism. German numerical and technical superiority gradually took its toll, however, and cleared the skies of enemy aircraft. Meanwhile German medium bombers and Stuka dive bombers attacked Polish troops and communications. Although actually a mediocre plane with poor speed, flimsy armor, and limited range, the Stuka worked well in this type of unopposed operation. With its fixed landing gear, the Stuka resembled a bird of prey. It was outfitted with a siren that unleashed a shrill, blood-curdling shriek as it swooped down on its victims. These features added to its impact as a weapon of terror.

Germany's most remarkable progress came in the south, where an armored corps, commanded by General Erich Höpner, sliced northeastward, reaching the outskirts of Warsaw on September 8. Another panzer corps, commanded by General Guderian, severed the Polish corridor and moved into East Prussia on September 3. The Poles fought gallantly but faced overwhelming odds. At times, when surrounded, Polish cavalry, armed with lances, actually charged German tanks rather than surrender. Confronted by these disasters, the Polish high command belatedly ordered a withdrawal of all remaining units to the Narew-Vistula-San river line.

The Germans received only one major scare. It came on September 9, when the Poles directed a determined counterattack against the flank of Rundstedt's forces to the west of Warsaw. But after heavy fighting, the Germans blunted the Polish thrust and drove on to meet Bock's forces pushing southward. This union encircled 170,000 Polish troops, completing the pincers movement outlined in Case White.

The final phase of the Polish campaign began on September 9. It took the form of another pincers movement, which closed near Brest-Litovsk on September 17 when Guderian's panzers,

swinging southward from East Prussia, met armored forces, commanded by General Ewald von Kleist, that had dashed northward from southern Poland. On the same day, Soviet troops invaded Poland from the east and quickly overran the remainder of the country. The late timing of this operation was due to the fact that the Soviets had not expected the German invasion to come so soon and were not prepared to strike earlier. A total of 90,000 Polish troops escaped into Hungary and Rumania, many of them eventually making their way to France and Britain, from where they carried on the fight.

Polish resistance continued for some time at various isolated points, including Warsaw. After reaching the suburbs of the capital on September 8, the Germans soon discovered that the narrow confines of street fighting were not well suited for attacks by armor. They resorted instead to artillery and aerial bombardment and finally launched an infantry assault on September 26. When the exhausted Polish garrison surrendered the following day, many of the people of Warsaw lay dead in the blazing ruins that comprised much of the city. The Polish capital had become the first of many European cities to experience such a fate. A few other isolated garrisons fought on in gallant but hopeless battles until as late as October 6.

The Germans had destroyed Poland with astonishing speed and thoroughness, even if the *Blitzkrieg* had not always functioned as flawlessly as Goebbel's propaganda machine insisted. In particular, the Luftwaffe had not completely perfected its support of the swiftly moving ground forces. Nevertheless, the *Blitzkrieg* had revolutionized warfare. Surprisingly, the Western Allies were slow to recognize this. They blamed Poland's inadequate military forces and faulty defensive plan for the disaster and assumed that it would be different when the Germans attacked in the west. The French began to have second thoughts about the potential of tanks, however, and hastily embarked on the creation of four armored divisions.

In keeping with their defensive strategy, France and Britain made no effort to stage an offensive against Germany while the *Blitzkrieg* was destroying Poland. The French launched only a minor probing action, despite the fact that Germany had only 25 weak reserve divisions in the west and a defensive system, the West Wall, which was far from complete and of negligible strength. But it was sufficient to impress the Western Powers, who persisted in calling it the Siegfried line after the legendary warrior of German mythology.

Ribbentrop and Soviet foreign minister Molotov met on September 28 to partition Poland. The Soviet Union gained slightly more than half of the country and about a third of the population as well as the oil fields. Germany, though receiving a smaller amount of territory, acquired roughly two-thirds of the people, the major industrial centers, the mining regions, and the best farmland. Hitler annexed approximately half of his share, as well as Danzig, directly to Germany. He designated the remainder the "Government General" and kept it under total German domination. This arrangement gave the Germans slightly more territory than the secret protocol of August 23 had provided, but in return the Soviets received a free hand in Lithuania, which the original agreement had conceded to Germany.

Hitler had intended even before the invasion to treat the Polish people with draconian harshness. The SS now served as the instrument of his policy with the essentially passive compliance of the army, although some officers proclaimed their distaste for what was euphemistically referred to as "housecleaning." This involved the wholesale executions of Polish army officers, aristocrats, clergy and intellectuals in a concerted effort to eliminate any vestige of a ruling class. The SS also shot many Jews, a preliminary to much more thoroughgoing measures later. The Nazis intended to reduce the remaining Polish population to the role of "slaves of the Greater German World Reich." As for the Soviets, they, too, executed captured Polish army officers and resorted to mass arrests of "undesirable political elements" who were deported to Siberia and other undesirable destinations in the Soviet Union.

Stalin had mixed emotions about the destruction of Poland. To be sure, the USSR had avoided involvement in the war against Germany and had gained over half of Poland and a claim to the Baltic states. But the awesome display of German military power had disturbed the Soviet dictator. He quickly set out to create as much of a buffer zone between the Soviet Union and Germany as

possible. In the next few weeks, he pressured Lithuania, Latvia, and Estonia into signing treaties that authorized the Russians to establish military, air, and naval bases on their territory.

Ultra

Although Poland had vanished from the map, the Poles provided the Allies with the basis for one of the great technological achievements of the war. It came in the realm of military intelligence and eventually enabled the Allies to intercept and decipher German military messages and produced a wealth of information on enemy strength and intentions.

During the 1920s the Germans had developed a highly sophisticated encyphering machine, called Enigma. It was so complex that the Germans became absolutely convinced that their cyphers could not be broken. In 1929, one of these machines, enroute from Berlin to the German legation in Warsaw, fell into the hands of Polish counterintelligence agents. They created an exact replica of the Enigma before allowing it to proceed to its destination and then set about breaking the German cypher. They succeeded in doing so by 1932 and read much German signal traffic during the 1930s. The Germans changed their cypher in late 1938, however, and the Poles had to undertake their task again. After Poland's defeat, many Polish cryptanalysts escaped to the West and took a few Enigma machines with them.

By April 1940, the British, with the help of the Poles, broke some of the new German codes. Unfortunately, various problems arose. All of this delayed putting their efforts to practical use for another year. Eventually, however, the achievements of the codebreakers proved most valuable to the Allied cause. They also became the best-kept secret of the war and earned the code name Ultra. Still confident that their cypher could not be broken, the Germans never recognized what had happened.

A Phony War of Real Danger

In stark contrast to the horror of the *Blitzkrieg* in Poland, Western Europe remained strangely quiet during the first eight months of the war. This inactivity prompted observers to conclude that the conflict was really a fraud. Americans called it the "phony war." To the French it was the *drôle de guerre* (literally, "odd little war"), and to the Germans the *Sitzkrieg* (sitting war). But the war was not as phony as it appeared. Hitler, in fact, was determined to strike in the west in the fall of 1939.

The French fully expected the Germans to attack, and Britain's military leaders agreed that Germany would strike, but Chamberlain did not expect Hitler to launch a major offensive and felt that time was on the Allies' side. The prime minister believed that the war would hurt the German economy and lead to a collapse of civilian morale. He failed to recognize that Hitler was also fighting a war of limited liability that would not require full mobilization of the economy. Germany also negotiated a second and more far-reaching economic understanding with the Soviet Union soon after the conquest of Poland. The Soviets agreed to provide Germany with grain, oil, and other raw materials in return for manufactured goods, including armaments. The Russians also supplied the Germans with rubber, tin, and other commodities that they imported from Southeast Asia.

In line with Chamberlain's vision of the fragile nature of Germany's economy as well as traditional British policy, the Allies instituted a naval blockade. But the blockade proved less effective than in World War I because of Germany's economic relationship with the USSR. The Germans countered the blockade with submarine attacks on Allied shipping, but their U-boat fleet was too small at this time to be much more than a nuisance. The British also used the period of the "phony war" to strengthen the Royal Air Force, especially their fighter planes.

Brauchitsch, Halder, and other generals were deeply concerned by Hitler's decision to attack in the west during the fall of 1939. Under no circumstances could an offensive begin before November, and this would mean a winter campaign, which they viewed as an invitation to disaster. Brauchitsch and Halder protested against the proposed offensive, but Hitler won the argument.

Hitler's intransigence led to a rebirth of the conspiracy against him that had surfaced during the Sudetenland crisis only to go into eclipse as a result of his triumph at the Munich conference.

This time the conspirators went so far as to plan Hitler's assassination. The conspiracy had its nerve center in the Abwehr (Armed Forces Intelligence) and its driving force in Colonel Hans Oster, an aide to Admiral Wilhelm Canaris, the Abwehr's chief. Canaris protected Oster in his efforts while keeping his distance from the actual plot. Oster gained the support of Halder, who again consented to lead a military coup following the assassination. In fact, for a time Halder carried a pistol in his pocket, intending to shoot Hitler, but he could not quite bring himself to kill an unarmed man.

As in 1938, Brauchitsch sympathized with the conspirators but refused to become directly involved. Other leading generals, including Bock and Rundstedt, also offered sympathy but declined to implicate themselves. But Halder, too, eventually lost his nerve, fearing discovery of the plot, and took no action. Indeed, as time passed, he became more optimistic about prospects for an offensive in the west. With his defection, the conspiracy failed for a second time.

Despite Hitler's insistence on an early offensive, bad weather forced repeated postponements, and in January 1940 a German courier plane, carrying documents pertaining to the plan of attack, flew off course and made a forced landing in Belgium. Belgian authorities seized some of the documents before the Germans on board could destroy them. The Germans feared that the incident had compromised the security of their operation, and this concern, along with continuing bad weather, resulted in postponement of the offensive until May.

The capture of the documents also contributed to a decision to scrap the original invasion plan and adopt a substitute that proved infinitely superior and played a vital role in Germany's success. The old plan, code-named Case Yellow, did not promise a decisive result and held out the possibility of a renewal of the stalemate of 1914–18. It provided for primary concentration of strength, including most of the armor, in Army Group B, commanded by General von Bock. His forces were to drive through the Netherlands and Belgium into northern France before halting at the Somme River. Army Group A, under General von Rundstedt, was to drive through southern Belgium and Luxembourg in support of Bock's spearhead.

The revised plan for Case Yellow owed its inspiration in part to General Erich von Manstein, Rundstedt's chief of staff. Cold in manner and extremely outspoken, Manstein won little acclaim for his personality, but he was probably the most brilliant of the German generals. Like Guderian, he had served at Verdun in 1916 and had developed a similar horror of static warfare. He offered his plan as a means of avoiding a repetition of such a dilemma. It called for the spearhead to be provided by Army Group A, which would receive additional strength, especially armor. Rundstedt's panzer forces were to drive through Luxembourg and southern Belgium and break into France near the fortress city of Sedan. Once they had accomplished this, they could pursue any of three options: swing eastward behind the Maginot line, drive toward Paris, or dash for the English Channel with the intention of cutting off Allied forces in northern France and Belgium. When the Germans finally launched their offensive in May 1940, they chose the third alternative, with amazingly successful results.

Manstein's plan also called for Bock's Army Group B to move through the Netherlands and northern Belgium as part of the overall forward movement and as a feint to lure the Allies into Belgium and away from the German spearhead. Brauchitsch and Halder originally resisted Manstein's plan as too bold. They feared an Allied counteroffensive against the German flank as Rundstedt's forces penetrated into northern France. Halder's opinion changed, however, as a result of a series of war games conducted by OKH during the winter. These confirmed that an armored thrust through the Ardennes offered the best chance of catching the Allies off balance and preventing a quick defensive response. Hitler, who

was toying with a similar plan, agreed, assuring adoption of the revised version of Case Yellow, which gained formal approval on March 15.

While the Germans debated the change in Case Yellow, the Allies put the finishing touches on their own plan, with which they intended to counter the expected attack. This was Plan D, or the Dyle Plan, referring to the Dyle River in Belgium. It provided for the advance of strong French and British forces to a line based on the Dyle and Meuse rivers in central Belgium. The Allies assumed that the main German attack would come, as in 1914 and as intended in the original Case Yellow plan, through the plains of northern Belgium. They dismissed the area of Luxembourg and southern Belgium as offering no serious threat because it contained the rugged Ardennes Forest. The French believed that armored forces could not maneuver successfully in this hilly, heavily wooded terrain. As a result, Plan D stipulated that the two strongest French armies and the British Expeditionary Force would advance to the Dyle and the Meuse in Belgium while two weaker French armies took up positions opposite the Ardennes. When Hitler unleashed his attack in May, the Allies thus unwittingly sent their best troops into the jaws of the German trap and left second-rate forces in the path of Rundstedt's spearhead.

While these developments were taking place in the opposing headquarters, the "phony war" continued along the Franco-German border. There were good reasons for inactivity. The Allies were waiting for the German offensive, and the Germans, while planning to attack during the fall and winter, were unable to do so because of the weather and the change in plan. Neither side could see any point in border skirmishes that would cause casualties without being decisive.

CHAPTER SIX

Complications in the North: Finland, Denmark, Norway

While the western front remained strangely quiet, a new conflict erupted in northeastern Europe. Though something of a sideshow, it soon attracted the attention of Germany and the Allies and led indirectly to another clash of arms in the far northwestern reaches of the continent.

The Russo-Finnish War

The initial northern conflict became known as the Russo-Finnish War (Winter War) and raged from November 30, 1939 to March 14, 1940. It resulted from Finland's refusal to grant certain concessions that the Soviet Union demanded in the fall of 1939. The Soviet demands reflected Stalin's fear that Finland might fall under German influence. Leningrad, Russia's second largest city, lay only 20 miles from the Finnish border on the Karelian Isthmus, a narrow neck of land that separated the Gulf of Finland on the west from Lake Ladoga on the east. It was within range of Finnish artillery. The Soviets insisted that the Finns cede a portion of the Karelian Isthmus to Russia, thus freeing Leningrad from the threat of artillery bombardment. This revision would have left Finland's chief defensive system, the Mannerheim line, in Soviet hands. The Soviets also requested other changes, including a 30-year lease on the port of Hangö for use as a Russian naval base. Hangö was less than 100 miles from Helsinki, the Finnish capital. In return for these concessions, Moscow offered to give Finland twice as much territory to the north of Lake Ladoga. The Finns agreed to most of the Soviet demands but refused the Hangö lease, contending that it was incompatible with their independence and neutrality to allow a foreign base on their territory.

Stalin responded to the Finnish refusal by sending a force of 30 divisions and six tank brigades across the border against a total of only nine Finnish divisions. Before the campaign ended, the Russians committed a total of 45 divisions. An overwhelming Soviet victory seemed certain. But the Russians had not anticipated their own bungling or the astonishingly heroic and effective Finnish resistance under the leadership of 72-year-old Field Marshal Carl von Mannerheim. Mannerheim had served as a cavalry officer in the army of the Russian tsar. But he took advantage of Russia's weakness in 1918 to lead Finland to independence and defeated the Soviet-backed Red forces in a Finnish civil war. As chairman of the Council of National Defense in 1933, he was responsible for constructing the fortifications that bore his name.

Finnish troops not only halted the Russian offensive but annihilated five Soviet divisions. The Russians had committed the blunder that the Germans had managed to avoid on the western front—an attack in the dead of winter. Although the Mannerheim line was not especially strong, the Red Army encountered difficulty with the forests, swamps, and lakes that abounded in the Karelian Isthmus, and its efforts to achieve a breakthrough failed miserably.

But far greater disasters befell the Russians when they attacked at several points to the north of Lake Ladoga in areas characterized by dense forests, thousands of lakes, few roads, and heavy snow. Soviet commanders ordered their troops deep into the frozen wastes. Russian mechanized forces, which were quite unsuited for this type of warfare, became strung out in long columns extending for many miles that offered inviting targets for Finnish troops wearing white uniforms and operating on skis. The Finns, gliding like ghosts through the snow, cut Soviet supply lines and ambushed isolated enemy forces. Russian

FIGURE 6-1   Finnish ski troops move forward on the Karelian Isthmus front. *(National Archives and Records Administration)*

troops also suffered terribly from the cold as temperatures fell as low as 30 degrees below 0 Fahrenheit. They even lacked "trigger finger" mittens and had to bare their hands to fire their weapons. When the Finnish attacks ended, thousands of frozen Soviet corpses littered the roads and forests of east-central Finland. Observers noted that the bodies were as hard as petrified wood with skin the color of mahogany.

By early January 1940, it was clear that the Russians had failed. Stalin now appointed Marshal Semyon Timoshenko to command the Finnish front. A Ukrainian, Timoshenko had served as a noncommissioned officer in the tsarist army during World War I but became a Red Army officer in the Russian civil war. Though not a brilliant commander, he was far superior to the inept Marshal Klementi Voroshilov, one of Stalin's close associates, who had directed the abortive operations against Finland in December. Timoshenko abandoned the ill-advised attacks north of Lake Ladoga and concentrated on breaking through the Mannerheim line. He carried out a massive buildup throughout January and finally opened his offensive on February 11. The Russians outnumbered the Finns 50 to 1 and had an enormous advantage in equipment. By early March, they had broken through the Mannerheim line. The Finns, realizing

that they were at the end of their resources and fearing an imminent Soviet drive on Helsinki, asked for an armistice on March 12.

The peace terms were more severe than the original Soviet demands. Most important, they required the Finns to cede the entire Karelian Isthmus as well as all their other territory along the shores of Lake Ladoga. Finland also granted the lease on Hangö. But the Soviet Union, a great power of 175 million people, had little reason for jubilation. Though ultimately victorious, it had suffered repeated humiliations at the hands of a nation of barely 4 million. Hitler, who had been dubious about Russian power all along, was now convinced that his neighbor to the east was no match for the Wehrmacht. The Winter War contributed significantly to his underestimation of the USSR as an enemy a year later. The Soviets, however, now set out to remedy the glaring weaknesses that the conflict had exposed in their military machine. And, although progress was far from complete when Hitler attacked them in 1941, their efforts ultimately did pay dividends.

The Finnish campaign had an important by-product—the opening of all of Scandinavia as a potential theater of operations. British and French leaders were filled with admiration for the gallant Finnish resistance and actually contemplated sending a small military force to help Finland. They also considered bombing the oil fields of the Caucasus Mountains. In view of the Western Powers' reluctance to take military action to help Poland, it is really quite astonishing that they should have considered such a foolhardy undertaking on behalf of Finland. It would have meant war with the USSR at the same time that the Allies faced the threat of a German offensive in the west. Furthermore, such limited aid would not have made the slightest difference in the final outcome of the Winter War. The Allied attitude revealed the extent of anti-Soviet feeling in both Britain and France.

If they were to provide direct assistance to Finland, the Allies needed to secure passage for their troops through neighboring Norway and Sweden, but the Norwegians and Swedes refused to grant permission. The Allies' also hoped to occupy the mines of northern Sweden, which provided the Germans with 40 percent of their iron ore supply. Much of the ore reached Germany from the port of Lulea on the Gulf of Bothnia, an arm of the Baltic, but the gulf froze during the winter, necessitating shipments by rail to Narvik on Norway's Atlantic coast. From Narvik, the precious ore went by ship through the Norwegian Leads, a sheltered passage between the highly indented coast and the open sea. Winston Churchill, now Britain's first lord of the admiralty, had urged the mining of the Leads to interfere with German ore shipments as early as September 1939.

Germany also coveted Norway as the world's only source of heavy water, which was produced at the Norsk hydroelectric plant in the southern town of Vemork. German scientists hoped to use heavy water as a moderator in a nuclear reactor that might lead to the creation of an atomic bomb. In heavy water the hydrogen atoms of ordinary water are replaced by atoms of heavy hydrogen (deuterium), giving the water a different chemical formula as well as different physical characteristics, including greater weight.

Focus on Scandinavia

Although the conclusion of the Winter War ended the possibility of sending troops to Finland, Churchill and other Allied leaders persisted in plans to mine the Leads. They also assumed that such action would provoke Hitler to undertake an invasion of Norway, and at the first indication of this, they planned to occupy Narvik and the other major ports on Norway's Atlantic coast. But in all of their various schemes for intervention in Scandinavia, the Allies seriously underestimated the number of troops they would need to carry out such an operation. They were also skeptical of Germany's ability to invade Norway successfully in the face of superior British naval power.

Hitler worried about Allied intentions in Scandinavia during the Winter War and became especially concerned about the potential disruption of Swedish iron ore shipments to Germany. In December, he ordered preliminary planning for the possibility of a preemptive German invasion of not only Norway but Denmark as well.

An incident occurred in February that helped persuade Hitler that a Scandinavian operation was necessary. On the night of February 16, the British destroyer *Cossack* intercepted the German tanker *Altmark* in Norwegian territorial waters. A party from the *Cossack* boarded the *Altmark* and rescued 300 British prisoners, the survivors from a number of ships that the German surface raider *Graf Spee* had sunk during the first few months of the war. The *Graf Spee's* commander had transferred the prisoners to the *Altmark*. The *Altmark* affair convinced Hitler that Britain would not respect Norwegian neutrality. Two days later, he ordered invasion preparations to be accelerated, and on March 1 he issued a formal directive for an attack on Denmark and Norway.

Hitler gave the OKW sole responsibility for the Scandinavian enterprise, and the OKH had no part in its development. It was the only major German campaign of the war that combined land, sea, and air operations and in which the navy played a decisive role. Hitler appointed General Nikolaus von Falkenhorst, who had commanded a corps in the Polish campaign, to direct the invasion. With the bulk of German strength earmarked for the invasion of Western Europe in May, Falkenhorst had only limited forces at his disposal. But he used them boldly and skillfully when the Scandinavian operation began on April 9.

The Soviet-Finnish Treaty of Stockholm, March 1940

The Conquest of Denmark and Norway

Denmark's meager army of 15,000 men was no match for the Germans, who caught the Danes completely by surprise and overran the country in a matter of hours. The Germans also enjoyed the advantage of surprise when they landed in Norway. The Norwegian defensive forces were small and seriously deficient in modern equipment, especially aircraft.

The invasion of Norway was an extremely risky undertaking. It involved transporting troops not only across the Skagerrak, the relatively narrow body of water between Denmark and Norway, but into the Atlantic as well in the face of British naval supremacy. The German plan called for landings at all major Norwegian ports—Oslo and Kristiansand on the Skagerrak and Bergen, Stavanger, Trondheim, and Narvik on the Atlantic coast. Allied naval units had laid mines in Norwegian coastal waters the day before the invasion and were still nearby. The British could also intervene with their home fleet, which was stationed at Scapa Flow to the north of Scotland. In addition, they maintained a small military force that was to seize Norway's major Atlantic ports if the Germans showed any indication of retaliating for the British mine-laying operation.

When the Germans actually launched their invasion fleet, British planes spotted German naval forces heading northward as early as the morning of April 7. But when the home fleet sailed seven hours later, its commander decided to leave the military force behind despite the plan to seize the Norwegian ports. British naval units were also uncertain of the exact location or destinations of the German invasion forces. To make matters worse, a savage storm impeded their search for the elusive enemy. Although elements of the rival fleets engaged in isolated skirmishes, no all-out battle took place, and the Royal Navy did not seriously interfere with the German landings.

Speed, precision timing, and luck all contributed to Germany's success. The OKW scheduled each landing to take place at approximately the same time. The first troops to land traveled on fast warships, which penetrated quickly into each port, and disembarked in most cases before the Norwegians could react. Reinforcements followed in slower transports. The initial invasion forces did not total more than 10,000 men, and the largest number at any one port was approximately 2,000. The Germans did not use panzer units, which were not well suited for the mountainous Norwegian terrain. But they did employ small numbers of tanks to support the infantry, and the armor performed well in this role.

The only serious threat to the invasion came at Oslo, where for a time the fate of the entire operation seemed to hang in the balance. Oslo lay at the northern end of Oslofjord, the body of water that linked the capital with the Skagerrak. At the

fjord's narrowest point, the old but formidable Oscarsborg fort guarded the approach to Oslo with 11-inch guns and torpedo defenses. These weapons combined to sink the new German cruiser *Blücher* when the invasion flotilla attempted to penetrate beyond the Oscarsborg. Confronted by this disaster, the other German ships turned back and disembarked their troops about 20 miles from Oslo.

The success of the assault now depended on a projected airborne seizure of the airfield outside the capital. Once the Germans had accomplished this, they planned to strengthen their initial force with troops ferried in by transport planes. But fog over southern Norway prevented them from carrying out the airborne operation. If the Norwegians had made a vigorous attempt to defend the capital and its airfield at this crucial point, they might have badly disrupted the German timetable. Instead, they abandoned the city without a fight. A small unit did try to hold the airfield, but a few German fighter planes managed to land, and the pilots, using their machine guns, held the defenders at bay until transports arrived with reinforcements. These troops quickly marched on Oslo and occupied the city.

Oslo was the key to the invasion. The Germans quickly moved out from the capital to link up with troops at the other ports, who were simply to hold their positions until the relief expeditions arrived. With the exception of the force at Narvik, all carried out their missions successfully. Narvik lay too far north. In the days following the landing there, British destroyers and the battleship *Warspite* sank 10 German destroyers and gained complete control of the neighboring waters. British troops landed near the town on April 14, but their commander proceeded with excessive caution, and they did not force the Germans out of Narvik until May 28. By then the Norwegian campaign was almost over.

Anglo-French forces also landed at two small ports in the general area of Trondheim—Namsos 125 miles to the north on April 14 and Åndalsnes 100 miles to the south three days later. They hoped to capture Trondheim and gain control of central Norway. But they launched this enterprise much too late and with a lamentable lack of planning. Although the Allies originally outnumbered the Germans in the Trondheim area

The German Invasion of Denmark and Norway, April 9, 1940

by 13,000 to 2,000, they lacked heavy equipment, including artillery and tanks. The French found it particularly embarrassing when they had to leave most of their equipment aboard a cruiser that proved too long to penetrate into the small harbor at Namsos. The Allies were also well beyond the range of fighter planes based in Britain. The Germans, by contrast, used transport planes to reinforce their Trondheim garrison and provided strong tactical air support for their forces in the field.

Trondheim now became the key to Norway's fate. The Allies hoped to dislodge the German garrison by a pincers movement from north and south. It was not to be. They had to divert British forces from Åndalsnes to aid hard-pressed Norwegian troops that were trying to prevent the Germans from penetrating up two narrow valleys toward Trondheim. But the British proved much too weak, and the Luftwaffe pounded the Allied troops mercilessly. Superior German strength forced them to fall back on Åndalsnes. Meanwhile, Allied units pushing south from Namsos toward Trondheim made little progress due to the mountainous terrain and heavy snow cover. It proved necessary to evacuate all British and French troops from the two little ports early in May. Despite continued fighting in the Narvik

FIGURE 6-2   German troops take shelter behind a tank during the Norwegian campaign. *(National Archives and Records Administration)*

area, the campaign was virtually over. The British finally abandoned Narvik early in June, and as they evacuated, a German naval force, including the battle cruisers *Scharnhorst* and *Gneisenau,* sank the aircraft carrier *Glorious,* two destroyers, and three merchant ships, sealing the Allied defeat.

The "ramshackle Norwegian campaign," as Churchill called it, had revealed woeful deficiencies in Allied strategic planning and tactical execution. German forces, in their first real engagement against the British and French, had out-thought, out-maneuvered, and out-fought their enemies. The entire Allied effort had been "too little, too late."

Germany had won another startling victory, adding to the developing myth of Wehrmacht invincibility. The triumph also secured concrete advantages for Germany. It removed any threat to the nation's northern flank and safeguarded access to Swedish iron ore. Germany had sealed off Sweden from the west, and the Swedes were in no position to be other than obliging suppliers of Germany's needs. In addition to iron ore, these included manufactured goods such as ball bearings as well as both warships and merchant vessels built in Swedish shipyards. The Reich also secured permission to use Swedish railroads to reinforce their stranded garrison at Narvik during

the fighting in Norway and later to transport men and materiel eastward to take part in the Russian campaign. The conquest of Norway also provided bases from which German bombers, submarines, and surface raiders could attack British ships. Finally, it hampered the British naval blockade by greatly expanding the area that the Royal Navy had to patrol.

The campaign was not without its disadvantages for Germany, however. The German navy suffered serious losses, including the sinking of half its 20 destroyers and three of its eight cruisers. In addition, Germany's two battle cruisers, and the pocket battleship *Lützow* were disabled for months. Some observers have argued since the war that had these naval forces been available after the fall of France, they would have greatly enhanced German prospects for an invasion of Britain. But in view of Britain's continued naval supremacy and the threat posed by British air power, it is doubtful that the addition of these ships would have been a critical factor in enabling the Germans to cross the English Channel. Hitler also felt obliged to maintain a large defensive garrison in Norway. In the following years he increased its size markedly because of his persistent fear of an Allied invasion—an assault that never came.

CHAPTER SEVEN

The Fall of France

Hitler launched his long-awaited offensive in the west on May 10, 1940. The Wehrmacht put Manstein's variant of Case Yellow into effect, and the Allies responded with Plan D. The result was a spectacular success for the Germans, who smashed their enemies with such speed and ease that even they were astonished. Despite adoption of the new plan, only Hitler had been completely confident of victory. The scope of Germany's overwhelming triumph and the rapid collapse of the French army stunned the people of France as well as the British, who now faced the German juggernaut alone. It also reverberated around the world and jolted the American people out of the complacency that their remoteness from Europe had fostered and triggered a new debate on whether the United States should extend aid to the hard-pressed British.

Comparative Military Strength

Germany's amazing victory led to the wide-spread belief that its forces were much stronger in numbers and equipment than those of the Allies. This was not true, at least not at the start of the campaign or in regard to all types of equipment. The Germans had 136 divisions on the western front, but they assigned 19 of these to General Wilhelm Ritter von Leeb's Army Group C, which remained in a defensive position opposite the Maginot line. This left 117 divisions, including 42 that the OKH held in reserve. Seventy-five divisions took part in the initial assault. Of these, 30 comprised Bock's Army Group B and 45 formed Rundstedt's Army Group A. Allied strength totaled 144 divisions: 101 French, 11 British, 22 Belgian, and 10 Dutch. These troops varied in quality, however, and were under four separate commands. France also tied down 36 divisions in the Maginot line, which the

Germans did not attack until it was hopelessly outflanked. The Allies, nevertheless, committed 81 divisions to meet the attack.

One of the great myths, which persisted throughout the war, was the belief that Germany enjoyed vast superiority in armor. The French estimated that the Germans possessed as many as 7,500 tanks, but in reality they had only 2,500, well over half of them inferior Panzer I and Panzer II models. The remainder consisted of relatively small numbers of Panzer III and Panzer IV models and about 350 Czech tanks. France had about as many tanks as Germany, perhaps more. Many of them, especially the Somua medium tank and the Char B-1 heavy tank, were superior in armor and firepower, although they tended to be slower and had a limited range. Britain had almost 300 tanks in France, including the Matilda, which was better armed and armored than any German tank except the Panzer IV. The fatal flaw was the Allied failure to concentrate their tank units. Though the French had six divisions of armor and seven motorized divisions prepared to advance into Belgium, they were only recently organized and French doctrine did not provide for massing them in a point of main effort as the Germans did. Almost half the French tank battalions were dispersed along the rest of the front, supporting infantry, while German tank battalions were components of the panzer divisions. Bock had three panzer divisions as well as one motorized division in Army Group B. Rundstedt's Army Group A deployed seven panzer and three motorized divisions, which formed the powerful spearhead of the German attack.

This powerful concentration of armor together with Manstein's daring operational plan and close tactical air support were the keys to the spectacular German victory. Thus, despite the Allies' quantitative and qualitative superiority, Germany's brilliant use of its tactical resources resulted in a swift breakthrough and envelopment of the bulk of the Allied forces in a startlingly brief period of time. Not only did this reduce the Allies to an inferior position in strength, but the speed with which it was accomplished inflicted a profound phychological shock on them as well.

Most historians of the 1940 campaign have contended that Germany completely outclassed France in the air. It now appears that this is somewhat misleading. In fact, the French possessed a total of 4,360 planes to 3,270 for the Germans, and for the most part France's fighters and bombers were comparable to or better than those of the enemy. Unfortunately, France deployed only one-fourth of its air strength against Germany. This was due in large part to a shortage of both air and ground crews. A prolonged disagreement between leaders of the armed forces over the mission of France's air power contributed to this problem. The army insisted on close tactical support of ground troops, but the air force favored a strategic role, stressing long-range heavy bombers. Thus, when the Germans struck in 1940, the French had only 583 fighters and 84 bombers actually assigned to the front. The remainder were in the process of being reequipped or were stationed in France's colonies. Additional Allied strength, most of it British, included 197 fighters and 192 bombers. But the Royal Air Force held back the bulk of its aircraft for the defense of Britain. Under the circumstances, the Luftwaffe did enjoy a considerable advantage with 1,264 fighters and 1,504 bombers.

The Politics of Leadership

France also suffered from a cumbersome army leadership structure. General Maurice Gamelin was the supreme commander of land forces. Though highly intelligent, he tended to be indecisive. Gamelin also had a low regard for the potential of Germany's panzer forces. Despite his lofty position, Gamelin delegated operational control of the forces in northeastern France to General Alphonse Georges, who made most of the actual decisions. The division of authority between Gamelin and Georges created confusion, and Gamelin was often ignorant of the exact situation at the front.

Both France and Britain faced the German offensive under new political leadership. Premier Daladier had provoked a crisis in the French parliament because of his failure to aid the Finns during the Winter War and had resigned in March. His successor was Paul Reynaud, whose voice had been one of those crying in the wilderness during the 1930s regarding France's need for armored divisions. Reynaud had also criticized French foreign policy prior to the war. He had urged more vigorous measures against Germany and, as finance minister since 1938, had been largely responsible for increasing arms production. Unfortunately, Reynaud lacked a large personal following in parliament, while Daladier continued to have a strong base of support. Reynaud needed to maintain Daladier's backing and felt compelled to keep him in the cabinet as minister of war even though the two men detested each other.

In Britain, Chamberlain also ran into trouble with Parliament as a result of his handling of the Norwegian campaign and resigned on the very day that the Germans attacked in the west. The new prime minister, Winston Churchill, had been prominent in British politics for four decades and had been first lord of the admiralty early in World War I. But Churchill had spent most of the 1930s as a political outcast, at first as the result of his opposition to the government's plan to extend limited self-government to India. Later he compounded his unpopularity by his outspoken criticism of Chamberlain's appeasement policy, especially the Munich agreement. But when the policy ended in failure with the outbreak of war in 1939, Churchill won vindication, and Chamberlain appointed him to his former position at the admiralty. Blessed with boundless self-confidence and determination as well as great charisma, a quicksilver mind, and a restless imagination, Churchill clearly had the potential to be a far better wartime leader than Chamberlain.

But the circumstances that prompted the change were ironic because Churchill, more than anyone else, had favored Allied intervention in Norway and, as first lord of the admiralty, held ultimate responsibility for the Royal Navy's failure to prevent the German invasion. At first, Churchill's position was similar to Reynaud's. He had no large parliamentary following of his own, while Chamberlain actually remained leader of Churchill's Conservative party and continued in the cabinet with effective control over domestic policy until October.

Reynaud had great contempt for General Gamelin. As he put it, Gamelin "might be all right as a prefect or a bishop, but he is not a leader of men." He was so dissatisfied with the army commander's conduct of the Norwegian campaign that he tried to dismiss him early in May. But Daladier and others in the cabinet opposed this action, and Reynaud resigned in disgust on May 9. During this crisis, Gamelin learned of Reynaud's criticism, and he, too, resigned. Thus, when the Germans attacked the next day, France technically had neither a government nor an army commander in chief. Under the circumstances, both men withdrew their resignations.

Sweep through the Low Countries

Hitler unleashed his *Blitzkrieg* in the early hours of May 10, striking the Netherlands, Belgium, and Luxembourg simultaneously and making rapid progress everywhere. The Dutch were no match for Bock's Army Group B and received little aid from the Allies. Germany completely dominated the air over the Netherlands and made extensive use of paratroops to capture bridges over the many rivers and canals, key to the Dutch defense system. Knifing through the country, the Germans forced the Dutch to capitulate within five days. An especially ugly incident occurred while negotiations were under way for the surrender of Rotterdam, the Netherlands' leading port. German bombers leveled the center of the defenseless city and killed 980 civilians. This raid became symbolic of German ruthlessness, but it now appears that due to a breakdown in communications, the Luftwaffe units involved actually were not aware that the surrender talks were taking place.

Bock's attack on Belgium encountered fiercer resistance because the Belgian army was larger and its defenses stronger than those of the Dutch. The Germans made rapid progress, nevertheless, and their capture of the supposedly impregnable Fort Eben Emael on the Albert Canal in eastern Belgium was especially impressive. An airborne force of only 85 men, transported by gliders,

landed unmolested on the spacious and undefended roof of the fortress. The Belgian garrison totaled 750 men, but all of them were inside the fort. Once the Germans had consolidated their position, they used special hollow charge explosives to blow up the guns and neutralize the defenders. Soon afterward, Bock's main forces pushed through to link up with the airborne troops and then advanced to the Dyle River.

Meanwhile, French and British forces swept rapidly into Belgium to their prearranged positions along the Dyle and Meuse rivers. As a result, they had unwittingly placed themselves in a perfect position to be outflanked by Rundstedt's Army Group A. Three panzer corps, which formed Rundstedt's spearhead, slammed through Luxembourg and the Belgian Ardennes in two days against slight resistance. By May 13, each of them had crossed the Meuse in northern France and by nightfall had torn open a gap 50 miles wide in the French front. Panic on the part of some French troops and hasty orders to withdraw from the Meuse contributed to the German success. The southernmost and strongest of the panzer corps, commanded by Guderian, made the crucial crossing near Sedan. Three experienced panzer divisions attacked just one French infantry division composed of inadequately prepared and poorly equipped reservists. The French assumed that the Germans would not try to cross the Meuse until their artillery arrived. Rather than wait, however, Guderian ordered repeated attacks by medium bombers and Stukas, which pinned down and demoralized the defenders, allowing German infantrymen to cross the river in rubber boats. They secured a bridgehead, and soon afterward, engineers constructed a pontoon bridge that enabled Guderian's tanks to cross and exploit the breakthrough. Despite this success, the French 3rd Armored Division attacked Guderian's left flank, creating a dangerous threat. Unfortunately for the French, General Charles Huntzinger, commander of the French 2nd Army, ordered it to pull back. Huntzinger feared that the Germans might swing around his forces in an effort to outflank the Maginot line.

This decision relieved the pressure on Guderian's forces and enabled his armor to dash toward the sea. It reached the channel coast on May 20 near the mouth of the Somme, trapping the Allied

KEY:

≡≡≡	Maginot Line Belt of Fortifications
■ ■ ■	Fortifications
╫╫╫	Canals
➜	Main German Thrusts

0   20   40
MILES

The German Invasion of Holland, Belgium, and Luxembourg, and the Penetration of the French Northern Defense Line, May 10–20, 1940

forces in Belgium and northern France. Progress would have been even more rapid had it not been for the fears of Guderian's immediate superior, General von Kleist, that he was advancing too fast and might be cut off by French counterattacks. Kleist ordered him to halt briefly on two occasions to allow the following infantry to catch up to the panzers or at least narrow the gap. Hitler also urged caution, as did General von Rundstedt. But the French mounted little in the way of serious counterattacks, largely because of the speed of Guderian's advance and their own commitment of so many troops to Belgium and the Maginot line. They did attack with their few armored

divisions but deployed them on a piecemeal basis, which diluted their striking power. The Germans destroyed them one by one.

One Allied counterattack did achieve a modest success. A force of 75 British Matilda tanks and supporting troops struck against the 7th Panzer Division, commanded by the soon-to-be-famous General Erwin Rommel, near the French city of Arras on May 21. The ungainly looking Matilda had acquired its nickname because of its resemblance to the popular comic strip character Matilda the Duck. The British caught the Germans by surprise and inflicted damage sufficient to make Rommel believe that he was being attacked by a much larger force. It was not until Rommel utilized lethal 88mm anti-aircraft guns in an anti-tank role that the attack ground to a halt. This British counterattack as well as that of the French 3rd Armored Division near Sedan demonstrate what the Allies might have accomplished had they concentrated their armor and struck with greater force against the exposed German flanks. If they had done so, the outcome of the campaign might have been different.

Escape from Dunkirk

As Guderian closed the trap on the Allies, Bock's troops forced them to abandon the Dyle line and retreat into western Belgium. The Allies found themselves in a steadily shrinking pocket between the two German army groups. They searched desperately for some way to break through the encirclement, but all their efforts failed. Three alternatives now confronted them: surrender, continue fighting until annihilated, or attempt to evacuate as many troops as possible by sea. Ultimately they chose the third option, largely at the insistence of General Lord Gort, the British commander, who recognized long before other Allied leaders that this was the only way to escape.

During World War I, Gort had gained a reputation for bravery that few could approach, being wounded four times and winning the Victoria Cross, Britain's highest military decoration. Nevertheless, many of his fellow officers believed that he was out of his depth in commanding a large force. But Gort proved to be the savior of the BEF when, on his own initiative and without notifying the French, he ordered his troops to fall back toward the English Channel on May 23. Gort based his decision not only on the obvious German threat but also on the deteriorating position of the Belgian army, which supported his left flank. Churchill, who was slower to recognize the seriousness of the Allied dilemma, did not formally authorize a withdrawal until three days after Gort's decision to fall back toward the sea.

The Allies' chances of a successful evacuation did not appear promising. Guderian, after reaching the coast, turned north toward the French channel ports—Boulogne, Calais, and Dunkirk. He hoped to take all three by a quick thrust. Elements of his force rapidly surrounded Boulogne

and Calais while others moved toward Dunkirk, but on May 24 Rundstedt ordered him to halt his armor less than 15 miles from his destination. Guderian, Brauchitsch, and Halder all protested, but Hitler supported Rundstedt's decision. He also assigned to Bock's troops, with their preponderance of infantry, the task of capturing Dunkirk despite the fact that they were over twice as far away from the city as Guderian's faster-moving tanks.

This decision became one of the most controversial of the entire war. Some critics have charged that Hitler halted the armor in a deliberate effort to allow the British to escape, hoping that their gratitude for this favor would result in a willingness to make peace. But this argument does not square with the facts, especially since Rundstedt, not Hitler, originated the order. It appears more likely that both Rundstedt and Hitler were convinced that the Allies could not carry out a large-scale evacuation, and thus they could not see any need to press on to Dunkirk with Guderian's armor. This is not as surprising as it might seem. The British were initially pessimistic about their chances. Even Churchill did not believe that they could hold Dunkirk for more than two days or that the Royal Navy could save more than 45,000 troops. Reynaud and his military leaders had no faith at all in an evacuation, and French forces were slow to fall back on Dunkirk. Many of them never made it. To make matters worse, the Belgian army surrendered on May 28. Rundstedt and Hitler were also concerned about the heavier tank losses that the Germans had sustained in recent days. Both men wanted to conserve their armor for the next step in the offensive, a drive southward toward Paris. Finally, Luftwaffe commander Hermann Goering insisted that German air power could destroy the Allied forces at Dunkirk, and for a time Hitler accepted this as a possibility.

By May 26, it had become obvious that Bock's infantry was making extremely slow progress toward Dunkirk, and Guderian received permission to resume his advance. But it was too late. The Allies had strengthened their defensive perimeter around the city, and the panzers could make little headway.

The Dunkirk evacuation began on May 26 and proved amazingly successful. Britain still ruled the sea, and the German navy, badly mauled in the Norwegian campaign, was not able to intervene in any substantial way. The Royal Navy recruited hundreds of small civilian pleasure craft to ferry troops from the beaches to the larger naval ships waiting offshore. Vessels of all kinds joined this strange little armada—fishing boats, motorboats, yachts, lifeboats, tugs, barges, paddle steamers, even a car ferry. Civilians from all walks of life manned them, from butchers to bankers. One of the yachts sailed with its owner, Commander C. H. Lightoller, the senior surviving officer of the *Titanic* disaster, at its helm. The small boats moved toward the beaches amid great confusion, sometimes nearly being swamped by waves in the wake of naval ships. They ventured as close as possible to shore while long lines of soldiers, exhausted from days of fighting and retreat, waded out to meet them, the leading ranks up to their shoulders in water. All of this unfolded as bombs exploded and shells whistled overhead, and the buildings of Dunkirk burned in the distance. While the tenacious Allied rear guard prevented the Germans from breaking through the defensive perimeter, the Luftwaffe attempted to thwart the evacuation by bombing and strafing. Although the Luftwaffe inflicted considerable casualties, it could not prevent the evacuation. The Royal Air Force did its best to hamper the German air attacks but failed to gain control of the air over Dunkirk and the surrounding beaches. The British carried out the evacuation despite German air superiority.

When the operation ended on June 4, a total of 338,000 Allied soldiers had escaped, 224,000 of them British, but they had to leave behind or destroy all of their heavy equipment. Also left behind were many members of the gallant rear guard, now condemned to years of captivity. Despite the brilliance of the achievement, Dunkirk certainly was not a victory, as Churchill recognized, but the climax to an epic defeat. It gave Britain a badly needed psychological lift, but it did nothing to prevent the fall of France. Moreover, the British forces that escaped from Dunkirk did not contribute directly to the salvation of Britain from German invasion. Naval and air power, along with the limitations of Germany's armed forces, saved the British in the summer and fall of 1940. But it is true that had the British lost their expeditionary force at Dunkirk, this disaster might have

destroyed their will to continue the war. The evacuated troops also provided the nucleus for the British army of the future.

The Conquest of France

When news of the German breakthrough at Sedan reached Paris on May 13, it caused near panic in the French government. Reynaud telephoned Churchill and sobbed, "We are beaten. We have lost the battle." Although the campaign had barely begun, Reynaud's words were prophetic. The disaster also led to Gamelin's dismissal on May 18. His successor was General Maxim Weygand, who had succeeded Marshal Pétain as commander in chief of the French army in 1931 and retired four years later. Gamelin persuaded him to return to active duty in 1939 as military commander in Syria. Although 73 years old, the general remained amazingly fit and still ran wind sprints. Weygand recognized from the start that he had inherited a hopeless situation.

Another change, and a fateful one, was Reynaud's appointment of Pétain, now 85, as vice premier. Reynaud took this step in an effort to inspire his people with memories of Pétain's stirring defense of Verdun in 1916. But Pétain, like Weygand, did not believe that it was possible to stop this German offensive. Instead, he used his position to undermine Reynaud and work for a separate peace.

While the fighting at Dunkirk was still in progress, Weygand tried to establish a defensive system along the Somme and Aisne rivers. But the "Weygand line" was manned by only 61 French divisions and one British, all of them infantry. At this point, the Germans did possess overwhelming superiority, both in men and armor. Weygand did not expect to stop the enemy but intended to fight one last battle to salvage French military honor. Starting on June 5, the OKH unleashed 95 divisions against the Weygand line and quickly broke through its weak defenses. Bock sent two spearheads toward Paris and another into Normandy to the northwest. Rundstedt directed his armor around the rear of the Maginot line.

As the Germans plunged deeply into the heart of France, Mussolini belatedly entered the conflict. Traditionally, historians have assumed that the Duce made the decision to stab his unfortunate neighbor in the back more or less on the spur of the moment. But it now appears that Mussolini had decided as early as April to declare war on France and Britain if and when Hitler struck in the west. He apparently expected another stalemate as in World War I and hoped for a negotiated peace in which Italy would be one of the participants. Instead, the unexpected success of the German *Blitzkrieg* convinced Mussolini that unless he acted, the conflict would end before Italy could claim any of the spoils. He declared war on June 10 but made no immediate attack.

Soon afterward, the French declared Paris an open city to spare it the horrors of Warsaw and Rotterdam, and on June 14 it fell to the Germans. The government fled to Bordeaux. As the situation worsened, panic gripped many French civilians. An estimated six to ten million refugees fled southward, clogging the roads and often impeding the army's retreat. They used any means of transport that they could find, including bicycles, carts, even hearses. Not a few were on foot. At times, German planes bombed and strafed the roads, killing many and creating utter chaos. Meanwhile, German spearheads raced on. While Rundstedt's armor swung behind the Maginot line, General von Leeb's Army Group C attacked the line frontally. Leeb, a rather cautious and unimaginative Bavarian who was noted for his skill in defensive warfare, had commanded Army Group C since before the start of the war. His forces had remained on the defensive along the Rhine while the army groups of Bock and Rundstedt had won glory in Poland and had smashed the Allies in Belgium and northern France. But now his troops drew the unenviable assignment of testing the vaunted French defensive system, which proved exceedingly formidable. Despite heavy shelling, it held out until the end of hostilities without the loss of a single major fortress.

With the Germans rapidly overrunning the country and the French army disintegrating, France's government split on the question of further resistance. Reynaud and his supporters wanted to fight on from the French colonial empire in North Africa, but Pétain and Weygand insisted on an armistice and gained the backing of a majority in the cabinet. Pétain succeeded Reynaud as premier on June 16 and quickly asked for a cease-fire, but almost a week elapsed before the armistice talks convened. In the meantime, the Germans continued to push southward.

Hitler imposed his armistice in the exact spot where Germany had submitted to the Allies in 1918—near Compiègne, to the northeast of Paris. He even ordered the same railway car, which had been the site of the earlier capitulation, moved from a museum for the occasion.* After attending the preliminaries of the surrender ceremony, he journeyed to the French capital, where, in silent contemplation, he viewed the tomb of Napoleon, his great predecessor in the art of conquest. Hitler's terms provided for German occupation of two-thirds of France, including Paris and the entire Atlantic coast. The rest of the country remained under French control, as did France's colonial empire and fleet. All of these arrangements were temporary, the final peace treaty being left until the end of the war with Britain.

The fall of France marked the end of the democratic Third Republic, which had been the French form of government since 1870. Pétain and a number of his colleagues disliked the republic, with its unstable multiparty system. In its place they created an authoritarian regime with Pétain as head of state. They also selected the small health resort city of Vichy as the capital of unoccupied France. Vichy contained a number of large hotels and casinos that could serve as government buildings. Stunned and humiliated by the speed and thoroughness of their defeat, the French faced the future with little hope that their country could survive as anything more than a satellite of an all-powerful Germany. Still, most of the French people rallied to Pétain and remained loyal to him for much of the existence of the Vichy regime. As the great hero of the defense of Verdun in World War I, he provided a link to France's glorious past. To many, he also symbolized conservative values and order. Conservatives saw Pétain as a bulwark against communism and the possibility of "Red revolution" in the wake of the army's shattering defeat. And a substantial number of the French were sympathetic to some aspects of Hitler's ideology, most notably his opposition to communism

---

*Shortly afterward the railway car was sent to Berlin where later it was destroyed by an allied bombing raid. A replica is now on display near Compiègne.

The German and Italian Invasions of France, May 10–June 24, 1940

and his attitude toward the Jews. A strong strain of anti-Semitism had long been present in French society.

The divisions within the French cabinet prior to Pétain's assumption of power mirrored those in French society. The far right of the political spectrum, including many military officers, had never embraced the Third Republic. Fear of the Soviet Union and the spread of communism had tended to divert attention away from the menace posed by Nazi Germany during the '30s, and this continued after the outbreak of war. To make matters worse, the French Communist party followed the line laid down by the Comintern in Moscow, making its loyalty to the republic tenuous at best.

Thus, when France entered the conflict, its people were far from united. Those on the far right opposed the war, and suffered from a defeatist mentality. The Communists, after briefly supporting the war, reversed their field after the Nazi-Soviet Pact went into effect. Not all those who opposed the conflict were from the far right or far left, however. Many were simply pacifists, opposed to war on principle. Memories of the horrors of World War I also contributed to anti-war feeling and defeatism. The strange "neither war nor peace" atmosphere of the Phoney War greatly increased social and political tensions and was marked by governmental repression of Communists. One historian has referred to the Phoney War as

FIGURE 7-1   Adolf Hitler expresses his joy on hearing of Marshal Pétain's request for an armistice. (*National Archives and Records Administration*)

"the bridge between the Third Republic and the Vichy regime."*

But one Frenchman chose not to capitulate. Charles de Gaulle, who had won promotion to general during the campaign and had served Reynaud briefly as undersecretary of war, refused to accept either the armistice or the Vichy regime. Instead he escaped to London, organized his own government in exile, and pieced together a "Free French" military force, primarily from troops in France's Central African colonies, which accepted his leadership.

France had fallen in just 35 days, but German armor had actually settled the issue within the first week. The keys to Germany's success clearly were (1) the revised plan of attack, (2) the Allied assumption that the Germans would strike through northern Belgium, and (3) the German use of concentrated armor in the thrust through the Ardennes. Had the Germans remained faithful to their original plan, the outcome might have been different. Allied superiority in tank quality

might have led to a German defeat or at least a stalemate. In fact, French mechanized forces did win an early victory over German panzers attached to Army Group B in a battle fought in eastern Belgium between May 12 and 14. They knocked out 160 German tanks, most of them Panzer Is and IIs, at the cost of 105 of their own. The French also made the mistake of sending their 7th Army into the southern Netherlands as part of Plan D. Had they retained it in its original role as a strategic reserve, it would have been in an excellent position to attack Guderian's flank near Sedan. General Huntzinger also made a crucial error when he ordered the withdrawal of the 3rd Armored Division, which had been striking against Guderian's forces. This decision effectively ended any hope of blunting the German spearhead. Throughout the breakthrough in the Ardennes and the dash to the sea, many German leaders, including Hitler, remained nervous, fearing an attack on their exposed flank.* But once they realized the magnitude of their victory, doubts about armored warfare vanished,

---

*Julian Jackson, *France: The Dark Years, 1940–1944* (Oxford: Oxford University Press, 2001), pp. 113–114.

*See Ernest R. May, *Strange Victory: Hitler's Conquest of France* (New York: Hill and Wang, 2000) for the challenging thesis that the German offensive almost failed.

FIGURE 7-2   Hitler and his entourage visit Paris following the French capitulation. (*AP/Wide World Photos*)

and an almost blind faith in the potential of the *Blitzkrieg* took their place.

A Spectacular Success

In a very real sense, Germany's smashing victory over France marked the peak of Hitler's success in World War II. Though more spectacular triumphs, still lay ahead, none could equal the impact of this one, both in Germany and throughout the world. Despite Germany's quick conquests of Poland, Denmark, and Norway, no one expected the astonishing swiftness and utter thoroughness of its crushing victory over the great French army, which had held out for over four years in World War I and eventually emerged triumphant, despite appalling casualties. Clearly, the *Blitzkrieg* had made this a far different war from its predecessor. It appeared as if the German war machine were invincible. The fall of France also opened a myriad of strategic possibilities for Hitler. Achieving a negotiated peace with Britain or a cross-channel invasion of the island kingdom headed the list. But occupation of the French coast also gave Germany access to the Atlantic for its submarines and surface raiders as well as a direct link to Franco's Spain. His alliance with Italy and the collaborationist policy of Vichy France provided the opportunity to move into North Africa and the Middle East. But all of these options also posed potential problems and challenges to German strategic planning. From this point, the war was to become increasingly complicated and final victory ever more elusive.

CHAPTER EIGHT

Britain Is Still an Island

In the aftermath of Germany's crushing victory over France, Hitler dominated the continent of Europe to an extent unmatched since the peak of Napoleon's power in the early nineteenth century. But he had not yet won the war because the British had not joined the French in seeking an armistice. Furthermore, Britain was still an island, separated from the continent by the English Channel and the North Sea and, thus, could only be invaded by a difficult amphibious assault.

What to Do about Britain?

In the euphoria that prevailed in the summer of 1940, however, Hitler was convinced that the British would have to make peace, eliminating the need for an invasion. Many observers around the world shared this view. Certainly the leaders of Vichy France did not expect Britain to survive for long. During the last days before the French capitulation, Churchill had made a grandiose offer of union between Britain and France, including joint citizenship for the peoples of both countries, if the French would continue the struggle. But the proposal met with little support in the French cabinet, and General Weygand remarked that France had nothing to gain from union with a country that would soon have its neck "wrung like a chicken's."

Even in Britain, contrary to popular myth, there was considerable support for a negotiated peace, particularly during the period between the French debacle at Sedan and the successful evacuation from Dunkirk. Chamberlain and Lord Halifax, the foreign secretary, both favored such a policy, and Churchill seriously considered this approach during May and early June. But on June 4, the day the last British soldiers escaped from Dunkirk, he spoke these defiant words in Parliament: "...we

shall defend our island whatever the cost may be, we shall fight on the landing grounds, we shall fight in the fields and in the streets, we shall fight in the hills; we shall never surrender." As time passed, support for a negotiated settlement faded among other British leaders, but it did not vanish for some time.

Germany put forth a number of peace feelers through neutral intermediaries, but the British ignored or rebuffed them all. Hitler finally made a personal appeal on July 19 in which he indicated that if Britain returned the German colonies it had received under the Versailles treaty and recognized Germany's domination of the continent, he would spare the British Empire. But to Churchill it appeared that Hitler visualized Britain as nothing more than a German satellite. He was not willing to consider peace on this basis.

Britain's reluctance to end the war left Hitler with no recourse but to force submission. But how was he to accomplish this? Although his fellow Germans sang the popular song "We Sail against England," it was not that easy. The Germans had failed to develop even the most rudimentary plan for an invasion. They also lacked the ships required to transport an invasion force of sufficient size, and the German navy was totally inadequate to protect such a force against the formidable British fleet. And despite the awesome power that the German army had displayed in defeating France, none of its troops possessed the training necessary to carry out such a highly specialized undertaking.

Admiral Raeder, the commander of the German navy, was highly pessimistic. The Royal Navy was greatly superior to the German fleet, and the Royal Air Force (RAF) would make an all-out effort to prevent Germany from gaining control of the air over the channel and potential landing grounds.

Without air supremacy, Raeder insisted, an invasion was not feasible. The German generals shared these concerns.

Hitler was hesitant, too. He was essentially continental in his thinking and feared the destruction of his army by the Royal Navy and the RAF. As he confessed to Raeder in a remarkably candid observation: "On land, I am a hero. At sea, I am a coward." He would authorize an invasion only if the Luftwaffe first eliminated British air power, thus allowing unhindered German air attacks on the Royal Navy. Although for a time he directed all German resources to the task of winning control of the air and preparing for an invasion, from as early as July, his mind was not focused solely on Britain. Instead, he turned his thoughts increasingly to the possibility of an attack on the Soviet Union.

Planning the Attack

Despite all these misgivings, on July 16, Hitler authorized the OKH to draft an invasion plan, which was given the code name Operation Sea Lion and the target date of August 15. In its original form, the plan was quite unrealistic and called for landings by 500,000 men on a front over 200 miles wide along Britain's southern coast. The OKH formulated Sea Lion without sufficient coordination with the navy, and Admiral Raeder was horrified when he saw the plan. He pointed out that the navy could provide neither the ships to carry the necessary troops nor sufficient warships to protect an invasion force on this scale. It would require vigorous effort even to scrape together enough vessels to transport a much smaller force. General Halder believed that such a reduced operation would be suicidal. As he put it, "I might just as well send the troops that have landed straight through the sausage machine." But he could hardly argue with Raeder's facts. Reluctantly, he revised the plan by reducing the landing area to the extreme southeastern corner of England and sharply cutting the number of troops. Halder and Brauchitsch also agreed to delay the invasion until September 15 to enable Raeder to assemble an improvised fleet of ships, barges, and tugs.

Before an invasion could start, of course, the Luftwaffe had to gain control of the air. But could the Luftwaffe succeed, and if so, could it finish the job quickly enough to allow the invasion to take place on schedule? Goering was extremely confident and even considered it possible to bomb Britain into submission without an actual invasion. The Luftwaffe's primary mission was to destroy the RAF fighter plane force. Once it had accomplished this, German bombers could attack British naval ships, coastal installations, and troops without fear of RAF interference. All German leaders considered the destruction of the British fighter force to be the absolutely essential prerequisite for an invasion.

Despite Goering's confidence, the Luftwaffe proved inadequate for its task. Essentially a tactical air force designed to support the army, it was undertaking a strategic mission that was beyond its capabilities. Also, the superiority of the Luftwaffe over the RAF was not as great as many believed at the time. Its chief strength consisted of two air fleets under the command of Field Marshals Albert Kesselring and Hugo Sperrle. Both men had started their careers in the army and had served in World War I. Kesselring participated in secret planning for the Luftwaffe during the 1920s and, after its creation, served as chief of staff from 1936 to 1937. Sperrle led the famous Condor Legion, which fought on Franco's side in the Spanish civil war. The combined strength of their air fleets included 1,200 high-level bombers and 280 Stukas, but the latter proved so vulnerable to British fighters that Kesselring and Sperrle quickly withdrew them from combat. For the first time, the Stuka faced fighters that could take advantage of its inadequate speed, armor, and armament.

The Luftwaffe also lacked long-range heavy bombers. Instead it had to make do with aircraft that had inferior bomb-load capacity and range. This weakness was the result of a combination of accident and deliberate choice. When the Luftwaffe came into existence in 1933, its first chief of staff, General Walter Wever, was convinced that in any future war, Britain would be among Germany's enemies. He recognized that Germany would need a strategic air force using long-range heavy bombers that could successfully attack British cities, especially those in the more remote areas. But Wever died in a plane crash in 1936 before he could carry out his plans. His successor, Kesselring, and other Luftwaffe leaders did not share Wever's enthusiasm for heavy bombers and questioned their accuracy from high altitudes. They preferred to concentrate instead on production of the Stuka and medium-range bombers—the Dornier 17, Heinkel 111, and Junkers 88—which could also serve as dive bombers. These were the aircraft that the Luftwaffe unleashed against Britain in the summer of 1940. They had to depend on fighter escorts during daylight. This meant that they could not advance much beyond London because of the limited range of the best German fighter, the Messerschmitt (Me) 109. Bombers could penetrate more deeply into British air space at night, without fighter escort, but night bombing was highly inaccurate.*

The two air fleets combined had 760 Messerschmitt 109s and 220 twin-engine Messerschmitt 110 fighters. Although the Me 110 had greater range than the Me 109, it proved a big disappointment because it was too heavy and unmaneuverable. All things considered, the Me 109 was superior to the British Hurricane and on even terms with the best British fighter, the Spitfire.

A third and smaller German air fleet operated from Norway and Denmark, which were too far away from Britain for this force to be effective. Its bombers depended on unwieldy Me 110s for escort because their British targets lay beyond the range of the Me 109. The RAF also received early warnings of their approach. As a result, this air fleet made only one major daylight attack, which the British repulsed with heavy losses.

Defending against the Luftwaffe

When the Luftwaffe launched its offensive, RAF Fighter Command possessed a total of 650 operational aircraft, mostly Hurricanes and Spitfires, but also including 100 obsolete models. The commander of this force was Air Marshal Hugh Dowding, whose reserved manner had earned him the nickname "Stuffy." Though lacking in charisma, he was popular with the fighter pilots, whom he affectionately called his "chicks." Dowding proved to be one of the major heroes of the Battle of

Britain. Before the war, he had fought to increase the size of the fighter force against the opposition of strategic air power enthusiasts in the RAF who had favored concentration on the production of long-range bombers. He had also been instrumental in the development of the Hurricane and the Spitfire. But despite his efforts, Dowding was concerned about Fighter Command's numeric inferiority. He feared the destruction of his force if he committed too many planes too early. To prevent this, he insisted on keeping a large number of fighters in reserve in northern and central Britain beyond the range of the Me 109.

This policy placed primary responsibility for fending off the Luftwaffe on Air Vice Marshal Keith Park's Fighter Command Group 11, which protected southeastern England, including London. A New Zealander by birth, Park shared Dowding's insistence on conserving Fighter Command's strength. He refused to commit his entire force against German formations approaching England and kept many fighters in reserve. As a result, the British planes that intercepted the enemy were usually badly outnumbered. Not surprisingly, this approach drew strong criticism, but Dowding and Park remained adamant until mid-September, when they finally increased the number of fighters committed to combat. Despite its unpopularity at the time, their cautious policy contributed significantly to Fighter Command's salvation and ultimate victory. It also came as a surprise to the Germans who had expected the British to commit all their fighters to southern England, leaving them without a reserve force.

British aircraft production increased greatly during the summer of 1940 and actually outdistanced German output by a considerable margin. This achievement was due primarily to the unrelenting efforts of Lord Beaverbrook, whom Churchill had appointed minister for aircraft production on May 14. Born in Canada, Beaverbrook was the publisher of the London *Daily Express*. He antagonized some RAF leaders, who criticized his single-minded emphasis on production of fighter planes. But Beaverbrook insisted that national survival depended on the construction of Spitfires and Hurricanes.

The British had another distinct advantage—radar (radio detection and ranging), which they had pioneered as early as 1935. Radar gave the RAF

---

*For an account of doctrines of air power, see Chapter 20.

FIGURE 8-1   Royal Air Force Spitfires patrol the British skies. *(AP/Wide World Photos)*

advance warning of the approach and direction of German planes. Much of its success was due to the efforts of scientist Robert Watson-Watt, who experimented with bouncing radio waves off distant planes and using the resulting echoes to detect their approach. Watson-Watt carried out his work with the help of a committee of scientists headed by Henry Tizard. Dowding recognized the importance of radar and cooperated in developing a chain of 21 radar stations along England's southern and eastern coasts.

Tizard was also active in the creation of an effective ground control system that directed fighter planes to intercept German aircraft on the basis of radar warnings. To supplement the radar stations, the British developed an observer corps, consisting of hundreds of aircraft spotters who alerted the ground control operation centers of the estimated number, altitude, speed, and bearing of incoming enemy forces. The combination of radar, observers, and ground control eliminated the need to maintain constant air patrols to detect German planes and enabled British units to avoid being caught on the ground. The Germans had developed radar, too, but they had focused on its offensive potential rather than using it in a defensive role. They failed to recognize how important it would be in the Battle of Britain.

Ultra reports were also available. They revealed that Hitler had ordered preparations for Operation Sea Lion and that the Germans encountered some problems in gathering tugs and barges for the projected invasion. The reports also provided information on the strength of the Luftwaffe and the location of its bases. But they often failed to indicate clearly actual bombing targets and exact timetables. In short, though useful during the Battle of Britain, Ultra was not of great value until considerably later.

With the threat of invasion now seemingly imminent, a significant transformation took place in the attitude of the British people, who were determined to defend their homeland. Churchill's leadership was a significant factor in this change. His masterful speeches and bulldog manner inspired confidence to a degree that Chamberlain could not remotely approach. Among his most memorable words were these, which he delivered soon after the fall of France:

> The Battle of France is over. I expect that the Battle of Britain is about to begin. Upon this battle depends the survival of Christian Civilization. Upon it depends our British life, and the long continuity of our institutions and our Empire.... Let us therefore brace ourselves to our duties, and so bear ourselves that, if the British Empire and its Commonwealth last for a thousand years, men will still say, "This was their finest hour."

The Battle of Britain

Germany's preliminary air operations began on July 10 and continued until August 6. They consisted of raids against British shipping and resulted in relatively little combat between the two fighter forces. It was not until August 8 that the Germans switched to attacks on British airfields with the intention of destroying the RAF fighter force. This shift marked the actual start of the Battle of Britain. The delay in launching this assault was due in part to the need to replace planes and pilots that the Germans had lost during the campaign in western Europe. The Luftwaffe also unleashed heavy assaults against radar stations on August 12 but seriously damaged only one. It failed to undertake any important follow-up raids against these installations, which must be considered a blunder of the first magnitude.

Despite the fact that the Germans had been conducting major raids against RAF fighter bases for almost a week, they did not officially launch their grand air offensive until August 13. They hoped to win mastery of the skies over Britain and the channel within four weeks to enable the invasion to commence by September 15. Intense aerial combat followed. Fighter Command absorbed considerable punishment, but it remained strong and replaced lost planes with new aircraft coming off the assembly line. Pilot losses were serious but perhaps not as critical as some observers have contended. The British secured replacements who performed well. And since the battle took place over Britain, many pilots were able to bail out of their planes and return to action. German losses were also high. During the crucial months of August and September, the RAF lost 832 fighters, and 532 more were damaged. The Luftwaffe suffered fewer fighter losses—668 destroyed and 436 damaged—but it also lost 500 bombers and 67 Stukas. The heavier toll of British fighters was due partly to the Me 109's superiority over the Hurricane. But the RAF's policy of making German bombers its primary target was also an important factor. This left British fighters more vulnerable to Me 109 attacks than would have been the case if they had concentrated on attacking German fighters.

Combat in the Sky

These figures on losses do not capture the reality of the aerial combat that produced them. Throughout most of August and September, dogfights between German and British fighters raged at frequent intervals in the skies over Britain. They often resulted in flaming death for the unsuccessful pilots, and many, who were shot down but survived, were badly injured or burned. German bomber crews were virtually defenseless, if deprived of their fighter escorts, and fell victim to RAF fighters in large numbers. Each of these desperate engagements were of short duration, however, because German fighters had only 20 to 30 minutes of flying time over British airspace before turning back. Some of them did not make it and had to ditch at sea or crash land before reaching their bases.

Fighter aces emerged on both sides. They included two veterans of the German Condor Legion—Colonel Werner Mölders, who accounted for 45 enemy planes by the end of November, and Major Adolf Galland, who recorded his fortieth "kill" on September 24. On the British side, Group Captain Stanford Tuck shot down 25 planes by the end of October, while Squadron Leader Douglas Bader was credited with 23 before being shot down over northwestern France and taken prisoner in the summer of 1941. Bader accomplished this despite having two artificial legs. He had lost both legs in a peacetime crash.

The Battle Continues

The Battle of Britain entered its second phase on August 24, when the Germans unleashed even more intense raids on Fighter Command bases. During the next week, the Luftwaffe shot down so many British fighters that the RAF losses actually outstripped production of replacement aircraft. The trend was dangerous, but the Germans also suffered significant losses and began to relax pressure on RAF airfields as early as September 4, when Goering diverted some strength to assaults on industrial cities and other targets.

Phase 3 of the Battle of Britain began on September 7. It featured a drastic change in tactics by the Germans, who abandoned their attacks on

KEY:

- ● Heavily Bombed Areas
- ▨ Industrial Areas
- ▲ Shipping Centers
- ✕ Armament Works
- ▽ Plane Factories
- ☐ Naval Bases
- - - - Main German Air Raid Routes

0   50 MILES   100 MILES

North Atlantic

ORKNEY IS.

Scapa Flow

SCOTLAND

Cromarty

ABERDEEN

DUNDEE

Donbristle

North Sea

Firth of Forth

GLASGOW

Firth of Clyde

Leith

EDINBURGH

LONDONDERRY

NORTHERN
IRELAND

BELFAST

Tynemouth

NEWCASTLE

SOUTH SHIELDS
SUNDERLAND
MIDDLESBROUGH

Gateshead

Darlington

Isle of Man

Scarborough

Irish Sea

York

DUBLIN

LIVERPOOL

LEEDS

MANCHESTER

SHEFFIELD

IRELAND

NOTTINGHAM

WATERFORD

DERBY

Gt. Yarmouth

BIRMINGHAM

NORWICH

Coventry

WALES

ENGLAND

Worcester

Ipswich

Reading

SWANSEA

LONDON

CARDIFF

BRISTOL

Dover

Margate

Folkestone

20 Miles

Dunkirk

SOUTHAMPTON

BOURNEMOUTH

CALAIS

BRIGHTON

Eastbourn

WEYMOUTH

PORTSMOUTH

FRANCE

PLYMOUTH

Falmouth

To Cherbourg
75 Miles ➤

To Havre
100 Miles ➤

The Battle of Britain, July–December 1940

Fighter Command bases in favor of direct raids on London. Goering made this decision with the support of both Hitler and Kesselring over the protests of Sperrle, who feared the change would ease pressure on Fighter Command just as its losses were reaching a critical point. The shift was due in part to Goering's concern that the Luftwaffe was not making rapid enough progress toward air supremacy. He believed that attacks on London would lure more British fighters into the sky over the capital, where they could be destroyed. But the shift was also due in part to Hilter's anger over the British response to a German raid on London on August 24. Although the Luftwaffe had refrained from direct attacks on the British capital previously, this was enough to prompt Churchill to order a retaliatory strike against Berlin, and during the next few days RAF Bomber Command carried out five raids on the German capital. They inflicted little damage but killed a few civilians and infuriated the Führer. Finally, the German leaders hoped that the bombing of London might weaken British civilian morale.

Critics have pointed to this change in tactics as the turning point in the Battle of Britain because it supposedly gave Fighter Command a new lease on life just as it had reached the verge of exhaustion. This is highly questionable. To be sure, the diversion ended the damage that the Germans had inflicted on Fighter Command airfields, but it did not lessen the number of RAF fighter engagements with the Luftwaffe. The raids on London certainly did not destroy the RAF, but it is unlikely that continued attacks on Fighter Command bases would have had this effect either. Goering pressed his assault on London for a week, climaxed by two especially heavy raids on September 15. But they did little serious damage and resulted in heavy German losses.

While the Luftwaffe and RAF battled for control of the air, Admiral Raeder and his staff did a remarkable job of assembling the ships and barges necessary to transport the invasion forces across the channel. But they could do nothing to ease the alarming shortage of escort vessels. Meanwhile, the British increased the strength of their army, and by the first week in September, 16 divisions guarded the landing areas. They were not at full strength in weapons, but they did have 800 tanks. RAF bombers also carried out raids during mid-September against German invasion craft in the French and Belgian channel ports and caused considerable damage. The cabinet also approved the use of poison gas against German troops if they succeeded in landing on the coast and could not be repelled by other means.

The failure of the Luftwaffe's attacks against London on September 15 convinced the Germans that their efforts to destroy RAF Fighter Command had failed. They had not achieved the all-important prerequisite for an invasion. On September 17, Hitler postponed Operation Sea Lion indefinitely. His decision really sounded the death knell for the project, because he soon shifted his attention away from Britain in favor of an invasion of the Soviet Union.

Luftwaffe attacks against Britain continued but without clear purpose. After September 15, the emphasis gradually shifted to night raids on the British capital. These attacks soon became known as the London "Blitz" and reflected the fact that RAF fighter attacks were hurting the Luftwaffe. Night raids made it more difficult for the RAF to shoot down German bombers and enabled the Luftwaffe to penetrate deeper into British airspace by sharply reducing the need for fighter escorts. But the shift also made it harder for German bombers to hit their targets and to destroy British fighters. At first, however, the Germans enjoyed considerable success with an offensive radar navigational device called *Knickebein* (crooked legs). It utilized intersecting radio beams from widely dispersed transmitters to guide bombers to their targets. British scientists were up to the challenge, however, and soon devised various means of disrupting the system. Night attacks increasingly took on the guise of terror bombing, designed to undermine Britain's will to fight.

British Civilian Morale

Contrary to a persistent myth, civilian morale during these raids was not always high. This was especially true during the early stages of the bombing of London, which focused on the docks of the city's East End. London's worst slums were also located here. For a time, strong resentment flourished among many "East Enders" over the fact that their neighborhood was being devastated, while the wealthier sections of the city remained virtually unscathed. Vehement protests also arose over the lack of bomb shelters. All of this gradually faded, and morale stiffened as other parts of London sustained major damage. One bomber, flying off course, even dropped a bomb into the courtyard of Buckingham Palace where King George VI and his family were in residence.

The lack of satisfactory bomb shelters was not limited to the East End. As a result, people began to crowd into London's subway (Underground) stations in search of refuge. Before long, whole families packed themselves into these "Tube" stations night after night. Although hot, humid, smelly, often mosquito infested, and always filled to capacity, they afforded protection and even a sense of comradeship to their nocturnal residents.

In November, Goering extended his raids to other cities and ports, starting with an attack that destroyed much of Coventry in the industrial Midlands. Over 400 bombers devastated the center of the city with incendiary and high-explosive bombs, killing more than 500 people and destroying a beautiful fourteenth-century Gothic cathedral. A new German radar device, X-Gerat, utilizing a more sophisticated beam that could operate on various frequencies to avoid jamming, contributed significantly to the destructiveness of the Coventry raid. For a time, the Luftwaffe again enjoyed more accurate bombing, but once again, the British devised an antidote. This time it came in the form of small radar sets installed in fighter planes. Assisted by ground control, they enabled the fighters to intercept enemy bombers with much greater success.

The assault on cities continued until late December, followed by a comparative lull during the winter. One of the worst of these raids struck London on December 29. Although only 136 bombers took part, their incendiaries set almost 1,500 fires, which destroyed a large area bordering St. Paul's Cathedral. Despite being hit by 28 incendiaries, the cathedral itself suffered only minor damage. The Luftwaffe resumed its offensive in earnest when better weather returned in March 1941 and carried out a series of heavy attacks for the next two months. This time, in addition to London, the Germans concentrated on port cities and the industrial centers of Birmingham and Manchester. But in May, the skies over Britain fell strangely silent as most of the Luftwaffe headed east to participate in the invasion of the USSR.

FIGURE 8-2 The dome of St. Paul's Cathedral still stands after a devastating Luftwaffe raid on London. (*UPI/Corbis/Bettmann*)

Both sides made wildly inflated estimates of enemy losses during the Battle of Britain, officially the period from July 10 through October 31. The British claimed a total of almost 2,700 enemy aircraft destroyed, while the Germans believed that they had accounted for slightly over 3,000 RAF planes. In reality, the Luftwaffe lost 1,882 fighters and bombers, the RAF 1,017 fighters, 118 bombers, and 130 Coastal Command aircraft for a total of 1,265.

Germany's air offensive had caused considerable damage and taken many lives, but it had not achieved its objectives of destroying RAF Fighter Command, preparing the way for invasion, or breaking the morale of the British people. This failure offered two lessons for those who were willing to learn. It demonstrated that a cross-channel invasion could not be improvised but had to be prepared well in advance with ample troops, equipment, landing craft, warships, and control of the air. Britain and the United States learned this lesson well—perhaps too well. The German failure also revealed that there were definite limits to the effectiveness of bombing cities, something that Britain and the United States were exceedingly slow to learn. Obviously, the Luftwaffe was not suited for such a mission, but the British and Americans later experienced disappointing results from strategic bombing of German cities, carried out by long-range bombers that they had designed especially for this purpose.

It is now clear that Germany's attempt to destroy RAF Fighter Command in the summer of 1940 was probably doomed from the start. The inadequacies of the Luftwaffe, the weakness of its planning, and the inconsistency of its approach combined to diminish greatly the possibility of success. And if these obstacles were not enough, Fighter Command was a formidable opponent.

The gallant British pilots who flew the Spitfires and Hurricanes denied control of the air to the Luftwaffe, and without this vital prerequisite, a cross-channel invasion was out of the question. Churchill's memorable words immortalized their contribution: "Never in the field of human conflict was so much owed by so many to so few."

CHAPTER NINE

The Plot Thickens:
The Mediterranean
and the Balkans

Germany's failure to defeat Britain in the fall of 1940 dulled the luster of the Wehrmacht's reputation for invincibility and posed the likelihood of a long war. The conflict between Germany and Britain had become a standoff. Although Germany could not invade Britain, the British were in no position to undertake an invasion of the continent. As time passed and both sides increased in strength, there would be little chance that this situation would change unless Britain gained allies. And when Hitler turned his attention in the fall of 1940 to planning his attack on the Soviet Union, he relegated Britain to second place in Germany's strategic considerations. Starting in the late summer of 1940, Hitler also embarked on a series of diplomatic initiatives designed to pressure the various countries of the Balkan area of Europe into alliance with Germany. Among other things, this would safeguard his southeastern flank prior to the invasion of the Soviet Union.

Complications in the Mediterranean

Hitler did want to exert some pressure on the British, however. Thus, he turned his attention to the Mediterranean where Britain possessed a number of important bases—at Gibraltar on Spain's southern coast, in Egypt, and other parts of the Middle East. But he did not want to commit too many resources to this task and always viewed the Mediterranean as a sideshow. As the war continued, however, he nevertheless became increasingly involved in this area as complications not of his making embroiled him in new commitments.

Hitler initially focused on capturing the British naval base of Gibraltar, which dominated the western entrance to the Mediterranean. This would require the approval of Franco, the Spanish dictator, for the passage of German troops through

Spain. Hitler also wanted to entice Franco into joining the Axis. But Franco demanded compensation in North Africa at the expense of France. This demand would obviously anger the Vichy French government, whose willing collaboration Hitler hoped to retain. Franco's ambitions also conflicted with those of Mussolini, who had designs on much of the same area, and clearly Hitler did not want to antagonize his new Italian ally. All of this led to confusion and ultimately disillusionment for Hitler.

Mussolini also dreamed of conquering both Egypt and Greece, and in the fall of 1940, he sent troops into both, anticipating easy victories. Instead, both turned into disasters and he became a laughingstock. Hitler had no choice but to come to his ally's rescue. Mussolini's blunders threatened Hitler's timetable for the invasion of the Soviet Union, scheduled for May 1941, and also jeopardized his hopes for bringing the Balkan countries under his control through diplomatic pressure alone.

The Question of Gibraltar

Hitler's interest in Gibraltar focused primarily on taking it away from Britain rather than acquiring it for Germany. In fact, in negotiating with Franco during the fall of 1940, he used it as bait for securing Spain's agreement to join the Axis and allow passage of German troops through the country. The Spanish had long dreamed of regaining Gibraltar, which the British had taken from them in 1704. But Franco wanted far more—the French North African colonies of Morocco and Algeria as well as a slice of French West Africa. Hitler was dismayed by the extent of these ambitions, especially because they would be opposed by the Vichy French. In addition, Mussolini coveted part of Algeria and a port on the Moroccan coast.

Mussolini also hoped to acquire other French possessions—the island of Corsica, the city of Nice on France's Mediterranean coast, the Alpine province of Savoy, and another North African colony, Tunisia. Because Hitler wanted to remain on good terms with all three countries, he favored deferring these claims until after the war. Hitler actually met with Franco at Hendaye in the French Pyrenees Mountains on October 23, 1940, but he gained neither Spain's adherence to the Axis nor permission for passage of German troops. Franco was by no means convinced that the Germans were going to win the war, especially in view of the failure of their air offensive against Britain. Hitler later told Mussolini that, rather than meet with Franco again, he would prefer to have three or four teeth pulled.

Although Hitler was clearly in a position to overrun the unoccupied portion of France, if necessary, he preferred the cooperation of Vichy, at least for the present. He even hoped to entice Pétain's government into an alliance with Germany. This seemed a real possibility in the fall of 1940 because of strained relations between the French and their former ally, Britain. Vichy leaders were outraged when elements of the Royal Navy actually attacked French ships in Algerian ports on July 3.

FIGURE 9-1   Winston Churchill gives his famous "V" salute outside the prime minister's residence in London. (*UPI/Corbis/Bettmann*)

The Mediterranean Theater of Operations, 1940–43

Churchill had become anxious that the French fleet might fall into German hands and ordered an operation against the large French naval force at Oran and the neighboring base of Mers-el-Kebir. He made this decision over the heated objections of British naval leaders, who warned that such action would have a disastrous impact on Anglo-French relations. Churchill instructed Admiral James Somerville to offer the French commander, Admiral Marcel Gensoul, the opportunity to join the British or take refuge in a distant colony. If he refused, Somerville's naval force was to attack. Gensoul chose to resist, and the British reluctantly opened fire, sinking one battleship, disabling three other capital ships, and killing over 1,000 French sailors. This incident triggered discussion in the French government of a possible declaration of war against Britain, but cooler heads prevailed, and France limited action to breaking diplomatic relations. The French also avoided an alliance with Germany, although they did follow a policy of collaboration on many issues.

North Africa: The Desert War

Instead of attacking Gibraltar, Hitler ultimately embarked on operations in the eastern Mediterranean, where he had not originally planned to become involved. This entanglement was due to Italy's attempts to conquer Egypt and Greece in the fall of 1940 and the disastrous failure of both. Mussolini was eager to move out of Hitler's shadow and demonstrate the prowess of his armed forces. He struck first in Africa, where prospects looked bright. Italian troops in Libya greatly outnumbered the British in neighboring Egypt, while Mussolini's East African army in Eritrea, Ethiopia, and Italian Somaliland dwarfed Britain's forces in British Somaliland, Kenya, and the Sudan. Although Egypt had been officially independent since 1922, Britain had retained a strong influence in this desert country as well as military, naval, and air bases.

Things started out well enough as Italian troops overran British and French Somaliland in August. Mussolini planned to follow this success by sending his Libyan army into Egypt with Marshal Rodolfo Graziani in command. Graziani had led one of the armies that overran Ethiopia in 1935–36 and served as viceroy of Italian East

Africa for two years before taking over the Libyan command in the summer of 1940. But Graziani was pessimistic about the proposed offensive. He recognized that his troops were deficient in armor as well as other motorized equipment. Lack of mobility was a serious shortcoming in the desert.

Graziani was painfully aware that Italy was not prepared for war. The nation's industrial base was the smallest of any of the industrialized powers, and it had to import most raw materials. The Italians received no material aid from Germany, which, of course, also relied heavily on imports. In fact, the two allies actually competed for such commodities as Rumanian oil. Mussolini had hoped that the war would soon end in victory for the Axis. Instead, he found himself in a struggle that gave every indication of being a long one. As it persisted, the weakness of the Italian economy became ever more apparent.

General Archibald Wavell led Britain's forces in Egypt as well as East Africa and Palestine. Wavell had lost an eye on the western front during World War I. The general won great popularity with his troops, who appreciated his frequent visits to front-line positions. In 1939, Wavell had undertaken the thankless task of organizing a Middle East command with limited resources but had managed to gain some reinforcements from India, New Zealand, and Australia.

Wavell tried to compensate for his numerical inferiority by dispersing his forces in packets along the Egyptian-Libyan border to give the impression that he was strong enough to cover the entire frontier. His troops also resorted to hit-and-run raids against the Italian positions. The bluff worked, and Graziani did not move across the border until September 13. But even then his heart was not in the enterprise, and he halted after reaching Sidi Barrani, 50 miles into Egypt. He established a series of fortified camps at this point and proceeded to build up a huge supply base for the next phase of the operation, an offensive toward Alexandria, Cairo, and the Suez Canal. But the Italian attack never came.

Instead, Wavell went over to the offensive himself on December 9. The British commander originally planned only a large-scale raid because he estimated that the Italians outnumbered his forces 80,000 to 36,000. He did enjoy an advantage in tanks, however, with 275 to only 120 for

The British Offensive against the Italians, December 7 and 8, 1940–February 9, 1941

the Italians. The British tanks included 50 heavily armored Matildas, which proved impervious to the Italians' inferior antitank weapons and played an especially important role. After one battle, the British counted 38 dents in the armor of a single Matilda, but none of the Italian shells had penetrated the tank's heavy skin. Italian tanks, by contrast, were death traps equipped with armor barely worthy of the name. British shells riddled them with holes. Wavell's forces were also much stronger in motorized transport.

Wavell was fortunate to have General Richard O'Connor as his field commander. O'Connor enjoyed the complete confidence of his men, and with good reason. He enjoyed a reputation for bold, imaginative tactics and soon proved to be a master at handling mobile forces in the desert.

O'Connor used his tanks to exploit a gap between two of the Italian fortified camps. He then attacked each camp from the rear, catching Graziani's forces completely by surprise and capturing 40,000 men. Those Italians, who managed to escape, fled back into Libya, where they took refuge in the coastal fortress of Bardia. But O'Connor's troops seized this stronghold early in January 1941 and took another 45,000 Italians prisoner. Anthony Eden, who had succeeded Halifax as British foreign secretary, greeted the fall of Bardia with a new version of Churchill's famous tribute to the RAF: "Never has so much been surrendered by so many to so few." The British moved on to encircle the port of Tobruk, which they captured on January 22 along with 30,000 more prisoners.

Despite these disasters, Graziani still had 20,000 men in eastern Libya, and they now fell back along the coast. In an effort to prevent their escape, O'Connor split his forces. One column pursued the retreating Italians, while a second spearhead of tanks and motorized infantry attempted to outflank them by cutting the coastal road at Beda Fomm. It did so by striking boldly across a 170-mile expanse of largely uncharted and extremely rugged desert. The soldiers who made this trek encountered terrible hardships, including sandstorms and freezing rain, but they reached Beda Fomm before the enemy. When the Italians arrived, the British attacked them from concealed positions and, after a desperately fought battle, captured another 20,000 prisoners. The British then moved on to El Agheila, about a third of the way across Libya. But on February 12, Churchill ordered Wavell to cease his offensive and divert part of his forces to Greece, where a new situation had developed as a result of Italy's invasion of that country.

Wavell's offensive had been amazingly successful. At the cost of fewer than 2,000 British casualties, it had accounted for a total of 130,000 prisoners. Britain's victory and Italy's disaster had been due in large part to differing approaches to the campaign. The British had recognized that the desert was similar to the ocean with its vast expanse of desolation. In such an environment, there really was no such thing as a continuous front. The key to victory was mobility, with tanks operating much as ships at sea. The far less mobile

Italians had to rely on static defense in the form of fortified camps, such as those near Sidi Barrani, or fortress towns such as Bardia and Tobruk. They tied down their forces in these strongholds, which proved vulnerable to the encircling maneuvers of the more mobile British.

As the full scope of the Italian defeat became apparent, Hitler decided to intervene to save what was left of Libya. But with plans already under way for the invasion of the Soviet Union, he had few troops to spare—only one light and one panzer division, both understrength. He chose General Erwin Rommel to lead this meager force.

Born in southern Germany to middle-class parents, Rommel had won acclaim during World War I for his personal heroism as a young officer who specialized in tactics of infiltration behind enemy lines. Hitler's willingness to adopt new and unorthodox military ideas quickly won Rommel's admiration, and Rommel's relatively humble origins endeared him to the Führer, who often felt uncomfortable in the company of aristocratic generals. Until 1939, Rommel had always been an infantry officer, but the success of the *Blitzkrieg* in Poland made him a true believer in armored warfare. Soon afterward, Hitler helped him obtain command of a panzer division. Despite his lack of previous experience with tanks, Rommel mastered armored operations in a remarkably brief time. Indeed, his division performed with conspicuous success during the 1940 campaign in Western Europe. Like Guderian, he believed in the swiftest possible exploitation of a breakthrough.

Rommel possessed exceptional ability to assess battlefield situations quickly and act decisively. At times he flew over the front in a reconnaissance plane to obtain a better overall picture. His favorite command position was at the head of his troops, often exposing him to enemy fire. Although usually outnumbered in manpower and equipment, he consistently outmaneuvered his opponents. He came to be greatly respected by the British. In fact, Churchill once paid tribute to him in Parliament as "a very daring and skillful opponent." Many of his fellow German officers, however criticized him as reckless. Nevertheless, the risks he took frequently caught the enemy by surprise and, given his numeric inferiority, were probably essential to his success.

Ultra reports alerted Wavell of Rommel's arrival and the strength of his forces. But Wavell was convinced that the Axis would not be able to launch an attack until at least May. In fact, the OKH ordered Rommel not to attack the British under any circumstances and to remain on the defensive. But Rommel was not one to play a passive role, and he decided to attack late in March, even before his full force had arrived. He recognized that the British were also weak. To give the impression of greater German strength, Rommel used dummy tanks mounted on Volkswagen chassis. He also retained five Italian divisions and enjoyed superiority in the air. His attack caught the British by surprise, and his troops defeated them in a series of brief encounters, forcing them to fall back in confusion all the way to the Egyptian frontier. The British suffered a severe blow when the Germans captured General O'Connor during the retreat. But Rommel was not able to pursue the British into Egypt because his forces were now in a vulnerable position at the end of a precarious supply line. The British also succeeded in holding Tobruk, which the Axis forces had bypassed in their drive to the Egyptian border. Tobruk posed a threat to Rommel's flank and deprived him of port facilities close to the front. It was now clear that the desert war had become a deadlock.

Meanwhile, the British enjoyed much greater success in East Africa, where they took the offensive against the Italians in January. One force pushed into Eritrea and Ethiopia from the Sudan, while a second invaded Italian Somaliland from Kenya. Although the Italians outnumbered Wavell's forces, they lacked modern equipment and were cut off from any hope of supply from Italy or Libya. The Allied forces moved with remarkable speed against weak resistance in Italian Somaliland and southern Ethiopia. In the north, the Italians put up a much tougher fight, but relentless British pressure forced them to retreat. By the end of May, Wavell's troops controlled virtually all of Italian East Africa and had also reconquered British and French Somaliland.

The Balkan Campaigns

Although Hitler could do nothing to save Mussolini's East African Empire because of its remote location, he did come to his fellow dictator's aid in the Balkans, where Italy had undertaken another ill-advised invasion in October 1940.

FIGURE 9-2   A German field artillery piece fires against a British position during the desert fighting. (*National Archives and Records Administration*)

This time Greece was the victim, but once again the operation turned into an Italian fiasco, one that jeopardized Hitler's own encroachment on the Balkans. During the previous summer, the Führer had resorted to diplomatic pressure to safeguard his Balkan flank and protect German access to Rumania's oil fields prior to the invasion of the USSR. Hitler was also concerned about Soviet expansion into the Balkans, which followed Germany's victory over France. With the French defeated, Stalin realized that his country was more vulnerable to a German attack. The Soviet dictator moved to extend the buffer zone between Russia and Germany by annexing Lithuania, Latvia, and Estonia and seizing the Rumanian provinces of Bessarabia and Northern Bukovina. The occupation of Bessarabia brought Red Army troops within 100 miles of the Rumanian oil fields at Ploesti, an important source of oil for the German war machine.

At about the same time, Hungary demanded the return of the province of Transylvania, lost to Rumania in the 1919 peace settlement. Bulgaria also insisted that the hard-pressed Rumanians cede the province of Southern Dobruja to them. Hitler feared that these disputes would lead to war between the Balkan states and that the Soviets might take advantage of this instability to extend their influence still more. To prevent this,

he assumed the role of mediator in these disputes while pressing all three Balkan powers to join the Axis. He awarded Hungary a large part of Transylvania and granted Southern Dobruja to Bulgaria. In return, he guaranteed Rumania's remaining territory and received the right to station German troops on Rumanian soil.

Hitler had accomplished all this without firing a shot, but the failure of Italy's invasion of Greece posed a new threat to the stability of the Balkans. The Führer had warned the Duce not to take action against Greece, and the Italian supreme command, which recognized the army's weakness in modern equipment, was equally opposed. But Mussolini was determined to strike and launched his attack from Italian-occupied Albania on October 28, despite the approach of winter and ominous weather forecasts. The Italians made good progress at first but were headed for trouble. Torrential rain fell as they penetrated down the mountain valleys of northwestern Greece. The small, poorly equipped but tough Greek army waited until the opportune time and then counterattacked. The Italians found themselves in an overextended position and exposed to murderous fire from artillery in the mountains above them. They also ran short of supplies due largely to the primitive Albanian infrastructure. Before long there was a complete logistic collapse. Meanwhile, Greek counterattacks cut the Italian columns to pieces and forced the survivors back into Albania. By the end of the year, the Greeks were in control of almost one-quarter of Albania, but their offensive bogged down in January and the struggle degenerated into a stalemate. Mussolini had suffered another humiliation, and the Greeks had won the admiration of much of the world, just as the Finns had done the previous winter.

Hitler feared that Mussolini's "regrettable blunder" would lead to the diversion of British forces from Egypt to help Greece. But with his attack on Sidi Barrani approaching, Wavell could not spare any troops, although he did send a small military mission and some aircraft in November. It was not until after the British had smashed the Italians at Beda Fomm that they considered it possible to send an expeditionary force. Churchill was dubious about the chances for success, but Eden, who had undertaken a fact-finding trip to Greece, favored intervention, as did Wavell. The prime minister took their advice and dispatched 58,000 British, Australian, and New Zealand troops to Greece. The force was much too small for the task and desperately weak in both tanks and aircraft.

Even before Britain's intervention, Hitler had decided to invade Greece to rescue his Italian ally and protect his Balkan flank. To facilitate this operation, he persuaded Bulgarian leaders to join the Axis and allow German troops to enter their country on March 1, 1941. With Rumania, Hungary, and Bulgaria all safely in the Axis camp and the invasion of Greece looming in the near future, the position of Yugoslavia became crucial. Hitler had been pressuring the Yugoslavs to join the Axis ever since the start of Italy's invasion of Greece, and the Belgrade regime finally agreed on March 25. But certain Yugoslav officers staged a coup that ousted the pro-German government. This heroic but rash act enraged Hitler, who now expanded his forthcoming operation against Greece to include Yugoslavia as well.

Germany unleashed *Blitzkrieg* against both countries on April 6. They proved remarkably effective, especially the attack on Yugoslavia, which the OKH improvised on short notice. Hitler ordered it to begin with a massive bombing attack on Belgrade as a special act of vengeance. After two days of repeated raids, the capital lay in ruins. The Germans sent 650,000 troops against the Yugoslavs, including the 2nd Army, which pounced from Austria and Hungary, and the 12th Army, which struck from Rumania and Bulgaria. Seven panzer divisions played a crucial role in the operation despite the rugged mountain terrain. On paper, Yugoslavia could assemble an army of more than a million men, but the rapid German onslaught prevented full mobilization. The Yugoslavs were also woefully lacking in modern equipment, including tanks and aircraft. German columns quickly sliced through the stricken country. The invasion also glaringly revealed the fundamental flaw in the Yugoslav state: the inability of the two main national groups, the Serbs and the Croats, to get along. They had squabbled since the founding of Yugoslavia. Now many Croats refused to join in what they considered to be a Serbian fight, and some cooperated with the Germans. Belgrade fell on April 12, and five days later the Yugoslavian army surrendered.

Although the Greek campaign took a little longer, the outcome was never in doubt. Greece was in a hopeless position, with the bulk of its army engaged in Albania. The Greeks also insisted on keeping most of their remaining forces along the Metaxas line, a defensive system opposite the Bulgarian border. The Metaxas line was vulnerable to a flanking attack by German troops penetrating into Greece from southern Yugoslavia. Unfortunately, the Greeks held fast to the Metaxas line and Albania, and when the Germans struck, they quickly penetrated behind both positions and cut off the Greek defenders. The remaining Allied forces were badly outnumbered and had to retreat southward toward Athens and beyond. The British had no choice but to carry out a Dunkirk-type evacuation. Again it was successful, and 43,000 troops escaped during the period April 23–May 1.

The Conquest of Crete

The Germans followed their conquest of Greece with an invasion of the Greek island of Crete, which lay 100 miles southeast of the mainland, on May 20. Originally, Hitler had not seriously considered an operation against Crete. But Goering convinced him of the need to undertake an airborne assault to prevent Britain from maintaining a base on the island. The Allies had over 30,000 men on

The Axis Conquest of Yugoslavia and Greece, April 1941

Crete, including 20,000 who had been evacuated from the mainland. But they were critically deficient in equipment and totally lacking in air support.

Germany's conquest of Crete was one of the most remarkable campaigns of the war because it employed only airborne troops. This was not the original intention, however. The Germans planned to carry out a seaborne landing at the same time as the assault from the sky. But British naval units intercepted two flotillas of small Greek ships that carried 7,000 German troops. They sank 14 of the ships and forced the remainder to flee back to their ports in Greece. The airborne operation might have failed, too, because the Allied commander on Crete, General Bernard Freyberg, commander of the New Zealand Division, received detailed information from Ultra of the impending seaborne and airborne landings. He also obtained a copy of the actual operational order for the invasion, which was recovered from a German plane that had crashed the day before the attack. This document clearly indicated that the airborne assault would be the main one. Unfortunately, Freyberg, a man of incredible courage who had won the Victoria Cross in World War I, drew the wrong conclusions. He remained primarily concerned about the amphibious operation, which, of course, never took place. As a result, he failed to defend adequately the all-important airfields that the Germans needed to capture if they were to reinforce their original airborne landing force.

Even so, it was a close call for the Germans. Goering and the other German planners had underestimated the size of the Allied garrison and deployed only 22,000 men to take the island. The first wave of parachutists and gliderborne troops numbered a mere 3,000, and the Allied defenders inflicted heavy casualties on them. But they pressed on relentlessly, with the help of complete air supremacy, and by the second day had captured the airfields that were their primary objectives. Once they had accomplished this, transport planes quickly flew in reinforcements. The British had to resort to another evacuation, the fourth in slightly more than a year. Again they were successful—16,000 men were saved. But the Germans paid a heavy price for Crete: 3,674 killed and over 2,000 wounded. Their casualties in this campaign were greater than those suffered in Yugoslavia and Greece combined. Indeed, Hitler considered the casualties so severe that he never again tried an airborne mission of such magnitude.

The Germans in Control

As a result of his various Balkan operations, both diplomatic and military, Hitler had gained complete control of southeastern Europe and had secured his flank for the invasion of the Soviet Union. As for the British, their intervention had been reminiscent of the Norwegian campaign and

represented another forlorn chapter in the continuing saga of "too little, too late." The decision to divert troops from North Africa to Greece had been a mistake. The forces involved had been too weak to prevent the German conquest and were sorely needed in Libya when Rommel appeared on the scene.

The spring of 1941 also witnessed dramatic events in the Middle East. In Iraq, the pro-German politician Rashid Ali and a group of army officers carried out a successful coup in April. Hitler promptly dispatched arms shipments to the new regime and received approval from Vichy France for German planes to land in neighboring Syria to refuel before moving on to Iraq. But Britain reacted to the coup by sending troops to Iraq from India and Palestine, forcing Rashid Ali to flee to Iran. The British proceeded to restore a friendly government to power in Baghdad.

Meanwhile, Britain had become concerned that the Germans might send troops into Syria. Actually, Hitler had no intention of doing so and quickly withdrew his aircraft. This really eliminated the need for Allied intervention, but Churchill was insistent. On June 8, British and Free French troops moved into Syria from Palestine and Iraq, and the Vichy government ordered its troops to resist. Fighting lasted for five weeks before the Vichy forces capitulated on July 14. Britain now controlled the entire eastern end of the Mediterranean with the exception of neutral Turkey. But after holding the world spotlight for several months, the Mediterranean now lapsed back into its true sideshow status. The war's main event had already begun on the plains of Russia.

CHAPTER TEN

Operation Barbarossa: Dream of *Lebensraum*

Hitler's invasion of the Soviet Union in June 1941 was his greatest blunder. The undertaking proved beyond Germany's capacities and, thus, was probably fatal in itself, apart from the fact that it created a two-front war. Hitler's only chance was a quick victory, but he lacked the power to accomplish this. The Soviets were almost certain to win a long war because of their greater resources in manpower, raw materials, and industrial potential.

The Decision to Invade the USSR

Given Hitler's basic objective of creating *Lebensraum* in the east, it was virtually inevitable that he would attack the Soviet Union eventually. But why did he strike in 1941 when Soviet neutrality assured him of peace in the east, as well as important supplies, while he continued his war against Britain? It appears that he decided to attack because he believed that the Soviets were too weak to prevent him from realizing his cherished dream. At the same time, he recognized that Britain was no threat to invade the continent in the west.

But Hitler justified his decision on the grounds that he could not trust the Soviets. His concern was not entirely fabricated. Hitler never felt completely secure from a Soviet attack while he was dealing with the Western Powers, and his fears increased in the summer of 1940 when the Soviets seized the Baltic states and the Rumanian provinces of Bessarabia and Northern Bukovina. Why the takeover of the Baltic states and Bessarabia should have come as any surprise is difficult to understand. Germany had agreed that they lay within the Soviet sphere of influence. But Northern Bukovina was another matter. The Germans had not conceded this territory to the Soviets. Reports of Soviet troop concentrations in the

newly annexed provinces increased the Führer's paranoia regarding a Soviet attack.

Germany's dependence on the Soviet Union for raw materials also worried Hitler, especially because Stalin insisted on payment in the form of armaments. In fact, early in 1940, Hitler had ordered that arms deliveries to the Soviets receive priority over those to the German army. He considered this drastic measure necessary to assure the continued flow of raw materials from the USSR. By the summer of 1940, supplies from the Soviets comprised 22 percent of Germany's total imports.

Finally, Hitler feared that Stalin might enter into an alliance with Britain and, in fact, suspected that Stalin was responsible for the British refusal to make peace after the fall of France. But, while Hitler warned of the danger of a Soviet attack in the future, there is no indication that he considered it imminent. In fact, he may have expressed his concern primarily to justify his own insistence on an invasion.

Despite Hitler's fears, there is no indication that the Soviets planned to attack Germany at any time in 1940 or 1941. It is true that in May 1941 Stalin expressed concern about deteriorating Soviet-German relations and warned of the possibility of a German invasion. He hoped to stave off such action by diplomatic means but feared that war would be inevitable by 1942. At that point, he believed that the Soviets would be strong enough to face Germany and might even have to initiate hostilities. But he clearly based this speculation on fear of German intentions and certainly did not plan to strike without provocation.

Hitler's own thoughts were clearly straying eastward well before the start of the Battle of Britain. As early as July 1940, he ordered OKH to submit plans for a possible campaign against the Soviets. Hitler declared that "to all intents and purposes the war is almost won." But he warned of the need to destroy the Soviet Union, thus depriving the British of their last potential continental ally. In his view, the defeat of the Soviets would also discourage the Americans from entering the war.

Hitler was convinced that such an undertaking would result in an easy victory. Never impressed by Soviet military power, he became thoroughly contemptuous of the Red Army after its dismal performance against Finland. He also believed that the Soviet government was unpopular and would collapse with the first few military defeats. As he proclaimed later, "You have only to kick in the door, and the whole rotten structure will come crashing down."

Thus, he believed that the time was ripe to translate his geopolitical and racial vision into reality by crushing the Soviets and creating his cherished *Lebensraum* for the German master race at the expense of the Slavic *Untermenschen*. Hitler informed his generals that the conflict would not be fought according to the traditional rules of warfare. He saw it as a war of "ideologies and racial differences." This approach manifested itself in the notorious "Commissar Order," which provided for the summary execution of political commissars, the Communist political officers attached to Soviet military units, and other Communist leaders. Red Army soldiers, bypassed by German forces, were not to be treated as prisoners of war but as partisans and were to be shot. In addition, Hitler was willing to see 20 to 30 million Soviet citizens die of starvation to provide food for the Wehrmacht. Although German military leaders insisted that they had opposed such measures and placed the blame solely on Himmler's SS, it is now clear that many of them were very much involved. General Erich Höpner, commander of one of the panzer groups in the invasion, clearly had no qualms when he wrote these words in May 1941:

> The war against the Soviet Union is an essential component of the German people's struggle for existence.... This struggle ... must therefore be conducted with unprecedented severity. Both the planning and the execution of every battle must be dictated by an iron will to bring about a merciless, total annihilation

of the enemy. Particularly no mercy should be shown toward the carriers of the present Russian-Bolshevik system.*

Military Strengths and Weaknesses

Neither the OKW nor the OKH opposed the invasion. They shared Hitler's view of Soviet weakness and were particularly scornful of the Red Army's showing in the Winter War. After studying the situation, Halder concluded that the Soviets would not be able to resist for more than eight to ten weeks.

Both Hitler and his generals were guilty of two serious errors. They woefully underestimated the obstacles involved in a Russian campaign and the strength of the Soviet armed forces. They also overestimated Germany's own power. The obstacles should have been obvious. The Soviet Union comprised an area greater than North America, and its huge population provided vast reserves of manpower. Its infamous winter weather mandated that the Germans would have to win the campaign between May and October. The inadequate Soviet roads and the fact that Soviet railway gauge was wider than that of Western Europe posed staggering logistic problems. The Germans faced the dilemma of converting the rail system to the narrower Western gauge. Germany's shortage of motorized transport also would create difficult supply problems in the vast expanse of the Soviet Union.

The Soviet armed forces had some serious weaknesses, but they also possessed remarkable strength, especially in manpower and quantity of equipment. The Red Army appears to have had the equivalent of 230 to 240 divisions, including 170 infantry divisions, as well as 33 cavalry and 46 armored and motorized brigades. Estimates of Soviet tank strength range from 10,000 to 24,000. Unfortunately, most of them were obsolete, but the Soviets had developed some outstanding new tanks—the heavy KV and the medium T34—that were superior to the best German models. The T34 was especially formidable. It was fast, armed with a 76-millimeter gun,

---

*Quoted in Omer Bartov, *Hitler's Army: Soldiers, Nazis, and War in the Third Reich* (Oxford: Oxford University Press, 1992), pp. 128–129.

and well armored. The Soviet air force contained at least 8,000 planes, including 2,000 fighters and 1,800 bombers, but only 800 in each category were modern.

The chief Soviet weakness was in military leadership. This was due largely to Stalin's extensive purge of the officer corps in the late 1930s in an effort to destroy any possibility of army resistance to his rule. Approximately 35,000 officers were either executed or imprisoned, most on trumped-up charges of treason. Those eliminated included three of five marshals, 14 of 16 army commanders, 60 of 67 corps commanders, and 136 of 199 division commanders. No fewer than 75 of the 80-man Supreme Military Council as well as all 11 vice commissars of defense were also liquidated or sent to prison camps. The purge had a devastating impact on the morale of the surviving officers, who obviously feared for their lives. It also required the wholesale promotion of junior officers to fill vacancies for which many of them were not qualified. Many of the top generals in 1941 were more notable for their political reliability than for their military prowess. Hitler and his generals were quite aware of the deplorable condition of the Soviet officer corps, which was yet another reason why they looked upon the Red Army with contempt.

Among the Soviet officers who were exceptions to the prevailing mediocrity or downright incompetence were Marshal Timoshenko and especially General Georgi Zhukov. Zhukov, the son of a peasant shoemaker in a small village near Moscow, began his military career as an enlisted man during World War I. His bravery twice won him the Order of St. George, Tsarist Russia's highest military decoration. With the coming of the revolution, he joined the Red Army and saw action as a cavalry officer in the civil war. He won Stalin's favor in the following years and became a specialist in armored warfare. Timoshenko had salvaged victory in the Winter War and, with Zhukov's help, had launched a desperately needed modernization of the Red Army that focused on the development of armored divisions. But their efforts encountered strong opposition among the less progressive elements in the Soviet leadership.

General Konstantine Rokossovsky was still another rising star. A victim of Stalin's purge of the officers corps, he only recently had been released after four years in prison. His captors had treated him brutally, breaking several ribs, smashing his toes with a hammer, and kicking out nine of his teeth, for which he later received steel replacements. The son of a Polish father and a Russian mother, he was drafted into the tsarist army during World War I. After joining the Red Army during the Civil War, he rose rapidly in rank before his arrest in 1937. During the struggle to come, he gained renown as Russia's finest tactical commander as well as the begrudging respect of the Germans, who referred to him as "the Dagger."

The Red Army's recent battle experience was not limited to the fiasco in Finland. The Soviets had fought Japanese troops along the disputed border between Manchuria and Soviet East Asian territories in 1938, and shortly before the outbreak of the European war, Zhukov had led a massive tank force to a resounding victory in the Battle of Khalkhin-Gol. This defeat stunned the Japanese who henceforth did not share the German assumption of Soviet weakness. Khalkhin-Gol may also have played a major role in Japan's decision to direct its future expansion toward Southeast Asia rather than against the USSR.

Stalin exercised supreme authority over the army and insisted that much of it be stationed far forward in the buffer area of Lithuania, eastern Poland, and Bessarabia. This placed the main Soviet armies in positions that were dangerously vulnerable to a German armored attack. Stalin's decision was due in large part to his fear that the peoples of the newly acquired Baltic States and Poland as well as those of the Ukraine might prove unreliable. But it also reflected Red Army doctrine, which insisted that any German invasion would be quickly halted and followed by a major Soviet counteroffensive.

German strength in 1941 was not appreciably greater than it had been during the campaign in the west in 1940. The OKH assembled 145 divisions for the invasion, including 102 infantry, 19 armored, and 14 motorized. Although the number of armored units had almost doubled from May 1940, this was deceptive because the quantity of tanks per division had actually declined by half. Overall tank strength, 2,500, remained the same as in 1940. But experience had shown the need for a higher proportion of infantry, and the panzer regiments now were equipped with Panzer IIIs and Panzer IVs. More divisions also provided greater operational flexibility. The Luftwaffe had 2,770 planes, including 1,085 bombers and 920 fighters. Its strength in both categories was actually lower than at the start of the Battle of Britain. This was due largely to losses suffered in the skies over Britain during 1940 as well as the diversion of units to the Mediterranean and the need to defend Germany against RAF bombing attacks.

Objectives and Strategy

Hitler and the OKH disagreed over objectives. To be sure, both considered the destruction of the Red Army in the shortest possible time as the primary aim. But the OKH believed that German forces should concentrate on the capture of the capital, Moscow, which also was an important industrial center and the hub of the Soviet rail network. Hitler gave priority to the conquest of the Baltic states and Leningrad in the north as well as the Ukraine, with its huge supplies of grain and iron ore, and ultimately the Caucasus oil fields in the south. The Führer was also anxious for German forces to link up with the Finnish army in the Leningrad area. Finland had allowed a small German force to enter its territory as early as September 1940 and agreed to join in the campaign against the Soviets to regain the land lost in the Winter War. The Finns also feared the possibility of another Soviet attack and realized that they could not afford to alienate both Germany and the USSR.

Despite the divergence in views of German leaders, Hitler approved a compromise operational plan on December 18, 1940. It was given the code name Operation Barbarossa, in honor of the medieval German emperor Frederick Barbarossa, who drowned while on a crusade in 1190 but, according to Germanic legend, was merely sleeping while awaiting the moment for the restoration of a glorious German empire. The plan provided for participation by three army groups. Army Group North, commanded by Field Marshal von Leeb, was to slash through the Baltic states toward Leningrad. It consisted of two infantry armies of 27 divisions and a panzer group of three armored divisions. Army Group Center, under Field Marshal von Bock, was to penetrate into Soviet-occupied Poland and Belorussia in the direction of Moscow. It was the largest army group with two infantry armies of 42 divisions and two panzer groups of nine armored divisions. Army Group South, led by Field Marshal von Rundstedt, was to drive through the Ukraine. Its strength included three infantry armies of 38 divisions and a panzer group of five armored divisions. Two Rumanian armies and a Hungarian corps were also to take part in the southern operation.

Army Group Center was to destroy the enemy in Poland and Belorussia and then shift its panzer forces to help Army Group North smash the enemy in the Leningrad area. After accomplishing this objective, the armor would return to the central front to resume the drive on Moscow. The OKH intended to start Operation Barbarossa on May 15, but the *coup d'état* in Yugoslavia and Hitler's decision to crush that country forced postponement until June 22. Original German plans had called for an invasion of Greece without using forces earmarked for Barbarossa, but the Yugoslav complication necessitated a diversion of strength. Even without the intervention in Yugoslavia, however, it is doubtful that the Russian campaign could have started in May. The spring of 1941 was extremely wet, and the rivers in eastern Poland were at flood stage until early June.

The Spectacular Invasion Begins

Hitler was supremely confident that the invasion would succeed. "When Barbarossa commences," he exclaimed, "the world will hold its breath and make no comment." At first, his optimism seemed justified. When the Germans struck on June 22, they caught Soviet troops totally off guard, even though Soviet agents had repeatedly warned Stalin of the impending invasion. The Soviets had an outstanding intelligence service, which included Richard Sorge, a German Communist who operated in Japan and had gained the complete trust of both German and Japanese officials in Tokyo. He not only alerted Stalin to the impending attack but even included the date of the invasion. Another Soviet agent in Switzerland, referred to as Lucy (for the city of Lucerne), confirmed the date and added details of the German operational plan. Churchill also sent Stalin personal warnings based on messages intercepted by Ultra and other sources. But the Soviet dictator refused to alert any of his commanders in the forward zone. Stalin apparently believed that Britain had instigated the warnings to stir up trouble between Russia and Germany and wanted to avoid any activity that might provoke the Germans. Although he finally allowed an alert to be sent early on June 22, it came far too late.

Germany also gained complete surprise from the air. The first bombers took off before the start of hostilities, flew at high altitudes to avoid detection, and then swooped down on unsuspecting Soviet air bases just as German troops crossed the border. More devastating air attacks followed. The Soviets lost an estimated 1,200 planes on the first day.

Operation Barbarossa made spectacular early progress. After the first week, the German propaganda ministry announced bombastically: "In seven short days, the Führer's offensive has smashed the Red Army to splinters.... The eastern continent lies, like a limp virgin, in the mighty arms of the German Mars." Chaos reigned among Soviet forces along much of the frontier. Ill-trained to fight defensively because Soviet military doctrine

focused almost totally on offensive warfare, they were stunned by the speed of the German advance and poorly led by many of their officers. Desperate counterattacks resulted in heavy casualties and usually failed. Red Army soldiers fought bravely and often to the death rather than surrender because to be taken prisoner, even in a hopeless situation, was considered treason. Nevertheless, many thousands ultimately had no recourse because of the speed of the German advance. Leeb's Army Group North drove 155 miles through Lithuania and into Latvia in the first five days, spearheaded by a panzer group commanded by General Höpner. Although Höpner had been active in the conspiracy against Hitler before the war, he had demonstrated great skill as a panzer corps commander in both the Polish and Western European campaigns. By July 10, his armor was within 80 miles of Leningrad, but at this point the drive bogged down due to heavily wooded terrain and supply problems.

Bock's Army Group Center also scored massive gains. Two panzer groups, one commanded by General Hermann Hoth on the left and the other by Guderian on the right, carried out two successive encirclements of large Soviet forces. Unlike Höpner, Hoth was a loyal supporter of Hitler, but he, too, had led panzer forces with considerable

FIGURE 10-1   German soldiers charge past an armored half-track vehicle and a burning farmhouse during the invasion of the USSR. *(Library of Congress)*

flair in Poland and Western Europe. Together they closed the first trap near Minsk in the area of the prewar Soviet-Polish border on June 26. They completed the second envelopment near Smolensk, 200 miles to the east, in mid-July. In all, Bock's troops captured 480,000 prisoners, and the Soviets suffered disastrous losses in armor. But as impressive as these victories were, they were less decisive than the Germans thought because many Soviets were able to escape before the pincers closed. Others eluded capture even after that because the panzers were so far ahead of the mass of infantry following on foot that the flanks of the encirclements were weakly held. Still, the Germans had covered 440 miles in 23 days and were only 200 miles from Moscow.

Progress was slower in the south as Rundstedt's forces moved toward Kiev with a panzer group, commanded by General von Kleist, in the vanguard. Although Kleist had worried over the rapid pace of Guderian's dash toward the English Channel in 1940, he had become a convert to armored warfare and had led a panzer group during the conquest of Yugoslavia. But he and Rundstedt encountered fierce Soviet resistance in the Ukraine as well as severe supply problems. Stalin had assumed incorrectly that the primary German attack would come in the south because of Hitler's desire to capture the area's economic resources. Thus, he had concentrated greater Soviet strength in the Ukraine than along the northern and central fronts.

Stalin's early response to the invasion was one of shock. In fact, the "man of steel" lost his nerve and withdrew into solitude for two weeks while the Germans thrust deeper into his country. Without its supreme leader, the regime drifted into confusion. Stalin finally emerged from his isolation to address the nation on July 3 in a dull, uninspiring voice. Despite his own dereliction of duty, he called for a relentless struggle against the enemy. When Stalin finally shook off the effects of his collapse, he and other Soviet leaders set out to overhaul their command structure. Stalin created the State Defense Committee (GKO), which consisted of five members of the ruling Politburo with Stalin as its chairman. It now assumed overall direction of the war effort. Stalin also established Stavka, the general headquarters of the Soviet supreme

command, which was directly subordinate to the GKO. The army general staff came under Stavka's supervision, and its chief of staff, General Boris Shaposhnikov, received a key position in Stavka. Henceforth, Stavka conceived basic strategy, while the general staff developed actual operational plans for the conduct of the war. But, even after this reorganization, Stalin continued to dominate the war effort and contributed to still more military disasters by his stubborn refusal to authorize troop withdrawals from untenable positions. He also persisted in blaming others for his own failures.

It was not until August 5 that the last resistance ended within the Smolensk pocket on the central front. Even before this it had been necessary for Bock's troops to halt their forward progress and establish an advance supply base. Army Group Center had outdistanced its supply line, and most of the infantry was still strung out far behind the armor. Meanwhile, the preinvasion dispute over strategy, which the compromise plan for Operation Barbarossa had temporarily settled, returned in a more virulent form on July 19. Hitler proposed to divert Hoth's panzer group from Army Group Center to help in the drive on Leningrad as the original plan had stipulated. But now he also wanted to shift Guderian's panzer group to the south, where the possibility of another huge encirclement loomed. Brauchitsch and Halder insisted that it would be wiser to keep the armor in the center for a drive on Moscow. Bock and Guderian agreed. They all contended that since Moscow was the decisive objective, the Soviets would commit their greatest strength to its defense. This posed the possibility of destroying much of the Red Army, which was the chief objective of Operation Barbarossa. The quarrel continued while Army Group Center fought off fierce Soviet counterattacks, but on August 20 Hitler ordered Hoth's armor northward and Guderian's to the south.

Critics have long contended that the generals were correct and that Germany may have lost the campaign and the war because of Hitler's refusal to allow an immediate drive on Moscow. But evidence now indicates that German supply problems were so severe that a major attack on the capital was probably not feasible until mid-September.

Hoth's panzers contributed to the encirclement of Leningrad, but Hitler did not intend to storm the city. He planned instead to starve it into submission. The siege began in September, and the suffering of Leningrad's population soon reached epic proportions. Perhaps as many as a million Leningraders worked incessantly to build a crude defensive perimeter around the city, including earthen walls, tank traps, pillboxes, and barbed wire entanglements. Many others volunteered for a paramilitary force, the People's Army. Despite having almost no training and few weapons, they received the grim assignment of plugging gaps in the army's defensive line. Some of them were armed only with containers of boiling water, which they threw at the enemy. Others ignited kerosene in an effort to slow the German advance. They suffered appalling casualties.

Although the Soviets were not able to lift the siege until early 1944, the worst of the ordeal occurred during November, December, and January of 1941–42. Food was in such short supply during this period that over 200,000 people died of starvation and diseases caused by malnutrition. The city depended on supplies that came by train from Moscow to Lake Ladoga and then by boat to the small port of Osinovets. From there the precious cargoes traveled another 35 miles by rail, a route within easy range of German artillery. But the Germans cut the Moscow-Leningrad railroad on November 9, and the Soviets did not regain control until a month later. Even after restoring the rail link, it was necessary to haul supplies across the frozen lake in trucks, many of which broke through the treacherous ice. Food became so scarce during the worst months of the siege that people resorted to devouring dogs, cats, rats, and melted-down wallpaper glue, as well as a horrible jelly made from sheep intestines. Many persons dropped dead in the streets, and since few had the energy to bury them, they often remained there. As hunger became more and more severe, some resorted to cannibalism, eating the flesh of corpses that they found in the streets or makeshift morgues. Leningraders also suffered horribly from the savage cold of the far northern winter. As stocks of coal and oil vanished, many froze to death.

Meanwhile, Guderian's panzer group took part in the encirclement of massive Soviet forces under the command of Marshal Semyon Budenny near Kiev, the capital of the Ukraine. Kleist's panzer group, which had driven to the southeast of Kiev, hooked north to link up with Guderian's armor, which was thrusting southward. Some have blamed Budenny, whom one observer described as a man "with an immense mustache but a very small brain," for the Soviet disaster. He had become a close associate of Stalin, rising to high rank through favoritism. But despite Budenny's meager qualifications for command, the real culprit in the debacle at Kiev was Stalin, who ordered Budenny not to withdraw his forces from their exposed position. This decision enabled the Germans to capture over 600,000 Russians. Hitler was ecstatic and called the encirclement the "greatest battle in the history of the world." It was certainly a brilliant victory, but it did not assure a triumphant outcome to the campaign.

The Germans did not complete the Kiev operation until September 26. While it was in progress, Hitler decided that the time had come for an attack on Moscow with the greatest possible strength. He restored the panzer groups of Hoth and Guderian to Army Group Center and also shifted Höpner's armor from Army Group North to take part in the offensive. At the same time, Hitler ordered Army Group South to advance toward Kharkov, the Donetz Basin industrial area in the eastern Ukraine, and Rostov, the gateway to the Caucasus oil fields.

Bock launched his drive toward Moscow on September 30. It featured armored thrusts by Hoth on the north, Höpner in the center, and Guderian on the south that quickly produced two new encirclements and the capture of another 600,000 prisoners. Hitler was convinced that the enemy would "never rise again." His optimism appeared well founded. Soviet forces remaining to the west of Moscow were outnumbered and lacking in heavy equipment.

The Soviets had suffered huge losses of war materiel since the start of the invasion. They had managed to offset this to some extent by a drastic effort to increase production between July and October. But as the Germans swept eastward, Soviet leaders had no choice but to dismantle industrial plants and evacuate them to safer locations. These included the region of the Volga River hundreds of miles east of Moscow as well as much more remote destinations—the Ural Mountains,

KEY:

▬▬▬▬	Moscow Highway
▼▼▼▼	Soviet Fortifications
••••••	Front Line June 21, 1941
– – –	Front Line July 10, 1941
–·–·–	Front Line Sept. 1, 1941
▬ ▬ ▬	Front Line Oct. 1, 1941
▰▰▰▰	Front Line Dec. 6, 1941
→	Main German Thrusts
▤	Soviet Pockets & Partisan Area
▨	Soviet Russia
⚓	Soviet Naval Base

0   100   200

The German Invasion of Soviet Russia, June 22–December 6, 1941

Western Siberia, and Central Asia. This was a formidable task that required exceptional planning and placed a tremendous strain on the railroad system. In all, the Soviets moved over 1,500 industrial enterprises to the east between July and November. Once they had completed this great evacuation, it was necessary to reassemble the industries as quickly as possible, under often very difficult conditions. Millions of workers had to make the long trek to the east, where they labored as many as 15 hours a day and experienced deplorable living conditions.

German troops also overran many of the Soviet Union's best food-producing regions, especially the Ukraine. As a result, the same areas that provided havens for the uprooted industries had to increase their food production drastically. This often involved the cultivation of crops that had never before grown in these regions. Once again, the results were remarkable.

In the aftermath of the great battles of encirclement, it seemed certain that Moscow would fall to a giant pincers movement. Hoth's panzers were to swing around the northern flank of the capital, while Guderian was to turn the southern flank. Höpner would continue his advance directly on the city. But now complications arose. Rain fell steadily during much of October, and in many places the advance mired in mud until November. Although the Germans were within 40 miles of Moscow at one point, they debated whether it might be wise to go over to the defensive.

The Soviets Turn the Tide

There was good reason for caution. The winter was about to start, German forces were depleted, and the supply situation was badly snarled. Yet some German generals believed that an all-out effort might crush the Red Army and feared that breaking off the offensive would result in a World War I–type stalemate. After much debate, the OKH finally proposed to resume the drive on Moscow, and Hitler agreed. The Germans based this decision, however, on inadequate knowledge of enemy strength. The Soviets had been moving in fresh divisions, including many Siberian units from East Asia. Stalin felt secure in weakening his East Asian forces because of Sorge's reports from

Tokyo that Japan would not intervene against Russia but intended to attack the United States. He also appointed Zhukov to take command of the Moscow front. Zhukov had no intention of committing his newly arrived troops to defend against the German offensive. Instead, he hoarded them to the east of the capital and planned to wait until the enemy drive had lost its momentum before unleashing a powerful counterstroke.

In the meantime, the troops that had survived the earlier German offensive had to defend Moscow. Again officials recruited hundreds of thousands of civilians to build three rings of defenses around the city. They also committed units of the People's Army to fill gaps in the line, and as at Leningrad, these poorly trained and ill-equipped auxiliaries fought bravely and suffered heavy losses. While the desperate struggle unfolded, Stalin delivered stirring speeches in which, instead of resorting to the usual Communist slogans, he appealed directly to the patriotism of the army and the people. He implored them to rally to the defense of Holy Mother Russia, and they responded with grim determination.

Army Group Center launched its final onslaught on November 15, but the drive made limited progress and ground to a halt by the end of November. The weather had deteriorated even before the start of the offensive, with temperatures dropping as low as 35 to 40 degrees below 0 Celsius, and heavy snow fell later in the month. Because of the lack of antifreeze, the Germans kept small fires burning under their tanks when they were not in use to prevent freezing. The men were without winter clothing and had to make do with what they could seize from the Soviets. During this operation, the Wehrmacht lost more soldiers to frostbite than to the Soviets. Dysentery created additional dangers. Many men suffered congelation of the anus while squatting to relieve themselves in temperatures as low as –60 degrees Celsius. The stabbing cold also froze food so solid that butter had to be cut with a saw, and horse meat proved impervious to the ax. If hot soup were not eaten promptly, it became cold in seconds and frozen in minutes.

The stage was set for the Soviet counter-offensive. The Red Army's first initiative came in the south. Timoshenko had replaced Budenny as commander on this front after the Kiev encirclement, and his troops forced Rundstedt to abandon Rostov on November 28. Zhukov launched far heavier attacks against the enemy flanks to the north and south of Moscow on December 5. Halder favored a retreat to a more or less prepared line. But Hitler insisted that the troops must form a number of strong points, called hedgehogs, around advanced supply depots and fight on even if surrounded. After the war, Halder blamed this decision for the heavy losses that the Germans suffered during the winter of 1941–42. But a number of other generals contended that Hitler actually saved the army from what would have been a rout if it had attempted a large-scale withdrawal.

The situation was precarious for a long time, and at one point there was a real danger that the Red Army might encircle Army Group Center. The Soviets did cut off some German troops, but they continued to hold out, and the Luftwaffe supplied them by air throughout the winter. Zhukov wanted to concentrate the bulk of the Red Army for an all-out assault on the Moscow front, which he believed might deal Army Group Center a fatal blow. But Stalin insisted that Soviet forces continue to attack on all fronts. This weakened Zhukov's striking power and helped the Germans to hold out. The Red Army also suffered heavy losses. This was inevitable against such a tenacious enemy, but it was also indicative of Zhukov's philosophy of war. He believed in hammering relentlessly at an objective, no matter what the cost in lives.

When the Soviet counteroffensive finally ground to a halt in March 1942, it was clear that the war on the eastern front had become a stalemate for the time being. It was also apparent that the struggle for the Soviet Union would be long and bloody.

Failure in the campaign led to a wholesale shake-up of Germany's military leadership. Rundstedt resigned in protest when Hitler refused to allow an additional withdrawal following the loss of Rostov. Soon afterward, Hitler dismissed both Guderian and Höpner for ordering unauthorized retreats. He lashed out with particular fury against Höpner, whom he stripped of his rank and ousted from the army. Bock gave up his command because of illness, and Leeb resigned early in 1942. An even higher luminary added his name to the roster of fallen generals when Brauchitsch asked to be relieved as commander in chief. His health had

deteriorated steadily under the strain of the campaign. Rather than appoint a successor, Hitler took over as commander in chief himself. Halder was the sole survivor in the army's top echelon.

Hitler's assumption of Brauchitsch's duties represented a serious encroachment on army responsibilities. Henceforth, he restricted the OKH to planning operations on the eastern front only and even there frequently intervened in command decisions. Elsewhere, the OKW exercised operational authority, and the OKW was, of course, very much under the Führer's control. The success of Hitler's "hold fast" policy before Moscow during the winter of 1941–42 also increased his belief in his own destiny. It set a dangerous precedent. In the future, when confronted by even more serious situations, he repeatedly relied on the same policy, with catastrophic results.

The Wehrmacht's failure to crush the Red Army in 1941 was fatal to Hitler's dream of *Lebensraum* and ultimately to the existence of the Third Reich. His invincible army had been stopped, its power blunted. It would never again be as formidable as it had been in June 1941. Even if it had been possible for Army Group Center to capture Moscow, there is little likelihood that the Germans would have won the campaign. There is no reason to believe that the Soviets would not have continued to fight on. The crucial mistake was the decision to attack the Soviet Union in the first place. The task was simply beyond Germany's resources.

Treatment of POWs

One of the most hideous aspects of Nazi policy toward Russia was the treatment of Soviet prisoners of war. Ironically, many Red Army soldiers, especially minorities, disliked the Soviet regime and went over to the Germans more or less voluntarily. But the SS subjected them to brutal treatment. Many starved, froze to death, or died from other causes. Almost 3.3 million Soviet prisoners perished in Nazi camps or in transit. When the war began to go against the Reich, the Germans changed this barbarous policy and used Soviet prisoners for labor. They even recruited some of them as soldiers, primarily members of minorities who still harbored grievances against the Soviet government. Although the number of such troops eventually reached substantial proportions, they never played an important role in Hitler's war effort. Only 10 percent of Red Army POWs survived the German camps, and sadly most of these were looked upon with suspicion by the Soviets and sent to Siberia where they were worked to death.

The Germans were not alone when it came to barbaric treatment of prisoners. The Soviets responded in kind. While the Red Army High Command did not sanction shooting prisoners, individual units did so spontaneously. It appears that 90 to 95 percent of German prisoners perished in the period 1941–42. In November 1941, Stalin proclaimed that it was necessary "to annihilate all Germans who penetrated as occupiers, down to the last man." By February 1942, however, Red Army leaders urged an end to this policy, and Stalin ordered that henceforth captive German soldiers were to be held as prisoners rather than slain.

CHAPTER ELEVEN

Hitler's New Order in Europe

Russia's unexpected counteroffensive had dealt Hitler's vision of *Lebensraum* in the east a shattering blow. But the dream was not yet dead. Indeed, efforts were under way to establish what Hitler called the New Order, not only in the areas of the Soviet Union that had fallen under German control but in the remainder of Nazi-dominated Europe as well. Hitler intended the New Order to apply ultimately to all the peoples of Europe, in ways that differed according to his view of the merits of each group as well as circumstances. The degree of accommodation and resistance among the conquered peoples also varied from country to country as did the attitudes and policies of the few remaining neutral European states.

In all occupied countries elements of collaboration as well as resistance coexisted. Generally resistance did not take substantial form until later in the occupation and then usually due to increasing harshness on the part of Nazi authorities. The first response of many people was one of shock, in large part due to the speed of the German conquest. Most people tried to adjust to the changed conditions and hoped to avoid getting into trouble. In some countries, numerous people actually admired Nazism. Fear of communism and a desire for order often motivated such persons. Others considered resistance useless and likely to lead to reprisals. As time passed, and it became clear that Germany would probably lose the war, this attitude waned, but most people still decided to sit out the war rather than resort to active resistance. Still others could see definite opportunities for economic gain and better treatment by collaborating. Resistance was, of course, a risky undertaking and often hampered by a lack of resources. In some countries the terrain did not provide sufficient shelter for resistance operations. The Nazis contributed to the growth of resistance movements

by such practices as forcing large numbers of men into their slave labor program. Neutral countries, such as Sweden and Switzerland, saw cooperation as the key to remaining free from German occupation as well as economic gain.

The Greater German Empire

The Germans were the chosen people in the New Order. But Germandom, in Hitler's mind, included not only the Germans of the Reich and the ethnic German minorities of Central and Eastern Europe but also the other Germanic peoples—the Scandinavians, the Dutch, the Luxembourgers, the German-speaking Swiss, the Flemish Belgians, and the English. He envisaged most of these peoples as members of a Greater German Empire. The English were the one possible exception to this. Hitler apparently intended to allow them to maintain their independence as an affiliated state, provided that they demonstrated a sufficiently positive attitude.

Hitler's approach to the Germanic peoples of Scandinavia and the Low Countries varied from area to area, but his final intent was to absorb all of them into the Greater Reich. When his troops overran Denmark in April 1940, he allowed the Danish government to continue administering the country, subject to German supervision. The Danes believed that a policy of accommodation to the conquerors was the only sensible approach. After the German invasion of Russia, the government allowed the recruitment of a volunteer *Frikorps Danmark* to fight against the Soviets, and in November 1941 it bowed to German pressure and adhered to the Anti-Comintern Pact. Werner Best, who became the top German official for Denmark in 1942, believed that a lenient policy would enable Germany to dominate the country peacefully. But his hopes fell afoul of rising anti-German feeling and increased sabotage activity by a resistance movement that had existed since 1940. All of this led to a crackdown in August 1943, complete with the imposition of military rule for the remainder of the war.

Hitler initially planned a similar policy of moderation for Norway, but Norwegian resistance to the German invasion shattered this hope. It was widely believed in Allied countries that wholesale treachery on the part of many Norwegians had paved the way for Germany's victory. The major culprit in this so-called "5th Column" was believed to be Vidkun Quisling, a man whose name became synonymous with traitor. In reality, there was no 5th Column. To be sure, Quisling, the leader of a Nazi-type political party, had visited Berlin in December 1939 and had urged Hitler to take over his native land. But the Führer had not seen fit to take him into his confidence regarding the projected invasion, and Quisling was as surprised as any other Norwegian when the Germans actually struck. He did move quickly to set up a collaborationist government in Oslo, however, which Hitler did recognize. But the regime proved so distasteful to most Norwegians that Hitler soon withdrew his support. Quisling regained Hitler's favor in 1942, however, and returned to his former position. He retained it until the end of the war, even though Hitler found him increasingly tiresome. Quisling visualized Norway as an independent client-state of the Reich. Hitler had no intention of allowing this, and Josef Terboven, the top German official in Norway, dominated the country. As in Denmark, a resistance movement came into existence soon after the German conquest. According to the media in the United States and Britain, it engaged in pitched battles with the Germans on a regular basis. In reality, its contribution was much less spectacular. Nevertheless, it had one major accomplishment to its credit—the raid on the Norsk hydroelectric plant at Vemork in February 1943, which temporarily cut off the supply of heavy water for Germany's nuclear research program. The Norwegians, who carried out this raid, were trained in Britain by the Special Operations Executive (SOE). Churchill had ordered the creation of this organization during the grim summer of 1940 with the stated intention of setting "Europe ablaze." Although the blaze was slow in

coming and never did fulfill the prime minister's high expectations, this raid was one of the SOE's most successful operations.

Norway's neighbor, Sweden, maintained its freedom from Nazi occupation, but if Hitler had won the war, it seems likely that it, too, would have disappeared into the Nazi empire. In the meantime, the Swedes cooperated with the Germans and profited from a brisk trade, including the iron ore so vital to Germany's war economy. Sweden also departed from its traditional neutrality to allow German troops to use Swedish trains enroute to Norway, at least on a limited basis.

The Führer originally intended to grant preferential treatment to Luxembourg, but Grand Duchess Charlotte and her government fled into exile and refused to cooperate. As a result, the Germans absorbed the country into the Reich administratively and economically.

In the Netherlands, Hitler originally hoped to gain the cooperation of the Dutch by treating them leniently, somewhat on the order of his initial policy in Denmark. But the swift departure of Queen Wilhelmina and the Dutch cabinet to Britain during the invasion in 1940 undercut this approach. Instead, Dutch officials continued to handle routine administration but took orders from Reich Commissioner Arthur Seyss-Inquart, who had been Hitler's instrument in the destruction of Austria's independence. Seyss-Inquart soon encountered a number of rivals for authority, however. These included the SS, the Foreign Ministry, and various economic organizations. Hitler intended eventually to incorporate the Netherlands into the Reich, and as the first step in this direction, German officials attempted to integrate the Dutch economy with Germany's. While considerable progress resulted, the competition between rival Nazi agencies also led to a great deal of inefficiency and confusion.

Not all of the Dutch were hostile toward the Germans, most notably a Dutch Nazi party, which reached a membership of 110,000. But its leader, Anton Mussert opposed absorption of his country into a Greater German Reich. He preferred a league of Germanic peoples that would include an independent Greater Netherlands, enlarged by the annexation of the Flemish-speaking areas of Belgium and northern France. Obviously, this did not meet with Hitler's approval, but the party proved useful to the Germans in rounding up Jews for deportation as well as helping to recruit volunteers for Waffen SS units and Dutch regiments that served on the Eastern Front. The majority of the Dutch became increasingly disenchanted with German rule and economic exploitation, however, and a resistance movement developed. Its scope of action was limited by the flat, open nature of the country's terrain.

Belgium posed a special problem because of its mixed population. Hitler recognized the Flemish-speaking people of northwestern Belgium as Germanic and, thus, worthy of absorption into his Greater Germany. The French-speaking Walloons, who lived in the southeast, had highly questionable Germanic credentials. Although a substantial number of the Flemish were sympathetic to the Germans, they were badly split into various nationalist parties. Staf de Clerc's Flemish National Union was the strongest of these, but de Clerc cherished a dream similar to that of Mussert in the Netherlands, in this case a Greater Flanders. Again, this obviously was at odds with Hitler's plans. The Germans also did not want to alienate the Walloons by tying themselves too closely to the Flemish, especially in view of the friendly attitude of Leon Degrelle, an extreme Walloon nationalist and an admirer of the Nazis. After the invasion of Russia, Degrelle even organized a Walloon brigade and served with it on the Eastern Front. Unlike Queen Wilhelmina and Grand Dutchess Charlotte, King Leopold refused to leave his people and remained in Belgium, referring to himself as a voluntary prisoner. The Belgian cabinet did escape to Britain and established a government in exile. A resistance movement also came into being but confronted many of the same problems as the one in the Netherlands. It is clear that Hitler ultimately planned to annex all of Belgium after the war.

Switzerland, like Sweden, remained free from occupation throughout the war. Hitler saw the German-speaking Swiss as the black sheep of Germandom because of their democratic government and what he viewed as their single-minded devotion to business. To him, Switzerland was "a pimple on the face of Europe." Nevertheless, immediately following the armistice with France in 1940, the OKH ordered planning for an invasion of Switzerland. Hitler intended to absorb four-fifths of the country into Germany while allowing Italy

to take the Italian-speaking portion in the south. But planning for Operation Sea Lion and later the actual attack on the Soviet Union relegated the Swiss project to the realm of what might have been. Like the Swedes, the Swiss profited from a vigorous trade with Germany throughout the war. They supplied the Reich with munitions and other manufactured goods as well as meat and dairy products. They also cooperated in other ways. In 1942, they closed their borders to Jews at the very time that the Holocaust was starting, in effect condemning those seeking refuge to a death sentence. Swiss banks also became depositories for funds looted from every country that fell under German domination during the war, including huge amounts from victims of the Holocaust. The Swiss refused to cooperate with postwar international efforts to recover these assets until the late 1990s.

The "Jewish Question"

If the Germanic groups were the chosen people in the New Order, the Jews were the damned. While the Nazis inflicted barbaric cruelty on other peoples who fell under their yoke and murdered vast numbers of them, none were subjected to the same type of systematic genocide as that which befell the Jews. Although the term is sometimes applied to many of the Slavs, it is the Jews whom we remember as victims of The Holocaust. From the time he came to power, Hitler clearly planned to expel the Jews from Germany and other territories that fell under his control. Whether he intended from the start to exterminate them is less clear.

The early Nazi approach focused on the imposition of numerous restrictions aimed at making life miserable for the Jews and encouraging their emigration from Germany. Some Jews did leave, but the majority stayed. Many simply lacked the financial means to flee. Others disliked the thought of abandoning their homeland and hoped that the persecution might be temporary. The situation deteriorated in 1935 as Nazi thugs attacked Jewish shops and beat up Jews in the streets. This trend culminated later that year in the promulgation of the Nuremberg Laws, which deprived Jews of German citizenship and prohibited marriage and sexual relations between Jews and ethnic Germans.

Persecution became more intense in November 1938 when a Jew assassinated an official of the German embassy in Paris. A wave of terror followed in Germany. The Nazis murdered 100 Jews, arrested 30,000 others, and engaged in the wholesale burning of synagogues and the destruction of Jewish shops. They broke so much glass in the process that this pogrom became known as *Kristallnacht* (Night of Crystal Glass). In the aftermath of *Kristallnacht,* the Nazis forced the Jewish community to pay a heavy indemnity, seized Jewish businesses, and required firms to dismiss Jewish employees. All of this led to a great increase in emigration during the remainder of 1938 and into 1939. The Nazis established a special agency to facilitate emigration in early 1939, but an estimated 140,000 Jews still remained in Germany, Austria and Czechoslovakia when the war erupted. The great majority of the Jews, who died in the Holocaust, however, were residents of countries not subject to German domination before the war.

With the outbreak of hostilities, Jewish emigration became extremely difficult, and the Nazis eventually resorted to deportation. At first they did little to implement this policy, other than to speculate on where to send the Jews. The most bizarre solution involved a plan to take over the island of Madagascar, a French possession off the southeast coast of Africa, and convert it into a permanent Jewish homeland. But the Germans were never able to gain control of Madagascar. Instead, they designated Poland as the dumping ground for Jews, but the process did not begin until the fall of 1941, when the Nazis launched a large-scale deportation program.

The Holocaust

Hitler and his associates ultimately chose extermination as the "final solution to the Jewish question," a ghastly process that is remembered today as the Holocaust. Traditionally, scholars, while not contending that the German people were blameless, attributed primary responsibility to Hitler, Himmler, and the SS. But studies gradually appeared, which indicated that Nazi anti-Jewish policies were widely accepted at virtually all levels of German society long before the war and the formulation of the final solution. During the 1990s some historians began to focus on the actions of German reserve police battalions, which were recruited from "ordinary" civilians and participated in killing Jews in Eastern Europe. Daniel Jonah Goldhagen charges that the willingness of members of these units to become executioners reflected a centuries-old and uniquely German "eliminationist" anti-Semitism that sought to eliminate Jews from participation in German society. Christopher Browning argues that Goldhagen exaggerates the murderous nature of anti-Semitism among the German population as a whole and ignores many factors that influenced the behavior of the police battalions that had little to do with hatred of the Jews. These included fear of punishment for not carrying out orders, peer pressure, and apathy. He contends that these men acted no differently than would those from other countries, if confronted by such an extreme situation. This controversy has sparked an ongoing debate among historians, not only on the issue of the police battalions but also on other questions involved in the Holocaust. It is now also clear that the German army was involved in committing atrocities against Jews and other peoples to a much greater extent than was once believed.

The concept of the final solution to the "Jewish question" appears to have taken shape gradually. The Germans put the preliminaries into effect in 1939, when 2 million Polish Jews came under German domination. The SS, under the direction of Reinhard Heydrich, the head of Himmler's security services rounded up Polish Jews and concentrated them in ghettos in large cities. It is not clear whether the original intention was extermination or expulsion. Death camps, as such, did not come into existence until much later. The task of concentration proved a formidable one, however, and the SS eased the problem by shooting many Jews, a practice that continued when the Germans invaded the Soviet Union in 1941. Special Action Group murder squads carried out this policy in the USSR on a much greater scale than in Poland. The most notorious massacre featured the shooting of 33,000 Jewish men, women, and children in a wood called Babyi Yar near Kiev. In all, the SS killed approximately 1.4 million Jews in this manner by the end of 1942.

The Nazis established the first ghetto in the Polish city of Lodz in October 1939. Others soon followed, most notably the Warsaw ghetto, which became the largest. The Germans provided for the formation of a Jewish Council (*Judenrat*) in each ghetto, composed of influential members of the Jewish community. These councils received the thankless task of administering the ghettos and ultimately filling quotas of Jews to be sent to the death camps. In this grim situation, the actions of the council members varied greatly, running the gamut of human behavior from slavish submission to open rebellion. The ghetto residents performed what amounted to slave labor for their captors. Fuel and food were in short supply, and deaths from malnutrition and epidemics of diseases were common. Mortality was especially high among children and the elderly. A steady influx of Jews deported from other countries led to badly overcrowded conditions and compounded the original problems.

During the spring of 1941, Heydrich and his underlings began to plan for the possibility of the "biological extermination" of the Jews. By the late summer and fall of 1941, it became apparent that this would be the form of the "Final Solution." On August 20, Goebbels wrote, "The Jews are the lice of civilized humanity. They must somehow be exterminated." The next step in the process toward the Final Solution, starting in December 1941, was the establishment of six actual death camps, using gas. Five of these were located in the Government General of Poland—Belzec, Chelmno, Maidanek, Sobibor, and Treblinka. But the largest was centered at Auschwitz in an area of southwestern Poland that Hitler had incorporated into the Reich. The commandant, Rudolf Höss, replaced gassing by carbon monoxide with the more deadly Zyklon-B crystals (hydrogen cyanide or prussic acid) at Birkenau (Auschwitz camp II) and could "process" 24,000 human beings in a day. Heydrich assumed responsibility for the extermination program, although Himmler retained overall supervision, and Adolf Eichmann handled the actual task of arresting and transporting Jews to the camps.

Heydrich and Eichmann were among the most sinister members of the Nazi hierarchy. Blond, tall, and well built with strong, indeed cruel features, Heydrich was one of the few party leaders who looked the part of the true Aryan. Ironically, this paragon of the Nordic "Blond Beast" was

probably not "racially pure." He allegedly had a Jewish grandmother. This did not prevent him from executing the Final Solution with cold-blooded efficiency. No less an authority than Hitler admiringly referred to him as "the man with the iron heart." It was Heydrich who convened the Wannsee Conference of Nazi officials on January 20, 1942 to coordinate the Final Solution. Eichmann lacked Heydrich's physical attributes but shared his devotion to duty. He rose gradually through the SS ranks and presided over the program that encouraged Jewish emigration and later enforced deportation.

If life was grim in the ghettos, it was far worse in the death camps. It was also often very short. Upon arrival, men and women were separated along with their children, boys going with their fathers, girls with their mothers. Herded into barracks, subsisting on meager rations, and subject to the brutality of sadistic guards, the inmates performed slave labor while awaiting their rendezvous with the gas chambers. Thousands of inmates became human guinea pigs in medical experiments performed by doctors such as Josef Mengele. Experiments included studies of the effects of freezing human beings or subjecting them to intense air pressure as well as sterilization of women. Some prisoners were deliberately infected with diseases such as typhus, while others were exposed to mustard gas and still others became victims of wounds that were allowed to become gangrenous. The Germans selected some Jews to be members of special units (*Sonderkommando*), which were responsible for herding inmates into the gas chambers and burning their bodies afterward, although SS personnel did the actual killing. Many *Sonderkommando* were eventually put to death as well.

Jews considered unfit for labor often were taken directly to the gas chambers, disguised as bath houses, where they were told to undress prior to taking showers. The unsuspecting victims, including many young children sometimes received towels to allay fears of what might await them. But once in the "showers," Zyklon-B crystals dropped through holes in the ceiling, releasing lethal gas. After a few minutes of increasing panic and agony, the victims died. Once the gas was pumped out of the chambers, the *Sonnderkommando* entered to carry out the grim task of extricating gold rings from fingers and gold fillings from teeth. The bodies were then transported to the crematoriums to be incinerated.

SS leaders referred to the killing of Jews euphemistically as "special treatment." At first they murdered only those who were unfit for work, but in the spring of 1942 they extended the principle to all Jews in Eastern Europe. In March 1943, the Nazis attempted to speed up the deportation of the remaining Jewish population from areas under direct German control as well as satellite states. Civilian authorities and ordinary citizens cooperated eagerly in some countries, while in others they attempted to foil the Nazi policy. Most of the small Jewish population of Denmark and over half of the Norwegian Jews escaped to neutral Sweden. About 50 percent of Belgian Jews, again a small number, and more than two-thirds of the 300,000 French Jews were also able to elude Nazi efforts to capture them, as were most of Italy's 50,000 Jews.

The Jewish populations of other countries were less fortunate. Nazi death camps took the lives of most of the surviving Jews of Poland and the German-occupied areas in the Soviet Union as well as the majority of those from the Netherlands, Yugoslavia, and Greece. Despite the resistance of the Hungarian government, the Germans ultimately secured the deportation of 500,000 Jews after Germany occupied Hungary militarily in 1944. Most of them died at Auschwitz. Although one of the most anti-Semitic countries in Europe, Rumania also resisted Nazi pressure to deport Jews to the death camps. This was due in large part to the fact that both Hungary and Italy had not cooperated in this endeavor, and the regime in Bucharest did not want to appear to be the "weak sister" among the Nazi satellite states. But this did not prevent the Rumanians themselves from carrying out mass murders of 260,000 Jews. In all, perhaps as many as 5.8 million Jews perished during the Holocaust. Their only crime was the fact that they were Jewish.

Although some commentators have expressed bewilderment that the Jews accepted their fate so docilely, resistance to the Nazi murderers was an exceedingly difficult undertaking. But many Jews did resist. The most notable example was the Warsaw Ghetto Uprising of April 1943 when a small, poorly armed resistance force lashed out against German efforts to liquidate the ghetto and send the remaining residents to death camps. It held out against much stronger German forces for 42 days. The Germans, commanded by SS officer Jürgen Stroop, used tanks, artillery, dynamite, and flamethrowers against the rebels, who finally retreated into the sewers and made a gallant last stand there. Revolts also took place in other Polish ghettos, and there were even uprisings in the Treblinka, Auschwitz, and Sobibor death camps. All of them failed, but they at least allowed those who participated to die with far more dignity than was the case in the gas chambers. Other Jews fought as partisans in Poland and the Soviet Union, and many joined the French resistance forces.

One of the horrible ironies of World War II was the timing of the Final Solution. The Nazis launched their extermination policy at almost the same time that the German army was suffering its first reverse in Russia and accelerated the killing in 1943 when it should have been clear even to Hitler that chances of a German victory were extremely remote. They were determined to finish the task before the war ended.

Many survivors have related accounts of ghastly incidents that took place during the Holocaust, but the following eyewitness description by a Jewish stoker at Auschwitz perhaps best captures the nightmarish horror of the crime against the Jews. It refers to a situation caused by the arrival at Auschwitz of over 400,000 Hungarian Jews in July 1944. Approximately 75 percent of them went to their deaths immediately, creating a serious problem for the camp's crematoriums, which lacked the capacity to process such a glut of bodies. The stokers had to burn many of the victims in open pits, which also created problems:

While in the Crematorium ovens, once the corpses were thoroughly alight, it was possible to maintain a lasting red heat with the help of fans, in the pits the fire would burn only as the air could circulate freely in between the bodies. As the heap of bodies settled, no air was able to get in from outside. This meant that we stokers had to constantly pour oil or wood alcohol on the burning corpses, in addition to human fat, large quantities of which had collected and was boiling in the two collecting pans on either side of the pit. The sizzling fat was scooped out with buckets on a long curved rod and poured all over the pit causing flames to leap up amid much crackling and hissing. Dense smoke and fumes arose incessantly. The air reeked of oil, fat, benzole and burnt flesh.*

Despite Nazi efforts to keep the extermination of Jews secret, as early as 1941 news of the mass murders began to penetrate into Germany as well as Allied and neutral countries. At first, the reports were greeted with disbelief. Even Jews in the United States and Britain were skeptical. By 1942, however, it gradually became clear that the reports were undoubtedly true. The response or lack of response of the Allied Powers to this genocidal policy has become a hotly debated topic among historians. The Soviet Union was not likely to divert its attention from the desperate struggle against the Germans raging on its own soil, even if Stalin had been concerned about the plight of the Jews. There is no evidence that he was. Britain also focused almost completely on the war, and the United States generally deferred to the British on Jewish policy until late in the conflict. Critics of the Western Allies, and they are numerous, contend that Britain and America refused to pursue a number of options that might have saved some of the Jews. They insist that the Allies should have pressed the Germans to release the Jews from captivity. This, to be sure was not done, but since Hitler was determined to exterminate the Jews, it is inconceivable that he would have responded to such entreaties. Even if he had, how would the Jews have been removed, and where would they have gone? It is highly unlikely that the neutral countries of Europe—Spain, Portugal, Switzerland, and Sweden—would have welcomed a mass influx of Jews. Clearly, the Allies could have made the effort, but in all probability it would have amounted to a public relations ploy.

Critics have focused especially on what they view as the failure of Britain and America to bomb railway lines leading into Auschwitz as well as facilities in the camp itself. There were good reasons, however, why this was never attempted. Auschwitz lay beyond the range of Allied bombers and fighters until late 1943 when British troops captured the Foggia airbase in southern Italy, and

the vastly-improved U.S. P-51 "Mustang" fighter became operational for long-range escort duty. Other death camps in Poland were even more remote. In fact, none of the various civilian groups concerned about the fate of the Jews proposed such an attack until May 1944. The U.S. War Department did not receive any proposals for this until June 18, and then only against a secondary line transporting Hungarian Jews to Auschwitz. Officials doubted if such a raid could actually put the line out of commission. Moreover, the Nazis completed the shipment of Jews from Hungary on July 9, sealing the fate of the proposal. The question of bombing Auschwitz itself posed a myriad of technical problems such as inadequate intelligence on the layout of the camp and the inaccuracy of so-called precision bombing. There was a very real danger that bombs, which were intended to destroy the gas chambers and crematoriums, would actually fall on barracks, killing rather than saving many of the Jews housed there. Indeed many Jewish groups opposed such raids because of this danger.

Finally, some critics have contended that late in the war Himmler and Eichmann initiated negotiations with Jewish contacts in which they offered to free large numbers of Jews in return for ransom. The most notable example was Eichmann's April 1944 proposal to free a million Jews in return for 10,000 trucks, which were to be used only on the Eastern Front. Some historians have denounced the Western Allies for not pursuing this option, but others consider such a deal unrealistic and shameful. It would have posed still another moral dilemma since it would cost the lives of Soviet soldiers in order to save Jews. Clearly, Stalin, already deeply suspicious of his Western allies, would have greeted news of such an arrangement with outrage, rightfully considering it a flagrant betrayal. Moreover, it is not at all clear that these proposals were really genuine. They would have to be carried out behind Hitler's back since he was obviously opposed to such a policy, and that would have been highly dangerous to the officials involved. Furthermore, if such an agreement actually did come to pass, there was no assurance that the trucks provided by the Germans would be used only on the Eastern Front.

The attitude of Pope Pius XII toward the Holocaust also has sparked controversy. Critics have

---

*Filip Müller, *Eyewitness Auschwitz: Three Years in the Gas Chambers* (New York: Stein & Day, 1979), p. 136.

taken him to task for his "silence" on the plight of the Jews during most of the war. Some have attributed this to an inability to grasp the scope of the disaster befalling the Jews. Others focus on the Pope's overriding concern for the preservation of the Catholic Church and a reluctance to jeopardize its position by antagonizing the Germans and Italian fascists. It was not until late in the conflict that the Pope's policy began to change, most notably in regard to the Church's participation in saving the majority of Italian Jews from falling into the hands of the Nazis. He also intervened in behalf of Hungarian Jews.

The Jews were not the only people to feel the full fury of Hitler's hatred. He condemned the Roma (Gypsies) to the same fate. The Roma apparently originated in India and over the centuries became dispersed throughout the world. They wandered about in small groups and refused to settle in one place. Hitler considered them "trash" fit only for extermination. The death camps claimed the lives of approximately 200,000 out of a total of 700,000 European Roma.

The New Order in Slavic Countries

Hitler also looked upon the Slavs with utter contempt. For them, the New Order ultimately held only the prospect of expulsion from their homelands, enslavement, or death. But during the war, Nazi policy toward the Slavs varied from country to country.

The Czechs of Bohemia and Moravia were the first Slavic people to fall under German domination. Hitler initially followed a moderate policy toward them because he valued their efforts in producing war materiel and because they cooperated with the Germans. The Czechs did so because they hoped to ensure their continued existence. They developed little in the way of a resistance movement, although former president Beneš did maintain an exile government in London. In Bohemia and Moravia, the Czechs carried out routine administration, but the real power remained in the hands of the German official who held the title of "Reich protector." Konstantine von Neurath, the former German foreign minister, was the first to hold this position. Himmler's protégé Karl Hermann Frank, a Sudeten German, served as Neurath's deputy but quickly built up his own rival power base.

At first, Hitler opposed any attempt to "Germanize" the Czechs, but Neurath and Frank persuaded him that Czechs who possessed "Germanic" characteristics were deserving of such an "honor." The majority of the Czechs, who were not eligible for Germanization, would face expulsion to the east when the convenient time came. Although the Germans developed this policy in secret, the Czechs soon became aware of its intent and grew restless. Hitler considered Neurath too weak to control the situation and replaced him with Heydrich early in 1942. Heydrich followed a carrot-and-stick policy that combined specific benefits to workers and peasants with harsh repression of any dissent. The incentives included increased wages for workers and higher crop prices for peasants. His approach proved effective, and the Czechs became increasingly docile. These developments alarmed the Czech government in exile and the British, who engineered a plot to assassinate Heydrich. They expected his death to provoke German vengeance, which would in turn kindle Czech resistance. The plot was successful; Heydrich fell victim to an ambush, and Nazi reaction was at least as brutal as expected. They totally destroyed two villages after shooting all the men and sending the women and children to concentration camps. The name of one of the stricken villages, Lidice, became a symbol for Nazi brutality. Contrary to the hopes of the British and the Czech exile regime, however, the German reprisals so thoroughly frightened the Czechs that resistance did not develop. Bohemia and Moravia remained remarkably quiet until the end of the war.

Slovakia had become an ally of Germany after the destruction of Czechoslovakia and even sent troops to fight in Russia. As a reward, Hitler allowed the Slovaks to keep their own government under Monsignor Josef Tiso, an admirer of Mussolini's Fascist system who had long opposed Slovakia's incorporation in Czechoslovakia. But despite Slovak collaboration, German economic and military influence increased and in 1944 provoked a revolt that the Germans crushed with some difficulty. Hitler now imposed complete German domination, although the puppet Slovak regime continued to function. He apparently planned expulsion to the east or extermination as the eventual fate of the Slovaks.

The Germans treated the Poles much more harshly than either the Czechs or the Slovaks. Poland had resisted, and Hitler was in no mood to be lenient. In an effort to deprive the Poles of a potential ruling class, the SS shot Polish intellectuals and clergy. They also planned to transfer the Poles from the incorporated territories to the Government General and replace them with German settlers. The Nazis actually began this process during the war with the deportation of 300,000 Poles. Former German residents of the Baltic states took their place and were joined later by large numbers of ethnic Germans whom the Nazis shifted from Russia, Rumania, and Yugoslavia. A great deal of confusion snarled the process, and both the Poles and many of the ethnic Germans did not relish their arbitrary transfer.

In addition to absorbing Poles who had lost their homes in the incorporated territories, the Government General had to accept large numbers of Jews and Roma. This huge influx of people created staggering administrative problems for Nazi officials and tremendous pressure on the already shattered Polish economy. Although the Nazis shipped many Poles to Germany to serve as laborers, the bulk of the population remained in the Government General and was subjected to savage oppression. The Germans set out to reduce education for Polish children to a bare minimum and placed severe restrictions on cultural activities in an effort to wipe out a sense of being Polish among the population. The Poles responded by conducting secret classes and doing everything possible to keep cultural vitality alive. An underground press urged the Poles to remain united, resist the Germans, and avoid collaboration. Hitler looked upon the Poles as "slaves of the German Reich." Many were literally worked to death or used as guinea pigs in medical experiments conducted in Nazi death camps.

Hitler appointed Hans Frank to head the administration of the Government General. Long an associate of Hitler, Frank quickly alienated both the Poles and his German associates, and various Nazi agencies soon challenged his power. Himmler and the SS dominated racial policy and supported a program of settling German colonists in the more favorable parts of the Government General while moving Poles to less desirable areas. Hitler apparently intended the final solution to the Polish question to include absorption of the entire Government General into the Reich, the resettling of the area with Germans, and the expulsion or extermination of Poles. The harsh nature of the German occupation led to the growth of resistance groups, many of which merged into the Polish Home Army. Soon after the German invasion of Russia, a Communist resistance organization also came into existence and became a rival to the non-Communist Home Army. The Germans reacted to acts of sabotage or the killing of German officials by shooting hostages and even wiping out whole villages.

Yugoslavia, another Slavic country, experienced varying types of treatment at the hands of the Germans. Hitler partitioned the country soon after completion of the German conquest in April 1941. He divided the northwestern area of Slovenia into German and Italian occupation zones and established the puppet states of Croatia and Serbia.

Many Croats had refused to resist the German invasion and thus became the most favored Yugoslav group. Hitler greatly enlarged Croatia by granting the Croats territories inhabited by Serbs including the province of Bosnia, which also contained Croat and Muslim populations. Ante Pavelich, leader of the extremist Croatian nationalist movement Ustaše, became head of the new state and followed slavishly pro-German and anti-Serb policies. He set out to expel or exterminate both Serbs and Jews within his territory and presided over such horrendous massacres that even the Germans were appalled. Estimates of the number of Serbs who lost their lives range from 350,000 to 750,000. Despite Pavelich's subservience, Hitler had actually designated Croatia as an Italian satellite and allowed Mussolini's forces to occupy Croatian territory along the Adriatic Sea. Hitler also maintained German troops in the eastern portion of the country, and when Italy abandoned the war in 1943, Wehrmacht units replaced the Italians in the coastal strip.

The Serbs also lost additional territory to Italy, Hungary, and Bulgaria, leaving a state smaller than pre-World War I Serbia. Hitler allowed a Serbian government under the leadership of General Milan Nedich, but the country remained subject to overall German military supervision. Nedich, a former Yugoslav minister of war, cooperated with the Germans because he feared the alternative might be the extermination of his people.

Soon after the German conquest, Colonel Draja Mihailovich, a former member of the Yugoslav general staff, organized a resistance movement, the Chetniks (from *cheta*, the 19th-century Serbian guerrilla band that had helped drive out the Turks). The Chetniks were primarily a Serbian patriotic front and failed to transcend the prewar Serb-Croat rivalry, even though it won the support of the British and later the Americans. Indeed, Mihailovich was especially bitter toward the Croats, whom he blamed for the disintegration of Yugoslavia and for the atrocities against Serbs. He visualized a restoration of a Serbian-dominated Yugoslavia after the war. The Partisans, a Communist resistance movement led by Josip Broz (better known as Tito), proved much more important.

Tito, who was born in Croatia, fought in the Austro-Hungarian army early in World War I. But the Russians captured him in 1915, and he remained a prisoner of war until the Russian Revolution. After his release, he remained in Russia, became a Communist, and saw action in the Red Army during the Russian civil war. When Tito returned to his homeland in 1923, he joined the outlawed Communist movement and became general secretary of the party in 1937. Due to the Nazi-Soviet Nonaggression Pact, he did not take the field against the Germans until after Hitler's invasion of the USSR. Unlike Mihailovich, Tito strove to create a national movement that would embrace all Yugoslav ethnic groups.

The Partisans also posed a much more serious problem for Hitler than the Chetniks. Mihailovich became concerned that by fighting the Germans, he would expose the Serbian people to reprisals. He also feared that if Tito grew too strong, Yugoslavia would become a Communist state after the war. Bedeviled by these two specters, Mihailovich cooperated with the Germans against Tito, but his policy proved disastrous. Not only did it fail to save his compatriots from savage repression, but it also weakened the Chetniks in the eyes of the Western Allies, who shifted their support to Tito during 1943. When the war ended, Tito controlled large areas of Yugoslavia. Mihailovich fell into his hands, was tried for

treason, and was executed. Tito became the ruler of a Communist Yugoslavia.

Occupation Policies in the USSR

Hitler's occupation policies in the Soviet Union were at least as ruthless as those he directed against the Poles and Serbs. He contended that Germany had but one obligation: "to Germanize the country by immigration of Germans, and to look upon the natives as Redskins." His reference to "Redskins" was an allusion to the United States' treatment of the native Americans, a policy he greatly admired. The Nazis pursued this approach not only toward the Russians but also the Belorussians, Ukrainians, and at least some of the inhabitants of the Baltic states. This policy cost Germany the cooperation of these peoples, especially the Ukrainians, many of whom had greeted the Germans as liberators from Soviet tyranny. Hitler ordered the elimination of all potential leaders as well as Jews and Roma, and for good measure he suggested that anyone "who looked in any way suspicious" should be shot.

The SS and the army, too, carried out his wishes with ruthless determination. Even before the invasion, the Nazis sought to demonize the Soviet regime and the various peoples who made up the population. Their propaganda portrayed Germany's aggression as if it were a preventive war designed to defend the German people from an inevitable attack by barbaric "Asiatic" hordes bent on the destruction of European civilization. It is not surprising then that the SS and the army put the principles of the infamous Commissar Order into effect with the utmost ferocity. The leadership of the army also indoctrinated its troops with this perverted view of reality. For example, General Hoth informed his soldiers in November 1941 that Germany's mission was "to save European culture from advancing Asiatic barbarism" and added that: "This battle can only end with the destruction of one or the other; a compromise is out of the question."

Much German-occupied territory in the Soviet Union remained under military administration because of its proximity to the front. Civilian authorities controlled only areas far enough to the rear to be considered safe. As in other occupied countries, German administration was a jumble of competing jurisdictions.

Officially, Alfred Rosenberg, the self-styled theoretician of the Nazi party, exercised full authority over the occupied areas. Although Rosenberg was of German descent, he had been born in the Baltic city of Tallinn in Tsarist Estonia and had fled to Germany to escape the revolution. Rosenberg became an associate of Hitler and appears to have influenced his ideas to some extent in the early 1920s. Hitler may have decided to appoint Rosenberg to his post because of his knowledge of the USSR—limited though it was, it was superior to that of most other Nazi leaders. But from the start, Rosenberg was able to exert little real control while various Nazi rivals challenged his authority.

Himmler and the SS especially operated as a law unto themselves and imposed a policy of terror in an attempt to cow the population into submission. Goering also assumed a lofty role that supposedly gave him control over economic exploitation. But others soon intruded and undercut Goering's position. These included Fritz Sauckel, the head of the slave labor program, and Dr. Fritz Todt, the minister of armaments and munitions.

Technically, Saukel remained under the authority of Goering as director of the Four-Year Plan, but in reality he wielded virtually unlimited power over recruiting laborers. Todt began as another of Goering's nominal subordinates under the Four-Year Plan and had been responsible for construction of the West Wall along Germany's western border. But when he became minister of armaments and munitions in 1940, he was no longer responsible to Goering and eventually began the process of converting Germany's economy to a full wartime basis. When he died in a plane crash in 1942, Albert Speer succeeded him and greatly accelerated the transformation. In the face of all this competition, Goering's actual control over the Russian economy was never extensive.

To increase the confusion still more, the Germans established two special regional administrations. The first of these supervised the Ostland, an area consisting of the Baltic states and western Belorussia; eastern Belorussia remained under military rule. Hitler selected Hinrich Lohse as Reich commissioner of the Ostland. Lohse had been a close associate of Rosenberg who had counted on his loyalty. But Lohse's primary aim was to build up his own power. In pursuit of this goal, he attempted to play off Rosenberg, Himmler, and Goering against one another.

Each of the Baltic states as well as Belorussia received its own subcommissioner who operated under Lohse's supervision. Wilhelm Kube, the subcommissioner of Belorussia, strove to increase his administrative autonomy and quarreled frequently with Lohse. He was fond of fair-haired Belorussian women and developed a virtual harem of "blondies," as he called them. He did not win their love, however, and one of them eventually killed him by means of an antipersonnel mine that she concealed in his bed.

The other special administration, under the direction of Erich Koch, supervised a large part of the Ukraine. The eastern Ukraine remained under military control, Koch has been described as a man of "monumental stupidity and arrogance." He followed relentlessly brutal policies and cooperated enthusiastically with the anti-Jewish campaign and slave labor program.

German occupation policies helped enlarge the Partisan movement in the Soviet Union, but this process took time. In 1941, most of the Partisans were soldiers who had been bypassed by the German advance and had managed to hold out in forests and swamps. It was not until 1942 that their numbers became notable, and a highly organized mass movement did not develop until 1943. This slow growth was due largely to the fact that the Soviet government and army were unable to devote much time to organizing Partisan warfare because of more immediate problems. Nevertheless, even during the 1941 campaign, small partisan hit and run attacks on German troop columns and garrisons created confusion and concern. This was especially the case during the Battle of Moscow when the Soviets sent units of regular troops behind German lines to augment partisan bands, swelling their number to 10,000.

Germany did not hold its Russian conquests long enough for Hitler to put his long-range program into effect, but he clearly intended to dominate everything as far east as the Ural Mountains. He also planned to annex the Baltic states, Belorussia, much of the Ukraine, and the Crimea. German colonists would have become the master race in this vast area, and the Nazi regime would have enslaved the native populations.

Hitler's Policy toward Italy

Nazi policy toward the Latin peoples of Europe was less clear-cut than that pursued in regard to the Jews and the Slavs. Hitler considered them to possess some Aryan blood but, alas, not enough to qualify as Germanic. Although Italy was a Latin country, Hitler had desired an alliance with Rome from an early date. To obtain that goal he refused to pressure Mussolini to cede the former Austrian territory of the South Tyrol, which contained a substantial German minority. Italy had obtained the South Tyrol in the 1919 peace settlement. His bond of friendship with Mussolini also extended to designating most of the Mediterranean as an Italian sphere of exploitation. But the ouster of Mussolini in July 1943, and Italy's surrender to the Allies shortly afterward put an end to Hitler's generosity. Henceforth, he thought in terms of annexing not only the South Tyrol but all Italian territory formerly belonging to Austria-Hungary and, perhaps, everything north of the Po River.

The Germans quickly occupied roughly two-thirds of the country after the Allies landed in the southern part of the peninsula at the same time as Italy's surrender.

Italy also witnessed the rise of a resistance movement. Dissatisfaction mounted with the early Italian military disasters in North Africa and Greece, and after the German invasion of Russia, Italian Communists became active in organizing strikes in northern Italy. A partisan movement came into being during the German occupation. The partisans harassed the Germans in the countryside and became especially active in the fighting in northern Italy during the last weeks of the war.

Collaboration and Resistance in France

Hitler's attitude toward the French, another Latin people, was initially far less forbearing. He took immediate steps to absorb Alsace-Lorraine back into Germany and planned to acquire a strip of French territory extending from the mouth of the Somme to the Swiss border. Until November 1942, Germany's relations with the French differed

from those with other defeated peoples because the armistice of 1940 had left part of France unoccupied. Technically, the Vichy regime continued to administer the entire country, but in Occupied France primary control lay with the German army. As usual, the SS and various Nazi economic agencies challenged this authority. Again this led to considerable chaos.

During 1940–41, Vichy leaders, such as Pétain and his chief minister Pierre Laval, considered a final German victory inevitable and thought that realism required French adjustment to a German-dominated Europe. Laval served four times as premier, but during his last term his attempt to concede Mussolini a virtual free hand in Ethiopia caused such a backlash that he resigned in early 1936. For the next four years, he receded into the political wilderness and grew extremely bitter toward the Third Republic. Pétain rescued Laval from near oblivion in June 1940 when he appointed him to be his deputy.

Admiral François Darlan succeeded Laval as the key man under Pétain during most of 1941 and early 1942. Darlan owed his powerful position to the fact that he was chief of staff of the navy, and the navy had emerged from the conflict almost unscathed. Even after the British attack on Oran and Mers-el-Kebir in the summer of 1940, it remained an important factor in European power politics. Britain's action against the fleet also helped bring Darlan's latent anti-British sentiments to the surface. Darlan followed a strongly collaborationist policy until Germany's fortunes began to fade in Russia. When he shifted to a less pliant approach, the Germans pressured him out of office. Laval returned to power and remained the dominant leader in Vichy until the end of the regime in 1944.

Most of the French people quickly rallied to the Vichy regime, in large part because they identified with Pétain, the hero of Verdun and a symbol of victory in World War I. The French also tended to blame the leaders of the Third Republic for the country's military debacle. Political conservatives had feared a Communist revolt in the wake of defeat and welcomed Pétain's government as a bulwark against the left.

The leaders in Vichy badly underestimated Hitler's ambitions. They still persisted in the belief that he was primarily interested in regaining the territories lost in World War I and in absorbing all Germans into the Reich. They also admired Germany's authoritarian government, which contrasted so vividly with the instability of the Third Republic. To them, collaboration was the key to negotiating a peace settlement that would be beneficial to France. This policy achieved little except for the gradual return of 600,000 of the 1.5 million French prisoners of war who had been interned in Germany.

There was no shortage of other collaborators. Many industrialists and businessmen were eager to obtain German orders for war materiel and other products. Workers wanted to keep their jobs even if this meant providing the recent enemy with goods. The Catholic Church had often been at odds with the Third Republic over its anticlerical legislation and welcomed the new government's pro-Catholic policies, especially in regard to education. On the extreme right of the political spectrum, several small political groups wanted to go beyond Vichy's more traditional authoritarian government to create a system modeled after those of Germany or Italy.

There were limits to Pétain's willingness to collaborate, however. He insisted on maintaining French control over both the fleet and the empire and refused to engage in military cooperation with Germany. He and his colleagues were less squeamish when it came to the Jews. In October 1940, the government passed a law excluding Jews from public office and some professions as well as providing for the internment of foreign Jews. Vichy also made no attempt to intervene against German roundups of Jews and by June 1942 even agreed to participate in them. Much of the population did not appear overly outraged by these actions. The majority of Catholic bishops also reacted weakly to the persecution of the Jews. Whatever their personal feelings toward the victims might be, their primary concern was to safeguard the position of the Church.

To be sure, not everyone was in favor of collaboration. Although for some time General de Gaulle won little support in France itself, a resistance movement did develop, but it remained weak for some time. As in many other countries, the Soviet Union's entry into the war galvanized Communists in France to join the resistance. Germany's forced labor program, again with Vichy's acquiescence, proved to be the chief catalyst to the growth of the Resistance.

The Germans sharply increased the number of French people required for labor service in 1943, but many evaded this fate by joining the Resistance. The Resistance took the name Maquis (French for "underbrush") and adhered to de Gaulle's Fighting French movement. Resistance units contributed to the success of the Allied invasion of Normandy in June 1944 by snarling German communications with innumerable acts of sabotage. Early that same year, the Maquis created a unified military force, the French Forces of the Interior (FFI). Though poorly equipped, the FFI reached a numerical strength equivalent to 15 divisions and succeeded in liberating much of central France after the Allied invasion.

As in other countries, the Germans punished acts of resistance with great ferocity. The most infamous of these took place in the small town of Oradour-sur-Glâne in central France in June 1944. It became even more notorious because it was the result of a mistake. A day earlier a Waffen SS officer fell victim to a sniper's bullet in a nearby town with a similar name. Seeking vengeance, an SS detachment swept into Oradour-sur-Glâne, shot the men and herded the women and children into a church where they burned to death when the Germans set the building on fire. In all, 642 persons died.

The ultimate success of the Resistance was a triumph for de Gaulle and his once forlorn movement. In the last few months of the European conflict, an actual combat army, the French 1st, took its place in the Allied line. As for de Gaulle, he was destined to be the dominant figure in France in the early postwar period and, after 12 years in the political wilderness, would emerge again as the founder and first president of France's Fifth Republic.

Nazi Policy toward Other Europeans

Spain, still another Latin country, was also in a unique position. Although the Spanish government had professed friendship to Germany, it had skillfully avoided an alliance. Hitler never forgave Franco for his duplicity. Even Franco's decision to dispatch a Spanish military force, the Blue Division, to fight on Germany's side in the Soviet Union did not eliminate his animosity. If Germany had won the war, Hitler probably would have pressed for the ouster of Franco and his replacement by a more pliable Spanish leader.

During the war, Spain, along with neighboring Portugal, declared a policy of neutrality. This did not prevent Spain from supplying Germany with war materiel as well as large amounts of wolfram, a vital ingredient in the production of armor-piercing shells. After the entry of the United States into the war, Franco set out to cultivate good relations with Washington, while maintaining his hostility to the "godless hordes" of the Soviet Union. As the war turned against Hitler, Spain continued to supply Germany, but its trade with the Allies soon eclipsed that with the Axis. Spain and Portugal were also important destinations for downed Allied airmen and agents as well as escaped prisoners and other fugitives on the escape route operated by Resistance workers. In addition, they, like neutral Switzerland, Sweden, Ireland, and Turkey, were centers for diplomatic contacts among the warring powers as well as hotbeds of espionage activity.

The Greeks were not related to the Germans, Slavs, or Latins, but they suffered terribly. After the conquest of Greece, Hitler placed the country primarily under Italian and Bulgarian occupation while retaining German control over certain strategically important areas. He also established a puppet Greek government that proved highly unpopular. When Italy left the war in 1943, German forces occupied the Italian-held area of Greece. A Greek resistance movement developed early in the occupation. It consisted of various rival groups, the most important of which was the Communist Greek Liberation Front (EAM) and its Greek People's Liberation Army (ELAS). The Germans responded to Greek resistance by shooting large numbers of hostages and annihilating entire villages. But an even greater horror came in the guise of famine due to persistent food shortages. More Greeks succumbed to starvation than to German firing squads.

Was Resistance Worth the Price?

Traditionally, those who served as members of resistance movements in Nazi-dominated Europe have been hailed as heroes and those who collaborated with the Germans vilified as traitors. More recently, however, some historians have questioned whether the resistance was really worth the price it cost in the lives of innocent civilians. Acts of resistance often resulted in the Germans shooting large numbers of hostages in reprisal. In some cases, the Germans even resorted to wiping out whole villages and deporting or killing all their inhabitants. Resisters also often resorted to the same type of atrocities that they decried when committed by the Germans. These included torture, mutilation, and murder of prisoners. This was especially true of partisan units in Russia and Yugoslavia.

Although, many collaborators acted out of desire for personal survival or political and economic gain, some did so because of fear that the alternative would bring down German wrath on their innocent neighbors. To be sure, the resistance performed valuable work in providing intelligence to the Allies in regard to German troop dispositions and strength as well as vital acts of sabotage and aiding the escape of both downed Allied airmen and fugitive Jews. But the question remains: Was the killing of one German soldier or even a handful worth the slaughter of 100 or more hostages? And, to be sure, Lidice and Oradour-sur-Glâne were not the only villages to be wiped out in German reprisals, as the people of Poland and the Soviet Union could attest.

Horror as State Policy

Theoretically, at least, the Nazis inflicted their multiple horrors on Europe on behalf of the German people. Their actions were in keeping with Hitler's basic aims—domination of Europe, creation of *Lebensraum,* and the expulsion or extermination of Jews and other "undesirables" from Nazi-occupied areas. Whether the German people were in favor of such hideous policies was irrelevant to Hitler. He neither confided in them nor sought their opinions. To be sure, the German people thrilled to the Wehrmacht's early victories and certainly were not ignorant of much of what followed in the wake of these conquests. The extent of that knowledge and the degree of complicity of the German people in these policies are a matter of heated debate, as the controversy over the "ordinary Germans" in the reserve police battalions who murdered Jews in Eastern Europe clearly indicates. At present, there would appear to be more confusion than clarity on this most troublesome issue. It is clear, however, that as the war continued, more and more Germans came to realize the enormity of these crimes. With this growing awareness, fear of retribution haunted them, strengthening their will to fight on in hope of delaying the day of reckoning. Certainly, when the war ended, few of them were willing to admit that they knew anything about these monstrous atrocities. Even with the passage of decades it remains difficult to comprehend that one of the world's most culturally advanced nations could have perpetrated these horrors as a deliberate policy of state. But it did.

CHAPTER TWELVE

America Enters the War

If the German military disaster in Russia were not enough, at the very time that the Red Army unleashed its massive counterstroke, Hitler committed his second blunder. He declared war on the United States, opening the prospect of a really serious two-front conflict. Hitler's decision marked the culmination of steadily deteriorating relations between the two countries since the outbreak of the war. This process of erosion unfolded at the same time that Japan and America had embarked on a collision course that led to hostilities in the Pacific.

Franklin Roosevelt

The administration of President Franklin Roosevelt had grown increasingly supportive of Britain in the struggle against Nazi Germany. But the president was reluctant to push matters too far, especially without assurance that American public opinion would be receptive to his policies. This approach was characteristic of Roosevelt's keen political instincts, which had been largely responsible for his unusually successful career. A member of a wealthy New York State family and a distant cousin of former President Theodore Roosevelt, he possessed boundless charm, good looks, and an effective speaking style. Roosevelt had served as assistant secretary of the navy during Woodrow Wilson's administration and had the misfortune of being the Democratic party's vice presidential candidate in the disastrous election of 1920. Despite an attack of polio that left both his legs crippled, he became governor of New York in 1928 and gained reelection by a landslide margin two years later. His great success earned him the Democratic presidential nomination in 1932, and he scored an overwhelming victory over President Herbert Hoover.

His administration gained congressional approval of a vast array of legislation designed to bring about recovery from the Great Depression while not interfering too greatly with the capitalistic economy. Although the country did recover to some extent, the depression continued throughout the 1930s. Roosevelt won reelection in 1936 by a huge majority.

In foreign policy, the president looked with concern at the expansion of German and Japanese power as well as Mussolini's conquest of Ethiopia but followed a cautious policy toward all three. The growth of American isolationism contributed to his reluctance to undertake any measures that might be interpreted as threatening to lead the country into war. For a time he attempted to win congressional acceptance of his right to impose embargoes on the sale of arms and other strategic materials to aggressor nations. But ultimately he accepted a series of three neutrality acts that Congress passed between 1935 and 1937. This legislation called for an immediate embargo on arms sales to all belligerents. The Neutrality Acts were the fruit of one of the supposed lessons of World War I. Those favoring their passage hoped that, by prohibiting arms sales, the country could avoid being gradually drawn into another European war. Hitler's seizure of Bohemia and Moravia and Mussolini's occupation of Albania in 1939 alarmed Roosevelt, and he made appeals to both dictators to refrain from further aggression. His attitude toward neutrality legislation also changed.

A Cautious Approach

When the European war broke out in September 1939, the American Neutrality Act of 1937 went into effect, placing an immediate embargo on arms sales, much to the distress of Britain and

France. Their blockade prevented Germany from buying arms from the United States, but the embargo had the same effect on them. Roosevelt recognized this and appealed to Congress to revise the Neutrality Act. Congress responded in November by repealing the embargo provision and authorizing the sale of arms on a "cash and carry" basis. This action allowed the Allies to buy arms and munitions and transport them in their own ships. But it barred U.S. vessels from carrying war materiel to Allied ports in an effort to avoid German submarine attacks on American shipping such as those that had brought the United States into World War I.

The fall of France and the German threat to Britain in the summer of 1940 caused many Americans to fear that Germany might attack the United States if the Nazis should defeat Britain and gain control of the British and French fleets. This concern led to growing support for the extension of aid to Britain. Hundreds of young men even joined the Royal Air Force to fight the Germans in the skies over Britain. But many still favored an isolationist approach and urged a policy of scrupulous neutrality. Very few Americans actually favored U.S. entry into the conflict, but the isolationists feared that by extending aid to Britain, America would eventually stumble into war. This difference in opinion led to a spirited debate between interventionists and isolationists.

Isolationists were far from a monolithic bloc. They ranged from idealists, who opposed war on moral grounds, to fascist organizations, with many gradations in between. Among the most outspoken were the demagogue Catholic priest, Father Charles Coughlin, who preached a pro-fascist line, and Charles Lindbergh, Jr., whose first solo flight across the Atlantic in 1927 had made him an international hero. While living in Europe during the 1930s, Lindbergh became deeply impressed by the strength of German airpower. After the fall of France, he was convinced that Britain would lose the war and insisted that America should avoid involvement in a hopeless cause. In one speech he proclaimed that he would rather be allied with Nazi Germany than with communist Russia. A number of pro-Nazi organizations came into being and tried to gain the support of German Americans. Among them, the German American Bund, led by Fritz Kuhn, was the most notable. Members of the Bund wore uniforms and gave the Nazi salute. They also sang songs of hate against the Jews. The America First Committee, founded in the fall of 1940, attempted to unite all the disparate groups. In Congress, a group of die-hard isolationists opposed all legislation designed to aid Britain or bolster U.S. defensive preparations. Interventionists organized the Committee to Defend America by Aiding the Allies and the Fight for Freedom Committee to counter the isolationists. Meanwhile, the bulk of Americans looked on with interest and not a little confusion as this debate persisted. Roosevelt agreed with the interventionists that the United States should extend aid to Britain and increase its own defensive preparations. But he continued to be extremely cautious and did not take the lead in these matters. Instead, interventionists in Congress secured passage of a whole series of measures to strengthen the armed forces, including a bill that would roughly double the size of the navy. This legislation culminated in the establishment of the first U.S. peacetime draft in the fall of 1940.

America also extended aid to Britain. Roosevelt and Churchill, who had met briefly during World War I, began to correspond soon after the outbreak of war. Their friendship became closer in the following months. The first fruit of this transatlantic relationship came when Roosevelt agreed to provide Britain with 50 overage U.S. destroyers for convoy duty. In return, Britain granted 99-year leases for American naval and air bases in British possessions in the Western Hemisphere, ranging from Newfoundland to British Guiana. This arrangement actually had limited immediate impact because many of the destroyers required repair before they were serviceable for convoy duty. The British also lacked experienced crews to operate them. But the agreement had great symbolic importance because it signified the start of closer cooperation between the United States and Britain.

Roosevelt reverted to a highly cautious approach during the presidential election campaign of 1940. But after winning reelection to an unprecedented third term, he felt able to offer greater aid to Britain. The key to this approach was the Lend-Lease Bill, which Congress passed in March 1941 over bitter isolationist opposition.

The British had been buying war materiel from the United States since the fall of 1939, but by the end of 1940, it appeared that they would soon exhaust their financial reserves. The Lend-Lease Act came to the rescue by authorizing the president to lend or lease arms and munitions to Britain with payment deferred until after the war.

The immediate impact of lend-lease was not spectacular. It accounted for only 1 percent of the arms and munitions used by Britain during 1941, although America provided much needed shipments of food, fuel, and other supplies. But ultimately the program extended $27 billion in assistance. The United States also authorized aid to the Soviet Union soon after the start of the German invasion. Again the immediate impact of aid to Russia was not great, but it steadily increased and by 1943 played an important role in the Soviet war effort. A rising flow of trucks and Jeeps was especially vital, providing the Red Army with much greater mobility in their later offensives. Vast quantities of food, strategic raw materials, clothing, medical supplies, and heavy machinery were also important as was war materiel such as aircraft, guns, and ammunition. This aid, of course, came at the expense of arms and equipment that could have been used by American forces. Lend-lease was consistent with the attitude of a majority of Americans. In January 1941, a public opinion poll indicated that 70 percent favored aid to Britain, even at the risk of war.

While the debate over lend-lease took place, American planners revised their strategic priorities in case of war. As early as June 1939, a joint army-navy board had formulated the so-called Rainbow plans to provide for various contingencies in case of war. These included Rainbow 5, which covered the possibility of U.S. involvement on the side of Britain and France in a war against Germany. Shortly after Roosevelt's reelection in 1940, navy planners drafted Plan Dog, which contended that America's chief priority was the defeat of Germany. This document stated that U.S. intervention in the European war was necessary to achieve this aim. At the same time, it insisted that American forces would have to assume a defensive stance against Japan in the Pacific. Both the president and the army accepted the navy proposal.

Growing U.S. Support for Britain

In January 1941, American military and naval leaders met with their British counterparts in Washington to explore contingency plans in case the United States should enter the war. These American-British conversations (ABC) took place in the greatest secrecy and lasted for two months. They came to the same conclusions as Plan Dog and emphasized the importance of the Atlantic lifeline between America and Britain. Officially, the ABC-1 agreement concerned only hypothetical developments, but it forged still another link in the tightening relationship between the two countries. It also contributed to the transfer of U.S. naval units from the Pacific to the Atlantic.

Throughout the summer and fall of 1941, America's role in support of Britain increased significantly. In April, U.S. forces occupied the Danish territory of Greenland after an agreement with the Danish ambassador in Washington. In July, American troops also took over Iceland, another Danish possession. They relieved British troops, which had occupied the island soon after the German seizure of Denmark. Both Greenland and Iceland became bases from which U.S. air and naval units could patrol the Atlantic.

In August, Roosevelt and Churchill met in a secret rendezvous on the British battleship *Prince of Wales,* off the coast of Newfoundland. There they drafted the Atlantic Charter, which, as a joint declaration of policy by a belligerent power and a technically neutral nation, was a remarkable document. Its idealistic terms upheld the right of all peoples to choose their own governments, affirmed Anglo-American dedication to peace "after the final destruction of the Nazi tyranny," and rejected any territorial aggrandizement as a result of the war. The Atlantic Charter was important because it symbolized growing Anglo-American solidarity. It also had propaganda appeal to the conquered peoples of Europe, encouraging them not to lose hope.

During July 1941, Roosevelt ordered U.S. naval and air units to patrol the Western Atlantic to warn Britain of the presence of German submarines, again hardly a neutral act. Although Hitler instructed his submarine commanders not to retaliate against American ships, some of them became so outraged by the effectiveness of these patrols that they did respond in anger. Early in

September, a German U-boat became involved in an engagement with the U.S. destroyer *Greer*, which had been tracking the submarine for several hours. It is not clear which vessel actually initiated hostilities, but neither suffered any damage. Roosevelt, nevertheless accused the Germans of a deliberate attack. Describing a U-boat as a "rattlesnake poised to strike," he authorized U.S. destroyers henceforth to employ a "shoot on sight" policy. In October, U-boats attacked two destroyers on convoy escort duty, damaging the *Kearny* and sinking the *Reuben James* with the loss of 115 lives. Roosevelt responded this time by persuading Congress to authorize the arming of U.S. merchant ships and allowing them to carry cargoes to Allied ports. Clearly, by the fall of 1941, the United States was, for all intents and purposes, a participant in the war, although on a limited basis. And each incident in the North Atlantic increased the likelihood of a full-fledged American commitment.

U.S.–Japanese Tension

War came to America not through developments in the Atlantic but because of growing friction between the United States and Japan in the Pacific. It was the culmination of a long history of fluctuating tension that began with the advent of the United States as a world power during the Spanish-American War in 1898. In the ensuing peace settlement, America forced Spain to cede Guam in the Central Pacific and the Philippines in East Asia. The acquisition of the Philippines created an American presence close to China, which at that time appeared to be at the mercy of the European powers and Japan. The United States feared that these countries would bar American commercial interests from China. In response to this concern, in 1899 Secretary of State John Hay formulated the Open Door policy, which sought to maintain U.S. access to the China market and, as modified in 1900, to preserve China's territorial integrity and independence.

At first, America viewed Germany and Russia as the chief threats to the Open Door, but when Japan defeated Russia in the Russo-Japanese War of 1904–5, the Japanese loomed as the greater peril. In 1911, U.S. leaders demonstrated their concern about the possibility of a conflict with Japan when they drew up War Plan Orange. This provided for American forces to hold out in the Philippines against a Japanese attack until the navy steamed across the Pacific to provide relief. The plan remained the basic U.S. strategy for a potential war with Japan until the adoption of the Rainbow plans in 1939. But even then it continued in existence in a modified form as Rainbow 3. Unfortunately, it failed to give sufficient consideration to the enormous logistic problems posed by the huge distances involved in such an operation. Its prospects became even more dubious when the Japanese seized the Caroline, Mariana, and Marshall islands from Germany during World War I. Japan's presence in the Central Pacific posed a serious threat to America's lines of communication with the Philippines.

The establishment of the Anglo-Japanese Alliance in 1902 also alarmed the United States. This agreement allowed Britain to shift most of its East Asian naval ships to their home base, and with the destruction of the Russian fleet in the Russo-Japanese War, Japan held the dominant position in Asian waters. In 1915, the Japanese took advantage of this situation to issue its "Twenty-One Demands," which would have transformed China into a virtual Japanese dependency. But strong American and British pressure forced Japan to back down on the most stringent of its demands, much to Tokyo's irritation. Japanese leaders found it puzzling that America was so fixated on access to the Chinese market when its trade with Japan was so much greater than with China. American immigration policy angered the Japanese even more, both in regard to its refusal to go along with Japan's cherished proposal for a racial equality clause in the Covenant of the League of Nations and the detested Immigration Act of 1924, which barred Japanese immigration into the United States. This humiliation remained vividly lodged in the Japanese collective memory.

Although relative tranquility prevailed in U.S.-Japanese relations during the 1920s, Japan's conquest of Manchuria in 1931 and invasion of China proper in 1937 caused growing American concern. Brutal incidents such as the rape of Nanking and the attack on the U.S. gunboat *Panay* also increased tension, as did Japanese interference with American and European trading rights. America extended some aid to China in the form of loans, arms sales, and eventually lend-lease supplies. The Chinese also won the hearts and minds of numerous Americans, especially the pressure group that came to be known as the China Lobby. Comprised of persons involved in Far Eastern trade, politicians, missionaries, and various admirers of the Chinese, this group pressured Congress to increase support for the Kuomintang regime. But until 1940, Washington tried to avoid any action that might lead to war with Japan, particularly in view of the deteriorating situation in Europe.

When the European war began, Japan had been fighting in China for over two years, and hostilities continued there while Hitler won his victories in Poland, Norway, and Western Europe. With the conquest of the Netherlands and the fall of France, Japan set out to take advantage of these countries in Southeast Asia, where Dutch authorities continued to rule the East Indies (now Indonesia) and the Vichy French administered Indochina. The Japanese pressured the Dutch to grant trade concessions and demanded that the French close supply routes through Indochina to China. They also gained Churchill's temporary agreement to prohibit aid from reaching Chiang's forces through Burma (now Myanmar), the British colony that bordered China on the southwest. The United States viewed these actions as a prelude to greater Japanese penetration into Southeast Asia and adopted a much tougher policy. In July, America imposed an embargo on exports of aviation fuel and the highest grades of iron and scrap steel to Japan. The Japanese refused to be deterred by these measures, however, and in September they extorted the Vichy regime's reluctant agreement to the stationing of Japanese troops in northern Indochina. The U.S. responded by imposing a complete embargo on the export of all grades of iron and steel scrap to Japan.

Washington's alarm increased still more when Japan joined Germany and Italy in signing the Tripartite Pact in September. This agreement provided that the three powers would assist each other "with all political, economic, and military means" if one of them were attacked by a power not involved in the European war or the Sino-Japanese conflict. The three powers specifically exempted the Soviet Union, which still enjoyed friendly relations with Germany at that time, from the terms of the pact. It appears that Hitler regarded this stipulation as a cover to disguise his growing interest in attacking the Soviets. But however the Führer may have viewed the pact, other governments saw it as a deterrent to America's entry into the war, either in Europe or Asia.

Japan continued to encroach on Indochina and established a protectorate over the entire colony in July 1941. This action clearly posed the likelihood of Japanese expansion into other parts of Southeast Asia and led to the most serious crisis to date in U.S.-Japanese relations. Roosevelt, acting on the recommendations of his top advisers, froze Japan's assets in the United States and enforced a trade embargo that went far beyond the 1940 restrictions. Britain and the Dutch took similar measures. Most important, the embargo cut off oil exports, which hit the Japanese particularly hard because they imported 88 percent of their oil. Without this vital commodity, Japan's war machine would grind to a halt. But Japan could solve this problem by gaining control of the Dutch East Indies which contained rich oil fields. If they seized British Malaya as well, they would gain four-fifths of the world's rubber supply and two-thirds of its tin.

Japanese Intentions in Asia

The Japanese believed that they would have to choose one of three alternatives: (1) abandon their ambitions in Southeast Asia and perhaps China as well; (2) work out a compromise with the United States that would involve resumption of trade at the price of some Japanese concessions; or (3) attack Dutch and British possessions in Southeast Asia and, probably, American bases in East Asia and the Pacific. If they struck at the Dutch East Indies and Malaya without neutralizing the Philippines, their supply lines would be vulnerable to air interdiction by U.S. bombers based on the principal Philippine island of Luzon. It thus appeared that the third option would necessitate attacks on the Philippines as well as the U.S. Pacific Fleet at Pearl Harbor on Oahu in the Hawaiian Islands.

Admiral Isoroku Yamamoto, commander in chief of the Japanese Combined Fleet, insisted that if Japan were to have any chance of success in a war with the United States, it must destroy the Pacific Fleet by a surprise assault. There was a precedent for such an attack. At the start of the Russo-Japanese War in 1904, Yamamoto's hero, Admiral Heihachiro Togo, had dealt a severe blow to a Russian fleet at Port Arthur, destroying two battleships and several cruisers. This operation had been the prelude to an even greater victory, the Battle of Tsushima, in which Togo's forces devastated a second Russian fleet. Yamamoto, who had lost two fingers in that struggle, was among the first Japanese naval officers to recognize the importance of airpower. He had overcome resistance from more conservative admirals to the development of aircraft carriers and now proposed use of carrier-based planes to attack American naval power in the Pacific.

Ironically, Yamamoto had long been an opponent of war with the United States. He had studied at Harvard University and served as a naval attaché in Washington, and he clearly recognized America's enormous industrial potential. But he believed that aggressive Japanese policies made war inevitable. Thus, he considered a lightning stroke to destroy the Pacific Fleet absolutely mandatory. He believed that this would secure a period of six months during which Japan could establish a powerful position in Southeast Asia and the Western Pacific. This should convince American leaders that they could dislodge the Japanese only through a long, bloody struggle. Yamamoto did not think the Americans would have the stomach for the sacrifices necessary to accomplish this and would seek a negotiated peace. This would confirm Japan's dominant position in East Asia. His plan was initially much too bold for most of the other top Japanese naval leaders, but he eventually won them over by persuasion and several threats to resign if he did not get his way.

The Japanese army favored war, but Premier Fumimaro Konoye preferred negotiations with the United States. Konoye was a member of an influential family and was a close friend of Emperor Hirohito. Konoye had served as premier at the time of the Japanese invasion of China but had resigned in 1938. He formed a second cabinet in the summer of 1940. Although generally considered a moderate, Konoye recognized the army's dominant influence over the government and shared its desire for Japanese hegemony in East Asia but doubted that war with America

would facilitate this. The army leaders agreed to let Konoye seek a diplomatic solution, but only with the stipulation that if diplomacy did not secure a settlement by mid-October, Japan would resort to hostilities.

In return for American relaxation of the trade embargo, Konoye offered to withdraw Japanese troops from Indochina after the conclusion of the war with China. He did not specify any terms for ending the conflict but did propose a meeting with Roosevelt to discuss a general settlement. His overtures inspired little enthusiasm in the American government, and both Secretary of State Cordell Hull and Secretary of War Henry Stimson favored a hard line, fearing that any sign of weakness would only encourage Japan in its expansionist designs.

A former Tennessee lawyer, congressman, and senator, Hull had gained his position in Roosevelt's cabinet largely because of his popularity with southern Democrats and his influence in Congress. Stimson had served as President Taft's secretary of war early in the century and as Hoover's secretary of state at the time of the Manchurian crisis. A Republican, he had received his appointment in 1940 as a result of Roosevelt's desire to gain bipartisan support for his foreign policy. Washington responded to Konoye's initiative on October 2 by informing Japan that a meeting between the president and the premier would be possible only after the Japanese had clarified their obligations under the Tripartite Pact. The Americans also asked for a clear-cut indication of Japan's intent to withdraw its troops not only from Indochina but from China as well.

Konoye's diplomatic initiative had failed, and when the army's time limit for negotiations expired on October 15, he resigned. The war minister, General Hideki Tojo, became premier. Although his personality was far from magnetic, Tojo was hardworking and intelligent. Indeed, the sharpness of his mind so impressed his fellow officers that they called him "the Razor." But he tended to view issues from the perspective of the army only, and had little knowledge of the rest of the world, a low regard for the United States, and a willingness to take risks. Before becoming war minister in 1940, he had served as chief of staff in the Kwantung Army and had been a brigade commander in the Sino-Japanese War. Unlike many generals, Tojo had no use for *gekokujo* and believed that junior officers should remain under the firm discipline of their superiors. This attitude won him the respect of conservative generals and civilian leaders alike. But not all members of the Japanese hierarchy were pleased with his appointment as premier. Yamamoto complained that he tended to act in an overly bold manner without a clear idea of the dangers that a conflict with America would pose for Japan.

Tojo favored war, but Emperor Hirohito insisted that the government "go back to blank paper" in its continued pursuit of an agreement with the United States. The cabinet bowed to his request and approved a new two-step approach. The first step, Plan A, called for a long-range agreement to guarantee economic equality for all powers, not only in China but throughout the world. It also offered to interpret the Tripartite Pact defensively if the United States refrained from taking advantage of this to enter the European war. Finally, the Japanese agreed to withdraw their forces from Indochina and parts of China. If the United States rejected Plan A, Japan would resort to the short-term Plan B, which proposed suspension of American aid to China and an end to economic sanctions. In return, Japan would refrain from any more aggressive actions in Southeast Asia, would withdraw its troops from southern Indochina, and would launch peace talks with China. After reaching a settlement with the Chinese, Japan would withdraw all its troops from Indochina. Army leaders only agreed to withdrawing troops from southern Indochina after bitter debate and considered this a major concession. If the United States rejected this offer, Japan would consider war the only option.

American Diplomatic Reactions

Both Roosevelt and Hull reacted cooly to Plan A. Hull also disliked Plan B, but the President was more receptive to it and suggested a response indicating willingness to continue negotiations, if for no other reason than to gain time to strengthen U.S. forces in the Pacific. Indeed, both General George C. Marshall, the army chief of staff, and Admiral Harold Stark, chief of naval operations, warned of the inadequacy of American forces and urged that the United States make a counterproposal.

Marshall, a graduate of Virginia Military Institute rather than West Point, had served as a staff officer on the western front in World War I. He became chief of staff in 1939 and proved a masterful organizer with special skill in the difficult but vital art of logistics. Cold and aloof with few personal friends and almost no sense of humor, Marshall possessed an exceptionally keen mind. Although willing to listen to the views of his subordinates, once he decided on a course of action, he adhered to it with steadfast determination. Among his many strong qualities was his ability to choose the best people for key positions. He had no patience with failure but was unusually loyal to those who produced results.

Stark became chief of naval operations the same year that Marshall assumed his post. He had held a number of command positions, both on the high seas and as a staff officer in Washington. Stark was an excellent planner but tended to be indecisive and lacking in forcefulness. He had two major achievements to his credit, however—drafting Plan Dog and securing congressional approval of a substantial increase in funding for the navy.

Hull drew up a counter proposal to Plan B based on Roosevelt's wishes that offered economic concessions in return for Japan's withdrawal from threatening positions and a halt to all aggressive action. But this plan encountered Chinese and British opposition. Hull accordingly scrapped it in favor of a much tougher proposal, the so-called ten point demand of November 26, that called for Japan to withdraw from both Indochina and China as a prerequisite for American agreement to unfreeze Japanese assets and resume trade. The Japanese viewed this as an ultimatum and on November 29 made their final decision for war.

American leaders had stiffened their attitude toward Japan during the summer and fall of 1941 in large part because they had obtained information from U.S. cryptanalysts who had broken Japan's top diplomatic cipher system, code-named "Purple," and were, thus, able to intercept secret messages. As a result, Roosevelt and his advisers were aware of Japanese proposals well before they received them officially. They also knew that Japan intended to go to war to achieve its aims if the United States did not accept Japan's terms. The process of intercepting and deciphering

Japanese messages was code-named Magic. Unlike Ultra, Magic could only reveal diplomatic secrets. The Americans had not yet broken Japan's naval and military ciphers. Roosevelt, Stimson, and especially Hull grew increasingly cynical about the possibility of negotiating a settlement as a result of the information they obtained from Magic. They became convinced that war was virtually inevitable when they read a particularly ominous message that pinpointed November 29 as the final deadline for negotiations and added that thereafter, "things are automatically going to happen."

In retrospect, the United States might have made a serious mistake by making China such a major factor in its approach to this diplomatic crisis. It is highly questionable whether China was vital to U.S. interests despite traditional American support for the Open Door policy and sympathy for the suffering of the Chinese people at the hands of the Japanese. This was especially true in view of the increasing likelihood that America would be drawn into the European war because of the volatile situation in the North Atlantic. And, as Plan Dog and the ABC1 agreement stated, Germany was the primary enemy. Moreover, much of U.S. naval strength was tied down in the Atlantic, and a Pacific war by its very nature would be a naval war. Both naval and army leaders were quite aware of this as well as America's overall military weakness and the need to build up strength. Marshall and Stark informed Roosevelt on November 25 that "the essential thing now is to gain time." Moreover, the U.S. was in no position to liberate China, and despite widespread belief in America that China should be treated as if it were a great power, the reality was quite different. The Kuomintang regime was corrupt, weak, and unpopular, while the Communists dominated much of the countryside, not to mention the presence of powerful Japanese occupying forces. Acceptance of Japan's Plan B as the basis for continued negotiations might have averted or at least delayed a two-front war. Indeed, Roosevelt initially was willing to respond to the proposal in this manner, but opposition from China and Britain persuaded the more rigid Hull to insist on Japanese withdrawal from, not only Indochina, but all of China as well as a prerequisite for resumption of economic relations. The Japanese

were especially alarmed by this because they interpreted it to mean withdrawal from Manchuria as well as China proper. This was apparently not Hull's intent, but he failed to make this clear. After the war several Japanese leaders involved in the decision-making process insisted that had they known that Manchuria was excluded, negotiations probably would have continued. The Japanese army's growing fervor for war and its dominant position in the power structure obviously complicated matters, but as long as the diplomatic process continued, at least the possibility of a negotiated settlement remained.

Preparations for War in the Pacific

The key factors in the forthcoming conflict in the Pacific were air and sea power, especially the ability to launch air strikes from aircraft carriers and attacks by submarines against enemy shipping. Although the British had used carrier-based planes against the Italian navy in the Mediterranean, the full extent of the revolution that air power posed for naval warfare did not become clear until the outbreak of the Pacific conflict. The Japanese had ten aircraft carriers, while their enemies had only three available in the Pacific, all U.S. carriers based at Pearl Harbor. In other aspects, the combined American, British, and Dutch naval forces in the Pacific nearly matched Japan's strength, but they were under three different commands and widely dispersed, and many of the Allied ships were inferior in quality. American and British remoteness from East Asia also made it exceedingly difficult for them to supply and reinforce their garrisons.

By far the strongest Allied naval force was the U.S. Pacific Fleet at Pearl Harbor. In addition to its three carriers, it contained eight battleships, including the old *Utah,* which had been converted to a target ship, seven heavy cruisers, and numerous smaller craft. If the Japanese could destroy this force, especially the carriers, they would gain naval supremacy in the Pacific. Their plan also called for simultaneous attacks on other Allied strongholds—the U.S. outposts of Wake Island and Guam in the Pacific and the British possessions of Malaya and Hong Kong on the Asian mainland. Additional attacks would follow against the Philippines, the Dutch East Indies, and the British colony of Burma.

To deliver the blow against Pearl Harbor, Japanese planners provided a striking force of six carriers with a complement of 360 planes. These consisted of high-level bombers, dive bombers, torpedo bombers, and fighters. Two battleships, three cruisers, and eight destroyers escorted the carriers. Admiral Chuichi Nagumo commanded this formidable armada. Nagumo had received the honor by virtue of seniority despite the fact that he had no previous experience with air power. Ironically, Nagumo had initially opposed the Pearl Harbor attack as too reckless. Indeed, Yamamoto's plan contained extremely dangerous elements. It required the striking force to travel 3,500 miles, without being discovered, according to a rigidly precise timetable. To avoid detection, the Japanese imposed absolute radio silence and charted the approach to Hawaii through a vast, lonely expanse of sea far from inhabited areas and regular shipping routes.

The Japanese also adopted certain technical innovations that they hoped would enhance their prospects for success. One of these arose out of concern over the shallow 40-foot depth of Pearl Harbor. They feared that torpedoes might sink so low that they would detonate on the bottom. To prevent this, the Japanese borrowed a method developed by the British—the use of more buoyant wooden fins, which prevented torpedoes from falling too far below the surface. They also attached fins to armor-piercing naval gun shells, which they substituted for bombs. The fins made the shells fall like bombs, but the shells could pierce the armor of warships much more effectively than bombs.

When the Japanese unleashed their attack on Pearl Harbor and nearby air and military installations on December 7, they took the Americans completely by surprise. This led to the birth of a conspiracy theory that still has its adherents who contend that Roosevelt and his associates deliberately provoked Japan into attacking the United States. These critics claim that by pursuing a hardline policy during the summer and fall of 1941, American leaders gave the Japanese no option. They also charge that the president and his top advisers had access to Magic-intercepted messages, as well as other sources of information, indicating that Pearl Harbor was a likely target. However, according to this scenario, they refused to warn naval and military leaders in Hawaii

because they wanted the attack to succeed. Proponents of this "back door to war" thesis insist that Roosevelt hoped the attack would create a wave of revulsion among the American people that would enable him to bring the United States into the war not only against Japan but, via the back door, Germany as well. The president supposedly pursued this devious policy because of popular opposition to America's entry into the European conflict by way of the Atlantic front door.

There is little evidence to support this conspiracy thesis. It is true that Roosevelt was becoming more actively involved in the Atlantic and in support of the British and Soviet war efforts. By late 1941, he also probably thought American entry into the European conflict was necessary, but it is likely that incidents in the Atlantic would have accomplished this eventually without help from Japan. It also is true that messages intercepted by Magic showed clearly that Japanese attacks were likely in early December, but the question was where. Naval intelligence had also begun to penetrate the Japanese navy's cipher well before the attack on Pearl Harbor. But U.S. cryptanalysts were able to decipher only about 10 percent of intercepted messages at the time. They did not complete the breaking of the cipher until early 1942. Various pieces of information, if considered in isolation, hinted of Japanese interest in Pearl Harbor, but they were too few and too unspecific to indicate that the Pacific Fleet was a Japanese target. Roosevelt and his aides instead considered the Dutch East Indies, Malaya, Hong Kong, and the Philippines to be the probable targets. Reports of a large Japanese buildup in Indochina bolstered this belief. If Nagumo had difficulty accepting the boldness of Yamamoto's plan to attack Pearl Harbor, it is not surprising that American leaders did not anticipate such a daring stroke.

But the fact that the Japanese caught Pearl Harbor completely by surprise does reflect negatively on American leaders. This is especially true with regard to their rigidly secretive attitude toward Magic. Intercepted messages were available only to the 10 highest-level civilian and military leaders. To maintain security, these leaders kept the breaking of the Japanese cipher secret even from Admiral Husband Kimmel, commander of the Pacific Fleet, and General Walter Short, the army commander in the Hawaiian

Islands. They did issue several communications to Kimmel and Short that warned of the general possibility of war, but they sent the last of these messages on November 27. Marshall and Stark feared that the dispatch of still more warnings might be too much like the boy who cried wolf. But Marshall did issue one final alert to Short on the morning of December 7, when Magic revealed Japan's intention to break diplomatic relations. Washington viewed this as a preliminary to war. A delay in transmission prevented this message from reaching its destination until after the attack on Pearl Harbor, however.

The roles of Kimmel and Short in preparing the naval and military forces in Hawaii for possible attack have also stirred controversy. Both men had taken over their commands in February 1941. Kimmel had earned a reputation for efficiency and discipline, though without noteworthy imagination or creativity. Navy leaders thought so highly of Kimmel that they selected him to command the Pacific Fleet despite the fact that he was junior to many other admirals. Short had served in the infantry for almost 40 years. His fellow officers considered him capable and highly conscientious rather than brilliant.

Although coordination between the two commanders appears to have been less than satisfactory, Kimmel did undertake long-range aerial reconnaissance of the waters off Oahu, but he directed his efforts primarily to the west and southwest of the island. This was in keeping with intelligence reports indicating that, if the Japanese attempted an attack, it would likely come from that direction. He also sent some patrols north of the island but lacked sufficient long-range aircraft to carry out this mission on a daily basis. Unfortunately, December 7 was one of the days this could not be done. Kimmel's predecessor, Admiral James O. Richardson, had not provided anti-torpedo nets for the warships anchored at Pearl Harbor because he feared that they would impede the fleet's ability to move quickly. When Kimmel succeeded Richardson, the navy department informed him that it also considered such defenses unnecessary because the shallow waters of Pearl Harbor would prevent a successful Japanese torpedo assault, a decision that proved disastrous. Kimmel did fail to issue a general alert after the U.S. destroyer *Ward* reported that it had attacked a

Japanese submarine near the entrance to Pearl Harbor on the morning of December 7. He believed that the incident was not serious enough to warrant such an action. Finally, Short's radar system was understaffed and lacked experienced personnel. Whatever their mistakes, it now appears that both men may actually have been primarily victims of bad luck rather than negligence. But both ultimately were held responsible for the disaster and relieved of command.

The Attack on Pearl Harbor

On the morning of December 7, 1941, two enlisted men, who were operating a mobile radar unit on the north end of Oahu, detected an unusually large number of aircraft approaching from the northwest. But when they reported their finding to the information center, an inexperienced lieutenant told them not to worry. He assumed that the planes were a flight of 13 U.S. B-17 bombers scheduled to arrive from California later that morning. Within a half-hour, the first wave of Nagumo's aircraft descended on Pearl Harbor. As they swooped in, Commander Mitsuo Fuchida, leader of the striking force, radioed Nagumo, "Tora! Tora! Tora!" (Tiger! Tiger! Tiger!), indicating that they had achieved complete surprise.

The Japanese had launched their planes from a point 220 miles northwest of Oahu, and their attacks were devastating. This was especially true of the first wave of torpedo bombers. Of the seven U.S. battleships in "Battleship Row," the Japanese sent four to the bottom and severely damaged the others. They sank three destroyers, the target ship *Utah*, and four small vessels. They also inflicted damage on three light cruisers, destroyed 160 aircraft, and disabled 128 others. Short had ordered the planes to be drawn up in tight formation on the airfields to make them less susceptible to sabotage. Unfortunately, this disposition left the aircraft much more vulnerable to Japanese bombers, which caught most of them on the ground. More than 2,400 American personnel lost their lives. Japanese losses totaled only 29 planes destroyed, along with their crews, and 70 planes damaged.

Pearl Harbor was a disaster for the Americans, but it could have been far worse. Nagumo's planes had put much of the Pacific Fleet out of action, but the three American carriers were not among the stricken ships. Two of them, *Lexington* and *Enterprise*, had left for other destinations, and *Saratoga* was undergoing repairs on the West Coast. Seven heavy cruisers were also at sea. Had the cruisers and especially the carriers been destroyed or seriously damaged, Japan would have won total supremacy in the Pacific. Of the stricken battleships, only two—*Arizona* and *Oklahoma*—were beyond hope of salvage. The shallowness of Pearl Harbor was largely responsible for this; the ships were merely grounded, not sunk. The Japanese also failed to destroy the navy's submarine base, fuel storage tanks, and repair and maintenance facilities. The loss of the fuel would have been especially disastrous.

When it became apparent that the American carriers were absent from Pearl Harbor, Commander Minoru Genda, Nagumo's air staff officer, urged the admiral to pursue additional operations. Unlike Nagumo, Genda was an expert on air power and an ace fighter pilot. Genda believed that Nagumo should locate the carriers at sea and destroy them. He also pressed for a follow-up raid on the fuel storage tanks and dockyards at Pearl Harbor. But Nagumo was overjoyed with his success and feared losses to his own carriers. As a result, he refused to take any more risks and ordered his striking force to return to its home base.

Japan had won a remarkable tactical victory, but it had not scored the great strategic triumph Yamamoto had gambled on. The admiral had gained time for Japan to establish a dominant position in Southeast Asia and the Western Pacific. But instead of convincing America of the futility of a long war, the attack on Pearl Harbor had the opposite effect. It united the government and the people in the determination to pursue the conflict to a victorious conclusion. Roosevelt went before a joint session of Congress on December 8 to deliver a grim but stirring speech. He referred to the previous day as "a date which will live in infamy" and called for a declaration of war. The House responded 388 to 1 in favor, the Senate unanimously.

The United States at War

But war had come only with Japan. Despite the "back door to war" thesis, Roosevelt had not asked for a declaration of war against Germany. To have responded to a Japanese attack on Pearl Harbor with such a request would have aroused

FIGURE 12-1   U.S. warships burn following the Japanese attack on Pearl Harbor.
(Navy Dept./National Archives and Records Administration)

considerable opposition both in Congress and among the American people. It was Hitler who decided the issue.

During the summer and fall of 1941, the Führer had become increasingly concerned that Japan might work out an agreement with the United States, thus freeing America to intervene in the European war. In an effort to prevent such an occurrence, Hitler had encouraged Japan to attack U.S. bases in East Asia and the Pacific. This would deflect American forces to that part of the world. He had even gone so far as to assure Japan that Germany would respond to such a Japanese initiative with a declaration of war against the United States. He also pressured Mussolini into extending a similar guarantee. These pledges of assistance went far beyond the obligations of either Germany or Italy under the Tripartite Pact. Hitler was ignorant of the fact that Japan intended to attack the United States, even without German support, because the Japanese did not see fit to inform him. Obviously it was to their advantage to keep him in the dark until he had committed himself to enter the struggle against America. But they refused to take him into their confidence even after he had given them his assurance.

Japan's assault against Pearl Harbor, thus, caught Hitler as much by surprise as it did the United States. But when the Japanese asked him to honor his pledge soon afterward, he complied without hesitation. On December 11, both Germany and Italy declared war. Hitler's decision provided the United States with the option of concentrating its strongest forces against either Japan or Germany. Roosevelt and his advisers chose Germany because they considered it to be the more formidable enemy, though of necessity they earmarked much of the navy for the Pacific.

It is quite remarkable that Hitler honored his commitment to Japan. He had certainly violated agreements in the past, and by ignoring this one he might have avoided a clash with America while the Japanese tied down U.S. forces in the Pacific. Apparently he declared war because he still expected the United States to concentrate its primary effort against Japan. It also appears that he anticipated American entry into the conflict in Europe in the near future because of escalating incidents in the Atlantic. Thus, from his perspective, it did not seem that he was actually risking much by a declaration of war. Some historians have argued that Hitler took this step because he underestimated the United States' potential strength, in part because of his belief that the Americans were a mongrel people. But this argument is not convincing in view of Hitler's insistence that German submarine commanders avoid any kind of provocation to the United States in the Atlantic and his efforts to embroil America with Japan in the Pacific.

However he rationalized his decision, it was still a blunder, second in importance only to his attack on the USSR. He had brought the United States, Britain, and the Soviet Union into a coalition against him. This alliance virtually assured that Germany would lose the war—provided that the Allies could overcome political and strategic differences, which soon appeared, and lingering distrust, especially between the Soviets and the Western Powers.

CHAPTER THIRTEEN

Japan Triumphant, December 1941–May 1942

Pearl Harbor was only the beginning. A series of even more disastrous Allied defeats followed in rapid succession. Yamamoto had promised that his surprise attack on the Pacific Fleet would gain six months for Japan to establish an impregnable position in Southeast Asia and the Pacific. The extent to which the havoc the Japanese had created at Pearl Harbor was responsible for their subsequent conquests is debatable. Nevertheless, their success did continue for almost six months. But Japan's newly won position did not prove impregnable. Once the United States had recovered from the shock of Pearl Harbor, it began to bring its enormous warmaking potential into play. American resources were far greater than those of the Japanese, and ultimately enabled the United States to turn the tide.

But the first six months belonged to Japan. Her victories were reminiscent in some respects of Germany's *Blitzkrieg* triumphs. They came with amazing speed and remarkable ease. Like the Germans earlier, the Japanese seemed invincible. The Allied response was also similar to the abortive efforts of Britain and France in the early months of the war—too little, too late.

Japanese Military Strength

Even more than Germany, Japan won victories with forces that were not particularly large. The Japanese army in December 1941 contained only 51 active divisions, although it possessed garrison troops and other units equivalent to 40 additional divisions. In all, Japan's available forces totaled 1.2 million men, and the military could draw upon an additional 2 million reservists, many of whom had seen service against the Chinese. But much of the army remained in China, leaving only 11 divisions for operations against Southeast Asia and the Pacific. The army also had its own air force, which included 2,000 first-line planes.

Japan's navy contained a formidable nucleus of ten carriers, six of which took part in the Pearl Harbor mission. Its 11 battleships included *Yamato,* whose 70,000 tons and nine 18.1-inch guns made it the world's largest and most powerfully armed ship. *Yamato* was so huge that each of its gun turrets was as large as a destroyer. Construction on a sister ship, *Musashi,* was nearing completion. Eighteen heavy cruisers, 21 light cruisers, 100 destroyers, and 63 submarines were also available. The navy possessed an air force of 3,000 planes. Although most Japanese aircraft were not of outstanding quality, the Mitsubishi A6M fighter, which the Japanese called the Zero, was exceptional and saw service with both the army and the navy. During the early months of the war, it outclassed Allied fighters, but unfortunately for the Japanese, it remained their standard fighter long after the Allies had developed superior models.

The Japanese army differed greatly from the German. It had no armored divisions and emphasized light tanks, small guns, and mortars. These weapons suited the amphibious operations that characterized Japan's war effort in Southeast Asia and the Pacific. The Japanese also enjoyed the benefit of local air supremacy and the element of surprise as well as far greater experience and superior training. Allied blunders and slowness to respond to Japanese initiatives played important roles, too, as did the Allies' marked tendency to underestimate the ability of Asiatic troops to stand up against Western forces.

Japanese Advances, 1941–42

War in Southeast Asia and the Pacific

In an effort to create some coordination among the widely dispersed Allied forces in East Asia, General Marshall urged the creation of a unified command structure. Roosevelt and Churchill agreed to his request at the Arcadia Conference in Washington during December. This was their first meeting since the entry of the United States into the war. With the help of their military staffs, they appointed General Wavell to direct the American, British, Dutch, and Australian Command (ABDA-COM). The area under Wavell's jurisdiction included the Dutch East Indies, Malaya, Burma, and the Philippines. In reality, he had almost no control of the Philippines, which remained under the command of the American General Douglas MacArthur. By the time Wavell reached his headquarters in the Dutch East Indies on January 10, 1942, the outlook was gloomy, to say the least.

Japan struck at numerous other targets on the same day as the assault on Pearl Harbor. These attacks included air raids on Wake Island and the Philippines and land operations against Guam, Hong Kong, Malaya, and the Philippines. Guam was the first outpost to fall. Its close proximity to the powerful Japanese base on the island of Saipan in the Marianas made its position hopeless. After two days of air attacks, the Japanese landed and quickly overwhelmed its defenders.

Over 1,000 miles to the east, Wake Island proved much harder to subjugate. Its tiny garrison of 447 marines, commanded by Major James Devereux, along with 75 naval and army signal corps personnel, fought valiantly with the help of a handful of marine fighter planes and a few 5-inch coastal defense guns and antiaircraft guns. Japanese planes and warships subjected the island to three days of bombing and shelling, starting on December 11. The Japanese also planned to land on Wake the same day, but their warships were greeted by heavy fire from the American coastal batteries and bombing attacks from the few surviving marine aircraft. Two Japanese destroyers were sent to the bottom and three other ships were damaged. This remarkable setback required the Japanese to send for reinforcements, including two of the carriers that had taken part in the Pearl Harbor raid.

Admiral Kimmel, who still commanded the U.S. Pacific Fleet at that time, countered by ordering a task force, centered around the carrier *Saratoga,* to relieve Wake. But soon after its departure, Admiral William Pye succeeded Kimmel temporarily as fleet commander. Pye feared the possibility of losing *Saratoga* and called off the operation on December 23. The Japanese landed on Wake the same day and encountered savage resistance from the outnumbered marines before finally forcing them to surrender. They marked their victory by machine-gunning wounded in the island's hospital and utilizing the able-bodied as slave laborers. The failure of the Wake relief expedition, coming so soon after the Pearl Harbor debacle, represented another severe blow to the U.S. Navy's morale although the heroism of Wake's

garrison won the admiration of the American people and even became the subject of a Hollywood film in 1942.

Hong Kong, still another isolated Allied base, fell before the end of December. Consisting of a group of islands and a small peninsula on the Chinese mainland adjacent to Japanese-held territory, Hong Kong's position, like Guam's, was hopeless. Japanese forces struck on December 8 and quickly drove the defenders off the mainland. They followed with an invasion of Hong Kong Island on December 18, captured its water supply, and split the garrison into two pockets. One of them surrendered on Christmas, the other the following day. Japanese soldiers, flushed with victory and angry over the casualties they had suffered, now plunged into an orgy of savagery, killing prisoners and raping nurses as well as civilian women.

Japan faced a more formidable task in the Philippines. Allied ground forces there were fairly numerous but varied in quality and were poorly equipped. General MacArthur led 31,000 regular troops, including 12,000 Filipinos, who served as part of the U.S. Army, and the inadequately trained Philippine army of 102,000. The so-called U.S. Asiatic Fleet contained only a few surface ships and 29 submarines.

MacArthur was a controversial figure before the war and has remained so ever since. The son of a Civil War hero, he won several decorations for bravery during World War I and became the youngest American general to command a division. He served as army chief of staff from 1930 to 1935. During the lowest point in the Great Depression, MacArthur committed a major public relations blunder when he led troops, using tear gas and tanks, to oust 2,000 World War I veterans from Washington. These men had been demanding early payment of their war service bonuses. In 1935, the general received an appointment as military adviser to the Philippines, which had become a commonwealth of the United States with limited self-government. He still held that post when Roosevelt recalled him to active service in 1941. MacArthur was intensely ambitious, extremely vain, and ardently fond of publicity. He habitually wore a gold braid–encrusted cap, carried a riding crop, and smoked a gigantic corncob pipe, all of which made him a prime target for photographers. MacArthur badly underestimated the Japanese as opponents and expressed great confidence that his forces could repulse any invasion. He did not expect the Japanese to strike before the spring of 1942.

Concern over American airpower on the main Philippine island of Luzon had been one of the primary reasons for Japan's decision to attack the United States. Actually, it was far less formidable than American leaders had intended. They had planned to station 165 heavy bombers on Luzon, but only 35 B-17 Flying Fortresses had arrived by the time the Japanese struck. A total of 104 P-40s, which were inferior to the Zero, and some obsolete models provided fighter support. Weak as it was, this airpower remained the key to U.S. plans to hold the Philippines as well as to attack Japan's supply lines. But the Japanese quickly eliminated this threat through a combination of their own initiative, American mistakes, and fortunate timing.

The Philippine Debacle

No one has ever satisfactorily explained why this disaster occurred. Since the war, the principal American actors in the drama—MacArthur; his able but domineering chief of staff, General Richard Sutherland; and the air commander, General Lewis Brereton—have all contradicted each other as to who was actually to blame. It is clear that all three men had received ample warning of the Pearl Harbor attack. It is also certain that on that same day, Brereton planned to stage a bombing raid against Japanese bases on Formosa and attempted to obtain permission to do so from MacArthur. But Sutherland refused to allow him to see the general, contending that MacArthur was too busy. This caused a delay, and the raid never took place.

Instead, when Japanese planes struck targets in northern Luzon, the bombers at Clark Field near Manila went aloft to avoid being caught on the ground. The main fighter force attempted, unsuccessfully, to intercept the enemy. When the U.S. aircraft returned to refuel, enemy planes did catch them on the ground, destroying 18 B-17s and 53 P-40s. This calamity took place even though radar had warned of the Japanese approach. Despite the confusion over this unfortunate series of events, ultimate responsibility lay with MacArthur as

commander of all forces in the Philippines. He failed to take the initiative in protecting his aircraft, and neither he nor Sutherland responded to Brereton's entreaties for prompt action. But it is also true that Brereton should have based his aircraft in Mindanao in the southern Philippines, where they would have been beyond the range of Japanese aircraft.

More raids followed during the next few days, and by December 17 only a handful of American fighters remained, while the surviving B-17s sought refuge in Australia. Japan had won total air supremacy in the Philippines. Japanese air attacks also devastated naval installations in Manila Bay and forced the flight of much of the Asiatic Fleet to Australia and the Dutch East Indies.

Japanese troops executed their first landings on Luzon's northern coast on December 8, but the main invasion did not come until December 22 at Lingayen Gulf, 150 miles north of Manila. General Mashaharu Homma commanded the invading force, which consisted of only two divisions. Homma was an unusual Japanese general. His interests were much broader than those of most of his fellow officers, extending to the arts. He was even an amateur playwright. Homma also shared Yamamoto's opposition to war with America, an attitude tantamount to heresy in the Japanese army. Nevertheless, he carried out the invasion with considerable skill.

The prewar American defensive plan called for a withdrawal to the Bataan Peninsula, which flanked Manila Bay on the west. But MacArthur had anticipated a landing at Lingayen Gulf and hoped to defeat the Japanese on the beaches. He also expected Washington to send a major relief expedition to his aid. MacArthur badly overestimated the ability of his own troops, especially the Philippine army. And clearly, after the Pearl Harbor disaster, any relief expedition to the Philippines was out of the question. The Philippine forces defending northern Luzon proved quite incapable of repelling the Japanese. By Christmas, the enemy was preparing to drive on Manila. The Japanese also made another major landing on the southeast coast of Luzon, which MacArthur had not anticipated. Manila now faced powerful Japanese invaders from both north and south.

MacArthur had only two options: withdraw into the mountains to concentrate on guerrilla activity or adopt the original plan and make a stand on Bataan. He chose the latter and ordered a fighting withdrawal. Despite great obstacles, his forces completed their retreat by early January 1942. But they were now bottled up on Bataan and the fortified islands near the entrance to Manila Bay. MacArthur's misguided decision to defend the beaches at Lingayen Gulf also created severe logistic problems. Instead of shifting food, medicine, and other supplies to Bataan, as stipulated in the prewar plan, he sent them north to the gulf. Most were lost, and the supplies that did reach Bataan were inadequate. The defenders of the peninsula soon found themselves on half-rations, and many of them fell victim to malaria and other tropical diseases.

MacArthur's troops made their initial stand near the northern end of the peninsula along a line anchored on the forbidding peaks of an extinct volcano. Homma's forces attacked this position on January 11, and two weeks of desperate fighting raged in appalling conditions. For a time the Americans gallantly repulsed repeated Japanese assaults, including suicide charges. But by January 26 the Japanese threatened to cut off the defenders near the coast. MacArthur ordered a retreat and was able to stabilize the front 20 miles to the south. Malaria and other diseases now decimated the Japanese, who also received orders to divert a division to take part in operations against the Dutch East Indies. By early March, Homma had only 3,000 men in the line and feared a counterattack. But the Americans failed to detect the extent of the enemy's weakness and were so plagued by illness and hunger themselves that they were in no condition to take offensive action. Instead, Japanese reinforcements arrived later in the month and rescued Homma from his dilemma.

MacArthur had been less than successful in his handling of the Luzon campaign. The disaster at Clark Field, the unfortunate decision to contest the beaches, and the problems it created for his forces when they reached Bataan provided ample justification for his dismissal. But he did not share the fate of Kimmel and Short. Instead, he emerged as a hero. The ability of his troops to hold Bataan for over three months contrasted vividly with the succession of defeats that Allied forces suffered

elsewhere. His publicity-oriented staff magnified his role, and the mass media widely disseminated news of his achievements. Roosevelt and Marshall even recommended him for the Congressional Medal of Honor. The American people, thankful for any relief from the persistent gloom of the weeks after Pearl Harbor, eagerly accepted him as a larger-than-life figure.

Clearly, under the circumstances, dismissal and retirement were out of the question. To leave him to face capture and imprisonment seemed equally impossible. Instead, on March 12, Roosevelt ordered MacArthur to leave the Philippines and make his way to Australia. After a perilous journey by sea and air, he reached his destination and announced dramatically, "I came through and I shall return." General Jonathan Wainwright, an old cavalryman who had directed the retreat from Lingayen Gulf, succeeded MacArthur as commander, but his prospects were grim. Disease and constantly declining rations had sapped the energy of his men, who had been reduced to virtual walking skeletons. A growing sense of hopelessness had also eroded their morale. MacArthur, who was well fed and safely ensconced on the fortified island of Corregidor, had paid only one visit to Bataan since December 24 and had grown highly unpopular with his troops. They referred to him sarcastically as "Dougout Doug." His departure did nothing to enhance his standing with them and weakened morale still more. On April 3, Homma opened his final offensive and quickly gained a breakthrough as Allied resistance disintegrated. Fighting on Bataan ceased on April 9. But Wainwright continued the struggle from Corregidor until May 5.

One of the most horrible incidents of the Pacific war followed immediately after the surrender of Bataan—the Bataan Death March. It resulted in part from a breakdown of Japanese arrangements for transporting and feeding the captured Allied troops. They had expected to take no more than 25,000 prisoners, but the actual number was over 75,000. As a result, many of the captives, already weakened and starving, had to walk the entire 55 miles to a railhead, where the Japanese directed them into overcrowded boxcars to complete the trip to the prison camp. Japanese treatment of the prisoners varied greatly. Some showed kindness,

Fourteenth Army
(Homma)

BATAN
8 Dec

——— XXX ———   US ARMY COMMAND
                BOUNDARIES
                AIRFIELDS

10 Dec

CAMIGUIN
10 Dec

10 Dec

LAOAG

APARRI

GONZAGA

Central

Kanno and
Tanaka Dets

VIGAN

TUGUEGARAO
12 Dec

**Main Japanese
landings**
22 December 1941

Cordillera

BONTOC

Cagayan

ILAGAN

Sierra

L u z o n

Madre

SAN FERNANDO
BAUANG

BAGUIO
24 Dec

BAYOMBONG

DAMORTIS

ROSARIO

TAYUG

LINGAYEN

CARMEN

Agno

Zambales Mts

SAN JOSE

TARLAC
30 Dec

CABANATUAN

IBA

GAPAN
30 Dec

Clark Field
PORAC
Del Carmen Field

SAN FERNANDO
2 Jan

CALUMPIT

24 Dec

DINALUPIHAN

OLONGAPO

MANILA
2 Jan

Nielson & Nichols Fields

Bataan
Peninsula

Manilla
Bay

Lamon
Bay

CAVITE

DAET

CORREGIDOR

MAUBAN

Laguna De Bay

ATIMONAN

TIAONG
29 Dec

SIAIN

CATANDUANES

Bicol Peninsula

BATANGAS

NAGA

BOAC

**12 Dec
Kimura Detachment**

LEGASPI

Mindoro

BURIAS

IROSIN

Sibuyan
Sea

0   MILES   100

0   KILOMETRES   150

SAN JOSE

The Japanese Invasion of Luzon, December 1941–January 1942

but many others resorted to brutality, beating stragglers and bayoneting or beheading those who had fallen. Over 7,000 died on the journey, more than 4,000 of them Filipinos. This manifestation of brutality in part reflected Japanese contempt for troops who chose to surrender rather than die in battle or commit suicide. But brutality was also a way of life to Japanese soldiers, whose superiors often treated them savagely. Not surprisingly, they responded with even more violent treatment of those who fell under their jurisdiction.

The Conquest of Malaya

Long before the end of resistance on Bataan and Corregidor, the Japanese had administered a defeat to the Allies that was far more devastating to their hopes and prestige: the conquest of Malaya and Britain's island fortress of Singapore at its southern tip.

British leaders had decided to build a naval base at Singapore in 1922, shortly after the Anglo-Japanese Alliance expired. They intended to base a fleet there as a deterrent to Japanese ambitions in Southeast Asia. To safeguard Singapore, they provided it with defenses that would repel any attack from the sea. But they built no fortifications on the north side of the island, despite the fact that this area offered little in the way of natural obstacles and lay across the narrow and shallow Strait of Johore from Malaya. The British did not consider such fortifications necessary. They assumed that the Japanese would not be so reckless as to try pushing their way through the supposedly impassable jungle of Malaya. Britain also established a number of airfields in Malaya that they intended to use as bases for the defense of Singapore. Unfortunately, funds were in short supply during the 1920s and 1930s, and with the outbreak of war in 1939, primary British concern focused on Europe and Britain. When Italy entered the conflict, the Middle East got second priority, leaving Singapore and Malaya a poor third on Britain's list of commitments.

Although British military leaders had asked for over 500 planes to defend Malaya and Singapore, only 158 were available when the Japanese struck, and most of them were obsolete. Despite their designation of Singapore as a naval base, the British

were unable to supply it with a permanent fleet. As war approached in late 1941, the only ships they could spare were the battleship *Prince of Wales* and the battle cruiser *Repulse*. But without a carrier or adequate land-based aircraft, these ships were dangerously vulnerable to air attack. The Admiralty opposed the decision to send the ships to Singapore. But Churchill stubbornly insisted, and they reached their destination shortly before the Japanese attacked Malaya. Their commander, Admiral Sir Tom Phillips, known as "Tom Thumb" because of his diminutive stature, had a long and distinguished career. Unfortunately, he had little recent sea experience, and perhaps even more ominous, he continued to insist that "bombers were no match for battleships."

Despite the obvious inadequacies of the British position, the myth developed that Singapore, the "Gibraltar of the Pacific," was impregnable, and nowhere was this belief stronger than in Singapore itself. The effect of the Singapore myth was not unlike that of the "Maginot mentality" in prewar France. The British also badly underestimated Japanese military capabilities. But not all British leaders were blind to Singapore's vulnerability to an attack from the north. General W. G. S. Dobbie, the army commander in Malaya during 1937–38, and his chief of staff, General Arthur Percival, insisted that the real danger to Singapore would come from Japanese landings in Malaya. Their appreciation led to a decision to extend the defense of Singapore to the whole of Malaya, but little was done to provide adequate defensive positions other than to build the airfields. Percival became commander in Malaya during the spring of 1941. Percival had led troops in World War I with considerable bravery and served in France during the debacle of 1940. Upon his return to Malaya, he recognized the weakness of his position. Although he possessed 89,000 troops, they were deficient in training and lacked modern weapons. Of these, only 20,000 were British; the rest of the force consisted of 37,000 Indians, 17,000 locally recruited soldiers, and 15,000 Australians. Given the vulnerability of the British position, they probably would have been wiser to focus on the defense of Johore state at the southern end of the Malay Peninsula and Singapore itself rather than all of Malaya.

Percival's opponent in the struggle for Malaya and Singapore was General Tomoyuki Yamashita. Yamashita was perhaps the best general in the Japanese army. He was also highly controversial. Some suspected him of complicity in the 1936 coup that had attempted to seize the government. Tojo had long regarded him as a dangerous rival. Yamashita deployed 70,000 troops, but a shortage of sea transport limited his initial force to only 17,000 men. They were among the best in the Japanese army, however, and possessed superior equipment.

On December 8, Japanese troops landed on Malaya's northeast coast. The first landing actually preceded the Pearl Harbor attack by more than an hour, because Malaya lay well to the west of the International Dateline and, thus, was a day ahead of Pearl Harbor time. Later that day, Admiral Phillips put to sea with *Prince of Wales, Repulse,* and four destroyers to raid enemy ships taking part in the invasion. But Phillips made the fatal error of moving north without air cover. Japanese high-level bombers and torpedo bombers attacked the British squadron on December 10 and sent both *Prince of Wales* and *Repulse* to the bottom, along with Phillips and 800 crewmen. With one blow, the Japanese had won supremacy in the waters off Southeast Asia.

On land, Yamashita's troops pushed southward with remarkable speed despite the heavy jungle and mountainous terrain. British commanders overestimated Japanese strength and were so fearful of being outflanked that they frequently ordered retreats before they were really necessary. The Japanese quickly captured the northern airfields, turning the supposed key to Singapore's defense against the British and assuring Japanese supremacy in the air. One Japanese column knifed southward along the east coast, while two others moved along the western shore. They consistently outmaneuvered and outwitted the enemy by infiltrating around their positions and carrying out a series of landings behind British lines. To facilitate their mobility, many of the Japanese sped southward on bicycles. When their tires suffered blowouts from the intense heat, they simply continued to ride on the rims. In fact, the clattering noise of the rims caused panic among some retreating Allied soldiers, who assumed that tanks were pursuing them. By January 31, the Japanese had driven the British out of Malaya and into Singapore.

Even after the disasters in Malaya, Percival still had 85,000 troops to defend the island. But morale was low, and many of the troops and much of the leadership were of questionable quality. The Japanese, by contrast, displayed their usual dash and enjoyed domination of the air. Percival also mistakenly thought that the Japanese would land on the northeast coast and thus placed his strongest force there. Instead, on February 8, they crossed the strait and quickly established a large beachhead on the northwestern shore. Although the defending force was twice as large as the attackers, the Japanese again outmaneuvered and outfought their opponents. They captured the island's main water supply and penetrated the suburbs of Singapore itself.

The Japanese were now experiencing a shortage of ammunition, and Yamashita feared that if forced into street fighting to take the city, they would lose the battle. To prevent this, he brazenly demanded that the Allied forces surrender. At first, Percival wanted to continue the fight, but his principal subordinate commanders urged capitulation in view of the loss of the reservoirs. When confronted by the specter of fire, sickness, and death as a result of the water shortage, Percival agreed, and fighting ceased on February 15. The surrender was a humiliating end for the "Gibraltar of the Pacific." It also dealt a mortal blow to British and, indeed, Western prestige among the peoples of Southeast Asia. Singapore had become such a symbol of European power in Asia that its fall shattered the myth of Western invincibility. Another wave of atrocities followed as Japanese soldiers bayoneted prisoners, including the wounded, and massacred many Chinese residents.

The East Indies: Dutch No More

The Dutch East Indies did not feel the sting of invasion until well after the initial assaults on the Philippines and Malaya. Japanese leaders recognized that the Dutch were far weaker than the Americans and British and concentrated on their stronger opponents first. But by early January 1942, the campaigns in the Philippines and

Malaya were clearly progressing toward victory, and the Japanese felt secure enough to strike at the East Indies and seize the long-coveted oil fields. They executed their first landings on January 11 on the northeastern coast of Borneo and a day later on the northern beaches of Celebes. In mid-February, Japanese troops landed on northern Sumatra. By the end of February, Japan controlled much of all three islands and had set the stage for an assault on Java, the principal island.

An Allied fleet of five cruisers and nine destroyers attempted to intercept the invasion convoy in the waters north of Java on February 27. The hastily assembled force included Dutch, U.S., British, and Australian ships and had no common tactical doctrine or signal code. It fell afoul of the enemy convoy's naval escort, consisting of four cruisers and 14 destroyers. Much of the ensuing Battle of the Java Sea took place after dark, and the Japanese were masters of night fighting. They sank two cruisers and three destroyers while suffering damage to just one of their own destroyers. The remaining three Allied cruisers managed to escape, only to succumb to other enemy naval units in the Battle of Sunda Strait off northwestern Java during the next two days. Japan had gained total supremacy in the waters around the island. Japanese troops landed at two points on Java's northern coast on March 1 and quickly overwhelmed the few defenders. Hostilities ended on March 8.

The Fall of Burma

While Japan was overrunning Malaya, Singapore, the Philippines, and the Dutch East Indies, its forces were also engaged in the conquest of Burma. This Texas-size British colony was strategically important because it bordered northern India on the east and contained the supply line to Chiang Kai-shek's Chinese forces. This route extended by rail and road from Rangoon, the capital and chief port, to Lashio 600 miles to the north and from there, via the Burma Road, to China. Japan's first penetration into Burma came as early as December 10 from neighboring Thailand. An independent country, Thailand had offered no resistance to the entry of Japanese

troops two days earlier. But the main invasion of Burma began 400 miles farther north on January 20 with a thrust toward Rangoon. Although Japanese forces were scanty, the British, Indian, and Burmese defenders were even weaker. Once again, the Japanese fought masterfully in the jungles, outmaneuvered the Allies and encircled Rangoon. But the defenders were able to escape through a gap in the Japanese forces. Rangoon fell on March 6.

The Japanese received reinforcements later in March and pursued the Allies northward up the country's three great river valleys. Chinese forces arrived in early April to help the British make a stand 150 miles south of Mandalay in central Burma. But a rapid Japanese advance up the Irrawaddy River and its tributary, the Chindwin, prevented this. Another Japanese column dashed toward Lashio. Allied forces now had no choice but to fall back toward the border of India, while the Japanese advanced up the Chindwin in an effort to cut off their withdrawal. The Allies won the race and reached the sanctuary of India by the middle of May, ending their 1,000-mile retreat from Rangoon.

As the Japanese advanced from Rangoon to Mandalay, their navy carried out a raid against the British naval base of Trincomalee on the island of Ceylon (now Sri Lanka) off the southeastern coast of India. Ceylon was vital strategically. If it should fall, the Japanese would menace not only southern India but also British supply lines around the southern tip of Africa to the Middle East, India, and Australia. To prevent this, Britain protected Ceylon with a substantial naval force, including three aircraft carriers and five battleships. Early in April, Admiral Nagumo led a Japanese task force, which featured five carriers and four battleships, into the Indian Ocean. He hoped to repeat his Pearl Harbor success, but British patrol planes warned Ceylon of the enemy approach. Although Nagumo's aircraft damaged port facilities and sank two cruisers and light aircraft carrier *Hermes,* most of the British fleet withdrew to safety.

The raid nevertheless convinced the British that their fleet at Ceylon was vulnerable to Japan's superior strength, and they diverted their ships to bases on the west coast of India and as far away as East

Africa. They also feared that the Japanese might send naval forces into the western Indian Ocean and threaten South Africa. To guard against such a possibility, they seized the port of Diego Suarez on French Madagascar in May and occupied the remainder of the island in September. The Japanese never again ventured even as far west as Ceylon.

By May 1942, Japan had reached the zenith of its power. Japanese forces dominated Southeast Asia and the Western Pacific. They threatened the Indian Ocean, Australia, and the Central Pacific. They had proved more than a match for their Western adversaries. But their days of victory were almost at an end.

CHAPTER FOURTEEN

The Struggle for the Initiative in the Pacific

The tide of battle in the Pacific began to turn when Japan suffered a series of setbacks between May and December 1942. The most spectacular of these took place at sea—the Battle of the Coral Sea in May, the Battle of Midway in June, and a series of bitter engagements in the waters off the Solomon Islands from August to November. Japanese fortunes on land also began to fade during the same period—on New Guinea and on Guadalcanal in the Solomons. By the end of the year, the balance had clearly shifted against Japan. But the United States had only tentatively taken the initiative. Many more months of bitter fighting and painfully slow progress lay ahead as Japan struggled to regain the upper hand. Not until late 1943 did the tide turn irrevocably against the Japanese. The key factor was America's far greater industrial base, which by then was in high gear and producing an ever increasing flow of ships, planes, and other kinds of war materiel that had not been available earlier. Japan, with its much weaker industrial capacity, could not even approach this remarkable achievement. Nevertheless, the first steps in the turning of the tide took place in 1942.

Japanese Strategy

Most of the first steps originated, not from American planning, but from Japanese initiatives that the army and navy high commands agreed to carry out only after a heated and prolonged debate over strategy. These arguments took place while Japan was winning victories in early 1942 and focused on proposals for possible operations in the late spring and early summer. Army leaders, who had insisted that Japan go to war with the United States in 1941, now were reluctant to engage in any major new offensives against America or Britain. They were more interested in an attack on the USSR if, as they expected,

Germany's projected summer offensive dealt the Soviets a mortal blow.

Naval leaders, who had been much more reluctant to go to war with America, now were eager to extend Japan's domination. But they did not agree on where to strike. Some urged the conquest of Ceylon, which would enable Japan to control the Indian Ocean and threaten India. Others preferred to thrust southward toward Australia. Still others insisted on striking eastward to seize Midway, an atoll over 1,000 miles northwest of Pearl Harbor. Admiral Osami Nagano, chief of the naval general staff, favored the second alternative. Admiral Yamamoto much preferred the third. Nagano was Yamamoto's superior and possessed the authority to overrule him. He had opposed Yamamoto's plan to attack Pearl Harbor, but after its success, he was reluctant to challenge him again.

Yamamoto won the argument, and Nagano agreed to an operation against Midway. He also abandoned thoughts of an invasion of Australia but nevertheless decided to seal off that continent partially before the Midway undertaking. He planned to accomplish this by capturing Port Moresby, on the southeastern coast of the island of New Guinea, and Tulagi in the southern Solomons. Japanese forces had landed at various points along the northern coast of New Guinea during the winter and spring and had seized the Admiralty Islands, New Britain, and New Ireland to the northeast as well as the northern islands of the Solomon chain. Once in control of New Britain, they took advantage of the outstanding natural harbor at Rabaul to build a powerful naval base. By extending their domination over the airfield at Port Moresby, the Japanese could protect Rabaul from air attack while securing a base from which to bomb northern Australia. By establishing a seaplane base on Tulagi, they could patrol the eastern waters of the Coral Sea between the Solomons and both New Guinea and Australia.

American Operations

Meanwhile, American leaders had reorganized the U.S. Navy's command structure. Shortly after Pearl Harbor, Admiral Ernest J. King became commander in chief of the U.S. Fleet, and Admiral Chester W. Nimitz took over as commander of the Pacific Fleet. King was a brilliant planner and administrator, but he was also arrogant and aloof. A veteran of the Spanish-American War, he had served as chief of staff in the Atlantic Fleet during World War I. While in this position, he developed a strong dislike of the British that, unfortunately, he never lost. King had commanded the Atlantic Fleet with distinction during 1941. The admiral viewed the war from a narrow focus that favored the navy's interest. He disagreed with the "Europe first" strategy and urged greater emphasis on the Pacific. Such an approach would certainly enhance the navy's role because naval power was the key to victory over Japan. Just as obviously, the army would be of primary importance in Europe. Indeed, King's insistence on the significance of the Pacific contributed greatly to the fact that it never became as secondary a theater of operations as Roosevelt and others had originally planned.

Nimitz, by contrast, was easygoing, well liked, and a team player. Roosevelt chose him over 28 senior officers to lead the Pacific Fleet, certainly one of his most inspired decisions. Nimitz's first task was to revive the fleet's shattered morale after the Pearl Harbor disaster, and he achieved this with remarkable speed. He did so largely by refusing to dismiss most of the members of Kimmel's staff and instead expressed complete confidence in them. They in turn gave him their complete loyalty. Nimitz proved to be a brilliant leader of men as well as a skilled strategist and tactician.

The new commander faced the awesome responsibility of holding a line from Midway to Australia against further Japanese encroachments with the relatively meager forces remaining after the Pearl Harbor attack. Their chief strength lay in the carriers *Saratoga, Lexington, Enterprise,* and *Hornet.* But a Japanese submarine damaged *Saratoga* in January 1942 and forced it to return to the U.S. West Coast for repairs. As its replacement,

Nimitz received *Yorktown* from the Atlantic Fleet. Fortunately for him, the Japanese navy was busy in the waters off Southeast Asia in the first few months of 1942 and made no move against his fleet.

Nimitz soon came into possession of another weapon that proved of tremendous value in the upcoming operations: Navy cryptanalysts had broken the Japanese naval code. By May, Nimitz possessed detailed information that made it clear that the Japanese intended to attack Midway as well as Port Moresby and Tulagi. Starting in the summer of 1942, it became standard practice to refer to information derived from the Japanese naval codes by the British name, Ultra. When the Americans broke the enemy's army code in the spring of 1943, this source of intelligence also came under the Ultra umbrella. The name Magic applied only to diplomatic ciphers.

While the Allies were suffering their depressing series of defeats during the first few months of 1942, Nimitz carried out minor offensive operations against the Japanese, with little success. Carrier-based planes from a task force commanded by Admiral William Halsey raided Wake and islands in the Caroline chain during February and Marcus Island, less than 1,000 miles from Tokyo, in March but inflicted only minor damage.

By far the most ambitious undertaking during this period was a daring attack by 16 army air force B-25 bombers on April 18. This force, under the leadership of Lieutenant Colonel James Doolittle, took off from the carrier *Hornet* 700 miles to the southeast of Japan and bombed Tokyo and several other Japanese cities. Most of the planes continued on to China where they either landed or crash landed. One wound up in the Soviet Union. Doolittle had already won fame for his daring peacetime exploits as a pilot and at one time held the world's record for air speed. His attack on Japan soon made him a national war hero. Although the raid did little damage, it provided a much needed psychological lift for the American people. It also came as a shock to the Japanese leaders and people, who had seen their sacred homeland violated by the enemy for the first time. Among those affected was Yamamoto, who feared that the raid indicated a gap in Japan's defenses that must be plugged. Roosevelt had quipped that the attack had originated from a secret base called

"Shangri-la," a reference to a mythical land that was the setting for the popular 1933 novel and 1937 film *Lost Horizon*. Yamamoto suspected erroneously that Midway might be Shangri-la. This belief reinforced his determination to strike at Midway and destroy the U.S. carriers.

Battle of the Coral Sea

Japanese leaders began their operations against Port Moresby and Tulagi in early May. They allotted strong naval forces to cover the landings, but this time the Americans were in a position to challenge them. Once his cryptanalysts had alerted Nimitz to the Japanese plan, he ordered a task force, under the command of Admiral Frank Jack Fletcher, to contest the enemy attempt to take Port Moresby. Fletcher's force included the carriers *Yorktown* and *Lexington*. Fletcher had no experience with carriers or airplanes before the war. He had this shortcoming in common with many of his colleagues, however, and it did not prevent him from gaining command of a carrier task force. Although popular with his fellow officers, he encountered criticism for poor seamanship and indecision during the abortive attempt to relieve Wake Island. One of Nimitz's staff officers later referred to him as "a big, nice, wonderful guy who didn't know his butt from third base."[*]

The Japanese occupied Tulagi without opposition on May 3. Meanwhile, the major invasion expedition headed southward from Rabaul toward Port Moresby under the protection of the light carrier *Shoho* and other naval units. At the same time, a more powerful task force converged on the Coral Sea from the Japanese base of Truk in the Carolines. It included the heavy carriers *Zuikaku* and *Shokaku*. The overall commander of the operation was Admiral Shigeyoshi Inouye, whose Fourth Fleet had attacked Guam and Wake in December. Inouye expected American naval units to intervene but assumed that his slightly stronger force would prevail. The Battle of the Coral Sea followed on May 7–8. It was the first naval engagement in history in which the opposing ships never came within sight of each other. Carrier-based planes provided all the firepower. The Japanese lost *Shoho,* and *Shokaku* sustained severe damage. On the American side, *Lexington* survived the effects of Japanese torpedoes and bombs but succumbed when a spark from a generator ignited gasoline fumes and caused a series of explosions. Japanese planes also seriously damaged *Yorktown.*

Tactically, the battle was a draw because the opposing fleets inflicted roughly equal punishment. But the United States won a strategic victory because Inouye became so concerned about his losses that he called off the landing at Port Moresby. Even more important, both *Shokaku* and *Zuikaku* had to return to Japan, the former for extensive repairs and the latter for fresh planes and pilots. Neither was available when Yamamoto's forces steamed for Midway. The Battle of the Coral Sea was not decisive, but it clearly marked a shift in momentum, one that continued.

Battle of Midway

The really crucial battle came at Midway. Yamamoto assumed that American naval forces would intervene in strength if Japan threatened Midway. This would provide the opportunity for the Combined Fleet to finish the job it had started with the Pearl Harbor attack—the destruction of the U.S. Pacific Fleet, especially its carriers. Yamamoto based his strategy on the premise that Japan would not be secure until it had eliminated the Pacific Fleet. His thinking was undoubtedly sound, but his plan was faulty.

Its most serious flaw was the provision for too many objectives. This diluted Japanese strength. Yamamoto called for a secondary assault on two of the Aleutian Islands, Attu and Kiska, which lay many hundreds of miles to the west of Alaska. Although he hoped this operation would divert U.S. ships and planes away from the Midway area, it shifted Japanese strength from the major objective as well. And his insistence on the occupation of Midway also distracted attention from the main purpose of the plan: to lure the Pacific Fleet into a showdown battle. His forces could accomplish this by their mere presence in the waters near Midway.

Yamamoto also failed to concentrate the strength he had earmarked for the Midway operation. His

---

[*]Gordon W. Prange with Donald M. Goldstein and Katherine V. Dillon, *Miracle at Midway* (New York: Penguin Books, 1983), p. 97.

plan provided for Admiral Nagumo's carrier striking force to perform two missions: an air strike against Midway's land-based aircraft and an attack on the Pacific Fleet when it intervened. Yamamoto was convinced that U.S. forces would not move westward until after the Japanese had taken Midway. But if the Americans should intervene earlier, they might catch Nagumo's force while his planes were assaulting Midway and his carriers were most vulnerable to air attack. Other Japanese naval units were to provide close support for the Midway invasion force. Meanwhile, Yamamoto himself planned to remain far to the rear with what he referred to as the Main Body, consisting of three battleships and supporting vessels. He intended to bring this force into action against the Americans when the opportune time came. But he placed the Main Body so far to the west that the showdown battle might be over before it could act.

Nagano and his naval staff pointed out many of these weaknesses. They discounted the importance of occupying Midway and warned that it was unlikely that the Japanese could again catch the Americans by surprise. But Yamamoto enjoyed such massive prestige that his plan won approval. The navy set early June as the target date for the attack on Midway. Yamamoto and other Japanese naval leaders also suffered from what they later described as "victory disease." They had grown so accustomed to winning one great triumph after another that they became arrogant and assumed that they would overcome all obstacles. Even the members of the naval staff who criticized Yamamoto's plan most vehemently never doubted that their forces would succeed.

Despite the flaws in Yamamoto's plan and the breaking of the Japanese naval code, Nimitz's forces were considerably weaker than those of the enemy. Yamamoto's total strength included four heavy carriers—*Akagi, Kaga, Hiryu,* and *Soryu*—and two light carriers as well as seven battleships, 15 cruisers, and 44 destroyers. To counter this huge armada, Nimitz had three carriers, eight cruisers, and 15 destroyers under the command of Admiral Fletcher. Two of the carriers, *Enterprise* and *Hornet,* formed the core of a task force under the command of Admiral Raymond Spruance. The hastily patched-up *Yorktown* provided the nucleus of a second small task force under Fletcher's direct control.

Nimitz had selected Spruance as a last-minute replacement for Halsey, who had to be hospitalized because of a severe skin condition. At first glance, Spruance might seem a poor choice. His prior sea experience had been as commander of destroyers, cruisers, and a battleship. He was, thus, a member of what naval aviators referred to disparagingly as the "gun club." Unlike the effervescent Fletcher and Halsey, Spruance had gained a reputation among other officers as cold and humorless. But he remained calm and cautious in action while demonstrating a flair for making the right decisions and taking advantage of opportunities. His performance in the forthcoming battle ended any doubts as to his ability.

Whereas Nimitz was aware of Japanese intentions and deployed his strength accordingly, Yamamoto was ignorant of the location of the Pacific Fleet. He assumed that Nimitz knew nothing of his plans and would not be able to intervene until after Midway had fallen. The Japanese also incorrectly believed that they had sunk *Yorktown* in the Battle of the Coral Sea, and Yamamoto expected to face, at most, two American carriers. His plan called for Japanese submarines to provide early warning of the Pacific Fleet's westward movement. However, due largely to the misconceived certainty that the Americans would not move prior to the Midway attack, the submarines were slow to take up their designated positions to the west of Oahu. When they finally did, U.S. naval forces had already passed far beyond that point and were waiting to ambush the enemy carrier striking force from the northeast.

Nagumo's fleet penetrated to within 250 miles of Midway on June 4. It launched an attack on the atoll while sending out reconnaissance planes to search for any U.S. ships that might be in the area. But the Japanese carried out their search with neither a sense of urgency nor their usual efficiency, and hours elapsed before they discovered the presence of American vessels. Meanwhile, Japanese planes damaged installations on Midway and destroyed 17 aircraft. They were preparing for a second attack when a search plane finally spotted elements of the Pacific Fleet. Before Nagumo could react to this unwelcome news, wave after wave of American torpedo planes attacked the Japanese carriers. But they failed to damage their targets and fell victim to Japanese Zero fighters and withering antiaircraft fire. They managed, nevertheless, to disperse the Zeros, and when U.S. dive bombers pressed home their attacks soon afterward, they scored several direct hits on *Soryu, Akagi,* and *Kaga,* turning them all into blazing hulks.

Only *Hiryu* remained, and its planes took off in search of the American carriers. They found Fletcher's flagship, *Yorktown.* The first wave of dive bombers scored three hits, and the second assault by torpedo bombers added two more. Even now *Yorktown* might have survived, but two days later, enemy submarine I-168 fired another pair of torpedoes into its side. This time there was no escape. But *Hiryu* was doomed, too. American dive bombers attacked and set it ablaze. Within a short time, the last of Nagumo's heavy carriers joined the three others on the bottom.

When Yamamoto received news of the Japanese disaster, he belatedly attempted to intervene with the battleships of his Main Body. He hoped to attack the Pacific Fleet in a night engagement. The Japanese had proved themselves masters in this type of encounter. But Spruance, who had succeeded to operational control of the Pacific Fleet when Fletcher had to abandon *Yorktown,* refused to risk his carriers and withdrew to the east. When Yamamoto discovered this, he, too, reluctantly pulled back. His Main Body, which had not fired a shot, might just as well have remained in Japanese waters.

Midway was a crucial victory for two reasons. It had foiled Yamamoto's second attempt to destroy the Pacific Fleet, and it had reduced Japan's overwhelming numerical advantage in carriers. Not only had the Japanese squandered four carriers, but they had lost 253 planes and their skilled pilots. Neither their carrier force nor their naval air power were ever the same after this demoralizing defeat. Nevertheless, the Japanese navy still remained powerful and for some time numerically superior to the Pacific Fleet. In the months that followed, the two enemies would struggle for supremacy on both land and sea, while the strategic initiative hung in the balance.

Small Victories, Big Defeats

Yamamoto's only success was the capture of Attu and Kiska in the Aleutians, but this was a dubious achievement. The Japanese forces, which occupied these remote and desolate northern islands, faced an ominous future after the defeat at Midway.

On land, the Japanese continued to hold the initiative, but their days of ascendancy were dwindling. After the failure of their plan to capture Port Moresby by a seaborne operation, they attempted to take it by land. This was no easy task. It involved pushing southward along a narrow, perpetually muddy trail, known as the Kokoda Track, which ran from Buna on New Guinea's northeastern coast across the rugged, rain-swept, and jungle-choked Owen Stanley Mountains. The Japanese pushed southward from Buna in late July and by August 26 had penetrated to within 30 miles of Port Moresby. But their drive bogged down due to supply problems, the difficult terrain, and stiffening resistance from Australian troops. In mid-September, they abandoned their attempt to take Port Moresby.

The Australians launched a counteroffensive on September 28 but encountered ferocious Japanese resistance and did not reach the Buna area until mid-November. Australian and American troops now slowly hammered away at skillfully constructed enemy defenses, featuring bunkers made from coconut tree logs. The Japanese fought with fanatical determination, preferring suicide charges to surrender, but eventually the Allies prevailed. Buna fell on January 2, 1943. It was now clear that the tide had turned against Japan in New Guinea.

Battles for the Solomon Islands

Even before the Japanese drive on Port Moresby had halted on the Kokoda Track, American forces had launched their first offensive in the southern Solomon Islands. Initially, U.S. leaders had merely intended to take Tulagi and neighboring Gavutu. But when they discovered that enemy troops had landed on nearby Guadalcanal and were constructing an airstrip there, they decided to attack it as well. Although Guadalcanal had been something of an afterthought, this little-known island became the site of a desperate struggle that lasted for six months.

Admiral Robert Ghormley, the U.S. naval commander in the South Pacific, held overall responsibility for the invasion. The site of Ghormley's headquarters was Nouméa, on the French island of New Caledonia, which had sided with de Gaulle.

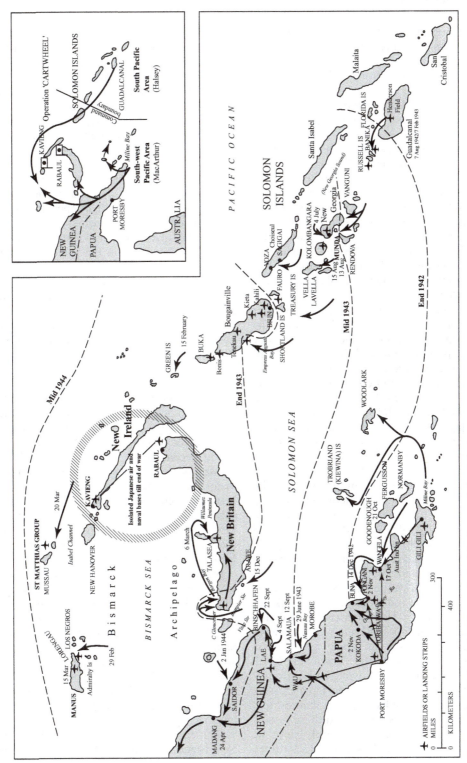

Eastern New Guinea, the Bismarck Archipelago and the Solomons

Although Nouméa lay 900 miles to the southeast of Guadalcanal, it was the nearest deep-water port with reasonably adequate facilities. Nouméa was also almost 6,500 miles from San Francisco. Its remote location from both the source of supplies and the fighting front, along with a chronic shortage of shipping, created a highly difficult logistic situation.

Ghormley had to make do with land and sea forces that were so slender and so hastily assembled that Operation Watchtower earned the nickname "Operation Shoestring". Eleven thousand marines, under the command of General Alexander Vandegrift, landed on Guadalcanal on August 7. Vandegrift was a quiet, modest man known for his fatherly concern for his troops. When first informed of his mission, he confessed that he had no idea as to the location of Guadalcanal. Smaller forces invaded Tulagi and Gavutu and by the next day had overcome the fierce resistance of their tiny garrisons. The Guadalcanal landing surprised the meager Japanese defenders, and they offered no opposition but withdrew into the jungle. They even abandoned their airstrip, which the Americans seized and christened Henderson Field after Major Loften R. Henderson, a marine pilot who had died at Midway.

Once Japanese leaders recovered from their initial shock, they set out to drive the marines into the sea and immediately dispatched reinforcements to Guadalcanal under the command of General Kiyotake Kawaguchi. A veteran of the Philippine campaign, Kawaguchi immediately recognized that Guadalcanal would become a vital point in the Pacific war and was determined to dislodge the Americans.

In the following weeks and months, Japanese troop transports and supply ships repeatedly made night runs down the narrow channel separating the western Solomons from the eastern islands in the chain. The Americans called this body of water "The Slot" and referred to the nocturnal Japanese naval missions under Rear Admiral Raizo Tanaka as the "Tokyo Express." Although the defeat at Midway had seriously weakened their carrier force, the Japanese still had a considerable advantage in battleships, cruisers, and destroyers. They used these vessels to escort their transports and supply ships as well as to bombard Henderson Field. At times

they also attempted to interdict American reinforcements and supplies that converged on Guadalcanal during daylight hours.

The struggle for Guadalcanal became largely one of supply, and the side that maintained its flow while cutting off the enemy's would ultimately win. The issue remained in doubt for months. Kawaguchi's troops launched savage attacks against marines defending Henderson Field. During the night of September 13, they tried repeatedly to break through a position that became known fittingly as Bloody Ridge. The marines repulsed them each time, killing over half the attacking force while suffering heavy casualties themselves. Early in October, General Harukichi Hyakutake, the Japanese commander in the Solomons, took personal control of the battle. But he was no more successful than Kawaguchi.

Guadalcanal was an abominable place to fight a war. Most of it consisted of rugged mountains, dense jungles, and malaria-ridden swamps. The heat and humidity were constant and oppressive. Both sides suffered from the appalling conditions and from some of the most ferocious fighting of the entire Pacific war. Despite continued fanatical Japanese attacks, which often featured suicide banzai charges, the marines held out night after night, week after week, month after month. Fresh army forces finally relieved the exhausted garrison in December.

Meanwhile, the rival fleets fought a series of six major naval engagements and many minor ones between August and November in an effort to gain control of the sea and win the battle of supply. Most of these encounters took place at night and involved primarily cruisers and destroyers. The Japanese continued to demonstrate their mastery of night fighting, utilizing trained night vision and searchlights, and took a heavy toll of American ships, although they, too, suffered serious losses. But two of the clashes occurred in daylight and featured attacks by carrier-based aircraft. Savo Sound, the body of water between Guadalcanal and Tulagi, claimed so many ships from both fleets that the Americans nicknamed it "Ironbottom Sound," because this large concentration of submerged metal skewed magnetic compasses, creating a navigation problem.

The first of these encounters, the Battle of Savo Island, unfolded on the night of August 8–9,

FIGURE 14-1   Marine landing craft head for the enemy shore after a combined naval and aerial bombardment (*National Archives and Records Administration*)

soon after the marine landings. It gained its name from the volcanic island at the entrance to "Iron-bottom Sound" and ended in a Japanese victory. A Japanese cruiser squadron overwhelmed a somewhat makeshift Allied force, sinking one Australian and three American cruisers and severely damaging another as well as several destroyers. The Japanese lost only one cruiser to a submarine attack after the battle ended. It was one of the worst defeats ever suffered by the U.S. Navy. But the Japanese missed an opportunity to destroy the American transports off Guadalcanal and Tulagi. Instead, with the approach of dawn, Admiral Gumichi Mikawa withdrew his ships because he feared air attacks by carrier-based planes. But Admiral Fletcher, who had led U.S. forces in the Coral Sea and at Midway, had already pulled back his three carriers—*Saratoga, Enterprise,* and *Wasp*—because he feared a Japanese air strike. Their departure left the transports completely exposed to an attack, which fortunately never came.

Fletcher was less timid in the Battle of the Eastern Solomons later the same month. His carrier planes intercepted an enemy supply convoy and its supporting carrier force. They sank the light carrier *Ryujo,* but Japanese aircraft damaged *Enterprise.* Marine planes from Henderson Field

also destroyed an enemy cruiser and a supply ship. Their losses convinced the Japanese that daylight runs were too risky, and they returned to the night-time Tokyo Express. But Japanese submarines remained a constant menace. Torpedo attacks mortally wounded *Wasp* and put *Saratoga* and the battleship *North Carolina* out of action until November.

In the Battle of Cape d'Esperance on the night of October 11–12, U.S. warships used radar to detect the approach of an enemy convoy off Guadalcanal's northwest coast. They sank a destroyer and a cruiser while losing a destroyer. Soon afterward, Admiral Nimitz concluded that the Guadalcanal operation required more aggressive and inspiring leadership than Admiral Ghormley was able to provide. He replaced him with Admiral Halsey.

The new commander was a man of action in the swashbuckling naval tradition, preferring to act quickly and boldly without too much thought for the consequences. He believed in carrying the fight to the enemy with unrelenting persistence. Unlike most of the leading American admirals at this time, Halsey was an aviator. When the war began, he was America's most experienced carrier task force commander. He was exceptionally outgoing and enjoyed the respect and love of his men. While Spruance, the victor of Midway, earned renown as "an admiral's admiral," Halsey was clearly "a sailor's admiral."

Halsey decided to bring the carriers into action again in an effort to gain the initiative. The result was another daylight encounter near the Santa Cruz Islands to the east of Guadalcanal on October 26. Aircraft from a task force commanded by Admiral Thomas Kinkaid, a veteran of the Battle of the Coral Sea, attacked and damaged the Japanese carriers *Zuiho* and *Shokaku*. But the Americans paid a heavy price as enemy planes sent the carrier *Hornet* to the bottom and damaged *Enterprise's* flight deck. The battle ended in a tactical victory for the Japanese, but their heavy losses in planes and pilots tended to nullify their advantage.

The fifth and decisive clash, the Battle of Guadalcanal, took place on November 12–15 near the entrance to Ironbottom Sound. A large Japanese force tried to protect a landing of reinforcements and supplies on Guadalcanal. A much smaller U.S. squadron rashly steamed forward to engage the enemy at close range. It crippled the old battleship *Hiei* and sank two destroyers while losing one cruiser and four destroyers. At this point both forces withdrew, but the following day the Japanese submarine I-26, which had already sunk the *Wasp,* torpedoed the light cruiser *Juneau,* which went down with the loss of 600 men, including the five Sullivan brothers. Torpedo planes from the carrier *Enterprise* finished off the *Hiei* the same day. That night Japanese cruisers bombarded Henderson Field, but on the 14th, navy and marine pilots sank a heavy cruiser and no fewer than seven troop transports. In the evening, the Japanese returned with the battleship *Kirishima,* four cruisers, and nine destroyers. This time they encountered two new American battleships—*Washington* and *South Dakota*—and four destroyers. At midnight another savage engagement followed as searchlight beams and the flashes of big guns illuminated the sky. The Japanese sank three destroyers and crippled *South Dakota,* but *Washington,* with its radar fire control, sank *Kirishima.* Soon after, the Japanese withdrew once again, leaving the U.S. Navy in control of the waters around Guadalcanal. At dawn on the 15th, American land and carrier-based planes destroyed the remaining four enemy transports.

Japanese forces tried again to land supplies on November 30, precipitating the sixth and final major battle. It took place off Guadalcanal's Tassafaronga Point. This time the Americans outnumbered the enemy. But again the Japanese demonstrated their skill in night fighting. They outmaneuvered the U.S. ships, sank a cruiser, and inflicted serious damage on three more at the cost of only one of their own destroyers. Despite this victory, Japanese leaders concluded that their navy could not continue to absorb losses like those they had been suffering since August and reluctantly agreed to abandon Guadalcanal. In early February 1943, they gradually and skillfully evacuated their forces despite U.S. naval superiority. By February 9, the Americans controlled the entire island.

Guadalcanal was in many respects as pivotal a victory as Midway. The United States had forced the Japanese out of the bitterly-contested island and before long would take the offensive up the Solomon chain. Although it had suffered heavy losses at sea, the U.S. Navy was able to obtain replacements and continued to press the attack in the following months. Japan was not so fortunate. The Japanese had staked a great deal on stopping this first Allied offensive and had failed. In the process, they had lost their reputation for invincibility in land warfare, and their naval power, so badly shaken at Midway, had suffered still another setback.

A War of Savage Hatred

The grim struggles on New Guinea and Guadalcanal also increased American hatred of the Japanese, which had been growing since the start of the war. The Japanese assault on Pearl Harbor, which Americans invariably referred to as a "sneak attack," was the most important factor in the prevailing view of the Japanese as treacherous and devoid of all decency. The Bataan Death March and reports of atrocities that accompanied Japanese conquests in East Asia and the Pacific also contributed significantly to the American image of the Asian enemy. Americans were especially outraged when a Japanese court condemned eight U.S. airmen to death for their participation in the Doolittle raid on Japan. These men had been captured after they crash landed in occupied China. Only three were actually executed, however, while the sentences of five others were commuted to life in prison. The film *The Purple Heart,* released in 1944, presented a dramatic and sensational account of this trial.

These examples of Japanese brutality combined with a long tradition of American racial prejudice toward Asians created a hatred far more virulent than that toward the Germans and Italians. Despite the enormity of German crimes against Jews and other peoples, Americans tended to distinguish between good and bad Germans rather than brand the entire population as brutal or degenerate. Such was not the case with their perceptions of the Japanese. They saw them as far different from other people—savage and bloodthirsty. Cartoonists habitually portrayed them as monkeys or apes. Virtually all Americans, both military personnel and civilians, called them "Japs," although marines in the Pacific often preferred "Japes." Hollywood films presented them as far more inhuman, sadistic, and treacherous than their German or Italian counterparts. In 1944, *Newsweek* quoted Admiral Halsey as contending that the "only good Jap is one who's been dead for six months." Ernie Pyle, the revered correspondent, who covered the war at close range both in Europe and the Pacific, after seeing a few Japanese prisoners, admitted that "they give me the creeps."*

Despite the American belief that only the enemy committed atrocities, some U.S. marines and soldiers in the Pacific shot Japanese wounded and prisoners and kept body parts as souvenirs, sometimes even fashioning necklaces and bracelets

*Quoted in John W. Dower, *War Without Mercy: Race and Power in the Pacific War* (New York: Pantheon Books, 1986), p. 78.

from their teeth. To be sure, Japan's military code, with its insistence on fighting to the death, banzai suicide charges, prohibition of surrender, and generally brutal treatment of prisoners and wounded contributed to this, as did the Japanese practice of booby-trapping their dead and wounded.

Hatred was a two-way street, however. Japanese soldiers and civilians tended to look upon their American enemies as self-indulgent, greedy, and bent on exploiting the peoples of Asia as well as opposing Japan's right to do the same thing. They also bitterly resented American opposition to Japan's proposal for a racial equality clause in the League of Nations Covenant as well as U.S. immigration policy with its anti-Japanese bias. Japan was not as overtly racist in its wartime propaganda as was the United States, however. Instead, official government policy stressed the supposedly unique qualities of the Japanese people, contending that they were more virtuous than Westerners because of their alleged descent from the gods as well as the purity and continuity of their ethnic blood and culture. Nevertheless, the Japanese media did seek to dehumanize the Americans, and their cartoons portrayed them as monsters or demons.

Nevertheless, the animosity between Japanese and Americans pales when compared to the unprecedented ferocity of the European war on the Eastern Front. There, of course, the conflict became a war of ideologies in which both sides participated in mass murder of prisoners of war and civilians alike on a regular basis. And, despite their mutual dislike, the Americans were able to adopt enlightened occupation policies in Japan when the war ended, and the Japanese accepted their fate with surprising resignation.

CHAPTER FIFTEEN

America Gains
the Initiative
in the Pacific

The bitter struggle for supremacy in the Pacific following the American victory at Midway persisted into 1943, and the outcome hung in the balance until late that year. Although the Allies continued to advance in the difficult terrain of both New Guinea and the Solomons, progress remained heartbreakingly slow, and Japanese resistance continued to be tenacious and fanatical. Meanwhile, the rival fleets battled for domination in the surrounding waters. Nevertheless, the Allies took an increasing toll of enemy resources on land and especially at sea and in the air. As time passed, America also transformed its vast industrial potential into actual production of ships, planes, and other weapons on a scale that Japan's smaller industrial base could not even approach.

Starting with an American amphibious assault on the Gilbert Islands in November, it became clear that the initiative had definitely passed to the Allies. In the following months Allied forces won victory after victory in New Guinea and the nearby islands, bringing them within striking distance of the Philippines, while a series of American operations in the Central Pacific brought them ever closer to Japan itself.

Questions of Strategy and Leadership

As this process unfolded, the United States and its allies grappled with vexing questions of strategy—where and how to strike at the enemy with greatest effect. They also confronted the problem of leadership. Should there be unity or division of command over operations in the vast Pacific? Since Britain devoted its strength overwhelmingly to the war in Europe and to a lesser extent to the defense of India and the proposed reconquest of Burma, the war in the Pacific became primarily an American responsibility. In view of this disparity,

American interservice and personal rivalries assumed key importance in the development of strategy.

Early in the conflict, when the Japanese still held the initiative, Admiral King and other naval leaders looked forward to the time when the United States could take the offensive. They visualized Admiral Nimitz as the supreme commander of this great enterprise. But General MacArthur, the hero of Bataan, had other ideas. His defense of the Philippines, though in many respects disastrously inadequate, had captured the imagination of the American people. Even though President Roosevelt had originally proposed one commander for the entire Pacific, MacArthur's dramatic escape from the Philippines and his great popularity contributed to the decision to divide responsibilities between the general and Nimitz.

MacArthur became commander in chief of Allied forces in the Southwest Pacific, an area that included Australia, the Solomons, New Guinea, the Bismarck Archipelago, the Philippines, and all the Dutch Indies except Sumatra. Nimitz, in addition to retaining his command over the Pacific Fleet, became commander in chief of the North, Central, and South Pacific theaters of operations. He also assumed direct command over the North and Central Pacific, while Admiral Ghormley carried out this duty in the South Pacific under Nimitz's overall direction. The Southwest Pacific, thus, became an army responsibility. The other Pacific areas became navy preserves. Britain retained operational control over Burma and the rest of Southeast Asia, including Sumatra.

During the first two years of the war, planning focused on the great naval base that enemy forces had created at Rabaul on the island of New Britain. Control of Rabaul enabled the Japanese to support their forces, which had penetrated into

New Guinea to the southwest and the Solomons to the southeast. In March 1942, Admiral King proposed a counteroffensive that would feature simultaneous drives through New Guinea and the Solomons before converging on Rabaul. Soon after the Battle of Midway, MacArthur urged a thrust directly on Rabaul without the preliminaries in New Guinea and the Solomons. He spoke of accomplishing this in less than three weeks with the aid of a naval task force. Clearly such a daring stroke was far beyond American capabilities at

this time. MacArthur probably realized this, but his proposal catapulted him into the forefront of the strategic debate. Once confronted by the objections of naval leaders, he quickly agreed that a more gradual approach was indeed preferable. He insisted that since such an operation would take place in his Southwest Pacific theater, it was only just that he should assume command. But King contended that since the participation of large-scale naval forces would be absolutely essential, Nimitz should be the commander.

Assault on Japan, 1942–45

King and General Marshall finally settled this argument by dividing responsibilities between Nimitz and MacArthur. They shifted the boundary between the Southwest and South Pacific commands slightly to the west to bring the southern Solomons within the latter area. Their agreement called for an advance in the Solomons by forces under Ghormley's command while MacArthur cleared the northeastern coast of New Guinea. When the two commanders had successfully carried out these tasks, they would launch converging attacks against Rabaul. The opening phase of this ambitious undertaking culminated in the capture of Buna on the New Guinea coast in January 1943 and the Japanese evacuation from Guadalcanal a month later.

The navy also favored a thrust through the Marshall, Caroline, and Mariana islands in the Central Pacific. King considered this the most direct route to the Japanese home islands. The key to the success of a Central Pacific strategy was the capture or neutralization of another major Japanese naval base, at Truk in the Carolines. MacArthur much preferred a drive along the northern coast of New Guinea followed by a thrust through the Philippines to Japan. Such an approach would, of course, take place within his Southwest Pacific theater, enabling him to make good his pledge to return to the Philippines.

The navy was probably correct in its belief that the Central Pacific offered the superior route. It certainly was more direct and would facilitate concentration of resources for maximum effect. And because the Marshalls, Carolines, and Marianas consisted of over 1,000 far-flung small islands, the navy could pick its invasion targets. The Japanese clearly could not defend all these islands but would have to stretch their forces thinly to provide for the defense of as many as possible. Finally, the conquest of the Marianas would bring the cities of Japan within range of American long-range bombers while isolating the Solomons, New Guinea, and Rabaul, leaving them to "wither on the vine" in the rear of the American onslaught.

Once again, this dispute over navy and army objectives resulted in a compromise. In April 1943, the Joint Chiefs of Staff opted for a two-pronged strategy that employed both the navy's Central Pacific approach and MacArthur's route. They based their decision in part on the belief that the expenditure in blood, materiel, and effort in the Solomons and New Guinea had been too great simply to terminate these operations. But they designated the Central Pacific as the primary theater and proposed to devote the lion's share of naval strength to this area.

Both offensives employed a bypassing technique. This involved capturing islands or parts of islands and then moving several hundred miles to other objectives, followed by another leap and then another. In the process, the two offensives bypassed many Japanese-held islands, kept the enemy guessing as to where the next blow would come, and made it most difficult for them to concentrate their forces effectively.

American Moves in the North Pacific

There was also the less important matter of the North Pacific. Japanese troops still held the barren, fog-shrouded Aleutian islands of Kiska and Attu, which they had seized at the time of the Battle of Midway. These forces, however, were too weak to attempt additional landings in the eastern Aleutians or Alaska. The United States probably would have been wise simply to allow them to remain on their bleak outposts while seeking more important objectives elsewhere. But fear that the enemy garrisons might pose a threat to Alaska led to the decision to invade Attu, the more weakly defended of the two islands, on May 11, 1943.

With a 5-to-1 advantage in numbers, the U.S. Army's 7th Division landed without opposition on two sides of Attu. But once ashore, the Americans found themselves subjected to savage artillery, mortar, and machine-gun fire. Snow and mud added to their difficulties as they slogged slowly inland. The defenders resisted grimly until the end of the month, engaging in repeated desperation charges. Almost the entire garrison of 2,600 men fought to the death or committed suicide. The Americans next turned their attention to Kiska. Bombers attacked the island repeatedly, starting in July. But when U.S. troops actually landed on August 15, they discovered that the Japanese had evacuated their garrison two weeks earlier under cover of fog.

Action in the Southwest Theater

Meanwhile, following the capture of Buna and Guadalcanal in early 1943, the Joint Chiefs of Staff again took up the thorny question of command in New Guinea and the Solomons. Since the northern Solomons lay within the boundaries of MacArthur's Southwest Pacific theater, the Joint Chiefs agreed that the general would exercise strategic command over both areas. But Admiral Halsey would retain tactical control in the Solomons under MacArthur's general directives. Halsey had succeeded Ghormley as commander of Allied forces in the South Pacific during the Guadalcanal campaign. The Joint Chiefs also laid down guidelines for the strategy that MacArthur and Halsey were to carry out during 1943. The two commanders then hammered out a final plan, code-named Operation Cartwheel, in April. It provided for MacArthur to persevere in his advance along New Guinea's northern coast and ultimately to undertake a landing on New Britain's western shore. At the same time, Halsey's forces were to push north, up the Solomons "ladder."

Before these operations could begin, MacArthur's air commander, General George C. Kenney, led his 5th Air Force to a rousing victory against a Japanese convoy in the Bismarck Sea to the north of New Britain. An exceptionally dynamic man, Kenney insisted on maintaining complete control over air operations himself. When MacArthur's chief of staff, General Sutherland, tried to interfere, he informed him in the most emphatic terms that when it came to air operations, he was the expert and Sutherland was the novice.

Land-based bombers had accomplished little in either the New Guinea or Guadalcanal campaigns before Kenney took over in August 1942. They had operated at high altitudes, in keeping with air force doctrine, but Kenney decided to experiment with low-level attacks by B-25 Mitchell medium bombers. These planes, named for the famous advocate of strategic airpower, General William ("Billy") Mitchell, were modified with eight .50 caliber machine guns in the nose for strafing and practiced skip-bombing runs during the fall and winter of 1942–43 from altitudes as low as 150 feet. By the end of the winter, they had mastered this art and were ready to try it on the enemy.

Their opportunity came when Ultra reports indicated that a Japanese convoy of eight troop transports and eight destroyers had left Rabaul on March 1 bound for New Guinea through the Bismarck Sea. Kenney sent B-17s to bomb the convoy from high altitude in the usual manner. But after two such attacks, which sank two transports, B-25s and other medium bombers zoomed in at low level the next day and sank five transports as well as four destroyers. PT boats finished off the last transport that night. Almost 3,000 enemy troops lost their lives. For the first time, land-based bombers had destroyed a Japanese convoy without the aid of naval forces. This placed a premium on such air power in the future and strengthened the American resolve to obtain advance air bases that would bring more remote Japanese strongholds within striking range of U.S. bombers.

Admiral Yamamoto now had to face the fact that the Americans were gaining air superiority in the Southwest Pacific. Yamamoto sought to reverse this trend by sending over 300 planes on a series of raids against Guadalcanal and Tulagi as well as Allied bases in New Guinea during April. But this effort proved ineffective, as the Japanese suffered aircraft losses at least equal to those that they inflicted on the Allies.

Some of the inexperienced pilots who took part in the operation believed that their efforts had been far more successful than was actually the case, however. Their optimistic reports misled Yamamoto, who decided to visit the northernmost island of the Solomons, Bougainville, to congratulate his supposedly victorious flyers. This proved a fatal mistake. American cryptanalysts intercepted messages containing detailed information on the admiral's trip. Eighteen P-38 Lightning fighters were waiting for his bomber and its escort of nine Zeros as they approached southern Bougainville on April 18. One of the P-38s shot down the admiral's plane, killing the architect of the attack on Pearl Harbor. Yamamoto had chosen his own successor, Admiral Mineichi Koga, as commander of the Combined Fleet. Though capable and efficient, Koga lacked his predecessor's strategic ability and adopted a conservative and unimaginative approach to the war.

By June 1943, Halsey and MacArthur were ready to launch their new operations in the

Solomons and New Guinea. The two key targets in the Solomons were New Georgia, which lay to the northwest of Guadalcanal, and Bougainville. Successful landings on these islands would enable Halsey's forces to bypass most of the remainder of the Solomons and provide air bases for raids against Rabaul.

The attack on New Georgia began with landings along the island's southeastern coast late in June. Americans also went ashore on neighboring Rendova Island. Within artillery range of southwestern New Georgia, Rendova provided a convenient jumping-off point for the major invasion near the chief Japanese base at Munda on July 2. Although the inexperienced 43rd Army Division went ashore without opposition, it soon encountered extremely rugged terrain and made agonizingly slow progress against Japanese forces, who held the high ground before Munda. The division's morale became so poor and combat fatigue cases so prevalent that Halsey had to send in two additional army divisions.

The Americans were not able to make a concerted effort to take the airfield at Munda until July 25. Numerous well-situated coconut-log-and-coral pillboxes barred their way. But incessant artillery, air, and naval bombardment gradually took a heavy toll on the defenders, as did that fearsome weapon, the flamethrower, which made its first extensive appearance in the Pacific war. By July 29, the highly capable and resourceful Japanese commander, General Noburu Sasaki, realized that additional resistance was futile and began to withdraw his forces to Kolombangara Island just to the northwest. Munda airfield fell to the Americans on August 5.

Halsey opted to bypass Kolombangara with its garrison of 12,000 troops, and on August 5, he sent 4,500 men ashore on lightly defended Vella Lavella, which lay to the northwest. These forces quickly occupied the island and confronted General Sasaki with the alternative of leaving his troops on Kolombangara to wither on the vine or withdrawing them to Bougainville. He chose the latter, and in late September and early October, the Japanese carried out a nighttime evacuation.

As in the Guadalcanal campaign, rival naval forces fought a series of engagements while the battle raged on New Georgia. In the first of these on July 6, a Japanese destroyer force sank the light cruiser *Helena* while losing two of its own ships. In another encounter on July 13, the Japanese lost a light cruiser but damaged three Allied cruisers and sank a destroyer. The final engagement came on the night of August 6–7 in the waters between Vella Lavella and Kolombangara. Six U.S. destroyers ambushed a squadron of four enemy destroyers and bested them at their own game, night fighting with torpedoes. They sent all but one of the Japanese ships to the bottom.

Halsey's final objective in the Solomons was Bougainville. If the Americans could gain a foothold there, they could establish airfields much closer to New Britain. This would enable fighter-planes using these bases to provide protection for Kenney's bombing raids against Rabaul. The key to a successful landing on Bougainville was to destroy Japanese air bases on the island. Planes operating from Munda carried out this task with great efficiency.

Halsey decided to bypass heavily defended southern Bougainville and strike at Empress Augusta Bay, about two-thirds of the way up the western coast. The 3rd Marine Division made the assault against weak opposition on November 1 and pushed inland. The Japanese commander, General Hyakutake, who had failed earlier to dislodge the Americans from Guadalcanal, had expected the landing to come in the south. He clung persistently to this belief even after the Americans had established a substantial perimeter at Empress Augusta Bay. His failure to send reinforcements eased the marine advance, although Japanese counterattacks did result in some heavy fighting. By the end of December, the Americans held an enclave ten miles wide and five miles deep and had built three airstrips.

On the first night of the American landing, Admiral Sentaro Omori attempted to attack the transports disembarking troops. He used two heavy and two light cruisers as well as six destroyers for this purpose, but they fell afoul of an American force of four light cruisers and eight destroyers, commanded by Admiral M. Stanton Merrill. In the Battle of Empress Augusta Bay that followed, Merrill's ships denied the Japanese access to the transports while sinking one light cruiser and a destroyer. After this rebuff, the Japanese squadron retired to Rabaul.

Admiral Koga responded to Omori's defeat by dispatching seven heavy cruisers, one light cruiser, and four destroyers from Truk to Rabaul, preparatory to another strike. But U.S. cryptanalysts intercepted messages pertaining to the operation and alerted Halsey. The admiral had no surface ships capable of dealing with such a large number of heavy cruisers and faced a potentially critical situation. He decided to use the only weapon he had, Task Force 38, which he had borrowed from Nimitz to support the Bougainville operation. Admiral Frederick Sherman, who had been captain of the carrier *Lexington* in the Battle of the Coral Sea, commanded this force. It included the carriers *Saratoga* and *Princeton*.

The United States had never tried a carrier strike against a base as powerful as Rabaul. But on November 5, Sherman's planes swooped in for a surprise attack, which, with the aid of considerable good luck, scored a remarkable success. While clouds protected *Saratoga* and *Princeton* from Japanese aircraft, U.S. planes had the benefit of bright sunshine over Rabaul. They damaged three cruisers and the same number of destroyers. The Japanese never again attempted to use heavy cruisers in this theater.

Pushing along New Guinea's Coast

While Halsey's forces invaded New Georgia and Bougainville, MacArthur continued operations along the New Guinea coast. His objectives were the villages of Salamaua and Lae about 175 miles north of Buna. Important preliminaries for this operation had started in January, when Allied aircraft transported an Australian brigade to strengthen Kanga Force, a guerrilla unit that had maintained an airstrip at the village of Wau, 25 miles southeast of Salamaua. These troops repulsed a Japanese effort to capture the airstrip and in February began to push the enemy back toward Salamaua.

In late June, American forces carried out a seaborne landing at Nassau Bay, 15 miles south of Salamaua. This operation opened a supply route to the Australians at Wau and also helped convince the Japanese that the Allies intended to deliver their main thrust toward Salamaua. In reality, their primary objective was Lae, about 25 miles to the north. Lae was the gateway to the Markham and Ramu river valleys, which extended almost 400 miles to the northwest. They formed

a relatively easy route to the important Japanese base at Madang. The campaign to take Lae and Salamaua was a grueling affair that featured an abundance of mountains and thick, rain-soaked jungle. Extreme heat and humidity as well as a variety of tropical diseases were ever present. Nevertheless, Australian and U.S. forces finally forced the Japanese to evacuate Lae and Salamaua by September 16.

During the remainder of September and October, Australian forces reached a point only 50 miles south of Madang. On January 2, 1944, U.S. troops landed at Saidor to the northwest in an effort to cut off the enemy retreat. Although the Japanese managed to avoid this fate by sidestepping the Americans with the help of inland trails, they lost almost a third of their original force of 7,000 men. Even those who survived suffered from disease and starvation. In late March, the Australians linked up with the Americans near Saidor. On April 24, Allied troops finally occupied Madang, but its capture proved anticlimactic. The Japanese had already evacuated to Wewak, nearly 200 miles to the northwest.

While the Australians continued the thankless task of pushing along New Guinea's seemingly endless coast, MacArthur staged a series of leapfrog amphibious operations. The first of these took place on April 22 at Aitape, 75 miles from Wewak, and Hollandia, 125 miles farther west. U.S. forces took the Japanese by surprise and quickly gained control of both objectives. Another landing seized the small, weakly defended island of Wakde, 130 miles from Hollandia, on May 17. Ten days later, U.S. forces went ashore on the larger island of Biak, 190 miles to the northwest. Biak became a nightmare. Its garrison was much larger than the Americans had expected, and the Japanese had fortified a multitude of interconnecting caves in the island's steep cliffs. The invaders had to dislodge the enemy from each of these strongholds with the help of TNT, flamethrowers, and ignited gasoline. Resistance finally ended in mid-August.

A Chain around Rabaul

In December 1943, while Allied forces were still struggling along New Guinea's coast, and Halsey's troops were establishing their perimeter at Empress Augusta Bay, MacArthur launched still another phase of Operation Cartwheel—the invasion of New Britain. Army troops executed an uncontested landing at Arawe, along the southern coast, on December 15 and successfully fought off Japanese counterattacks. On the day after Christmas, marines easily gained a foothold at Cape Gloucester, near the island's northwestern tip. But they had to overcome a Japanese force entrenched on a nearby hill as well as torrential monsoon before securing their position.

By the end of 1943, the Allies menaced Rabaul from the western end of New Britain as well as from Bougainville and New Georgia. They subjected the great base to repeated air attacks during the months which followed, but they abandoned their original plan for a seaborne assault in favor of bypassing Rabaul. It had gradually become evident that an invasion was not necessary. The great base had been effectively neutralized.

On February 29, 1944, MacArthur's troops provided the last major link in the chain that the Allies were forging around Rabaul when they landed on Los Negros in the Admiralty Islands, almost 200 miles northwest of New Britain. Aerial intelligence had indicated that the island contained only a weak defending force, but in reality it totaled 4,000 men. Fortunately for the Americans, the enemy troops were on the opposite end of the island. By the time the Japanese were able to counterattack, the landing force had firmly established itself.

The Central Pacific Offensive

Meanwhile, Nimitz had opened his Central Pacific offensive. He had been able to assemble far larger naval forces than were available for the various phases of Operation Cartwheel. By October 1943, the 5th Fleet, under Admiral Spruance, consisted of eight carriers, seven battleships, seven heavy and three light cruisers, and 34 destroyers. Despite the loss of four carriers during 1942, *Saratoga* and *Enterprise* were still afloat and had recovered from assorted injuries. The navy had also received six new *Essex*-class carriers, which were faster, more maneuverable, and better armed than the older carriers. In addition, the Pacific Fleet was putting into service another half-dozen light carriers of the *Independence* class. Actually converted cruisers, these vessels were

equal in speed to the larger carriers but could carry only half as many planes. Carrier aircraft had also improved. American designers had studied a captured Japanese Zero and had developed their answer to this famous fighter, the F6F Hellcat. Not only did the Hellcat possess better armor and armament, but also it could both outclimb and outdive the Zero.

The original plan for the Central Pacific offensive called for American forces to bypass the Gilbert Islands, the southeasternmost point in the Japanese defensive perimeter, and strike directly at the Marshalls. But American strategists ultimately decided that it would be best to gain bases in the Gilberts first to provide steppingstones to the Marshalls.

Spruance held overall command of the operation in the Gilberts. Admiral Richmond Kelly Turner led the naval assault force, including the transports, landing craft, and supporting warships, which would actually be responsible for getting the troops ashore. Marine General Holland Smith would take command of the troops once they were ashore. Turner's marked tendency to try to control operations even after the ground forces went into action became the source of friction between himself and Smith. Both "Terrible Turner" and "Howlin' Mad" Smith were formidable personalities, and their jurisdictional squabbles contributed little to the smoothness of the operation.

The Taking of Tarawa and Makin

The objectives of the invasion were two small atolls—Tarawa, near the center of the Gilberts, and Makin, at their northwestern extremity. Plans called for attacks on both targets on November 20, 1943. Tarawa's defenses were much more formidable than those of Makin. They included a garrison of 5,000 men under Rear Admiral Keiji Shibasaki, as well as eight-inch gun batteries housed in concrete and coconut log bunkers. Tarawa consisted of a number of islands and coral reefs surrounding a 15-mile-long lagoon.

The key point was the elongated island of Betio, which stretched for $2^{1}/_{2}$ miles but measured only 800 yards at its widest point. Betio contained the majority of the Japanese defenders and had the protection of a coral reef that surrounded it on all sides. Moreover, the November tides at Tarawa were unpredictable. In fact, an expert on the island's tides warned that the water would not be deep enough to allow landing craft to pass over the reef and urged postponement of the invasion until December. But other former residents of Tarawa insisted that there would be sufficient clearance. Spruance refused to postpone the invasion, a decision that proved to be a mistake.

Although warships and land-based aircraft blasted Tarawa with the heaviest bombardment ever to precede an invasion up to that time, the Japanese defenses withstood this frightful tattoo. Worse, the warning about the reef turned out to be true. New amphibious tractor landing craft (amtracs), which were capable of climbing over the reef, carried the first three waves of marines to the beach with relatively little trouble. But the troops that followed were not so fortunate. Since there were too few amtracs, they had to make do with deep-draft landing craft. These became caught on the reef, and the marines had to wade through shoulder-high water for hundreds of yards to reach the beach. Many of them fell victim to Japanese fire. Even those who had landed earlier found themselves pinned down on the beach. By nightfall, 5,000 men had landed, but 1,500 of them were dead or wounded. The marines clung to a beachhead that did not exceed 300 yards in depth.

More savage fighting took place the next day, but the marines, with the help of flamethrowers and TNT, gradually forced the defenders back. The tide also finally increased in depth, allowing the landing of artillery, while naval guns and carrier planes blasted the Japanese positions. By the third night, the marines had pushed the enemy into the western end of the island. The Japanese now resorted to desperation attacks, which the Americans repulsed with heavy losses. Resistance ended on the afternoon of November 23.

"Bloody Tarawa" had been a rude shock, not only to the marines of the 2nd Division, who experienced the battle, and those who had planned it but to the American people as well. It had cost over 1,000 dead and more than 2,000 wounded, a terrible price for such a small atoll. After the battle, when General Smith observed the tremendous strength of the Japanese defensive positions, he expressed his amazement that his men actually were able to take them. "By God, those marines

just kept coming," he declared. "Many of them were killed, but more came on. It looks beyond the realm of a human being that this place could have been taken." The Japanese had suffered a far worse fate. Only 17 of them survived.

The assault on Makin also proved more difficult than expected. Although army troops, who greatly outnumbered the defenders, were able to establish a beachhead against little resistance, they found their progress inland slowed by snipers. The pace of the advance quickened the next day, but the Americans did not gain complete control of the atoll until November 23.

The Leap to Kwajalein

Possession of Tarawa and Makin set the stage for the next operation, a thrust northwestward into the Marshall Islands. Spruance, Turner, and Smith, who were to repeat the roles they had played in the Tarawa operation, assumed that the invasion target would be in the eastern Marshalls, which lay closest to the Gilberts. All three men were horrified when Admiral Nimitz informed them that he intended to leap ahead 400 miles to attack Kwajalein atoll in the center of the island chain. They warned that such a daring operation would expose both ships and landing force to bombing attacks from the many Japanese air bases in the Marshalls. But Nimitz's decision was not as wild as his dumbfounded subordinates thought. He had received Ultra reports that clearly indicated that the Japanese were expecting an attack against the outer Marshalls and were making their troop dispositions accordingly.

Nimitz did agree to Spruance's demand that Task Force 58, commanded by Admiral Marc Mitscher, carry out raids against airfields in the Marshalls. Unlike most U.S. naval commanders at this time, Mitscher was actually an aviator and proved a master at handling carriers. He also took a keen personal interest in his men, who in turn held him in exceptionally high regard. But Mitscher's carriers had to return to Pearl Harbor for refitting and could not undertake their mission until January 1944. In the meantime, army and navy planes, operating from airstrips on Tarawa and Makin, began the process of pounding the enemy bases. When the task force returned, it made quick work of the remaining Japanese aircraft.

Kwajalein possessed defenses comparable to those of Tarawa, but the invading Americans outnumbered the Japanese 41,000 to 8,000. On February 1, two marine regiments landed on Roi and Namur islands at the northern end of the atoll's lagoon, while two army regiments went ashore on Kwajalein island itself in the extreme south. The Japanese did not contest the landings, and the preinvasion bombardment was more prolonged and devastating than at Tarawa. The marines made rapid progress on Roi and Namur, and by the end of the second day, resistance had ended. The troops that landed on Kwajalein advanced more slowly and did not complete their operations until February 4. The conquest of the atoll cost far fewer casualties than Tarawa—373 dead and 1,500 wounded.

The Neutralization of Truk

Nimitz's next objective was Eniwetok atoll, at the far western edge of the Marshalls. His original timetable did not call for its capture until May. But the surprisingly easy victory at Kwajalein had justified the admiral's boldness and inspired a longing to take risks in other commanders. Spruance, Turner, and Smith urged an assault on Eniwetok as quickly as possible. They knew that the island was lightly defended but feared that this situation would not last long. Nimitz was in complete agreement. But one great danger confronted such an undertaking: Eniwetok lay within striking distance of Japanese air and naval forces at the great base of Truk in the Carolines. Even though Koga had withdrawn the bulk of his naval forces after the fall of Kwajalein, any attempt to take Eniwetok would be dangerous unless American air power neutralized Truk first. On February 17–18, Mitscher's carrier planes delivered repeated strikes against Truk, which destroyed 200 aircraft, sank eight warships and 24 merchant vessels, and damaged one carrier. The raids ended Truk's value as a major base.

In stark contrast to the ease with which Mitscher's flyers shattered the legend of Truk's invincibility, the conquest of Eniwetok proved a tougher task than anticipated. The Japanese had created a system of interlocking trenches, foxholes, and pillboxes that resembled a spiderweb. They greeted the invaders with heavy machine-gun and

FIGURE 15-1   Dead Japanese soldiers litter the ground near the entrance to a reinforced dugout on Tarawa. (*U.S. Department of Defense Visual Information Center*)

mortar fire, and as usual, the majority of the defenders fought to the death. Four days passed before resistance ended.

The quick succession of U.S. victories in the Gilberts and Marshalls as well as the neutralization of both Rabaul and Truk stunned Japanese leaders. A number of the close associates of the late Admiral Yamamoto feared the war was lost. Even Tojo appears to have believed that the wisest course would be to seek peace but feared to broach the subject in view of the fanatical attitude of most army officers.

Assault on the Marianas

The capture of Kwajalein and Eniwetok gave the Americans effective control over the Marshalls and left the remaining Japanese garrisons on islands in the chain to wither on the vine. Nimitz and Spruance now planned to bypass Truk and the other Caroline Islands and leap forward all the way to the Marianas, over 1,000 miles northwest of Eniwetok. Their objectives were Saipan, Tinian, and Guam, which contained the three largest Japanese

garrisons in the Marianas. Unlike the atolls of the Gilberts and Marshalls, the Marianas were substantial islands that lay only 1,200 miles from Japan. Their capture promised to open a multitude of objectives to Allied planners: an assault on the Philippines to the west, a northward thrust toward the Bonin Islands, within 700 miles of Japan, and the establishment of air bases from which long-range bombers could attack Japanese cities.

In addition to his 5th Fleet, Spruance had 127,000 troops available for the invasion, by far the largest force yet committed to any operation in the Pacific. Mitscher's task force attacked Japanese air bases for months prior to the invasion and virtually destroyed enemy air power in the Marianas.

Nimitz chose Saipan, the northernmost of the three major islands, as his first objective. Admiral Turner again commanded the amphibious force that made the assault, and General Smith led the ground forces. Mitscher's battleships hammered the island for two days before the actual invasion, and Turner's warships added their bombardment on the morning of the landings, but

FIGURE 15-2   A marine (center) falls victim to a sniper as Japanese troops open fire on a U.S. patrol on Saipan. *(Corbis/Bettmann)*

neither eliminated the enemy defenses. When two marine divisions landed on the southwest shore on June 15, they encountered fierce opposition and did not consolidate their beachhead until nightfall. During the next two weeks, with the help of army reinforcements, they fought their way northward to the main enemy defenses, which extended across the center of the island.

Admiral Nagumo, who had led the Japanese carrier striking force to its rousing victory at Pearl Harbor and its grim defeat at Midway, commanded the defending forces. Although the Japanese resisted desperately, the Americans ground slowly northward. On July 6, Nagumo and the island's army commander, General Yoshitsugu Saito, both took their own lives in an effort to encourage their troops to make a final attack. This assault came on the night of July 6–7 in the form of suicidal charges that decimated the remaining troops. But one last gruesome chapter remained—the mass suicide of perhaps as many as 8,000 civilians in the last hours of the battle. They threw themselves off cliffs on the northern tip of the island, touched off grenades against their bodies, or simply walked into the ocean to drown.

While the marines were pushing northward on Saipan, an even more dramatic struggle took place in the skies over the Philippine Sea, the portion of the Pacific between the Marianas and the Philippines. Admiral Koga had died in an airplane crash in April, and Admiral Soemu Toyoda had taken over as commander of the Combined Fleet. A much more aggressive leader than Koga, Toyoda reacted to the news of the impending invasion of Saipan by ordering Admiral Jisaburo Ozawa to move from the Philippines with his 1st Mobile Fleet to destroy American naval units off the Marianas. Ozawa had long been a leading advocate of carrier warfare. Next to Yamamoto, his American opponents considered him the most skillful Japanese admiral of the conflict.

When Spruance received reports of Ozawa's approach, he dispatched Mitscher's task force along with additional ships from the 5th Fleet to repel the enemy challenge. American strength included seven heavy and eight light carriers and a large number of battleships, cruisers, and destroyers. The Japanese countered with five heavy and four light carriers and a smaller supporting force. Ozawa launched an air strike on the morning of June 19, but American radar alerted the task force to the enemy's approach. U.S. fighters intercepted the Japanese planes 50 miles to the west. The Americans enjoyed a big numerical advantage with a total of 956 planes, including 475 fighters. The Japanese had only 222 fighters out of a total of 473 aircraft.

To make the discrepancy even greater, American pilots were better trained and more experienced. They had alternated between periods of combat and intervals in which they had served as flight instructors. This practice enabled them to give new pilots the benefit of their experience and expertise. The Japanese, by contrast, had committed their veteran pilots to a steady diet of combat. By the summer of 1944, few of them were left.

Japanese aircraft carried out four mass attacks on Mitscher's task force, but few of them were able to penetrate the U.S. fighter screen. They inflicted minor damage to just one vessel, the battleship *South Dakota*. Their own losses were staggering—275 of the 373 planes actually engaged. Only 29 American aircraft failed to return safely to their carriers. The Battle of the Philippine Sea was so one-sided that it earned the nickname "the Great Marianas Turkey Shoot." To add to Japanese woes, two American submarines, *Albacore* and *Cavalla*, sank the carriers *Shokaku* and *Taiho*. *Shokaku* was a veteran of the Pearl Harbor raid; *Taiho* was the largest carrier in the Japanese navy.

Despite this great victory, the Americans did not discover the location of Ozawa's fleet until the afternoon of June 20. Unfortunately, it was 340 miles to the east, a distance that made it unlikely that many American planes would have enough fuel to return to their carriers after attacking the enemy ships. Those that did make it back would have to land in the dark, a most dangerous assignment. This predicament was due to Spruance's concern before the battle began that Ozawa might divide his fleet and send one force to attack the transports off Saipan. To prevent such a possibility, he had refused Mitscher's request to close in on the enemy. Instead Spruance had ordered the task force to fall back toward Saipan.

Despite the danger to his aircraft, Mitscher was determined to attack the Japanese fleet. Given the problems involved, the results were good. Dive bombers and torpedo planes sank the carrier *Hiyo*, badly damaged three others, and destroyed

65 enemy aircraft. But 80 U.S. planes failed to make it back to their carriers or crashed while landing. Mitscher, defying both navy doctrine and possible enemy submarine attacks, ordered all ships to turn on their lights to guide the returning pilots to their destinations. Rescue ships and planes recovered the majority of the crews who had ditched at sea the next day.

Spruance's decision to turn back toward Saipan rather than to keep Task Force 58 moving toward the enemy fleet has caused continuing controversy. Some have argued that had he sent Mitscher farther west, his planes might have virtually destroyed the enemy carrier force. Others have contended that under the circumstances, Spruance acted correctly. They point to the fact that by keeping their distance, no American ships were lost, while the Japanese sacrificed their aircraft in vain. Regardless of which view is correct, it is clear that the Americans had administered a crippling defeat to Japanese naval air power, one from which it would never recover.

Even before the fall of Saipan, U.S. planes and ships pounded Tinian, which lay just to the southwest. The actual invasion came on July 24, when the same two marine divisions that had made the initial landings on Saipan went ashore on the north end of the island and encountered little opposition. The Japanese had expected the assault to come in the south, where they had massed the bulk of their strength. Again, the Japanese fought with blind heroism. But this time, the marines were able to overrun the island in only eight days.

Marine and army forces had actually landed on Guam three days before the start of the invasion of Tinian. Unlike the situation on Tinian, the enemy resisted the landings, and the Americans moved inland only after heavy fighting. Once again the Japanese withdrew to the northern end of the island, where they made another suicidal last stand. Organized fighting ended on August 1, but mopping up operations continued in parts of the island until the end of the war.

The loss of the Marianas and the disastrous Battle of the Philippine Sea represented a shattering blow to Japanese hopes of winning the war. Nine days after the fall of Saipan, Tojo and his government accepted the consequences of defeat and resigned. General Kuniaki Koiso succeeded Tojo and formed a new cabinet, which shouldered the task of halting the American momentum. Prospects were far from bright. The United States was now in a position to strike at the Philippines, an action that would threaten Japan's oil supply from the East Indies. American engineers were already transforming the airfields of the Marianas to accommodate the new B-29 Superfortress bombers. The range and bomb capacity of these giant planes gave them the capability of bringing death and destruction on a massive scale to the crowded and inflammable cities of Japan.

CHAPTER SIXTEEN

The Tide Turns in Russia: Stalingrad and Beyond

It is clear that 1941 was the crucial year of the war because of the failure of the German offensive in the Soviet Union and the entry of the United States into the conflict. But it was in 1942 that the war began to turn against the Axis, not only in the Pacific, but in the Soviet Union as well. Yet during much of the year, Germany again held the initiative on the plains of Russia and seemed poised for the knockout blow that had eluded the Wehrmacht in 1941. This success proved to be a prelude to disaster, however, and the Germans were in full retreat before the end of the year. They were still strong enough to challenge again in 1943, but their last bid for supremacy ended with their failure in the epic Battle of Kursk in July. After that, Germany's defeat became a virtual certainty.

New German Goals in the USSR

In the USSR, the Soviet winter counteroffensive bogged down by February 1942, and the Germans were able to recover from the sledgehammer blows that had sent them reeling in December and January. Hitler planned to wrest the initiative from the Soviets by the summer. But the Germans lacked sufficient strength to attack on the scale of the 1941 campaign. Hitler decided instead to concentrate on the south and abandoned the possibility of a second attempt to capture Moscow. His primary aim in the 1942 campaign was economic—the capture of the Caucasus oil fields. This would cut off the Soviets from their chief source of petroleum and greatly increase German oil supplies. But it also meant that Hitler was abandoning the stated objective of Operation Barbarossa a year earlier—the destruction of the main Soviet forces, which still lay before Moscow.

The Germans planned a three-step operation. Phase 1 called for an encirclement of Soviet troops to the west of the Don River by two powerful components of Army Group South. Field Marshal von Bock, now recovered from the illness that had sidelined him during the winter, had taken over command in the south. General Hoth's 4th Panzer Army provided the spearhead of the northern arm of the planned encirclement, with General Friedrich von Paulus's 6th Army to its right. These forces were to drive toward Voronezh on the Don and then dash southeastward along the river's west bank toward the industrial city of Stalingrad on the Volga River. General von Kleist's 1st Panzer Army formed the southern spearhead and was to advance north of Rostov and link up with Hoth's column. After completing this encirclement, Hoth and Paulus would execute phase 2 by establishing a blocking position on the Volga near Stalingrad to protect the southern force, which would carry out phase 3, the drive to the Caucasus.

When Paulus took over as leader of the 6th Army, it marked his first actual field command. He had served as chief of staff of the 10th Army during the campaigns in Poland and Western Europe. Paulus became Halder's deputy in October 1940 and participated in the planning for Operation Barbarossa. In fact, he had conducted war games prior to the 1941 invasion that demonstrated clearly that the *Blitzkrieg* would encounter severe supply problems and that German forces were barely adequate to capture Moscow. Halder had ignored his ominous warning. Paulus proved better suited to staff work than leadership in the field.

The German army on the eastern front had fallen below its strength at the start of the 1941 campaign by 350,000 men and now depended on Rumanian, Hungarian, and Italian units for support. These satellite troops were of lower quality and morale and lacked adequate equipment. Even

Closing the Ring, 1942–45

the German troops were inferior to those of June 1941. The bitter fighting of the hot summer of 1941 and the terrible winter that followed, along with partisan attacks and disease, had taken their toll. Total tank strength was slightly less than at the start of the 1941 campaign, but the OKH had concentrated a large part of it in the south. Germany still had not developed a tank that was a match for the Soviet T34. The Soviets also had encountered difficulty in replacing their tremendous losses in armor.

The Germans planned to eliminate a Soviet salient in their line south of Kharkov as a preliminary to the summer offensive. But before they could act, the Red Army staged an offensive from the salient with the intention of recapturing

Kharkov, the hub of the German communications network in the south. This Soviet operation actually proved a boon to the Germans, who had been building up their strength along the flanks of the salient. Soviet intelligence had failed to detect this. Stalin and Timoshenko, the Russian southern front commander, had insisted on this offensive over the opposition of both Zhukov and Shaposhnikov, the chief of staff. Timoshenko launched his offensive on May 12. The Soviets advanced swiftly at first and made a deep penetration, increasing the vulnerability of their position. On May 17, the Germans struck the enemy flank from the south and within a few days had cut off the Soviet spearhead, capturing 240,000 prisoners and destroying over 600 tanks. Timoshenko had asked for permission to pull back before the Germans sealed off his forces, but Stalin and Stavka had refused.

Another preliminary to the main German offensive came in the Crimea, the peninsula that juts into the Black Sea from the Ukraine. The 11th Army under General von Manstein, who had been so prominent in planning the Ardennes breakthrough in 1940, had conquered most of the Crimea during the fall of 1941. But Manstein's forces had failed to capture the Soviet naval base of Sevastopol, which remained secure behind three belts of powerful permanent defenses. Manstein received reinforcements and strong air support in the spring and on June 7, he unleashed another offensive against Sevastopol, but again the Soviets resisted furiously. Despite incessant air attacks, and shelling by two huge siege mortars, one of which hurled shells weighing over 2 tons, and a railway gun that fired 5-ton rounds, Sevastopol did not fall until July 3.

The disastrous failure of the Red Army's attempt to take Kharkov seriously weakened the Soviets in the south, and when the Germans opened their major offensive (Case Blue) on June 28, they rapidly swept forward. Timoshenko's badly depleted forces, desperately short of armor, had to fall back quickly. Stalin remained convinced

FIGURE 16-1   Josef Stalin, the Soviet dictator. *(UPI/Corbis/Bettmann)*

that the Germans intended to strike their major blow at Moscow and concentrated the bulk of his strength in defense of the capital. Once again he disregarded intelligence reports that the offensive would come in the south.

Hoth's 4th Panzer Army drove 100 miles in eight days, reaching the Don near Voronezh, which the Germans planned to secure as the anchor for their eastern flank. But the Soviets defended Voronezh stubbornly, and Bock persisted in efforts to take the city before sending Hoth's panzers southward along the Don to form the northern pincer of the planned encirclement of enemy forces. This helped Timoshenko carry out a successful withdrawal toward Stalingrad. Several days elapsed before the 4th Panzer Army headed south. Hitler became disenchanted with Bock's slow progress and replaced him with General Maximilian von Weichs. He also split Army Group South into two separate commands—Army Group B in the north under Weichs and Army Group A to the south under Field Marshal Wilhelm List. Weichs had been a corps commander in the Polish and Western European campaigns and led the 2nd Army in the invasions of Yugoslavia and Russia. List had commanded the 14th Army in Poland and the 12th Army in both the Ardennes breakthrough and the Balkans.

Meanwhile, Kleist's 1st Panzer Army moved eastward to form the southern wing of the encirclement. But the Soviets withdrew here, too, and the Germans took few prisoners. Hitler assumed that the Red Army was fleeing in panic instead of executing an organized withdrawal and ecstatically proclaimed that "the Russian is finished," to which Halder responded, "I must admit, it looks like it." In his euphoria, the Führer decided that it was now possible to drive toward the Caucasus without first securing the German flank at Stalingrad.

In keeping with this new approach, Hitler ordered Army Group A to swing southward with the 1st Panzer Army in the lead. He also ordered the 4th Panzer Army to abandon its drive on Stalingrad and assist Kleist's forces with their crossing of the Don east of Rostov. The less mobile Sixth Army, with its preponderance of infantry, received the task of capturing Stalingrad. The simultaneous pursuit of these two objectives and the diversion of the 4th Panzer Army proved to be serious mistakes. If left to continue their drive on Stalingrad,

Hoth's forces might have reached the city before the Soviets had consolidated their position there. And it soon became clear that the 1st Panzer Army did not need help crossing the Don as it made rapid progress against weak Soviet resistance. By August 9, it had streaked 200 miles southeast of Rostov and had reached the Maikop oil fields in the Caucasus foothills.

But now the Germans once again split their forces, one column moving east toward the Grozny oil fields and another hooking west in an effort to clear the Black Sea coast. Again it was a case of too many objectives. Both drives stalled because of a shortage of fuel, difficult mountain terrain, and stronger Soviet resistance. The Germans continued to try to break through during September, October, and November, without success. They had stretched themselves to the limit. Army Group South had originally been responsible for a 500-mile expanse of the front. As a result of the summer offensive, German forces in the south now had a dangerously long front stretching 1,300 miles.

As the Germans penetrated into the Caucasus, they reached the lower slopes of 18,481-foot Mount Elbrus, Europe's highest peak. A team of climbers could not resist the temptation and, braving fog and blizzards, scaled the giant mountain and planted a German flag near its summit.

The Struggle for Stalingrad

While Army Group A was driving toward the Caucasus, the 6th Army advanced slowly in the direction of Stalingrad. In the process, it created a long, vulnerable flank along the Don, which was guarded by weak satellite troops. The Soviets also retained a number of bridgeheads on the western bank of the river, and these provided strong positions for possible counterattacks. Hitler finally diverted the 4th Panzer Army back to the Stalingrad operation, but it was too late for a speedy conquest. Soviet resistance stiffened as the Germans neared the city in late August, and the war of movement came to an end.

The Soviet position was still highly precarious. During August, Stalin made major leadership changes. He ordered General Andrei Yeremenko to form a new army group in the Stalingrad area from reserve divisions. Yeremenko was still another former tsarist army soldier who had become an officer in the Red Army during the civil war. He had emerged as one of Stalin's chief troubleshooters and participated in the defense of Moscow in 1941. More important, Stalin called upon General Zhukov once again to come to the rescue. Although Timoshenko had conducted the retreat with reasonable skill, his name came to be associated with defeat. Zhukov, by contrast, had gained fame as the "savior of Moscow." In late August, Zhukov replaced Timoshenko as overall commander in the south.

General Vasili Chuikov was responsible for the actual defense of Stalingrad itself. Chuikov acted with extreme decisiveness. He had been serving as a military attaché in China when the invasion began and did not return to the Soviet Union until March 1942. Since then, he had seen little action, but he had studied German methods closely. His observations convinced him that the enemy disliked close combat and would not perform well in street fighting. Upon taking up his new command, he notified his superiors that "we shall either hold the city or die there."

Chuikov organized a skillful defense, and the Germans resorted to battering-ram tactics. They also bombed and shelled the city incessantly, reducing it to a wasteland of utter destruction. The Germans encountered extreme difficulty in moving through this sea of rubble, and the struggle deteriorated into a myriad of hellish small battles around Soviet strongpoints. At times the fighting even extended into the city's sewers. The ruins also provided ideal hiding places for deadly snipers on both sides. Nevertheless, the Germans gradually drove the Soviets back, street by street, block by block, building by building, sometimes room by room. The struggle became a colossal battle of attrition, and Stalingrad became a symbol for both sides. Stalin was insistent that the city that bore his name should not fall. Hitler became so mesmerized by the thought of taking Stalin's city that he kept hammering away despite heavy casualties and the erosion of his armor, which was not well suited for this type of close-quarters conflict in support of infantry. Ironically, Stalingrad was not a vital objective. The Germans could have established their block on the Volga much more easily to the south of the city. Nevertheless, by early November they held nine-tenths

of Stalingrad. But their position took the form of a
salient with long, inviting flanks to the north and
south of the city.

The Soviets, too, suffered serious losses, but
they were in a better position to replace them
because of their greater manpower reserves. Soviet
leaders had conscripted vast numbers of men after
the invasion of 1941. By the fall of 1942, this policy
had produced numerous fresh, well-trained divisions. Soviet war production had slumped drastically between October 1941 and the following
spring as a result of the large-scale evacuation of
industry to the Urals and other areas. But by early
fall, factories were turning out a much greater flow
of equipment. This was due in large part to concentration on only a few types of tanks, trucks,
and artillery that could be easily mass-produced
and round-the-clock manufacturing schedules.

Meanwhile, relations between Hitler and some
of his top generals became increasingly strained.
He dismissed List on September 9 and took over
command of Army Group A himself. Even more
significant, he ousted Halder as chief of staff late
in September and replaced him with General Kurt
Zeitzler, a younger, less experienced, and more
pliable officer who had started the Russian campaign as a colonel. Zeitzler had gained a reputation as an expert in logistics and a dynamic
problem solver. Rising quickly in rank, he won
the admiration of Hitler, who elevated him to
chief of staff over many senior generals.

While the struggle for Stalingrad raged on into
the fall, Zhukov followed the same approach he
had used with success at Moscow a year earlier. He
deliberately kept reinforcements for the Stalingrad
garrison to a minimum in order to mass as much
strength as possible opposite the weak Rumanian
forces that held the flanks of the Stalingrad salient.
On November 19, Zhukov launched his counterstroke, Operation Uranus.

An army group under General Nikolai Vatutin's
command delivered the first blow against the
Rumanian 3rd Army to the northwest of Stalingrad.
Vatutin had started the war as deputy chief of staff
and had stymied Bock's attempt to seize Voronezh
early in the 1942 offensive, helping to prevent the
encirclement of Timoshenko's forces. Vatutin's
troops struck the Rumanians from a large bridgehead on the west bank of the Don, quickly tore
a gaping hole in their front, and then swung

**German Sixth Army Trapped and Destroyed at
Stalingrad, Nov. 23, 1942–Feb. 2, 1943**

southeastward. The next day, a second army
group, commanded by Yeremenko, shattered the
Rumanian 4th Army to the south of Stalingrad and
raced northwestward. The Soviet spearheads came
together 45 miles west of the city on November 23,
sealing off the 6th Army and one corps of the 4th
Panzer Army.

Paulus asked permission to abandon Stalingrad and attempt to break through the encirclement, but Hitler refused. Memories of his "hold
fast" order of the previous year were still fresh.
The Führer informed Paulus, "I am not leaving
the Volga!" He thought of Stalingrad as a super
hedgehog and ordered the Luftwaffe to supply the
trapped forces by air, as it had done with isolated
strong points called hedgehogs in the winter of
1941–42. But this time the Luftwaffe failed. To
supply Stalingrad was a far greater task, and its
earlier efforts had eroded both planes and pilots.
Prolonged periods of violently stormy weather
also snarled operations.

Hitler ordered Manstein, now a field marshal, to
lead an expedition to reestablish contact with the
Stalingrad garrison. Manstein launched his attempt
on December 12 and made fairly good progress at
first, but he could not possibly succeed unless the
6th Army attempted to break out and link up with

his forces. Hitler refused to allow this, and Paulus himself seemed to have had no confidence in his army's ability to carry out such a difficult undertaking at this late date. The whole question of the relief of Stalingrad became academic when the Soviets unleashed another offensive (Operation Saturn) on December 16. This time they smashed through the Italian 8th Army, and lunged from the Don toward Rostov with the intention of cutting off all German forces to the south, including Army Group A, which was still fighting in the Caucasus. Even Hitler could see the danger of a far worse disaster than Stalingrad. He ordered his troops in the threatened areas to retreat, and they managed to escape the impending trap.

German forces isolated at Stalingrad now found themselves in a hopeless position. They continued to hold out against increasing pressure, but the Soviets split them into two pockets in late January 1943. Hitler ordered the defenders to fight to the last man. He also promoted Paulus to field marshal, partly as a bribe to continue the struggle, but also to remind him that no German field marshal had ever surrendered. But the Germans were exhausted and short of food, medicine, and other supplies. Indeed shortages were so severe that Paulus actually cut off food supplies to approximately 30,000 wounded men, who could not be evacuated, in order to give healthy soldiers a better chance of survival. Many wounded men also froze to death while awaiting treatment. The Germans could not avoid surrender, however, and fighting ceased on February 2. Some Germans attempted to escape to the west. Only one of them actually succeeded; ironically, he fell victim to a mortar shell 24 hours after reaching the apparent safety of the German line. Hitler viewed the surrender as a betrayal. He railed against Paulus, vowing never to appoint another field marshal and complaining that it was shameful for him not to have committed suicide. The Führer also insisted that his troops should have shot themselves with their last bullets.

In all, the Germans lost over 200,000 troops at Stalingrad, including 90,000 prisoners. Only 5,000 of the latter would ever see Germany again. The disaster was one of the war's great turning points. Henceforth, with few exceptions, the Germans would remain on the defensive on the eastern front.

The Germans on the Defensive

After the disaster at Stalingrad and the retreat from the Caucasus, no real hope remained that Germany could achieve an offensive victory over the Soviet Union. The Wehrmacht had twice shown itself unable to overcome the twin obstacles of the USSR's vast distances and Soviet staying power. By early 1943, it was clear that the Red Army was superior in materiel as well as in numbers. Germany's only hope now lay in a defensive strategy that would inflict such severe losses on the Red Army that Stalin might be willing to seek a negotiated peace. But visions of victory still danced in Hitler's head. He was not interested in a negotiated settlement, only in winning the war. Instead of assuming a defensive posture, the German army resorted to a massive and ultimately disastrous offensive in July 1943—the Battle of Kursk. If Germany's defeat at Moscow in 1941 had shattered Hitler's dream of a quick, decisive victory, and Stalingrad had sounded the death knell for an offensive approach, Kursk destroyed even the possibility of a successful defensive strategy. From that point the initiative passed permanently to the Soviets, and throughout the remainder of 1943 and 1944 the Red Army relentlessly drove the Germans westward. By the end of 1944 it was poised within striking distance of Germany itself.

The Germans managed to escape the trap that the Soviets had tried to spring on their armies in the Caucasus, but Red Army forces pushed them back to the starting point of their 1942 offensive and for a time drove well beyond this line. Two factors prevented an even more catastrophic defeat. As the Soviets moved west, they faced the same problem that the Germans had encountered during the 1941 and 1942 offensives. Their supply lines became badly overextended while the enemy fell back on its main supply bases. Also, Field Marshal von Manstein proved himself a master of defensive warfare. He succeeded in holding Rostov long enough to enable large German forces to escape the Red Army spearhead that threatened to cut them off. Then, in February 1943, just as the Soviets appeared to be on the verge of dealing a death blow to the whole German position in the south, he delivered a brilliantly conceived counterattack. The Red Army had captured Kharkov and was driving toward the Dnieper River, but in the process it had created a deep salient with long, vulnerable flanks. Manstein sensed his opportunity and thinned out his forces in the path of the Russian advance while massing his panzers to the south and north of the overextended Soviets. He then attacked the enemy flanks and forced the enemy to retreat. His troops recaptured Kharkov and drove beyond.

Other developments bolstered the German cause. One of the most important was Hitler's appointment of Albert Speer to the position of minister of armaments in 1942. Within a year, Speer had placed German industry on a basis approaching a full wartime footing, and his efforts greatly accelerated production of tanks and other weapons until well into 1944. Hitler also brought General Guderian back to active duty as inspector general of armored troops in February 1943. Speer and Guderian worked together to increase the quantity and improve the quality of German armor. Their efforts led to the adoption of two new models, the Tiger and the Panther. The Tiger was a heavy tank with thick armor, wide tracks, and a powerful 88-mm gun. The Panther, a medium tank with a high-velocity 75-mm gun, was faster and more maneuverable than the Tiger and eventually was equal or superior to the Soviet T34. Unfortunately, it suffered from various mechanical problems at first, including an alarming tendency to catch fire. It was not until the winter of 1943–44 that the Panther's designers overcame these "teething" problems.

German numerical inferiority after Stalingrad not only sounded the death knell for an offensive strategy but cast serious doubt on the possibility of a static defense as well. The Wehrmacht simply lacked the strength to defend the entire front, which sprawled from Leningrad to the Black Sea. The only hope for a successful strategy lay in an elastic defense. Such an approach required extensive withdrawals to shorten the front. As the Germans pulled back, they hoped to be able to lure the Soviets into an overly aggressive pursuit. This could create the opportunity for counterattacks similar to the one that Manstein had used to such good effect in February. Both Manstein and Guderian favored this approach. They believed that it offered the only chance to wear down the Soviets to a point that might erode their will to

continue the war and open the way to a negotiated peace.

Operation Citadel

Manstein proposed such a strategy for the spring of 1943. The southern portion of the front in the Ukraine took the form of a large German bulge that jutted precariously eastward, well beyond the northward extension of the battle line. Manstein assumed that the Soviets would try to cut off this salient in the spring and urged that the Germans fall back toward the Dnieper when the Soviets struck. He hoped to entice the Soviets into overextending their advance. Then, when they were most vulnerable, he would attack their flank near Kiev. If all went well, the Red Army would suffer a disastrous defeat. But such an operation would necessitate abandoning the mineral-rich Donetz Basin, and Hitler was unwilling to give up this valuable territory.

Instead, the Germans adopted an alternative and much less imaginative plan that ultimately proved catastrophic. It focused on another salient, this time an enemy bulge that extended around the city of Kursk to the north of Kharkov. The OKH feared that the Soviets would stage their spring offensive from this position and urged that it be eliminated by simultaneous attacks against its northern and southern flanks. Manstein had actually suggested such an undertaking soon after his victory at Kharkov. He had insisted that the assault begin in April, before the Soviets could build up their defenses in the salient. But a series of delays forced postponement of the offensive until July.

The German plan, Operation Citadel, called for Field Marshal Günther von Kluge's Army Group Center to attack the salient from the north while Manstein's troops struck from the south. General Zeitzler, the chief of staff, and Kluge were the foremost advocates of Citadel. Guderian was dead set against it from the start, and Manstein's enthusiasm cooled when it became clear that delays would be involved. Hitler had strong misgivings, too. At one point, he told Guderian, "Whenever I think about this attack my stomach turns over." Guderian responded, "In that case your reaction is the correct one. Leave it alone!" Unfortunately for the Germans, Hitler eventually bowed to the arguments of Zeitzler and Kluge.

Kluge and Guderian were old and bitter rivals. Before succeeding Bock as head of Army Group Center, Kluge had commanded the 4th Army in Poland, France, and the 1941 Russian campaign. He considered Guderian to be bold to the point of recklessness and once charged that the panzer leader's operations "always hang by a thread." At one point Kluge challenged Guderian to a duel, but Hitler ordered the two generals to reconcile their differences.

Unfortunately for Hitler and his generals, the Soviets soon learned about the entire plan from their spy network and took elaborate defensive measures. Marshal Zhukov, the hero of Moscow and Stalingrad, once again directed Soviet planning. He intended to follow his usual approach: wear down the attacking Germans and then direct powerful counterstrokes against their flanks. To facilitate this plan, the Soviets laid deep mine fields, behind which they concentrated vast quantities of artillery and antitank guns as well as large reserves of armor. Their efforts created a prodigiously strong defensive position that extended 65 miles in depth. An army group commanded by General Rokossovsky, who had led a corps in the Ukraine, an army in the Battle of Moscow, and an army group at Stalingrad, defended the northern portion of the salient. General Vatutin, another veteran of the Stalingrad encirclement, directed another army group along the southern flank.

When the Germans finally launched Operation Citadel on July 5, they unleashed an exceptionally powerful force of 17 panzer divisions. Despite the magnitude of their effort, the Red Army outnumbered them in manpower 1.3 million to 900,000 and enjoyed an advantage in tanks of 3,300 to 2,700. Soviet superiority in artillery was even more marked—20,000 to 10,000. The Germans soon encountered heavy losses in the mine fields, which the Soviets had situated in such a way as to channel enemy armor directly into artillery and antitank fire.

The struggle became a great battle of attrition along a front that seldom exceeded 15 miles in width. It was the greatest clash of armor of the entire war, with almost 3,000 tanks on the field at the peak of the fighting. It was also one of the bloodiest and most hideous of the many horrendous battles on the Eastern Front. Many German infantrymen insisted that it was the worst they

had experienced. Soviet artillery took an especially grim toll of German armor. The 3rd Panzer Division lost all but 30 of its 300 tanks, and several other panzer divisions suffered similar losses. The Germans did little more than dent the Soviet defenses. Both sides suffered exceptionally heavy losses, but whereas the Soviets could sustain theirs, the Germans were less fortunate. For them, Kursk was fatal. On July 12, Hitler ordered his generals to break off their attacks.

His action did not come a moment too soon, because the Red Army opened a powerful counteroffensive the same day. They attacked the enemy flank to the north of the Kursk salient and threatened to cut off the German forces, which had been advancing southward. On August 3, the Soviets delivered another blow against the Germans

The Battle of Kursk, July 1943, and the Subsequent Soviet Offensive

to the south of the salient and thrust toward Kharkov. The great industrial city changed hands for the fourth and last time on August 22 as General Ivan Konev's troops drove the enemy westward. Konev was another general who rose to prominence during the war. His fame ultimately became second only to that of Zhukov. Konev had followed the usual route of future Soviet commanders. A noncommissioned officer in the tsar's forces, he joined the Red Army in 1918, winning renown for his guerrilla exploits in Siberia during the civil war. He had assumed command of the Moscow front just in time to take the blame for the disasters of October 1941. For a time he appeared headed for oblivion, but Zhukov came to his rescue and made him his deputy. He became an army group commander in 1943. Despite Zhukov's kindness, Konev later became his chief rival.

The Soviets rolled on toward the Dnieper and crossed the river near Kiev at the end of September. Instead of halting their advance to organize a conventional crossing, their spearhead units simply stormed across the river with the help of small boats and improvised rafts. They established several bridgeheads on the west bank before the Germans could consolidate their defense. By early November, the Red Army had recaptured Kiev.

The Germans Begin to Crumble

If the failure at Stalingrad had ended all hope for a German offensive victory, the disaster at Kursk and the subsequent Soviet counteroffensive eliminated any chance for a successful defensive struggle. Hitler's panzer forces never fully recovered from the triphammer blows of the summer and fall of 1943. And despite Speer's amazing achievement in increasing German tank production, it did not keep pace with Soviet output of armor. During 1944–45, Germany produced 8,400 tanks, a figure almost three times greater than the entire armored force that had launched the Russian campaign in 1941, but the Soviets produced 10,000 T34s alone during 1944. Russian industry turned out vast quantities of other arms as well, including greatly improved aircraft, guns, mortars, and automatic infantry weapons.

By this time, American industry had also made the transition to a full wartime basis. In addition to providing a steadily accelerating flow of materiel to

their own armed forces, the Americans sent increasing lend-lease aid to Russia. This included all types of equipment, food, and other supplies. Most significantly, America provided more than 375,000 trucks, over 50,000 Jeeps, and almost 9,000 tractor vehicles, including half tracks used to haul Soviet artillery, as well as vast quantities of spare parts. This gave the Red Army much greater mobility and hastened their ultimate victory.

In the aftermath of the Kursk debacle, Germany also found it impossible to replace its manpower losses, whereas the Soviets were able to draft large numbers of men from the areas they recaptured. The Red Army also absorbed partisan units that had been operating behind enemy lines. If the Soviets harbored any doubts about their ability to win the war before the Battle of Kursk, they had none afterward.

The staggering defeat at Kursk struck Hitler with tremendous impact. He now withdrew in relative isolation, with only a few people in attendance, and found refuge in his own dream world. The catastrophe increased his distrust of the generals. After all, Kursk had been their idea, not his. The OKH had planned the operation, and Zeitzler had talked him into overcoming his own doubts. In the future, he relied more and more on his own intuition. But even though he had been right about Kursk, he now returned to the rigid "stand fast" mentality that had led to the Stalingrad encirclement and soon contributed to new disasters. The first of these occurred when the Führer rejected Manstein's plea that he evacuate the 17th Army from the Crimea. His refusal enabled the Soviets to cut off this force in November.

The Soviets Roll On

Meanwhile, the Red Army continued to drive westward. In January 1944, it penetrated into the southeastern corner of prewar Poland. The same month also witnessed the lifting of the 900-day siege of Leningrad. In early February, Soviet troops, operating from bridgeheads west of the Dnieper, attempted to cut off a German salient around the town of Korsun. Konev sent a spearhead slashing northwestward, while Vatutin swung to the southeast. The two forces came together on February 3, trapping almost 75,000 Germans. Konev received a promotion to the rank of marshal as his reward.

FIGURE 16-2   Soviet partisans in action behind the German front. (*Library of Congress*)

Vatutin was not so fortunate. He died of wounds inflicted by a band of Ukrainian nationalists soon afterward.

In March, Konev launched an incredible operation, his "mud offensive," which took place during the worst part of the spring thaw in the Ukraine. It provided ample evidence of the growing skill of Red Army commanders and violated all the rules of war. Playing on the advantage of complete surprise, it resulted in another great Soviet victory. The keys to this achievement were the wide-tracked T34 tank, with its center of gravity located in the midsection of the vehicle, and the American four-wheel-drive truck; both were able to perform efficiently in the abominable conditions. Before the month was over, the Soviets swept into Bessarabia in prewar Rumania. These defeats so enraged Hitler that he dismissed both his army group commanders in the south, Manstein and Kleist. Despite their many brilliant contributions to Germany's efforts in Russia, they could not accomplish the impossible.

A lull set in on the eastern front in April. But the Soviets resumed the offensive with even greater vigor in Belorussia on June 23, a little over

two weeks after the start of the Anglo-American cross-channel invasion of France. Once again Marshal Zhukov held overall command. This time he enjoyed a 4-to-1 superiority in manpower and a 6-to-1 advantage in armor. With the possible exception of the Battle of Kursk, this was the most carefully prepared Soviet offensive of the war. It caught Army Group Center off guard and stabbed deep into the German rear, destroying 25 divisions with a total of 350,000 men. The disaster was greater than Stalingrad. Soviet forces now proceeded to liberate the last remnants of Soviet soil from German control and threatened the Baltic states. They also overran most of eastern Poland. By late August, troops under Rokossovsky's command had reached the outskirts of Warsaw.

The Warsaw Uprising

The arrival of the Soviet spearhead in the vicinity of the Polish capital triggered one of the great tragedies of the war—the Warsaw Uprising. The Polish Home Army, an anti-Communist resistance force affiliated with the London-based Polish government in exile, attempted to seize Warsaw before the Red Army entered the city. This action represented the culmination of gradually deteriorating relations between the London Poles and Moscow.

General Wladislaw Sikorski had personally organized the Polish exile regime in Paris during the fall of 1939. Sikorski, who had commanded the forces that had halted the Red Army's attempt to capture Warsaw during the Russo-Polish War in 1920, had also recruited an 82,000-man military force, largely from Poles who had been working as miners in France. With the French capitulation in 1940, Sikorski moved his government and army to Britain.

Sikorski had established diplomatic relations with Moscow after the German invasion of the Soviet Union. Stalin had been eager to accept any offers of friendship at that time, but he was not willing to agree to Sikorski's plea for a restoration of Poland's prewar eastern border after the conflict. His refusal contributed to continuing tension between the Soviets and the Poles. This worsened dramatically in April 1943, when Germany announced the discovery of the bodies of 4,300 Polish army officers in the Katyn Forest near Smolensk. The Germans charged that the Russians had murdered these men while this area had been under their control. Many Westerners believed that the Germans had actually committed the atrocity, but Sikorski's government asked for an inquiry by the International Red Cross. Stalin reacted to this by angrily breaking off relations with the Poles. It is now certain that the Soviets were indeed the culprits.

Shortly after the severing of relations, Sikorski died in a plane crash, and Stanislaw Mikolajczyk succeeded him as prime minister. Mikolajczyk was a moderate of peasant stock who had fought the Germans in 1939 before escaping to the West. He tried to persuade his colleagues that they had no choice but to seek an understanding with the Soviets. But he lacked Sikorski's prestige and authority, and anti-Russian members of his cabinet refused to follow a conciliatory policy.

When the Soviets smashed into Poland during their 1944 summer offensive, they recognized the Communist-dominated Polish Committee of National Liberation, which established itself as a provisional government in the city of Lublin. They also arrested members of the Home Army in areas that fell under their control. The Soviet presence and the existence of the Lublin regime badly undercut the London Poles' claim to be the legitimate government of Poland. It was this combination of events that led to the decision to launch the Warsaw Uprising. If the Home Army could gain control of Warsaw, it would provide Mikolajczyk's government with a power base in Poland. Whether it could maintain that position once the Red Army arrived in strength was another matter. At best, the operation was an act of desperation.

The Warsaw Uprising began on August 1, and General Tadeusz Bor-Komorowski's Home Army forces soon captured half the city. The general's name originally had been simply Komorowski, and he had served as a cavalry leader during the German invasion of Poland. Soon afterward, he had persuaded Sikorski to allow the formation of an underground home army and became its commander in 1943. The general had assumed the name Bor as a cover and subsequently retained it. Despite their initial success, the Poles could not defeat the German garrison without help from the Red Army, but Rokossovsky halted his advance along the Vistula River to the east of Warsaw.

Critics have charged that Stalin deliberately refused to allow his troops to come to the rescue and thus enabled the Germans to destroy the Home Army. Although it is true that the Soviet dictator had no sympathy for Bor-Komorowski's forces and was not sorry to see the Germans crush the revolt, the Soviet failure to act appears to have been due to less sinister factors. When Rokossovsky's troops reached the vicinity of Warsaw, they were suffering from exhaustion and severe supply problems. They were especially deficient in bridging equipment, which was necessary for a crossing of the Vistula. It appears that Rokossovsky had no choice but to halt. Indeed, the whole massive offensive into Poland had lost its momentum by this time. When the Soviets did attempt to force their way across the river in mid-September, the Germans repulsed the attack.

Anglo-American leaders hoped to drop supplies by air to the beleaguered Poles, but for several weeks Stalin would not allow their planes to land on Russian airfields to refuel for the return trip. When he finally granted permission for one such operation, it proved a dismal failure. By this time, the Germans had recaptured much of the city, and most of the supplies fell into their hands. Without outside help, the Poles were doomed, and on October 2 the survivors of the horrible ordeal surrendered. In the process of crushing resistance, the Germans committed savage atrocities against Warsaw's population. They set fire to buildings and shot down many thousands of men, women, and children. When the fighting ended, Hitler ordered the total destruction of what was left of the city. The Germans also shipped 150,000 civilians to the Reich as slave laborers and sent the remaining 550,000 to concentration camps. Not a single Pole remained in the wasteland of demolished buildings that had once been Poland's capital.

Soviet Successes in the Baltic States and the Balkans

Zhukov's sweepingly successful offensive against Army Group Center had also threatened to outflank Army Group North in the Baltic states. But the Soviet high command left the actual task of clearing Estonia, Latvia, and Lithuania to other Red Army forces. A major offensive began on September 14 with the objective of breaking through to the Baltic coast near Riga, the Latvian capital. Field Marshal Ferdinand Schörner, the commander of Army Group North, was a staunch supporter of the Nazi regime as well as a tough and resourceful officer. He managed to evacuate his forces from Estonia and northern Latvia but encountered increasing pressure from General Ivan Bagramyan's troops, which were thrusting through Lithuania. Bagramyan had seen most of his previous service in the Ukraine. He had narrowly missed being captured in the 1941 Kiev encirclement and had commanded an army in the Battle of Kursk. His troops reached the Baltic to the southwest of Riga on October 10 and captured the city five days later. The bulk of Army Group North was now trapped in a pocket in the Courland Peninsula of western Latvia.

Guderian, who had succeeded Zeitzler as chief of staff in July, urged Hitler to evacuate Schörner's forces by sea. Hitler flatly refused, insisting that by staying in the Courland Pocket, Army Group North would divert Soviet strength away from other operations. Guderian pointed out that these troops would be far more useful in defense of the eastern approaches to Germany. As usual, Hitler won the argument. Although some units were

evacuated later, 26 divisions remained in Courland until the end of the war.

The collapse of Germany's position in the East led to the rapid defection of its satellites during the late summer of 1944. On June 10, Red Army troops had opened attacks against Finland in the Karelian Isthmus. By June 20, the Finns asked for an armistice. But both the negotiations and the Soviet offensive bogged down for the next two months. It was not until September 19 that hostilities finally ceased. The Soviet terms were roughly those that had ended the Winter War four years earlier, with some relatively minor changes. Finland's timely exit from the conflict allowed it to avoid occupation by Soviet forces.

Rumania, Bulgaria, Slovakia, and Hungary had all been seeking to desert the Axis for some time. Rumania was the first to succeed. On August 20, Soviet army groups, commanded by Marshals Rodion Malinovsky and F. I. Tolbukhin, converged on the Axis troops defending northeastern Rumania. They broke through to the Danube River and cut off 12 German divisions. Malinovsky had won fame for his part in repulsing Manstein's attempt to relieve the German troops trapped in the Stalingrad pocket. This had required leading his army on a forced march that covered 125 miles in five days through a howling blizzard. As an army group commander, he had played a major role in expelling the enemy from the Ukraine. Tolbukhin had commanded an army in the encirclement of Stalingrad. Later his army group had contributed to the first sweep across the Ukraine and the reconquest of the Crimea.

When the Red Army began its offensive, Rumania's King Michael, with the support of army leaders, ousted the pro-German premier, Marshal Ion Antonescu, and announced the end of hostilities. In their surrender terms, the Soviets forced the Rumanians to return Bessarabia and Northern Bukovina to the USSR. But in return, they supported Rumania's claim for the restoration of Hungarian-occupied Transylvania to Rumanian sovereignty. A Rumanian coalition government, consisting of both Communist and non-Communist ministers, took office, but it was disunited and inefficient. By February 1945, the Soviets had pressured the formation of a new regime that was essentially Communist.

After their disaster in Rumania, the Germans faced a hopeless position in much of the Balkans.

A vast open flank lay in the path of the Soviet juggernaut. Germany's remaining forces in Rumania fell back to the west and abandoned both the Ploesti oil fields and Bucharest, the capital, before the end of September. There was now nothing to prevent the Red Army from overrunning Bulgaria while other Soviet forces penetrated into Yugoslavia. On October 20, they joined with Tito's Partisans to capture Belgrade, the Yugoslav capital.

These developments made the position of the German troops in Greece highly precarious. Retreat northward was the only option if they were to avoid being cut off by the Soviet advance. They had to carry out their withdrawal over extremely poor roads, which Tito's forces subjected to repeated attacks. But they did escape. The German departure left a political vacuum in Greece, and Churchill dispatched British troops to fill it. They landed in Greece on October 4 and occupied Athens nine days later, just after the Germans had evacuated. A coalition Greek government took over administration of the country, but its prospects were bleak. Large guerrilla bands, including many Communists, roamed over much of the country. The regime could maintain itself in power only with British military support.

In Slovakia, disenchantment with the German alliance led to a revolt by Slovak partisans in September. The Slovaks hoped that Red Army troops would soon join them, but the Soviets had to cross the rugged Carpathian Mountains, which the Germans defended tenaciously, and did not reach Slovakia until October. By then the Germans had crushed the revolt.

Hungary, the last of the Nazi satellites, also looked for a way out of its dilemma. When the Soviets made their first penetration into Rumania in March 1944, Hitler sent German troops to stiffen Hungary's will to resist. But with the defection of the Rumanians from the Axis camp in September, Hungarian dictator Admiral Nicholas Horthy tried to secure an armistice. Hitler responded with his usual quickness. He dispatched an SS unit to kidnap Horthy and recognized a new pro-Axis Hungarian regime. The Führer's efforts proved less successful in halting the relentless advance of the Red Army. The Soviets broke into the Hungarian Plain in October and reached the suburbs of Budapest on November 4. Axis forces defended the Hungarian capital stubbornly, but by late December, the Soviets had encircled the city.

The year 1944 had been one of unrelieved disaster for the Germans on the Eastern Front. The Red Army had ousted them from the USSR, most of the Baltic states, half of Poland, and all but the northern fringes of the Balkans. It had even occupied the extreme eastern border area of East Prussia, the first Soviet penetration of Germany's prewar territory. But Hitler's forces were not yet finished. By late December, the Soviet steamroller had ground to a halt. This lull was due less to German defensive efforts than to Russian logistic problems, however. And it was not destined to last for long. Stalin's forces were planning to unleash a new series of powerful blows early in 1945.

CHAPTER SEVENTEEN

The Tide Turns in North Africa: El Alamein to Tunisia

The war reached another turning point in October 1942, even before the start of the Soviet counteroffensive at Stalingrad. This one involved the defeat of Rommel's Axis forces at El Alamein in Egypt. Even though it came in a much less important theater of operations, it has received at least as much attention as the German debacle in Russia. But, as in the Pacific and Russia, the Axis held the initiative during much of 1942. And, once again its victories proved to be a prelude to disaster. Before the end of the year, Rommel's vaunted Afrika Korps was in full retreat across Libya and faced still another danger from the west. Anglo-American forces had invaded the French colonies of Morocco and Algeria in early November and had driven eastward into Tunisia. There the Axis would make its last desperate stand in Africa in a struggle that would last until May 1943 and would end with another mass surrender.

The "Sideshow" in North Africa

Hitler had always considered North Africa as a sideshow. Once he committed himself to the invasion of the Soviet Union, the North African campaign represented a drain on German resources, which he hoped to keep as slight as possible. Some observers have pointed to this as a great missed opportunity on Hitler's part. They argue that had he been willing to concentrate on North Africa, he might have conquered Egypt and the Suez Canal and driven on to seize the oil fields of the Middle East. Rommel certainly thought so. He pleaded repeatedly for reinforcements and more equipment to enable him to complete the conquest of Egypt and advance beyond. But Hitler and the Wehrmacht leaders chose to keep him on a short leash while concentrating on the Eastern Front. In reality, even if Hitler had been willing and able to allot

greater resources to this theater, it appears highly doubtful that the Germans could have conquered Egypt, not to speak of the Middle East, because of the huge logistic problems involved.

The distance from Tripoli, the main Axis port in western Libya, to the British naval base at Alexandria in Egypt is over 1,300 miles, more than twice the distance from the prewar Soviet-Polish border to Moscow. The port of Tripoli had limited capacity, and the Germans had to transport supplies from there for hundreds of miles along a single road. Rommel was also short of trucks. There were other ports east of Tripoli, but they were all far inferior in capacity. Coastal shipping was also in short supply. These logistic facts made it impossible for the Germans to supply large forces and extremely difficult for them to supply the troops they did have in North Africa. British air and naval forces, operating from the island of Malta south of Sicily, also harassed Rommel's supply line across the Mediterranean. The Axis considered an invasion of Malta to eliminate this threat, but nothing came of it. They did, however, subject the island to intense bombing and inflicted severe damage on British convoys attempting to supply Malta.

After Rommel's 1941 spring offensive bogged down along the Libyan-Egyptian border, he tried repeatedly to dislodge the British force that held Tobruk, the bypassed port on his left flank. But the British clung tenaciously to the town, in large part to prevent the Axis from obtaining a port close to the front. Although the acquisition of Tobruk certainly would have helped Rommel, it actually had limited importance because of the harbor's inadequate capacity and the Axis shortage of coastal shipping.

The British hoped to regain the initiative, and General Wavell made an attempt to oust the Axis forces from their border positions and relieve the Tobruk garrison in May. But Rommel proved as skillful in defense as he had in offensive operations, and the attack failed. Meanwhile, Churchill had sent reinforcements, including tanks, to Egypt and prevailed upon Wavell to undertake a second and more powerful offensive in June. The British employed a flanking movement, which caught Rommel by surprise, but then followed up with direct attacks against Axis armor and antitank guns at Halfaya ("Hellfire") Pass. Although they were at a considerable numerical disadvantage in tanks, the Axis forces handled their armor much better than the British, who still tended to group their tanks in packets rather than in large concentrations. The Germans also effectively adapted their 88-millimeter antiaircraft gun for use as an antitank weapon. British Matilda tanks, which had been so efficient against the Italians, proved vulnerable to the 88. Rommel's troops forced the British to withdraw back to Egypt.

Churchill considered Wavell's handling of the operation to be overly cautious and replaced him with General Claude Auchinleck. Wavell actually exchanged positions with Auchinleck, who had been commander in chief in India and had spent most of his career there. He had also commanded operations in northern Norway in 1940 and later organized the defense of southern Britain against the invasion that never came. Quiet and popular with his men, he was receptive to new ideas but, like most British generals at this time, knew little about armored warfare. Auchinleck soon obtained reinforcements and formed the new 8th Army. But he bluntly resisted Churchill's insistent prodding for another offensive until he considered his forces strong enough to defeat Rommel and relieve Tobruk.

Auchinleck chose General Alan Cunningham to lead the 8th Army. The brother of the Mediterranean Fleet commander, Cunningham came to Egypt from East Africa, where he had directed the victory over the Italians earlier in 1941. But he had accomplished this famous exploit with much smaller forces and had no experience handling large armored units. During the following months British strength grew steadily, giving them a greater numerical superiority than they had enjoyed in their June offensive. British tanks were considerably more plentiful than those of the Germans, but they were inferior in quality to Rommel's Panzer III and Panzer IV models.

Auchinleck finally launched his offensive on November 18 with the intention of relieving Tobruk, but heavy fighting erupted around the Sidi Rezegh escarpment. Again the Axis forces outclassed their opponents in the use of armor. Rommel boldly directed a column around the British southern flank, hoping to shake Cunningham's confidence and force another withdrawal. He succeeded at first. Cunningham, whose morale had reached a low ebb, believed the battle was lost. But Auchinleck refused to break off the offensive. He replaced Cunningham with General Neil Ritchie and ordered the 8th Army to hold its ground. Rommel, now in a highly vulnerable forward position and still at a disadvantage in strength, had no choice but to fall back, enabling the British to relieve Tobruk. His flight continued throughout December all the way to El Agheila, the point from which he had launched his offensive the previous spring.

Meanwhile, the outbreak of war in East Asia led to the shift of two Allied divisions and an armored brigade as well as four fighter squadrons from North Africa to Southeast Asia. Rommel sensed that conditions were favorable for a counterattack, which he delivered on January 21, 1942. His forces outmaneuvered the British and forced them to withdraw to a fortified position running southward from Gazala, about 35 miles west of Tobruk. Here Rommel once more encountered supply problems, and a lull developed in the campaign while both sides built up their strength and prepared to take the offensive in the spring.

Rommel Drives into Egypt

Rommel struck first. He unleashed a major offensive on May 26. Although he had obtained some reinforcements, he was still inferior to the British in armor but now had air superiority. He also had another advantage. Axis intelligence had broken the code used by the U.S. military representative in North Africa, which provided detailed information on British intentions and troop dispositions. Rommel used another wide flanking attack in an attempt to swing north to the sea and cut off the British defenders. Auchinleck had received Ultra warnings of the impending assault, although they gave no help as to where the Axis would strike. He nevertheless guessed correctly that Rommel would combine an attack in the center with a thrust around the desert flank. Auchinleck recommended that Ritchie mass the bulk of his armor so that he could direct it in strength wherever it was most needed. But Ritchie ignored this advice and left his tanks scattered in various areas. Indeed, Ritchie lacked the experience to command in the field at this critical moment. He had served ably as a staff officer for 20 years but had not held a battlefield leadership role since World War I. Auchinleck had originally intended his appointment to be temporary and had actually directed field operations himself in the crucial days immediately following Cunningham's dismissal.

When Rommel opened his offensive, he soon realized that his forces were not strong enough to complete their initial thrust. Accordingly, he switched to a defensive position and lured Ritchie into attacking him. The Axis troops then made effective use of their antitank guns to wear down the British, who suffered such heavy losses in piecemeal assaults that Rommel was able to resume his offensive. Ritchie withdrew toward Egypt while one British force fell back on Tobruk.

This time Rommel attacked the town before the British could consolidate their position. His troops quickly overran the defenders and captured 35,000 prisoners as well as vast quantities of fuel, food, and drinking water on May 21. These supplies enabled them to thrust deeply into Egyptian territory. They reached El Alamein, 60 miles west of Alexandria, on June 30. Hitler rewarded Rommel for his dramatic success by promoting him to field marshal.

Auchinleck was determined to make his stand at the El Alamein position. It was ideal for defense, taking the form of a 36-mile bottleneck between the Mediterranean to the north and the impassable salt marshes and soft sand of the Quattara Depression to the south. This meant that the Axis forces could not outflank El Alamein and thus could only take it by frontal assault. Auchinleck dismissed Ritchie and took over personal command of the 8th Army. He was able to consolidate his defenses while Rommel encountered problems. The supplies, which the Germans had captured at Tobruk, were dwindling, and they were running short of armor.

Rommel tried, nevertheless, to break through at El Alamein in early July. But Auchinleck's forces

FIGURE 17-1   Field Marshal Erwin Rommel confers with two Italian generals in North Africa. *(AP/Wide World Photos)*

held firm, although their subsequent counterattack failed to dislodge the Axis troops. This struggle, the First Battle of El Alamein, to a considerable extent marked the turning point of the North African campaign, even though Rommel remained dangerous until August. It represented a personal triumph for Auchinleck and a major contribution to the ultimate Allied victory. In the months that followed, Britain sent a stream of reinforcements and supplies to the 8th Army, including many American Sherman and Grant tanks, which mounted 75-mm guns. The British also regained predominance in the air.

Despite Auchinleck's success in stopping Rommel in the First Battle of El Alamein, the disasters that had preceded this victory and the failure of his counterattack afterward led to his ouster. Churchill appointed General Harold Alexander commander of the entire theater and placed General Bernard Montgomery in charge of the 8th Army. Alexander exuded an aura of contagious confidence. At age 25, he had commanded a battalion on the western front in World War I, being wounded three times and winning numerous decorations for bravery. In 1940, he guided the final stages of the Dunkirk evacuation before directing the defense of southern Britain. He took over command in Burma in 1941, just in time to supervise the long, arduous retreat to India. Although his new position made him Montgomery's superior, Alexander actually exercised little control over the headstrong leader of the 8th Army.

Montgomery, like General MacArthur, possessed an outsized ego and loved to be the focus of publicity. But if anything, he was more arrogant, certainly far more abrasive, and clearly the most controversial British general of the war. The son of an Anglican bishop, he had served on the western front in World War I and almost succumbed to a sniper's bullet. The war's carnage convinced him of the need for organization, training, and caution in military operations. He also took a deep personal interest in his soldiers' welfare and, in return, earned their devotion. "Monty," as he became known to the public, commanded a division in the BEF during 1940 and later all forces engaged in the defense of southwestern Britain. He also shared MacArthur's fondness for unusual headgear, but he preferred an Australian slouch hat and later a beret to the American's gold-bedecked cap.

These changes occurred in mid-August, just before Rommel's last attempt to gain a breakthrough at El Alamein. His plan involved another "right hook" maneuver followed by a thrust northward toward the sea. In addition to his usual numerical disadvantage in armor, Rommel suffered from poor health. He directed his attack against the Alma Halfa Ridge, a position that, ironically, Auchinleck had strengthened with a deep belt of fortifications before his dismissal. Montgomery also used a defensive plan that Auchinleck had devised. When Rommel's offensive failed, Montgomery claimed that the plan was his own and refused to grant any credit to his predecessor. Montgomery also had the help of detailed Ultra reports that indicated where Rommel would attack and the forces he would use. This struggle forced Rommel into a permanent defensive stance.

The Second Battle of El Alamein

Montgomery was a master of the "set-piece" battle, an offensive in which the commander plans everything down to the last detail and amasses overwhelming manpower and materiel. If he had counterattacked immediately following the Battle of Alma Halfa, he might have cut off the German spearhead, which was in a highly vulnerable position. But Montgomery chose to eliminate any possibility of failure and refused to take action for almost two months. When he finally attacked in the Second Battle of El Alamein on October 23, his troops outnumbered the Axis forces 230,000 to 80,000. He also enjoyed an advantage in armor of 1,200 to 500, and only 210 of Rommel's tanks were of high quality. British command of the air was also overwhelming. Ultra reports continued to aid Montgomery as well. They provided information that enabled British submarines and aircraft to sink Axis shipping with cargoes bound for North Africa. Montgomery also gained a clear picture of Axis strength and morale, both before the offensive began and while it was in progress.

The British opened their offensive with an enormous artillery barrage that, though destructive, eliminated any chance of surprise. When the battle began, Rommel was not in Egypt. He had fallen victim to a severe case of boils, a common desert malady, and had flown to Germany for treatment. He did not return until two days after the start of the struggle. The bottleneck nature of the El Alamein position made it extremely difficult for attacking forces to maneuver under any circumstances. But Montgomery compounded the problem by concentrating most of his strength against a four-mile stretch of front near the northern end of the line. This enabled the Germans to bring firepower to bear against British armor, which also suffered heavy casualties in the extensive enemy mine fields. British tank losses were four times greater than those of their opponents, but the Axis could not afford even this ratio of attrition. By November 2, Rommel realized that he must retreat if he were to avoid total disaster. But Hitler, true to his "hold fast" mentality, delayed the withdrawal for two days.

Despite Rommel's earlier spectacular victories, his handling of this retreat was probably his greatest achievement. But he accomplished it only by taking over Italian motorized transport and ungallantly leaving most of his allies behind. Their sacrifice enabled 40,000 men to escape. The 8th Army followed, but Montgomery's pursuit lacked boldness. If he had acted with more vigor, he might have destroyed Rommel's forces. He did make several attempts to outflank the fleeing enemy, but these were too tentative and did not penetrate deeply enough to get the job done. Instead, Rommel was able to retreat into Libya. Meanwhile, in early November, British and American forces landed in French Morocco and Algeria and moved toward Tunisia, threatening the Afrika Korps from the

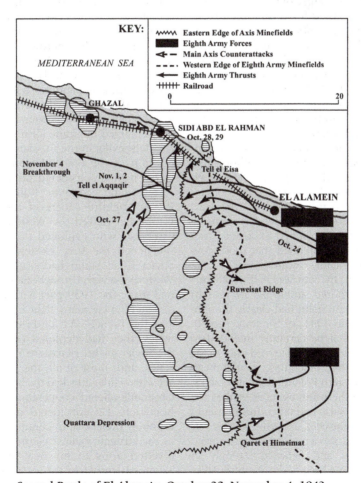

Second Battle of El Alamein, October 23–November 4, 1942

west. This time there was no halt at El Agheila as the Axis troops continued their flight across Libya to Tripoli and beyond. By the end of 1942, Hitler's dream of victory in Egypt had faded into the grim prospect of total expulsion from North Africa. But to the British, the victory at El Alamein enabled them to finally breath easier and dare to hope for continued success. As Churchill noted: "This is not the end, nor is it even the beginning of the end, but it is, perhaps, the end of the beginning."

Problems of a Marriage of Convenience

The Allied invasion of French North Africa was actually the fruit of a disagreement over strategy that began soon after the entry of the United States into the war and persisted for several months. It reflected the often contentious and somewhat fragile nature of the Allied coalition. The alliance of Britain, the United States, and the Soviet Union was just as much a marriage of convenience as the Nazi-Soviet Pact of 1939. It came into being in 1941 because all three powers had the same enemy, at least in Europe. Russia had not yet entered the war against Japan.

Britain and the United States enjoyed substantial agreement on basic war aims. And although the Western Allies frequently disagreed on strategy, they maintained a remarkable degree of cooperation. Both were democracies, detested the Nazi regime, and wanted to establish free governments in the countries that they planned to liberate from German rule. They also intended that those governments would be friendly toward them.

The Soviet Union, by contrast, had a totalitarian regime that harbored ambitions in Eastern Europe. To what extent Stalin had clearly thought out those ambitions in 1941, or for some time to come, is not clear. But he certainly intended to restore the Soviet borders that had existed prior to the German invasion. This, of course, would mean Russian control of eastern Poland, the Baltic states, Bessarabia, and Northern Bukovina as well as the territories that the Soviets had taken from Finland in the Winter War. However, as ruthless as he was as dictator, Stalin was also a realist who recognized the limits of power and believed strongly in spheres of influence. As long as the Western Allies acknowledged the Soviets' right to fulfill their war aims in Eastern Europe, he appears to have been willing to extend the same recognition to Britain and America in Western Europe and the Mediterranean.

Coalitions are notoriously difficult to hold together, and this one contained the seeds of disintegration from the start. Soviet historians argued that a cold war between Russia and the West had existed for many decades before the period that we now refer to by that name. They contended that the Cold War was merely put on hold during World War II to facilitate the defeat of the common enemy, only to flourish anew in the war's aftermath. To be sure, the Western Powers had looked upon Russia with distaste and distrust well before the twentieth century. Both Americans and British had denounced the tsarist regime as an absolute monarchy in an age of rising democracy. Britain also had long feared Russian encroachment toward the Mediterranean, in the Middle East, and on the fringes of India as well as in East Asia. The United States disapproved of Russian ambitions in China. These concerns had been pushed to one side during World War I when all three powers fought Germany, but they emerged in a new form with the triumph of the Bolsheviks in the Russian Revolution and the creation of the Soviet Union. For its part, the tsarist regime considered Britain and the United States to be economic bullies that threatened Russia's rightful sphere of influence. Later, the Bolsheviks viewed the Western Powers as hated capitalists who exploited the working class and threatened the very existence of the fledgling Soviet state. Stalin had been suspicious of the Western Powers throughout the 1930s, and he had made the 1939 pact with Hitler in the hope of watching Germany fight it out with the British and the French. As for Britain and the United States, they had deplored the Nazi-Soviet Pact, the Soviet seizure of eastern Poland and the Baltic states, and, most of all, the invasion of Finland. Yet when Hitler attacked the Soviet Union in 1941, Churchill offered cooperation to Stalin without hesitation. He considered alliance with Russia infinitely preferable to continued British isolation in the struggle against Germany, and he quickly diverted arms to his new ally. Roosevelt also extended lend-lease aid to Stalin even before the U.S. entry into the conflict.

Both Britain and the United States approached the war, at least in part, as a moral crusade against Hitler and Nazism. The Atlantic Charter reflected this attitude. But the two countries differed on their interpretations of the document. Roosevelt saw the charter as having worldwide implications, including the right of British colonies to obtain independence. Churchill viewed it as applying only to nations that had lost their independence during the war. Stalin does not appear to have taken the charter seriously.

In December 1941, Churchill and the British chiefs of staff traveled to Washington to confer with Roosevelt and the U.S. service chiefs in the Arcadia Conference. These leaders confirmed the "Europe first" approach to the war, which the Allies had laid down in January, and stipulated that the Pacific and East Asia would remain of secondary importance until the defeat of Germany. The Allies also agreed to form a unified Anglo-American high command that would operate in Washington. This combined chiefs of staff organization consisted of the top military and naval leaders of the two countries. But since the British chiefs would be in Britain most of the time, Field Marshal Sir John Dill, a former army chief of staff, would remain in Washington as London's permanent representative.

During the Arcadia Conference, the Americans noted the close coordination that existed among the British chiefs of staff compared to their own lack of cooperation. The British had established a chiefs of staff committee, consisting of Churchill's representative, General Hastings Ismay, and the heads of the three services—Field Marshal Alan Brooke (army), Admiral Sir Dudley Pound (navy), and Air Chief Marshal Sir Charles Portal (RAF). The United States had only the loosely linked Joint Board, which provided little real coordination.

In the aftermath of the conference, the Americans formed a joint chiefs of staff organization. It included General Marshall, Admiral King, and General H. H. Arnold, the head of the Army Air Force, as well as Roosevelt's personal representative, Admiral William Leahy, a former chief of naval operations. This body henceforth provided overall direction to the American war effort, under Roosevelt's supervision.

Britain and America confronted a dilemma in the unmistakable fact that the Soviet Union carried the predominant burden of the war against Germany from 1941 to 1944. This proved embarrassing to Roosevelt and Churchill and was a deterrent to their hopes of modifying Soviet ambitions in Eastern Europe. They were hardly in a position to be demanding on this point, given the magnitude of the Soviet war effort.

The lack of a massive Western contribution in 1942 angered Stalin, especially during the summer and fall, when the Germans were driving toward Stalingrad and the Caucasus. To be sure, the British were fighting Rommel in North Africa, but this was a sideshow, involving relatively small numbers. The desert struggle was also far away from Germany and could bring little direct relief to the Soviet Union. Britain did begin heavy bombing raids against German cities in 1942, but despite extensive damage inflicted by these attacks, they had relatively little impact on Germany's war industries.

Allied Differences on Strategy

Stalin insisted that Britain and the United States open a second front by undertaking a cross-channel invasion of Nazi-occupied France in 1942. Such an operation would place them in a position to drive directly on Germany and force Hitler to divert troops from the eastern front. U.S. leaders, including Secretary of War Stimson and General Marshall, shared Stalin's interest in a cross-channel assault. They argued that once established in western France, the Allies could thrust toward the heart of Germany by the shortest route. To them, every other potential theater of operations was of secondary importance. The British, however, preferred a more flexible approach, which recognized the need to invade Western Europe but also emphasized the exploitation of other opportunities, especially in the Mediterranean.

This division of opinion reflected long-standing differences regarding strategy in the two countries. Since the Civil War, American military leaders had focused almost entirely on the belief that the chief objective of strategy was the destruction of the enemy's ground forces and that everything else must be subordinated to this. The American approach was preeminently a military one and relegated political and economic considerations to secondary importance. British leaders had traditionally given much greater weight to these factors. Their approach reflected Britain's worldwide political and economic interests as well as its dominant position on the high seas. During the wars of the eighteenth and early nineteenth centuries, the British had created alliances, in which their continental allies assumed most of the burden of land combat. This freed Britain from the need to recruit a mass army and enabled it to pursue a peripheral strategy with the aid of its powerful navy. The British struck at various enemy strongholds and in the process often acquired additional territories for their empire. Britain also used its navy to enforce a blockade, strangling enemy trade. World War I had been something of an exception to this approach, in that Britain had adopted conscription to create a mass army for the first time. This did not prevent it from nibbling at the periphery, however, most notably the unsuccesful Churchill-inspired attempt to seize the Turkish straits leading to the Black Sea and Russia. Memories of the awful carnage on the Western Front had made the British fearful of another bloodbath and less than enthusiastic about a cross-channel invasion.

In keeping with his preference for a peripheral strategy, Churchill broached the possibility of an Allied landing in French North Africa during the Arcadia Conference. At that time, Auchinleck's British 8th Army was pursuing Rommel across eastern Libya toward El Agheila. Churchill proposed that Allied troops occupy the French colonies of Morocco, Algeria, and Tunisia, which bordered Libya on the west. This would threaten Rommel's rear and, it was hoped, lead to his expulsion from Africa. Roosevelt was sympathetic to such an undertaking, and the two civilian leaders and their military staffs agreed that this would be the major operation in 1942. They indicated that any invasion of the European mainland would have to wait until 1943.

But the failure of Auchinleck's offensive to gain decisive results and Allied setbacks in East Asia dashed hopes for an early invasion of French North Africa. The Japanese triumphs necessitated the diversion of ships, troops, and planes to the Pacific and delayed the possibility of an assault against the French possessions.

In the weeks that followed the Arcadia Conference, American military leaders became increasingly skeptical of the proposed North African operation. Stimson, Marshall, and General Dwight Eisenhower, the chief of the War Department's operations division, agreed that such an undertaking would only divert strength away from a cross-channel invasion of Europe. They developed an alternative plan in March 1942 that called for an immediate buildup of Allied strength in Britain preliminary to a cross-channel invasion in the spring of 1943 (Operation Roundup). But they also saw the possibility of a smaller landing on the coast of France (Operation Sledgehammer) as early as the fall of 1942. They recommended the latter if it proved necessary to divert German troops away from the Eastern Front or if other developments posed the likelihood of a successful undertaking of this type.

Initially, the British response was favorable, and they accepted the proposal in principle. But from the start, top British leaders, especially Field Marshal Brooke, had strong reservations about Sledgehammer. After studying the possibility of an invasion in 1942, Brooke came to the conclusion that the Allies were not strong enough to undertake such an operation. Specifically, he pointed to shortages of troops, equipment, and landing craft. Brooke had succeeded Dill as army chief of staff shortly before the Arcadia Conference. Previously, he had commanded a corps in France and had skillfully conducted the evacuation of BEF troops from Dunkirk. Brooke felt little confidence in the strategic sense or command ability of his American allies and quickly emerged as the foremost British opponent of a cross-channel invasion.

Brooke gained Churchill's support for his opposition to Sledgehammer, and the prime minister pressed Roosevelt to abandon plans for a possible cross-channel operation in 1942. In its place he urged a return to the original proposal to land in French North Africa. Although the debate continued for weeks, Roosevelt eventually accepted Churchill's argument. His decision angered Marshall, and the general now sided with Admiral King and urged Roosevelt to resist the proposed North African operation and, if necessary, abandon the "Europe first" strategy and concentrate on the Pacific. But his effort failed. Roosevelt had definitely abandoned Sledgehammer and insisted that Western forces undertake an offensive somewhere in the general European theater in 1942. He could see no alternative to North Africa.

Roosevelt made his decision in part because of his desire to convince the Soviets that the Western Allies were determined to fight the Germans. But he also realized that many Americans favored gaining revenge for Pearl Harbor by concentrating on the Pacific, and he hoped to involve them emotionally in the war against Hitler. All these factors led to a compromise. Roosevelt ordered the military to go along with a North African invasion (Operation Torch), and he continued to view Europe as the crucial objective. But he also agreed to divert stronger forces to the Pacific, and during 1942 and most of 1943, more American forces operated in the Pacific than in the European theater.

Critics have contended since the war that Churchill was fundamentally opposed to any invasion of Western Europe, but this is probably an exaggeration. To be sure, the prime minister remembered the bloodbath on the western front in World War I and wanted to avoid another. Such fears certainly played an important part in his opposition to Sledgehammer. But his primary concern appears to have been to avoid a cross-channel invasion until the Allies had become strong enough to ensure success. Considering the improvised nature of the German plan for an invasion of Britain in 1940, Churchill's opposition to Sledgehammer was not unfounded. But whether it was wise to shift strength to the Mediterranean instead of focusing all efforts on a buildup for an

invasion of France in 1943 is another matter. Once Churchill and Roosevelt made the decision to intervene in French North Africa, prospects for a cross-channel operation in 1943 plummeted, and the likelihood of the Allies' becoming bogged down in a Mediterranean strategy increased sharply.

Churchill believed that the West could plan both a Mediterranean and a cross-channel strategy and exploit the one that offered the best chance of success. But American military leaders viewed Churchill's policy as one designed to secure Britain's political and economic interests in the Mediterranean. Certainly Churchill was a staunch believer in the need to maintain the British Empire on the strongest possible basis after the war. But it is unlikely that this motive alone sufficiently explains his actions. Critics have also argued that he was primarily interested in keeping British losses as small as possible and allowing the Soviet Union to pay the chief cost in blood. Stalin, the most vehement of these critics, charged that the Western Allies were content to see the Soviets fight a war of attrition against Germany. Again, it is clear that Churchill was concerned about casualties on the scale of World War I. But he was also determined to keep the Soviets in the war and feared that Stalin might seek a separate peace if it appeared that Britain and the United States were not making a serious effort to defeat Nazi Germany.

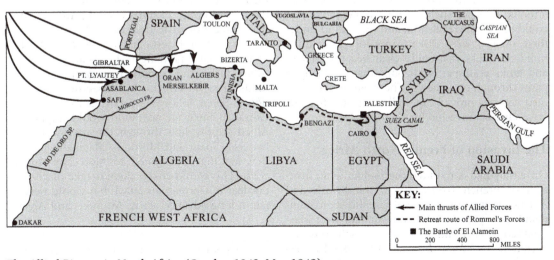

The Allied Pincers in North Africa (October 1942–May 1943)

British reluctance to undertake a cross-channel invasion increased as a result of an abortive raid on the French channel port of Dieppe on August 19, 1942. The British planned this operation as an experiment to determine if they could capture an enemy port and hold it for a limited time. A force of 5,000 Canadian troops attacked the port itself, while a thousand British Commandos and 50 American Rangers attempted to knock out coastal batteries that flanked the city. The German defenders greeted the Canadians with merciless fire and prevented them from crossing the sea wall. No fewer than 68 percent of the Canadians were killed, wounded, or missing, a statistic that created lasting bitterness in Canada. Dieppe was an especially well-fortified point, and the Allies made the landing in daylight without sufficient preliminary bombardment. This bloody failure convinced the British that they had been correct about Sledgehammer and probably weakened their resolve to undertake Operation Round-up in 1943.

But the Dieppe raid also taught the Allies some valuable lessons regarding the conduct of amphibious operations. It proved clearly that they could not take a fortified port by direct assault from the sea. This realization led to the eventual creation of artificial harbors that ships could tow across the channel. Dieppe also demonstrated the need to provide strong and continuous naval fire from close range against enemy coastal defenses. Finally, it led the British to devise specialized armored vehicles such as amphibious tanks that could be launched offshore and reach land under their own power. Other innovations included bulldozer tanks that could clear beach obstacles and tanks equipped with flails that could open paths through mine fields. These and other modified vehicles proved especially helpful when the cross-channel invasion finally took place.

The Invasion of French North Africa

Once they had committed themselves to an invasion of French North Africa, the British and Americans appointed General Eisenhower to command the operation. Eisenhower had won Marshall's confidence and been given this lofty position despite being junior to many other Allied generals. This was quite remarkable, considering that he had never before held a field command. But he had gained a reputation as a first-class staff officer. Eisenhower had grown up in the small Kansas town of Abilene, where his father toiled as a creamery worker. Young Dwight pursued the same occupation until he won appointment to West Point by virtue of his strong performance in a competitive examination. "Ike," as his friends called him, missed the opportunity to see combat in World War I when the conflict ended just before his departure for France. During the interwar years Eisenhower served twice as an assistant to MacArthur. He became chief of the war plans division in 1941.

Eisenhower owed his selection as commander of the North African operation in part to his planning and organizational skills. Perhaps even more important, he possessed a rare talent for blending diverse personalities harmoniously in a common enterprise. First and foremost a team player, he proved particularly adept at securing cooperation between American and British officers who often did not like each other. His outgoing personality, twinkling eyes, and broad grin captivated everyone who met him. As General Montgomery later remarked, he had "the power of drawing the hearts of men towards him as a magnet attracts the bits of metal. He merely has to smile at you, and you trust him at once."*

The Allies soon disagreed on the scope of the invasion. Churchill wanted to restrict the landings to Algeria and to extend them as far east as the port of Bône, 75 miles from the Tunisian border. Some British leaders favored landings even farther east at Bizerta in Tunisia. But Marshall worried about the danger of Axis air power if an Allied task force ventured so deeply into the Mediterranean. He also feared German intervention in Spain, followed by a thrust to the Strait of Gibraltar. Such an operation would imperil the Allied supply line through the narrow passage between Spain and Morocco. Marshall proposed that landings be limited to Morocco's Atlantic coast. This would enable them to take place without fear of German air attack but would necessitate a long advance across Morocco and Algeria.

---

*Field Marshal the Viscount Montgomery, *Memoirs* (New York: Signet, 1959), p. 483.

Eisenhower agreed with the British and opposed Marshall on this question.

Eisenhower and the British were undoubtedly correct, but this dispute ended in a compromise. The Allies agreed to land at Casablanca in Morocco and at Oran and Algiers in Algeria. But they dropped plans to assault either Bône or Bizerta. The failure to land farther east eliminated the opportunity for a quick sweep into Tunisia. This ultimately prolonged the North African campaign for six months and precluded any chance for a cross-channel invasion in 1943.

If the Allies could convince French military and naval commanders in North Africa not to resist the landings, they would gain a quick, bloodless victory. But many of the French officers were loyal to Vichy, which followed a policy of collaboration with Germany. Some also harbored a strong anti-British bias. This was especially true of naval leaders, who bitterly remembered the Royal Navy's attack on French warships at Oran and Mers-el-Kebir in July 1940. The British, accordingly, kept in the background as the Americans attempted to line up French support. But the Americans went about their task in an extremely cautious manner, fearing that they might alert the wrong people and jeopardize the invasion. And while some of the French leaders were sympathetic to the Allied cause, they worried about reprisals from their Vichy superiors and hesitated to commit themselves. Not surprisingly, the Americans failed to accomplish their mission.

Another vexing problem was the question of de Gaulle. Strong animosity existed between the military leaders loyal to Vichy and the Free French. The British and Americans excluded de Gaulle from any part in the planning and refused to use Free French forces in the landings. Roosevelt and the Americans especially considered de Gaulle to have little support in either France or North Africa. Instead, Allied leaders pinned their hopes on another French general, Henri Giraud, as the man who could rally the French once the landings had been made. Giraud, who had lost a leg in World War I, had commanded the French 7th Army during the debacle of 1940. He had made a dramatic escape from a German prison early in 1942 and was living in southern France. To facilitate this scheme, an Allied submarine brought Giraud to Gibraltar. But he had no authority in North Africa, and French officers there felt no loyalty to him. To complicate matters still more, Admiral Darlan, the commander in chief of all French armed forces, was in Algiers when the invasion took place on November 8.

The French resisted all three landings, but opposition was strongest at Casablanca, where coastal batteries and the battleship *Jean Bart*'s 15-inch guns caused problems for both the invading troops and naval ships offshore. Resistance was weakest at Algiers, which surrendered on the first day. Eisenhower's deputy, General Mark Clark, quickly opened negotiations with Darlan in an attempt to halt hostilities, and his efforts culminated in a deal on November 10. Darlan agreed to order French forces to cease firing and join the Allies. In return, Eisenhower recognized the admiral's control over French administration in North Africa. Hitler responded to these developments by sending German troops into previously unoccupied France.

Darlan also "invited" Admiral Jean de Laborde, the commander of the French High Seas Fleet at Toulon on France's Mediterranean coast, to join the Allies in Algeria. Unfortunately, de Laborde hesitated, and when the Germans mined the entrance to Toulon harbor, he scuttled his fleet to prevent it from falling into their hands.

The decision to deal with Darlan embarrassed the Allies because he had been one of the most active collaborators in the Vichy regime and was intensely anti-British personally and a right-wing authoritarian politically. Eisenhower made the decision, with the backing of Churchill and Roosevelt, to save lives and speed the conquest of French North Africa. But Darlan's ascendancy came to an end when he fell victim to an assassin's bullet on Christmas Eve.

Allied leaders recognized Giraud as his successor, but de Gaulle angrily challenged this decision. In frustration, Roosevelt and Churchill worked out a compromise that provided for the two generals to cooperate in a French Committee for National Liberation. Giraud proved totally inept politically, however, and de Gaulle easily outmaneuvered him. Within a year, Giraud had resigned, leaving de Gaulle in full control. The whole episode made de Gaulle highly resentful, and his relations with the British and Americans remained strained.

FIGURE 17-2   American troops fire a howitzer during the North African fighting. (*U.S. Army Signal Corps Photo/National Archives and Records Administration*)

The Tunisian Campaign

The Allied failure to land farther east than Algiers enabled Hitler to send troops across the 100-mile strait between Sicily and Tunisia to seize the major Tunisian ports of Tunis and Bizerta. The Germans encountered no opposition because Admiral Jean Ésteva, the French resident-general, refused to switch his allegiance to Darlan and remained loyal to Vichy. They quickly established a defensive perimeter. It extended from 25 miles west of Bizerta southward through mountainous terrain to the Mareth line, a defensive system that the French had constructed opposite the Libyan border. This enabled the Germans to provide a refuge for Rommel's troops, which were already in full retreat from El Alamein.

Meanwhile, the Allied forces that had landed at Algiers moved eastward. Airborne troops occupied Bône on November 12 and penetrated into Tunisia four days later. They reached a point within 12 miles of Tunis on November 28, but there the drive bogged down due to bad weather, a serious supply problem, a shortage of motorized transport, and fierce German resistance. The Allied attempt to seize Tunis and Bizerta quickly had failed. Indecisive fighting continued throughout December and January 1943.

Rommel ended his long retreat across the desert and reached the sanctuary of the Mareth line at the end of January. He now prepared to defend southern Tunisia against Montgomery's pursuing 8th Army while General Hans-Jurgen von Arnim commanded German troops in the north. Arnim had led a panzer division and later a corps on the eastern front. Hitler selected him for the Tunisian assignment because of his reputation for ruthlessness and his ability to get things done. But from the start, he and Rommel, who detested each other, engaged in jurisdictional disputes. Arnim opposed Allied forces under the leadership of the British general Kenneth Anderson, who had commanded a division in the Dunkirk evacuation as well as the unsuccessful attempt to capture Tunis and Bizerta. Noted for his stern and humorless manner, which did not endear him even to his own compatriots, Anderson soon encountered problems with his allies. The French objected to serving under a British officer, and General Lloyd Fredendall, the commander of the U.S. II Corps, disliked the British in general and Anderson in particular.

MEDITERRANEAN SEA

BIZERTA

Cape Bôn

BÔNE

British First Army
CONSTANTINE

TUNIS

TUNISIA

French XIX Corps

LE KEF

SOUSSE

TEBESSA

KAIROUAN

US IInd Corps

KASSERINE PASS

SFAX

ALGERIA

GAFSA

GABES

MARETH LINE

KEY:
◄— Main Allied Thrusts
◄- - Main Axis Counteroffensives
▲▲▲ Main Axis Defense Lines
0   100 MILES

British Eighth Army

TRIPOLI-
TANIA

The Battle of Tunisia, December 1942–May 1943

Eisenhower had exercised little direct control over the campaign, being absorbed in a myriad of political problems stemming from the Darlan deal and relations with French authorities in North Africa. He did warn the commanders in the field against taking risks, however, and clearly intended no further offensive action until reinforcements and more equipment arrived. Criticism mounted over his failure to provide a firm hand and hasten the conquest of Tunisia. For a time it appeared as if General Alexander would replace him. But Roosevelt and Churchill agreed to retain him in command. They also made Alexander his deputy.

As soon as Rommel arrived at the Mareth line, he concluded that continued defense of Tunisia was hopeless. He flew to Germany to try to persuade Hitler of this, but the Führer refused to sanction an evacuation. The field marshal returned to Tunisia to await the arrival of Montgomery, who had encountered supply problems and had paused to clear the port of Tripoli before proceeding on to assault the Mareth line.

This delay enabled Rommel to attack U.S. forces in mountainous west-central Tunisia during mid-February. If he could weaken them sufficiently, he could confront Montgomery without fear of an American attack on his rear. But he also hoped to gain a strategic victory by breaking

through to the supply base at Tebessa in Algeria, just across the Tunisian border. He believed its capture would force the Allies to retreat into Algeria. If all went well, he even visualized an armored thrust northward to Bône to cut off the Allies in Tunisia.

In reality, Rommel's offensive fell far short of these ambitious goals. It failed in part because the Germans had not created a united command structure in Tunisia. Rommel had no jurisdiction over Arnim's forces in the north, and Arnim refused to provide additional armor to enable the attack to be delivered in full strength. Despite these obstacles, Rommel scored an impressive early success. Not only were the American forces in his path inexperienced, but they also suffered from unsatisfactory training, poor discipline, and indifferent leadership. Eisenhower had long harbored doubts about Fredendall's abilities but, unfortunately, had hesitated to replace him.

Although the Allies received Ultra reports indicating that a German offensive was coming, they expected an attack in the north only. Actually, Arnim did plan to carry out such an assault independent of Rommel's operation. This mistake coupled with lax American precautions enabled Rommel to catch them by surprise. The Germans easily brushed aside the forces defending Faid Pass with new heavy "Tiger" tanks mounting an 88-mm gun, while Rommel prepared to strike directly at Tebessa. But his superiors were skeptical of such a daring plan. Instead, they ordered him to pursue a more limited objective by thrusting northwestward through the Kasserine Pass toward Thala and Sbiba. Ironically, if they had allowed Rommel to drive on Tebessa, he probably could have captured the supply base and threatened the entire enemy position in Tunisia. The Allies did not believe that he would be so bold as to advance in that direction. They expected him to do exactly as his superiors had ordered, and they arrayed their strongest forces in the path of his thrust toward Thala and Sbiba.

Rommel's panzers quickly broke through the poorly deployed U.S. forces defending Kasserine Pass. Panic gripped many of the Americans who fled in disorder, only to be killed or taken prisoner. But, despite this victory, the Germans were not strong enough to overcome the Allied troops blocking his progress toward Thala and Sbiba. He had no choice but to retreat through the pass. American forces had suffered a rude shock, but they had demonstrated their ability to rally from adversity and had contributed to the eventual failure of the German plan. Nevertheless, their initial setback had filled the British with concern about their combat ability. Alexander, who took over direction of field operations in Tunisia following the reverse at Kasserine Pass, believed that the Americans should play a secondary role during the remainder of the campaign. But Eisenhower refused to agree to this and insisted that they assume a major part in the final offensive.

Eisenhower also replaced Fredendall with General George Patton. He ordered Patton to tighten discipline and instill fighting spirit in the II Corps. Patton, who had commanded the landings on Morocco's Atlantic coast, succeeded brilliantly in this task. Patton's ego vied for prominence with those of Montgomery and MacArthur. He also shared their flamboyance and loved to wear two ivory-handled pistols. When America entered World War I, Patton served on General Pershing's staff in France. Later he became commander of armored forces and suffered a leg wound during the last American offensive. General Marshall appointed him to lead an armored brigade in 1940, and he entered the war as America's most accomplished and vigorous proponent of mechanized warfare. Autocratic, outspoken, and controversial, Patton did not care much for his British allies but cultivated cordial relations with the French.

Rommel now hoped to divert his armor to the southeast for an offensive against the British 8th Army before all of Montgomery's troops reached Medenine, opposite the Mareth line. But he encountered delays, and Ultra alerted Montgomery to the impending assault, including the exact date. The British rushed additional forces into position and prepared strong antitank defenses. When Rommel launched his attack on March 6, Montgomery's artillery inflicted heavy losses on enemy tanks and forced the Germans to fall back to the Mareth line. Once again, Rommel urged Hitler to evacuate Tunisia before it was too late. But the Führer had grown tired of Rommel's entreaties, which he considered defeatist. Hitler relieved him of his command, placing all Axis forces in Tunisia under Arnim's control.

The Final Push in Tunisia

In the weeks that followed, the Allies increased their strength and prepared for the final push. Montgomery delivered the major opening assault on March 20. He began with an ill-advised frontal attack against the Mareth line, followed by a thrust around the right flank of the Italian and German forces. His direct action failed, but the flanking maneuver succeeded. The Axis troops found themselves in danger of being cut off. They abandoned the Mareth line and retreated northward along the coast while Patton's U.S. II Corps applied pressure from the west.

By the middle of April, Allied forces had pushed the enemy back to a hilly perimeter around Tunis and Bizerta. Total Allied control of the air made it impossible for the Axis either to supply or evacuate their troops, which now were greatly inferior in numbers and equipment to their opponents'. Ultra provided such detailed and accurate information that Allied aircraft were able to destroy most of the German cargo planes that tried desperately to carry out supply missions. The combination of Allied air and naval power, Ultra, and the Italian navy's critical shortage of fuel also eliminated any possibility of rescue by sea. Although the Germans and Italians again fought tenaciously, by early May they could no longer withstand the mounting Allied pressure. They abandoned both Tunis and Bizerta and withdrew into the Cape Bon Peninsula to the east. With virtually no fuel or ammunition, their position was hopeless. On May 13, the last Axis forces surrendered. A total of 170,000 prisoners went into captivity, a disaster that some Germans referred to with grim humor as "Tunisgrad." In reality, more Axis soldiers surrendered here than at Stalingrad. In both battles, the Germans had tried to hold out in untenable positions, but had failed, in part because of their inability to keep open their lines of communication and supply due to insufficient air power. The disasters in Russia and North Africa represented a clear turning of the tide. They marked the start of mounting pressure on Germany as it attempted to fight enemies that were growing in strength on multiple fronts while its own power continued to decline.

Clearly, Hitler's decision to send troops to Tunisia was a blunder because of the sacrifice of so many soldiers. But it also lengthened the Allied operation in North Africa to such an extent that the British and Americans were unable to shift forces to Britain in time for a cross-channel invasion in 1943. Churchill and Roosevelt actually confirmed this outcome when they met in a conference at Casablanca in January 1943 while the struggle for Tunisia was still far from complete. Roosevelt accepted Churchill's proposal that the Allies concentrate on additional offensive operations in the Mediterranean during 1943, specifically, an invasion of Sicily. In return, Churchill approved a massive buildup for a cross-channel invasion in 1944.

During the Casablanca conference, Roosevelt also announced, with Churchill's prior agreement, that the United States and Britain were resolved to accept unconditional surrender as the only basis for peace with all the Axis powers. The two leaders intended the declaration as a means of convincing the Soviets that the Western Allies were serious about the war with Germany. They also hoped that it would deter Stalin from possibly seeking a separate peace.

Critics have branded the unconditional surrender declaration a serious mistake. They have contended that it provided the Germans with a propaganda windfall. Indeed, Nazi propaganda minister Joseph Goebbels did warn the German people that in view of this policy, they must continue to resist fanatically or be completely dominated by the vindictive Allies. The declaration may also have weakened the cause of a revived German conspiracy against Hitler. This included both civilians and military officers who hoped to kill Hitler, overthrow the Nazi regime, and seek a negotiated peace. Clearly, the demand for unconditional surrender made the conspirators' hope for a negotiated settlement highly dubious. But it is likely that even without the declaration, the Nazi regime would have maintained its absolute control over Germany, crushed the conspiracy's efforts to seize power, and fought the war to the bitter end.

One thing is clear, however. The declaration did not satisfy Stalin. The Soviet leader was furious when he heard that the Western Allies had postponed the cross-channel invasion. Assurances of unconditional surrender did nothing to reduce his suspicions that Britain and America were content that the Soviet Union should continue to bear the brunt of the war against Germany. The decision to postpone the assault on Western Europe also weakened the ability of Churchill and Roosevelt to argue against Soviet ambitions in Eastern Europe.

CHAPTER EIGHTEEN

Probing the Underbelly: Sicily and Italy

The invasion of North Africa and the lengthy Tunisian campaign had inevitably drawn the Allies into a Mediterranean strategy. Unless their forces were to remain idle for a year, they would have no choice but to attack what Churchill inaccurately referred to as the "soft underbelly" of Europe. But initially, there was no agreement on where they should strike. Sicily was the obvious target. It lay only 100 miles from Tunisia and a mere two miles from the toe of the bootlike Italian peninsula. Its conquest would clear the central Mediterranean for Allied shipping. But some Allied planners favored an assault on Sardinia, which lay 150 miles north of Tunisia and 200 miles northwest of Sicily. Only weak Axis troops were present in Sardinia, and its capture would open the possibility of an invasion of the Italian mainland to the north of Rome or even a landing on the southern coast of France.

A number of factors persuaded Roosevelt and Churchill to choose Sicily over Sardinia. Allied fighter planes operating from Malta could provide air cover for a Sicilian operation, and the shorter distance from Tunisia to Sicily would make an invasion armada less vulnerable to enemy air and submarine attacks. Sicily also offered easier Allied access to mainland Italy. But the Allies made no decision regarding a follow-up operation against the Italian coast. The British favored such an enterprise, but the Americans were reluctant to commit themselves in advance to any undertaking that might endanger the promised buildup for the cross-channel invasion of France in the spring of 1944.

The Allied Invasion of Sicily

Anglo-American planners paved the way for the invasion of Sicily with an elaborate hoax that later became the basis for a book and a film titled *The Man Who Never Was*. It involved the corpse of a vagrant, who had died of pneumonia. British agents removed the body from a morgue and provided it with a uniform complete with various papers identifying the bearer as a major in the British Royal Marines. A submarine then deposited the body along the coast of Spain where it washed ashore with a courier's briefcase attached to its belt. The case contained "official" documents indicating that the Allies planned to invade Sardinia or Greece. This information soon fell into the hands of German agents, who notified Berlin. Hitler responded by diverting troops to Greece. He had already sent reinforcements to Sardinia. Ultra quickly alerted Allied leaders that the enemy had taken the bait. These diversions as well as the loss of so many Axis soldiers in Tunisia resulted in a shortage of manpower for the defense of Sicily. But Mussolini was reluctant to allow additional German divisions to come to the rescue. The Duce feared that such an influx would give Germany a commanding position in his country. When Hitler offered to send five panzer divisions to Italy, Mussolini indicated that he could manage with three. The Germans finally sent all five, two of them going to Sicily.

Churchill and Roosevelt agreed that Eisenhower would serve as supreme commander of the Sicilian operation, Alexander as actual field commander. Alexander led an army group that included Montgomery's British 8th Army and the U.S. 7th Army under Patton. The plan for the invasion (Operation Husky) provided for the 8th Army to strike against the southeastern coast near the port of Syracuse while Patton's forces landed on the island's southern beaches. Ultra reports gave Allied leaders an accurate picture of Axis strength on the island and detected the arrival of the two German panzer divisions.

The Italian Campaign, July 1943 to the End of 1944

Italian troops defended the Sicilian coast while Field Marshal Kesselring, Hitler's commander in Sicily and southern Italy, held the less numerous but more mobile German forces in reserve. The Allies carried out the invasion on July 10 and caught the defenders off guard. Axis leaders had anticipated landings on the southwestern coast. They also did not expect the invasion to come when it did because of poor weather and high surf. The Italians were sick of the war, and several divisions collapsed almost immediately, some virtually without firing a shot. Montgomery captured Syracuse and drove northward along the east coast toward the port of Messina on the Strait of Messina, which separated Sicily from the toe of the Italian peninsula. Patton's forces pushed inland toward the center of the island.

Operation Husky designated Montgomery's drive as the main spearhead because it was closest to Messina. If he could take the city quickly, he would make it difficult, perhaps impossible, for the Axis to evacuate to the Italian mainland. Kesselring was quite aware of this and prepared to make his

FIGURE 18-1   A U.S. cargo ship explodes off the coast during the Allied invasion of Sicily. *(U.S. Coast Guard Photo/National Archives)*

stand south of Mount Etna, a huge volcano whose slopes lay in the path of the 8th Army's advance. Montgomery also played into Kesselring's hands by pausing to regroup his forces before pushing northward. This enabled the Germans to strengthen their defenses, and when the British resumed their drive, they made slow progress. The original plan called for Patton merely to protect Montgomery's left flank, but the American general chafed under this restriction, and he persuaded Alexander to authorize his forces to drive north to the sea, thus cutting Sicily in two. Patton did not tell Alexander that his real objective was to capture the great port of Palermo considerably farther west, followed by a drive along the northern coast to take Messina. Four days later, on July 22, his troops entered Palermo, much to Alexander's surprise. The speed of his advance made Patton a hero in America, and the press hailed him as "Old Blood and Guts."

Most accounts have portrayed the campaign from this point as a race between Patton and Montgomery to see which army could reach Messina first. It is now clear that there was no race. In reality, Montgomery realized that due to the strength of the German position confronting him, it was most unlikely that he could beat Patton to Messina. Indeed, Montgomery invited Patton to a meeting on July 25 during which he proposed, to Patton's amazement, that the 7th Army push on to capture the vital port and hopefully cut off the Germans facing the 8th Army. But tenacious German resistance stalled Patton's advance as it had already foiled Montgomery. Kesselring nevertheless realized that his badly outnumbered forces could not hold the Allies for long. He prevailed upon Hitler to withdraw as many troops as possible to the mainland while his rear guard fought an effective delaying action. The evacuation began on the night of August 11 and continued under cover of darkness for the next week. Patton finally reached Messina on August 17, but his entrance was anticlimactic. The Germans had gotten away.

Patton's elation over the capture of Messina proved to be short-lived. This was due to two incidents that occurred as his troops were advancing along the northern coast. On the first occasion, while visiting a field hospital, Patton encountered a soldier who had suffered no wounds. Assuming that he was malingering, the general accused him of cowardice and slapped his face. In reality, the man was afflicted with malaria and dysentery. A week later, when visiting another hospital, Patton ran across another soldier with no wounds but this time suffering from battle fatigue. The general again flew into a rage, called the man a coward, slapped him across the face, and even threatened to shoot him. He had to be restrained by the head of the hospital. News reports of this incident reached America and led to demands for the general's dismissal. Eisenhower shunned such a drastic remedy, but he did reprimand Patton and ordered a public apology. Under the circumstances, there was no chance of Patton's participating in the invasion of Italy, and many believed that his career was over. These postmortems proved premature, but he did not command another army until the summer of 1944.

Consequences of Allied Success in Sicily

Control of Sicily cleared the Mediterranean for Allied shipping and opened the way for an invasion of the Italian mainland. But the campaign also provided another vivid demonstration of German defensive brilliance and flair for executing fighting withdrawals. It should have been clear to Allied leaders that the enemy would be equally adept in defending Italy, where the terrain was even more difficult. Despite the success of the *Blitzkrieg* in the early years of the war, the power of a skillful defense still remained a factor of great importance.

The invasion of Sicily also led to Mussolini's fall from power. The war had been one long nightmare for the Duce, and the Italians had become ever more disillusioned with his leadership. With the expulsion of the Axis from Africa and the threat of an Allied invasion of Italy's home territory, opposition increased in the army and even within the Fascist party. The assault on Sicily convinced these dissidents that Mussolini must go, and on July 24 they moved against the once mighty dictator. King Victor Emmanuel III dismissed him as premier, and the police placed him under arrest. The aging Marshal Pietro Badoglio took his place. Badoglio had served as chief of the Italian supreme command from 1925 until 1940, when he became the scapegoat for the failure of the invasion of Greece. But Mussolini was not yet finished. On September 12, German commandos, led by Lieutenant Colonel Otto Skorzeny, landed in gliders on the mountaintop where he was held prisoner, rescued him, and escaped by plane. Hitler now installed the Duce as ruler of a puppet Fascist state in northern Italy.

Soon after becoming premier, Badoglio dissolved the Fascist party and formed a government without political affiliation. He also opened secret negotiations for an armistice. This was no easy task. He wanted to switch sides and join the British and Americans in ridding Italy of the Germans, but the Allies, primarily at American insistence, clung to their doctrine of unconditional surrender. This divergence in aims slowed progress toward an agreement. At the same time, Badoglio tried to assure the Germans that he would remain loyal to the Axis cause. Hitler refused to be deluded by this stratagem. He sent additional German troops into northern Italy and the area around Rome to defend against the expected Allied invasion. To complicate the situation still more, American leaders did not agree to an invasion of the Italian mainland until July 20. The wholesale Italian surrenders in Sicily convinced them that they might be able to carry out a limited operation with relative ease. The late date of this decision meant that several weeks of preparation would be necessary before the Allies could act.

Negotiations with the Badoglio regime also sparked a controversy similar to the one that had erupted after the Darlan deal in North Africa. Both the new premier and King Victor Emmanuel III had close links to Mussolini. The king's continuation on the throne offended many people in Allied countries as well as in Italy. But Churchill saw the monarchy as a source of stability and a bulwark against communism. He strongly favored dealing with the new government, and Roosevelt acquiesced. Negotiations finally concluded in an agreement on September 3 that fell short of unconditional surrender. It provided for Italy to hand over its navy, merchant marine, and air force to the Allies. The Italians also agreed to become a cobelligerent against Germany.

Onto the Mainland

The decision to invade the Italian mainland marked the start of the final lengthy stage of the Mediterranean strategy that had begun with the invasion of North Africa. Despite his earlier commitment to a cross-channel invasion, Churchill definitely appears to have lost his taste for such an enterprise by the summer of 1943. This was probably due in part to his concern over the defensive prowess the Germans had demonstrated in Tunisia and Sicily. The prospect of another World War I–type bloodbath in France, never far from his thoughts, now loomed larger. But he also believed that Allied operations in the Mediterranean had opened a much more promising strategy against the "soft underbelly" of Europe. He favored launching a vigorous offensive in Italy as well as providing aid to Yugoslav Partisans under Marshal Tito and attempting to bring Turkey into the war as an ally. The Americans did not share the British enthusiasm for an ambitious campaign in Italy, because they feared that this would divert strength from a cross-channel invasion in 1944. They insisted on a limited commitment.

It now appears that the area north of Rome offered the best choice for an invasion site. Kesselring believed that an assault there would have resulted in a German withdrawal from the southern half of Italy. But the Allies considered an operation so far north to be too risky and chose to strike farther south. The invasion involved three landings. In the first of these, forces of Montgomery's 8th Army crossed the Strait of Messina on September 3 and established a beachhead on the toe of the boot. Six days later, other elements of the 8th Army went ashore near the Italian naval base at Taranto on the instep of the boot. At the same time, General Mark Clark's Anglo-American 5th Army landed at Salerno, south of the great port of Naples.

Clark had recently enjoyed a meteoric rise from obscurity by gaining the backing of both Marshall and Eisenhower shortly before America's entry into World War II. Clark became Ike's deputy for the North African campaign and at age 46, became the youngest lieutenant general ever to serve in the U.S. Army. Clark possessed boundless energy and ambition. He also courted publicity and was frequently abrasive in his dealings with colleagues.

The Allies had chosen Salerno as an invasion site after a heated debate. Clark and other Americans preferred to outflank Naples by landing to the north of the city. This site would also reduce the distance to Rome, and its nonmountainous terrain posed the possibility of a rapid advance inland. The British insisted on Salerno because the area north of Naples lay outside the range of Allied fighter planes operating from Sicily. Unfortunately, the beaches near Salerno were ringed by mountains, which gave the Germans a strong defensive position.

Montgomery prepared the way for his landing on the toe of the boot with an enormous barrage from 600 guns based in Sicily as well as 120 naval guns. Although impressive, it proved totally unnecessary because the Germans chose not to contest the assault. But they did slow the British advance by skillful demolitions along the narrow roads leading north. The landing at Taranto also encountered no resistance. But the troops which went ashore at Salerno were not so fortunate. When the Germans heard the delayed announcement of Italy's surrender on September 8, their forces raced southward. They quickly disarmed Italian troops along the way and moved to block the Allied advance toward Naples and Rome. The Salerno operation ran into trouble initially from just one understrength panzer division. This unit held the mountains overlooking the beaches and rained down murderous artillery fire on the exposed Allied troops. A determined German counterattack threatened to force the invaders into the sea. By the third day of the operation, the situation looked grim. Only two U.S. artillery battalions blocked the Germans from breaking through to the sea at one point. Rear echelon soldiers found themselves pushed into service to man a last-ditch line of defense. But the intervention of Anglo-American artillery, air power, and naval bombardment prevented a disaster and allowed Clark to consolidate his beachhead.

It was not until the advance elements of Montgomery's forces reached the Salerno area on September 16, after a slow advance from the south, that the Germans began to fall back toward Naples. The Allies had hoped to take Naples three days after the Salerno landings but were not able to capture the city until October 1. British troops gained another important prize when they seized the major Italian air base at Foggia on the eastern side of the peninsula. Its capture enabled the Allies to dominate the skies over Italy and carry out bombing raids against targets as far away as Austria and the Balkans. German forces also evacuated Sardinia in late September and Corsica in early October.

FIGURE 18-2   Italian civilians look on as a wounded American soldier receives medical treatment. (*U.S. Coast Guard Academy*)

Kesselring continued to make good use of Italy's ideal defensive terrain. The Apennine Mountains extended down the center of the peninsula, creating formidable barriers to the Allied advance. Innumerable rivers provided additional impediments, especially since heavy rains turned them into swollen torrents. The vision of "sunny Italy" soon faded from the minds of both Allied and German soldiers. The valleys oozed with mud that made progress painfully slow. In the barren, rock-strewn mountains, the men had to contend with cold, snow, and a lack of cover. For supplies, they depended on mules, which carried them until the slopes became too steep, at which point soldiers took over and hauled them the rest of the way. In such conditions, armor was of little use. The struggle became one of opposing foot soldiers, often in hand-to-hand combat. The weary perseverance of the American GIs in the face of this misery as well as endless monotony was reflected in Sergeant Bill Mauldin's cartoons of "Willie" and "Joe" in the army newspaper *Stars and Stripes*. Mauldin became a great favorite of the soldiers along with war correspondent Ernie Pyle, who lived with them and shared their misery. Pyle wrote vividly about what it was really like at the front in Italy:

> Our troops were living in almost inconceivable misery. The fertile black valleys were knee-deep in mud. Thousands of the men had not been dry for weeks. Other thousands lay at night in the high mountains with the temperature below freezing and the thin snow sifting over them. They dug into the stones and slept in little chasms and behind rocks and in half-caves. They lived like men of prehistoric times, and a club would have become them more than a machine gun. ...
>
> The front-line soldier I knew lived for months like an animal, and was a veteran in the cruel, fierce world of death. Everything was abnormal and unstable in his life. He was filthy dirty, ate if and when, slept on hard ground without cover.*

During the fall and early winter, the Allies slogged northward from one river to another until they bogged down before the main German defensive position less than 100 miles from Rome—the Gustav line—in January 1944. Kesselring

---

*Ernie Pyle, *Brave Men* (New York: Holt, 1943), p. 98.

anchored this powerful line on Monte Cassino, which dominated the Liri and Rapido river valleys. A famous medieval abbey crowned the summit of the mountain, and the town of Cassino sprawled on its lower southern slope. General Heinrich von Vietinghoff's 10th Army defended the Gustav line. Vietinghoff had skillfully commanded a panzer corps in the Russian campaign and now proved a master of defensive warfare. He had led the German forces against the 5th Army at Salerno and directed the retreat that had so effectively delayed the Allied advance.

Changes in Allied Command and Strategy

A major change took place in the Allied command structure at the end of 1943. Eisenhower moved to London to become supreme commander of the long-delayed cross-channel invasion, with Montgomery as his field commander. Alexander remained in charge of Allied forces in Italy, while General Oliver Leese took over the 8th Army and Clark continued to lead the 5th Army. Leese had studied under Montgomery at Staff College and became one of his closest associates. He had served as an 8th Army corps commander at El Alamein as well as in Tunisia, Sicily, and Italy.

In a dramatic attempt to break the deadlock, the Allies made an amphibious landing behind the German front on January 22. They struck near the resort town of Anzio, which lay just 33 miles south of Rome. The operation took the Germans by surprise, and the attacking forces gained a beachhead against virtually no resistance. For a time, they imperiled the entire German position in Italy.

In planning the operation, General Alexander had intended that the invading troops advance rapidly to the Alban Hills 20 miles from the coast. This action would cut German communications between Rome and Cassino and force the enemy to abandon the Gustav line. But General Clark expected Kesselring to react quickly, as he had at Salerno, and ordered General John Lucas, the commander of the operation, to move inland only after building up strength in the beachhead. Lucas, a highly cautious and insecure man who lacked experience as a leader in the field, needed little encouragement to stand fast. Despite the remarkably successful landing, Clark refused to alter his decision, although Ultra intelligence revealed that German reinforcements would not arrive for a week. Kesselring did, however, converge nine divisions in eight days against the three American divisions and prevented expansion of the beachhead. Instead of threatening the rear of the Gustav line, the Allies found themselves pinned down by incessant artillery fire, including 280-mm shells from the railway gun dubbed "Anzio Annie" by the GIs.

On February 19, Clark replaced Lucas with General Lucien Truscott. The new commander had trained the first American Ranger battalion, which he had modeled after the elite British Commando units. Truscott provided much more vigorous leadership, but for the time being he and his troops had no choice but to remain on the defensive.

At the same time as the Anzio landing, Clark carried out a major attempt to gain control of the relatively wide valley of the Liri River. He and Alexander hoped that this would enable the Allies to outflank Monte Cassino on the southwest and link up with the beachhead. But American troops could not maintain a foothold across the Rapido River near its junction with the Liri and suffered heavy casualties. Later in January, Clark ordered the capture of Monte Cassino itself, which he believed was crucial if the advance were to continue. American units crossed the Rapido and penetrated the northern outskirts of the town of Cassino but failed to take the mountain.

In early February, a New Zealand corps under General Freyberg, who had led the unsuccessful defense of Crete in 1941, relieved the exhausted Americans. Freyberg's corps contained General Francis Tuker's Indian Division. The acid-tongued Tuker urged an operation to outflank Monte Cassino rather than a frontal assault. But since his superiors insisted on a direct attack, he demanded that heavy bombers destroy Monte Cassino Abbey as a prerequisite. Allied soldiers firmly believed that the Germans were using the building as an observation post. Freyberg supported Tuker, and Alexander bowed to the New Zealander's pressure. Alexander feared that unless the bombing took place, Freyberg would pull his corps out of the line. For some time, many people in New Zealand had been demanding that their troops return

home. But General Clark, Freyberg's immediate superior, argued against bombing the abbey. He doubted that the enemy was using it for observation. Alexander insisted, however, and Clark finally agreed. On February 15, over 200 bombers pulverized the renowned structure—to no avail. The Indian attempt to storm Monte Cassino failed, with heavy casualties as the price. Ironically, the Germans had not used the building as an observation post, although they had maintained a presence nearby. But they now moved into its ruins, which provided effective cover for mortars and machine guns.

The Allies renewed their efforts in March. Again they placed their faith in air power. This time they sent 500 bombers against the town of Cassino as a prelude to a ground attack that would seize Cassino before the dazed German survivors could recover from the terrible pounding. One thousand tons of high explosives obliterated the town, but when the bombardment ceased, the German defenders repulsed the attacking troops. The bombing actually hindered Allied progress by blocking Cassino's narrow streets with huge heaps of rubble.

The deadlock did not end until May, when Alexander moved much of the British 8th Army from the eastern end of the front to the Cassino area, where it worked in cooperation with the 5th Army. The Allies now enjoyed an advantage of 20 divisions to only 7 for the Germans. Starting on May 11, they ground slowly forward, and this time they were successful. Soldiers from a number of Allied nations made major contributions.

French troops, under General Alphonse Juin, executed a crucial flanking operation through rugged mountains southwest of the Liri. Kesselring and Vietinghoff had left this area lightly defended because they considered it impassable. Juin had long opposed the bloody attempts to take Monte Cassino by frontal assault. Despite a paralyzed right arm, a memento of World War I, he had led a division in the 1940 retreat to Dunkirk. He later commanded Vichy forces in North Africa. But his sympathies lay with the Allies, and he joined them after their landing in 1942. Juin now emerged as the man of the hour. His forces penetrated the Gustav line and threatened the entire enemy position. The Germans began to fall back. British forces took the town of Cassino, while a

Polish corps outflanked Monte Cassino on the north. After another bitter struggle, the Poles reached the summit and captured the ruins of the abbey on May 18.

Five days later, reinforced American troops in the Anzio beachhead launched an attack that Alexander hoped would take the town of Valmontone and cut off the enemy retreat from the Gustav line. But Clark was thinking of another objective—Rome. He wanted American troops to have the honor of capturing the Eternal City. Clark ignored Alexander's orders, and his staff directed Truscott to move toward Rome, even though Ultra reports indicated that the capture of Valmontone would likely result in a disaster for the German 10th Army. Truscott reluctantly complied. This decision allowed Kesselring to extricate his troops from danger, and he declared Rome an open city to spare it from destruction. American forces occupied the capital on June 4.

The Germans withdrew toward another prepared defensive position 150 miles to the north— the Gothic line, which stretched across the peninsula beyond the cities of Leghorn (Livorno) and Florence. They based this line on one of the last ridges of the Apennines to the south of the great plain extending northward to the Po River. By making skillful use of a series of strong mountain positions as he retreated, Kesselring prevented the Allies from reaching the Gothic line until late in August.

Allied leaders also weakened Alexander's striking power by diverting seven divisions to take part in an invasion of southern France (Operation Anvil-Dragoon). Churchill and Alexander were not keen on Anvil-Dragoon, preferring to push the offensive in Italy. Alexander insisted that if allowed to continue at full strength, he could capture the remainder of Italy and follow with a drive toward Vienna by way of the Ljubljana Gap in northern Yugoslavia. Since the war, critics of Anvil-Dragoon have contended that shifting these forces prevented Alexander from reaching Vienna and breaking into the Hungarian Plain ahead of the Soviets. This argument assumes a great deal. Although the retention

of these troops might have resulted in the liberation of most of the remainder of Italy in 1944, it seems highly unlikely that a quick thrust toward Vienna would have followed. In view of the spectacular tenacity of German defensive efforts in the Apennines, it is difficult to see how the Allies could have expected anything other than excruciatingly slow progress through the various ranges of the Alps that blocked the route to the Austrian capital.

Despite their reduction in strength, Alexander's forces surprised Kesselring in September and fought their way through the Gothic line. But once beyond it, they continued to encounter difficult mountains as well as boggy terrain and an abundance of rivers. German resistance stiffened, and although the Allies pressed their attacks throughout the fall, they made little progress. In late December, they decided to forgo additional offensive operations until the spring of 1945. Another grim winter in Italy's icy mountains lay ahead.

The Italian campaign remains extremely controversial. Its supporters contend that operations on the mainland pinned down 20 German divisions that might otherwise have opposed the Soviets or the cross-channel invasion. They insist that this alone made the Allied effort in Italy worthwhile. But other observers question whether the heartbreakingly slow advance up the peninsula was worth the price in blood and destruction of so much of the country. They contend that an Anglo-American presence in Sicily, Sardinia, and Corsica alone probably would have forced Hitler to concentrate substantial strength in Italy to guard against invasion. The Germans maintained 24 divisions in the Balkans in large part to resist a potential assault on this area, which did not face as direct a threat as Italy. These critics argue that once Allied troops had gained control of the southern portion of the peninsula, Germany could not have avoided a considerable commitment there. They question whether the Allies showed good judgment in hammering away at such formidable defensive positions as the Gustav line. It would appear that they are correct. There was no strategic objective worthy of such an approach.

CHAPTER NINETEEN

War in the Atlantic

Germany started World War II in a formidable position both on land and in the air, but its navy clearly suffered in comparison to the fleets of Britain and France. Indeed, the Allies' advantage on the high seas was greater than it had been during World War I. It became even more pronounced with America's entry into the conflict. But as the war continued, it became obvious that Germany's only chance of defeating the British lay in the Atlantic Ocean. This was due to Britain's dependence on the importation of vast quantities of food, raw materials, military supplies, and equipment. If the Germans could reduce that flow to a critical level, they might yet force the British to abandon hostilities. The key to such a possibility was the submarine (*Unterseeboot* in German—*U-boot* for short, and *U-boat* in English). If Germany could produce enough of these U-boats and sink enough Allied ships, they might get the job done. Conversely, the key to Britain's survival was the development of antidotes for this submarine menace. The ongoing struggle to achieve these opposing aims became known as the Battle of the Atlantic.

The Balance of Power at Sea

When the war began, the Germans possessed 57 submarines, only 22 of them suitable for operations in the Atlantic. The remainder were intended for duty in coastal waters or for training. Admiral Raeder, the commander in chief of the German navy, and Admiral Karl Dönitz, commander of the submarine service, realized that such a meager force could not inflict decisive damage. And since both the army and the Luftwaffe received production priority over the navy, a large U-boat force would not be available for at least two years. In addition, Raeder hoped to strengthen his surface

fleet, which also diverted resources from U-boat construction.

Raeder, who had received the navy's top post five years before Hitler came to power, wanted a balanced fleet that would include a large submarine force as well as a formidable surface component with numerous battleships. There was one major flaw in his approach, however. Such a fleet would only begin to assume powerful dimensions in 1943 and would not reach completion until 1948. Much of the problem was due to Raeder's belief in Hitler's claim that there would be time for a major construction program before the outbreak of war. He also accepted the Führer's assurances that Britain would remain neutral.

But since hostilities came in 1939, and because, contrary to Hitler's soothing words, Britain was arrayed against Germany, the surface fleet was also at a hopeless disadvantage in relation to the Royal Navy. It included three "pocket battleships"—*Deutschland, Admiral Scheer,* and *Admiral Graf Spee.* These vessels were products of the limitation of German naval construction under the Treaty of Versailles to warships of 10,000 tons or less. The pocket battleships actually exceeded this restriction by 2,000 tons but were of light construction and possessed six 11-inch guns, which made them more powerful than most faster ships and faster than most vessels that were better armed. German naval leaders intended them as surface raiders that would prey on enemy merchant shipping. Other elements of the surface fleet included two battle cruisers of almost 32,000 tons—*Scharnhorst* and *Gneisenau*—as well as eight cruisers and 21 destroyers. Two 42,000-ton battleships of the latest design—*Bismarck* and *Tirpitz*—along with the heavy cruiser *Prinz Eugen* were under construction and would not be available until 1941.

By contrast, the Royal Navy had 15 capital ships and another five battleships under construction. The British also possessed 62 cruisers, seven aircraft carriers, 178 destroyers, and 56 submarines. France contributed five battleships, two battle cruisers, 19 cruisers, two carriers, 69 destroyers, and 75 submarines. With this discrepancy in their favor, the Allies instituted a blockade of Germany, but it initially proved less than successful because the Germans were able to obtain most of the raw materials they needed from the Soviet Union and Eastern Europe.

The U-Boat: Key to Victory?

Unlike Raeder, Dönitz had assumed all along that Britain would fight Germany in the next war and recognized that the submarine was the only weapon that could be decisive against the British in the North Atlantic. He had served for two years on submarines during World War I. This experience prompted him to push hard during the interwar years for the formation of a large U-boat force. Dönitz worked tirelessly to perfect submarine tactics that featured mass attacks on enemy convoys. Far more approachable than the austere Raeder, Dönitz enjoyed extremely close relationships with his subordinates.

When the war began, Dönitz did what he could with his limited forces to launch a submarine campaign against the Allies. Its first victim was the British passenger liner *Athenia*. Although the facts are still not completely clear, the commander of U-30 apparently mistook the vessel for an auxiliary cruiser and torpedoed it. Loss of life was relatively light: Of 1,417 aboard, 112 perished. British leaders denounced the Germans for committing a deliberate atrocity, but Hitler actually deplored the sinking of the *Athenia,* and he ordered his submarine commanders to refrain from any further attacks on passenger ships. The Führer hoped to entice Britain and France to make peace once Germany had defeated Poland. This made him reluctant to precipitate any incidents that might provoke continued hostility on their part.

German U-boats scored a number of successes in the following months. The first of these came on September 17 with the sinking of the British aircraft carrier *Courageous*. The most spectacular occurred on the night of Friday, October 13,

when *U-47*, commanded by Lieutenant Commander Günther Prien, penetrated the Royal Navy's main base at Scapa Flow in the Orkney Islands north of Scotland. The submarine sank the battleship *Royal Oak* and escaped without a scratch. U-boats also took a heavy toll of British shipping, considering their small numbers. By March 1940, they had sunk 222 ships, a total of 886,000 tons. But the Germans paid a stiff price, losing 15 of their precious few U-boats.

Germany enjoyed the advantage of having broken the Royal Navy's cipher before the war. This gave the Germans valuable information on British naval dispositions. Although the Admiralty developed protection for its cipher by the fall of 1940, the Germans compensated for this by breaking the British and Allied merchant ship code. This provided their U-boats with detailed intelligence on merchant traffic and contributed to many sinkings until the summer of 1943.

Combating the U-Boat

The British resorted to the convoy system, which they had used to good advantage in World War I. This involved grouping large numbers of merchant ships and escorting them by warships, especially destroyers. But Churchill, as first lord of the admiralty and later as prime minister, was not convinced of the value of close escort of convoys. He preferred wide sweeps by naval ships to hunt down submarines. In line with his desires, warships split their duties between escorting convoys and running search-and-destroy missions. The results were disappointing. U-boat sinkings were few, while the skeleton escorts had difficulty fending off submarine attacks on convoys. Churchill proved hard to convince, however, and did not change his policy until 1942, when convoys received larger close escorts.

Escort vessels were fortunate to have the assistance of sonar (*sound navigation and ranging*), a high-frequency device that could detect submerged U-boats. The British called this system asdic (*antisubmarine devices investigation committee*). But asdic was not a miracle weapon. It could not detect submarines on the surface, and U-boats usually attacked at night while surfaced. It could detect the range and bearing of submerged submarines, but it could not determine their depth. U-boats were

Battle of the Atlantic, 1940–43

often able to escape destruction by diving to 400 feet, thus avoiding depth-charge patterns.

An additional 900,000 tons of Allied shipping fell victim to mines and surface raiders from the outbreak of the war to the end of February 1940.

Indeed, for a time a new weapon, the magnetic mine, loomed as the greatest menace of all to the British. At first, it proved impervious to mine sweeping because, unlike conventional mines, which were extended from anchors by cables, the

FIGURE 19-1 A Royal Navy destroyer crewman looks out on the ships of an Atlantic convoy. *(Library of Congress)*

magnetic mines came to rest on the bottom in shallow water. When a ship's steel hull passed over such a device, it interfered with the earth's magnetic field and triggered the mine. Unfortunately for the Germans, the British soon discovered a remedy by attaching cables to their ships that set off electrical charges and desensitized the hulls of the vessels.

The most dramatic episode in the early days of the war at sea came in connection with attacks by surface raiders. Two of the pocket battleships, *Deutschland* and *Admiral Graf Spee,* had penetrated into the Atlantic shortly before the war. They received service from tanker supply ships that waited for them at prearranged locations in waters off the usual shipping routes. *Deutschland* sank only two vessels before returning to Germany. Hitler had worried about the propaganda effect of losing a ship named *Deutschland,* so after its return, he promptly renamed it *Lützow,* after the flagship of the German battle cruiser squadron in the Battle of Jutland.

Graf Spee was more fortunate, at first. Operating in the South Atlantic and the Indian Ocean, where there were fewer Allied warships, it found easy prey, sinking nine merchant ships. But on December 13, *Graf Spee* encountered a small Allied squadron consisting of the heavy cruiser *Exeter* and two light cruisers, *Ajax* and *Achilles,* off the coast of South America. Although the pocket battleship outgunned all three enemy vessels and thus could shell them safely from long range, its commander, Captain Hans Langsdorff, made the mistake of closing on his adversaries. In the ensuing battle, *Graf Spee* disabled *Exeter,* which had to break off the action, but Langsdorff's ship also sustained some damage. He decided to put in for repairs and refueling at Montevideo, the capital of Uruguay and a major port on the estuary of the Plate River. This proved to be his second mistake. The Uruguayan government responded to British diplomatic pressure by terminating the vessel's stay before the repairs had been completed.

In the meantime, the heavy cruiser *Cumberland* joined *Ajax* and *Achilles,* which were waiting offshore. Langsdorff now faced three options: internment for the duration of the war, another battle with the British cruisers, or scuttling his ship. He chose the third. On December 17, *Graf Spee* steamed out into the Plate estuary where scuttling charges tore the ship apart. Langsdorff and his crew took refuge across the river in Buenos Aires, Argentina. The captain wrapped himself in an imperial German flag to show his contempt for Hitler and shot himself in his room the next night.

Despite the losses that the Germans had inflicted on Allied shipping during the first six months of the war, U-boat attacks were not yet more than a highly annoying nuisance. Nevertheless, Britain's prospects in the war at sea received two serious blows during the summer of 1940: the fall of France and the entry of Italy into the conflict. Not only would the British lose the support of France's sizable navy, but Churchill feared that it would fall under Germany's control, greatly altering the balance of power on the high seas. It was this grim prospect that prompted Churchill to order the attack on French naval vessels at Mers-el-Kebir and Oran in July. Ironically, the operation, which naturally worsened relations between Britain and a recent ally, was quite unnecessary. Vichy leaders were determined to keep their fleet in French hands.

The Struggle for the Mediterranean

The Italian navy was another matter. A formidable presence in the Mediterranean, it included two modern 35,000-ton battleships, four old but modernized 23,000-ton battleships, 18 cruisers, more than 60 destroyers, a similar number of torpedo boats, and 100 submarines. This submarine force was the largest of any of the belligerents'. Italian surface ships generally were faster and possessed longer-range guns than their British counterparts. Their chief weakness was their relatively thin armor, which made them vulnerable to direct hits. Italy's numerical superiority was a source of deep concern to Admiral Sir Andrew Cunningham, the commander of Britain's Mediterranean Fleet based at Alexandria in Egypt, and Admiral Sir James Somerville, who commanded Force H based at Gibraltar.

Cunningham had gained a reputation as an aggressive destroyer commander during World War I but by 1937 appeared headed for retirement. The worsening international situation spared him this fate and led to his appointment to the crucial Mediterranean post before the outbreak of war. Somerville actually had retired in 1938 after a short illness but returned to service in 1939. He helped organize the Dunkirk evacuation and took over Force H after the fall of France.

On the night of November 11, 1940, the British carrier *Illustrious* launched an attack by 21 Swordfish bombers against the Italian naval base at Taranto. The Swordfish were antiquated fabric-covered, open-cockpit biplanes, and their lack of speed made them highly vulnerable to antiaircraft fire. They could deliver their strike only at night. Ten of the Swordfish dropped flares to illuminate the harbor and bombed shore installations. The remaining 11 launched torpedoes against the ships lying at anchor. They knocked one modernized old battleship out of action permanently and crippled two other battleships, including the new 35,000-ton *Littorio,* as well as two cruisers. The disaster forced Italian naval leaders to shift all remaining major ships to Naples and other, more remote ports on Italy's western coast, where they would be safe from British attack. In January 1941, German dive bombers, in their first action in the Mediterranean, gained a considerable measure of revenge for their ally's defeat at Taranto when they disabled *Illustrious.*

Cunningham's fleet scored another triumph in March 1941, shortly before the German invasion of Greece and Yugoslavia. An Italian squadron, led by the new battleship *Vittorio Veneto* and comprising 8 cruisers and 13 destroyers, attempted to intercept a British convoy transporting ground forces to Greece. But British cryptanalysts had broken the Italian naval cipher and provided Cunningham with vital information on the enemy's intentions. In an engagement fought off Cape Matapan, the southernmost tip of the Greek mainland on the 28th, British torpedo bombers from the aircraft carrier *Formidable* and twin-engined Blenheim bombers from Crete damaged *Vittorio Veneto* and crippled the heavy cruiser *Pola.* Admiral Angelo Iachino returned to Taranto with his battleship, but that night Cunningham's battleships finished off *Pola* as well as two other heavy cruisers and two destroyers.

Despite the disasters of Taranto and Cape Matapan, the Italian navy had far greater success escorting Axis troop and supply convoys to North Africa. Italian submarines and light surface units, working in cooperation with German and Italian aircraft, also made it exceedingly difficult for British convoys to reach the island base of Malta. Lying only 70 miles south of Sicily, Malta posed a problem for Axis convoys because it lay astride their route to Libya. The British maintained a small number of cruisers and destroyers there as well as an air contingent. These forces attacked Axis convoys during the summer of 1941 and resulted in Raeder's decision to shift six U-boats to the Mediterranean. The submarines proved effective, sinking the carrier *Ark Royal* and the battleship *Barham*. But the Italians carried out the most spectacular operation of that year when a submarine launched three slow-moving, electrically operated torpedoes near Alexandria in December. Two frogmen guided each torpedo through the harbor's defenses and deposited them under the battleships *Queen Elizabeth* and *Valiant* and a tanker. Explosions destroyed the tanker and seriously damaged both battleships.

German planes also began to attack Malta in January 1942, and the British reinforced the island's meager air strength in June. Many have hailed Malta as a critical factor in Britain's eventual victory in North Africa, but they may have exaggerated its importance. Approximately 86 percent of all materiel shipped to Axis forces arrived safely in Libya between 1940 and November 1942, and the British suffered heavily in their efforts to keep the island supplied. They paid their highest price in ships and lives in August 1942, when a large naval force escorted a convoy of 14 merchantmen from Britain to Malta by way of the Strait of Gibraltar. Axis submarines and air attacks sank all but five of the supply ships as well as the aircraft carrier *Eagle,* two cruisers, and a destroyer and severely damaged another carrier and two more cruisers. Malta may have been more of a liability than an asset.

The Battle of the Atlantic Continues

Meanwhile, Germany's victories in Norway and France in the spring of 1940 had provided bases on the Atlantic for submarine and surface raiders as well as aircraft. French bases proved superior to those in Norway because of the greater size of the harbors and their proximity to British shipping lanes. The Germans built concrete submarine pens up to 30 feet thick that were impervious to air attack in French ports. Air bases in France and Norway also provided Germany with its only opportunity to experiment with a long-range bomber, the Focke-Wulf 200 Kondor, which was actually a converted airliner and transport plane. Although the Kondor was slow and vulnerable to fighter planes, during 1940 and much of 1941 British convoys lacked such fighter support. This enabled Kondors along with medium bombers to destroy 580,000 tons of shipping in 1940 and over a million tons in 1941. With the advent of British escort aircraft carriers in September 1941, this threat quickly diminished.

Although U-boats were still not numerous enough to constitute a war-winning force, they sank over 1.6 million tons of shipping from June to November 1940, a period that U-boat crews referred to as the "happy time." These losses worried the British, whose naval resources were stretched dangerously thin. Escort vessels were at a premium, but the development of the corvette, a small vessel of only 925 tons, helped ease the problem. Britain produced large numbers of them in relatively short order. Though lacking the speed and punch of destroyers, corvettes greatly strengthened convoy escorts.

Sinkings tapered off during the winter of 1940–41 because of the difficulty that submarines encountered in bad weather but mounted again in the spring and summer. Dönitz made increasing use of "wolf pack" tactics, which employed a number of U-boats working together. Usually, one submarine would locate a convoy and alert other U-boats in the area by wireless. They would then attack the convoy at night while operating on the surface, where they had an advantage in speed over most escort vessels.

Despite the persistent submarine and bomber menace, aid from North America helped brighten Britain's outlook. The Royal Canadian Navy created an escort force in June 1941 that provided protection for convoys between Newfoundland and Iceland. In April, the United States established air bases in Greenland, and in July, U.S. forces relieved British troops in Iceland. During July, Roosevelt ordered American naval and air forces to patrol the western Atlantic and warn British convoys of the presence of German submarines. The United States's lend-lease program also included constructing both naval ships and merchantmen for Britain as well as providing refitting facilities for British ships in American ports. In September, America undertook the responsibility of escorting convoys to a midocean meeting point where British escorts took over, and in November, Congress authorized the arming of U.S. merchant ships and allowed them to carry cargoes to belligerent ports.

Britain also benefited from Ultra. The German naval cipher had proved especially difficult to break, but in May 1941, a British destroyer crew captured submarine *U-110's* cipher machine and code books. The destroyer had severely damaged *U-110* and its commander had ordered his men to abandon ship after setting demolition charges. But these had failed to detonate. This stroke of fortune enabled the Royal Navy to amass a vast glut of information on U-boat strength and positions as well as plans for attacking convoys. Although this intelligence certainly did not end the submarine menace, it helped prevent the Germans from achieving greater success.

During the period from April to December 1941, Axis submarines sank over 1.5 million tons of shipping, but only one-third of the victims were members of convoys. A definite decline in sinkings occurred between October and December, and it appeared that the British might be getting the better of the Battle of the Atlantic. But this improvement was short-lived.

It was also during the period 1940–41 that German surface raiding reached its peak. Disguised merchant ships led the way, starting in April 1940. These were equipped with 5.9-inch guns that gave them the firepower of most light cruisers. They also carried torpedoes and received supplies from ships that waited for them in quiet waters. Seven of these raiders sailed at various times between March 1940 and November 1941. They accounted for 65 merchantmen with a total tonnage of 435,000. But with the aid of detailed Ultra intelligence, British warships sank three of them and, starting in the summer of 1941, hunted down and destroyed most of their supply ships.

Ironically, German surface warships were less productive, due largely to their shorter range and Hitler's reluctance to allow them to take risks. The pocket battleship *Scheer* enjoyed the most success. It sank 16 merchant ships totaling 99,000 tons as well as an armed British merchant cruiser between October 1940 and April 1941. The cruiser *Hipper* carried out two raids in late 1940 and early 1941, sinking nine vessels of over 40,000 tons. And during the first three months of 1941,

the formidable battle cruisers *Scharnhorst* and *Gneisenau* destroyed 22 ships with a total tonnage of 116,000 before taking refuge in the French port of Brest.

Bismarck's First and Last Voyage

By far the most famous of these sorties, though certainly not the most successful, was that of the newly commissioned battleship *Bismarck* and the heavy cruiser *Prinz Eugen* in May 1941. Under the command of Admiral Günther Lütjens, these powerful ships left Bergen, Norway, on May 21 and ventured into the Atlantic. RAF reconnaissance planes discovered them the same day and alerted the British main fleet. The cruisers *Norfolk* and *Suffolk* sighted the German ships in the Denmark Strait between Iceland and Greenland on May 23, while the battle cruiser *Hood* and the new battleship *Prince of Wales* closed in for a showdown. *Prince of Wales* was still undergoing tests on her armament and, in fact, sailed with construction workers on board. *Hood* was Britain's largest ship but dated from 1920 and had poor armored protection. In the predawn twilight of May 24, the opposing ships opened fire at a range of 14 miles. A shell from *Bismarck* plunged through *Hood's* weak deck armor and into a magazine. The ship immediately blew up, killing all but three of the crew of 1,400. Both *Bismarck* and *Prinz Eugen* also hit *Prince of Wales* with several shells, forcing it to break off action.

The two German ships continued on their way, with *Norfolk* and *Suffolk* shadowing them at a safe distance until the main British fleet, some 300 miles away, could arrive. But *Bismarck* had suffered damage from *Prince of Wales'* shells, most notably an oil leak that forced Admiral Lütjens to abandon his raid into the Atlantic and head for the French port of St. Nazaire at reduced speed instead. Lütjens sent *Prinz Eugen* ahead, and that ship reached Brest on June 1.

Although *Bismarck's* pursuers lost contact on May 25, a Catalina flying boat discovered the ship the following day. Soon afterward, Swordfish torpedo planes from the carrier *Ark Royal* attacked *Bismarck,* and one of the torpedoes jammed the ship's rudder, leaving the vessel helpless. When the British battleships *King George V* and *Rodney* finally caught up with the stricken vessel, they pounded it with armor-piercing shells and left it a flaming hulk. The cruisers *Norfolk* and *Dorsetshire* attempted to finish the job with torpedoes, but they proved ineffective against *Bismarck*'s strong armor. The ship did not finally succumb until the crew scuttled it to prevent the pride of the German navy from being captured by the British.

Dorsetshire and a destroyer lingered to pick up survivors. They had rescued 110 of *Bismarck*'s 2,300-man crew when *Dorsetshire* sighted a German submarine. The two ships looked to their own safety and steamed away at high speed. The U-boat's untimely appearance ironically condemned many German sailors who were still in the water to death. The submarine could save only three. The loss of *Bismarck* for all practical purposes ended the efforts of German surface craft to play a major role in the Battle of the Atlantic.

But *Scharnhorst, Gneisenau,* and *Prinz Eugen* all remained at Brest. Although well situated for additional sorties into the Atlantic, they were also vulnerable to Allied air and naval attack and remained immobilized until February 1942. By that time, Hitler had become convinced that the Allies planned to invade Norway and insisted that the three cruisers leave Brest and take up positions in northern waters. The only way in which they could possibly accomplish this was by a danger-ous dash through the English Channel, where the British would almost certainly attack them. The Germans, accordingly, carried out mine-sweeping and radar-jamming operations in advance, and the cruisers left Brest with a destroyer escort on the night of February 11. When daylight came, they were only halfway through the channel. Despite Ultra warnings that the Germans were planning a channel dash, the British did not detect the ships until late in the morning. German fighters fought off RAF attacks, and the squadron continued its escape. Although both *Scharnhorst* and *Gneisenau* struck mines and suffered minor damage, all three ships found refuge in German ports.

Russia's entry into the conflict in June 1941, while clearly a major turning point in the war, added to the drain on British naval resources. Churchill shifted a large number of ships to trans-port war materiel to the Soviets. The transforma-tion of the United States into a full-fledged belligerent in December 1941 also greatly enhanced Britain's prospects. But Japanese attacks on British possessions in East Asia compounded Britain's already heavy naval commitments and led to the loss of two more capital ships—*Prince of Wales* and *Repulse* in December 1941. Moreover, many American vessels, which had been cooperating with the British in the North Atlantic, now served their own country. And ships under construction in the United States that might otherwise have gone into the British navy or merchant marine joined the U.S. Pacific Fleet.

Crisis and Resolution in the North Atlantic

The Battle of the Atlantic reached its most critical stage during 1942. Admiral Dönitz estimated that sinkings of Allied shipping must average 700,000 tons per month if the Germans were to win the struggle. They had averaged only 180,000 tons during 1941. In an effort to reach this goal, Dönitz sent as many U-boats as he could spare to American waters. Although the number actually operating there never exceeded a dozen, they accounted for almost half the tonnage that submarines sank between January and April and took an especially heavy toll of tankers. One of the chief reasons for this remarkable success was the U.S. Navy's reluc-tance to group merchant ships in convoys unless they were protected by strong escorts of warships. Since the latter were in short supply, they refused to organize convoys at all, making merchant ves-sels easy prey for U-boats. A lack of trained crews and officers added to the problems. To make mat-ters worse, for some time the United States did not impose a blackout on eastern seaboard cities. Merchant ships and tankers, silhouetted against this brightly illuminated background, provided per-fect targets for U-boats operating at night. Subma-rine commanders later looked back on this period as the "second happy time" and the "American shooting season."

Allied losses during February, March, and April hovered near the 500,000-ton mark. In May, they rose to 600,000 and in June exceeded Dönitz's magic number of 700,000. The Germans also con-tributed to this success by changing the cipher used by their submarines in February. British cryptanalysts were not able to penetrate the new cipher until December, although they continued to detect other enemy naval messages. Belated

American adoption of the convoy system and improved antisubmarine methods cut July sinkings to under 500,000 tons. The new techniques included a refined airborne radar that made it possible for aircraft to locate U-boats on the surface at night and attack them with the aid of searchlights. But the Germans adjusted to this by installing receivers in their submarines that could detect the impulses emitted by the radar of approaching enemy planes. This enabled the U-boats to dive before the aircraft arrived. In the summer of 1942 the Allies also began to place high frequency radio detectors (HF/DF or "Huff-Duff") on their escort ships. These devices enabled them to locate U-boats through their radio transmissions.

The Germans increased their submarine strength to over 300 in August, about half of which were operational. These included larger vessels that had a range of 30,000 miles and could dive much deeper than earlier models. Sinkings once again climbed over 500,000 tons in August and continued to increase during the following months, reaching a high of over 700,000 in November. During all of 1942, the Allies lost 1,664 ships with a tonnage of almost 7.8 million to all causes, over 80 percent to submarines. These losses ran almost a million tons ahead of new Allied shipping that came into service during 1942.

Early in 1943, Hitler angrily threatened to scrap all German surface ships after the failure of an attack by a force of cruisers and destroyers on a Russia-bound convoy in the Barents Sea. Admiral Raeder responded by resigning as commander in chief of the navy, and Dönitz succeeded him. The new commander vowed to step up the U-boat campaign and managed to persuade Hitler not to eliminate the surface fleet. After a lull during December 1942 and January 1943, due largely to bad weather, submarine attacks increased in February and reached alarming proportions during the first three weeks of March, when wolf packs accounted for over 600,000 tons.

But sinkings declined precipitously, starting in the last week of March and continuing into April and May. The key to this abrupt change was a new coordinated antisubmarine offensive instituted by British Admiral Sir Max Horton, who became commander in chief of Allied naval forces in the western approaches to the British Isles in November 1942. A submarine commander during World

FIGURE 19-2   A depth charge explodes as a U.S. warship hunts an enemy submarine. (*National Archives and Records Administration*)

War I, Horton had been in charge of British home-based submarines since 1940. His knowledge of underwater craft as well as his great drive and willingness to experiment served him well in his new position. He devised methods that brought much greater pressure to bear on U-boats, and he proved more than a match for Dönitz. The restored ability of Ultra to decipher German messages flowing between U-boat captains and Submarine Command proved of crucial importance. Without it, Horton would not have been able to direct his offensive with such pinpoint accuracy. Ultra information also convinced the Admiralty that the enemy had penetrated its convoy code and led to the adoption of a replacement, which proved secure.

Horton developed large support groups of destroyers and frigates, small warships that were faster than corvettes. These support groups aided convoy escorts by hunting down and destroying submarines operating in nearby waters. Horton also provided increased air support from both escort carriers and shore-based aircraft. These planes had the advantage of a new and revolutionary short-wavelength radar that German U-boats could not detect. Finally, improved depth charges and new rocket weapons also contributed to the remarkable reversal of fortunes. Not only did it become more difficult for U-boats to sink ships, but they found themselves hounded as never before. The climax came in May, when the Germans lost 41 submarines. This toll was so prohibitive that on May 23, Dönitz withdrew his forces from the North Atlantic. During the summer of 1943, the Allies built more ships than they lost. They had won the Battle of the Atlantic.

But the struggle was not yet over. Dönitz devoted himself to enlarging and improving the quality of his submarine force. He and his colleagues introduced the snorkel, a collapsible air intake and exhaust release mast that barely protruded above the surface and enabled submarines to remain continuously submerged. The homing torpedo, which was acoustically attracted by an enemy ship's propellers, also came into operation. But the Allies foiled this formidable weapon by developing the foxer, a device that a ship towed at a safe distance behind it. The foxer made more noise than the vessel's propellers and thus diverted homing torpedoes from their real targets.

The Germans also developed a formidable new submarine, the Walter type. This was a large U-boat that could remain underwater indefinitely. Thanks to a special perhydrol fuel, it was capable of such high speeds when submerged that it could outdistance most escort vessels. But it encountered a multitude of "teething" problems that proved so difficult to overcome that none of this type of submarine ever saw action. Two other smaller models, both equipped with snorkels, did go into mass production during the winter of 1944–45. But by that time it was much too late.

Dönitz resumed the submarine offensive in September 1943, but it accomplished little, while the Allies destroyed 25 U-boats during the first two months. In early 1944, the Germans sank only three ships but lost 37 of their own craft. Dönitz found these results so discouraging that in March he halted operations against convoys until the new submarines would be able to go to sea in strength—a day that never came.

Supply Routes to Russia

Allied aid also continued to flow to Russia, utilizing three routes. The first was via the Arctic Ocean to the north of Norway and the USSR, bound for the ports of Murmansk and Archangel. The second extended through the Indian Ocean and Persian Gulf to Iran and then across the Caspian Sea. British and Soviet troops had occupied Iran in August 1941. The third, and least known, stretched across the North Pacific to the Soviet port of Vladivostok. In this case, the U.S. had taken advantage of Russian neutrality in the war against Japan by transferring some of its merchant ships to the Soviet flag, thus enabling their safe passage across the Pacific.

The Arctic route was by far the most dangerous. Here, too, both German U-boats and surface ships attempted to intercept convoys bound for Murmansk and Archangel. The Germans also had air and naval bases in Norway. In addition to submarines, by 1942 Germany had gathered most of its surface craft in Norwegian waters, including the battleship *Tirpitz,* the pocket battleships *Scheer* and *Lützow,* and the heavy cruiser *Hipper.*

Allied convoys had to make much of the voyage to the Russian ports without benefit of air cover. The most severe German attacks came between March and July 1942, culminating in the tragic destruction of convoy PQ 17, which left Britain late in June. Admiral Sir Dudley Pound, the commander of the Royal Navy, received information that *Tirpitz* had put to sea with the apparent intention of attacking the convoy. Pound ordered the escorting cruisers to withdraw from the convoy, fearing that they would fall victim to the German battleship. He also ordered the merchant ships to scatter. But Hitler, fearing the loss of *Tirpitz,* insisted that it return to base. German submarines and aircraft carried out the mission instead and did so with deadly efficiency, sinking 23 of the 36 merchantmen.

Sobered by this disaster, the Allies did not dispatch another convoy until September, despite Stalin's bitter protests. The next convoy, PQ 18, received a much stronger escort, and although German U-boats and aircraft sank 13 ships, they suffered heavy losses themselves. A few convoys also made the Arctic run during the winter of 1942–43. But in March, the British halted this traffic for several months due largely to the critical situation in the Atlantic. When convoys resumed in November, they received more powerful escorts than ever before, including carriers.

In late December, *Scharnhorst* and its supporting destroyers attempted to intercept convoy JW55B. But the British battleship *Duke of York* and three cruisers received detailed Ultra reports of the German movements and laid a trap. They pummeled *Scharnhorst* with fire from their big guns. The battle cruiser proved extremely difficult to sink, however. It took direct hits from an estimated 25 shells and 11 torpedoes to send the vessel to the depths of the frigid Arctic. Only 36 of its crew of nearly 2,000 survived.

The last blow to German surface power came with the crippling and later the sinking of *Tirpitz*. In September 1943, British midget submarines X-6 and X-7 damaged the huge battleship, which lay at anchor in northernmost Norway, putting it out of action for six months. Carrier-based planes attacked the vessel again in April 1944 and inflicted minor damage. RAF heavy bombers crippled it in September, and a second attack in November finally settled the issue. Six-ton bombs ripped into *Tirpitz*'s hull and set off a magazine. Soon afterward, the ship capsized, carrying almost 1,000 men to the bottom.

No Guaranteed Victory

Of the 1,170 submarines that Germany possessed during the whole of World War II, the Allies destroyed 784. In all, U-boats sank 2,828 Allied merchant ships, comprising a tonnage of over 14 million. Allied shipping losses in the Atlantic and European theater of operations from all causes totaled 21.6 million tons. Had the Germans been able to develop their new submarines earlier and bring them into action in large numbers, the outcome of the Battle of the Atlantic might have been different. If the Allies had been able to speed up their timetable and employ some of their ultimately decisive methods at an earlier date, their victory might have come sooner. Since neither development came to pass, it was, as the Duke of Wellington said of his victory over Napoleon at Waterloo, "a damned close-run thing."

CHAPTER TWENTY

Target Germany: The Allied Bombing Offensive

Of all the terrible new weapons that gained their baptism of fire in World War I, the one that most captured the popular imagination was the bomber. Although its actual importance was negligible during the 1914–18 conflict, it inspired a ghastly vision: the mass destruction of cities by a rain of bombs in a future war. The public was not alone in entertaining this apocalyptic view. Some military theorists also came to believe that the advent of the airplane had revolutionized warfare and that bombers would win the next conflict with little or no aid from other forces. They referred to this cataclysmic form of warfare as strategic bombing.

Strategic Bombing

A raid by 14 German Gotha aircraft on London in June 1917 had a special impact on British appraisals of the potential of strategic bombing. It had this effect even though, by later standards, it inflicted few casualties—162 persons killed and 432 wounded. Other raids of limited scope followed until May 1918. Together they helped convince some British leaders that in the future, large formations of long-range bombers would be able to pound an enemy into submission.

This notion gained its strongest support in the fledgling Royal Air Force, which came into existence as a service independent of both the army and navy in April 1918. The RAF's first chief of staff, General Hugh Trenchard, became an outspoken enthusiast for strategic air power during the 1920s.

In America, General William ("Billy") Mitchell also championed the cause of strategic bombing during the same period, but he was less successful in gaining acceptance of his ideas. There was no independent air force in the United States; the army and navy retained their own air arms and tended to regard Mitchell as an irresponsible visionary.

The man who many later credited with having the greatest influence on the theory of strategic air power was the Italian general Giulio Douhet. In a book that appeared in 1921, Douhet preached that bombers held the key to victory in a future war. He visualized bombing raids that would paralyze industry and civilian morale and make continued resistance impossible. But his influence may not have been as great during the 1920s and 1930s as is commonly believed. A complete English translation of his work did not appear until 1942 in the United States and 1943 in Britain.

Although a German translation of Douhet appeared in 1935, theories of strategic bombing played little role in the Luftwaffe's approach to aerial war. To be sure, General Wever, the first German air chief of staff, saw the need for a large force of long-range bombers and pressured the Dornier and Junkers aircraft firms to develop prototypes of such planes, but his death in 1936 ended progress in this direction. Instead, his successors devoted themselves to the creation of a tactical air force that would work closely with the army in its *Blitzkrieg* operations. Certainly, the Luftwaffe performed well in this role in the early campaigns of World War II. But its failure to develop a strategic bombing force was one factor that contributed to the futility of Germany's effort to knock Britain out of the war in 1940.

Even in Britain, where enthusiasm for strategic bombing ran highest, the RAF made little progress toward the development of an adequate bomber force prior to the war. This was due in part to the government's reluctance to provide the necessary funds. Disagreement also developed over the type of bomber that should be produced. As the war approached, the RAF still had a preponderance of light bombers that were unsuitable for strategic bombing. It also became obvious that Britain needed a strong fighter-plane force to defend the country against German air attacks. The simpler design of fighter planes also made it possible to produce them more quickly than the larger and more complex bombers. In 1939, the government gave priority to the creation of 18 new fighter squadrons, a decision that played a vital role in the RAF's victory over the Luftwaffe the following year.

When the war started, Britain was clearly at a numerical disadvantage in bombers, compared to Germany. This contributed to the realization that the RAF would be unable to inflict serious damage on German cities for the foreseeable future. British leaders concluded that it would be better to avoid provocative raids that might result in heavier retaliatory strikes on British cities. Nevertheless, the government went ahead with plans to develop four-engine long-range bombers. It had ordered prototypes of the future Stirling, Halifax, and Lancaster bombers as early as 1937. Although these planes were not available when the war began, they would devastate Germany later in the conflict. And despite this slow development, strategic bombing enthusiasts never slackened in their faith regarding the war-winning potential of heavy long-range bombers. Their single-minded approach led them to downplay the benefits to be gained from the creation of a tactical air arm that would work in close support of the army and navy. The British and German air forces thus approached the war with completely different philosophies.

The RAF exponents of strategic bombing also greatly underestimated the difficulties that lay in wait for bombers. They thought in terms of precision raids in daylight and assumed that it would be relatively easy to find and destroy targets. To say the least, this was wildly optimistic. Indeed, accurate navigation to targets and the ability to hit them, if they were reached, proved difficult when World War II began.

In the early stages of the conflict, neither Germany nor the Western Allies engaged in any large-scale raids on the cities of their chief opponents. To be sure, the Luftwaffe attacked Polish cities, especially Warsaw, and later destroyed the center of Rotterdam. But both of these operations were, to some extent, extensions of the German doctrine of tactical support for the army.

British air activity during the period of the "phony war" consisted primarily of dropping leaflets over German cities at night and infrequent daylight bombing attacks on naval targets. The most ambitious of the latter raids occurred in December 1939. Twenty-two Wellington bombers attacked enemy shipping along Germany's North Sea coast. But the two-engine Wellingtons inflicted little damage, and only seven of them made it home. Heavy losses in other daylight attacks on similar targets led to a decision in April 1940 to restrict bombing to nighttime raids.

During the Battle of Britain, Germany, of course, attempted to carry out a strategic mission with a tactical air force. It failed either to destroy RAF Fighter Command, the vital prerequisite for an invasion, or force Britain out of the conflict through bombing attacks alone. When German aircraft dropped a few bombs on London in August 1940, they caused little damage. But Churchill ordered a retaliatory strike on Berlin, and during the next few days, RAF Bomber Command carried out five raids on the German capital. They inflicted negligible damage. Indeed, only 29 of the 105 bombers that participated in the first raid actually found Berlin, a clear indication of the difficulties of aerial navigation. But the raids fulfilled their major mission: to make a gesture of Britain's willingness to strike back.

They also had an unexpected result. Hitler's anger over these violations of the sacred German capital contributed to the Luftwaffe's shift away from attacks on Fighter Command bases to direct attacks on London. The ensuing raids against the British capital and other cities during the next few months represented the most prolonged bombing assault in history up to that point, even though their results were disappointing.

German raids on cities also helped eliminate whatever squeamishness British leaders might still have harbored regarding the bombing of German cities. But the same problems persisted—an inadequate striking force as well as the technical problems of navigation and precision. An extremely inaccurate raid by 134 bombers against the railroad center of Mannheim in mid-December provided ample evidence of the lack of precision. Still, Bomber Command was the only British weapon capable of acting offensively against Germany.

During 1941, the British clung to the belief that they could carry out successful precision raids. But indications of woeful inaccuracy continued to mount. By the fall of that year, British air leaders, including Chief of the Air Staff Sir Charles Portal, came to the conclusion that area bombing offered the best opportunity to direct a decisive blow at Germany. This would involve striking at the center of German cities in an effort to inflict such heavy damage and casualties that enemy morale would crack, forcing an end to the war.

Portal was a true disciple of Trenchard and had directed Bomber Command prior to assuming the RAF's top post in late 1940. A man of great intelligence, efficiency, and capacity for work, Portal struggled with a shortage of aircraft at first, but he ultimately presided over a vast wartime expansion of the air force. This growth made possible the adoption of the strategic bombing policy in which he so strongly believed. Portal and other RAF leaders downplayed the failure of the Luftwaffe to break British morale in 1940–41. They attributed this in large part to the absence of strategic aircraft. To avoid a similar mistake, they visualized the creation of a British force of 4,000 heavy bombers capable of destroying Germany's will to resist within six months. They also assumed that enemy fighters would not be able to prevent night attacks any more than RAF fighters had stopped German night raids in 1940–41.

But Churchill doubted that area bombing would secure the desired result and warned that the Germans might improve their defenses against night attacks. He contended that only daylight bombing against industry held the possibility of real progress. This would only be feasible, however, if the RAF sharply reduced the size of the German fighter-plane force. In other words, control of the air was the key to a meaningful strategic bombing campaign. Unfortunately, the RAF could not accomplish this with its Hurricane and Spitfire fighters, which lacked the range to penetrate deeply into Germany. Moreover, the RAF staff believed that available technology made it impossible to develop new long-range fighters capable of escorting bombers over Germany in daylight.

Churchill's fear of stronger enemy defenses proved prophetic. Improved radar enabled the Germans to detect the approach of British aircraft and direct night fighters to the attack. Luftwaffe aircraft now also used a precise short-range radar that allowed them to find their targets much more easily. British losses mounted, but the results of their bombing did not improve.

Britain Takes the Offensive

Despite growing doubts about the potential of strategic air power, its supporters won out. Churchill found his own pessimism countered by the glowing optimism of his chief scientific adviser, Lord Cherwell, and the air staff opted for a policy of area raids against cities in February 1942. The appointment of Air Marshal Arthur Harris to the post of commander in chief of Bomber Command that same month provided the final ingredient. During World War I, Harris had served as a bugler in the army before joining the Royal Flying Corps and winning the Air Force Cross for bravery. He now became the high priest of strategic bombing.

Described as "ruthless, relentless, remorseless," Harris approached the war with total devotion to the principle of breaking civilian morale through 1,000-plane raids that would lay waste city after city. Despite mounting evidence to the contrary in the following months and years, "Bomber Harris" never faltered in this belief. He worked tirelessly to build up a huge force of four-engine bombers capable of carrying large bomb loads of ever-increasing destructiveness. His efforts were enhanced by the development of Gee, a radio device that aided navigation and enabled bomber crews to identify their targets with greater accuracy. Bomber Command also enjoyed access to a vast stream of information from Ultra. This intelligence proved useful in regard to the strength, location, and intentions of German fighter forces. It also provided details about weather over Germany and the enemy's radar system.

The first step in Harris's intensive campaign began in late March 1942, when 234 bombers attacked the German Baltic port of Lübeck. This raid featured the RAF's first use of large quantities of incendiary bombs, which destroyed the city's center, including many beautiful medieval buildings. But the attack resulted in little damage to either the port or industry. Raids against another Baltic port, Rostock, followed on four consecutive nights in April. Once again, incendiaries wiped out the medieval beauty of the old city but had a negligible impact on military targets. These assaults so enraged Hitler that he resorted to Luftwaffe attacks against a number of lovely historic English cities—Exeter, Bath, Norwich, York, and Canterbury.

In late May, the bomber offensive took a huge leap into the realm of destructiveness when Bomber Command carried out the first 1,000-plane raid against Cologne. Again, this massive force devastated the center of the city but had little effect on outlying industrial areas. The attackers lost 40 aircraft. Two days later, over 900 planes struck the great industrial city of Essen in the Ruhr, but heavy cloud cover prevented serious damage. Thirty-one bombers failed to return. Later that month, a force of comparable strength bombed the North Sea port of Bremen, but again bad weather conditions reduced the impact. The Bremen mission was the last of this scope until 1943. These raids had failed to break civilian morale.

Despite the disappointing results of these raids, British support for strategic bombing escalated during 1942. The number of planes involved and the tonnage of bombs dropped helped fire the imagination of leaders and common people alike, as did an increase in the number of four-engine Lancasters, by far the best British bomber. Other promising developments included improved navigational capabilities and the use of Pathfinder, a force of planes that preceded the main body of bombers to find and illuminate target areas with flares. On a more ominous note, however, German fighter-plane production rose from 3,744 in 1941 to 5,515 during 1942.

The Americans Join In

With America's entry into the war, the United States Army Air Force (USAAF) loomed as a new and potentially powerful addition to the bombing offensive. The first units of the U.S. 8th Air Force arrived in May 1942 and began operations in August. Their contribution remained limited at first because American bomber strength was relatively small. U.S. planes did not penetrate beyond France, Belgium, and the Netherlands. But America possessed the capability to increase its bomber force drastically and also had two fine aircraft—the B-24 Liberator and, especially, the B-17 Flying Fortress. Both were four-engine heavy bombers that bristled with machine guns.

In contrast to their British allies, American leaders rejected area bombing of cities aimed at breaking civilian morale. They much preferred precision bombing of industrial and other military targets, using the superior Norden bombsight. Unfortunately, precision bombing required raids during daylight hours, which greatly increased danger to the attacking planes. But the Americans believed that their heavily armed formations of bomber group combat boxes could defend themselves alone against enemy fighter planes. They also expected to hit their targets much more accurately than the British. It soon became evident that they were overly optimistic on both counts. German fighter pilots inflicted heavy losses on U.S. bombers. Like the British before them, the Americans also found that their raids were far less accurate than they had anticipated. Unlike the British, they persisted in raiding targets in daylight.

This approach dominated the thinking of the man who commanded the USAAF, General H. H. Arnold. One of America's pioneer aviators, Arnold had learned his flying from the Wright brothers. He became head of the Air Corps in 1938 and laid the groundwork for the vast wartime expansion of U.S. air power. Although Arnold's nickname "Hap" reflected a sunny personality, he was deadly serious in his belief that air power held the key to victory. His efforts had helped earn the air force equality with the army and navy, although technically it remained attached to the former. The first commander of the 8th Air Force, General Carl ("Tooey") Spaatz, and General Ira Eaker, who succeeded him in late 1942, were also longtime fliers. Together they had set an endurance record when they remained aloft for almost 151 hours in 1927. They also shared an intense faith in daylight strategic bombing.

Ultra proved especially helpful to the USAAF's efforts. Daylight precision bombing required much more information on targets than did Bomber Command's nighttime area raids. Ultra also gave an accurate picture of damage inflicted and the progress of German repairs.

Roosevelt and Churchill agreed at the Casablanca conference in January 1943 that Allied air forces would continue both approaches to strategic bombing. This would be referred to as Operation Pointblank, the CBO—Combined Bomber Offensive, or "Round the Clock Bombing." American precision attacks would seek to destroy German industry, while RAF area raids would concentrate on undermining civilian morale. Starting in March and continuing until July, the British blasted the industrial cities of the Ruhr. These raids, known collectively as the Battle of the Ruhr, caused widespread destruction but did not seriously impede German industrial production.

The Destruction of Hamburg

By far the most devastating and horrible raids in this phase of the war took place during the period from July 24 to August 3, 1943, with Hamburg as the target. Almost 800 RAF bombers delivered the first attack on the night of July 24–25. Many factors conspired to bring ruin to Germany's greatest port and second largest city. The night was clear, the target was well marked by Pathfinders, and a new device, called Window, badly confused German radar signals. Window consisted of strips of tinfoil (chaff) that bomber crews dropped in bundles at intervals of one minute. So successful was this device that only 12 aircraft failed to return. The bombers dropped high-explosive, incendiary, and newly developed phosphorus bombs on Hamburg, causing widespread destruction.

Far worse disasters lay ahead for the stricken city, however. American bombers added to the devastation in the next two days, even though they suffered heavy losses from German fighter attacks. The greatest horror came on the night of July 26–27. The previous raids had virtually paralyzed Hamburg's firefighting capabilities. When RAF bombers returned to rain another deluge of incendiaries and phosphorus bombs on the city, they started innumerable fires, which all converged to form a firestorm. A $1\frac{1}{2}$-mile-wide column of superheated air rose 8,000 feet into the sky, sucking in the air from the surrounding area and suffocating thousands of people. The conflagration's intense heat turned air raid shelters into ovens and literally baked alive thousands of persons who had taken refuge in them. Temperatures rose to over 1,000 degrees Fahrenheit, and winds reached nearly 300 miles per hour.

But of all the hideous forms of death that the citizens of Hamburg suffered, the most terrible fate befell several hundred who were spattered by showers of phosphorus. Phosphorus clings tenaciously to any surface it touches, including human flesh, and continues to burn as long as it remains exposed to oxygen. Even when smothered by sand or water, it flares into flame again once the cover is removed. Many victims of this horror threw themselves into the Alster River, where they had to choose between slowly dying in agony from flaming phosphorus or drowning.

A fifth attack followed on the night of July 29–30, and a final one took place on August 2–3 as a sort of melancholy postscript to this orgy of destruction and death. In all, the raids wiped out nine square miles of the city and killed at least 60,000 persons. Another 750,000 found themselves homeless.

Bomber Command struck at many other German cities during 1943, culminating in a series of 16 devastating raids on Berlin that began in November and continued until March 1944. But all of the terrible raids of 1943 and early 1944 had relatively little impact on Germany's productive capacity, and despite the horror that gripped the country after the Hamburg raids, they failed to destroy civilian morale. Once the initial shock wore off, the German people steeled themselves to their fate. There was little else they could do.

Even more discouraging to the British were the increasing losses that their bombers suffered in the raids after Hamburg. The Germans developed an improved airborne radar, which was not subject to jamming by Window, as well as new night-fighting tactics. These innovations once again restored the balance in favor of the defense. To make matters worse, the Germans increased fighter-plane production during the first half of 1943, reaching a peak of 2,316 a month by June. This accomplishment was largely due to techniques employed by Albert Speer, the minister for armaments and war production, including remarkably quick repair of bombing damage and dispersal of industry. German industry also concentrated on production of just two types of fighter—improved versions of the Me 109 and the newer Focke-Wulf 190.

The U.S. 8th Air Force, to its credit, recognized the need to destroy the German aircraft industry, and during 1943 concentrated its attacks primarily on targets related to the production of fighters. They did succeed in reducing German aircraft production to some extent during the second half of the year but suffered heavy losses in the effort. The most disastrous of these raids occurred in October, when 291 Flying Fortresses attacked the ball bearings factory at Schweinfurt in central Germany. Repeated German fighter attacks from head on destroyed 60 bombers and damaged 138. It was now clear that daylight bombing could not succeed unless large numbers of long-range fighter planes escorted the bombers. Until late in 1943, Allied fighters such as the P-47 Thunderbolt lacked the range to penetrate deeply into Germany. Luftwaffe fighters simply waited until the escorts had to return to their base and then pounced on the bombers.

The Allies Regain the Upper Hand

The answer to the Allied dilemma came in the form of a fighter escort plane with vastly increased range—the formidable P-51 Mustang. Although the P-51 had been available since 1940, the USAAF had rejected the plane at first because of its underpowered engine. Now equipped with a new high-performance engine, it proved to be the finest prop-powered fighter plane of World War II. It was superior to German fighters in speed and maneuverability and could now escort bombers to Berlin.

From April to September 1944, the Allies gave top priority to aerial attacks in support of the cross-channel invasion. To accomplish this, they diverted heavy bombers from their strategic mission to aid the medium bombers and fighter bombers of General Lewis Brereton's U.S. 9th Air Force and Air Marshal Sir Arthur Coningham's British 2nd Tactical Air Force. Their chief targets prior to the actual landings were the French railroad network and bridges leading to the projected landing site. These raids snarled the communications system so badly that when the invasion began, the Germans found it extremely difficult to move reinforcements and supplies to the beachhead. Once the Allied armies gained a foothold on the French coast, the air forces provided tactical support by attacking a multitude of targets at the front as well as in the German rear.

Brereton had been MacArthur's air commander in the Philippines and a central figure in the controversy over the destruction of most of the American planes on Luzon soon after Pearl Harbor. He was the architect of the "bridge-busting" campaign prior to the invasion. Coningham had served as a fighter pilot on the western front during World War I and had been RAF commander in North Africa as well as leader of Allied air forces in Sicily and Italy. He believed strongly in close cooperation between air and ground forces but often quarreled with General Montgomery, who looked down on the RAF's contribution. General Elwood ("Pete") Quesada, who had gained prominence as a fighter commander in North Africa, served under Brereton as leader of the 9th Tactical Air Command. Quesada was a much more avid believer in close support of ground troops than Brereton. He quickly won the admiration of army officers for his cooperative attitude and the brilliant success of his operations.

Meanwhile, the Germans concentrated on the development of new weapons that they hoped might turn the tide against the Allies. One of the potentially most useful of these was the Messerschmitt 262 jet-propelled fighter. It had been undergoing trials since 1942 and by the summer of 1943 was ready for mass production. With a speed in excess of 500 miles per hour, the Me 262 would have outclassed every Allied fighter, including the Mustang. It might have forced the Allies to abandon their mass bombing raids on Germany.

But Hitler thought in terms of offensive rather than defensive weapons. Despite the protests of General Adolf Galland, commander of the Luftwaffe's fighter arm, he insisted that the plane be converted into a fighter-bomber. Galland later commented that "one might as well have given orders to call a horse a cow!" Hitler hoped that large numbers of these aircraft would smash the Allied cross-channel invasion when it came. But the Germans did not complete this conversion until after the Allies had successfully landed on the French coast. Even then, the aircraft were available in only small numbers. Finally, in September 1944, Hitler allowed some of the Me 262s to be used as fighters. By then it was much too late, and there were too few of them to make an impact. This revolutionary plane never became a real factor in the war. The British had been working on a jet aircraft, too, and it actually became operational shortly before the end of the war in Europe.

A week after the Allies began their cross-channel invasion on June 6, 1944, Hitler unleashed the first of his "vengeance weapons" against Britain. This was the V-1, a pilotless jet-propelled plane with a warhead containing a ton of high explosives.

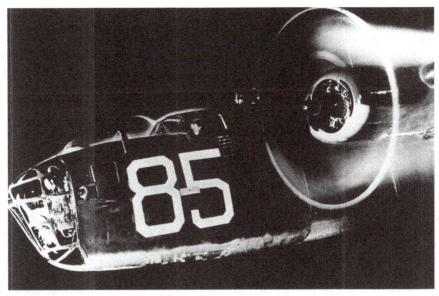

FIGURE 20-1   An American bomber during a night mission. (*U.S. Air Corps/National Archives*)

During the next few weeks, the Germans launched thousands of these "buzz bombs" from sites along the channel coast against London and other British cities. Hitler sent an even more terrifying weapon, the V-2, against Britain from launching sites in the Netherlands, starting on September 8. The V-2 was an actual rocket and also carried a one-ton warhead. It reached a speed of 3,600 miles per hour upon reentering the atmosphere and could not be intercepted. Both the V-1 and the V-2 were terror weapons as well as means of gaining some measure of vengeance for Allied bombing raids against German cities. Hitler hoped that they might have a decisive impact on the course of the war, but even though they killed almost 9,000 persons, their effect fell far short of expectations. The V-2 also proved exceptionally costly and diverted precious resources from the production of fighter-planes badly needed for the defense of the Reich.

The V weapons did succeed in forcing the Allies to divert a large portion of their bombers to attacks on launching sites. Although these raids may have delayed the V-1 attacks for three or four months, they did not prevent the eventual onslaught. Raids against launching sites continued, but the Germans switched to smaller sites that were even more

difficult to hit. Gradually the Allies came to realize that the only real remedy for V weapon attacks was to overrun the launching sites.

During the summer of 1944, a difference of opinion developed among Allied leaders over bombing targets. Air Chief Marshal Sir Arthur Tedder, the deputy supreme commander in Europe, favored raids on the German communications network. The great success of such attacks in France prior to the cross-channel invasion convinced him of the value of this approach. But General Spaatz, the commander of all U.S. strategic air forces in Europe, believed that raids on Germany's oil supply would be even more effective. Spaatz had already directed American bombers to attack oil objectives during the spring of 1944. General Nathan Twining's U.S. 15th Air Force bombed Rumania's Ploesti oil fields from its bases in Italy during April. The 8th Air Force, now commanded by General James Doolittle, the hero of the 1942 raid on Tokyo, sent its bombers against German synthetic oil plants in May. These raids increased in frequency after the cross-channel invasion and had a definite effect on German oil production. They were so successful that British bombers also began to strike at oil targets.

But the really crucial phase of the bombing offensive began in November 1944 with the establishment of oil plants as first-priority targets and communications as second-priority. Raids against synthetic oil production, coupled with the Soviet capture of the Ploesti oil fields in August, caused an alarming drain on German oil stocks. Although Speer's ceaseless efforts resulted in some improvement, the overall trend was critical for both the Luftwaffe and the army. The Luftwaffe found it more and more difficult to obtain fuel for training flights, which sharply reduced its ability to put fighters into the air. This, coupled with the growing domination of the Mustang fighter, gradually resulted in Allied supremacy in the skies over Germany.

The assaults on German communications targets developed more slowly, but in February and March 1945, these operations became shatteringly effective. The flow of raw materials to German industry diminished to a trickle. With the Soviet capture of eastern Germany's major industrial area of Upper Silesia in February, German dependence on the Ruhr became far greater. But raids on communications, along with RAF attacks on the Ruhr itself, virtually paralyzed the area's ability to produce war materiel. By April, Allied bombers were hard-pressed to find suitable strategic targets and devoted their efforts to tactical support of the ground forces that were overrunning Germany.

But terror raids continued to figure prominently in the bombing offensive. Not only Bomber Command but the USAAF as well took part in devastating attacks on major German cities, including Berlin, Stuttgart, Nuremberg, Leipzig, and Munich. This wave of destruction culminated in a series of tragic raids on the beautiful city of Dresden. Renowned for its glorious Rococo architecture, Dresden had previously escaped devastation and contained little of strategic importance. The city's prewar population of 630,000 had increased dramatically with the influx of over 200,000 refugees fleeing from the Red Army, which had already penetrated eastern Germany. Several factors contributed to the decision to strike against Dresden. Churchill favored an attack as a means

FIGURE 20-2   An aerial view of the devastation that Allied air power inflicted on Mannheim, Germany. (*National Archives and Records Administration*)

of impressing Stalin with the awesome power of Anglo-American air might as well as a demonstration of Western determination to cooperate with the Soviet offensive. As an almost untouched urban center, Dresden also provided Allied leaders with a tempting target in keeping with the policy of smashing enemy cities.

On the night of February 13–14, over 800 British bombers dropped huge quantities of incendiaries and high-explosive bombs on the city, creating a hideous firestorm similar to the one that had tormented Hamburg a year and a half earlier. If this were not enough, 300 American planes rained additional devastation on the flaming target the following day, and 200 more U.S. bombers struck again on February 15. Over 35,000 persons died in the raids. Little remained of the once lovely city.

Was It All Worthwhile?

The Allied strategic bombing offensive has remained one of the most controversial episodes of World War II. Over 400,000 German civilians lost their lives as a result of attacks on targets within the Reich's pre-1938 borders. At least another 400,000 suffered injuries. By comparison, Britain lost only 65,000 civilians to German bombing attacks. Allied bombs destroyed 30 to 80 percent of 50 major German cities. But the price was high: 40,000 Allied planes destroyed and 160,000 airmen dead. Did all the destruction and slaughter visited upon Germany's cities really affect the war to an extent that justified such drastic measures? Did the results offset the heavy casualties suffered by Allied bomber crews?

Raids on German industry clearly did not destroy the Reich's ability to produce war materiel during 1943–44. In fact, German aircraft production rose from the previous high of 10,898 in 1943 to 25,285 in 1944. Tank production also increased sharply. But, without Allied raids, Germany would have possessed the potential to increase production even more. Allied bombing cut Germany's projected output of tanks by 35 percent and aircraft by 31 percent in 1944. The bombing offensive also forced the Germans to divert fighter aircraft from the various fronts to defend the Fatherland and left them no choice but to concentrate on

production of fighters at the expense of bombers. Indeed, bomber output dropped to only 18 percent of Germany's overall aircraft production by the end of 1944. This clearly reduced the threat of bombing attacks on Allied ground forces. By 1944 Germany had diverted one-third of artillery production to antiaircraft guns, an action that left its army at a huge disadvantage in firepower. As many as two million men who might otherwise have seen combat against Allied troops also had to serve in antiaircraft crews and civil defense roles. Allied bombing attacks on the French rail and road networks prior to D Day also contributed significantly to the success of the Normandy invasion.

Despite the benefits of direct attacks on industry, area bombing of cities certainly failed in its major purpose—to destroy German civilian morale and the will to resist. Nevertheless, it did weaken morale and created an atmosphere of great sorrow and insecurity among German civilians. Obviously, a steady menu of death, destruction, and fear must take its toll.

It was not until the Allies focused on oil and communications targets late in the conflict that strategic bombing really had a paralyzing effect on Germany's ability to wage war. But by that time the outcome was no longer in doubt. It is possible that concentration on these targets earlier might have shortened the struggle, but such an approach was not feasible until the advent of long-range fighters in large numbers for escort duty. These were not available until early 1944. Without such escorts, large-scale raids deep into Germany against oil and communications targets would certainly have resulted in losses as prohibitive as those suffered in raids on cities.

Ironically, despite the infinitely greater emphasis on strategic bombing, tactical air power in support of ground troops probably made at least as significant a contribution to victory. But it, too, was sometimes guilty of overkill as in the massive attacks on Cassino and the French city of Caen. These raids actually caused more difficulty for the advancing Allied troops than for the German defenders. They created so much havoc that Allied tanks and supply vehicles could not penetrate through the huge mounds of debris that clogged the streets of the devastated towns.

CHAPTER TWENTY-ONE

Total War and the Home Fronts

World War I had led to the creation of a new concept—total war. It had gradually taken shape after the initial dreams of speedy victory had died in the face of the reality of a prolonged and bloody conflict. Total war involved a close interrelationship between a nation's economy, its technology, and the mobilization of its civilian population for the purpose of winning the war. Although many aspects of total war had been present in earlier conflicts, World War I was the first instance in which governments attempted to integrate them all completely and in a most determined manner. The degree to which the various warring powers succeeded in securing the total mobilization of their economic and human resources varied considerably. World War II witnessed a similar attempt by the belligerents to harness their resources totally in the interest of victory. Again, the extent of their efforts and their achievements differed markedly.

Germany: From Limited Liability to Total War

One might think that Nazi Germany, as a totalitarian state, would have been the most ambitious and the most successful in preparing its economy and people for total war. But the bureaucratic confusion that characterized the Third Reich, coupled with Hitler's dream of waging a war of limited liability, retarded its progress for years. In keeping with Hitler's long-standing fear of a breakdown of civilian morale similar to that which had occurred in Germany during World War I, he insisted that much of German industry concentrate on the production of consumer goods. By the time that something approaching an all-out effort was underway, it was too late. The war was already lost.

Goebbels's propaganda ministry did quickly mobilize the press, radio, and film to foster support for the war, but the results were disappointing at first. Goebbels as well as Hitler and other Nazi leaders were disturbed by reports of Germans glumly watching their troops as they marched through Berlin soon after the invasion of Poland. Their reaction contrasted sharply with the almost ecstatic response to the outbreak of World War I.

It was not until the Wehrmacht won its early victories and especially the spectacular *Blitzkrieg* triumph over France in the spring of 1940 that German confidence flourished. The failure to knock Britain out of the war and, most notably, the invasion of the Soviet Union the following year, however, brought the return of doubt and fear. Once again, the early German successes on the eastern front, trumpeted so bombastically by Goebbels, only made the setback before Moscow more discouraging. A sudden increase in the number of wounded soldiers on the streets of German cities provided an especially sobering reminder that all was not well at the front.

With the resumption of German offensive activity during the summer of 1942, the propaganda barrage picked up in intensity, rekindling dreams of victory. But even Goebbels could not disguise the loss of the 6th Army at Stalingrad. The advent of British bombing raids on German cities added an even greater blow to civilian morale, particularly the horrors of the firestorm that engulfed Hamburg in 1943. Goebbels took advantage of the Allied unconditional surrender proclamation in January of that year to try to stiffen civilian resolve to fight to the bitter end. The extent to which this propaganda windfall actually changed popular devotion to the war effort is by no means certain, however.

The German economy, geared to Hitler's rearmament "in breadth" approach, did not come close to total mobilization until 1942. By then, the growing difficulties on the eastern front gave Germany little option but to move in that direction. At this point Dr. Fritz Todt, minister of armaments since 1940, gained greater authority to deal with the overall economy, but he had only begun the process of converting industry to total war when he died in a plane crash early in 1942. Albert Speer succeeded him and immediately took up the task with exceptional energy and great success.

Speer loomed as a curious exception to most of the Nazi leaders who surrounded Hitler and basked in his reflected glory while seeking their own aggrandizement. By contrast, Speer viewed himself as an artist and technician operating beyond the realm of politics. While clearly aware of the monstrous nature of Nazism and Hitler's policies, he considered them irrelevant to the sphere in which he worked and attempted to isolate himself from them. Speer had joined the Nazi party as a young architect in 1931 and soon came to the attention of the Führer. His flair for organization and innovation prompted Hitler to choose him as Todt's successor at the age of 36. Speer quickly set out to increase production dramatically, develop new and better weapons, improve transportation, and eliminate waste. By 1943, he had placed the Reich's economy on what approached a full wartime level.

Despite Speer's efforts, much of German industry was still producing consumer goods. Speer also faced competition and obstruction from the many governmental and party organizations that played roles in the economy. His most notable adversary was Fritz Sauckel, who controlled industrial manpower in his capacity as plenipotentiary for labor mobilization. Sauckel successfully resisted Speer's attempt to take charge of all labor in Germany as well as in occupied countries in the interest of greater efficiency and a more thorough mobilization of resources.

German Utilization of Labor

By this time the Wehrmacht's incessant demands for manpower had created an acute shortage of German males available for the production of war materiel. Two sources could be tapped to help alleviate this problem—foreign slave laborers and German women. Although Speer had no qualms about slave labor, he disagreed with Sauckel on how this resource should be utilized. In Speer's view, it would be more effective to develop industries in occupied countries, thus creating a more contented work force by allowing foreign laborers to remain in their homelands. Sauckel insisted on rounding up foreign workers and shipping them to Germany as slave laborers, a practice that provided little incentive for the workers and instilled in them an intense hatred of their Nazi masters. By 1944, over 5 million slave laborers toiled in wretched conditions, Polish and Russian women making up the majority of them. Another 2 million prisoners of war, the largest portion from the Red Army, also were mobilized.

As early as April 1942, Speer urged that women be recruited for industrial jobs. But Hitler and Sauckel both resisted, holding steadfastly to their belief that a woman's place was in the home. This was in keeping with German tradition. It had long been held that women's role could be summed up in three words—"children, church, kitchen." It was not until 1943, when it was obvious that the war was not going well, that women, 17 to 45 years of age, were required to register for compulsory labor. Although the initial response from women, who tended to remain faithful to traditional gender roles, was far from enthusiastic, they gradually answered the call. They became increasingly prominent in war industries and eventually were more numerous than male workers, but their number never rose above 50 percent of the female population. Their wages also hovered more than 25 percent below those of men.

It was not only in war industries that women moved into jobs formerly reserved for men. Hannah Reitsch, a devoted Nazi, gained renown as a test pilot and became a favorite of Hitler. She was so dedicated to the Führer and the Nazi cause that in February 1944, she allegedly urged the use of suicide pilots, who would crash rockets into their targets, and even volunteered to fly the first mission. As the war went from bad to worse for Germany, and the Wehrmacht became even more desperate for manpower, women began to take over air defense tasks, serving in the detection and charting of approaching Allied planes as well as members of searchlight crews. By 1945, they had graduated to operating antiaircraft guns. Many died while trying to repel enemy bombers.

In February 1943, soon after the Stalingrad debacle, Goebbels proclaimed a campaign of total war in an address to a crowd of Nazi enthusiasts in Berlin's Sportpalast. During his speech, he shouted, "Do you want total war?" His audience, carefully selected for its loyalty and zeal, thundered back, "Yes!" But the results of this attempt at total mobilization proved highly disappointing. Despite the ringing support expressed at the Sportpalast, party functionaries did not flock to the factories. Indeed, Martin Bormann, Hitler's deputy, refused to allow party workers to be recruited for work in war industries. Party leaders also saw to it that their wives were appointed to positions that did not actually exist. In the crowning act of folly, the Nazis also continued to use thousands of able-bodied members of the SS to round up and transport Jews to death camps.

Goebbels tried again to mobilize Germany in a total war effort in July 1944. Now that it was much too late, he enjoyed more success. Stringent measures went into effect in an eleventh-hour attempt to cheat fate. The age limit for compulsory labor for women rose to 50, and all males, ages 16 to 65, were required to register, while younger children found themselves liable for agricultural work. But although Speer managed to eliminate many of the restrictions that had formerly hampered his efforts, he could not accomplish the impossible, and when Allied air power began to concentrate on attacking oil and communications targets, the increasing fuel shortage made attempts to increase production meaningless.

Another Nazi stratagem that failed to fulfill the hopes placed in it was the *Volkssturm* (People's Storm), a paramilitary defense force. Made up of boys as young as 16 and men as old as 60, it was viewed by Hitler as a last-ditch effort to stem the Allied tide. Created in November 1944, the few units that came into existence were poorly equipped and barely trained. Those that saw action usually disintegrated quickly.

The Decline of Living Standards

While Germany's leaders bickered and did what they could to bolster the war effort, life for the civilian population declined. Although shortages of such things as meat, fish, fruit, and heating coal arose quickly in cities, they were kept within bounds by Germany's ability to exploit the countries that fell under its control. Foodstuffs especially were diverted from the occupied nations, while the native populations suffered from hunger, and slave laborers and inmates of the concentration and death camps were starved. With the gradual loss of the conquered areas and the deterioration and eventual paralysis of the transportation network, shortages of virtually everything became the norm.

As the tempo of Allied air raids accelerated, more and more civilians experienced the ordeal of the British during the Blitz of 1940–41, but on a much greater scale. They crowded into bomb shelters, which offered little protection from direct hits and often became crematoriums during incendiary raids. In 1943, the government began to resort to large-scale evacuations of nonessential civilians from cities, but this influx of hungry urbanites did not please many in the rural population. When the Red Army penetrated into the Reich in the last months of the war, many Germans fled in terror, fearing Soviet reprisals for the atrocities inflicted on their people. Many of those who remained behind were killed, while thousands of women and young girls were raped and often murdered. Clearly Hitler's early promises of a glorious future for the German people had grown hollow.

Resistance in Germany

Not everyone in Germany was in favor of the Nazi regime or the continuation of the war. In fact, an anti-Nazi, antiwar opposition movement had developed in Germany well before the war. It began with civilian opponents on the left of the political spectrum. But both Social Democrats and Communists were so weakened by early Nazi moves against them that they accomplished nothing. A number of conservatives also opposed Hitler from an early date. These people disliked democracy and favored a traditional authoritarian government, but they detested the Nazi regime and Hitler's reckless foreign policy. Carl Goerdeler, the former mayor of Leipzig, became the chief link between them and disaffected members of the army officer corps. Despite their opposition to Hitler, these conservatives believed that Germany had a right to its pre–World War I borders as well as Austria and the Sudetenland. They clung to their desire to retain these territories long after it should have been apparent that the Allies would never allow such gains, even if the resistance succeeded in ridding Germany of Hitler.

Another opposition group, the Kreisau Circle, consisted chiefly of members of the aristocracy. Named after the estate of one of its leaders, it originally disavowed German territorial gains and hoped to improve relations with both France and Poland. As time passed, however, some of its members also expressed a desire to retain the German-populated areas that Hitler had taken. Military involvement in the opposition waxed and waned according to the fortunes of war in the early years of the conflict but blossomed anew when the invasion of the Soviet Union soured. Starting in 1942, various plots to assassinate Hitler developed and led to an actual attempt on the Führer's life in July 1944.*

Less violent sources of opposition developed within the churches. Although they had originally rallied to the support of the Nazi regime, relations between the church and the state remained tenuous. The Nazis were fundamentally opposed to the Christian moral code, but, Hitler was reluctant to push this hostility to the point of alienating Christians. Once the war began, he hoped to maintain both Protestant and Catholic support and ordered an end to anti-Christian activity, but tension mounted nevertheless. Religious opposition to the regime eventually focused on the Nazi policy of extermination of the mentally ill and retarded. Clemens von Galen, the Catholic archbishop of Munster, delivered a sermon in 1941 that somewhat belatedly denounced the Nazi practice of euthanasia. Hitler was so concerned about antagonizing the Catholics that he terminated the program shortly afterward. Unfortunately, the church refrained from making similar attacks against the policy of exterminating Jews.

Soon after coming to power, the Nazis attempted to unite all Protestant churches under a pro-Nazi group called the German Christians, which gained a dominant position and pushed through a number of reforms, including the purging of non-Aryan clergy. A group of pastors, led

by Martin Niemöller, who had been a U-boat commander in World War I, and including the theologian Dietrich Bonhoeffer, refused to accept these changes and protested secular interference in church affairs. Out of this dissent, a new Confessional church came into being, but the Gestapo moved against some of its leaders. Niemöller was to languish for years in a number of concentration camps. Bonhoeffer became an active conspirator against Hitler and lost his life in this cause. Hitler eventually curbed the German Christians in hope of gaining greater unity among the Protestants. Henceforth, the Protestant churches offered no more than passive resistance. The Jehovah's Witnesses were the most consistently anti-Nazi religious group. They steadfastly refused to cooperate with the regime and suffered severe persecution.

A small resistance movement also developed among some students at the University of Munich, who formed the White Rose group in the spring of 1942. Led by Hans Scholl, his sister Sophie, and Christoph Probst, the members of the White Rose printed and distributed pamphlets denouncing the Nazis and the war they had launched. Although characterized by perhaps the purest motives of any of the opposition groups, their efforts had no real effect. Their short history came to an especially poignant end when the Gestapo arrested the Scholls in the winter of 1943. They lost their heads to the guillotine soon afterward.

Britain: Toward Total Mobilization

The responses of Britain and the United States to the challenge of total war posed a dramatic contrast to the confused and uneven German approach to the same task. Despite Hitler's accusation that they were soft and decadent, the Western democracies proved able to mobilize their resources far more completely, in a much more rational manner, and with exceptional dedication.

At first, however, Britain approached the conflict with less than an all-out effort. To be sure, Parliament passed an Emergency Powers Act in September 1939 that gave the government authority to control the economy in the interest of winning the war. But, in keeping with Chamberlain's vision of a war of limited liability, the British hoped to keep their military commitment to a minimum, placing their faith instead in the naval blockade, the strength of the French army, and the Maginot line. British war industries did not operate at full capacity for many months. In fact, much of British industry remained devoted to the production of consumer goods, and automobile dealers proudly displayed their new models for 1940. As late as the spring of that year, unemployment still hovered at 1 million, while the government had done little to stockpile food and raw materials. The strange atmosphere of the "phony war" did not stimulate a sense of urgency.

The greatest concern in Britain, as it had been during the interwar years, focused on the threat of aerial attack. Accordingly, the government adopted measures to strengthen British air defenses and to deal with damage caused by bombing and fires. It also launched a program of the evacuation of mothers and their children from the cities. Over 3 million of them quickly found refuge in rural areas and small towns, but most returned home when weeks and then months passed without air raids. The government also established new ministries for economic warfare, food, shipping, and information.

The real change in Great Britain came as a result of the debacle in France in 1940 and the looming threat of bombardment and invasion. The first step occurred with Churchill's ascent to power and his formation of a coalition cabinet as well as a war cabinet similar to those of World War I. One of Churchill's most important appointments was his selection of Lord Beaverbrook for the new post of minister of aircraft production. Beaverbrook, of course, greatly accelerated the production of Spitfire and Hurricane fighters during the Battle of Britain. His efforts also contributed significantly to the vast increase in bomber production.

Under the direction of the famous economist John Maynard Keynes, the government embarked on a massive program to harness the entire economy to the formidable task of winning the war. It began with an ambitious survey of all the economic and human resources of the country. When completed in April 1941, this study enabled the government to make the most efficient use of national resources. Virtually the entire economy came under government direction, while railroads and ports were subject to actual government management. A nationwide system soon went into effect to provide for the allocation of all kinds of

resources, price controls, and the rationing of a large variety of commodities, including food.

In late 1941, Parliament empowered the government to conscript all men, 18 to 50, for either the armed forces or industrial and other types of essential service. In March 1941, the government required women, ages 19 to 40, to register for war work and raised the upper limit to 45 in the fall of 1942. In Britain, too, few men were enthusiastic about interfering with what were considered to be the proper roles for women, especially those who were married. Not all women were keen about this either. When the age limit was extended to 50 in 1945, there were protests over the "conscription of grandmothers." At first, the influx of women into war industries proceeded on a voluntary basis. Actual conscription of women progressed slowly, but by mid-1943, all women, 19–30, were liable for service, and a million and a half women were employed in "essential industries." Women met discrimination from male-dominated trade unions and often worked only part-time and in unskilled jobs. Their wages also lagged behind those of male workers, and at their peak were only 53 percent of those for men. Despite these impediments, women did enjoy greater financial independence because of their wartime employment. Nevertheless, the cause of women's rights made little progress during the war, although their wartime experience may have increased the self-confidence of women and may have provided some impetus to the flowering of the women's movement in later years. Approximately 500,000 other women served in auxiliary military roles—in the Women's Land Army, Women's Royal Naval Service, Women's Auxiliary Air Force, and Auxiliary Territorial Service.

A vast expansion of war industries took place, and from 1940 to 1942 Britain produced more tanks and aircraft than Germany. Only with the beginning of the transformation of the Nazi economy in 1942 did this situation start to change. The amount of British land under cultivation also increased impressively, as every available patch of ground was soon transformed into a garden plot.

In keeping with the coalition nature of the government, Ernest Bevin, a Labour party and trade union leader, received the post of minister of labor. Bevin acted as a virtual dictator over labor allocation and regulation. But, despite stringent controls over the work force, Britain experienced little unrest among its workers. Patriotism, satisfaction over the end of unemployment, widespread respect for Bevin, overtime pay, price controls, and a general improvement in the standard of living all contributed to relative tranquility.

Britain's massive investment in the war placed a serious strain on the country's financial resources. Half the national output of goods and services went into the war effort, while exports dropped dramatically and imports of food and other commodities accelerated sharply. In an effort to control inflation and avoid borrowing, the government sought to pay for as much as possible through increased taxation. By 1941, the basic tax rate reached 50 percent of earnings, and corporate excess profits were taxed at 100 percent. But this was not nearly enough. Britain had borrowed heavily from Commonwealth countries and the United States as its gold reserves dwindled alarmingly to pay for imports. The introduction of American lend-lease aid in 1941 did help to ease this problem but at a price.

The United States drove a hard bargain, gaining an end to restrictions on American trade with Commonwealth members, the acquisition of most of Britain's investments in foreign countries, and limitations on British exports. In 1942, the United States also obtained Britain's acceptance of a Reciprocal Aid Agreement, which established "reverse lend-lease." This required the British to provide material aid of various kinds to American forces stationed in Britain, ultimately amounting to $6 billion. In proportion to the British national income, this represented as high a figure as lend-lease did to the American national wealth.

Life in Wartime Britain

The British civilian population suffered far less from bombing than did the Germans and was able to avoid the horrors of land warfare altogether. But it did sustain 300,000 casualties, including 65,000 dead, as well as destruction from bombing and the later V weapons. British civilians also had to put up with wartime austerity—shortages, rationing, and queuing to obtain items in short supply. Mutual experiences, such as waiting out air raids in crowded shelters, and shared responsibilities, such as serving as air raid wardens and fire spotters, helped bring people from various walks

of life together and break down class divisions. For example, lower-class refugees from large cities often took up lodgings with middle-class families in small towns.

The recognition that all classes were sharing in the great crusade to defeat Hitler also led to a new interest among political leaders in social reform. The tremendous growth in the scope of state activities in running the war and mobilizing the economy opened the prospect of a greater role for the government in regard to social problems after the conflict. Churchill's Conservative party as well as the Labour and Liberal parties shared this interest in the welfare of society, although Labour was the most vocal.

But it was Lord Beveridge, a Liberal, who was the driving force behind a famous report that appeared in 1942 calling for a system of insurance that would guarantee at least a subsistence level of income for all citizens as well as medical care and what amounted to "cradle to the grave" security. The government endorsed many of the Beveridge Report's findings the following year.

In keeping with the precedent of World War I, the British postponed parliamentary elections until the end of the European war, although one should have been held as early as 1940. In the meantime, the coalition government provided a role for all parties in directing the country.

While the German invasion, so feared by the British people in 1940, never came to pass, another invasion of sorts left its mark on Britain. This was the great influx of American GIs during the buildup for the Allied invasion of Western Europe. As welcome as the U.S. alliance was, the British found it difficult to cope with the sheer numbers of Yanks in their midst, not to mention the brash behavior of many of them as well as their enormous interest in British females. As one Cockney comedian joked, there were only three things wrong with the Yanks, they were "overpaid, oversexed, and over here." Many British women welcomed the attention that they received from the American visitors, however, and no fewer than 70,000 of them eventually became war brides. As for the GIs, they tended to find their British hosts a bit too reserved for their taste, British wartime food without taste, and British beer much too warm. Despite these and other sources of irritation, the GIs and their British hosts got along much better than the leaders of their respective armies and governments had feared.

The American Giant Awakens

While Britain's mobilization for total war was remarkable as well as far more extensive and efficient than that of Nazi Germany, the British clearly did not have the huge economic resources or the vast population of the United States. Of all the belligerent powers, America was to perform the most prodigious feats in producing implements of war. Of key importance in this exceptional transformation was the fact that when the war began its industrial facilities were not being utilized to anything close to their full potential due to the lingering effects of the Great Depression. Despite the fact that it produced more steel than any other country on the eve of the outbreak of the European conflict, it was only using one-third of its capacity. Ten million men were still unemployed in 1939. But U.S. industry had become more efficient during the 1930s with the introduction of new techniques and equipment. The government had also approved measures that set the stage for a great expansion in output by authorizing the doubling of the navy's strength in 1940 and planning to increase vastly the size of the air force. All of this meant that, once the United States entered the conflict, it could accelerate production without creating an undue strain on industry. At the same time, it would finally end the severe unemployment that had persisted for more than a decade.

Along with this immense industrial potential, the country became a full participant in the war with a totally united people. The Japanese attack on Pearl Harbor had seen to that. It ended the conflict between isolationists and interventionists that had grown increasingly heated during 1940 and 1941. Large numbers of men rushed to the recruiting offices to volunteer for the armed forces. Before long, new patriotic songs such as "Remember Pearl Harbor" gained popularity. Somewhat later, "Praise the Lord and Pass the Ammunition" became a big hit.

Measures against Japanese-Americans

Unfortunately, as a part of this rush to unity, paranoia blossomed in the form of an irrational fear of the Japanese living in the United States. Soon after

Pearl Harbor, this hysteria reached a crescendo in West Coast states. Fear of invasion and sabotage by an enemy "fifth column" led to demands that Japanese-Americans be interned in camps for the duration of the war. Few people argued against this shameful violation of the civil rights of U.S. citizens. President Roosevelt bowed to this pressure and in February 1942 approved an army order providing for the removal of 112,000 Americans of Japanese ancestry and resident Japanese aliens from their homes. These unfortunate victims had no choice but to abandon their jobs, businesses, and farms and submit to internment in ten relocation centers, such as Topaz and Manzanar, in seven Western states. Although starting in 1943 the government allowed 35,000 Japanese-Americans to leave the camps in return for loyalty oaths and agreements not to settle on the West Coast, the camps remained in operation until January 1945. Some Nisei (those born in the United States of immigrant Japanese parents) did join the American army and, as the 442nd Regimental Combat Team fighting in Italy, became the most decorated U.S. unit in the war.

The government did not take any measures against Germans and Italians who were American citizens except those charged with specific acts of disloyalty. But it did require enemy aliens to register, and those who were considered to be dangerous were also interned. Only 1,228 Germans and 232 Italians found themselves subjected to this kind of treatment, however. Most Italians gained their release within a few months of Italy's surrender, while the Germans remained confined until the end of the conflict.

The great sense of unity that the attack on Pearl Harbor had instilled in the American people soon manifested itself in various other forms of patriotic expression. It was present in the war bond drives and civil defense preparations for the unlikely possibility of enemy air attacks and in scrap metal drives, which proved more useful for providing a sense of participation in the war effort than for any real material advantage.

The number of men and women in the armed forces rose dramatically, eventually totaling 15 million. The draft had already increased the army's strength to 1.6 million by the time the Japanese attacked Pearl Harbor. This number climbed to 8.3 million by the end of hostilities in 1945. The navy also grew from 325,000 to 3.4 million.

FIGURE 21-1   Mountains form a dramatic background for the grim reality of life in a war relocation camp for Americans of Japanese ancestry. (*National Archives and Records Administration*)

Mobilization of U.S. Industry

American industry saw to it that these vastly increased armed forces were equipped with enormous amounts of weapons and other materiel. Automobile plants soon converted their facilities to produce tanks, trucks, jeeps, and aircraft. Shipyards turned out staggering numbers of vessels of all kinds, from aircraft carriers and battleships to transports and merchantmen. The efforts of Henry J. Kaiser, a California industrialist who earned the nickname "Sir Launchalot," were especially notable. Kaiser built vast shipyards on the West Coast and greatly reduced the amount of time needed to construct ships. By 1945, tonnage had increased by 42 percent. Among the vessels produced was the Liberty ship, a new type of merchantman that could be built in 10 days with prefabricated sections. Later, the larger and swifter Victory ships appeared. Also important were landing craft, such as the LSI (landing ship infantry) and LST (landing ship tank), which came into service in abundance. Aircraft production rose from less than 6,000 in 1939 to over 96,000 in 1944. Not only did the United States satisfy the voracious demands of its own armed forces, but it also supplied its allies with war materiel of all kinds and in huge quantities. It was an achievement of truly epic proportions.

Such a gigantic transformation of the economy required centralized direction on a significant scale, although the American system did not come close to matching that of Britain. The vast scope of the war effort, coupled with Roosevelt's managerial style, led to a proliferation of agencies dealing with various aspects of mobilization. This resulted in considerable confusion and problems of divided authority. Soon after Pearl Harbor, Roosevelt appointed Donald Nelson, a Sears, Roebuck executive, to head the War Production Board (WPB). Subject only to the president's supervision, Nelson possessed the power to allocate resources and regulate production. Unfortunately, he proved so easygoing that he could not prevent the army and navy from bypassing the WPB and dealing directly with large corporations. Nevertheless, Nelson did ban the production of many items he considered nonessential, including automobiles for civilian use, refrigerators, and most other electric appliances. In addition, he halted housing construction except for homes for defense workers.

Roosevelt also created the Office of Economic Stabilization (OES), headed by his friend James Byrnes, a former senator from South Carolina. Byrnes received the authority to control prices, wages, profits, and rents. In May 1943, Roosevelt elevated Byrnes to direct the newly formed Office of War Mobilization (OWM), which had vast powers over the entire home front. Despite the mushrooming agencies, overlapping jurisdictions, and bickering that marked the American war effort, remarkable progress came with astonishing speed. During 1942, U.S. production equaled that of all Axis powers. In 1943, it was one and a half times as great and, in 1944, twice the output of Germany and Japan combined.

American Minorities in the War

The sudden and spectacular expansion of industrial activity led to an urgent need for labor. This ignited a great increase in population mobility, including the shift of 1.2 million people to the West Coast states, a trend that continued after the war. About three-fourths of those on the move came from the South. With so many men going into the armed forces, opportunity beckoned for numerous people who had been previously unemployed or engaged in menial labor. Among them were large numbers of black people. They migrated from the South to seek jobs in the industrial cities of the North and on the West Coast. Unfortunately, they also encountered discrimination. Roosevelt issued an executive order establishing a Fair Employment Practices Committee, but the committee suffered from poor funding and a meager staff. Although some progress was made, especially in government employment, discrimination on the part of both management and labor unions persisted. Nevertheless, by the end of the war, blacks filled 8 percent of the jobs in war industries, up from only 3 percent in 1942 and approaching the proportion of blacks in the national population—10 percent.

Blacks also served in the armed forces, but the army and navy both segregated them in all-black units and, for the most part, assigned them to menial tasks. They faced discrimination, not only on military installations but also from residents of nearby communities. Some cafes in the South refused to allow them to sit at lunch counters but

admitted German prisoners of war without protest. Army and naval leaders were reluctant to send blacks into combat, in part because many of them were illiterate, a deficiency due primarily to the abysmal state of educational opportunities for blacks in the South. But they also questioned the ability of blacks to perform under fire. Only two black infantry divisions were activated—the 92nd and the 93rd, although a few other smaller tank and artillery units also were created. At first, they served only under white officers, but recruitment and training of black officers progressed during the war. Nevertheless, black officers could command only black soldiers. The two black divisions did not see combat until 1944, the 92nd in Italy and regiments of the 93rd in the Pacific. The navy relegated most black sailors to shore duty, especially as stevedores loading ships. In August 1944, it began to assign some blacks to auxiliary ships in a move toward integration. Blacks also served in the air force, most of them in support units or as manual laborers. But some became pilots and were later referred to as the "Tuskegee Airmen" because they trained at Tuskegee, Alabama. The first unit to be activated was the 99th Pursuit Squadron. Three others followed (the 100th, 301st, and 302nd), and all eventually comprised the 332nd Fighter Group. They proved their skill and courage while escorting bombers from Italian bases.

American Indians, as Native Americans were called at the time, served in all branches of the armed forces. When the war ended, their number had reached 25,000, almost 22,000 of them in the army. Unlike the blacks, they were not members of segregated units. Over 400 men from the Navaho tribe volunteered for duty in the marine signal corps and served as "code talkers" in the Pacific. In this capacity, they transmitted messages in their own native Navaho language, which was totally unknown to the Japanese, reducing the time to encode and decode signals by half. Another Indian marine, Corporal Ira Hayes, was one of the six men immortalized in the famous photograph of the flag-raising on Iwo Jima.

The Role of American Women

The United States never resorted to conscripting women into the wartime labor force, but roughly 2 million women did move into jobs in defense industries. Although government propaganda immortalized "Rosie the Riveter" in wartime posters as the symbol of the American woman's role in the war effort, only a few actually performed this type of specialized work. As in Britain, most women carried out unskilled tasks, such as welding. Again, as in Britain, their wages remained lower than those of male workers, and they often encountered hostility when they moved into positions previously reserved for men. Despite these problems, many women enjoyed their newly found independence. Others harbored no desire to join them in such poorly paid, unskilled jobs. In a poll conducted in 1943, a majority of women expressed no interest in working in a war industry. The overall increase in female employment was not as great as might be expected, only rising from 25 to 36 percent of the work force. Women also entered the armed forces. During 1942, the government formed what became the Women's Army Corps (WAC), as well as equivalents in the navy (WAVES), coast guard, (SPARS), and marines. The latter contingent never received a nickname, and the marine corps reacted with hostility to the suggestion that they be called "marinettes." A total of 215,000 women eventually enlisted in the four branches of the military. They served in a variety of noncombatant positions, although 38 WASPs (Women's Air Service Pilots) died while ferrying planes and towing targets.

Feeding the Nation and More

With the help of unusually good weather during much of the war, farmers harvested the largest crops in history and achieved equally impressive results in meat production. It was vital that they did, because they had to provide food, not only for the armed forces and civilians of the United States but for America's allies as well. Once Allied forces landed in Europe, they also assumed the obligation of feeding the liberated peoples. To accomplish all this was an enormous achievement, comparable to that in the realm of industrial production. Although farmers urged that prices for agricultural commodities be allowed to rise to their natural levels, Roosevelt warned that this would lead to runaway inflation. He insisted on price controls coupled with government subsidies to farmers instead. Farm income doubled

between 1940 and 1943. Despite the upsurge in farm production, the prodigious demand for food led to the imposition of rationing. The government limited the distribution of such items as meat, butter, sugar, coffee, and canned goods, as well as nonfood products including gasoline and tires. The combination of price controls and rationing retarded inflation and facilitated a more equitable distribution of scarce commodities. Such measures could not overcome human nature and the desire for profit, however, and as in all other belligerent countries, some people sold rationed items on the black market for significantly higher prices. Shortages also developed in many unrationed commodities.

It was one thing to boost production to unprecedented levels, it was another to pay for it. World War II cost the government more than $300 billion, compared to only $32 billion for World War I. Roosevelt hoped to finance much of this through increased taxation but encountered opposition in Congress. Nevertheless, Congress did raise income and excise taxes. It also provided for a graduated percentage tax increase according to personal income, sharply higher corporation taxes, and a 95 percent tax on profits in excess of prewar expectations. In all, taxes paid for 40 percent of the war's cost. The government attempted to cover as much as possible of the remainder through the sale of war bonds to American citizens. A series of eight war bond drives ultimately accounted for about three-fifths of the total expenditures. Despite all of these measures, the federal deficit rose from $49 billion in 1941 to $259 billion in 1945.

Unlike Britain, which faced a much more direct threat, elections continued as usual in the United States. A congressional election in 1942 resulted in substantial Republican gains in both the House and the Senate. In 1944, Roosevelt, although weary and suffering from heart disease and high blood pressure, ran for a fourth term. He defeated Thomas E. Dewey, the Republican governor of New York, but the margin of victory, 3.6 million votes, was his smallest.

The Soviets Rebound from Disaster

The Soviet Union shared some of the same weaknesses that plagued Germany in meeting the challenge of total war. Like the Nazi regime, the Soviet

FIGURE 21-2   American women put finishing touches on the noses of bombers at Douglas Aircraft's plant in Long Beach, California. (*National Archives and Records Administration*)

dictatorship in theory exercised total control over all aspects of life, but unlike Germany, this domination extended to the economy. Yet in reality, it too suffered from divided authority, inefficiency, and confusion. Although the state directed a centralized economy, the sheer size of the country and excessive bureaucratic procedures necessitated that many decisions be made on the local level. In the process, local officials often circumvented the cumbersome formal system. The Soviets had also failed to devise a detailed strategic plan for dealing with a possible German invasion or mobilizing the economy for total war. When Hitler launched Operation Barbarossa in 1941, these weaknesses played a major role in the early Soviet disasters.

Just as Hitler often bore responsibility for German mistakes and defeats, Stalin contributed in no small way to the catastrophic setbacks of 1941–42. The Soviet dictator's disregard for human life in his ruthless pursuit of victory was perhaps the most important factor in the appalling losses suffered by the Red Army not only in the early months but in the later triumphant phases of the war as well. Stalin's refusal to heed the many warnings of a German attack, along with his insistence

on maintaining so many troops close to the border, his obsession with reckless counterattacks, and his refusal to authorize evacuations from untenable positions, repeatedly placed Soviet troops in jeopardy. During the prewar period, he had also failed to provide for any kind of overall coordination of Soviet forces. This oversight created confusion and an almost total absence of centralized control during the first days of the invasion. It was not until the establishment of the GKO as a war cabinet and Stavka as a general military headquarters that coordination began to take the place of chaos.

Even then, Stalin dominated both bodies and played the major role in the deployment of troops that led to the disastrous encirclements at Kiev in 1941 and Kharkov in 1942. "But for Stalin," two authorities on the Soviet war effort have charged, "it may well be argued, the Germans would never have reached Moscow or Leningrad, the Caucasus or Stalingrad." *

---

*John Barber and Mark Harrison, *The Soviet Home Front, 1941–1945: A Social and Economic History of the USSR in World War II* (London: Longman, 1991), p. 54.

Stalin and the Soviet government also made serious mistakes in their failure to provide plans to mobilize the Soviet economy for war. To be sure, much of the country's industrial resources were already producing war materiel, but no master plan existed for the coordination of the entire economy, and Soviet leaders had failed to disperse industries to areas in the deep interior. As a result, well over half of the Soviet Union's industrial capacity lay in regions that fell to the enemy by the fall of 1941. Naïvely trusting in the Red Army's ability to stop an invasion quickly, the Soviets also did not devise a plan to evacuate industry from the threatened areas. They finally had to improvise such measures in the most unfavorable conditions and in many cases were unable to carry out the task before the arrival of the Germans. Nevertheless, the Soviets did achieve notable results from their evacuation program.

While the evacuation of industry played a significant role, it was certainly not the only factor in the process of placing the economy on a total war basis. The conversion of nonmilitary industry to war production was of key importance. This task also required speed and took place largely through local improvisation with relatively little centralized direction. Although this approach provided badly needed war materiel in the short run, the lack of overall planning led to excessive concentration on this kind of production. It had the unfortunate by-product of dangerously restricting the output of steel, fuel, and other resources necessary for continuing production of war materiel in the future. As a result, the economy fell into a serious crisis during the first half of 1942.

A severe shortage of labor also developed when many skilled workers entered the army. It grew even worse as the terrible losses in military personnel mounted, necessitating wholesale replacements, while many workers were trapped in enemy-occupied areas. It became necessary to recruit unskilled laborers to replace skilled workers, with a corresponding decline in quality and efficiency. This supply of labor came largely from teenage boys, men over 50, and women. A similar shortage of workers afflicted agriculture. The peasantry had provided by far the largest proportion of recruits for the army even before 1941. To fill the resulting void in farm workers, women became the major source of labor in the production of food. By 1944, they provided almost 75 percent of the rural work force and three-fifths of the industrial workers. But their tradition-minded male superiors denied them access to most administrative and managerial positions.

Although estimates vary, perhaps a million women also served in the Red Army or in partisan units. At first, they filled noncombatant roles, but by the summer of 1942, they began to appear at the front, many as members of air defense crews. But some saw action in the infantry and armored forces as well. Women also served in the air force, and many saw combat. Lilya Litvak won fame as a fighter ace by shooting down 12 German planes before being killed in 1943. When the war ended, most women were quickly demobilized and their contribution to victory largely ignored by Soviet officials, despite the fact that 86 women had won the Hero of the Soviet Union medal.

Prisoners also constituted a large portion of the labor force. These included both political prisoners and actual criminals, who worked as slave laborers in industry, construction, mining, and farming. Perhaps more than 250,000 of them labored in appalling conditions, and many died because of hunger and other privations as well as savage discipline. The Soviets used other prisoners in penal battalions attached to the Red Army. These unfortunate men performed especially dangerous duties and suffered the heaviest casualties of any Soviet military units.

Hunger Stalks the Land

The Soviets also faced an enormous food crisis. They contributed to this themselves by failing to provide adequate food supplies for cities, such as Leningrad and Moscow, and by burning crops in an effort to impede the German advance. But, while this scorched earth policy had little impact on the enemy, it deprived the Soviet people of much needed food. The German conquest of the country's best agricultural land, especially in the Ukraine, severely aggravated the crisis, as did the labor shortage. Hunger and even death by starvation stalked much of the country. Soviet officials resorted to drastic measures to combat the problem, such as restricting ration cards to only those involved in some way with the war effort. Citizens without cards had to rely on the kindness of family members or friends if they were going to eat. The Soviets also appealed to the United States for aid, and America responded by sending large-scale shipments of food as well as trucks and railroad rolling stock to transport the precious cargo. Soviet food production continued to lag far below prewar levels throughout the conflict. This decline reached bottom in 1943, as the Red Army recovered more and more territory formerly occupied by the Germans. For the time being, however, much of this land, devastated by either combat or the retreating enemy, could not be cultivated, while many more people had to be fed in the liberated areas.

During 1942, it became obvious that the economy was so badly disrupted that the government had to adopt a more centralized system to coordinate all areas of production. The chief mechanism for this transformation was a subcommittee of the GKO called the Operations Bureau. Even at this point, much of the old, informal network of improvisation continued to function but with much closer supervision and a new system of priorities.

The Great Patriotic War

The magnitude of the danger created by the German invasion and the early disasters led to a change in policy regarding the role of the Communist party. During the prewar period, the government had identified the achievements of the regime with the party and downplayed nationalism. But soon after the outbreak of war, Soviet leaders portrayed the struggle in patriotic rather than ideological terms. They referred to the conflict as the Great Patriotic War and warned of the danger to Holy Mother Russia. Stalin addressed the country in stirring patriotic speeches and even cited the heroic deeds of heroes from the wars of the tsarist period.

Stalin also sought a reconciliation with the Orthodox Church, which had been subjected to persecution and had been sinking more and more into oblivion since the revolution. In return for assurances of total allegiance to the state, the church gained the right to conduct services on a reasonably free basis. This had the effect of rallying devout citizens to the support of the regime and the war effort, but it also kindled a religious revival that survived even in the postwar years,

when Stalin watered down some of the wartime concessions that had been granted to the church.

During the early months of defeat, Stalin tended to identify the war effort with the government as a whole rather than with himself. But when the Soviets began to gain the initiative and staged their increasingly successful offensives, he saw to it that he gained the lion's share of credit. Propaganda soon reverted to its prewar portrayal of Stalin as the personifacation of the Soviet Union, but this time it created a variation on the theme—Stalin as a larger-than-life war leader and the symbol of victory. In the eyes of many Soviet citizens, he emerged as a popular hero for the first time. Indeed, despite his early catastrophic failures and continuing disregard for human life, Stalin did contribute significantly to the ultimate triumph. He learned from his mistakes and provided increasingly intelligent and undeniably firm leadership.

But Soviet citizens played an even greater role in winning the final victory in supplying millions of people for both the armed forces and for industry and agriculture, where they produced the weapons and food that were essential for success. Most of them suffered from hunger and other privations as the standard of living plummeted. Many others, who languished for years under German occupation or in prison camps, fared far worse. Those unfortunate Soviet soldiers who fell captive to the Germans and survived this terrible ordeal found themselves treated as traitors after their liberation, because Stalin had decreed that surrender was tantamount to treason. During World War II, no country suffered as severely from start to finish as did the Soviet Union. While not all of its inhabitants rallied to the unconditional support of the regime, they all faced one glaring truth: the terrible fate that awaited them if the Germans won the war. This helped unite them in an effort that often took the form of a genuine crusade against the hated invader.

Not all Soviet citizens viewed the war as a patriotic crusade, however. This was especially true of members of the many national minorities. Large numbers of Ukrainians, Belorussians, and inhabitants of the former Baltic states initially welcomed the Germans as liberators. The brutal reality of Nazi racial policy soon turned many of them against the invaders, but some continued to collaborate, including substantial numbers who served in military units formed by the Germans. Among these armed formations was the Russian Liberation Army, led by the disillusioned former Soviet general Andrei Vlasov. But most of its soldiers were Russian prisoners of war who preferred the prospect of serving the Germans over dying from starvation or exposure in Nazi prison camps. Despite its lofty name, Vlasov's army accomplished nothing, and Vlasov himself eventually fell into Soviet hands and was executed.

The most notable example of cooperation between non-Russians and Germans took place in the Caucasus during its relatively brief period of occupation in 1942. Here the German army remained in control of administration because of the area's proximity to the front and ruled with moderation, while keeping the SS and other Nazi agencies at bay. This enlightened approach led to close relations between the invaders and various small ethnic groups. When the Germans withdrew, however, the Soviets instituted a reign of terror, executing prominent collaborators and deporting the remainder of these minorities to Central Asia. Deportation to Central Asia or Siberia was also the fate of the Volga German minority of eastern Russia as well as the Tartars of the Crimea. Most of these unfortunate people were victims of guilt by association rather than actual collaboration.

Japan: Conflict of Interest

If Germany and the Soviet Union suffered from the problems of lack of coordination, bureaucratic inefficiency and confusion, Japan was plagued even more by such difficulties. Its army and navy engaged in an extreme case of interservice rivalry at the expense of the overall war effort. Thus, while attempting with considerable success to press the entire population into total war, Japan ironically found its progress toward full mobilization stymied by those who were most determined to fight the war to a victorious conclusion. It also faced a number of limitations on what it could accomplish under any circumstances. Japanese industrial resources, while considerable, paled by comparison to those of the United States. This was the case when the war began and continued to accelerate as it progressed. In 1941, the United States possessed a population almost twice as large as Japan's, an industrial potential at least seven

times greater, and raw materials perhaps 78 times more plentiful. And while America enjoyed immense productivity in agriculture, Japan still featured small plot cultivation, making it at least as dependent on food imports as Britain.

Although people in the United States and Britain looked upon Japan as a dictatorship in which Tojo's authority was as great as that of Hitler, in reality the Japanese premier probably wielded less direct power than did either Churchill or Roosevelt. While he also served as war minister and at times as foreign minister as well as minister of commerce and industry, he always had to compete with a number of influential former premiers and aristocrats close to the emperor. Most important, the army general staff continued to exercise its traditional independence. In his new roles, Tojo was only a political leader, and real authority in Japan still lay with the army hierarchy. When Tojo finally attempted to bridge the gap by assuming the post of chief of staff of the army in February 1944, it was far too late to prevent Japan from spiraling ever closer to defeat. But it was not only the army that followed an independent course, for the navy also operated as a law unto itself.

The most critical factor in weakening Japan's war effort was the ongoing feud between the army and navy, which resulted in an almost total lack of coordination between them. The officer corps of each had utter contempt for the other, and hatred between the families of military and naval leaders in many cases dated back for generations. The two branches of service were more interested in competing with each other than in joining forces against the common enemy. The results were catastrophic. This vicious rivalry had an especially baneful effect on attempts to mobilize industry for the maximum and most efficient production of war materiel.

Officially, the ministry of commerce and a cabinet planning board were to work with industrial leaders to develop policy for the production and distribution of supplies to the army and navy. Their efforts came to nothing, however, because neither service would cooperate. Each withheld information and dealt directly with industrial firms to fulfill its needs without any consideration of the overall conduct of the war. Soon after the conflict started, the government established civilian agencies for each industry in an effort to control and coordinate production, but they also failed to prevent the army and navy from going their separate ways. Later a new munitions ministry, headed by Tojo himself, tried to bring order to this chaos, but to no avail.

The most lamentable examples of this destructive rivalry developed in the aircraft industry and in regard to oil supplies. Bickering over the design and production of planes as well as duplication of effort led to the underutilization of available industrial facilities. In 1943, Japan produced only 10,000 aircraft despite having the potential to turn out more than 50,000. The army managed to gain control over 85 percent of the oil supply from the East Indies, even though its needs were limited. This confronted the navy, which was dependent on oil to fuel its ships, with a critical shortage that seriously hampered its operations. The army even built its own tankers and later started to construct submarines, allegedly for the purpose of supplying its far-flung garrisons, a decision that accomplished nothing.

Japan's Labor Policies

As in other belligerent countries, labor shortages plagued Japanese industry. The army's insistence on drafting skilled workers, especially from industries producing materiel for the navy, did nothing to improve the situation. Students and women as well as Korean and Chinese slave laborers and Allied prisoners of war replaced these vital workers. Women were pressed into service despite the strongly held view that women should be restricted to producing children and caring for their families. In 1942, government leaders, including Tojo, expressed emphatic opposition to employing women in war work, but in 1943, they had no choice but to make women liable for labor service. In 1944, over 14 million women were employed in various occupations and played important roles in factories and mines, working in some cases as much as 16 hours a day. Although clearly intended as a temporary expedient, the release of women from their traditional role helped to instill in them a new attitude that prepared them for important changes in their position in the postwar era.

Over 800,000 Koreans and 38,000 Chinese "contract" workers were also conscripted for labor in factories and mines. Despite bombastic propaganda about Japan's plans to create a new order in which all the peoples of East Asia would enjoy a far better life free from Western oppression, the Japanese treated the Koreans and Chinese with extreme brutality and often worked them to death. An estimated 60,000 Koreans and 7,000 Chinese died under their tender care. On one occasion, police crushed a revolt of Chinese workers, who rose up in desperation against their savage treatment, and killed 418. Most of the victims were literally flogged to death. Approximately 20,000 Allied prisoners of war suffered similar mistreatment while performing forced labor in the Japanese home islands. At least 60,000 other Allied prisoners, half of them British, were forced to work on the construction of a notorious railroad linking Burma with Thailand. They were joined in this monumental task by 300,000 civilian slave laborers imported from Indonesia, Malaya, Burma, and China. In addition to suffering from the usual Japanese brutality, these workers contended with intense heat, monsoon rains, a variety of virulent tropical diseases, and a host of often lethal jungle creatures. An estimated 60,000 men died while working on this infamous project. The construction of one of the bridges along the 260-mile route inspired Pierre Boulle's less than factual novel *The Bridge on the River Kwai*, which was later made into an Academy Award–winning film. When the surviving Allied prisoners and slave laborers were finally liberated from their prison camps in various parts of the Japanese Empire, most of them were little more than living skeletons. In recent years, hundreds of these victims have sued the Japanese government as well as privately owned industrial and mining firms in an attempt to gain some measure of compensation for the suffering they endured.

Despite the interservice rivalry, the lack of overall coordination of economic planning, and the shortage of labor, Japan built up its heavy industry. It also reduced the number of small and medium-sized firms, which strengthened the big industrialists. In the process, the Japanese increased their total industrial production by one-fourth between 1940 and 1944. Unfortunately for them, this did not begin to approach the massive rise in American industrial output. Between 1941 and 1944, for example, the Japanese turned out almost 59,000 aircraft, while the United States produced 262,000. Japan's per capita productivity actually dropped significantly as a result of the loss of skilled workers to the services.

The shortage of labor also took its toll in agriculture. Again, women along with old men and young boys and girls stepped into the breach. They managed to prevent a decline in domestic rice production until 1945, but imports fell off alarmingly due to crop failures in Korea and the growing impact of American submarine and air attacks on shipping. Fish, another important element in the Japanese diet, also became increasingly scarce as fishermen entered the service and fishing became more dangerous as American forces moved ever closer to the Japanese home islands. Hunger rose accordingly, as did the prevalence of disease associated with malnutrition. To encourage greater food production, the government reduced the rents of tenant farmers, who improved their position relative to landlords, a change that helped prepare the way for postwar land reform. The Japanese also used every available bit of land to grow food, much as the British were doing. Rationing, which was a major factor throughout the war, increased in stringency with the worsening of shortages of virtually everything. As in other warring countries, the black market flourished, and those in charge of its operations were able to obtain scarce commodities and sell them for huge profits.

The "Valley of Darkness"

The final death blows to Japan's economy came in the form of the massive fire bombing of the country's major cities in 1945 and the escalation of the American submarine campaign, which strangled the Japanese supply line to Southeast Asia. By the summer of 1945, many thousands of Japanese civilians had paid the ultimate price for the attack on Pearl Harbor, and millions of others were homeless and suffered from mounting privations and bleak prospects. The fire bombing raids clearly weakened civilian morale and shattered faith in a victorious conclusion to the conflict. Nevertheless, egged on by propaganda, the people persisted in their willingness to resist the enemy to the death. To this end, the government organized civilian volunteer groups during the last few months of the conflict to prepare for the expected American invasion of the sacred home islands. These units prepared defensive positions and were to participate in the actual fighting once the enemy was ashore. Their armament for this task was unlikely to have much impact, consisting of bamboo spears and carpenter's awls. Because raw materials were in such short supply due to the U.S. submarine attacks, some industrial workers were released from their jobs and also joined the volunteer units.

While Japan did not utilize concentration camps such as those of Nazi Germany or forced labor camps such as those of the Soviet Union, various types of civilian as well as military police maintained close surveillance of the activities of the people. Paranoia over dissent and possible espionage also increased, although almost no overt resistance to the war existed. The government subjected newspapers and other publications to rigid censorship and engaged in an ambitious propaganda effort to glorify Japan's early victories, while either ignoring or distorting the rising number of defeats. For example, survivors of Japanese ships sunk in the Battle of Midway found themselves placed in seclusion upon their return to Japan to prevent dissemination of the news of the disaster. For years the people received a steady diet of bombastic proclamations insisting that ultimate success was assured. Eventually, however, it became impossible to disguise the scope of the debacle that was befalling Japan. As city after city fell victim to destruction from fire bombs, the Japanese people needed no confirmation from the government that the end was near. Japan had descended into the "Valley of Darkness" long before the atomic bombs devastated Hiroshima and Nagasaki.

CHAPTER TWENTY-TWO

Cross-Channel Invasion at Last: D Day to the German Border

Controversy continues to this day on the question of whether the Western Allies could have carried out a successful cross-channel invasion of France in 1943. Some observers contend that such an operation was definitely within Anglo-American capabilities. They argue that had Roosevelt and Churchill followed this approach and avoided embroilment in the Mediterranean, they would have shortened the war and Western troops would have liberated much more of Europe than they subsequently did in 1944–45. But most commentators insist that conditions were not conducive to a successful invasion before 1944. To support their position, they point to the German submarine offensive, which took a heavy toll on Allied shipping until the spring of 1943, as well as shortages of ships, landing craft, troops, and equipment. They also insist that the campaigns in North Africa, Sicily, and Italy provided valuable combat experience that many Allied troops, especially American, needed before starting a cross-channel operation.

In rebuttal, proponents of a 1943 invasion convincingly argue that the Allies did possess sufficient ships and landing craft before 1944, but in the wrong places—the Mediterranean and the Pacific. They contend that the Allies could have avoided this dilemma had they remained faithful to their original plan to strike across the channel. These critics also demonstrate that the Allies could have provided enough men and materiel for an invasion by the spring of 1943. Although they admit that many of these troops would not have had actual battle experience, they believe that German weakness in the west would have offset this deficiency. Hitler had only 49 divisions in France, most of them of second-line quality, and was especially short of tanks during 1943. A year later, he had assembled 58 divisions and was considerably

stronger in armor. German defenses along France's Atlantic coast were also much weaker in 1943 than in 1944, and the Allies would have enjoyed air superiority. The chief question that casts doubt on the possibility of a successful 1943 operation was the threat posed by German submarines to Allied shipping in the Atlantic. Clearly it was still a serious problem in early 1943, whereas it had virtually ceased to exist in 1944. Whether it was critical enough to have prevented assembling sufficient troops and materiel for an invasion is by no means clear.

In the final analysis, it is impossible to answer definitively the question of whether an invasion in 1943 would have led to victory or a serious setback for the Allies. We do know, however, that when the invasion finally came in 1944, it took place despite the continued doubts of many British leaders. British interest in the Mediterranean had increased since the agreement at the Casablanca conference to undertake a cross-channel invasion in 1944. Churchill reaffirmed his commitment to an invasion of Western Europe at both the Washington Trident Conference in May and the Quadrant Conference at Quebec in August. But he also argued for an extension of operations into northern Italy. In fact, the British war cabinet agreed in October that the Italian campaign should have priority and voiced its opposition to promising a cross-channel operation in May 1944.

Teheran and Allied Strategy

Churchill's attachment to the Italian campaign contributed to American skepticism regarding British intentions. This concern did not finally subside until November 1943, when Roosevelt, Churchill, and Stalin agreed on the basic details of the cross-channel invasion at the Teheran conference. This was the first face-to-face meeting of all three Allied leaders, the "Big Three." It took place in the capital of Iran, a country that Soviet and British troops had occupied jointly in the summer of 1941 to facilitate the transit of Western aid to Russia and to safeguard Allied access to the Iranian oil fields. At first Churchill continued to push for extended operations in the Mediterranean and postponement of the cross-channel invasion (Operation Overlord). But Stalin supported the Americans and insisted on Overlord. The Soviet dictator had long been suspicious of Anglo-American sincerity about opening a second front in Western Europe and still feared that his allies might seek a separate peace, leaving the USSR to face Germany alone. He had repeatedly pressed them to move faster to undertake an invasion and either failed to grasp or was indifferent to the monumental logistic problems involved in a cross-channel invasion. Confronted by the opposition of both of his allies, Churchill reluctantly agreed that the cross-channel invasion would have top priority in 1944, while the Italian campaign would be relegated to secondary importance. They also agreed that American troops would undertake an invasion of southern France to coincide with Overlord but on a lesser scale.

It was also at Teheran that Roosevelt made his decision to appoint Eisenhower supreme commander of the Allied expeditionary forces that would carry out the invasion. Western leaders had already agreed that an American would serve in this post because the United States would ultimately commit larger forces to the conquest of Western Europe than the British. But Eisenhower's appointment came as a surprise to Churchill and Stalin, both of whom would have preferred General Marshall. Roosevelt chose Eisenhower largely because he considered Marshall irreplaceable as chief of staff.

The decision proved especially beneficial to the Allied cause. Eisenhower possessed the ability to get along with both American and British leaders. These qualities were of vital importance in the man who was responsible for holding the Western coalition together. British Air Marshal Sir Arthur Tedder served as Eisenhower's deputy. Another team player, Tedder had developed a close relationship with Eisenhower in the Mediterranean. He had commanded British air operations in North Africa, Sicily, and Italy, with impressive results.

Tedder possessed a common touch that made him popular with his subordinates. Montgomery was given command of the Allied ground forces that were to make the landings on the French coast as well as responsibility for much of the planning for the invasion.

By 1944, the Western Allies had produced vast amounts of war materiel that were essential if the invasion were to be successful. This materiel was available not only for the cross-channel invasion, but for the war effort in the Mediterranean and the Pacific as well. Nevertheless, Operation Overlord received first priority, and the buildup of equipment and supplies in Britain mounted throughout the months preceding the actual landings on the French coast.

Preparing for the Invasion

The Allies chose the coast of Normandy for the invasion site. Several important factors influenced their decision. Normandy contained two important ports—Cherbourg to the west and Le Havre to the east—either of which would be valuable for supplying the invading troops. The projected landing areas also lay to the east of the Cotentin Peninsula, which jutted northward into the English Channel, protecting the beaches from the prevailing westerly winds. Ultra had informed Allied leaders that the Germans expected the invasion to come at the Pas de Calais, 200 miles to the northeast and only 20 miles from England across the Strait of Dover. The Allies also knew that the Germans had erected stronger defenses and stationed a larger proportion of their troops there than in Normandy. Finally, the British ports across the channel from Normandy were larger and could handle much greater ship and troop concentrations than those opposite the Pas de Calais.

Six divisions formed the initial seaborne landing force—three American, two British, and one Canadian. The Americans represented the nucleus of the U.S. 1st Army, commanded by General Omar Bradley, and were to land near the eastern base of the Cotentin Peninsula and drive toward Cherbourg. In stark contrast to the flamboyant Patton, Bradley was unassuming and colorless. Although considered to be lacking in imagination by some, his quiet efficiency won the respect of his fellow officers. Bradley had missed active service

Allied Invasions of Europe, 1944–45

during World War I and did not gain his first field command until 1941. When Patton took over the 7th Army, Bradley replaced him as commander of the II Corps in the last stages of the Tunisian campaign and in Sicily. Marshall and Eisenhower chose him for the 1st Army post largely because of his administrative ability.

The British and Canadians, the advance guard of General Miles Dempsey's British 2nd Army, were to land farther east near the mouth of the Orne River and capture the important road junction of Caen, which was to serve as the anchor point for the beachhead. Dempsey, like Bradley, was quiet but able. He had served as a corps commander in Sicily and Italy and was one of the few British generals who did not resent Montgomery's interference with operations in the field.

Shortly before these troops went ashore, two American airborne divisions were to land to the west of the U.S. beachheads to provide flank cover, while one British airborne division was to carry out the same mission to the east of the Anglo-Canadian landings. Reinforcements would arrive as soon as the assault units had secured a foothold on the coast.

Until Bradley's troops captured Cherbourg and repaired the damage that the Germans were certain to inflict on port facilities, the invasion force would rely on two prefabricated concrete harbors called Mulberries. Allied ships were to tow the Mulberries across the channel in sections and put them into place off the Normandy coast. They were also to lay pipelines that would provide badly needed fuel. Preparations for the invasion took many months to complete, including the transportation of 1.5 million American soldiers across the Atlantic and from the Mediterranean. Six hundred warships and over 4,000 transports and landing craft formed the greatest invasion armada in history. A total of 12,000 planes provided support for the operation.

Meanwhile, the Germans made preparations to resist the expected invasion. Field Marshal Rundstedt had returned from the inactive list to command all German forces in the west. But the actual leader of the ground forces (Army Group B) in the northern third of France, Belgium, and the southern Netherlands was Field Marshal Rommel. Rommel set out to create as powerful a combination of obstacles as was possible along the coastline—the so-called "Atlantic Wall." His biggest problem was his ignorance of where the Allies would actually strike. As a result, he ordered defenses built on every beach where a landing might be made. This necessitated the expenditure of many precious resources fortifying beaches that would never be attacked. He ordered almost 4 million mines laid as well as the construction of massive numbers of underwater obstacles, thousands of bunkers and casements, some housing 155-mm guns. The underwater obstacles proved especially important because they forced the Allies to land at low tide to prevent landing craft from snagging them. This reduced Allied options as to the timing of the invasion because they needed to land at dawn and would have the benefit of low tide on only a few days a month. German leaders did not agree as to where the invasion would come. Hitler guessed correctly that the target would be Normandy. But Rundstedt and Rommel expected the Allies to attack the Pas de Calais because of its proximity to England. This seemed consistent with the cautious Allied strategy in North Africa and Italy. The Pas de Calais was also closer to Germany and its industrial heartland, the Ruhr. But Hitler's concern about Normandy did lead Rommel to strengthen the defenses there.

Allied leaders also went to elaborate lengths to convince the Germans that an American army, under Patton's command, was present in southeastern England. Its obvious objective, if it existed, would be the Pas de Calais. They even constructed a dummy headquarters, supply depots, and railroad sidings in this area. Bombing raids in the months preceding the invasion also avoided Normandy to help persuade the Germans that it would not be the invasion target. The double agent Juan Pujol (code name Garbo) also fed the Germans false information, indicating that the Allies were going to land at the Pas de Calais. The Germans, who held Garbo in high esteem, accepted his appraisal as genuine. Even after the actual landings in Normandy, Garbo still persuaded the Germans that these were just a feint to divert attention away from the main assault at the Pas de Calais. Ultra reported that these deceptions had reinforced enemy certainty that the assault would come at the Pas de Calais. Meanwhile, air attacks concentrated on the French rail and road networks, including the bridges over the Seine River to the east and the Loire River to the south of Normandy. This interdiction bombing sealed off the invasion site, which made it extremely difficult for the Germans to reinforce their Normandy garrison.

Eisenhower faced a myriad of problems in determining when to actually launch the invasion. Among them were the need for a reasonably calm sea and sufficiently good visibility to enable bombers and naval guns to sight their targets prior to the landings. Even more daunting were two absolutely essential factors that had to occur in combination: a late rising moon to allow airborne forces to carry out their missions, and a low tide just after dawn to enable seaborne troops to land successfully. These two critical requirements would be present in tandem on June 5, 6, and 7, but after that not until July. Eisenhower initially chose the 5th as D Day, but stormy weather threatened to delay the operation indefinitely. German leaders in France were convinced that they had nothing to fear for the foreseeable future. This false sense of security prompted Rommel to visit Germany to celebrate his wife's birthday. Several other German generals left their coastal commands to participate, ironically, in a war game simulating an Allied invasion. In contrast, the horrendous weather plunged Eisenhower and other Allied leaders into gloom. But on the evening of June 5, RAF Group Captain J. N. Skagg, the chief Allied meteorologist, informed them that conditions would improve during the next few hours and would continue until about noon on the 6th. After conferring with his commanders, Ike, already worn down by extreme tension and an overwhelming sense of responsibility, silently weighed his options and then announced his momentous decision: "I'm quite positive that we must give the order. I don't like it, but there it is. I don't see how we can do anything else." June 6 would be D Day.

The Invasion Begins

German certainty that the weather would delay the invasion and the absence of so many commanders from their posts contributed to the surprise of the Allied landings. Even after they began, Rundstedt persisted in his belief that the main attack would come at the Pas de Calais. Ironically, Hitler, who had originally predicted that Normandy would be the invasion site, now agreed with Rundstedt. The relatively small number of Allied divisions that took part in the initial assault convinced him of this. Thus the German leaders at first refused to divert forces from the 15th Army in the

Pas de Calais to bolster the front in Normandy. Rundstedt did seek permission to shift two panzer divisions from reserve to Normandy. But Hitler was sleeping when his headquarters received this request, and no one was willing to wake him. Twelve precious hours elapsed before Rundstedt received approval, and several more passed before the divisions actually departed for the beachhead.

The Allies planned to carry out Operation Overlord in three stages. They referred to the first of these as the break-in, which included the actual landings and consolidation of the beachhead. The second was the buildup. This focused on expanding the beachhead and increasing the size of the invasion force. Finally came the breakout, which the Allies were to execute when the buildup was complete. It involved punching through the German defenses around the beachhead and breaking out in the direction of the German border.

Allied forces executed the break-in stage successfully, starting on D day, June 6. Before the American amphibious landings took place, the 82nd and 101st Airborne Divisions dropped inland to control the approaches to the beaches. They made their drops under cover of darkness, and the paratroopers were badly scattered, but groups of

them caused confusion among the Germans and distracted their attention from the beaches. Some accidentally came down over the town of Ste.-Mere-Eglise. Helplessly exposed to fire from the German defenders, many of them were killed before ever reaching the ground. One particularly unfortunate soldier was sucked into a fire that was raging in a nearby building. Two others landed on the roof of a church. One of them managed to escape, while the other hung by his suspension lines from the steeple and pretended to be dead for over two hours. To add to his ordeal, he was temporarily deafened by the constantly clanging church bell located just a few feet from his head. In another preliminary action, three companies of Rangers scaled Pointe-du-Hoc, a sheer 100-foot cliff 10 miles west of Omaha Beach, the easternmost of the two American landing sites. Their mission was the destruction of a battery of 155-mm guns. Despite heavy casualties, they made it to the top only to find, much to their horror, that the guns were not there. The Germans had removed them, apparently to protect them from bombardment. Nevertheless, the Rangers later discovered the guns as they fought their way inland and disabled them. The price had been high—all but 50 of the 200 Rangers had been either killed or

FIGURE 22-1   American troops head for the coast of Normandy on D day, June 6, 1944. (*U.S. Coast Guard Academy*)

wounded. But their great sacrifice prevented the massive guns from shelling the invasion armada and landing beaches below.

The amphibious landings at Omaha Beach encountered every conceivable problem. Omaha's terrain was by far the most difficult of any of the landing sites. The beach itself was relatively narrow and was dominated by a steep and heavily fortified bluff. Below the bluff stretched a sea wall and an antitank ditch as well as an extensive swampy area, all of which blocked access to five ravines that formed the only routes leading from the beach to the top of the bluff. All sorts of problems arose before the invasion force ever reached shore. The navy launched many landing craft too far out, and the choppy sea swamped them, taking a heavy toll of men, tanks, and artillery. Once the invaders reached the shore, they encountered devastating enemy fire. Many never made it out of their landing craft. Those who did found themselves pinned down on the beach with very little cover. As one soldier later put it, "Our life expectancy was about zero." Utter chaos reigned for hours before the Americans finally managed to breach the sea wall and gradually made their way to the top of the bluff. Approximately 2,500 Americans lost their lives on Omaha Beach that day. The Americans who landed at Utah Beach to the west encountered fewer obstacles and far fewer casualties, although here, too, they moved inland more slowly than expected.

British and Canadian troops landed at Gold, Juno, and Sword beaches to the east of Omaha Beach and advanced several miles with relatively little difficulty. But they failed to fulfill their major objective for the first day, the capture of the key communications center of Caen, when counterattacked by the 21st Panzer Division. This enabled the enemy to establish strong defensive positions to the north of the city as reinforcements arrived. The 12th SS Panzer Division was the first of these. Comprised of fanatical teenagers who were members of the Hitler Youth, it was led by equally motivated veterans of the Eastern Front. The division soon collided with Canadian troops and might have broken through their position except for the timely intervention of Allied naval fire. The Germans did take several hundred Canadians prisoner and proceeded to murder them in a flagrant display of Nazi zeal. Once German leaders

realized that Normandy was actually the main invasion target, they became convinced that the Allies planned to attempt their breakout from the Caen area. It does appear that Montgomery had originally considered an operation of this type. But strong German resistance and slow Allied progress prevented such a strategy. Instead, the final Allied plan called for the British and Canadians to maintain maximum pressure on the Germans at Caen to give the impression that the main breakout attempt would come there. The Americans were to execute the actual breakout at the opposite end of the beachhead.

Slightly over 100,000 Allied troops reached shore during the first two days. General Friedrich Dollmann's German 7th Army, which was responsible for the defense of Normandy, possessed six infantry divisions and one panzer division at first. Dollmann had commanded this army since the outbreak of the war. His forces had taken part in the conquest of France but had found themselves relegated to garrison duty during the following four years. Within ten days, Allied manpower in Normandy had increased to over 500,000, and by July 1, almost a million men were inside the beachhead. During the same period, the Germans built up their strength to 14 divisions, 9 of which were panzer divisions.

The first major American objective was to pinch off the Cotentin Peninsula and capture Cherbourg. Despite strong German resistance, they finally took the city on June 27. But the Germans destroyed the port installations and blocked access to the harbor with sunken ships. As a result, the Allies were not able to use the port until July 16 and did not complete clearing operations until the end of September.

Not only did Rommel expect the British to execute the breakout attempt, but he was also especially concerned about the terrain on the eastern end of the beachhead. It consisted of a rolling plain, stretching from Caen to Falaise 25 miles to the south, and it was ideally suited for armored attacks. Rommel seemingly had less to fear from the Americans, who had to contend with the extremely difficult "hedgerow country" to the west of Caen. High earthen banks, topped by thick hedges, lined the fields and roads of this region, providing the Germans with a deep belt of perfect defensive positions. Heavy fighting followed for several weeks, especially at Caen and Saint-Lô, a small city that was the key point in the projected American breakout. Although the Germans resisted tenaciously, the Allies gradually wore them down.

The buildup of Allied strength in Normandy led to the creation of two army groups by the end of July. The 21st Army Group, under Montgomery's command, consisted of Dempsey's British 2nd Army and General Henry Crerar's new Canadian 1st Army. Crerar, who had spent the interwar years strengthening his country's small army, had served as chief of staff and as a corps commander in Italy. The 12th Army Group, led by Bradley, included the 1st Army, now commanded by General Courtney Hodges, and the newly activated 3rd Army, headed by Patton, who by this time had overcome the disgrace of the slapping incidents in Sicily. Hodges had gained high rank despite being dismissed from West Point because he failed geometry. Undeterred by this setback, he enlisted as a private, quickly gained a commission, and won the Distinguished Service Cross during World War I. Although Bradley considered him a masterful tactician, some of his associates criticized him for not exerting enough control over his subordinates.

The German command structure experienced even more far-reaching changes. Hitler dismissed Rundstedt early in July when the field marshal expressed pessimism regarding the chance of pushing the Allies back into the sea. Rommel suffered injuries when a British plane attacked his staff car on July 17, ending his role in the defense of Normandy. The Führer called on Field Marshal von Kluge, the former commander of Army Group Center on the Eastern Front, to succeed both Rundstedt and Rommel.

An Attempt on Hitler's Life

These developments coincided with an unsuccessful attempt to assassinate Hitler on July 20, the final chapter in a conspiracy that had begun before the war and persisted into the conflict. When the tide turned against Germany in Russia, a small group of officers on the Eastern Front concluded that it was necessary to end the war and that this would be possible only if Hitler were eliminated. They planned no fewer than six attempts to kill him in 1943, but all of their efforts misfired.

Colonel Klaus Schenck von Stauffenberg, who had lost his right hand, two fingers on his left hand and an eye in Tunisia, carried on their mission with the help of officers in Berlin and on the Western Front. Stauffenberg became the key figure in the July 20 attempt on Hitler's life, which took place at the Führer's "Wolf's Lair" headquarters at Rastenberg in East Prussia. He attended the meeting in his capacity as chief of staff of the Replacement Army, which had responsibility for training troops. After placing a briefcase containing a bomb under the conference table, he excused himself and made his escape. When the bomb exploded a few minutes later, it killed four men and wounded 20 others. But the table's heavy oak top and stumplike support absorbed enough of the blast to spare Hitler.

Stauffenberg and his fellow conspirators had planned to follow the assassination by seizing control of the government in Berlin and seeking an end to the war. But officers who remained loyal to Hitler received word that he was still alive and quickly arrested Stauffenberg and several others, effectively crushing the plot. They shot Stauffenberg and his immediate associates shortly thereafter. But most of the conspirators were not so fortunate. Hitler took his revenge on them in the weeks that followed. High-ranking officers and civilians had to endure thunderous denunciations from the rabid Nazi judge Roland Freisler, who presided over perfunctory trials and handed out predetermined sentences. Many of the condemned were hanged by piano wire suspended from meat hooks. Hitler ordered the executions to be filmed so that he could view the victims' death agonies at his leisure. From all accounts, he found this entertainment immensely satisfying. Among those implicated in the conspiracy were Kluge and Rommel. Both committed suicide.

Hitler had already replaced Kluge with Field Marshal Walther Model, a veteran of the Eastern Front whose loyalty to the Führer had remained unshaken. A blunt, outspoken officer of middle-class background, Model led a panzer division in the 1941 invasion of the Soviet Union. He subsequently became known as "the Führer's fireman" for his ability to halt Soviet offensives. He commanded all three army groups on the Eastern Front in succession during 1943–44. Model was not afraid to stand up to Hitler and at times even ignored his orders.

Another important change took place at almost the same time as the attempt on Hitler's life, although there was no connection between the two incidents. General Zeitzler, the OKH chief of staff, had become so frustrated by his confrontations with Hitler that he asked to be allowed to go on sick leave. The Führer was so enraged by this request that he dismissed Zeitzler from the army and refused to allow him to wear his uniform. He appointed General Guderian to succeed him.

The attempt on his life increased Hitler's suspicion of even generals who remained loyal to him. And the fact that he had cheated death added to his conviction that he was a man of destiny who would somehow overcome the enormous problems that confronted him.

The Allies Break Out

Meanwhile, back at the front, the Americans took Saint-Lô on July 18, and the British finally completed the capture of Caen two days later. The long-awaited breakout (Operation Cobra) began on July 25. After an intense aerial bombardment, Bradley launched an offensive by the 1st Army along a narrow front south of Saint-Lô. The Germans, still convinced that the British would make the breakout attempt, persisted in keeping most of their panzer divisions near Caen, thus contributing to the American success. Ultra kept Bradley informed of the relatively weak forces in the path of his troops. General J. Lawton Collins's VII Corps provided the 1st Army's spearhead. Collins had proved himself as a division commander on Guadalcanal, where he had earned the nickname "Lightning Joe." An exceptionally vigorous officer, he became famous for his ability to move his troops quickly. He had skillfully directed the capture of Cherbourg and now scored a breakthrough at Saint-Lô. His forces cleared the way for a thrust to Avranches, at the western base of the Cotentin Peninsula.

The 3rd Army exploited the gap that the 1st Army had created. Patton sent two armored divisions sweeping westward into Brittany in the hope of capturing the Breton ports, while the rest of his army wheeled to the east and began to drive across France, against little opposition. The attempt to capture the Breton ports failed because the Germans defended them skillfully in an effort to deny the Allies the use of their facilities. The American breakthrough threatened the entire German position in Normandy and seemed to dictate a general withdrawal to the Seine. But instead of pulling back, Hitler ordered an assault against the American flank at Mortain near Avranches. The attack failed, and the German 7th Army now found itself in a highly precarious situation. Elements of the 1st Army were swinging eastward around its southern flank, while the British and Canadians were pressuring it from the north.

Bradley hoped to prevent an enemy retreat by sending elements of both the 1st and 3rd armies north through Argentan to link up with the Canadian 1st Army, which struck south by way of Falaise. But the trap did not close quickly enough. Although the Americans made rapid progress at first, Bradley ordered them to halt because he feared that they would collide with the Canadians in the open field. The Canadians, who encountered stronger resistance, also advanced more slowly than hoped, and Montgomery failed to reinforce them with British troops. This combination of factors enabled 35,000 enemy soldiers to escape before the pincers closed on August 19. Nevertheless, 10,000 Germans died in the Falaise pocket, and another 50,000 surrendered. The slaughter became so concentrated in the battle's final stages that Eisenhower referred to the pocket as a "killing ground." Even the German forces that had escaped fell back on the Seine mauled and demoralized.

Now, when it was too late, Hitler authorized the 15th Army to move south from the Pas de Calais in an attempt to stabilize the front. But it accomplished little and became intermingled with the fleeing remnants of the 7th Army, compounding the confusion. Meanwhile, Patton's forces crossed the Seine and rolled toward the German border. Their rapid progress eliminated any chance of a German stand along the Seine.

The Southern Invasion: Anvil-Dragoon

While the Battle of the Falaise pocket raged and Patton's troops rampaged through the French countryside, Allied forces landed on France's Mediterranean coast. Eisenhower originally intended this operation to take place at the same time as the invasion of Normandy, but a shortage of landing craft forced its postponement for over two months. The British opposed the operation, which originally had the code name Anvil, because the plan called for the diversion of troops from Italy. Eisenhower and other American leaders insisted, however, and the invasion began on August 15 with the new code name Dragoon. General Alexander Patch's U.S. 7th Army went ashore between the French naval base of Toulon and the resort city of Cannes. A veteran of World War I, Patch had commanded the army forces that relieved the marines at Guadalcanal.

The invaders made rapid progress against weak opposition, and moved inland. French troops, under General Jean de Lattre de Tassigny, landed soon afterward. De Lattre had served in the defense of France in 1940 and had refused to buckle under to either the Germans or the Vichy regime during the following months. His outspokenness cost him a ten-year prison sentence, but he escaped to Britain in 1943 and later commanded French troops in North Africa. De Lattre's forces joined with the Americans to capture Toulon as well as the great port of Marseille. The Allies soon received word from Ultra of Hitler's order for all German troops in southern France to withdraw northward. This information enabled them to pursue the enemy up the valley of the Rhone River with great confidence and vigor. Their progress was so swift that on September 12, they made contact with the U.S. 3rd Army north of Dijon in eastern France.

Few operations have received more criticism than Anvil-Dragoon. Most appraisals have insisted that it was unnecessary and prevented the exploitation of the situation in Italy. But the capture of Marseille alone made the undertaking worthwhile, especially in view of the failure to capture the Breton ports. From September through January, the Allies unloaded more supplies at Marseille than at any other port.

The Allies' Swift Advance

As the German position in western France disintegrated following the breakout from Normandy and the Falaise pocket disaster, all Allied armies streaked forward. Paris now lay in the path of the U.S. 1st Army, but Eisenhower planned to bypass the great city. He wanted to avoid street fighting, which might destroy the beautiful capital and cause heavy casualties. If Paris fell, the task of supplying its huge population with food would also create a serious logistic problem. The French, both within and outside the city, decided the issue. French Forces of the Interior rose in revolt against the Paris garrison, and de Gaulle demanded that Eisenhower send troops to relieve the poorly armed Resistance units. While the supreme commander hesitated, General Jacques Philippe Leclerc, commander of the French 2nd Armored Division, acted.

Leclerc had been one of the first officers to rally to de Gaulle in 1940. He won fame in December 1942 by marching a Free French regiment from the central African colony of Chad through over 1,200 miles of desert to join the British at Tripoli. Now the independent-minded general defied orders and sent a force toward Paris. Bowing to the inevitable, Eisenhower approved his action. But Leclerc's troops progressed more slowly than expected, and Bradley dispatched American units to join in the liberation. Paris fell on August 25. Like Rome, the City of Light had escaped serious damage, but it had been a close call. Hitler had ordered the commandant of Paris, General Dietrich von Choltitz, to defend the city and ultimately to reduce it to "a field of ruins." Although Choltitz did defend Paris up to a point, he could not bring himself to destroy it and surrendered to the French instead. Huge throngs of ecstatic Parisians plied the Allied troops with flowers, wine, and kisses and cheered as they marched in triumph down the famous Champs Élysées.

Soon after the liberation of Paris, the British 2nd, Canadian 1st, and U.S. 1st armies all knifed into Belgium while Patton drove into Lorraine. By September 15, most of Belgium and Luxembourg had fallen into Allied hands, and the German border was only a few miles away. But the Allies outdistanced their supply lines, and shortages, especially of fuel, began to develop. The "Red Ball Express" truck companies, whose personnel were 60 percent black, transported gasoline and other supplies from the beaches to the front. But despite their exceptional efforts, it became clear that all the armies could not continue their breakneck progress. Accordingly, Montgomery urged a single-thrust strategy with the British 2nd and U.S. 1st armies driving toward the Rhine and the Ruhr while the Canadians and Patton's troops halted to conserve supplies. But Eisenhower insisted on a broad-front strategy with both army groups moving forward more or less simultaneously. The supreme commander prevailed, and his decision sparked a controversy that still continues. Montgomery contended that it prevented not only the encirclement of the Ruhr but also a thrust all the way to Berlin.

Evidence now indicates that Montgomery was probably correct regarding the feasibility of a quick drive to the Rhine. The Germans had little strength in the path of such an operation, and the Allies probably had sufficient supplies to service the forces of Dempsey and Hodges or, conversely, those of Patton. But it does not appear that a Rhine crossing was possible, and certainly Montgomery was wildly optimistic about prospects for an advance to Berlin. The Allies clearly lacked the capability to supply such an ambitious enterprise.

Although the capture of Marseille eased the supply problem, the Allies badly needed a major port close to the front. The obvious choice was the Belgian city of Antwerp, one of Europe's largest ports. Allied leaders were elated when Antwerp fell to the British on September 4 with its port intact. The British had advanced so rapidly that the Germans were unable to block the harbor or destroy its facilities. But to take the city was not enough. Antwerp lay on the Scheldt River, 60 miles from the North Sea, and the Germans still controlled the Belgian and Dutch territory that bordered the river's estuary.

Eisenhower obtained warnings from Ultra that Hitler planned to hold the estuary and thus deny the use of Antwerp to the Allies. He therefore gave the highest priority to clearing the approaches to the Scheldt and provided Montgomery with ample supplies for this purpose. A quick thrust might have accomplished this before the Germans could consolidate their defenses there. It might also have trapped the remnants of the German 15th Army. The speed of the Allied advance had pinned them into a pocket on the southern bank of the Scheldt's estuary. But Montgomery's mind was on another objective, and he made no effort to carry out this mission. His failure to act allowed most of the enemy troops to evacuate across the river. This battered but substantial force was then able to participate in the defense of the Netherlands. A German rear guard also continued to hold the Scheldt estuary and prevented its clearing until the end of November. Until then, Antwerp was useless to the Allies.

FIGURE 22-2 Allied Supreme Commander General Dwight Eisenhower (right) confers with Generals Ralph Royce (left) and Omar Bradley (center). (*National Archives and Records Administration*)

The Push to Cross the Rhine

Instead of focusing on the vital objective of clearing the Scheldt estuary, Montgomery conceived a much more ambitious undertaking—a massive airborne operation aimed at crossing the Rhine in the Netherlands. If the Allies could accomplish this, they would not only hurdle the formidable river barrier that guarded Germany but would outflank the northernmost fortifications of the West Wall along the German-Dutch border. They would also be able to threaten German V-2 rocket-launching sites in the Netherlands. But the proposed operation would require the Allies to cross four other rivers and three canals before they reached the Lower Rhine at Arnhem. If it were to succeed, Anglo-American airborne troops would have to seize the bridges over these water obstacles while British land forces drove northward to relieve them. The distance to the most remote bridge at Arnhem was 64 miles.

Montgomery gained Eisenhower's approval for his plan, which was given the code name Operation Market-Garden. It was an exceptionally bold undertaking and required unusually precise timing. To compound the risk, Ultra detected the presence of two SS panzer divisions near Arnhem. But neither Montgomery nor Eisenhower was willing to call off the operation. The plan called for the U.S. 101st Airborne Division to capture the bridge across the Maas, the Dutch part of the Meuse, southernmost of the three major rivers, near Eindhoven. This division, nicknamed Screaming Eagles, also would take a number of bridges over lesser streams and canals. The American 82nd ("All-American") Airborne Division was to seize the span over the Waal River, a branch of the Rhine, farther north near Nijmegen. The British 1st Airborne Division, called the Red Devils because its men wore maroon berets, drew the most difficult assignment of all. It had to capture the northernmost bridge across the Lower Rhine at Arnhem.

Market-Garden began on a clear September 17 with daytime landings. But it soon encountered bad weather that delayed the dropping of some of the paratroops. Even more serious, Ultra proved correct; the two German panzer divisions were indeed in the vicinity of Arnhem, although they were refitting and not at full strength. This posed a serious menace to the 1st Airborne Division.

The British compounded the dilemma by dropping their forces too far from the objective. This enabled the Germans to split them into two segments and prevent the capture of the bridge. One group of 500 men, commanded by John Frost, a 31-year-old lieutenant colonel who carried a fox-hunting horn into battle, managed to seize the northern approach to the span. But it was too weak to move across without aid from the main force. The 82nd Airborne also had difficulty capturing the bridge over the Waal. If the Americans had moved toward this objective immediately upon landing, they would have encountered only a few enemy sentries. Instead, they concentrated on taking the high ground near Nijmegen first. By

Operation Market-Garden, September 17–25, 1944

the time they advanced toward the river, the Germans had sent reinforcements and held the bridge for three days. Only after a bloody crossing of the Waal in flimsy canvas boats was the 82nd able to secure the bridge.

The British XXX Corps, comprising the relief force, had to move through swampy terrain along one narrow road that the Germans subjected to artillery fire. These obstacles, among others, prevented it from advancing as rapidly as anticipated. Ultimately, the relief force came to the rescue of all the airborne troops except those at Arnhem. As General Frederick Browning of the I British Airborne Corps had warned, the bridge there proved a "bridge too far." After nine days of heavy fighting, only 2,400 of the original 9,000 Red Devils managed to break through enemy lines and escape. The failure of Market-Garden ended Allied hopes of crossing the Rhine in 1944.

Shortly before the start of this operation, Hitler had reappointed Rundstedt to his former position as German supreme commander in the west. Rundstedt and especially Model, still in command of Army Group B, managed to scrape together enough forces to reconstruct the front. They did so not only in the Netherlands but also opposite Hodges, who was probing beyond the Belgian border into Germany, and Patton, whose drive was counterattacked by the 5th Panzer Army and bogged down in Lorraine. The 1st Army drove to within a few miles of the German border city of Aachen on September 15 but was unable to complete its capture until October 21. Despite the great success of the Allied summer offensive, the Germans were not yet finished in the west any more than in the east.

The Importance of D Day

It is sometimes said that D day was the most important day of World War II and that the success of the landings in Normandy meant that Hitler would lose the war. This would appear to be something of an exaggeration. Clearly D day was the most important day of the war for the Western Allies, and it certainly hastened the final defeat of Germany. But it would appear that the Germans had already lost the war on the Eastern Front—at Moscow, Stalingrad, and Kursk—long before the Western Allies landed in France. Nevertheless, D day was exceptionally important. If the invasion had failed, the Americans and British might not have tried again. They might have shifted their focus back to Italy and the Mediterranean with dubious prospects. Even if they did try again to land in Western Europe, this would have taken time, and the Red Army would have continued to push the Germans back. Its massive victory in Belorussia shortly after D day is evidence of this. All of Germany and much of Western Europe might have fallen to the Soviets. The success of the D day invasion and the subsequent drive across France, Belgium, and into the Netherlands assured that this would not happen.

CHAPTER TWENTY-THREE

The End of the Thousand-Year Reich

Allied frustration increased in the late fall of 1944 as German resistance stiffened all along the Western Front. The failure of Operation Market-Garden had stymied British progress in the Netherlands, and American forces also encountered problems. Hodges's 1st Army came up against the "dragon's teeth" concrete antitank obstacles and pillboxes of the West Wall and the difficult terrain of Germany's Hürtgen Forest south of Aachen. The battle to take this dense and dismal forest became the bloodiest and most protracted since the hedgerow fighting in Normandy. To the south, Patton's 3rd Army had to struggle through the hilly country of Lorraine before reaching the West Wall in the coal-mining region of the Saar. Still farther south, General Jacob Devers' recently formed 6th Army Group, consisting of Patch's 7th and de Lattre's 1st French Army, contended with the Vosges Mountains, a long, low range along the western border of Alsace. But even though dreams of a quick triumph had vanished, certainty of ultimate victory remained high. Eisenhower and his commanders continued to prepare for the thrust to the Rhine and beyond.

The Battle of the Bulge

But Hitler had one final trump to play—one last offensive. This counterstroke was strictly the Führer's idea, and its ambitious scope appalled both Rundstedt and Model. Hitler envisioned a variation on the theme of an earlier triumph. He chose to strike in the Ardennes once again, recognizing that it was the weak point in the Allied line, just as it had been the French Achilles' heel in 1940. But this time, rather than penetrating into France, he planned to send his armor across the Meuse River all the way to Antwerp. If he could accomplish this, he would isolate Montgomery's forces from the American armies to the south.

To fulfill his grandiose dream, Hitler rashly weakened German strength on the Eastern Front to provide a powerful striking force for the Ardennes operation. It included General Josef Sepp Dietrich's 6th SS Panzer Army on the north, General Hasso von Manteuffel's 5th Panzer Army in the center, and the refurbished 7th Army of General Erich Brandenberger on the south. Dietrich had been a close associate of Hitler's since the early days of the party, when he had led the Führer's SS bodyguard. He later commanded a panzer division on the Eastern Front as well as an armored corps in Normandy. Dietrich lacked the skill and imaginative leadership of the aristocratic Manteuffel who had gained an impressive reputation as a panzer corps commander in Russia. Brandenberger, another veteran of panzer warfare, had taken over the 7th Army following the disasters of the summer. He had shown considerable ability in plugging weak points in the German line during the autumn fighting. In all, the OKW amassed 24 divisions, including 10 panzer, an armored force larger than the one that had executed the great Ardennes breakthrough in 1940.

Considering the ease with which the Wehrmacht had slashed through the Ardennes $4\frac{1}{2}$ years earlier, it is remarkable that the Allies failed to take greater precautions to protect this portion of the front. Although the Germans had clearly shown that they were still dangerous in a defensive role, Allied leaders did not consider them capable of a major counteroffensive.

Only four American divisions from Hodges's 1st Army held the Ardennes front, and Allied leaders were oblivious to the impending onslaught. The chief factor that contributed to their lack of concern was Hitler's insistence on complete radio silence in connection with the operation. Ultra was thus unable to read any messages indicating

The German Offensive in the Ardennes, December 16–31, 1944 (The Battle of the Bulge)

specifically that an assault was coming in the Ardennes. But Ultra and other sources did detect the transfer of panzer divisions and fighter-planes from the Eastern Front to the west. Eisenhower, Hodges, and other generals interpreted this buildup as preliminary to a possible attack to the north of the Ardennes near Aachen. More significantly, Ultra also intercepted numerous messages in which Model called for detailed aerial reconnaissance over the Ardennes. The Allies refused to give sufficient credence to these reports, an oversight that ranks as one of the great intelligence failures of the war.

Operation Autumn Fog opened with a predawn artillery barrage on December 16. It was a complete surprise. English-speaking German commandos infiltrated behind U.S. lines and caused great confusion. Dressed in American uniforms, they cut telephone lines, changed road signs, and killed military policemen in charge of directing troop convoys. They spread fear among American personnel, who began to suspect everyone and subjected strangers to informal questioning. Queries ranged from asking the identity of major league batting champions to the names of state capitals. Although this approach proved reasonably successful, even genuine Americans didn't know all the answers. At one point, General Bradley had to

confess ignorance when asked to identify the husband of popular movie star Betty Grable. But his interrogator let him pass anyway. On another occasion, Bradley responded correctly that Springfield was the capital of Illinois, only to be told that the answer was really Chicago!

Members of the 1st SS Panzer Division inspired still more fear by murdering Americans who fell into their hands early in the offensive. The most notorious massacre occurred near the town of Malmédy, where German machine-gun and pistol fire took 86 lives.

German armor overwhelmed badly outnumbered American forces along a 70-mile front and rumbled on toward the Meuse. Allied leaders were slow to grasp the gravity of the situation, and the enemy benefited from the low overcast, which prevented Allied air power from intervening. But American units stubbornly defended two road junctions in eastern Belgium—St. Vith and Bastogne. Although St. Vith fell on December 22, Bastogne continued to hold out. When Eisenhower finally recognized that the German attack was a major operation, he ordered the U.S. 101st Airborne Division to reinforce the town's garrison. German troops surrounded Bastogne and issued an appeal for the defenders to surrender. General

Anthony McAuliffe, the acting American commander, limited his response to one word: "Nuts!"

When the skies finally cleared on December 23, Allied fighter bombers decimated enemy armored spearheads. The Germans, who were also experiencing a severe fuel shortage, had no choice but to break off their offensive the following day. Manteuffel's 5th Panzer Army had penetrated to within five miles of the Meuse. It was now apparent that Hitler's dream of reaching Antwerp had been far too ambitious. His great counteroffensive had merely created a bulge in the Allied line 65 miles deep and 45 miles wide.

Meanwhile, for the purpose of greater efficiency, Eisenhower transferred the U.S. 1st and 9th armies, which lay to the north of the bulge, to Montgomery's 21st Army Group. The 9th Army, commanded by General William Simpson, had entered the Allied line in November between the British on the north and the 1st Army on the south. Its first units had seen action in the bloody fighting that led to the capture of the Breton port of Brest in September. Marshall selected Simpson personally for this command. Although Eisenhower and Bradley would have preferred Collins, both soon came to appreciate Simpson's quiet, uncomplaining, and efficient professionalism.

This change left only Patton's 3rd Army to the south of the salient in Bradley's 12th Army Group. Although the decision contributed to much better coordination of U.S. and British forces in the north, Montgomery's arrogant attitude worsened already strained relations between him and the Americans. As one of Montgomery's own staff officers remarked, he "strode into Hodges's headquarters like Christ come to cleanse the temple."

Allied forces soon struck against the flanks of the bulge. Most notably, Patton executed one of the most remarkable feats of the war when he pivoted two of 3rd Army's three corps 90 degrees northward from Lorraine toward Bastogne. Despite intense cold, snow, and icy roads, his 4th Armored Division relieved Bastogne on December 26. To the north of the salient, Collins's VII Corps struck southward toward Houffalize on January 3, 1945. It soon became obvious to Manteuffel and Rundstedt that they must withdraw from the dangerously exposed salient. But Hitler, true to his "hold fast" mentality, refused. The Allies forced the Germans to give ground, nevertheless, and inflicted severe

casualties. By the end of January, they had eliminated the bulge. Hitler had sacrificed his last reserves and his greatest concentration of armor in an enterprise that never had a chance of success. He had delayed the final Allied offensive in the west, but he would have precious little strength left to meet the attack when it came in early 1945. His disastrous failure in the Battle of the Bulge also dealt a severe blow to German morale on the Western Front. And he had played into Soviet hands by weakening his forces in the east.

The Struggle for the Colmar Pocket

Hitler did not limit his offensive operations to the Ardennes. Just before midnight on December 31, he unleashed seven infantry and three panzer divisions against Devers's 6th Army Group. Devers had commanded U.S. forces in Britain prior to Eisenhower's arrival and then moved to the Mediterranean, where he supervised the invasion of southern France. The Germans delivered their attack southward astride the Vosges Mountains toward the Saverne Gap, with a supporting thrust from the so-called Colmar pocket, a large bridgehead that they had retained on the west bank of the Rhine. Containing the city of Colmar, it lay to the south of Strasbourg, the provincial capital of Alsace. This offensive had two major aims. Hitler hoped to force Eisenhower to divert 3rd Army troops away from their attacks against the southern flank of the Bulge. He also wanted to maintain a strong foothold in Alsace, which he considered part of Germany. Allied leaders received ample warning of the attack from Ultra. But the shift of Patton's army to the north had required Patch and de Lattre to stretch their forces thinly to protect a considerably broader front.

When the Germans struck, American forces were driven back but finally held along the Moder River. By January 25, the Germans broke off their offensive and began to transfer some of their best divisions to the Eastern Front. It had not been necessary for Eisenhower to divert strength away from Patton to hold the line. Meanwhile, French and American forces had opened a counterattack against the southern flank of the Colmar pocket five days before the end of the enemy offensive. The French captured Colmar on February 2, and the Allies eliminated the last vestiges of the pocket one week later. Once again Hitler had squandered resources and failed to gain any lasting advantage.

The Soviet Assault on Poland

Long before the Western Allies had eliminated the Bulge and the Colmar pocket, Soviet forces unleashed a gigantic offensive in Poland. The Red Army originally planned this operation to coincide with the major Anglo-American assault in the west. Hitler's Ardennes counterstroke had delayed the latter but in the process had thinned out German forces opposite the Red Army to a dangerously low point. In December, German intelligence reported a buildup of 225 Soviet divisions and 22 armored corps along the front from the Baltic to the Carpathians. But Hitler insisted on continuing his Ardennes operation rather than shifting forces back to the Eastern Front. He even refused Guderian's request for evacuation of the 26 German divisions that the Soviets had cut off in Latvia's Courland Peninsula.

Hitler's blindness to the danger in Poland led him to transfer two panzer divisions from there to take part in an attempt to break the Russian encirclement of Budapest. Although the Germans penetrated to within 12 miles of the Hungarian capital in late January, a Soviet counterattack forced them to abandon their offensive. After savage street fighting, Red Army troops completed their conquest of Budapest on February 14.

While Hitler focused on the relief of Budapest, the Soviet high command prepared to deliver its blow in Poland. Three army groups assembled along the Vistula River—Rokossovsky's Second Belorussian Front to the northeast of Warsaw, Zhukov's First Belorussian Front to the south of the city, and Konev's First Ukrainian Front in extreme southern Poland. In all, the Soviets concentrated 1.5 million men, 3,300 tanks, 28,000 guns, and 10,000 aircraft. The Germans could muster only 596,000 men, 700 tanks, 8,200 guns, and 1,300 planes.

The Red Army launched its massive offensive on January 12. Konev struck from a bridgehead on the west bank of the Vistula, about 100 miles south of Warsaw. Zhukov attacked just below the Polish capital and swung behind the city. To the north, Rokossovsky wheeled toward East Prussia and Danzig. The three spearheads tore open a 200-mile gap in the German front and rolled on relentlessly. Zhukov seized Warsaw on January 17, and Konev's troops penetrated into the province of Silesia, Germany's second most important industrial area, on January 20. Three days later, they crossed the Oder River near Breslau. Rokossovsky reached the Baltic east of Danzig on January 26, cutting off the German defenders of East Prussia. This proved to be the prelude to one of the least known operations of the war: the epic evacuation of an estimated two million people from various Baltic ports, far in excess of the 338,000 men rescued at Dunkirk. Nevertheless, Soviet submarines torpedoed several ships jammed with soldiers and refugees, the majority of whom died in the Baltic's icy waters. The most horrendous of these disasters occurred when submarine S-13 fired two torpedoes into the former passenger liner *Wilhelm Grustloff*. At the time, the Germans estimated that at least 6,000 persons died, but a recent computer-generated estimate puts the toll at over 9,600. Either way, it remains the worst maritime disaster in history, far exceeding the 1,517 lives lost in the much more famous sinking of the *Titanic*.

After taking Warsaw, Zhukov rolled westward and sliced into Germany. On January 31, his forces reached Kustrin on the Oder. Within a week, they crossed the river and established two sizable bridgeheads, one only 33 miles from the suburbs of Berlin. Zhukov now encountered serious supply problems. Konev was more fortunate, at least for the time being. On February 9, his forces drove northeastward from their bridgeheads across the Oder and a week later were just 60 miles from Berlin. But the Germans continued to hold out in bypassed Breslau. Hitler also shifted several divisions from the western front to bolster his defenses on the Oder. To make matters worse for the Soviets, a sudden thaw turned many of the roads to mud and melted the ice on the Oder.

By pushing forward so rapidly, Zhukov's armies had created a salient with a long, vulnerable northern flank. Relatively strong German forces still held much of the province of Pomerania, which lay between the Soviets and the Baltic. Guderian planned to stage a counterattack from this area in the hope of pinching off the advance Soviet units on the Oder. He urged that General von Weichs, a veteran of the 1941 and 1942 campaigns in Russia, lead the assault. Much to his astonishment, Hitler insisted on Himmler, who had neither military training nor skill. By this time, the Führer so distrusted army generals that he preferred a loyal Nazi as commander, whatever his qualifications. Guderian also requested that Sepp Dietrich's 6th SS Panzer Army, which had broken off the Ardennes offensive, be shifted to Pomerania to take part in the counterattack. Again Hitler refused and instead sent Dietrich's forces to Hungary. Not surprisingly, when Guderian launched his counterstroke on February 15, it was far too weak to achieve his objective.

But the German attack made Stalin nervous, and he ordered Zhukov and Rokossovsky to eliminate the threat from the north before attempting to move farther west. German forces had to fall back to three strong points on the Baltic coast—Danzig, Gdynia, and Kolberg. It was not until March 30 that the last of them, Danzig, surrendered.

Meanwhile, Hitler ordered his troops in Hungary, bolstered by the arrival of the 6th SS Panzer Army, to launch the final German offensive of the war. He hoped to protect the oil fields in western Hungary by driving to the Danube River and threatening Budapest. The attack began on March 5 and made some progress but soon fell afoul of muddy conditions, a fuel shortage, and stronger Red Army forces. By March 15, the Soviets had regained the initiative, and Marshal Tolbukhin's army group started an offensive. The Germans resisted stubbornly for three days, but when Soviet troops threatened to cut off their escape route, they fell back precipitously. Their retreat became a rout, and Tolbukhin's forces pursued them across the Austrian border. The Soviets reached the outskirts of Vienna on April 4 and, after six days of street fighting, occupied the entire city.

As the Red Army penetrated into Germany and Austria, many civilians fled in panic. There was good reason for their flight, as Soviet political officers had exhorted Red Army soldiers to take vengeance on the German population. Many of the troops needed little or no persuasion. They were vividly aware of the atrocities that the Germans had perpetrated in the Soviet Union, and now, after years of savage fighting, they had finally reached the homeland of the hated enemy. But most of the German people did not flee and felt the invader's wrath. Soviet soldiers shot some of them and raped many women, including the very young and the very old.

Amid all these disasters and growing chaos, Hitler decided to rid himself of Guderian. The general had always been outspoken and was never afraid of Hitler, qualities that the Führer actually admired. But in recent weeks, the quarrels between the two men had deteriorated into shouting matches. On March 28, Hitler sent Guderian on sick leave and replaced him with General Hans Krebs, a much weaker personality who had no thought of disagreeing with Hitler.

The Yalta Conference

Early in February, with the Soviets already less than 40 miles from Berlin and the Western Allies still recovering from their rude shock in the Ardennes, Roosevelt, Churchill, and Stalin met in their second "Big Three" conference at the seaside resort of Yalta in the Crimea. With the Red Army in control of most of Eastern Europe and seemingly poised to strike directly at Berlin, Stalin participated from a position of great strength, and the Western Allies were quite aware of it. Roosevelt also hoped for Soviet participation in the war against Japan as well as cooperation between the two countries in the postwar era. In pursuit of these objectives, he worked more closely with Stalin than with Churchill, much to the latter's chagrin. To some extent this reflected the obvious decline in Britain's stature in the Allied coalition, but it was also due in part to continuing American suspicion of British imperialist ambitions. The Americans also realized that the Soviets would be in control of Eastern Europe when the war ended and hoped to avoid alienating Stalin by being too demanding regarding this area. This did not mean that all would go smoothly, and the tendency of both sides to cast their arguments in ideological terms helped to create tension that would continue after the conference ended.

The Big Three agreed to the American-sponsored Declaration on Liberated Europe, a rather forlorn attempt to moderate Soviet intentions in Eastern Europe. It provided for the establishment of coalition governments containing Communists and non-Communists in all liberated countries as well as free parliamentary elections. Churchill and Roosevelt also recognized the USSR's claim to

The Last Battles on Three Main European Fronts—Eastern, Western, and Southern—February 1–May 7, 1945

eastern Poland and agreed that the border should run generally along the line that British foreign secretary Lord Curzon had proposed in 1919. They also essentially accepted Stalin's demand that Poland and the Soviet Union divide East Prussia and that the Poles receive additional compensation east of the Oder. In return, the Western leaders won Stalin's agreement that the London Poles would be represented in the Polish Liberation Committee and that free elections would determine Poland's future government.

As for Germany, the three men affirmed their intention to divide the country into occupation zones for each of the major allies as well as allotting a smaller zone for France. The Soviet zone would include most of eastern Germany. They also provided for the division of Berlin into occupation zones and declared their dedication to disarming Germany as well as punishing war criminals and eliminating Nazi influence. Finally, Stalin demanded extensive reparations from Germany to compensate for wartime losses and to help rebuild the Soviet economy. Churchill and Roosevelt managed to defer the actual amount until after the war.

The Allied Drive to the Rhine

After the failure of Hitler's Second Ardennes offensive, logic dictated a German withdrawal to the Rhine. The Reich's only hope of holding out against the Western Allies' might was to defend the great river barrier. German forces were not powerful enough to attempt a stand west of the Rhine. Not only had they suffered from the fearful pounding in the Ardennes, but their leaders had shifted much of their remaining strength to try to stem the Soviet flood. Hitler nevertheless insisted that his troops contest every inch of German soil. They would fight to the west of the Rhine.

The Allied plan for clearing the Rhineland provided for three separate operations. In the north, Dempsey's British 2nd and Crerar's Canadian 1st armies would strike southward, while Simpson's U.S. 9th Army was to thrust northward to meet them. In the center, Hodges's 1st Army, now restored to Bradley's 12th Army Group, would drive toward Cologne and Bonn on the Rhine and then pivot southward along the river. It was to link up with Patton's 3rd Army, which was to swing along the north bank of the Moselle River toward the Rhine. Farther south, Patch's 7th Army would move northward to make contact with Patton's forces near Koblenz.

The British and Canadians opened this ambitious plan with an enormous artillery barrage on February 8. The offensive also featured a joint U.S.-British airborne drop (Operation Varsity) that in some ways was larger than that of Operation Market-Garden. The paratroopers seized a key area of high ground, but despite their efforts, the ground forces encountered bitter resistance as well as flooded terrain, which slowed their progress. They did not reach the Rhine until February 21. Simpson's forces suffered from even greater obstacles. They had to cross the Roer River to launch their attack, and the Germans opened the gates of a dam upstream, flooding the area. The Americans had to wait two weeks before the waters subsided sufficiently for them to negotiate the remaining barrier in assault boats. On March 4, they finally made contact with the Canadians.

The 1st Army opened its offensive on February 26 when Collins's VII Corps crossed the Roer with a dual mission: to protect Simpson's left flank and to capture Cologne, which fell on March 5. Although much of the city lay in ruins, its great twin-spired Gothic cathedral, despite some damage, remained intact. Meanwhile, the 1st Army's III Corps moved toward Bonn and Remagen, 15 miles farther south.

At Remagen, a platoon of the 9th Armored Division accomplished one of the most incredible feats of the war. It stormed the Ludendorff railroad bridge on March 7 and, despite heavy enemy fire, succeeded in seizing its objective. The Germans had tried to blow up the span; two preliminary explosions had caused some structural damage, but the main charge had failed to detonate. The Americans quickly established a bridgehead on the west bank of the Rhine, and within 24 hours, 8,000 men were across the river. It was the only bridge along the entire course of the Rhine that the Germans failed to destroy. Ironically, its capture came on the ninth anniversary of the German occupation of the Rhineland. Hitler reacted to the Remagen disaster by dismissing Rundstedt as commander in chief on the Western Front for the second and last time. Kesselring, the commander in Italy, succeeded Rundstedt. General von Vietinghoff took Kesselring's place in Italy.

The armored spearhead of Patton's 3rd Army dashed 65 miles along the north bank of the Moselle and reached the Rhine in less than three days. On March 14, Patton sent his XII Corps southward across the Moselle and along the Rhine. The Germans had expected him to swing north to exploit the Remagen bridgehead, and his maneuver took them by surprise. At the same time, Patch's 7th Army struck northward through the Saar to link up with Patton. By March 25, all organized resistance west of the Rhine had ceased. Hitler's decision to fight in the Rhineland had cost him dearly. The Allies had mauled his forces and had taken 290,000 prisoners. As the struggle for the Rhineland unfolded, German morale, which had been so strong for so long, began to crack.

The Remagen bridgehead was located in one of the most rugged areas of the Rhine, one that the Allies had not intended as a major crossing point. But once the 1st Army gained its foothold there, Eisenhower moved quickly to expand it. In part, he did this to draw German troops away from other portions of the Rhine's east bank and ease the task of establishing additional bridgeheads. The 3rd Army gained the first of these when it secured a foothold southwest of Frankfurt on March 22. The Germans, who had managed to retreat across the river, had blown up the bridges but were too few, too disorganized, and too demoralized to offer any real resistance.

FIGURE 23-1   A convoy of U.S. 7th Army trucks rolls past wrecked buildings in Augsburg, Germany. (*National Archives and Records Administration*)

Patton had carried out his bold crossing deliberately to "jump the Rhine" before Montgomery, who was still planning an operation that Eisenhower had intended as the main crossing. The British commander had massed 25 divisions from the 2nd and 9th armies preparatory to an assault across the river to the north of the Ruhr. Before launching this pile-driver blow on March 23, he subjected the east bank of the Rhine to a colossal pounding from 3,000 artillery pieces as well as aerial bombardment. Considering the fact that only five weak German divisions guarded the landing area, this proved more than adequate. The Germans offered little resistance. Allied airborne troops also dropped behind enemy lines once the operation began and contributed to its overwhelming success. By March 27, all seven Allied armies were across the great river, and the way to the Reich's heartland lay open.

Crushing the Axis in Italy

Germany was not the only place where catastrophe beckoned the Nazi regime. In Italy, a three-month lull in Allied offensive operations came to an end early in April. The Allies outnumbered the enemy 2 to 1. They enjoyed the same margin of superiority in artillery and a 3-to-1 advantage in tanks. In addition, they had recently received much up-to-date equipment and abundant supplies. Allied air power also dominated the skies.

British troops opened their attack on April 9 with a frontal assault along the Senio and Reno rivers coupled with an amphibious operation across Lake Comacchio, a large body of water near the Adriatic coast. By April 18, the 8th Army had broken into the broad plain of the great Po River. Meanwhile, the 5th Army opened its attack across the last remaining mountain ridges south of the plain on April 14 and achieved a breakthrough three days later.

Vietinghoff had committed most of his forces to the front line and was unable to establish a new defensive position. He urged Hitler to authorize a retreat to the Po, but the Führer, as usual, refused. Finally, on April 20, Vietinghoff ordered a withdrawal himself. But by that time it was too late. Allied armored forces swept toward the river and cut off many Germans. The entire Axis position in Italy had collapsed.

As the Axis disasters mounted, Mussolini attempted to escape to Switzerland with his long-time mistress, Clara Petacci. But Italian partisans cut short their flight on April 28 and shot them both to death. They brought their bodies to Milan and dumped them in a large square, where a mob of vengeful Italians trampled and spat on the corpses. One well-placed kick broke the former Duce's jaw. When this grisly ritual ended, partisans strung wire around the forlorn couple's feet and hung them upside down from a steel girder, where they remained on display for some time. Thus, the man who had once dreamed of creating a new Roman Empire perished in total degradation.

All that remained was the surrender of the surviving Axis troops. Actually, General Karl Wolff, head of the SS in Italy, had opened secret negotiations for capitulation through neutral Switzerland as early as February. He had encountered a myriad of obstacles, however, and had been unable to conclude arrangements before the start of the final Allied offensive. Now, as it became obvious that nothing could prevent total defeat, Vietinghoff joined Wolff in seeking an end to the struggle. German representatives signed an unconditional surrender agreement on April 29, and the document became effective on May 2.

The Allies Overrun the Reich

Meanwhile, the stage was set for the final German collapse in the Reich itself. The establishment of multiple Allied bridgeheads on the east bank of the Rhine accelerated the disintegration of German forces. The great North German Plain lay in the path of the Allied leviathan, and although occasional river barriers remained to be crossed, they were still a considerable distance to the east. The badly outnumbered, exhausted, and demoralized soldiers of the Wehrmacht were nearing the end of their tether. Equipment was breaking down, supplies were running low, and Allied planes roamed at will over the stricken Fatherland. Fuel shortages became so critical that tanks could not move and planes could not fly.

The next Allied objective was the Ruhr. Its neutralization would deal a death blow to German industry. Elements of Simpson's 9th Army dashed around the Ruhr's northern flank, while units of Hodges's 1st Army swept around the sprawling industrial complex from the south. The two arms of the envelopment came together at Lippstadt on April 1, trapping all of Model's Army Group B and two corps of Army Group H, which defended northern Germany. Hitler characteristically proclaimed the Ruhr a fortress to be defended to the last man and the last bullet. But it was not a fortress, and its garrison was in no condition to carry out prolonged resistance. For the next two weeks, the encircling forces applied increasing pressure on the defenders and secured their capitulation on the 19th. A total of 325,000 Germans surrendered. Among those who did not was Model, who preferred suicide to captivity.

Even while the Battle of the Ruhr pocket was raging, other elements of both 9th and 1st armies were stabbing deeply into the heart of Germany. The creation of the Ruhr pocket had left a yawning void in their path with only scattered German units between them and the Elbe River far to the east. Simpson's spearhead reached the river on April 11 and by April 13 had secured a bridgehead on the east bank only 50 miles from Berlin. It appeared that the road to the German capital was open. Simpson urged that he be allowed to push on to Berlin. But Eisenhower ordered him to halt while Allied armies "cleaned up" the flanks to the north and south. The American advance now shifted to the southeast toward Leipzig, Chemnitz, and Dresden. It also focused on Bavaria and Austria, where Hitler supposedly planned to make a last stand in a National Redoubt centered in the Alps. On April 16, the Soviets launched their long-awaited final offensive against Berlin and encircled the city ten days later.

Eisenhower's decision to halt Simpson's advance became still another of the controversial issues of the war. Critics, especially Simpson and Montgomery, charged that had Ike allowed the 9th Army to continue its drive, it would have reached Berlin before the Soviets. But only Simpson's spearhead had reached the Elbe, and its tanks were running low on fuel. Most of his forces were still far to the west. The Americans had fewer than 50,000 men and little artillery in their advance positions. The Red Army, by contrast, had been massing troops and supplies on the Oder for weeks and were only 33 miles away from the city. Had Simpson attempted to continue his push toward Berlin, the Soviets would almost certainly have speeded up the timetable for their offensive against the capital. With two bridge-heads to the west of the Oder and 1,250,000 men and 22,000 artillery pieces in position, it seems likely that they would have reached Berlin in force before the Americans.

When he made his decision to halt, Eisenhower recognized the weakness of Simpson's advance forces as well as the far greater strength of the Soviets. He also knew that the Big Three had agreed to divide Germany into occupation zones after the war and that Berlin would lie within the Soviet zone. Even if American forces had been able to take the city, this agreement would have required their withdrawal from the portion reserved for the Soviets as well as from territory east of the Elbe. At this point, Eisenhower also considered both the Leipzig-Dresden area and the National Redoubt more important military objectives for the Western Allies than Berlin, which he assumed would fall to the Red Army.

In reality, the National Redoubt was a myth. Although American leaders had long speculated on the possibility of a last-ditch stand by die-hard Nazis in the south, the Germans never planned such a desperate scenario. But Propaganda Minis-ter Goebbels had learned of this American illusion in late 1944 and did everything he could to encourage his enemies in their belief. He was remarkably successful. Although U.S. intelligence wavered between skepticism and acceptance, Eisenhower became convinced that the possibility of a redoubt had to be assumed. Bradley was even more certain of its existence. Both men feared that unless American troops moved into this area quickly, SS forces and other Nazi fanatics might prolong the war for months, perhaps even years.

Allied forces were now lunging forward every-where. Crerar's Canadian 1st Army liberated most of the remainder of the Netherlands and occupied the northwestern portion of Germany. Dempsey's British 2nd Army reached Lübeck on the Baltic on May 3, effectively sealing off Denmark to the north-west from the advancing Soviet armies. In the south, the French 1st Army crossed the Rhine and drove toward western Austria. Patch's 7th Army seized Nuremberg, site of the Nazi party rallies, on April 20; then hooked south to take Munich, the party's birthplace, ten days later. It captured Hitler's mountain retreat at Berchtesgaden on May 4.

Patton's 3rd Army drove into eastern Germany and crossed the Czech border on April 25. With only weak German forces between his tanks and Prague, Patton asked permission to push on to the Czech capital. Eisenhower refused, indicating that it, like Berlin, was now a political rather than a military objective and lay in the path of the Red Army's advance. There seems little doubt that Patton could have reached Prague first, because the Soviets were considerably farther away and encountering stronger resistance. Instead, elements of the 3rd Army swung southward into Austria and soon discovered that there was no National Redoubt. Prague fell to the Red Army on May 9.

The Nazi Death Camps Fall

As Allied armies converged from east and west, they began to occupy the Nazi death camps in Poland and the concentration camps of the Reich itself. SS units attempted to destroy the evidence of their monstrous deeds in the Polish camps. Although not always successful in this endeavor, they did blow up the huge crematoriums at Auschwitz. SS guards herded many of the surviving inmates westward and shot large numbers along the way. Soviet troops had captured Maidanek, Sobibor, Treblinka, and Belzec during their 1944 summer offensive and overran Auschwitz and Chelmno in January 1945. They found horrific evidence of the mass slaughter perpetrated by the Nazis in these camps as well as some survivors, many of whom were near death. Moscow publicized some of this but downplayed the fact that the overwhelming majority of the vic-tims were Jews. Nevertheless, the fate of the Jews soon became known throughout the world, and the names of the camps became synonymous with murderous brutality.

The rapid advance of Allied forces in the west engulfed the concentration camps of Germany before the SS could destroy them. One by one, they also revealed their terrible secrets, including huge piles of corpses and the living skeletons of the survivors as well as torture chambers and strangling rooms where guards hung prisoners with short nooses attached to rows of hooks. There were also lamp shades, purses, and gloves made from human skin. Photographs and films brought much of the impact of these horrors home to the people of Britain and America.

FIGURE 23-2   The heaped corpses of political prisoners at the Belsen concentration camp symbolize the brutality of the Nazi regime. (*AP/Wide World Photos*)

High Drama in Berlin

But the greatest drama of all unfolded in Berlin. Hitler had shifted his headquarters to the capital from East Prussia when the Soviets opened their January offensive. With the approach of enemy troops, he took refuge in an underground bunker near the Reich's Chancellery building. The once mighty conqueror had become a physical wreck during the years of defeat. He had developed a stoop, suffered from tremors in his limbs, and dragged his left leg when he walked. The pressure of directing the war effort, lack of sleep, and nervous exhaustion all contributed to this deterioration. He had also fallen under the influence of a quack doctor, Theodore Morell, who convinced him that the answer to his health problems lay in frequent injections of powerful drugs as well as a variety of pills. These remedies actually made his condition worse. The injuries that the Führer suffered in the attempt on his life in July 1944, though not serious, also weakened him.

Despite his failing health, Hitler cowed his associates with the violence of his wrath and retained the power of life and death over every

German from the highest generals to the lowliest members of society. His capacity for hatred and his morbid fascination with destruction grew more pronounced as the certainty of final defeat became ever greater. In March 1945, he ordered Speer to supervise the destruction of everything that might be useful to the Allies as they advanced into Germany. His list included bridges, dams, factories, mines, railroads, and rolling stock. He visualized a total scorched-earth policy. Speer balked at this and told Hitler that the war was lost and that nothing should be done to jeopardize the survival of the German people. The Führer was not impressed:

> If the war is to be lost, the nation also will perish. … There is no longer need to consider the basis for even a most primitive existence. On the contrary, it is better to destroy even that, and to destroy it ourselves. The nation has proved itself weak, and the future belongs to the stronger Eastern nation. Besides, those who remain after the battle are of little value; for the good have fallen.*

---

*Quoted in H. R. Trevor Roper, *The Last Days of Hitler* (London: Pan Books, 1952), p. 88.

Appalled at the prospect of such senseless destruction, Speer set out to sabotage the Führer's orders and succeeded to a considerable degree. Although Germany emerged from the war in a thoroughly battered condition, the devastation was not as total as Hitler, the self-proclaimed embodiment of the German nation, had desired.

Hitler was still in the bunker when the Red Army launched its final offensive on April 16. The Soviet plan provided for Zhukov's forces to outflank Berlin from the north while Konev's troops swung around from the south. The assault began with the most intensive artillery barrage of the war, featuring a concentration of one gun every 13 feet. The Germans fought desperately, but within two days, the Soviets had broken through and poured like a torrent toward and around the capital. The two wings of the pincers met to the west of Berlin on April 25. Other Red Army forces dashed westward and on the same day met elements of the U.S. 1st Army near Torgau on the Elbe.

Although Hitler's aides had urged him to leave Berlin even before the start of the Red Army offensive, he refused and remained in his bunker after the Soviet jaws closed. Even now he visualized a miraculous turnabout in the war and continued to talk about counteroffensives using divisions that existed only on paper. He clutched at the few straws that still seemed available. The most notable example occurred when President Roosevelt died of a cerebral hemorrhage on April 12, four days before the Soviets opened their drive on Berlin. Both Hitler and Goebbels saw a parallel between Roosevelt's death and the demise of the Russian tsarina Elizabeth in 1762 during the Seven Years' War, when Frederick the Great was king of Prussia. At that time, the Russians were threatening to capture Berlin, but following the tsarina's death, her successor chose to make peace with Frederick instead. Hitler now saw himself as a modern-day Frederick. He and Goebbels hoped that Roosevelt's successor, Harry Truman, might be the architect of a negotiated peace with Germany. Both men continued to believe that sooner or later the Western Allies would fall out with the Soviets and join Germany in an anti-Communist crusade. Their expectation proved totally unfounded. Truman was determined to fight the war to the victorious conclusion so close at hand.

Red Army troops penetrated into Berlin's suburbs on April 22, and the German capital won the dubious designation of "fortress" from the Führer. The struggle for the German capital became much like that for Stalingrad $2\frac{1}{2}$ years earlier. The German garrison fought with fanatical dedication while Hitler did what he could to spur them on. But his cause was beyond redemption. The Soviets pushed forward and by April 26, they were less than a mile from Hitler's bunker. The city, already devastated by years of Allied air attacks, sank into total ruin from the effects of Red Army artillery and the savage fighting.

The Bitter End

As the days passed, Hitler's last illusions about a miraculous turning of the tide slipped away. Realizing that the end was near, he lashed out with particular fury at those whom he held responsible for his defeat—the German officer corps, the German army, the German people. Then he received the unkindest cuts of all. The first came from Goering, who had moved his headquarters to the Bavarian Alps. Misinterpreting instructions from Hitler, Goering announced that he was assuming the power to negotiate with the Allies. This so enraged Hitler that he ordered Goering arrested. Soon afterward, he received a report that Himmler, who was in northern Germany, had attempted to open peace negotiations. Even the man whom Hitler referred to as *treue Heinrich* (loyal Heinrich) had proved guilty of treachery.

By April 29, Hitler had resigned himself to death, but he still had unfinished business. First he married his longtime mistress, Eva Braun. Then he drafted his political testament in which he expelled Goering and Himmler from the party as traitors and appointed Admiral Dönitz president and commander in chief of the armed forces. The following day, Hitler retired to his suite, where he and his bride committed suicide—she by poison, he by a pistol shot through the mouth. Aides burned their bodies in the Chancellery garden. Goebbels and his wife poisoned their six children soon afterward and then took their own lives. On May 2, the last fighting ended in Berlin. The shattered, flaming city was a suitable setting for Hitler's *Götterdämmerung* (twilight of the gods). The Soviets paid a high price for the capture of Berlin. Although estimates vary, it appears that they suffered over 300,000 killed, wounded, and missing. German military casualties are unknown, but the Soviets claim to have taken 134,000 prisoners. Perhaps 100,000 civilians lost their lives during the struggle. Red Army soldiers also engaged in an orgy of rape in the aftermath of the battle. Estimates of rape victims range from 95,000 to 130,000.

The war in Europe was not yet over, but it would linger only a few more days. On May 2, Dönitz asked for a separate peace with the Western Allies, indicating his intention to continue the war against the Soviets. The Americans and British refused. Unconditional surrender was the only option. It finally came in a schoolhouse in Reims, France, at 2:41 on the morning of May 7. A second ceremony followed in Berlin the next day as Allied and German military leaders met to ratify the earlier agreement. World War II in Europe was over, and with it Hitler's "Thousand-Year Reich" expired. It had lasted 12 years.

CHAPTER TWENTY-FOUR

War on the Periphery: China, Burma, India

While Allied forces converged on Germany from east and west and U.S. forces carried out their island-bypassing operations in the Southwest and Central Pacific, fighting also took place in China, Burma, and even along the frontier of India. The Americans referred to this vast area as the China-Burma-India theater (CBI). But this designation gave the impression of greater unity in Allied operations in Southeast and East Asia than was actually the case. In reality, Chiang Kai-shek retained command in China, and the British exercised authority in India and in attempts to reconquer Burma. Starting in 1942, small American ground forces and larger air contingents operated from bases in India but remained strictly under U.S. jurisdiction. Cooperation among the three Allies was often far from close, and a great deal of mutual distrust prevailed.

American and British aims in the CBI also diverged on the question of the role that China should and could play in the war. Indeed, U.S. policy toward China strongly shaped Allied strategy and led to operations in Burma, which the British did not wish to undertake. And since the entire area lay on the periphery of the struggle against Japan and was far from crucial, the decision to devote so much effort to it was clearly a mistake.

The Chinese Situation

Although of secondary importance in the Pacific war, China had long held a strange fascination for American leaders and people alike, and this continued until well into the conflict. When the Japanese attacked Pearl Harbor in 1941, Chiang Kai-shek's forces had not fought a major battle since 1938. But the entry of the United States into hostilities convinced the Kuomintang leader that

Japan would lose the war. He did not intend to risk his troops in fighting against the Japanese if he could avoid it. He preferred to conserve them for the postwar era, when he would face the formidable task of restoring his control over all of China. And he intended to settle his old score with the Communists.

At best, Chiang's army was a flimsy affair. Much of it was poorly trained and equipped and under the leadership of warlords whose allegiance to the government in Chungking was questionable. Chiang did maintain a substantial number of higher-quality divisions under his own control, but he used many of them to blockade the Communists in an effort to cut them off from foreign aid. The Communists, ironically, were the only Chinese force that dedicated itself to fighting the Japanese. Their guerrilla tactics also proved effective in bringing much of the countryside under their control while restricting the enemy increasingly to the cities. The Kuomintang regime became more corrupt and inefficient during the interminable war. Its members devoted themselves primarily to advancing their own personal interests and paid little attention to the pressing economic and social evils that afflicted the Chinese people. Even had they possessed the will to deal with these problems, the pressures of war sharply limited their ability to do so.

Despite the depressing reality of China's situation, U.S. leaders pursued a policy toward that country that came close to wishful thinking. Roosevelt sympathized with China's desire to free itself from foreign influence—not merely Japanese but Western as well. He believed that the weakening of British, French, and Dutch colonialism in all of eastern Asia would facilitate this. But, nevertheless, the president looked forward to a close postwar relationship with China that would favor U.S. economic interests.

Roosevelt did not base his outlook solely on self-interest, however. He visualized China as a great power in the postwar era and believed that it deserved to be treated as one while the fighting raged. A great power must have a strong army, and Roosevelt intended to provide Chiang with U.S. military equipment, supplies, and advisers to help him make the best use of his abundant population. The president feared that if such assistance were not forthcoming, China might collapse or seek a separate peace. Lend-lease aid had begun to flow to the Chinese even before the attack on Pearl Harbor. It had traveled over the Burma Road from Lashio in eastern Burma to Chungking. But the fall of Burma in 1942 cut this route, and the United States resorted to an airlift of supplies over the world's highest mountain range, the Himalayas, which separated India from China. The Americans called this barrier "the Hump." Roosevelt and other U.S. leaders also saw China as a possible strategic objective after the conquest of the Philippines. It would provide a formidable jumping-off position for a seaborne assault on Japan as well as air bases for bombing raids against Japanese cities.

Many of the American people shared Roosevelt's sympathy for China and looked upon Chiang not as the dictatorial head of a corrupt regime but as a great national hero and the leader of a government that enjoyed strong support from the Chinese people. The "China lobby" helped create and perpetuate this distortion.

The establishment in China of a small air contingent, the American Volunteer Group (AVG), shortly before the attack on Pearl Harbor, contributed to the prevailing view. The AVG consisted of mercenary pilots whom Colonel Claire L. Chennault, a retired U.S. Army air officer, had recruited to fight in the service of China. After Pearl Harbor, it also participated in the defense of Burma and fashioned a remarkable record despite its dependence on P-40 fighters that were inferior to the Zero. Chennault minimized this disadvantage by using fighters operating in pairs and diving on their opponents from higher altitudes. The group soon earned the nickname "Flying Tigers" because of the painted tiger shark's teeth that adorned the noses of its planes. The AVG's exploits came as a relief to the American people, who were weary of a steady diet of defeat in the early months of the war. They even inspired a film, *Flying Tigers*, starring John Wayne. The AVG later became a part of the U.S. Fourteenth Air Force, operating from bases in southeastern China.

Not all Americans were uncritical of Chiang. Those who were most familiar with China warned that he and the Kuomintang regime were not what they seemed to be and that the Chinese army was not much better than a rabble. Churchill and the British, while not lacking in sympathy for China and the Chinese, also did not share the popular American view and were alarmed by Roosevelt's policies. They did not see China as a potential great power, a major factor in the war, or even a likely candidate for collapse or a separate peace.

In his effort to bolster the Chinese, Roosevelt sent General Joseph W. Stilwell to China early in 1942. Stilwell received his appointment largely because of his extensive service in the U.S. embassy in China and his fluency in Chinese. Chiang appointed him to serve as his chief of staff. But in addition, the general received command of all U.S. forces in the China-Burma-India theater as well as serving as Roosevelt's personal representative to Chiang and administrator of lend-lease aid. This multitude of responsibilities caused much confusion.

To make matters worse, Stilwell and Chiang did not get along. Chiang's suspicion of foreigners and his stubbornness were legendary, and Stilwell's acerbic personality had earned him the nickname "Vinegar Joe." Stilwell did not share Roosevelt's faith in Chiang, to whom he referred in private as "Peanut." But he did take seriously his mission to transform the Chinese army into a major factor in the war. Since Chiang had no intention of cooperating in this impossible task, it is not surprising that the two men often quarreled.

Stilwell also found himself closely involved in developments in Burma, which bordered China on the southwest. He arrived in Chungking in March 1942 during the British retreat from Rangoon. Chiang placed him in charge of Chinese forces that were assisting the British in Burma in an effort to keep open China's supply route from the West. Stilwell soon discovered that the Chinese operated with little regard for his orders. His troops became victims of the general Allied collapse, and the capture of Lashio cut the Burma Road, preventing their retreat into China. Instead they fled through the nightmarishly difficult mountains and dense jungle of northern Burma, eventually finding refuge in India. As Stilwell put it, they had suffered "a hell of a beating."

British Raids on Burma

Once the Japanese had conquered Burma, they had reached the limit of their planned expansion in Southeast Asia. Despite Allied fears to the contrary, they had no intention of invading India. Stilwell, who disliked the British and had been highly critical of their direction of the Burma campaign, called for an offensive to oust the enemy from the country as soon as possible. The British commander in India was Field Marshal Wavell, who had driven the Italians out of Egypt in 1940 and had assumed the hopeless task of commanding Allied forces in Southeast Asia during the early days of the Pacific war. Wavell recognized that his resources would not allow for such an ambitious undertaking. He did agree to a limited attack designed to capture the coastal area of Arakan, bordering India on the southeast. But when the thrust into Arakan began in December 1942, it progressed slowly. Many of the Allied troops had little experience, were poorly trained, and suffered from both malaria and low morale. When the Japanese counterattacked, they forced the Allies back to their original line by May 1943.

One bright episode helped to reduce Allied gloom. In late 1942, Wavell established a commando force of 3,000 men under the leadership of General Orde Wingate. Eccentric and unorthodox, Wingate was an inspirational leader who had utter contempt for most of his superiors. Although he was given to sudden and extreme changes of mood and had once attempted suicide, he had conducted successful guerrilla operations behind Italian lines during the British conquest of Ethiopia. Wingate referred to his commandos as "the Chindits." He took this name from the Chinthe, a mythical beast, half-lion and half-eagle, whose likeness adorned many Burmese temples. To Wingate, this creature symbolized his belief in close ground-to-air coordination as the key to successful guerrilla operations. He divided his British and Indian forces into seven columns, which moved into northern Burma in

The Burma Theater

February 1943 and, with the help of supplies dropped by cargo planes, raided enemy outposts and communications.

The Chindit raids were more of a nuisance than a major problem for the Japanese. They also resulted in the loss of one-third of Wingate's men, and many of the survivors were so weakened by disease and malnutrition that they could never return to combat. But this exploit did show that Allied troops could hold their own in jungle fighting with the Japanese and enhanced morale. The Chindits also devised jungle warfare techniques that Allied commanders successfully applied to later operations by larger formations. Wingate especially demonstrated that large-scale air supply was absolutely essential for troops operating in a vast wilderness such as Burma.

India's Internal Instability

While struggling with the Japanese in Burma, Britain also had to contend with problems in India. A nationalist movement had developed there during the early twentieth century. Under the leadership of Mohandas Gandhi, it had pursued a nonviolent policy of civil disobedience and moral pressure in its quest for independence. Gandhi and his followers, most notably Jawaharlal Nehru, had revitalized the Congress party, which was founded in 1885 but had long remained small and ineffectual. Under Gandhi and Nehru, however, it attempted to unite all Indians under one banner. Gandhi also became a Hindu spiritual figure who devoted himself to a life of prayer, meditation, and fasting. Dressed in the loincloth and shawl worn by the lowliest Indians, Gandhi became known as "Mahatma" (Great Soul) and symbolized the struggle for freedom.

But as time passed, India's basic religious division between Hindus and Muslims created an impediment to the Congress party's pursuit of independence. Although the Hindus were by far the most numerous of the many religious groups

FIGURE 24-1 Mohandas Gandhi, the spiritual leader of Indian nationalism. (*AP/Wide World Photos*)

that made up the population, the Muslims comprised the overwhelming majority in certain areas, especially in the northwest. The Muslims also found a leader of great ability and determination—Mohammed Ali Jinnah. Although Jinnah originally supported the aims of the Congress party, he eventually came to believe that if India gained independence as one state, the Muslims would find themselves in the position of a neglected, perhaps even persecuted minority. This concern led him to break with Congress and to assume leadership of another party, the Muslim League. Jinnah and the League favored division of the country into a Hindu India and a Muslim Pakistan. Gandhi, Nehru, and the Congress party remained totally opposed to such a policy.

By the early 1930s, Britain recognized that it could not avoid granting extensive concessions to Indian nationalism. The Government of India Act of 1935 provided for a parliamentary government complete with Indian ministers, but control over foreign affairs and defense remained in British hands. The Congress party found this unsatisfactory and demanded full dominion status. Despite its objections, Congress went along with the legislation as a stopgap measure.

When World War II began in 1939, the British, with their control over foreign policy, declared that India was at war with Germany. While Gandhi, Nehru, and certain other Congress leaders shared Britain's outrage over the policies of Nazi Germany, they did not believe that India had sufficient cause to go to war. They also protested the manner in which the British had brought India into the conflict. Their ministers resigned from the government, while Gandhi, true to his pacifist beliefs, condemned participation in any war as immoral. Nevertheless, elements of the Indian army, much of which was Muslim, served with distinction on Britain's side in North Africa and the Middle East.

With Japan's conquest of Malaya and Burma, the war came to India's doorstep. And as evidence of British weakness mounted, nationalist agitation increased. Britain realized that further concessions were inevitable and in March 1942 appointed Sir Stafford Cripps as a special envoy to seek an agreement. Cripps proposed that upon conclusion of the war, a constituent assembly would draft a constitution for India with complete freedom to create an independent state. In return, Congress would rejoin the government and support the war. But the proposal also provided that if the Muslims expressed their desire to secede from India, they would be allowed to create a separate state of Pakistan. Congress found such a partition completely unacceptable, and Gandhi planned to call for a nationwide movement of civil disobedience.

Before Gandhi could act, the government arrested him and the other Congress leaders. They remained in custody for the duration of the war in relative comfort. Ironically, Gandhi, a man renowned for his humble lifestyle, found himself installed in a sumptuous palace. These arrests sparked widespread civil disorders in Bombay as well as in other parts of the country. Unrest continued to flare until September when the death toll from the violence reached 750. With the Congress leaders temporarily out of the picture, Jinnah worked feverishly to build up support for the Muslim League among the Muslim population and, while cooperating with the British, continued to strive for the postwar creation of an independent Pakistan.

Indian nationalist opposition of a far more violent type came from outside India. The architect of this policy was Subhas Chandra Bose, a former Congress leader who had turned to extremism. Bose fled India early in 1941 and made his way to Germany, where he fell under the spell of Nazism. He believed that only an authoritarian system could create a unified Indian state. In 1943, he left Germany by submarine to assume leadership of a Free India movement that Japan was organizing among Indians in Southeast Asia as part of a plan for a "Greater East Asia co-prosperity sphere." When Bose arrived in Singapore, he took over the leadership of a government for Free India as well as the small Indian National Army, which consisted mostly of prisoners of war who had enlisted to escape the miserable conditions in Japanese penal camps. Such motivation was hardly likely to fill them with fervor for Bose's cause.

The Co-Prosperity Sphere

The concept of a co-prosperity sphere had originated before the attack on Pearl Harbor and visualized a new order for East Asia. Supposedly designed to free Asians from Western imperialism,

in reality it was largely a propaganda device to mask Japanese domination of the region. Although Japan sponsored "free" governments in China, Indochina, Malaya, Burma, and the Philippines, these were nothing more than puppet regimes that never gained the allegiance of a majority of their respective populations. The tendency of the Japanese army to treat these peoples with contempt and often with brutality also helped undermine this endeavor. Among other outrages, the Japanese army forced more than 100,000 women to become "sex slaves" for their troops. Some of them had to service as many as 30 men a day. This practice began as early as 1932 during one of Japan's early operations in China and at first utilized Japanese prostitutes. It was intended to reduce the number of rapes committed by soldiers and maintain discipline. But, as the demand increased, the army resorted to kidnapping women from other countries under Japanese rule, 80 percent of them from Korea. Subjected to barbarous treatment during their enslavement, these "comfort women" often suffered continuing shame when they returned home, ostracized by their own compatriots. In recent years many of these unfortunate victims have filed suit against the Japanese government for being forced into prostitution.

The Units of Death

The Japanese engaged in even more sinister activities in the realm of biological and chemical warfare, again to the sorrow of fellow Asians. Soon after the conquest of Manchuria in 1931, Shiro Ishii, a Japanese military doctor, created a secret organization of scientists that became known as Unit 731. Headquartered in the Manchurian city of Harbin, Unit 731 sought to perfect various forms of biological warfare and used human beings as guinea pigs to test the effects of deadly diseases such as plague, cholera, anthrax, and haemorrhagic fever. At first, it used prisoners but later expanded its web to include slave laborers and even women and children. The Japanese referred to these subjects as "maruta" (logs). The victims of their experiments endured hellish suffering before they died. Unit 731 cooperated with another scientific detachment, 516 Chemical Warfare Unit, which specialized in the testing of chemical weapons. It subjected still more human guinea pigs to the horrors of mustard gas and cyanide. The Japanese also carried out malnutrition experiments in which human subjects were starved and required to perform various physical tasks while scientists studied how long it took them to die. If all of this were not hideous enough, vivisection specialists dissected living human bodies, usually without benefit of anesthesia.

Ishii and his associates planned to use balloons to transport disease-carrying devices that would drift over the Pacific and release their lethal cargoes over the United States, creating epidemics that would ravage the population. The Japanese did actually launch about 200 balloons that landed in the United States, Canada, and Alaska in late 1944 and early 1945. Fortunately, none of them carried any bacteria, but they were equipped with incendiary devices, designed to ignite forest fires. Most of these failed to detonate, but two did, killing a woman in Montana and six fishermen in Oregon.

Allied Squabbles over Strategy

While Britain struggled with the troubled situation in India, the Allies continued to wage war in Burma and quarreled over strategy. To Roosevelt and his advisers, the reopening of a land supply route to China held first priority. To accomplish this, Allied troops must first reconquer northern Burma. This would enable the construction of a road from Ledo in India to China, facilitating the flow of supplies to Chiang and the buildup of Chennault's 14th Air Force operating from Chinese bases. But the Americans also wanted to reopen the old Burma Road and to recapture Rangoon. Until the Allies controlled the port of Rangoon and the railroad that extended northward to Lashio, any land supply route to China would be inadequate.

British leaders doubted that reopening the land supply route was worth a full-scale operation in the jungles of Burma. Indeed, they questioned whether providing more supplies to China would really benefit the Allied cause. They much preferred amphibious operations against the East Indies, which would threaten Japan's oil supply. But neither sufficient naval forces nor landing craft would be available for such an enterprise until late 1944. American leaders tended to attribute the British position to an unwillingness to shoulder a

rightful share of the war against Japan. Churchill and his advisers were especially sensitive to such criticism, given the scope of U.S. operations in the Pacific. This placed them at a disadvantage in the strategic debate, and they gradually yielded to American demands for an offensive in Burma.

As a major step in this direction, Allied leaders agreed on the need for a supreme commander in Southeast Asia. In August 1944, they chose Admiral Louis Mountbatten, who had been serving as Britain's chief of combined operations. A cousin of King George VI, Mountbatten was only 42 years old and had a gift for maintaining close personal relations with both his British subordinates and American officers. In another change, General Auchinleck, who had succeeded Wavell in control of North African operations in 1941, now took over his post as commander in India. Wavell moved "upstairs" to the political office of viceroy in India.

In preparation for the impending offensive in Burma, Allied reinforcements reached India and resulted in the establishment of the 14th Army with General William J. Slim in command. Slim, who had experienced the harrowing retreat from Burma in 1942, was perhaps the only British officer to earn the respect of both Stilwell and Wingate. He possessed a sincere concern for the welfare of his men, a trait that won him their wholehearted devotion. The Allies planned their major attack in the north, where engineers were to build the Ledo Road. Indeed, construction on the Indian portion of this supply route had begun as early as December 1942.

The Campaign to Retake Burma

The offensive started in October 1943 as two Chinese divisions under Stilwell's command thrust down the Hukawng River toward the major communications center of Myitkyina on the Irrawaddy River. But Japanese resistance stalled their advance. In February 1944, Stilwell sent an American guerrilla force, under the leadership of General Frank Merrill, to carry out a series of operations behind Japanese lines. This unit consisted of volunteers who had trained with the Chindits. It soon acquired the name "Merrill's Marauders." Wingate also launched a second Chindit operation in March but lost his life in a plane crash soon afterward.

Although the Marauders captured the Myitkyina airfield in May, both raider forces suffered heavy casualties while the Japanese and monsoon rains delayed the fall of Myitkyina until August. Its capture opened the way for the extension of the Ledo Road, and the herculean efforts of American engineers as well as Indian and Chinese laborers resulted in completion of the project in January 1945.

General Slim launched a second Arakan offensive in January 1944, only to be halted again by Japanese counterattacks. But this time Slim withdrew into a series of strongholds that received supplies by air. The new approach proved so successful that the enemy forces had to break off their assault.

Meanwhile, General Renya Mutaguchi's 15th Japanese Army invaded India in mid-March. This operation was in part a delayed response to the first Chindit raids, which had persuaded the Japanese that their hold on northern and central Burma was precarious. Mutaguchi hoped to seize the communication centers of Kohima and Imphal near the Burmese border. An especially aggressive officer, Mutaguchi possessed vast determination but little common sense. He plunged into his invasion of India with woefully inadequate supplies and scant regard for the dangers that lay ahead. Nevertheless, his forces advanced quickly, and early in April they surrounded both Kohima and Imphal. Their success might have been still greater had Ultra reports not warned the British that the Japanese were planning an offensive. Slim ordered the two garrisons to hang on with the aid of airlifted supplies.

The badly outnumbered defenders of Kohima fought one of the most courageous battles of the war and held out for two weeks until a relief expedition arrived. Imphal's garrison was considerably larger but also confronted much stronger Japanese forces. The siege lasted 88 days while both sides, especially the Japanese, ran dangerously short of supplies. When the British finally broke the encirclement on May 12, the remnants of Mutaguchi's starving and disease-weakened troops fell back into Burma.

Bose's Indian National Army participated in the Japanese invasion. The nationalist leader hoped that the operation would result in a triumphal march that would lure thousands of Indians to his cause.

But his troops displayed a dismal lack of fighting spirit and an alarming fondness for desertion.

Although the struggle for Kohima and Imphal took place in India, it was the most decisive engagement of the Burma campaign. It cost the Japanese 50,000 troops and severely weakened their ability to resist when Slim launched a major offensive in mid-November. The Allies now had the advantage of a greatly improved supply system, numerical superiority, and control of the air. They forced the Japanese back toward the Irrawaddy River. General Hoyotaro Kimura, the Japanese commander in Burma, hoped to smash the Allied forces as they crossed the Irrawaddy north of Mandalay. But Slim anticipated this and made his major crossing farther south against weak opposition on February 13, 1945. Once across, Indian troops dashed for Meiktila and captured the town on March 3, cutting road and rail communications to Mandalay, 75 miles to the north. By the end of March, Kimura accepted the inevitable, abandoned Mandalay, and retreated southward from Meiktila.

The road to Rangoon now lay open. But Slim was encountering supply problems, and it appeared doubtful that he could reach the capital before the start of the monsoon season. On May 1, Mountbatten came to the rescue by launching Operation Dracula, which featured both amphibious and airborne landings south of Rangoon. Caught between these forces and the main Allied column to the north, the Japanese evacuated Rangoon. The Allies occupied the city on May 3.

Meanwhile, Stilwell had opened a drive southward from Myitkyina in October. But soon afterward he had one quarrel too many with Chiang, who demanded his dismissal. Roosevelt had no choice but to comply. He appointed the much more tactful General Albert C. Wedemeyer to take Stilwell's place. But before long, Wedemeyer was sending messages reminiscent of Stilwell's in which he complained of Chiang's deviousness and lack of cooperation. Nevertheless, his forces pushed forward and on March 7 captured Lashio, the western terminus of the Burma Road.

A Change of Plans for China

Ironically, now that the Allies had regained control of the original supply route, Roosevelt and his advisers abandoned their former high hopes for

Chiang and China. America's swift advances in the Pacific had undercut the country's strategic importance, while events inside China had left U.S. leaders totally disillusioned with Chiang and his regime. All of this made it clear that the British had been right. The conquest of Burma and the supply route to China had not been worth the investment in blood and materiel.

Indeed, Japan's position in China became much stronger as the result of an offensive that its troops began in April 1944. This operation aimed at capturing the 14th Air Force bases in the southeastern part of the country. Attacks by General Chennault's planes on Japanese shipping had become a source of growing concern to Tokyo. The Japanese offensive made remarkable progress and by the end of November, most of Chennault's bases were in enemy hands, and the Japanese at long last had created a land link between northern China and Southeast Asia. But, as always in China, the war dragged on—at least for a few more months.

CHAPTER TWENTY-FIVE

The Collapse of Japan

By the late summer of 1944, there was no question that the war had turned irretrievably against Japan. Although most Japanese leaders were unwilling to accept this fact, they could find little reason for optimism. The Japanese were still in the ascendancy in China, but this hardly made up for the disastrous erosion of their position in the Central and Southwest Pacific and even Burma. Far worse disasters lay ahead. The Americans soon embarked on a series of new operations that left Japan on the brink of total collapse.

The Return to the Philippines

MacArthur, after securing his series of bases along New Guinea's northern coast, focused his attention on the reconquest of the Philippines. He had originally planned to invade Mindanao in the southern part of the archipelago before moving northward toward the principal island of Luzon. But in September, Halsey executed a carrier strike against the Philippines that indicated that Japanese air power in the islands might be weaker than expected. Halsey now urged that American forces bypass Mindanao and instead capture Leyte on the eastern edge of the central Philippines. MacArthur and Nimitz both agreed, but the Pacific Fleet commander also insisted on a preliminary attack against the Palau Islands, which he desired as an advance base to support the Leyte landing. The Palaus lay 500 miles to the southeast of Mindanao. The decision to attack the Palaus proved to be a mistake.

On September 15, when the 1st Marine Division went ashore on the island of Peleliu, which contained the main airfield in the Palaus, they soon discovered that American planners had greatly underestimated the difficulties involved. Instead of the quick victory that had been expected, the battle

became a nightmare. The northern portion of the island consisted of a series of jagged coral ridges separated by precipitous gorges. These ridges were full of interconnecting caves that the Japanese had reinforced with concrete. They were virtually impervious to preliminary shelling and bombing. Even with the help of army reinforcements, the marines were not able to root out the last Japanese from this labyrinth of caves until November 26. In addition to the horrendous terrain, the heat was unbearable, with temperatures soaring as high as 115 degrees. Despite 6,000 American casualties, possession of Peleliu did not contribute significantly to the success of the Leyte operation.

Ten days prior to the invasion of Leyte, Halsey led his 3rd Fleet in a series of carrier raids against Luzon and Formosa as well as the Ryukyu Islands, which stretched 600 miles from Japan toward Formosa. The 3rd Fleet was actually the 5th Fleet under different command. During the summer of 1944, Nimitz adopted the practice of alternating the fleet's commanders and staffs. When Admiral Spruance was in charge, it was the 5th Fleet, and Halsey and his staff planned their next operation. When Halsey took over, it became the 3rd Fleet, and Spruance and his staff prepared their next campaign. Likewise Admiral Mitscher's carrier task force operated as Task Force 58 when with the 5th Fleet and as Task Force 38 when with the 3rd Fleet. This procedure enabled Nimitz to get the most action out of the fleet.

Halsey's raids met a determined response from both land-based aircraft and Admiral Ozawa's carrier planes. But once again the Japanese fared badly, losing over 500 planes to only 79 for the Americans. Nevertheless, inexperienced Japanese pilots who survived the battle believed that they had actually sunk large numbers of U.S. ships and reported a great victory. In reality, they had damaged only two cruisers and a carrier. Although Japanese naval leaders later discovered that the pilots' claims were wildly inflated, they neglected to inform the army high command, which continued to believe that much of the U.S. fleet lay at the bottom of the Pacific. This delusion emboldened army leaders to change their strategy for meeting the invasion of the Philippines. They had planned to mass most of their troops in defense of Luzon. Now they decided that they could make a major stand on Leyte.

The Americans assembled an impressive force for the invasion of Leyte. Admiral Thomas Kinkaid commanded the 7th Fleet, which was responsible for transporting and protecting the actual assault force, General George Krueger's 6th Army. Halsey's 3rd Fleet provided the covering naval force, including Mitscher's fast carrier task force, now 17 carriers strong. Kincaid had led forces in the Coral Sea, Midway, and Guadalcanal actions as well as in the Aleutians. Krueger was born in Germany and moved to America with his parents as a boy. A veteran of the Spanish-American War, he had commanded troops in the New Britain and New Guinea campaigns.

On October 20, Krueger's forces landed at three points along the coast of Leyte Gulf, the body of water bordering the island on the east. They encountered little opposition and by nightfall had secured a substantial beachhead. Early in the afternoon of the first day, MacArthur and a small party waded ashore in knee-deep water after their landing craft ran aground a short distance from the beach. This scene provided photographers with one of the most famous pictures of the war. Soon afterward, MacArthur made a brief statement over a radio transmitter in which he announced, "People of the Philippines, I have returned!"

The Battle of Leyte Gulf

But the real drama took place during the following days, not on Leyte itself but in the surrounding waters—the Battle of Leyte Gulf, the greatest naval struggle of all time. Despite its mauling in the Battle of the Philippine Sea, the Japanese navy still hoped to destroy the Pacific Fleet in the decisive battle it had been seeking since the start of the war. To accomplish this, Admiral Toyoda devised a master plan that provided for the entire Combined Fleet to converge on the Philippines.

Admiral Ozawa's Northern Force moved south from Japan as a decoy to lure Halsey's 3rd Fleet away from Leyte. Although it included Japan's four surviving carriers, they had a combined strength of only 110 aircraft. At the same time, two Japanese task forces rushed northward from the Singapore area, made their way through the congested waters of the Philippines, and headed for Leyte Gulf from two directions. Their mission: to destroy the American transports and supporting warships. One of them, Admiral Takeo Kurita's powerful Force A, contained the superbattleships *Yamato* and *Musashi* as well as three other battleships, 12 cruisers, and 15 destroyers. It was to penetrate San Bernardino Strait, which separated Luzon from Samar, an island just to the northeast of Leyte. At the same time, Admiral Shoji Nishimura's Force C, including two battleships, a heavy cruiser, and four destroyers, would steam through Surigao Strait to the south of Leyte. Admiral Kiyohide Shima's Second Striking Force, consisting of three cruisers and four destroyers, was to push south from Japanese waters to assist Nishimura. Toyoda's plan was bold and imaginative but was also highly complex, required exceptionally precise timing, and exposed the Japanese fleet to great danger, especially in view of its lack of carrier-based planes. The forces converging on Leyte Gulf had to depend completely on land-based aircraft, which proved quite unreliable.

On October 23, two U.S. submarines sighted Kurita's force and alerted Halsey. They also sank two heavy cruisers and disabled a third. Kurita continued into the Sibuyan Sea to the south of Luzon, where planes from Mitscher's task force attacked *Musashi* the next day. The huge ship suffered no fewer than 19 torpedo and 17 bomb hits, which finally sent it to the bottom. Three other battleships sustained damage, but to the north U.S. light carrier *Princeton* was sunk by a dive bomber from Luzon. After this rude reception, Kurita turned back to the west, and his maneuver convinced Halsey that he was giving up the struggle. But after dark, Kurita moved once again toward San Bernardino Strait.

U.S. carrier aircraft spotted Force C the same day, and Admiral Jesse Oldendorf set out to intercept it with six older battleships, including five survivors of the Pearl Harbor attack, as well as eight cruisers and a large destroyer force. A night engagement followed in which Oldendorf arrayed his cruisers and battleships across the entrance to Surigao Strait while his destroyers and PT boats penetrated into the narrow body of water. The smaller craft made skillful use of their torpedoes, destroying the battleship *Fuso* and three destroyers and slightly damaging Admiral Nishimura's flagship, the battleship *Yamashiro*. Despite this disaster, Nishimura proceeded with his remaining three vessels in column formation. Oldendorf's waiting line of cruisers and battleships finished off *Yamashiro* and crippled both the cruiser *Mogami* and a destroyer. Soon afterward, Shima's force ventured into the strait, but when it encountered the blazing wreckage of several of Nishimura's ships, Shima wisely retreated.

Meanwhile, Halsey, assuming that he had nothing to fear from Kurita's Force A, abruptly shifted his 3rd Fleet northward to intercept Ozawa's carriers. He did not even bother to leave a covering force at San Bernardino Strait and failed to bring this to the attention of Admiral Kinkaid, the 7th Fleet commander. Kinkaid, assuming that Halsey had left his Task Force 34, which included six new battleships, as a rear guard, took no further action. As a result, only Admiral Clifton Sprague's weak force of five small escort carriers, three destroyers, and four destroyer escorts lay between Kurita and Leyte Gulf.

When Kurita emerged from San Bernardino Strait on the morning of October 25, he proceeded southward and discovered Sprague's ships off Samar. The little escort carriers were too slow to outrun Kurita's formidable armada but moved away as quickly as possible while launching air strikes against the pursuing enemy. Kurita mistakenly thought that he had fallen upon the big U.S. carriers and dashed forward to destroy them. He moved too fast. His ships became separated, and the engagement became a confused melee, reducing the tremendous striking power of his superior force. Torpedo attacks by Sprague's destroyers as well as planes from Admiral Felix Stumpf's escort carrier group, which lay to the south, also helped to disrupt the Japanese. Although Kurita's ships sank the escort carrier *Gambier Bay* and two destroyers, three Japanese cruisers also went to the bottom. Nevertheless, Kurita continued to enjoy an overwhelming advantage in firepower and seemed on the verge of annihilating the Americans.

But instead of moving in for the kill, he hesitated, apparently fearing intervention from Mitscher's task force, and finally decided to withdraw through San Bernardino Strait.

Contrary to Kurita's fears, Mitscher was still far to the north with Halsey, who refused to divert any ships to the south for some time after receiving news of the threat to Sprague's forces. He was determined to destroy Ozawa's carriers, and success eventually rewarded his persistence. Mitscher's planes sank all four, including *Zuikaku*, the last survivor of the Pearl Harbor striking force, as well as five other ships. Halsey was about to overtake the rest of Ozawa's ships when he received a query from Admiral Nimitz, who was concerned about the looming disaster in Leyte Gulf, "Where is Task Force 34?" Halsey angrily diverted his six battleships and a carrier group to intercept Kurita's squadron, but the Japanese had already fled.

The Battle of Leyte Gulf had dealt a death blow to Japan's naval power. Four carriers, three battleships, six heavy and four light cruisers, and nine destroyers littered the ocean's floor—26 Japanese ships lost to only six American. The Japanese had also lost 500 planes. But, ironically, Toyoda's master plan had almost worked. If Kurita had continued his assault on Sprague's escort carriers, he almost certainly would have destroyed them as well as the transports and supply ships. Halsey had blundered by not leaving a force to guard San Bernardino Strait. He had been fortunate that Kurita had placed discretion ahead of valor.

Shortly before the end of the three-day struggle, the Japanese introduced a new weapon, one that soon became terribly familiar to American sailors—the kamikaze. A suicide unit composed of pilots who deliberately crashed their bomb-laden planes into American ships, the Kamikaze Special Attack Corps owed its existence to the disastrous decline of Japan's airpower. *Kamikaze*, meaning "divine wind," referred to the typhoons that had destroyed the fleet of the Mongol ruler Kublai Khan, saving Japan from invasion in the thirteenth century. Admiral Takijiro Onishi, who commanded the 1st Air Fleet, believed that kamikaze attacks were the only way to inflict meaningful damage on U.S. ships and morale. Such assaults posed special defensive problems. It was extremely difficult to stop a crash dive completely. Even if crippled, a kamikaze plane might

The Battle of Leyte Gulf, October 1944

still hit its target. Although the first suicide attack damaged an Australian cruiser on October 21, the main assault came four days later against the hard-pressed U.S. escort carriers. It caught the Americans by surprise, sinking the escort carrier *St. Lo* and damaging four others.

Progress on Land

While the opposing fleets fought their desperate battle, American troops on Leyte soon encountered stronger opposition. General Yamashita, who had gained the nickname "Tiger of Malaya" as a result of his brilliant conquest of that British colony, now commanded Japanese forces in the Philippines. He had favored massing his troops on Luzon for an all-out struggle there. But his superior, Field Marshal Count Hisaichi Terauchi, the commander for all of Southeast Asia, insisted that Yamashita shift as many men as possible to Leyte. This delayed the American advance but did not save Leyte.

The XXIV Corps drove south from the beachhead and then swung inland, reaching the western coast on November 1. Almost simultaneously, the X Corps swept through the Leyte Valley to the northern coast. The two forces were now in position to converge on Ormoc, the chief enemy base on the western coast. But General Krueger paused to consolidate his position in the north before thrusting into the mountains protecting Ormoc. This delay enabled the Japanese commander, General Sasaki Suzuki, to establish a strong defense in the rugged heights. Incessant rain also hampered the American advance. But on December 7, the third anniversary of the Pearl Harbor attack, the 77th Division executed a surprise landing south of Ormoc and seized the town three days later. Although this maneuver really decided Leyte's fate, Japanese units held out in various parts of the island until as late as May 1945. On December 15, MacArthur sent troops ashore on lightly held Mindoro, just to the south of Luzon. They made rapid progress, and engineers immediately began to construct airfields from which U.S. planes could support an operation against Luzon itself.

MacArthur chose Lingayen Gulf, the site of the major Japanese landing in 1941, as his invasion target on Luzon. General Yamashita's hopes for an all-out struggle in defense of the island perished when Terauchi ordered him to divert so many troops to Leyte. Yamashita accordingly withdrew most of his remaining forces to the mountainous interior to fight a delaying action and did not contest the landings at Lingayen Gulf, which took place on January 9, 1945. But kamikaze planes sank the escort carrier *Ommaney Bay* and damaged another as well as two battleships and five cruisers. These attacks were especially hard on American morale because the great Leyte Gulf victory had seemingly ended the enemy's ability to interfere with amphibious operations. Americans also found it difficult to comprehend the mentality that motivated suicide attacks. In reality, not all kamikaze pilots were willing volunteers. Many of them joined only after experiencing intense pressure from their superiors.

After Krueger's 6th Army had consolidated its beachhead, the I Corps pushed slowly north and east in mountainous terrain against the strongest concentration of Yamashita's forces. The XIV Corps had an easier task driving southward through open country. It reached Clark Field on January 23 but did not secure the base until over a week later. Soon afterward, two motorized "flying columns" of the 1st Cavalry Division dashed for Manila and penetrated the city's suburbs on February 3. As U.S. forces moved into Manila, they occupied three prisoner of war camps and liberated 8,500 Americans. Many of the prisoners were on the verge of starvation and suffered from malaria, dysentery, and other diseases. In late January and early February, elements of General Robert Eichelberger's 8th Army landed without resistance to the north of Bataan Peninsula. Eichelberger was serving as commandant of West Point when the war began. He took over the task of capturing Buna in December 1942 and commanded troops in many of the subsequent operations along the New Guinea coast.

In contrast to the relatively easy thrust to Manila, the actual conquest of the capital became a long, arduous struggle. Yamashita had ordered his troops to abandon the capital, but Admiral Sanji Iwabachi, who commanded the naval forces there, refused to comply. Instead, navy and army units resisted savagely. Manila experienced widespread devastation, and its population suffered horribly. Almost 100,000 civilians died, including many who fell victim to Japanese atrocities reminiscent of the rape of Nanking. The last fighting did not end until March 3.

Meanwhile, the Americans who had landed north of Bataan moved quickly southward. All of Bataan was under their control by late February. The Japanese attempted to hold Corregidor in an effort to block access to Manila Bay, but the Americans surprised them with a combined amphibious and airborne assault on February 16 and captured most of the island within ten days. Now MacArthur's forces confronted the task of eliminating Yamashita's strongholds in the mountainous interior of Luzon. This necessitated another slow, bloody campaign, which continued with diminishing intensity until the end of the war.

The Agonizing Fight for Iwo Jima

Even before MacArthur's forces had taken Manila, Nimitz had launched another invasion in the Central Pacific. This time the objective was the small island of Iwo Jima in the Volcano group of the Bonin Islands. The Bonins stretched from near Japan to within 300 miles of Saipan. The name "Volcano" was apt. All of the islands were of volcanic origin and were, to say the least, uninviting. Iwo Jima, which means "Sulfur Island," was no exception. Various writers have described Iwo, when seen from the air, as resembling a pork chop. Mount Suribachi, a 550-foot dormant volcano, dominated the island's narrow southern end. The wider northern half consisted of a plateau that rose as high as 350 feet and contained a series of jagged volcanic ridges. Both uplands possessed innumerable caves. The Japanese had reinforced them with concrete, adding a large number of bunkers and blockhouses. They had fortified these positions with big naval guns, mortars, and machine guns. An intricate network of tunnels connected the caves and fortresses as well as underground quarters for the troops.

Between the two upland areas lay a connecting stretch of lower-lying terrain that contained two airfields and the island's only beaches. These were no ordinary beaches. Instead of sand, they consisted of volcanic ash, so soft that men sank into it up to their ankles. This made walking difficult and running almost impossible. Just beyond the beaches, a series of volcanic terraces rose abruptly to a height of 15 feet. The combination of the soft

ash and these steep obstacles created a serious problem for amphibious vehicles and tanks attempting to move inland. In addition, the Japanese had ringed the beaches with bunkers, blockhouses, and pillboxes. The island, less than 5 miles long and $2\frac{1}{2}$ miles across at its widest point, also abounded with bubbling sulfur pits, which created a pervasive acrid smell. As one observer later remarked it was "like hell with the fire out."

American leaders coveted this dismal volcanic outcrop because it lay only 660 miles from Tokyo. Its capture would eliminate attacks by Japanese fighter planes operating from the island against B-29s en route from the Marianas to raid Japanese cities. American fighters could then use the same bases to provide escort protection for the Superfortresses. Iwo also had potential as an advance base for the bombers themselves. Finally, the airfields would provide a useful haven for crippled aircraft unable to make it back to their bases in the Marianas. The Joint Chiefs of Staff set the original invasion date for January 2, but the slow conquest of Leyte delayed the assault until February 19.

Months of bombing did little to soften up Iwo's defenses. But the postponement of the invasion enabled the Japanese to reinforce their garrison

Battle of Iwo Jima, February–March 1945

until it reached a total of 21,000 men. American leaders knew that the island was well defended, but they were not aware of how strong it really was. Three days of shelling by Spruance's 5th Fleet failed to eliminate the island's well-protected defenses, although the barrage did knock out many of the installations around the beaches.

General Tadamichi Kuribayashi, the highly capable and realistic Japanese commander, had no intention of contesting the landing. He had learned from earlier defeats that such tactics did not work against an enemy that possessed naval and air supremacy. He preferred to wait until the Americans had landed and then rake the beaches with fire. Thus, when General Harry Schmidt's V Marine Amphibious Corps went ashore on February 19, it initially encountered much greater difficulty from the soft volcanic ash and steep terraces than from the Japanese. But the marines, virtually unprotected on the exposed beaches, soon came under murderous fire, and their casualties mounted alarmingly as they inched forward. Nevertheless, by nightfall, the 5th Division had fought its way across the narrowest part of the island, isolating Mount Suribachi. Kuribayashi had not started his barrage soon enough. Too many troops, tanks, and other equipment had landed. All he could do now was to exact as heavy a price as possible.

Despite ferocious opposition, Schmidt's troops clawed their way slowly up the slopes of Mount Suribachi, and a patrol reached the summit on February 23. Soon afterward, Associated Press photographer Joe Rosenthal happened to be present as four marines hoisted an American flag and hastily snapped what became the most famous picture of the war.

The capture of Mount Suribachi lifted the spirits of the Americans, but the campaign had barely begun. With about half the island under their control, the marines now confronted the grim task of conquering the rugged terrain of the northern plateau with its myriad of fortified caves. Kuribayashi realized that suicide charges would be much more costly to his own troops than to the Americans. He was determined to avoid the temptation and insisted that his forces defend the island from their concealed positions. This proved highly effective in slowing the American advance.

Again, as on Biak and Peleliu, flamethrowers and TNT proved the surest weapons against these powerful defenses. Some Japanese soldiers volunteered to be human booby traps, strapping explosives to their bodies and lying in the paths of unsuspecting flamethrowing tanks. The bloody struggle continued for weeks as the marines cleared all but two pockets on the extreme northern part of the island. Then, with all hope gone, the remnants of the Japanese garrison did resort to a series of suicide attacks. Fighting ended on March 23.

As Admiral Nimitz observed, "uncommon valor was a common virtue" on Iwo Jima. Thirty percent of the marines who saw action on the island became casualties. Almost 6,000 died and over 17,000 suffered wounds. No fewer than 27 marines received medals of honor, 13 of them posthumously. Virtually the entire Japanese garrison perished, including General Kuribayashi. Iwo may not have been worth the price. It proved less effective as a B-29 base than American leaders had expected, and since the air force shifted to night bombing raids against Japan, fighter support was not really necessary. Iwo's primary value came to be as a base where many crippled B-29s found safety.

The Costly Struggle for Okinawa

Iwo Jima was one of two enemy island bastions that Admiral Nimitz planned to take during the first half of 1945. The other was Okinawa, which lay in the center of the Ryukyu Islands, only 350 miles from Kyushu, the southernmost of the major Japanese home islands. Sixty-seven miles long and varying in width from 2 to 18 miles, Okinawa contained airfields as well as two excellent anchorages and would provide an ideal base for an invasion of Japan.

The island was beyond the range of American land-based planes but relatively close to enemy airfields on Kyushu, Formosa, and the other Ryukyus. This meant that Spruance's 5th Fleet would be vulnerable to attack by Japanese planes. In an attempt to eliminate this threat, aircraft from Mitscher's carriers as well as a newly arrived British task force raided these bases prior to the invasion. But despite their efforts, the Japanese still had 700 planes available when the assault on Okinawa began on Easter Sunday, April 1.

Admiral Turner was in charge of the overall expeditionary force, while General Simon Bolivar Buckner, Jr. commanded the 10th Army, which made the actual landing. Buckner, the son of a Confederate army general, had previously led U.S. troops in the Aleutians. His force of 180,000 men included both army and marine units. The 5th Fleet provided the heaviest preinvasion bombardment of the Pacific war, but Japanese defenses survived almost unscathed. Nevertheless, the landings on the southwestern side of the island went extremely well against only token opposition. Marine forces reached the east coast the next day, cutting the island in two.

Things had gone so well on Okinawa during the first week that Admiral Turner radioed Nimitz, "I may be crazy but it looks like the Japanese have quit the war, at least in this sector." To which, the far less optimistic commander of the Pacific Fleet replied sarcastically, "Delete all after 'crazy.' " There was good reason for the lack of resistance. General Mitsuru Ushijima, the clever and determined Japanese commander, planned to employ the same strategy that Kuribayashi had used on Iwo Jima. He realized that he could neither prevent the landing nor defend all of Okinawa. Instead, he chose to abandon the northern three-fourths of the island and make his stand in the southern portion, which contained the two main towns, Naha and Shuri. The entire area abounded with limestone cliffs and ridges honeycombed with caves and pillboxes connected by tunnels and bristling with the strongest Japanese artillery concentration of the war. The garrison numbered 120,000 men, the largest that U.S. forces encountered during the entire Pacific conflict.

On April 9, army troops collided with Ushijima's powerful defensive line to the north of Naha and Shuri. Six weeks of desperate fighting followed before the Americans forced the enemy back to the last ring of defenses. During the next ten days, they made slow progress as 12 inches of rain drenched the island, but on May 31, Ushijima withdrew for a final stand in the cave-studded ridges and ravines of extreme southern Okinawa. Another month of bloodshed lay ahead before the Americans overcame the last remnants of Japanese resistance. Again, U.S. forces paid a heavy price for Okinawa—over 12,000 killed and 36,000 wounded as well as the largest number of "combat fatigue" cases in the Pacific war. As usual, most of the defenders lost their lives, but for the first time, several thousand Japanese soldiers actually surrendered. Both

FIGURE 25-1   A U.S. marine receives Communion from a Catholic chaplain after the capture of Mount Suribachi on Iwo Jima. (*National Archives and Records Administration*)

commanders were among the dead. Ushijima committed suicide; Buckner fell victim to a shell burst that sent a piece of coral ripping into his chest. The campaign claimed still another prominent American when Pulitzer Prize–winning war correspondent Ernie Pyle fell victim to a Japanese machine gun bullet on the neighboring island of Ie Shima. Both GIs and Home Front mourned his passing.

While this ordeal unfolded on Okinawa, the Japanese subjected the 5th Fleet and offshore shipping to the war's most sustained and destructive kamikaze assault. Spruance arrayed large numbers of destroyers in an outlying arc around the island to detect Japanese planes on radar and alert the carriers and other units of their approach. The gallant crews of these "radar pickets" bore the brunt of the attacks. The Japanese timed the start of the kamikaze offensive to coincide with a sortie

by elements of their surface fleet. On April 6, the superbattleship *Yamato* left Japanese home waters accompanied by a light cruiser and eight destroyers. They had only enough fuel for the voyage to Okinawa. *Yamato* was to attack the 5th Fleet and then beach itself on the shore, where its 18-inch guns would support the island's garrison. It was a suicide mission and did not get far. U.S. submarines soon spotted the fleet and alerted Mitscher's task force. Three hundred planes repeatedly attacked the Japanese ships to the southeast of Kyushu, sinking *Yamato*, the cruiser, and four destroyers.

Despite the failure of this final sortie of the Japanese navy, kamikaze and conventional air attacks continued for weeks. In all, they sank 34 ships and damaged over 350. Among those that sustained damage were the veteran carrier *Enterprise*, four other flattops, and ten battleships.

Battle of Okinawa, April–June 1945

FIGURE 25-2 U.S. servicemen pay their last respects to three dead comrades during a shipboard memorial service. *(United States Marine Corps)*

The Pacific Submarine War

Although American leaders considered the conquest of Okinawa as only a preliminary to the projected invasion of the Japanese home islands, it turned out to be the last major amphibious operation of the war. But another campaign had virtually drawn to a close as well. This was a submarine offensive against Japanese merchant shipping. Although it received few headlines, it ultimately made as great a contribution to victory as the exploits of the land forces and the surface fleet. But almost two years passed after Pearl Harbor before it produced any important results.

For some time, Americans continued to think primarily in terms of submarine attacks on Japanese warships rather than on merchantmen and were slow to change their focus. As a result, during 1942 and early 1943, Japanese merchant traffic between Southeast Asia and the home islands encountered relatively little difficulty. Defective torpedoes also contributed to the American dilemma. It gradually became apparent that these weapons suffered from both inaccurate depth control and faulty firing mechanisms. Technicians solved the depth problem in August 1942, but they did not remedy the last of the firing-pin shortcomings until 13 months later.

Ultra reports on the movements of Japanese merchantmen and tankers gradually persuaded naval leaders that these ships would be easy prey for submarines. Vice Admiral Charles Lockwood, commander of the Pacific Fleet's submarine force, adopted "wolf pack" tactics, which proved highly effective. In addition, much improved submarines became available in large numbers by late 1943. The Japanese also failed to provide adequate escort vessels to protect their convoys. Japan's naval leaders had underestimated the potential of submarine attacks, and the poor showing of the Americans during 1942 and much of 1943 had done little to rouse them to action.

Sinkings by submarines increased during the second half of 1943, and by the end of 1944, half of Japan's merchant fleet lay at the bottom of the sea. Submarine attacks had virtually cut off the home islands from the natural resources of Southeast Asia. The interdiction of oil supplies was particularly disastrous for Japan's surviving air and naval units. When the war ended in August 1945, only 1.8 million tons of Japanese merchant shipping remained afloat, out of a total of 9.4 million used during the conflict. Submarines had accounted for 60 percent of the sinkings. They had achieved what German U-boats had failed to accomplish in their campaign against Britain.

The Japanese never made a concerted effort to cut American supply lines by submarine attacks, even though the links between the United States and the fighting areas of the Pacific were perilously long. Thus, America's massive industrial and logistic achievements continued to provide the basis for victory without any real challenge in the sea lanes. This was due in part to the Japanese view that submarines should be used primarily against warships. But it was also partly the result of the growing practice of diverting large numbers of submarines to transport supplies to bypassed garrisons in the Pacific.

Fire from the Sky

Disaster also afflicted Japan from the air. Although it did not develop as soon as on the land and sea, when it finally struck, it did so with savage fury. The agent of destruction was the B-29 Superfortress, which was much heavier and faster than the B-17 and carried a far greater bombload. When B-29s became available for combat in early 1944, American forces were still far away from the Marianas, and the bombers could only operate from bases in China as part of General Kenneth Wolfe's 20th Bomber Command. But Wolfe encountered many problems. His bases were totally dependent on air supply via "the Hump" and had to compete with Stilwell's ground forces and Chennault's 14th Air Force for the rather meager supplies that made it to China. Persistent mechanical defects also kept many of the B-29s grounded.

Wolfe was not able to launch a raid against Japan until June 14, 1944, when over 60 B-29s struck the huge iron and steel complex at Yawata. They delivered their attack from high altitude, according to the prevailing doctrine of precision bombing, but the assault was far from precise and inflicted little damage. It did result in large headlines in American newspapers, which made leaders and the public alike eager for additional raids against the home islands. But due to his many troubles, Wolfe was slow to comply, and this led

General "Hap" Arnold to replace him with General Curtis LeMay, a veteran of the strategic bombing offensive against Germany.

At age 39, LeMay was the youngest major general in the U.S. Army Air Force. He believed fiercely in the potential of high-level precision bombing. But all efforts to translate his faith into reality met with disappointment. B-29s continued to do little serious damage to Japanese industry. Strong winds and heavy cloud cover made precision bombing extremely difficult. In January 1945, LeMay assumed leadership of the 21st Bomber Command in the Marianas but continued to encounter the same disappointing results.

Reluctantly, the general concluded that he must change his approach. He decided to use incendiary bombs against enemy cities that contained many dwellings of flimsy wooden construction. The Japanese also housed much of their industry in small workshops in these highly inflammable residential areas. By this time, a particularly nasty type of incendiary was available. It contained napalm, a jellied form of petroleum that exploded upon impact and spread like a torrent, engulfing all before it. To provide greater accuracy, LeMay sharply reduced bombing altitude, and he stripped the B-29s of their machine guns to increase speed. Since the raids would take place at night, he believed that the faster-moving planes had little to fear from Japanese antiaircraft fire. The bomber crews did not share his confidence.

On March 9, 1945, over 300 B-29s dropped huge quantities of incendiaries on Tokyo from altitudes as low as 4,900 feet. Exploding napalm ignited rivers of fire, and strong winds whipped them into a vast inferno that destroyed 16 square miles of the city and incinerated almost 85,000 persons. The temperature of the holocaust reached an incredible 1,800 degrees Fahrenheit. An enormous incandescent glow illuminated the sky while human beings burst spontaneously into flame, metal melted, and canals boiled furiously. This was the largest inferno ever ignited by a single bombing attack. More than 80,000 people perished and over 40,000 were injured. The tremendous heat created such air turbulence that some bombers had difficulty maintaining control and were sucked into the fires. But over all, B-29 losses were light. More firebombing raids followed in rapid succession. Nagoya, Osaka, Kobe, Yokohama, and many other cities fell victim to the same type of horror. Over all, firebombing raids took an estimated 240,000 to 300,000 Japanese lives. Ostensibly, these raids aimed at destroying Japanese industry, and, to be sure, they did knock out an ample portion, but they were clearly terror raids, designed to weaken Japanese morale. Although the United States had been hesitant to resort to firebombing against German cities, it abandoned its reservations when it came to raining down fiery death on urban areas of Japan. In the wake of these raids, millions fled the cities, seeking refuge in the countryside. The flight of so many people hampered Japanese industrial production still more.

Both Sides Woo the Soviets

By the spring of 1945, Japan's economy was a shambles, and at least some Japanese leaders realized that the country could not continue the war for long. Lack of raw materials had cut steel output to less than 100,000 tons per month. Production of aircraft had declined disastrously, and planes that did come into service were starved for fuel. Similar shortages also immobilized the remnants of the navy and verged on paralyzing the entire transportation system. Food stocks dwindled alarmingly.

Although Japanese Premier Koiso publicly supported a vigorous war effort, he secretly opened diplomatic contacts with the Soviet Union, hoping to secure a negotiated peace. But Stalin was not interested in acting as mediator, and Koiso's government could not survive the multitude of disasters that befell Japan. In early April, Baron Kantaro Suzuki, a 78-year-old retired admiral and hero of the Russo-Japanese War of 1904–5, became premier. Suzuki apparently favored an end to the war, but many army and navy leaders still thought only in terms of fighting to the bitter end.

In the face of such opposition, the pursuit of peace was a tricky business. Like Koiso, Suzuki openly stated his support for the war, but behind the scenes his foreign minister, Shigenori Togo, looked for a way to end the conflict. Togo favored negotiations with the United States, but Suzuki, insisted on reviving Koiso's indirect approach through the USSR despite the Soviet refusal to renew its nonaggression pact with Japan at virtually the same time that Suzuki became premier. Again, Stalin declined to cooperate.

The United States and Britain had long sought Soviet participation in the war against Japan once the Allies had defeated Germany. Soviet intervention in Manchuria would make it difficult for the Japanese to shift forces from there to help defend the home islands. Stalin had given his promise to enter the East Asian conflict at the Teheran conference in November 1943 and had outlined the concessions he expected in return. He presented more specific demands, which Roosevelt and Churchill accepted, at the Yalta conference in February 1945. These included acquisition of the southern half of Sakhalin, a large island just to the north of Japan, as well as the Kuriles, a chain of much smaller islands stretching northeastward from Japan to the Soviet Union's Kamchatka Peninsula. He also asked for a lease on Port Arthur and special rights in the nearby port of Dairen on the Manchurian coast. Russia had controlled all of these territories, except the Kuriles, until Japan seized them in the Russo-Japanese War. Finally, Stalin insisted on joint Soviet-Chinese administration of the Manchurian railroads. Since the war, critics have attacked this agreement as a betrayal of China and a boon to Soviet expansionism. No doubt it was. But realistically, there is no question that Stalin was in a position to enforce his will on the areas involved, regardless of whether the United States and Britain concurred.

Advent of A New Age: The Atomic Bomb

Ironically, the need for Soviet intervention may have become academic on the morning of July 16, 1945, when the United States detonated the first atomic bomb in the White Sands desert near Alamogordo, New Mexico. The ensuing explosion created a huge fireball and a cloud of smoke that rose more than eight miles into the sky. Dr. J. Robert Oppenheimer, leader of the team of scientists that had been largely responsible for developing the bomb, watched the dawn of the atomic age with both fascination and horror. It reminded him of a passage from the *Bhagavad-Gita*, the great Sanskrit poem of India: "If the radiance of a thousand suns were to burst at once into the sky, that would be like the splendor of the Mighty One.... I am become Death, Shatterer of Worlds."

This dramatic spectacle marked the culmination of developments in physics that had begun early in the twentieth century and led to revolutionary progress in the late 1930s. Scientists discovered that splitting the nucleus of the uranium atom would produce enormous energy and release particles that would in turn trigger a chain reaction in other atoms, creating an even greater amount of energy. They also recognized that it was theoretically possible to harness this vast energy in a bomb of appalling power, but that the technical problems and expense involved would be prodigious.

German physicists were particularly active in this process of discovery, and some of them fled the tyranny of Hitler's regime. Fearing that Nazi Germany would produce an atomic bomb, they brought the matter to Roosevelt's attention in 1939. The president appointed a committee of scientists to study the problem, and in 1940, he and Churchill agreed to pool Anglo-American resources in this endeavor. But it was not until after America's entry into the war that a special unit of army engineers, headed by General Leslie Groves, assumed the devilishly difficult task of actually creating an atomic bomb. This top-secret undertaking was code-named the Manhattan Project. Groves worked closely with Oppenheimer's team, which also contained British scientists, at Los Alamos, New Mexico. The obstacles were staggering, but by the summer of 1945, the bomb was ready.

President Truman, who had succeeded to the presidency after Roosevelt's death in April 1945, received news of the successful test while he was in Germany, conferring with Stalin and Churchill at the Potsdam conference. This was the last of the Allied summit meetings, and, indeed, before it ended, only Stalin remained of the wartime Big Three. Churchill departed for home ten days after the conference began to await the results of Britain's first parliamentary election since 1935. He never returned. Instead, Clement Attlee, the leader of the Labour party, which won an unexpected landslide victory, took his place as prime minister and at Potsdam.

Roosevelt and Churchill had never informed Stalin of the Manhattan Project, and Truman was not prepared to do so now. He had watched with growing concern as the Soviets tightened their control over Eastern Europe. However, Truman did casually mention to Stalin that the United State had "a weapon of unusual destructive force." The Russian leader blandly indicated his satisfaction but did not press for details. In reality, he was already quite knowledgeable about the bomb. Klaus Fuchs, a German scientist who had fled his homeland to become a British subject and later a member of Oppenheimer's scientific team, had supplied Soviet agents with extensive information on the project.

Stalin also belatedly informed Truman of the peace overtures that the Japanese had been making. But this came as no surprise to the president because Magic intercepts of Japanese diplomatic messages had kept him abreast of their efforts to obtain peace. It was quite clear that the combination of submarine and air attacks as well as Japanese defeats in the Pacific had weakened Tokyo's resolve to continue the war, but the intercepts also indicated determination to resist. This stiffened American opposition to a negotiated peace, and on July 26, the Allies issued a joint declaration calling on Japan to accept "unconditional surrender" or face "prompt and utter destruction."

The Japanese reply to this appeal was vague, but Truman and his advisers interpreted it as a rejection and decided to go ahead with plans to drop an atomic bomb on a major Japanese city. They compiled a list of urban centers that had escaped fire-bombing and, thus, would provide a dramatic demonstration of the bomb's terrible power. The leading candidate was Hiroshima, a city of 340,000 located on the southeastern coast of Honshu, Japan's principal island.

With Colonel Paul Tibbets, Jr., at the controls, a B-29, named Enola Gay after the pilot's mother, took off from Tinian early on the morning of August 6, carrying a 9,000-pound nuclear bomb with the destructive power of 20,000 tons of TNT. The weather over Hiroshima was ideal as Enola Gay approached. Shortly before 8:15 A.M., an ungainly object hurtled out of its bomb bay doors. When it reached a point 660 yards from the ground, a blinding flash illuminated the sky, and a split second later, a gigantic fireball burst over the stricken city. Shock waves of unbelievable force followed, leveling almost everything in their path. The unearthly sight inspired copilot Robert Lewis to enter a terse, "My God!" in his log book. A tower of purple, orange, gray, and black smoke churned upward, topped by a cloud in the shape of a mushroom. It ultimately reached an altitude of 55,000 feet. Below, 60 percent of Hiroshima had virtually disappeared. Perhaps as many as 100,000 persons died instantly and as many more perished in the following days, weeks, and years from injuries and the effects of radiation.

Forcing Japan's Surrender

Later on that fateful day, Truman warned the Japanese that unless they surrendered, more cities would experience the same horror. The Suzuki government reacted to the disaster by stepping up its unrealistic efforts to persuade the Soviet Union to help arrange peace. Stalin's response was a declaration of war on August 8, three months after Germany's surrender, as promised at Yalta. He had been massing 1.5 million men along the Manchurian border for months. The once formidable Kwantung Army, which defended Manchuria, had seen much of its strength siphoned off to bolster the defense of Japan and other fronts. Three Soviet armies under Marshal Alexander Vasilevsky knifed swiftly into Manchuria from both east and west.

Secretary of War Stimson was troubled by the horror of the Hiroshima cataclysm and urged Truman to make a peace overture to Japan. But the president was determined to stand on the Potsdam Declaration, and since the Japanese had not agreed to surrender, they would experience the horror of a second atomic bomb. This time the target was Nagasaki, a city of 250,000 on Kyushu's western coast. Although the second bomb was more powerful than the first, it produced less spectacular results. The explosion on August 9 flattened Nagasaki's center and killed 35,000 people, but the surrounding hills limited the area affected.

The combination of the two atomic bombs and the Soviet Union's entry into the war convinced many Japanese leaders that they had no choice but to surrender. In fact, the Supreme War Council, which had overall responsibility for directing the military effort, was debating acceptance of the Potsdam Declaration even before the second bomb struck Nagasaki. But the six-member council remained split, despite learning of the second A-bomb. Three members led by Premier Suzuki would accept, but the other three, led by General Korechika Anami, the war minister, voiced intense

opposition. Emperor Hirohito broke precedent and the deadlock the day after the Nagasaki disaster by personally requesting that the council and cabinet consent to the declaration with the sole proviso that the emperor should retain his position. On August 10, the government relayed its acceptance on this basis.

Some American leaders still opposed the retention of the emperor, especially James F. Byrnes, who had recently become secretary of state. To Byrnes and others, the emperor symbolized the hated militaristic clique that dominated Japan. But Stimson realized how greatly the Japanese revered their emperor and believed that granting this concession was the only way to assure peace and avoid massive American casualties in an invasion of Japan. On August 11, the leaders reached a compromise that allowed the Japanese to keep their emperor but subjected his authority to an Allied supreme commander of occupation forces. The drama was not yet over, however. Japanese military leaders still opposed surrender, and the supreme council debated the matter for three days. Once again, Hirohito, encouraged by his closest adviser Marquis Koichi Kido, decided the issue. He tearfully urged acceptance of surrender and asked that the cabinet prepare a message to this effect that he would record for broadcast to the nation the next day. The cabinet members, almost overcome by emotion, agreed.

A group of young fanatical army officers made one last attempt to prevent surrender. They broke into the imperial palace grounds, seeking to destroy the recording of the emperor's message, and hoped to coerce the government into continuing the war. It was a final act of *gekokujo*. But this time there was too little support from higher officers. The coup failed. Although not involved in the coup, Anami chose to commit suicide rather than accept surrender. Admiral Onishi, who had been stockpiling kamikaze planes and fuel for one last all-out effort to prevent an American invasion, also took his own life as did many others. They remained faithful to the *Bushido* code of death before dishonor.

In his radio broadcast on August 15, the first time his people had ever heard his voice, Hirohito declared that he feared the "obliteration of the Japanese nation" by the "new and most cruel bomb," making it necessary to end the war.

When the announcement of Japan's surrender reached the United States, one of the most spontaneous celebrations in history erupted. Men, women, and children rushed into the streets and headed, as if by prior agreement, for the center of every town and city in America. They milled around in elated excitement for hours. The war was over. The mood in Japan was quite different—a combination of shock, shame, and relief. As the emperor had said in his address to the people, it was necessary to endure "the unendurable" and bear "the unbearable."

To the American people, August 14 was V-J Day, the moment of victory over Japan. But officially the war did not end until September 2, when the Japanese formally signed the document of surrender aboard the huge U.S. battleship *Missouri* in Tokyo Bay. General MacArthur, whom Truman had appointed Allied supreme commander, presided. During the ceremonies, he spoke these words, which reflected the feelings of everyone present as well as millions of people around the world:

> It is my earnest hope and indeed the hope of all mankind that from this solemn occasion a better world shall emerge out of the blood and carnage of the past—a world founded upon faith and understanding—a world dedicated to the dignity of man and the fulfillment of his most cherished wish—for freedom, tolerance and justice.

Postmortem: Was Atomic Force Necessary?

The question of whether it was necessary to use the atomic bomb to force Japan's surrender has remained probably the most controversial issue of World War II. Truman and other American leaders contended that they resorted to the bomb to shorten the war and save American lives. They also insisted that both the Hiroshima and Nagasaki bombs were necessary to convince the Japanese that further resistance was suicidal. From their perspective, dropping the second bomb might foster the mistaken belief among Japan's leaders that America had the bomb in mass production. These arguments formed the basis for the traditional interpretation of this question, which many historians still accept.

In later years, however, revisionist historians have charged that the bomb was not needed to end the war and that Japan could not have resisted for long. They contend that the United States not only should have paid more attention to Tokyo's peace overtures but should have taken the initiative by guaranteeing the emperor's throne. At the very least, they feel that Washington should have warned the Japanese of the bomb's existence and staged a demonstration of its destructiveness. Some also contend that U.S. leaders used the bomb not to force Japan's surrender but to impress the Soviets with America's awesome new power and to persuade Stalin to moderate his policies in Europe.

Some of these revisionist arguments are persuasive. There is strong evidence that Japan could not have long avoided surrender. The submarine blockade and the firebombing attacks had sharply reduced the country's ability to make war and had caused great suffering. Indeed, total casualties from the incendiary raids were far greater than those inflicted by the atomic attacks. The United States Strategic Bombing Survey after the war stated flatly that Japan could not have continued the struggle beyond the end of 1945, even without the use of the bomb.

It also is true that the United States made no effort to capitalize on Japanese overtures or to take any diplomatic initiative to secure peace. Truman and his advisers questioned the seriousness of the Japanese feelers to the Soviets. A direct approach to Washington might have had more impact. American leaders also doubted that the tentative peace initiatives really represented the position of the Japanese military. Indeed, there was good reason for this lack of conviction, because many of the enemy's top army leaders opposed acceptance of the Potsdam Declaration, and only the emperor's personal intervention settled the matter. Finally, the Japanese had consistently fought to the bitter end in the Pacific and American leaders expected even greater fanaticism and bloodshed in defense of the sacred home islands.

It is difficult to accept the contention that Truman and his advisers used the bomb to impress the Soviet Union rather than to end the war. Certainly, by the summer of 1945, they were concerned about the USSR's dominant position in Eastern Europe, but there is no indication that they intended to challenge it at that point. Perhaps American leaders hoped that the weapon's awesome power might help restrain Moscow's actions regarding the remainder of Europe, but this is not clear. However unnecessary the bomb may have been in forcing the Japanese surrender, it does not appear that the leaders in Washington were convinced of this. They probably believed sincerely that their action would save American lives. Planning for the invasion of the Japanese home islands called for landings on Kyushu (Operation Olympic) in November 1945, followed by an assault on Honshu (Operation Coronet) in March 1946. The Joint Chiefs of Staff estimated that American casualties would be over a quarter of a million. They projected this from the fanatical resistance on Okinawa, where 35 percent of U.S. forces became casualties. The medical staff of General Krueger's 6th Army, scheduled to implement Olympic, was preparing for 490,000 casualties, including 147,500 killed in action. Japanese casualties would simply be astronomical.

Probably it is best to consider the decision to drop the bomb in the context of the steadily escalating vindictiveness and brutality that marked the Allied war effort. This was the case not only against the Japanese but against the Germans as well. Once the British resorted to area bombing of Germany's cities, it was only a step to the firebombing of Hamburg and Dresden. Even the Americans, despite their protests against such an approach, had joined in area bombing of German cities by 1945. Hatred for the Japanese was even more pronounced. Neither the American people nor their leaders could forget the attack on Pearl Harbor, the Bataan Death March, or the fanatical Japanese resistance on island after island. U.S. leaders also became increasingly dedicated to the cause of unconditional surrender, which they believed would prevent a resurgence of Japanese militarism. When conventional strategic bombing of Japanese cities failed, it was but another step to area bombing with incendiaries. It is by no means certain that inflicting death by napalm was more humane than incinerating with nuclear bombs. The decisions to destroy Hiroshima and Nagasaki would seem to have been the last logical elements in the growing crescendo of hatred and destructiveness—undoubtedly terrible, perhaps morally indefensible, but, unfortunately and tragically, understandable.

Aftermath

World War II had finally ended, but its effects lingered. Some actually had their origin in the legacy of World War I. Others were of more recent vintage. Much of the world felt their impact, even areas that had not been directly involved in the conflict. As is the case with most wars, many of the issues that provoked hostilities were not really solved. Others were.

The Physical Costs of the War

World War II was the most costly conflict in history, in terms of both casualties and destructiveness as well as wealth expended. Casualty figures remain notoriously controversial, but perhaps 21 million military personnel lost their lives. Civilian deaths are even harder to pin down but may number 38 million, among them almost 6 million Jewish victims of the Holocaust as well as over 200,000 Roma (Gypsies).

The USSR suffered by far the most grievous total losses—an estimated 10 million military and 19 million civilian dead. Germany, too, paid a high price for Hitler's ambitions—almost 5 million soldiers killed along with over a million civilians. China also suffered horribly. Estimates vary widely, but military deaths may number 2.5 million, and as many as 20 million civilians may have perished as well. Japan's military and civilian fatalities numbered about 2.5 million. France, Britain, and Italy each suffered over 400,000 deaths, including both military and civilian. Poland lost 300,000 military personnel and over 6 million civilians, including almost 3 million Jews. Yugoslavia's death toll reached 400,000 soldiers and more than a million noncombatants. As in World War I, the United States remained free of destruction, but U.S. battle losses totaled 290,000.

The war had also uprooted perhaps as many as 30 million people from their homes in Europe, including those who had served as slave laborers or had survived the Nazi death and concentration camps. These unfortunate victims became known as "displaced persons" in the postwar era. In addition, the end of the war brought wholesale population shifts on a deliberate basis. Germans were the chief victims of this practice. Poland expelled 9 million of them from the territory east of the line formed by the Oder and Neisse rivers and from the southern two-thirds of East Prussia. The Poles had received these lands as compensation for the loss of eastern Poland to the USSR. Czechoslovakia also ousted the 3 million Sudeten Germans, thereby finally solving the Sudetenland question.

Total direct and indirect costs of the war in monetary terms may have reached as high as $4 trillion. Destruction was present almost everywhere in Europe as well as in North Africa. Unlike the situation after World War I, Germany had suffered extensive devastation, and all its major cities lay in ruins. If World War I had disrupted the European economy, the conflict of 1939–45 had brought it to a virtual standstill. In many countries, the industrial complex, communications network, and natural resources were in a state of desolation. Prewar patterns of trade were in total disarray, as were the financial and monetary systems. Inflation was rampant. The fighting had sharply curtailed food production, and starvation and disease stalked large areas of the continent.

In Asia, China bore the scars of eight years of conflict, and another four years of civil war lay just ahead. But, except for Burma and the Philippines, much of Southeast Asia had experienced little direct destruction since 1942. Most of the fighting had taken place on islands with small populations and primitive economies. Japan had not been so fortunate. The rain of death from the skies had destroyed large portions of its major cities.

Prosecuting War Criminals

The victorious Allies were determined to bring to justice the leaders who had been responsible for starting the war and the atrocities that followed. In the case of Germany, the two main culprits had escaped the ignominy of standing trial. Hitler, the man most responsible for the war and its horrors, was dead. So was Himmler, who like his Führer had resorted to suicide. But many German leaders were still alive, and most of them were in Allied custody. The United States, Britain, the Soviet Union, and France agreed in August 1945 to establish an international military tribunal to try the most important of them.

It convened in Nuremberg, the site of the former Nazi party rallies, in November 1945 and brought forth indictments against 24 German leaders. Among the best known were Goering, Ribbentrop, Speer, Generals Keitel and Jodl, and Admirals Raeder and Dönitz. They also included Alfred Rosenberg, the self-styled Nazi theoretician; Ernst Kaltenbrunner, who had succeeded Heydrich as chief of the Nazi security police; and Fritz Sauckel, the head of the slave labor program. The two men who had served as Hitler's deputies were on the list as well. The first of these, Rudolf Hess, had been officially the number three man in the Nazi hierarchy until May 1941. At that time, he had crashlanded an Me 110 fighter plane on British soil in an ill-advised attempt to negotiate peace. The second, Martin Bormann, had succeeded Hess and had disappeared in Berlin after Hitler's death. It is likely that he died trying to escape to the West.

The trial lasted until October 1946 and resulted in death sentences by hanging for 11 of the defendants, including Goering, Ribbentrop, Kaltenbrunner, Rosenberg, Sauckel, Keitel, and Jodl as well as Bormann *in absentia*. Hess and Raeder received life sentences, Speer 20 years, and Dönitz 10 years. Shortly before his scheduled execution, Goering cheated the rope by biting into a cyanide capsule that he had concealed on his person. A series of trials of less important Nazi officials also took place in the various occupation zones. The most notable of these in the American zone resulted in 24 death sentences and 116 prison terms.

In Japan, another international tribunal tried 40 leaders on charges of war crimes. In November 1948 seven of them received death sentences, including former Premier Tojo, who had failed in a suicide attempt prior to his arrest. Eighteen others received prison sentences. Fumimaro Konoye, who had preceded Tojo as premier, avoided arrest by taking poison. Other trials took place in various parts of Japan's former empire. Among the most notable defendants was General Yamashita. A court in Manila found the Tiger of Malaya guilty of condoning atrocities in the Philippines and sentenced him to death in December 1945.

General Ishii and his Unit 731 colleagues, who had engaged in medical experiments on human beings, were much more fortunate. After the war Ishii made a deal with the United States that gave them immunity from prosecution in return for turning over the records of their research into American custody. U.S. officials were determined to prevent them from falling into the hands of the Soviets or Chinese Communists.

Despite the enormity of the crimes involved, the tribunals have received much criticism. Some have questioned whether international courts had any legal standing since there was no world state. They also pointed out that the defendants, despite their undoubted complicity in barbaric policies, had actually broken no existing international laws. The proceedings were, thus, of a retroactive or *ex post facto* type, which neither the British nor the American legal system recognized. There was also the question of Allied behavior during the war. Were the Russians not guilty of aggression against Poland, the Baltic states, and Finland? Did they not commit mass murder in the shooting of the Polish officers in the Katyn Forest as well as atrocities against the population of eastern Germany? Did they not attack Japan without provocation in the last days of the war? What of the Anglo-American terror-bombing raids against Germany and the American firebombing of Japanese cities? What about Hiroshima and Nagasaki?

Former occupied countries of Europe also took action against leaders who had collaborated with the Germans. In Norway, Quisling, the man whose name had become synonymous with treason, died before a firing squad. In France, Pierre Laval, the chief collaborator during much of the Vichy regime's existence, met a similar fate. A French court also found Marshal Pétain, the World War I hero and Vichy's head of state, guilty of treason and sentenced him to death. But Charles de Gaulle, France's provisional president, commuted the sentence to life imprisonment in recognition of Pétain's earlier service.

Political Repercussions

The war also transformed the power structure of the world. World War I had started this process with the disintegration of Austria-Hungary. World War II banished five other countries from the ranks of the great powers—France, Italy, Germany, Japan, and even Britain. Although Britain had been one of the three major Allied powers, it had become painfully clear that it was the junior partner and lacked the size, population, and resources of the USSR and the United States. Even though Britain had suffered less destruction than the Soviet Union or Germany or even France, the British had paid a fearful price for victory. The nation was deeply in debt, its resources depleted, and its share of the world market but a memory.

Now only two great powers remained—the United States and the Soviet Union—and they were really superpowers, towering above all other nations and posing the possibility of a world split into two rival blocs. Furthermore, they were divided ideologically. America became the champion of capitalism and liberal democracy, the USSR of communism and totalitarianism. But as time passed, the United States came to support many countries that, though anti-Communist, were far from democratic. In the process, the distinction between the "free world" and the "totalitarian world" became fuzzy.

The war had created two vast power vacuums, one in Europe, the other in East Asia. In Europe, this was the logical conclusion to another legacy of World War I—the creation of a power vacuum in the central and eastern portions of the continent. For a time, Nazi Germany had filled that vacuum, but by 1945, the Red Army held most of Eastern and Central Europe by right of conquest.

Since 1945, many critics have attacked Roosevelt and to a lesser extent Churchill, for supposedly allowing the Soviets to dominate Eastern Europe. As proof they have pointed to arrangements that the two Western leaders made with Stalin during the last months of the war. Indeed, it is true that they did grant certain concessions, but these were only in keeping with the reality of the Red Army's presence in Eastern Europe.

Churchill had essentially acknowledged the Soviet claim to eastern Poland at the Teheran conference in November 1943. Actually, the prime minister, like many other British leaders, had always been skeptical about Poland's claim to much of this area because the population was primarily Ruthene and Belorussian rather than Polish. Churchill also recognized that there was nothing that either he or Roosevelt could do to keep the Baltic states out of Soviet hands. As for Roosevelt, he attempted to establish a close personal relationship with Stalin, which he hoped would persuade the Soviet leader to be reasonable about Eastern Europe. The president firmly believed that Soviet cooperation with the West was necessary for postwar stability in the world.

Soviet Influence in Eastern Europe

By late 1944, Churchill was growing alarmed at the Red Army's increasing control of Eastern Europe. In an attempt to salvage something, the prime minister suggested a division of influence in the Balkans during a visit to Moscow in October 1944. Stalin seemed receptive, and in a surprisingly casual manner, the two leaders agreed that the Soviets should enjoy 90 percent interest in Rumania and 75 percent in Bulgaria. The West would have to be content with 10 and 25 percent, respectively, in these countries but would hold a 90 percent advantage in Greece to the Soviets' 10 percent. Churchill and Stalin proposed a 50–50 division of interest in Hungary and Yugoslavia. To Churchill's chagrin, Roosevelt found this agreement a glaring example of the spheres-of-influence approach to power politics, which he detested.

Although the agreement did not extend to Poland, Churchill clearly realized that little could be done to save the cause of Mikolajczyk's Polish government in exile. Stalin's support for the Polish National Liberation Committee in Lublin and the failure of the Warsaw Uprising had sealed the fate of the London Poles. Mikolajczyk was in Moscow at the time of Churchill's meeting with Stalin and recognized the need to make concessions to the Soviet Union. But his colleagues in the government in exile refused, and he resigned as premier. Soon afterward, Churchill washed his hands of the stubborn London Poles and recognized the Lublin government the following January.

At Yalta in February 1945, Churchill and Roosevelt recognized the USSR's claim to eastern Poland and accepted Stalin's proposal that Poland and the Soviet Union divide East Prussia and that the Poles receive additional compensation to the east of the Oder. In return, Stalin agreed to representation for the London Poles in the Polish Liberation Committee as well as free elections to determine Poland's future government.

Despite Western concessions, the presence of the Red Army was the determining factor in Soviet domination of Eastern Europe. The only way in which the United States and Britain could possibly have changed this situation was by resorting to military action. Neither country was prepared to attempt such a drastic solution. Even had they considered attempting to expel the Red Army from Eastern Europe, there was no assurance that they could have done so in a conventional war. At best, a stalemate would probably have resulted. It is true that by the summer of 1945, the United States had a monopoly on the atomic bomb, but only the lunatic fringe believed that nuclear war was the answer to the dilemma. Moreover, atomic weapons remained in short supply for several years.

Critics have also contended that Western troops could have liberated much of Eastern Europe before the Red Army. Some have charged that the United States and Britain made a fatal error by not invading the Balkans in 1943 or 1944. But such an operation would have been political in nature, and U.S. leaders were eager to secure military victory by the quickest and most direct manner—a cross-channel invasion of Western Europe. They were not interested in political objectives on Europe's remote southeastern periphery. Certainly their thinking was sound militarily. Any assault on the Balkans would also have encountered extremely mountainous terrain, providing the Germans with ideal defensive positions similar to those in Italy.

Since the war, the myth has developed that Churchill actively urged such a policy from a relatively early date. In reality, he never proposed anything more than aid to Tito's Partisans in Yugoslavia, the occupation of the island of Rhodes in the Aegean Sea, and efforts to entice Turkey into the war. He did, of course, order British troops into Greece in 1944, but this operation took place only after the Germans had begun to withdraw from the country. Otherwise, Churchill supported General Alexander's questionable dream of a thrust through northeastern Italy toward Vienna and the Hungarian Plain.

Some have also charged that Western forces could have beaten the Red Army to Berlin in April 1945. But this is highly questionable because the Soviets had massive forces less than 40 miles from the German capital at that time, while just the spearheads of General Simpson's U.S. 9th Army were within striking distance. Only in the case of Czechoslovakia was there a real opportunity for U.S. forces to push farther east. Indeed, they probably could have taken Prague before the Soviets. Whether Czechoslovakia would have remained outside the Soviet orbit in the long run is by no means clear, however.

Soviet-dominated territories fell into two categories in the postwar era—those that the USSR annexed directly and those that became satellite states. The former consisted of the areas that Finland had ceded to the Soviets, the Baltic states, the northern third of East Prussia, eastern Poland, Ruthenia, the easternmost province of Czechoslovakia, and the Rumanian provinces of Bessarabia and Northern Bukovina. The Allies concluded peace treaties with Finland and Rumania in 1946 that confirmed their territorial losses. Britain and America never officially recognized the annexation of the Baltic states, although informally both Roosevelt and Churchill had realized at least as early as 1944 that this was inevitable.

As compensation for the loss of its eastern territory, Poland received the southern two-thirds of East Prussia and the area of Germany east of the Oder-Neisse line. The Americans and British approved the Polish occupation of these territories at the Potsdam conference. But they insisted on deferring actual determination of Poland's borders until the Big Three could agree on a peace treaty for Germany. As it turned out, the Allied powers never drafted a treaty, and the territories remained under Polish control. In its new form, Poland was 20 percent smaller than it had been in 1939, but the land received from Germany was considerably more valuable than that lost to the Soviet Union. The added territory included the ports of Danzig and Stettin and the rich industrial area of Silesia.

Poland became a Soviet satellite, along with East Germany, Czechoslovakia, Hungary, Rumania, and Bulgaria. The subjugation of these countries occurred despite Stalin's agreement at Yalta to the establishment of coalition governments in all liberated countries, as well as free parliamentary elections. Although coalition governments did come into existence, Communists held most of the key positions in these regimes. As time passed, they increased their control and gradually squeezed out the non-Communists. The exact manner in which this took place varied from country to country, as did the tempo of change. But a Communist monopoly on the vital cabinet post of minister of the interior, which controlled the police, usually contributed to the process. Although local Communists were primarily responsible for the transformation, the Red Army's presence in each country certainly served as a deterrent to any active resistance to the takeovers.

The Communists modeled the regimes of the satellite states closely after the Stalinist system in the USSR. They allowed no opposition parties and kept tight control over all aspects of life, including state-controlled economies. Bowing to Soviet pressure, they granted concessions that enabled the USSR to exploit their countries economically. Each government also followed foreign policies that dovetailed closely with that of Moscow.

Yugoslavia was an exception to this pattern. Although Soviet troops had helped drive the Germans from the country, Tito's Partisans had carried out most of this task. Thus, the Red Army never played the role it had assumed in other countries. Instead, Tito and his Communist followers dominated Yugoslavia from the start. With the cooling of East-West relations, Stalin tried to increase Soviet influence over Tito's regime. But the Yugoslav leader refused to acquiesce. When the USSR applied economic pressure, instead of buckling under, Tito turned to the West for aid. In the years that followed, Yugoslavia remained Communist but enjoyed independence from both blocs.

Albania was another exception. When the Germans withdrew in late 1944 to avoid being cut off by the Red Army, local Communists, with help from Tito's Partisans, fought Albanian non-Communists and established a provisional government. In the process, Yugoslavia's influence became so strong that it threatened to convert Albania into a satellite.

To avoid this, Enver Hoxha, the Albanian Communist leader, turned to the USSR for support, and Stalin was happy to oblige. Hoxha proceeded to wipe out all opposition to his rule, established a thoroughly Stalinist system, and linked his country closely to Moscow.

Finland was still another exception. Not only did the Finns remain free from Soviet domination, but they also continued as a non-Communist, democratic state. They owed this independence largely to their ability to make peace with the Soviets in 1944 before the Red Army could penetrate deeply into the country. Stalin was willing to allow Finland to enjoy its freedom, provided that it retained close relations with the USSR. Under the circumstances, the Finns followed a policy of economic cooperation and friendship with their huge neighbor to the east.

U.S. Aid to Western Europe

During the immediate postwar years, while the USSR consolidated its control over Eastern Europe, most of Western Europe emerged with democratic governments and badly strained economies. The United States and Britain allowed the Western European countries to handle their own affairs. Indicative of this is the fact that in two of these countries, France and Italy, large Communist parties flourished. In view of the lagging economic recovery of Western Europe, non-Communists feared that continued distress might lead to growing Communist strength. The French restored a form of government similar to the Third Republic. This Fourth Republic experienced many of the same problems, especially a multiparty system and chronic political instability. The Italians abolished their monarchy in 1946 and established a republic that also suffered from a multitude of parties and an unstable parliamentary system. The United States viewed the situation in both countries with growing concern.

But the American government looked with far greater distress at developments in Greece and Turkey, which bordered the Soviet satellites. A civil war had plagued Greece intermittently since 1944. It featured a sizable group of rebels under Communist leadership who opposed the corrupt and reactionary Greek government. Neighboring Bulgaria, Yugoslavia, and Albania provided aid to the Communists. But Stalin scrupulously honored his 1944 arrangement with Churchill, which had given Britain a free hand in Greece in return for a similar Soviet advantage in Rumania and Bulgaria. British forces had propped up the Greek government since 1944, but in early 1947 Britain indicated that due to financial difficulties, it would have to withdraw its troops in the near future. Meanwhile, Turkey was having trouble with the Soviets, who demanded the return of border areas that had been Russian before 1918. They also asked for the right to share in the defense of the straits linking the Black Sea with the Mediterranean.

This combination of developments led President Truman to announce in early 1947 that henceforth the United States would "support free peoples who are resisting attempted subjugation by armed minorities or by outside pressures." In the same speech, the president proposed to provide economic aid to both Greece and Turkey as well as military advisers and equipment. The president's speech was tremendously significant because in proclaiming what came to be known as the Truman Doctrine, he launched an entirely new approach to foreign policy. America had definitely abandoned its traditional peacetime aloofness from European affairs. The Truman Doctrine represented the official start of the American policy of containment, which attempted to prevent Soviet expansion and the spread of communism.

Later the same year, Secretary of State George Marshall, the U.S. army's wartime chief of staff, proposed a program for the economic rehabilitation of Europe. Officially titled the European Recovery Program, it was soon being referred to as the Marshall Plan. Concern over the economic woes of Western Europe and fear of increasing Communist strength in France and Italy motivated the program. In its inception, the plan offered economic aid to all of Europe, including the Soviet Union.

The USSR and its satellites actually responded to the offer with some interest, but when the United States demanded a survey of the economic resources of recipient countries, Moscow turned against the program and pressured the satellites to follow suit. Thus, when the Marshall Plan went into effect in 1948, it was primarily a Western European enterprise, although it also extended to

Greece and Turkey. The venture proved remarkably effective. Between 1948 and 1951, the United States provided credits and goods to European countries amounting to over $12 billion. This infusion of aid greatly stimulated recovery. Industrial production in Western Europe soon equaled prewar levels and by 1951 had surpassed them by 41 percent. The Marshall Plan also laid the basis for Western European economic integration. It required the recipient countries to cooperate in solving mutual economic problems as a prerequisite for aid. This led to a series of joint economic ventures that resulted in the establishment of the European Economic Community (EEC) or Common Market in 1957. Since then the member nations have moved steadily toward both economic and political integration, culminating in the Maastricht Treaty of 1992, which created the European Union, and the introduction of a common currency, the euro, in 2002.

The Cold War

The expansion of Soviet domination in Eastern Europe and the American response in bolstering Greece, Turkey, and Western Europe divided the continent into rival power blocs. The increased tension between them became known as the Cold War. Both the Soviet Union and the United States contributed to the process.

It is not surprising that the growth of Soviet control in Eastern Europe inspired concern in the West, especially the brusque manner in which this took place. But it is also not surprising that the Soviets were determined to regain the territory they had taken from Finland, the Baltic states, Poland, and Rumania during 1939–40, all of which had belonged to the Russian Empire before World War I. Stalin had repeatedly insisted on this while the war raged. And it is understandable that he desired Communist governments in Poland, Rumania, and Bulgaria. Both Poland and Rumania had been hostile to the Soviet Union throughout the interwar years. Rumania had also participated in the invasion of the USSR and had even helped itself, with German consent, to a slice of Soviet territory adjacent to Bessarabia. Bulgaria, though never actually declaring war against the Soviet Union, had joined the Axis. Stalin's original intentions toward Czechoslovakia and

Hungary are less clear. But local Communists took matters into their own hands and ruthlessly established their complete control.

Stalin believed that the USSR's sacrifices in the war against Germany, which were infinitely greater than those of the Western Allies, entitled it to a dominant position in Eastern Europe. It seemed to him that the Americans and British should realize this and not interfere. In return, he was willing to grant them a free hand in Western Europe and the Mediterranean. His attitude toward Greece was a graphic example of his belief in spheres of influence. There is no indication that he ever thought in terms of extending Soviet control into Western Europe. Certainly such an attempt would have resulted in war with America and Britain. The Soviets could hardly have benefited from a conflict against their former allies in the aftermath of the appalling struggle with Germany.

But the British and especially the Americans were not convinced that Stalin had no ambitions in Western Europe. They tended to view him as another Hitler bent on the subjugation of the entire continent. Again not surprisingly, they took measures to guard against this possibility. In the process, there appears little doubt that they overreacted to the perceived menace.

The Cold War in its early stages focused above all on Germany. According to the wartime and immediate postwar agreements, the Soviets and the Western Allies divided Germany into occupation zones. They also divided Berlin, but the German capital lay deep within the Soviet zone, making Western access dependent on Soviet cooperation. Supposedly all four occupying powers were to cooperate on matters of mutual concern, including the drafting of a peace treaty that would determine Germany's permanent fate. But there proved to be little cooperation, except on such obvious issues as disarmament, punishment of war criminals, and elimination of Nazi influence.

The question of reparations proved particularly thorny. The USSR insisted on extensive reparations to compensate for wartime losses and to help rebuild the Soviet economy. The Western Powers considered these demands excessive. Stalin looked on the Western attitude as hostile and simply decided to take whatever he considered necessary from within the Soviet zone. This involved dismantling German factories and shipping machinery to

the Soviet Union as well as exploitation of other German resources. The Soviets treated their zone as a self-contained economic unit. Britain, the United States, and France also disagreed with the Soviets on the type of German government that should emerge from the period of occupation. They desired a Western-style democracy with a capitalistic economy. The Soviets wanted a Germany in which Communist influence would be strong.

A number of conferences involving the foreign ministers of the occupying powers failed to resolve any of the major issues. By late 1946, the British and Americans abandoned all hope of cooperation with the Soviets and merged their zones under one administration. They also began to strengthen the western German economy. In March 1948, they pressured the French to merge their zone and announced the intention to create a federal government for all of West Germany. Preparations began for an assembly that would draft a constitution for the proposed state. In June, the Western Powers introduced a new West German currency. The Soviets objected strenuously to these actions by cutting off Western rail and highway access to Berlin through the Soviet zone. The Western Powers resorted to an airlift of supplies by hundreds of cargo planes, which carried thousands of tons of supplies into Berlin every day.

The Berlin blockade lasted for almost a year, but in May 1949, the Soviets admitted defeat by restoring Western land access to Berlin. The lengthy crisis represented the first serious confrontation between East and West in the Cold War and symbolized a hardening of positions on both sides. A West German state came into existence in May 1949, and the Soviets responded by creating a Communist East German republic in their zone. These actions confirmed the division of Germany.

Another symbol of the Cold War came into being while the Berlin blockade was still in effect. This was the North Atlantic Treaty Organization (NATO), a collective security alliance under American leadership aimed at defending Western Europe against a possible Soviet attack. Most of the Western European nations joined, as did Canada. The question of West German membership in NATO soon became the subject of strenuous debate. Clearly the new German state would greatly strengthen the alliance, but European NATO members, especially France, feared a rearmed Germany. Despite this

concern, West Germany became a member of
NATO in 1955 and received the right to develop an
army, which became part of the alliance's military
force. The USSR responded to West Germany's
admission by creating the Warsaw Pact later in
1955. This was the Eastern European counterpart
to NATO and included East Germany.

The descent into the Cold War became even
more ominous when the Soviets tested an atomic
bomb in 1949 and began to develop a nuclear
arsenal. In the years that followed, the two sides
entered into an arms race that eventually featured intercontinental ballistic missiles armed
with nuclear warheads. These sinister weapons
increased alarmingly, not only in number but also
in striking power. The Hiroshima atomic bomb,
the equivalent of 20,000 tons or 20 kilotons (KT),
of TNT had shocked the world in 1945. But by
1954, the United States had tested a hydrogen
bomb with the force of 20 million tons or 20
megatons (MT) of TNT. It also became painfully
clear that fallout in the form of radioactive dust
from these weapons could contaminate the entire
globe, posing the prospect of a war without win-
ners or even survivors.

The Spread of Democracy

Although Western observers in the postwar era
tended to focus their attention on the triumph of
communism in Eastern Europe, democracy also
scored impressive victories in countries that had
experienced dictatorship during the interwar and
wartime years. The horrible examples of fascism
in Italy and Nazism in Germany helped convince
many people in both countries that there were far
worse things than democracy. Despite their earlier
lack of success with such governments, this time
both countries made their new democratic systems work. Austria, too, overcame the legacy of
the Dollfuss-Schuschnigg dictatorship and Nazi
rule and fashioned a viable democracy.

The war also led to the establishment of a
new world peacekeeping organization, the United
Nations. To a large extent, President Roosevelt had
provided its inspiration. Similar in many respects
to the ill-fated League of Nations, the UN suffered
from many of the same shortcomings. Except in
unusual cases, it could take no action that either of
the superpowers opposed. On the rare occasions

when the United States and the USSR reached
agreement on substantive issues, they usually did
so outside the United Nations. But within its
limitations, the organization performed useful
work, especially in attempting to mediate disputes
between lesser powers.

While the Cold War was taking shape in
Europe, dramatic changes also occurred in Asia.
Japan followed Germany and Italy into the ranks
of the democratic powers under the tutelage of the
United States and, specifically, General MacArthur
in his capacity as Allied supreme commander. The
United States, which had played the major role in
the Pacific war, had no intention of sharing the
occupation of Japan with any other power. To be
sure, the Americans agreed to the establishment of
a four-power control council, but MacArthur actually governed the country. The general's first task
in converting Japan into a democracy was to
transform the emperor from a god to a constitutional monarch, and he persuaded Hirohito to
renounce his supposed divine origin. In April
1946, MacArthur authorized elections for a constituent assembly, which drafted a new constitution. This document did not meet with his approval,
however, so he issued his own version, which the
assembly dutifully ratified.

Parliamentary elections took place in 1947, and a
Japanese government came into being shortly thereafter. Its decisions remained subject to MacArthur's
veto until the occupation ended in 1951. Although
the new democracy contained elements borrowed
from the American constitution, it bore a greater
resemblance to the British system, which was more
in keeping with earlier Japanese parliamentary institutions. The constitution renounced Japan's right to
make war or maintain armed forces. (In later years,
the Japanese did agree to cooperate with the United
States by establishing a small military force for their
own defense.) MacArthur and his staff also presided
over an ambitious land reform program that granted
the former hard-pressed tenant farmers ownership
of their land.

Japan's empire was a casualty of the war. In
addition to the loss of the Kurile Islands and
southern Sakhalin to the USSR, Japan returned
Manchuria and Formosa to China and relinquished
control of Korea. The United States received the
Mariana, Caroline, and Marshall islands as trust
territories under United Nations supervision.

FIGURE A-1   The grim specter of the nuclear mushroom cloud haunted the postwar world. *(U.S. Air Force)*

Civil War in China

Change also came to China, but in a more violent way. Soon after the war, the old animosities between the Kuomintang and the Communists erupted once again in civil war. This time the Communists were in a much stronger position. They held extensive territory in the north, especially Manchuria, and their armies also operated in much of the countryside to the south. But they received little support from the Soviets. Stalin's association with Mao Tse-tung, the Chinese Communist leader, had never been close, and he disliked Mao's independent attitude. For the time being, he continued to recognize Chiang's regime and cooperated with the American airlift of Kuomintang troops, which had taken over the cities of Manchuria following Japan's surrender. However, he did nothing to prevent the Communists from acquiring Japanese war materiel.

Although the United States supplied arms and military advisers to Chiang, there was little it could do to prevent erosion of the Kuomintang position. Chiang tried to hold Manchuria after Soviet troops pulled out in 1946. But the Communists controlled the countryside and were able to

recruit large numbers of peasants for their army, which fought with considerable enthusiasm. Chiang's own forces suffered from poor leadership and low morale, and the corrupt and inefficient Kuomintang regime failed to capture the allegiance of the masses. The Communists had conquered most of Manchuria by the spring of 1947 and possessed much of China north of the Yangtze River by the summer of 1948. They overran the remainder of the mainland during 1949, and Chiang withdrew to Formosa, accompanied by his best troops.

As was so often the case with China, a great deal of misinformation circulated in the United States. Much of it was due to propaganda by the "China lobby" as well as by Republican leaders, who charged that President Truman and his Democratic administration had betrayed China. In reality, nothing could have saved Chiang's decadent regime. Most Americans also believed that the Communist victory had been due primarily to Soviet aid, but actually Stalin had hedged his bets until the last moment and had provided no direct support to Mao's forces. He did not even recognize the Communist regime until it had proclaimed itself as the People's Republic of China in October 1949. And although the Soviets did provide military aid to the Communists after that, relations remained cool. Mao resented the cautious Soviet attitude, while Stalin viewed the Chinese leader as a rival.

The Communists lacked the naval strength to carry out an invasion of Formosa. Instead, Chiang was able to maintain his dictatorial power over the island and with it the myth that somehow in the future he might be able to regain control over the mainland. Since the United States continued to recognize his regime as the legal government of China, this helped prevent the development of normal American relations with Communist China for many years.

Events in Korea Lead to War

The drama in China soon became intertwined with events in Korea, which adjoined Manchuria. When the war ended, American forces occupied Korea south of the 38th parallel while Soviet troops occupied the area to the north. Rival Korean regimes soon developed in each sector. In the south, Syngman Rhee, an authoritarian politician, headed a government dominated by conservative landowners, many of whom had cooperated with the Japanese. In the north, a Communist regime came into existence under the leadership of the guerrilla leader Kim Il-sung. Unlike the situation in China, the Soviets trained and equipped a North Korean army.

A Soviet-American commission considered the problem of reunifying the country but could reach no agreement. By 1949, Soviet and American troops had withdrawn, leaving the two Koreas to fend for themselves. Rhee's government became more dictatorial and unpopular as it imprisoned many of its liberal political opponents. In the north, the Communist regime confiscated the estates of the large landowners and distributed the land to the peasants.

On June 25, 1950, North Korean soldiers crossed the 38th parallel and drove rapidly southward, spearheaded by Soviet-provided T34 tanks and Yakovlev fighter-planes. Only the intervention of American troops, under United Nations authorization, prevented a Communist unification of the country. United Nations forces, under General MacArthur's command, clung to a perimeter around the port of Pusan on the southeastern coast. After substantial American reinforcements arrived, they took the offensive in September. MacArthur carried out a brilliant amphibious landing near Inchon, far to the northwest, that threatened to cut off the Communist troops near Pusan and forced them to retreat. Before the end of the month, American and South Korean forces had reached the 38th parallel. But instead of halting at the border, they pursued the enemy northward with the avowed intention of uniting all of Korea under Rhee's government. As they approached the Yalu River, which separated Korea from Manchuria, the Chinese Communists became alarmed by an American presence so close to their border. In late November, they launched a massive attack across the Yalu and sent the UN forces reeling back into South Korea. The war finally ended in a deadlock in July 1953, with the border between North and South fixed near the 38th parallel.

American leaders feared that the Communist invasion of South Korea might be the prelude to a similar operation by Russia against Western Europe. The decision to admit West Germany into NATO was a direct result of this concern. Events in Korea also led the United States to extend the protection of the 7th Fleet to Chiang's regime in Formosa. This action completed the reversal of an earlier policy that had stated that neither Formosa nor Korea was vital to American interests. The Korean conflict, in addition to confirming the permanent division of Korea, signified the extension of both the Cold War and the American policy of containment to East Asia. U.S. relations with the Soviet Union and Communist China had suffered a serious setback.

Withdrawal from Empire

Elsewhere in Asia, and in Africa and the Middle East, the war fatally weakened European imperialism and led to the collapse of the British, French, and Dutch empires. Japan's invasion of China

The Korean War, 1950–53

in 1937 and subsequent curtailment of Western economic influence there had started the process. The eventual Japanese defeat and the Communist victory in the civil war assured that neither the West nor Japan would ever again dominate China. Japan's seizure of French Indochina and conquest of the Dutch East Indies, Malaya, Singapore, and Burma also dealt a severe blow to European prestige. Even though the French, Dutch, and British restored their administrations over these possessions after the war, none of them was able to maintain control.

Britain withdrew from India in 1948 after presiding over the partitioning of the country into two independent states—India and Pakistan. The Netherlands left the East Indies and recognized the new nation of Indonesia in 1949. France abandoned Indochina in 1954 after failing to defeat Communist guerrilla forces in a prolonged conflict. Even American military intervention in the following years could not prevent the consolidation of three Communist states—Vietnam, Laos, and Cambodia—in the former French colony.

France found it impossible to maintain power in its North African possessions. Morocco and Tunisia both gained independence in 1956, and Algeria followed suit in 1962 after eight years of brutal warfare with the French. By 1960, the last of France's sub-Saharan colonies became independent as well. Britain also gradually relinquished control over its various African possessions during the 1950s and '60s, and Belgium withdrew from the Congo in 1960. Unfortunately, the future of these new states was often marked by poverty, disease, government repression, and civil strife.

In the Middle East, France begrudgingly withdrew from Syria and Lebanon in 1946, and Britain recognized Jordan's independence the same year. But the thorniest problem of all pertained to Palestine, where roughly 1,300,000 Arabs and about 600,000 Jews co-existed. The Zionist movement had long sought the establishment of a Jewish state in Palestine, and, in the wake of the of the Holocaust, accelerated its agitation in hope of creating a homeland for Europe's surviving one million Jews, some of whom were immigrating illegally into Palestine. Palestinian Arabs opposed all of this and gained the support of the Arab League, composed of various Arab states. Britain, caught in the middle and plagued by its postwar

economic distress, announced its intention to end its mandate in Palestine and, with American support, turned to the UN for a solution to the dilemma. In late 1947, the UN opted for partition of Palestine into two states—one Arab, the other Jewish. The Arab League rejected this and chose to settle the matter by force. Fighting persisted off and on until an armistice was finally signed in early 1949. Thus was born the new state of Israel, which had actually gained territory during the war. Some 900,000 Palestinian Arabs had become refugees in bordering Arab states. Despite the armistice, the Arab League refused to recognize the existence of Israel and demanded repatriation of the refugees. After three more wars in the following decades, Egypt and Jordan came to terms with the Israelis, but other Arab states did not. Arab bitterness toward the United States, which had supported the Jewish cause, also lingered. As the years passed, this volatile situation became intertwined with growing Western dependence on Middle Eastern oil as well as the rise of extremist Muslim fundamentalism and terrorism.

The End of the Cold War and Beyond

For many years the Cold War between Russia and the West appeared likely to continue without end, as did the superpower status of both the USSR and the United States. But the Cold War experienced a thaw following the death of Stalin in 1953. And though this process ebbed and flowed in the following decades, it came to a dramatically unexpected end during the late '80s and early '90s with the internal collapse of the Soviet Union and the disintegration of its dominant position in Eastern Europe. Behind its seemingly powerful facade, the Soviet state suffered from economic stagnation, while its bloated military forces devoured a huge portion of the country's resources, and the inefficient, corrupt and unpopular regime, saddled by an enormous bureaucracy, proved incapable of solving its problems. When Mikail Gorbachev came to power in 1985, he tried to restructure the government and the economy and relaxed Soviet control over Eastern Europe. But his reforms led to a chain reaction of events both in Russia and the satellite states. By 1991, the Soviet Union as such no longer existed, the satellites as well as the non-Russian republics had become independent, and Russia's days as a superpower had ended.

The position of the United States also deteriorated. Although remaining the world's leading military power, its postwar economic domination proved relatively short-lived. It faced increasingly powerful competition from Japan, Western Europe, and more recently from China, India, and other Asian countries. The U. S. trade deficit mounted alarmingly, and the value of the dollar, once the world's premier currency, plunged. In addition, the rise of extremist Islamic fundamentalism has posed a threat not even envisioned when the Allies celebrated their victory in 1945. America and, to a lesser extent, its allies, now must wage a struggle against terrorism that is far different from the one they fought in World War II. It is one without the traditional battle lines that characterized earlier conflicts and features an enemy that is often unseen, highly difficult to combat, and more than willing to die for its beliefs. Hopefully, it ultimately will prove as successful as the one waged against the aggression of Nazi Germany and Imperial Japan.

Additional Reading

General

Bennett, Ralph, *Ultra in the West* (London: Hutchinson. 1979).

Butler, J. R., Gwyner,. J. M. A., Ehrman, John, and Howard, Michael, *Grand Strategy* (London: HMSO, 1956–1972).

Churchill, Winston, *History of the Second World War,* 6 vols. (Boston: Houghton Mifflin, 1948–54).

Calvocoressi, Peter, and Wint, Guy, *Total War* (London: Penguin, 1972).

Wesley Frank, and Cate, James Lea, eds. *Army Air Forces in World War II,* 7 vols. (Chicago: Chicago University Press, 1948–55).

Drea, Edward J., *MacArthur's ULTRA: Code-breaking and the War Against Japan* (Lawrence: KS: University of Kansas Press, 1992).

Greenfield, Kent Roberts, and Conn, Stetson, eds., *The United States Army in World War II,* 75 vols. (Washington: Government Printing Office, 1944–1981).

Keegan, John, *The Second World War* (New York: Viking, 1989).

Lewin, Ronald, *American Magic: Codes, Ciphers, and the Defeat of Japan* (New York: Farrar, Straus, and Giroux, 1982).

———, *Ultra Goes to War* (London: Hutchinson, 1978).

Liddell Hart, B. H. *History of the Second World War* (New York: Putnam, 1971).

Morrison, Samuel Eliot, *History of the United States Naval Operations in World War II,* 15 vols. (Boston: Little Brown, 1947–1962).

Murray, Williamson, and Millett, Allan R., *A War to Be Won: Fighting in the Second World War* (Cambridge: Harvard University Press, 2000).

Overy, Richard, *Why the Allies Won* (New York: Norton, 1995).

Roskill, S. W., *The War at Sea, 1939–1945* (London: HMSO, 1954–61).

Webster, Sir Charles, and Frankland, Noble, *The Strategic Air Offensive Against Germany, 1939–1945* (London: HMSO, 1961).

Weinberg, Gerhard L., *A World at Arms: A Global History of World War II* (Cambridge: University Press, 1994).

Chapter 1: World War I: The Great Turning Point

Albertini, Luigi, *Origins of the War of 1914,* 3 vols. (New York: Oxford University Press, 1952–57).

Beckett, Ian F. W., *The Great War, 1914–1918* (Harlow: Longman, 2001).

Fischer, Fritz, *Germany's Aims in the First World War* (New York: Norton, 1967).

Gilbert, Martin, *The First World War: A Complete History* (New York: Henry Holt, 1994).

Keegan, John, *The First World War* (New York: Knopf, 1999).

Kramer, Alan, *Culture and Mass Killing in the First World War* (Oxford: Oxford University Press, 2007).

Lyons, Michael J. *World War II: A Short History* (Englewood Cliffs, N. J.: Prentice Hall, 2004).

Ritter, Gerhard, *The Sword and the Scepter,* 4 vols. (Princeton Junction, N. J.: Scholar's Bookshelf, 1970–88).

Schmitt, Bernadotte, and Vedeler, Harold, *The World in the Crucible, 1914–1919* (New York: Harper & Row, 1984).

Chapter 2: The Legacy of World War I

Bessel, Richard, *Germany after the First World War* (Oxford: Oxford University Press, 1993).

Boemke, Manfred F., Feldman, Gerald D., and Glazer-Schmidt, Elizabeth, eds., *The Treaty of Versailles: A Reassessment After 75 Years* (Cambridge: Cambridge University Press, 1998).

Cohen, Warren I., *America's Response to China: An Interpretive History of Sino-American Relations* (New York: Wiley, 1971).

Duus, Peter, Meyers, Ramon H., and Peattie, Mark R., eds., *The Japanese Informal Empire in China, 1895–1937* (Princeton: Princeton University Press, 1989).

Iriye, Akira, *The Origins of the Second World War: Asia and the Pacific* (London: Longman, 1987).

Keynes, John Maynard, *The Economic Consequences of the Peace* (New York: Harcourt, Brace, 1920).

Kleine-Albrandt, W. Laird, *The Burden of Victory: France, Britain, and the Enforcement of the Versailles Peace, 1919–1925* (Lanham. Md.: University Press of America, 1995).

MacMillan, Margaret, *Paris 1919: Six Months That Changed the World* (New York: Random House, 2002).

Marks, Sally, *The Illusion of Peace: International Relations in Europe, 1918–1933* (London: St. Martin's, 1976).

Moore, Sara, *Peace Without Victory for the Allies, 1918–1932* (New York: Berg, 1994).

Offner, Arnold A., *The Origins of the Second World War: American Foreign Policy and World Politics, 1917–1941* (New York: Praeger, 1975).

Sharp, Alan, *The Versailles Settlement: Peacemaking in Paris, 1919* (London: Macmillan, 1991).

Trachtenberg, Marc, *Reparations and World Politics* (New York: Columbia University Press, 1980).

Chapter 3: The Rise of the Dictators

Arendt, Hannah, *The Origins of Totalitarianism* (New York: Harcourt, Brace & World, 1966).

Binion, Rudolph, *Hitler among the Germans* (New York: Elsevier, 1976).

Bix, Herbert, *Hirohito and the Making of Modern Japan* (New York: Harper Collins, 2000).

Bracher, Karl Dietrich, *The German Dictatorship* (New York: Praeger, 1970).

Brozat, Martin, *The Hitler State* (London: Longman, 1981).

Burleigh, Michael, *The Third Reich: A New History* (New York: Hill and Wang, 2000).

Bullock, Alan, *Hitler: A Study in Tyranny* (New York: Harper & Row, 1964).

Carr, Edward H., *A History of the Soviet Union,* 7 vols. (New York: Macmillan, 1950–71).

Cassels, Alan, *Fascism* (Arlington Heights, Ill.: AHM Publishing, 1975).

Chamberlain, William Henry, *The Russian Revolution, 1917–1920,* 2 vols. (New York: Grosset & Dunlop, 1935).

De Felice, Renzo, *Interpretations of Fascism* (Cambridge: Harvard University Press, 1977).

Drea, Edward J, *In the Service of the Emperor: Essays on the Imperial Japanese Army* (Lincoln: University of Nebraska Press, 1998).

Friedrich, Carl J., and Brzezinski, Zbigniew, *Totalitarian Dictatorship and Autocracy* (New York: Oxford University Press, 1966).

Gentile, Emilio, *The Origins of Fascist Ideology, 1918–1925* (New York: Enigma Books, 2005).

Hitler, Adolf, *Hitler's Secret Book* (New York: Grove Press, 1958).

_____, *Mein Kampf* (London: Hurst and Blackett, 1938).

Iriye, Akira, *After Imperialism: The Search for a New Order in the Far East, 1921–1931* (Cambridge: Harvard University Press, 1963).

Jansen, Marius B., *The Making of Modern Japan* (Cambridge: Harvard University Press, 2000).

Kershaw, Ian, *Hitler,* 2 vols. (New York: Norton, 1998–2000).

_____, and Lewin, Moshe, eds., *Stalinism and Nazism: Dictatorships in Comparison* (Cambridge: Cambridge University Press, 1997).

Mack Smith, Denis, *Mussolini* (London: Weidenfeld & Nicolson, 1981).

Minichiello, Sharon, *Retreat from Reform: Patterns of Political Behavior in Interwar Japan* (Honolulu: University of Hawaii Press, 1984).

Morgan, Philip, *Italian Fascism, 1919–1943* (New York: St. Martin's, 1995).

Overy, Richard, *The Dictators: Hitler's Germany, Stalin's Russia* (London: Allen Lane, 2004).

Stern, J. P., *Hitler: Führer and People* (Berkeley: University of California Press, 1974).

Ulam, Adam, *The Bolsheviks* (New York: Collier Books, 1965).

_____, *Stalin: The Man and His Era* (New York: Viking, 1973).

Waite, Robert, *The Psychopathic God: Adolf Hitler* (New York: New American Library, 1977).

Chapter 4: The Road to War

Alpert, Michael, *A New International History of the Spanish Civil War* (New York: St. Martin's, 1994).

Baer, G. W., *Test Case: Italy, Ethiopia and the League of Nations* (Stanford, Calif.: Hoover Institute Press, 1977).

Bell, P. M. H., *The Origins of the Second World War in Europe* (London: Longman, 1986).

Boyle, J. H., *China and Japan at War, 1937–1945* (Stanford, Calif.: Stanford University Press, 1972).

Brooke-Shephard, Gordon, *Anschluss: The Rape of Austria* (London: Macmillan, 1963).

Burgwyn, James H., *Italian Foreign Policy and War in the Interwar Period, 1918–1940* (Westport, Conn.: Praeger, 1997).

Carley, Michael Jabara, *1939: The Alliance That Never Was and the Coming of World War II* (Chicago: Ivan R. Dee, 1999).

Chang, Iris, *The Rape of Nanking: The Forgotten Holocaust of World War II* (New York: Basic Books, 1997).

Crozier, *The Causes of the Second World War* (Oxford: Oxford University Press, 1997).

Emmerson, J. T., *The Rhineland Crisis, 7 March 1936* (Ames, Ia.: Iowa State University Press, 1977).

Haslam, Jonathan, *The Soviet Union and the Struggle for Collective Security in Europe, 1933–1939* (New York: St. Martin's, 1984).

Hildebrand, Klaus, *The Foreign Policy of the Third Reich* (Berkeley: University of California Press, 1984).

Hochman, Jiri, *The Soviet Union and the Failure of Collective Security* (Ithaca: Cornell University Press, 1984).

Jackel, Eberhard, *Hitler's World View: A Blueprint for Power* (Cambridge: Harvard University Press, 1981).

Knox, MacGregor *Common Destiny: Dictatorship, Foreign Policy, and War in Fascist Italy and Nazi Germany* (Cambridge: Cambridge University Press, 2000).

Mack Smith, Denis, *Mussolini's Roman Empire* (New York: Viking, 1976).

McDonough, Frank, *Neville Chamberlain, Appeasement and the British Road to War* (Manchester: Manchester University Press, 1984).

Morley, James, ed. *China Quagmire* (New York: Columbia University Press, 1983).

———, ed., *Japan Erupts: The London Naval Conference and the Manchurian Incident, 1928–1932* (New York: Columbia University Press, 1984).

Parker, R.A.C., *Chamberlain and Appeasement: British Foreign Policy and the Coming of the Second World War* (New York: St. Martin's, 1993).

Rich, Norman, *Hitler's War Aims: Ideology, the Nazi State and the Course of Expansion* (New York: Norton, 1973).

Rothwell, Victor, *Origins of the Second World War* (Manchester: Manchester University Press, 2001).

Taylor, A.J.P., *The Origins of the Second World War* (New York: Atheneum, 1961).

Weinberg, Gerhard L., *The Foreign Policy of Hitler's Germany*, 2 vols. (Chicago: University of Chicago Press, 1970–80).

Youli, Sun, *China and the Origins of the Pacific War, 1931–1941* (New York: St. Martin's, 1993).

Chapter 5: *Blitzkrieg* in the East, *Sitzkrieg* in the West

Bethell, Nicholas, *The War Hitler Won: The Fall of Poland* (New York: Holt, Rinehart and Winston, 1972).

Bond, Brian, *Liddell Hart: A Study of His Military Thought* (London: Cassell, 1977).

Carroll, Bernice A., *Design for Total War: Arms and Economics of the Third Reich* (The Hague: Mouton, 1968).

Guderian, Heinz, *Panzer Leader* (New York: Da Capo, 1996).

Halder, Franz, *The Halder War Diary, 1939–1945* (Navato, Calif.: Presidio Press, 1988).

Kennedy, Robert M., *The German Campaign in Poland, 1939* (Washington: Department of the Army, 1956).

Manstein, Erich von, *Lost Victories* (Chicago: Henry Regner, 1958).

Milward, A.S., *The German Economy at War* (London: Athlone Press, 1965).

Reid, Brian Holden, *J.F.C. Fuller: Military Thinker* (New York: St. Martin's, 1988).

Chapter 6: Complications in the North: Finland, Denmark, Norway

Ash, Bernard, *Norway, 1940* (London: Cassell, 1964).

Dildy, Doug, *Denmark and Norway, 1940: Hitler's Boldest Decision* (Oxford: Osprey, 2007).

Kersaudy, Francois, *Norway, 1940* (Lincoln: University of Nebraska Press, 1998).

Mannerheim, Karl von, *Memoirs* (New York: Dutton, 1954).

Moulton, J.L., *A Study of Warfare in Three Dimensions: The Norwegian Campaign of 1940* (Athens, Ohio: The Ohio University Press, 1967).

Tanner, V.A., *The Winter War: Finland against Russia, 1939–1940* (Stanford, Calif.: Stanford University Press, 1957).

Van Dyke, Carl, *The Soviet Invasion of Finland, 1939–40* (London: Cass, 1997).

Ziemke, E.F., *The German Northern Theater of Operations, 1940–1945* (Washington: Department of the Army, 1959).

Chapter 7: The Fall of France

Chapman, Guy, *Why France Fell: The Defeat of the French Army in 1940* (New York: Holt, Rinehart and Winston, 1968).

Doughty, Robert A., *The Seeds of Disaster: The Development of French Army Doctrine, 1919–1939* (Hamden, Conn.: Archon, 1986).

———, *The Breaking Point: Sedan and the Fall of France, 1940* (Hamden, Conn.: Archon, 1990).

Gelb, Norman, *Dunkirk: The Complete Story of the First Step in the Defeat of Hitler* (New York: Morrow, 1989).

Gunsberg, Jeffrey A., *Divided and Conquered: The French High Command and the Defeat of the West, 1940* (Westport, Conn.: Greenwood Press, 1979).

Horne, Alistair, *To Lose a Battle: France, 1940* (London: Macmillan, 1969).

Kirkland, Faris R., "The French Air Force in 1940: Was It Defeated by the Luftwaffe or by Politics?" *Air University Review* (September–October 1985).

May, Ernest B., *Strange Victory: Hitler's Conquest of France, 1940* (New York: Hill and Wang, 2000).

Shennan, Andrew, *The Fall of France, 1940* (London: Longman, 2000).

Shepperd, Alan, *France 1940: Blitzkrieg in the West* (Westport, Conn.: Praeger, 2004).

Taylor, Telford, *The March of Conquest: The German Victories in Western Europe, 1940* (New York: Simon & Schuster, 1958).

Chapter 8: Britain Is Still an Island

Ansel, Walter, *Hitler Confronts England* (Durham, N.C.: Duke University Press, 1960).

Churchill, Randolph S., and Martin, Gilbert, *The Life of Winston Churchill,* 8 vols. (Boston: Houghton Mifflin, 1966–86).

Dempster, Derek, and Wood, Derek, *The Narrow Margin: The Battle of Britain and the Rise of Airpower, 1939–1940* (London: Hutchinson, 1961).

Dobinson, Colin, *AA Command: Britain's Anti-Aircraft Defences of World War II* (London: Methuen, 2001).

Fleming, Peter, *Operation Sea Lion* (New York: Simon & Schuster, 1957)

Parkinson, Roger, *Summer, 1940: The Battle of Britain* (New York: David McKay, 1977).

Ray, John, *The Battle of Britain: New Perspectives* (London: Arms and Armour, 1994).

Taylor, Telford, *The Breaking Wave* (New York: Simon & Schuster, 1967).

Terraine, John, *A Time for Courage: The Royal Air Force in the European War, 1939–1945* (New York: Macmillan, 1985).

Wright, Robert, *Dowding and the Battle of Britain* (London: MacDonald, 1969).

Chapter 9: The Plot Thickens: The Mediterranean and the Balkans

Cervi, Mario, *The Hollow Legions: Mussolini's Blunder in Greece, 1940–1941* (Garden City, N.Y.: Doubleday, 1971).

Ciano, Galeazzo, *The Ciano Diaries, 1939–1943* (Garden City, N.Y.: Doubleday, 1946).

Connell, John, *Wavell: Scholar and Soldier* (London: Collins, 1964).

Cruikshank, Charles, *Greece, 1940–1941* (London: Davis-Pointer, 1976).

Forty, George, *Battle of Crete* (London: Allan, 2001).

Fraser, David, *Knight's Cross: A Life of Marshal Erwin Rommel* (London: Harper & Collins, 1993).

Knox, MacGregor, *Hitler's Italian Allies: Royal Armed Forces, Fascist Regime, and the War of 1940–43* (Cambridge: Cambridge University Press, 2000).

Mitchum, Samuel W., *Triumphant Fox: Erwin Rommel and the Rise of the Afrika Korps* (New York: Cooper Square/National Book Network, 2000).

Pitt, Barrie, *The Crucible of War: Western Desert, 1941* (London: Jonathan Cape, 1980).

Puzzo, Dante A., *Spain and the Great Powers, 1936–1941* (New York: Columbia University Press, 1962).

Schreiber, Gerhard, Stegemann, Berndt, and Vogel, Detlef, *The Mediterranean, South-East Europe, and North Africa, 1939–1941* (Oxford: Clarendon Press, 1995).

Van Creveld, Martin, *Hitler's Strategy: The Balkan Clue, 1940–1941* (Cambridge: Cambridge University Press, 1973).

Warner, Geoffrey, *Iraq and Syria, 1941* (Newark, Del.: University of Delaware Press, 1976).

Chapter 10: Operation Barbarossa: Dream of *Lebensraum*

Bartov, Omer, *Hitler's Army: Soldiers, Nazis and War in the Third Reich* (Oxford: Oxford University Press, 1992).

Bellamy, Chris, *Absolute War: Soviet Russia in the Second World War* (New York: Knopf, 2007).

Clark, Alan, *Barbarossa: The Russian-German Conflict, 1941–1945* (London: Weidenfeld, 1995).

Erickson, John, *The Soviet High Command: A Military-Political History, 1918–1941* (London: Macmillan, 1962).

———, and Dilks, David, eds., *Barbarossa: The Axis and the Allies* (Edinburgh: Edinburgh University Press, 1994).

Glanz, David, *Stumbling Colossus: The Red Army on the Eve of War* (Lawrence: University of Kansas Press, 1988).

———, *Barbarossa: Hitler's Invasion of Russia, 1941* (Charleston, S.C.: Tempus, 2004).

———, and House, Jonathan M., *When Titans Clashed: How the Red Army Stopped Hitler* (Lawrence: University of Kansas Press, 1995).

———, *The Siege of Leningrad, 1941–1944: 900 Days of Terror* (London: Spellmount, 2001).

Gorodetsky, Gabriel, *The Grand Delusion: Stalin and the German Invasion of Russia* (New Haven: Yale University Press, 1999).

Megargee, Geoffrey P., *War of Annihilation: Combat and Genocide on the Eastern Front* (Lanham, Md.: Rowman & Littlefield, 2005).

Overy, Richard, *Russia's War: Blood and Snow* (New York: TV Books, 1997).

Suvurov, Viktor, *Icebreaker: Who Started the Second World War?* (London: Hamish Hamilton, 1990).

Van Creveld, Martin, *Supplying War* (Cambridge: Cambridge University Press, 1977).

Whymant, Robert, *Stalin's Spy: Richard Sorge and the Tokyo Espionage Ring* (London: I.B. Tauris, 1996).

Chapter 11: Hitler's New Order in Europe

Arad, Yitzak, Belzec, Sobibor, *Treblinka: The Operation Reinhard Death Camps* (Bloomington: Indiana University Press, 1987).

Bankier, David, *The Germans and the Final Solution: Public Opinion Under Nazism* (Oxford: Blackwood, 1992).

_____, and Gutman, Israel, eds., *Nazi Europe and the Final Solution* (New York: Berghahn Books, 2008).

Bauer, Yehuda, *Rethinking the Holocaust* (New Haven: Yale University Press, 2001).

Bennett, Rab, *Under the Shadow of the Swastika: The Moral Dilemma of Resistance and Collaboration in Hitler's Europe* (New York: New York University Press, 1999).

Blood, Phillip, *Hitler's Bandit Hunters: The SS and the Nazi Occupation of Europe* (Washington: Potomac Books, 2006).

Browning, Christopher, *Ordinary Men: Reserve Police Battalion 101 and the Final Solution in Poland* (New York: Harper Collins, 1992).

Burrin, Philippe, *France Under the Germans: Collaboration and Compromise* (New York: The New Press, 1996).

Cesarani, David, *Becoming Eichmann: Rethinking the Life, Crimes, and Trial of a "Desk Murderer"* (Cambridge, Mass.: DaCapo Press, 2006).

Dallin, Alexander, *German Rule in Russia, 1941–1945* (London: Macmillan, 1975).

Dawidovicz, Lucy, *The War against the Jews, 1933–1945* (New York: Holt, Rinehart and Winston, 1985).

Dederichs, Mario, *Heydrich: The Face of Evil* (London: Greenhill Press, 2006).

Fleming, Gerald, *Hitler and the Final Solution* (Berkeley: University of California Press, 1984).

Goldhagen, Jonah, *Hitler's Willing Executioners: Ordinary Germans and the Holocaust* (New York: Knopf, 1996).

Gutman, Yisrael, and Berenbaum, Michael, *Anatomy of the Auschwitz Death Camp* (Washington: United States Holocaust Museum, 1994).

Hilberg, Raul, *The Destruction of the European Jews, 1933–1945* (New York: Holmes & Meier, 1985).

Homze, Edward J., *Foreign Labor in Nazi Germany* (Princeton: Princeton University Press, 1967).

Jackson, Julian, *France: The Dark Years, 1940–1944* (Oxford: Oxford University Press, 2001).

Laquer, Walter, *The Terrible Secret: Suppression of the Truth about the Final Solution* (Boston: Little Brown, 1980).

Lukacs, Richard C., *The Forgotten Holocaust: The Poles under German Occupation, 1939–1945* (New York: Hippocrene Books, 1997).

Mastny, Vojtech, *The Czechs under Nazi Rule: The Failure of National Resistance, 1939–1942* (New York: Columbia University Press, 1971).

Mazower, Mark, *Inside Hitler's Greece: The Experience of Occupation, 1939–1944* (New Haven: Yale University Press, 1993).

Paxton, Robert O., *Vichy France* (New York: Knopf, 1972).

Petrow, Richard, *The Bitter Years: The Invasion and Occupation of Denmark and Norway, April 1940-May 1945* (New York: Norton, 1979).

Phayer, Michael, *The Catholic Church and the Holocaust, 1930–1965* (Bloomington: Indiana University Press, 2000).

Rich, Norman, *Hitler's War Aims: The Establishment of the New Order* (New York: Norton, 1973).

Ridley, Jasper, *Tito* (London: Constable, 1994).

Rossiter, Margaret L., *Women in the Resistance* (New York: Praeger, 1986).

Rubinstein, William, *The Myth of Rescue: Why the Democracies Could Not Have Saved More Jews from the Nazis* (New York: Routledge, 1986).

Stafford, David, *Britain and European Resistance* (London: Macmillan, 1980).

Tomasevich, Jozo, *War and Revolution in Yugoslavia, 1941–1945: Occupation and Collaboration* (Stanford: Stanford University Press, 2001).

Warmbrunn, Werner, *The Dutch under German Occupation* (Stanford: Stanford University Press, 1963).

_____, *The German Occupation of Belgium, 1940–1945* (New York: P. Lang, 1993).

Wyman, David S., *The Abandonment of the Jews: America and the Holocaust, 1941–1945* (New York: Pantheon Books, 1984).

Chapter 12: America Enters the War

Butow, Robert J. C., *Tojo and the Coming of the War* (Princeton: Princeton University Press, 1961).

Casey, Steven, *Cautious Crusade: Franklin D. Roosevelt, American Public Opinion, and the War against Nazi Germany* (New York: Oxford University Press, 2001).

Dallek, Robert A., *Franklin D. Roosevelt and American Policy, 1932–1945* (New York: Oxford University Press, 1979).

Doenecke, Justus D., *Storm on the Horizon: The Challenge of American Intervention, 1939–1941* (Lanham, Md.: Rowman & Littlefield, 2000).

Heinrichs, Waldo, *Threshold of War: Franklin D, Roosevelt and American Entry into World War II* (New York: Oxford University Press, 1988).

Kennedy, David M., *Freedom From Fear: The American People in Depression and War, 1929–1945* (New York: Oxford University Press, 1999).

Langer, William L., and Gleason, S. Everett, *The Challenge of Isolation, 1937–1940* (New York: Harper & Row, 1952).

_____, *The Undeclared War, 1949–1941* (New York: Harper & Row, 1953).

Layton, Edwin T., Pineau, Roger, and Costello, John, *"And I Was There": Pearl Harbor and Midway-Breaking the Secrets* (New York: Morrow, 1985).

Marshall, Jonathan, *To Have and Have Not: Southeast Asian Raw Materials and the Origins of the Pacific War* (Berkeley: University of California Press, 1995).

Prange, Gordon W., *At Dawn We Slept: The Untold Story of Pearl Harbor* (New York: McGraw-Hill, 1981).

_____, *Pearl Harbor: The Verdict of History* (New York: McGraw-Hill, 1986).

Reynolds, David, *From Munich to Pearl Harbor: Roosevelt's America and the Origins of World War II* (Chicago: I..R. Dee, 2001).

Sarles, Ruth, *A Story of America First: The Men and Women Who Opposed U.S. Intervention in World War II*, Bill Kauffman, ed. (New York: Praeger, 2003).

Smith, Michael, *The Emperor's Codes: The Breaking of Japan's Secret Ciphers* (New York: Little Brown, 2000).

Worth, Ronald H., *No Choice but War: The United States Embargo against Japan and the Eruption of War in the Pacific* (Jefferson, N.C.: McFarland, 1995).

Chapter 13: Japan Triumphant, December 1941–May 1942

Allen, Louis, *Burma: The Longest War, 1941–1945* (New York: St. Martin's, 1985).

_____, *Singapore, 1941–1942* (London: Cass, 1993).

Connaughton, Richard, *MacArthur and Defeat in the Philippines* (New York: Overlook Press, 2001).

Costello, John, *The Pacific War, 1941–1945* (New York: Rawson Wade, 1981).

Evans, Donald C., *The Japanese Navy in World War II* (Annapolis: Naval Institute Press, 1986).

Gailey, Harry A. *The War in the Pacific: From Pearl Harbor to Tokyo Bay* (Novato, Calif.: Presidio Press, 1995).

Harries, Meirion, and Harries, Susie, *Soldiers of the Sun: The Rise and Fall of the Japanese Imperial Army* (New York: Random House, 1991).

James, D. Clayton, *The Years of MacArthur*, 2 vols (New York: Houghton Mifflin, 1972–75).

Lundstrom, John, B., *The First South Pacific Campaign: December 1941–June 1942* (Annapolis: Naval Institute Press, 1976).

Petillo, Carol Morris, *Douglas MacArthur: The Philippine Years* (Bloomington: Indiana University Press, 1981).

Swinson, A. J., *Defeat in Malaya* (New York: Ballantine, 1970).

Willmott, H. P., *Empires in the Balance: The Japanese and Allied Strategies to April 1942* (Annapolis: Naval Institute Press, 1982).

Young, Donald J., *The Battle of Bataan* (Jefferson, N.C.: McFarland, 1992).

Chapter 14: Struggle for the Initiative in the Pacific

Bergerud, Eric M., *Fire in the Sky: The Air War in the South Pacific* (Boulder, Colo.: Westview Press, 2000).

Buell, Thomas B., *A Biography of Admiral Earnest J. King* (Boston: Little Brown, 1980).

_____, *The Quiet Warrior: A Biography of Admiral Raymond A. Spruance* (Boston: Little Brown, 1974).

Dower, John W., *War without Mercy: Race and Power in the Pacific War* (New York: Pantheon, 1986)

Dull, Paul S., *A Battle History of the Imperial Japanese Navy, 1941–1945* (Annapolis: Naval Institute Press, 1978).

Frank, Richard B., *Guadalcanal: The Definitive Account of the Landmark Battle* (New York: Random House, 1990).

Hiroyuki, Agawa, *The Reluctant Admiral: Yamamoto and the Imperial Navy* (Tokyo: Kodansha International, 1979).

Hoyt, Edwin Palmer, *Blue Skies and Blood: The Battle of the Coral Sea* (New York: Eriksson, 1975).

Iriye, Akira, *Power and Culture: The Japanese-American War, 1941–1945* (Cambridge: Harvard University Press, 1981).

Linderman, Gerald, *The World Within War: America's Combat Experience in World War II* (New York: Free Press, 1997).

Mayo, Lida, *Bloody Buna* (Garden City, N.Y.: Doubleday, 1975).

Parschall, Jonathan, and Tully, Anthony, *Shattered Sword: The Untold Story of the Battle of Midway* (Washington: Potomac Books, 2005).

Potter, E. B., *Bull Halsey* (Annapolis: Naval Institute Press, 1985).

_____, *Nimitz* (Annapolis: Naval Institute Press, 1976).

Prados, John, *Combined Fleet Decoded: The Secret History of American Intelligence and the Japanese Navy in World War II* (New York: Random House, 1995).

Prange, Gordon W., *Miracle at Midway* (New York: Penguin, 1982).

White, Geoffrey, M., and Lindstrom, Lamont, *The Pacific Theater: Island Representations of World War II* (Honolulu: Hawaii University Press, 1989).

Willmott, H. P., *The War With Japan: The Period of Balance, May 1942–October 1943* (Wilmington, Del.: Scholarly Resources, 2002).

Yamagouchi, Midori, and Quinn, Joseph L., *Listen to the Voices from the Sea* (Scranton. Pa.: University of Scranton Press, 2000).

Chapter 15: America Gains the Initiative in the Pacific

Alexander, Joseph H., *Utmost Savagery: The Three Days of Tarawa* (Annapolis: Naval Institute Press, 1995).

Belote, James and William, *Titans of the Seas: The Development and Operations of American Carrier Task Forces during World War II* (New York: Harper and Row, 1975).

Denfield, D. Colt, *Hold the Marianas: The Japanese Defense of the Mariana Islands* (Shippensburg, Pa.: White Mane, 1997).

Dunnigan, James F., *Victory at Sea: World War II in the Pacific* (New York: Morrow, 1995).

Garfield, Brian, *The Thousand-Mile War: World War II in Alaska and the Aleutians* (Fairbanks: University of Alaska Press, 1995).

Hayes, Grace P., *The Joint Chiefs of Staff and the War against Japan* (Annapolis: Naval Institute Press, 1982).

Koburger, Charles W., *Pacific Turning Point: The Solomons Campaign, 1942–1943* (Westport, Conn.: Praeger/Greenwood, 1995).

Lorelli, John A., *To Foreign Shores: U. S. Amphibious Operations in World War II* (Annapolis: Naval Institute Press, 1995).

Miller, John, *Cartwheel: The Reduction of Rabaul* (Washington: Office of the Chief of Military History, 1959).

Reynolds, Clark G., *The Fast Carriers: The Forging of an Air Navy* (New York: McGraw-Hill, 1968).

Spector, Roland A., *The Eagle against the Sun: The American War with Japan* (New York: Free Press, 1985).

Taffee, Stephen R., *MacArthur's Jungle War: The 1944 New Guinea Campaign* (Lawrence: University of Kansas Press, 1998).

Y'Blood, William T., *Red Sun Setting: The Battle of the Philippine Sea* (Annapolis: Naval Institute Press, 1980).

Chapter 16: The Tide Turns in Russia: Stalingrad and Beyond

Adair, Paul, *Hitler's Greatest Defeat: The Collapse of Army Group Centre, June 1944* (London: Arms & Armour, 1994).

Beevor, Anthony, *Stalingrad: The Fateful Siege, 1942–1943* (New York: Penguin Books, 1995).

Borowiec, Andrew, *Destroy Warsaw! Hitler's Punishment, Stalin's Revenge* (Westport, Conn.: Praeger, 2001).

Cross, Robin, *Citadel: The Battle of Kursk* (New York: Sharpendon, 1993).

Davies, Norman, *Rising, '44: The Battle for Warsaw* (London: Macmillan, 2003).

Erickson, John, *The Road to Stalingrad* (New York: Harper & Row, 1975).

_____, *The Road to Berlin* (Boulder, Colo.: Westview Press, 1983).

Glantz, David M., *Colossus Reborn: The Red Army at War, 1941–1943* (Lawrence: University of Kansas Press, 2005).

_____, *From the Don to the Dnepr: Soviet Operations, December 1942–August 1943* (London: Cass, 1991).

_____, and House, Jonathan M., *The Battle of Kursk* (Lawrence: University of Kansas Press, 1999).

Gorbachevsky, Boris, and Glantz, David M., *Through the Maelstrom: A Red Army Soldier's War on the Eastern Front* (Lawrence: University of Kansas Press, 2008).

Grenkevich, Leonid D., *The Soviet Partisan Movement, 1941–1944* (London: Cass, 1999).

Haywood, Joel S. A., *Stopped at Stalingrad: The Luftwaffe and Hitler's Defeat in the East, 1942–1943* (Lawrence: University of Kansas Press, 1998).

Herring, George, *Aid to Russia, 1941–1946: Strategy, Diplomacy, and the Origins of the Cold War* (New York: Columbia University Press, 1973).

Jukes, Geoffrey, *Hitler's Stalingrad Decisions* (Berkeley: University of California Press, 1985).

Mitchum, Samuel W., *The German Defeat in the East, 1944* (Westwood, Conn.: Praeger/Greenwood, 2001).

Muller, Rolf-Dieter, and Ueberschar, Gerd R., *Hitler's War in the East: A Critical Assessment* (Oxford: Berghan Books, 1995).

Rauss, Erhard, *The Anvil of War: German Generalship in Defense on the Eastern Front* (London: Greenhill, 1994).

Zawodny, J. K., *Death in the Forest: The Story of the Katyn Forest Massacre* (London: Macmillan, 1971).

Ziemke, Frederick, *Moscow to Stalingrad: Decisions in the East* (Washington: Center for Military History, 1987).

Chapter 17: The Tide Turns in North Africa: El Alamein to Tunisia

Alexander, Sir Harold, *The Alexander Memoirs* (London: Cassell, 1962).

Ambrose, Stephen E., *Eisenhower, Soldier, General of the Army, President-elect, 1890–1952* (New York: Simon & Schuster, 1983).

Bradley, Omar, and Blair, Clay, *A General's Life: An Autobiography* (New York: Simon & Schuster, 1983).

Carver, Michael, *Dilemmas of the Desert War: A New Look at the Libyan Campaign, 1940–1942* (Bloomington: Indiana University Press, 1986).

Chalfont, Alun, *Montgomery of Alamein* (New York: Atheneum, 1976).

Connell, John, *Auchileck* (London: Cassell, 1959).

D'Este, Carlo, *World War II in the Mediterranean, 1942–1945* (Chapel Hill, N. C.: Algonquin Books, 1990).

Edmonds, Robin, *The Big Three: Churchill, Roosevelt, and Stalin in Peace and War* (New York: Norton, 1991).

Eisenhower, Dwight D., *Crusade In Europe* (Garden City, N. Y.: Doubleday, 1948).

Feis, Herbert, *Churchill, Roosevelt, Stalin: The War They Waged and the Peace They Sought* (Princeton: Princeton University Press, 1967).

Kimball, Warren, *Forged in War: Roosevelt, Churchill, and the Second World War* (New York: Morrow, 1997).

Lewin, Ronald, *Rommel as Military Commander* (New York: Ballantine, 1970).

———, *Life and Death of the Afrika Korps* (London: Batsford, 1977).

Lucas, James, *War in the Desert: The Eighth Army at El Alamein* (New York: Beaufort Books, 1983).

MacDonald, Charles B., *Mighty Endeavor: The American War in Europe* (New York: Morrow, 1986).

Messenger, Charles, *The Tunisian Campaign* (London: Ian Allen, 1982).

Montgomery, Bernard, *Memoirs* (New York: Signet, 1959).

Patton, George S., *War as I Saw It* (Boston: Houghton Mifflin, 1947).

Perry, Mark, *Partners in Command: Dwight Eisenhower and George Marshall in War and Peace* (New York: Penguin, 2007).

Pogue, Forrest C., *George C. Marshall,* 3 vols. (New York: Penguin, 1964–73).

Reynolds, David, ed., *Allies at War: The Soviet, American, and British Experience, 1939–1945* (New York: St. Martin's, 1994).

Sainsbury, Keith, *The North African Landings, 1942* (Newark, Del.: University of Delaware Press, 1976).

Schowalter, Dennis, *Patton and Rommel: Men of War in the Twentieth Century* (New York: Berkley Caliber, 2005).

Stoler, Mark, *Allies and Adversaries: The Joint Chiefs of Staff, the Grand Alliance, and U. S. Strategy in World War II* (Chapel Hill: University of North Carolina Press, 2000).

Watson, Bruce, *Exit Rommel: The Tunisian Campaign, 1942–1943* (Westport, Conn.: Praeger, 1999).

Chapter 18: Probing the Underbelly: Sicily and Italy

Atkinson, Rick, *The Day of Battle: The War in Sicily and Italy, 1943–1945* (New York: Henry Holt, 2007).

Blumenson, Martin, *Salerno to Cassino* (Washington: Office of the Chief of Military History, 1969).

Brooks, Thomas R, *The War North of Rome, June 1944–May 1945* (Cambridge, Mass.: DaCapo Press, 2003).

Botjer, George, F., *Sideshow War: The Italian Campaign, 1943–1945* (College Station: Texas A & M Press, 1996).

Clark, Lloyd, *Anzio: Italy and the Battle for Rome—1944* (New York: Atlantic Monthly Press, 2006).

Deakin, F. W., *The Brutal Friendship: Mussolini, Hitler and the Fall of Italian Fascism* (New York: Harper & Row, 1962).

D'Este, Carlo, *Anzio and the Battle for Rome* (New York: Harper-Collins, 1991).

———, *Bitter Victory: The Battle for Sicily, 1943* (New York: Dutton, 1988).

———, *Patton: A Genius for War* (New York: Harper Collins, 1995).

Hapgood, David, and Richardson, David, *Monte Cassino* (New York: Congdon & Weed, 1984).

Higgins, Trumbull, *Soft Underbelly: The Anglo-American Controversy over the Italian Campaign, 1943–1945* (New York: Macmillan, 1968).

Macksey, Kenneth, *Kesselring,: German Master Strategist of the Second World War* (London: Greenhill Press, 1996).

Monsoor, Peter R., *The GI Offensive in Europe: the Triumph of the American Infantry Divisions, 1941–1945* (Lawrence: University of Kansas Press, 1999).

Porch, Douglas, *Path to Victory: The Mediterranean Theater in World War II* (New York: Farrar, Strauss & Giroux, 2004).

Tobin, James, *Ernie Pyle's War: Eyewitness to World War II* (New York: Free Press, 1997).

Chapter 19: War in the Atlantic

Bekker, Cajus, *Hitler's Naval War* (London: Doubleday, 1974).

Bercuson, David Jay, and Herwig, Holger, *The Destruction of the Bismarck* (New York: Overlook Press, 2001).

Blair, Clay, *Hitler's U-Boat War: The Hunters, 1939–1942* (New York: Random House, 1996).

Cunningham, Arthur, *A Sailor's Odyssey* (London: Hutchinson, 1951).

Donitz, Karl, *Memoirs: Ten Years and Twenty Days* (London: Weidenfeld and Nicolson, 1959).

Ireland, Bernard, *The Battle of the Atlantic* (Washington: Naval Institute Press, 2003).

Jackson, Robert, *The Royal Navy in World War II* (Shrewsbury: Airlife, 1997).

MacIntyre, Donald, *The Battle of the Atlantic* (London: Leo Cooper, 2006).

———, *The Battle for the Mediterranean* (New York: Norton, 1975).

Raeder, Erich, *My Life* (Annapolis: Naval Institute Press, 1960).

Sadkovich, James, *The Italian Navy in World War II* (Westport, Conn.: Greenwood Press, 1996).

Van der Vat, Dan, *The Atlantic Campaign: World War II's Great Struggle at Sea* (New York: Harper & Row, 1988).

Von der Porten, Edward, *The German Navy in World War II* (New York: Thomas Y. Crowell, 1988).

White, David Fairban, *Bitter Ocean: The Battle of the Atlantic, 1939–1945* (New York: Simon & Schuster, 2007).

Chapter 20: Target Germany: The Allied Bombing Offensive

Bekker, Cajus, *The Luftwaffe Diaries* (London: MacDonald, 1996).

Biddle, Tami Roberts, *Rhetoric and Reality in Air Warfare: The Evolution of British and American Ideas about Strategic Bombing, 1914–1945* (Princeton: Princeton University Press, 2002).

Crane, Conrad C., *Bombs, Cities, and Civilians: American Airpower Strategy in World War II* (Lawrence: University of Kansas Press, 1993).

Copp, DeWitt S., *Forged in Fire: Strategy and Decisions in the Air War over Europe, 1940–1945* (Garden City, N. Y.: Doubleday, 1982).

Daso, Dik A., *Hap Arnold and the Evolution of American Airpower* (Washington: Smithsonian Institution, 2000).

Davis, Richard G., Carl A., *Spaatz and the Air War in Europe* (Washington: Smithsonian Institution, 1994).

DeBruhl, Marshall, *Firestorm: Allied Airpower and the Destruction of Dresden* (New York: Random House, 2006).

Garrett, Stephen A., *Ethics and Airpower in World War II: The British Bombing of German Cities* (New York: St. Martin's Press, 1993).

Hastings, Max, *Bomber Command* (New York: Dial Press, 1979).

Levine, Alan J., *The Strategic Bombing of Germany, 1940–1945* (Westport, Conn.: Praeger, 1980).

Middlebrook, Martin. *The Battle of Hamburg* (New York: Charles Scribner's Sons, 1980).

_____, *The Schweinfurt-Regensburg Mission* (New York: Penguin, 1985).

Neilland, Robin, *The Bomber War: Arthur Harris and the Allied Bombing Offensive, 1939–1945* (London: Murray, 2001).

Neufeld, Michael J., *The Rocket and the Reich: Peenemünde and the Coming of the Ballistic Missile Era* (New York: Free Press, 1995).

Overy, R. J., *The Air War, 1939–1945* (New York: Stein and Day, 1980).

_____, *Why the Allies Won,* Chapter 4 (New York: Norton, 1995).

Robertson, Scott, *The Development of RAF Strategic Bombing Doctrine, 1919–1945* (Westport, Conn.: Praeger, 1995).

Schaffer, Ronald, *Wings of Judgement: American Bombing in World War II* (Oxford: Oxford University Press, 1985).

Thomas, Hugh, *Overlord: General Pete Quesada and the Triumph of Tactical Airpower in World War II* (New York: Simon & Schuster, 1995).

Chapter 21: Total War and the Home Fronts

Addison, Paul, *Churchill and the Home Front, 1900–1955* (London: Pimlico, 1994).

Baird, Jay W., *The Mythical World of Nazi Propaganda, 1939–1945* (Minneapolis: University of Minnesota Press, 1974).

Balfour, Michael, *Propaganda in War, 1939–1945: Organizations, Policies, and Publics in Britain and Germany* (London: Routledge and Kegan Paul, 1979).

Barber, John, and Harrison, Mark, *The Soviet Home Front, 1941–1945: A Social and Economic History of the USSR in World War II* (London: Longman, 1991).

Beck, Earl R., *Under the Bombs: The German Home Front, 1942–1945* (Lexington: University of Kentucky Press, 1986).

Calder, Angus, *The People's War: Britain, 1939–1945* (London: Cape, 1969).

Cohen, Jerome, B., *Japan's Economy in War and Reconstruction* (Minneapolis: University of Minnesota Press, 1949).

Conquest, Robert, *The Nation Killers: Soviet Deportation of Nationalities* (London,. Macmillan, 1970).

Cook, Haruko Taya, and Cook, Theodore F., *Japan at War: An Oral History* (New York: The New Press, 1992).

Fussell, Paul, *Wartime: Understanding and Behavior in the Second World War* (Oxford: Oxford University Press, 1989).

Gebney, Frank, ed., *Senso: The Japanese Remember the Pacific War* (London: M. E. Sharpe, 1995).

Goodwin, Doris Kerns, *No Ordinary Time: Franklin & Eleanor Roosevelt: The Home Front in World War II* (New York: Simon & Schuster, 1994).

Harrison, Mark, *Accounting for War: Soviet Production, Employment, and the Defence Burden, 1940–1945* (Cambridge: Cambridge University Press, 2002).

_____, *The Economics of World War II: Six Great Powers in International Comparison* (Cambridge: Cambridge University Press, 1998).

Havens, Thomas R. H., *Valley of Darkness: The Japanese People and World War Two* (New York: Norton, 1978).

Homan, Lynn, and Reilly, Thomas, *Black Knights: The Story of the Tuskegee Airmen* (Gretna, La.: Pelican Publishing, 2001).

Ineaga, Saburo, *The Pacific: World War II and the Japanese, 1931–1945* (New York: Random House, 1978).

Jeffries, John W., *Wartime America: The World War II Home Front* (Chicago: I. Dee, 1996).

Johnson, Eric A., *Nazi Terror: The Gestapo, Jews and Ordinary Germans* (New York: Basic Books, 1999).

Kitchen, Martin,. *Nazi Germany at War* (London: Longman, 1995).

Linz, Susan, ed., *The Impact of World War II on the Soviet Union* (Totowa, N. J.: Rowman and Allanheld, 1985).

Milward, Alan S., *The German Economy at War* (London: Athlone Press, 1965).

_____, *War, Economy and Society, 1939–1945* (Berkeley: University of California Press, 1977).

Morehouse, Maggi M., *Fighting in the Jim Crow Army: Black Men and Women Remember World War II* (Lanham, Md: Rowman & Littlefield, 2000).

Moskloff, William, *The Bread of Affliction: The Food Supply in the USSR during World War II* (Cambridge: Cambridge University Press, 1991).

Overy, Richard, *War and Economy in the Third Reich* (Oxford: Oxford University Press, 1994).

Reynolds, David, *Rich Relations: The American Occupation of Britain, 1942–1945* (New York: Random House, 1995).

Rupp, Leila J., *Mobilizing Women for War: German and American Propaganda, 1939–1945* (Princeton: Princeton University Press, 1978).

Shillony, Ben-Ami, *Politics and Culture in Wartime Japan* (Oxford: Oxford University Press, 1981).

Smith, Malcolm. *Britain and 1940: History, Myth, and Popular Memory* (London: Routlege, 2006).

Soviak, Eugene, ed., *A Diary of Darkness: The Wartime Diary of Kiyoshawe Kyosi* (Princeton: Princeton University Press, 1980).

Steinert, Marlys, *Hitler's War and the Germans* (Athens, Ohio: Ohio University Press, 1977).

Taylor, Sandra C., *Jewel of the Desert: Japanese American Internment at Topaz* (Berkeley: University of California Press, 1993).

Thurston, Robert W., and Bonwetsch, Bernd, eds., *The People's War: Responses to World War II in the Soviet Union* (Urbana: University of Illinois Press, 2000).

Townsend, Kenneth, *World War II and the American Indian* (Albuquerque: University of New Mexico Press, 2000).

Tsurumi, Shunsuke, *An Intellectual History of Wartime Japan* (London: KPI Limited, 1986).

Weatherford, Doris, *American Women and World War II* (New York: Facts on File, 1990).

Weglyn, Michi, *Years of Infamy: The Untold Story of America's Concentration Camps* (Seattle: University of Washington Press, 1996).

Grigg, John, *1943: The Victory That Never Was* (New York: Hill and Wang, 1980).

Hart, Russell A., *Clash of Arms: How the Allies Won in Normandy* (Boulder, Colo.: Lynn Riener, 2001).

Harvey, A. D., *Arnhem* (London: Cassel, 2001).

Lamb, Richard, *Montgomery in Europe, 1943–1944: Success or Failure?* (New York: Franklin Watts, 1984).

Levine, Alan J., *From the Normandy Beaches to the Baltic Sea: The Northwest Europe Campaign, 1944–1945* (Westport, Conn.: Praeger/Greenwood, 2000).

Lewis, Adrian, R., *Omaha Beach: A Flawed Victory* (Chapel Hill: University of North Carolina Press, 2001).

McKee, Alexander, *Caen: The Anvil of Victory* (London: Souvenir Press, 1964).

Messenger, Charles, *The Second World War in the West* (London: Cassel, 1999).

Middlebrook, Martin, *Arnhem 1944: The Airborne Battle, 17–26 September* (London: Viking, 1994).

Mitchum, Samuel W., *The Desert Fox in Normandy: Rommel's Defense of Fortress Europe* (Westport, Conn.: Greenwood, 1994).

Murray, G. E Patrick, *Eisenhower versus Montgomery: The Continuing Debate* (Westport, Conn.: Praeger/Greenwood, 1996).

Wadell, Steve R., *United States Army Logistics: The Normandy Campaign, 1944* (Westport, Conn.: Greenwood, 1994).

Weigley, Russell F., *Eisenhower's Lieutenants: The Campaign of France and Germany, 1944–1945* (Bloomington: Indiana University Press, 1981).

Wilt, *The Atlantic Wall: Hitler's Defenses for Fortress Europe, 1941–1945* (New York: Enigma Books, 2004).

———, *The French Riviera Campaign of August 1944* (Carbondale: Southern Illinois Press, 1981).

Chapter 22: Cross-Channel Invasion at Last: D Day to the German Border

Ambrose, Stephen, *D-Day, June 6, 1944: The Climactic Battle of World War II* (New York: Simon & Schuster, 1994).

Blakoski, Joseph, *Utah Beach: The Amphibious Landing and Airborne Operations on D-Day, June 6, 1944* (Mechanicsburg, Pa.: Stackpole Books, 2005).

Blumenson, Martin, *Breakout and Pursuit* (Washington: Office of the Chief of Military History, 1961).

———. *The Battle of the Generals: The Untold Story of the Falaise Pocket: The Battle That Should Have Won World War II* (New York: Morrow, 1993).

D'Este, Carlo, *Decision in Normandy* (New York: HarperCollins, 1994).

Dunn, Walter S., *Second Front Now—1943* (University, Ala.: University of Alabama Press, 1980).

Fest, Joachim, *Plotting Hitler's Death: The German Resistance to Hitler, 1933–1945* (London: Weidenfeld, 1996).

Chapter 23: The End of the Thousand Year Reich

Ambrose, Stephen, *Eisenhower and Berlin, 1945: The Decision to Halt on the Elbe* (New York: Norton, 1967).

Astor, Gerald, *The Bloody Forest: Battle for the Huertgen* (Novato, Calif.: Presidio Press, 2000).

Beevor, Anthony, *The Fall of Berlin 1945* (New York: Viking, 2002).

Bechloss, Michael R., *The Conquerors: Roosevelt, Truman, and the Destruction of Hitler's Germany, 1941–1945* (New York: Simon & Schuster, 2002).

Buhite, Russell D., *Decisions at Yalta: An Appraisal of Summit Diplomacy* (Wilmington, Del.: Scholarly Resources, 1986).

Clemens, Diane, *Yalta* (London: Oxford University Press, 1970).

Cole, Hugh M., *The Lorraine Campaign* (Washington: Department of the Army, 1966).

Dupuy, Trevor Nevitt, *Hitler's Last Gamble: The Battle of the Bulge, December 1944–January 1945* (New York: Harper Collins, 1994).

Hastings, Max, *Armageddon: The Battle for Germany, 1944–1945* (New York: Knopf, 2004).

Le Tissier, Tony, *Race for the Reichstag: The 1945 Battle for Berlin* (London: Frank Cass, 1999).

MacDonald, Charles B., *The Last Offensive* (Washington: Office of the Chief of Military History, 1973).

Ryan, Cornelius, *The Last Battle* (New York: Simon & Schuster, 1966).

Toland, John, *The Last 100 Days* (New York: Random House, 1966).

Trevor-Roper, Hugh R., *The Last Days of Hitler* (New York: Collier Books, 1962).

Weinberg, Gerhard L., *Visions of Victory: The Hopes of Eight World War II Leaders* (Cambridge: Cambridge University Press, 2005).

Zumbro, Derek, *Battle for the Ruhr: The German Army's Final Defeat in the West* (Lawrence: University of Kansas Press, 2006).

Chapter 24: War on the Periphery: China, Burma, India

Campbell, A. F., *The Siege: A Story from Kohima* (London: Allen, 1956).

Daws, Gavan, *Prisoners of the Japanese: POWs of World War II in the Pacific* (New York: Morrow, 1994).

Evans, G. C., and Brett-James, Anthony, *Imphal* (London: Leo Cooper, 1976).

Harris, Sheldon H., *Factories of Death: Japanese Biological Warfare, 1932–1945, and the American Coverup* (London: Routledge, 1995).

Iriye, Akira, and Cohen, Warren, eds., *American, Chinese, and Japanese Perspectives on Wartime Asia, 1931–1945* (Wilmington, Del.: Scholarly Resources, 1990).

Jones, Francis Clifford, *Japan's New Order in East Asia: Its Rise and Fall* (London: Oxford University Press, 1962).

Lewin, Ronald, *Slim: The Standard-bearer* (London: Leo Cooper, 1976).

Matthews, G. F., *Reconquest of Burma, 1943–1945* (Aldershot, U. K.: Gale, 1966).

Moon, Pederel, *Gandhi and Modern India* (New York: Norton, 1968).

Ogburn, Charlton, *The Marauders* (New York: Harper and Row, 1959).

Prefer, Nathan N., *Vinegar Joe's War: Stilwell's Campaigns for Burma* (Novato, Calif: Presidio, 2000).

Rooney, David, *Wingate and the Chindits: Redressing the Balance* (London: Arms and Armour Press, 1994).

Schaller, Michael, *The U.S. Crusade in China, 1938–1945* (New York: Columbia University Press, 1979).

Slim, William, *Defeat into Victory* (London: Cassel, 1956).

Tanaka, Yuki, *Japan's Comfort Women: Sexual Slavery and Prostitution during World War II and the U.S. Occupation* (London: Routledge, 2002).

Terraine, John, *The Life and Times of Lord Mountbatten* (London: Hutchinson, 1968).

Tuchman, Barbara, *Stilwell and the American Experience in China, 1911–1945* (New York: Macmillan, 1970).

Williams, Peter, and Wallace, David, *Unit 371: Japan's Secret Biological Warfare in World War II* (New York: The Free Press, 1989).

Chapter 25: The Collapse of Japan

Allen, Thomas B., and Polmar, Norman, *Code-Name Downfall: The Secret Plan to Invade Japan and Why Truman Dropped the Bomb* (New York: Simon & Schuster, 1995).

Aperovitz, Gar, *Atomic Diplomacy: Hiroshima and Nagasaki* (New York: Vintage Books, 1966).

_____, *The Decision to Use the Atomic Bomb, and the Architecture of an American Myth* (New York: Knopf, 1995).

Belote, James and William, *Typhoon of Steel: The Battle for Okinawa* (New York: Harper and Row, 1970).

Blair, Clay, *Silent Victory: The U.S. Submarine Warfare against Japan* (Philadelphia: J. B. Lippincott, 1975).

Brooks, Lester, *Behind Japan's Surrender: The Secret Struggle That Ended an Empire* (New York: McGraw-Hill, 1968).

Cutler, Thomas J., *The Battle of Leyte Gulf, 23–26 October 1944* (New York: Harper Collins, 1994).

DeRose, James, *Unrestricted Warfare: How a New Breed of Officers Led the Submarine Force to Victory in World War II* (New York: John Wiley, 2000).

Feis, Herbert, *The Atomic Bomb and the End of World War II* (Princeton: Princeton University Press, 1966).

Frank, Richard B., *Downfall: The End of the Imperial Japanese Empire* (New York: Random House, 1999).

Friedman, Kenneth I., *Afternoon of the Rising Sun: The Battle of Leyte Gulf* (Novato, Calif.: Presidio, 2001).

Hallas, James H., *The Devil's Anvil: The Assault on Peleliu* (Westport, Conn.: Praeger/National Book Network, 1994).

Hastings, Max, *Retribution: The Battle for Japan* (New York: Knopf, 2008).

Inoguchi, Rikihei, Nakajima, Tadashi, and Pineau, Roger, *The Divine Wind: Japan's Kamikaze Force in World War II* (Annapolis: Naval Institute Press, 1994).

Kakehashi, Kumiko, *Letters from Iwo Jima* (London: Weidenfeld & Nicolson, 2007).

Kerr, E. Bartlett, *Flames Over Tokyo: The U. S. Army Air Force's Incendiary Campaign against Japan, 1944–1945* (New York: Donald I. Fine, 1991).

Leckie, Robert, *Okinawa: The Last Battle of World War II* (New York: Viking/Penguin, 1995).

Maddox, Robert James, *Weapons for Victory: The Hiroshima Decision Fifty Years Later* (Columbia: University of Missouri Press, 1995).

Newcomb, Richard F., *Iwo Jima* (New York: Holt, Rinehart and Winston, 1965).

Ogura, Tayofumi, *Letters from the End of the World: A First Hand Account of the Bombing of Hiroshima* (New York: Oxford University Press, 2001).

Parillo, Mark P., *The Japanese Merchant Marine in World War II* (Annapolis: Naval Institute Press, 1993).

Rhodes, Richard, *The Making of the Atomic Bomb* (New York: Simon & Schuster, 1996).

Roleff, Tamara L., ed. *The Atom Bomb* (San Diego: Greenhaven. 2000).

Skates, John Roy, *The Invasion of Japan: The Alternative to the Bomb* (Columbia: University of South Carolina Press, 1994).

Smith, Robert Ross, *Triumph in the Philippines* (Washington: Department of the Army, 1963).

Werrell, Kenneth P., *Blankets of Fire: U. S. Bombers Over Japan during World War II* (Washington: Smithsonian Institution, 1996).

Aftermath

Backer, John H., *The Decision to Divide Germany* (Durham, N.C.: Duke University Press, 1978).

Burma, Ian, *The Wages of Guilt: Memories of War in Germany and Japan* (New York: Farrar, Strauss and Giroux, 1994).

Dower, John W., *Embracing Defeat: Japan in the Wake of World War II* (New York: Norton, 1999).

Elwood, David W., *Rebuilding Europe: Western Europe, America and Postwar Reconstruction* (Oxford: Oxford University Press, 1992).

Feis, Herbert, *From Trust to Terror: The Onset of the Cold War, 1945–1950* (New York: Norton, 1970).

Gaddis, John L., *The Cold War: A New History* (New York: Penguin, 2005).

———, *Strategies of Containment: A Critical Appraisal of American National Security Policy during the Cold War* (New York: Oxford University Press, 2005).

Grimal, Henri, *Decolonization of the British, French, Dutch and Belgian Empires, 1919–1963* (Boulder, Colo.: Westview, 1978).

Harbutt, Fraser J., *The Iron Curtain: Churchill, America and the Origins of the Cold War* (New York: Oxford University Press, 1986).

Hoopes, Townsend, and Brinkley, Douglas, *FDR and the Creation of the UN* (New Haven: Yale University Press, 1997).

McCagg, William A., *Stalin Embattled, 1943–1948* (Detroit: Wayne State University Press, 1978).

Millett, Alan R., *The War for Korea, 1945–1950: A House Burning* (Lawrence: University of Kansas Press, 2005).

Milward, Alan S., *The Reconstruction of Western Europe, 1945–1951* (Berkeley: University of California Press, 1984).

Minear, Richard H., *Victor's Justice: The Tokyo War Crimes Trials* (Princeton: Princeton University Press, 1971).

Pepper, Suzanne, *Civil War in China: The Political Struggles, 1945–1948* (Berkeley: University of California Press, 1978).

Perry, John C., *Beneath the Eagle's Wings: Americans in Occupied Japan* (New York: Dodd, Mead, 1980).

Persico, Joseph E., *Nuremberg: Infamy on Trial* (New York: Viking, 1994).

Schwartz, Thomas Alan, *America's Germany: John McCloy and the Federal Republic of Germany* (Cambridge: Harvard University Press, 1991).

Tinker, Hugh, *Race, Conflict and the International Order: From Empire to the United Nations* (New York: St. Martin's, 1977).

Westad, Arne Odd, *The Global Cold War: Third World Interventions and the Making of Our Times* (Cambridge: Cambridge University Press, 2007).

Williams, William A., *The Tragedy of American Diplomacy* (New York: Dell, 1962).

Yergin, Daniel, *The Shattered Peace: The Origins of the Cold War and the National Security State* (Boston: Houghton-Mifflin, 1977).

Zubok, Vladislav, and Pleshakov, Constantine, *Inside the Kremlin's Cold War: From Stalin to Khrushchev* (Cambridge: Harvard University Press, 1996).

Index